Ancient Lives

Ancient Lives is an engaging and accessible textbook that introduces complete beginners to the fascinating worlds of archaeology and prehistory through sites of key significance and the world's first civilizations.

Opening with an introduction to the basic principles, methods, and theoretical approaches of archaeology, the book then provides a summary of world prehistory from a global perspective, exploring human origins and the reality of life in the prehistoric world. Later chapters explore the development of agriculture and animal domestication, and the emergence of cities and state-level societies across the globe. The new edition updates and reflects the latest thinking through numerous updates of case studies, discoveries, and advances in methods and theory. In addition to comprehensive revisions throughout the book, new sections on the relevance of archaeology to contemporary society and issues are included.

Ancient Lives continues to be a comprehensive and essential introduction to archaeology and is an ideal textbook for students studying archaeology and prehistory for the first time.

Nadia Durrani is a best-selling archaeological writer. The former editor of *Current World Archaeology* magazine, she is also the long-standing co-author of Brian Fagan's portfolio of textbooks. Her other books include *Climate Chaos: Lessons on Survival from Our Ancestors* (with Fagan), which won the 2023 COSMOS award for Italy's best popular science book. She studied archaeology and anthropology at Cambridge University, has a PhD from University College London, and is a Fellow of the Society of Antiquaries, UK.

Brian M. Fagan (1936–2025) was one of the world's leading archaeological writers and an internationally recognized authority on world prehistory. In addition to writing textbooks, he wrote dozens of general books including *The Adventure of Archaeology*; *A Little History of Archaeology*; and *The Great Warming: Climate Change and the Rise and Fall of Civilizations*. He studied at Cambridge University and was Emeritus Professor of Anthropology at the University of California, Santa Barbara, USA.

Ancient Lives

An Introduction to Archaeology and Prehistory

Eighth edition

Nadia Durrani and Brian M. Fagan

Routledge
Taylor & Francis Group
NEW YORK AND LONDON

Designed cover image: Getty Images

Eighth edition published 2027
and by Routledge
605 Third Avenue, New York, NY 10158

by Routledge
4 Park Square, Milton Park, Abingdon, Oxon, OX14 4RN

Routledge is an imprint of the Taylor & Francis Group, an informa business

First edition published by Prentice Hall 2000
Seventh edition published by Routledge 2020

British Library Cataloguing-in-Publication Data
A catalogue record for this book is available from the British Library

ISBN: 9781032972220 (hbk)
ISBN: 9781032972206 (pbk)
ISBN: 9781003592754 (ebk)

DOI: 10.4324/9781003592754

Typeset in Sabon
by codeMantra

To
Carol Ellick with affection

and Nancy Roberts
also with affection and with thanks
for many kindnesses and the
"Eureka moment" that resulted in *Ancient Lives*

Brief Contents

Contents

Preface

Golden pharaohs, lost cities, grinning human skeletons: Archaeology is the stuff of romance and legend! Many people still think of archaeologists as adventurers and treasure hunters, like Indiana Jones of Hollywood movie fame seeking the elusive Holy Grail. These enduring images go back to the late nineteenth century, when archaeologists like Heinrich Schliemann could still find lost civilizations like Troy and excavate three royal palaces in a week. Today, a few, if any, archaeologists are like Indiana Jones. They are scientists, not adventurers, as comfortable in an air-conditioned laboratory as they are on a remote excavation site. The development of scientific archaeology from its Victorian beginnings ranks among the greatest triumphs of twentieth-century science.

Archaeology has changed our understanding of the human experience in profound ways. A century ago, most scientists believed that humans were no more than 100,000 years old. Today, we know that our origins go back over 6 million years. Our predecessors assumed that the Americas were settled about 10,000 years ago and that farming began around 6,000 years ago. New excavations date the first Americans to at least 15,000 years ago and the beginnings of agriculture by 12,000 years ago. Most important of all, archaeology has changed our perceptions of ourselves and our biological and cultural diversity. Welcome to the fascinating world of archaeology and prehistory!

Ancient Lives is a celebration of the only scientific discipline that studies human biological and cultural evolution over enormously long periods of time. These pages explore more than six million years of the human past.

About *Ancient Lives*

This book is divided into two halves, and into seven parts as well. The first seven chapters cover the basic methods and theoretical approaches of archaeology. The remainder of the book takes a journey through prehistory, from human origins to those dramatic moments when Spanish conquistadors gazed upon the Aztec capital in the Valley of Mexico and at the wealth of the Inca civilization in the Andes. The remaining parts subdivide these broad themes into more manageable chunks.

Part 1, "Archaeology: Studying Ancient Times," consists of four chapters. These chapters define archaeology and prehistory, introduce the nature of the archaeological record, discuss the ways in which archaeologists date the past, and examine ancient technology and ways of obtaining food.

Part 2, "Ancient Interactions," focuses on people and their interactions, on the study of ancient religious beliefs, and on the all-important topic of explaining the past.

Part 3, "The World of the First Humans," beginning with Chapter 8, starts the narrative of human prehistory with a discussion of human origins and the spread of archaic peoples out of tropical Africa after 2 million years ago. Part 3 ends with an analysis of the controversies surrounding the origins of modern humans—*Homo sapiens*, us, the "wise person." Part 4, "Modern Humans Settle the World," contains just one chapter, Chapter 10, which covers the thousands of years of migration that took modern humans from our African homeland into every corner of the Old World, and, by 15,000 years ago, into the Americas.

In Part 5, "The First Farmers and Civilizations," the story continues in the Old World with the beginnings of farming in southwestern Asia, and later in other parts of Asia. It was farming that led to the last great migrations of *Homo sapiens* to the offshore islands of the Pacific Ocean. Chapter 12 discusses the beginnings of civilization—complex, state-level society—in Mesopotamia and Egypt. Chapter 13 describes the origins of Asian civilization, culminating in the stupendous Khmer states of Cambodia.

Part 6, "The Ancient Americas," moves to the Western Hemisphere and follows developments after first settlement of the Americas in Chapter 14, telling the early story of maize, the staple crop of Native American agriculture. Chapters 15 and 16 recount the multifaceted histories of civilization in Central America (Mesoamerica) and the Andes region of South America, respectively.

Finally, Part 7, "Finale," provides a frank appraisal of the future of archaeology and of career prospects in archaeology, the subject of a brief essay in Chapter 17. A glossary of technical terms, sites, and cultures follows the final chapter.

The Philosophy Behind *Ancient Lives*

Writing a textbook such as *Ancient Lives* is a constant exercise in compromise and making decisions as to what to include and what to omit. *Ancient Lives* is designed as a first text in archaeology and prehistory that seeks to engage the reader in a complex enterprise, to explore some of the dimensions of archaeology and human prehistory at a fundamental level. For the archaeology section (Chapters 1–7), we have made unashamed use of our own extensive fieldwork and laboratory experience, of years of visiting other archaeologists' excavations and surveys, to give a sometimes unavoidably arid subject matter greater immediacy. At the same time, these seven chapters draw on methods and examples from all parts of the world, for this is what the prehistory in the next nine chapters is all about. Remember that archaeology and prehistory are global enterprises, not just a product of Europe, North America, and Mexico. The beginner should enjoy archaeology and prehistory, with all the attendant global diversity of field experience and intellectual problems.

The seven methods and theory chapters make use of examples from the Americas, Africa, Europe, and Asia, from the earliest archaeological sites to modern urban trash deposits. There are numerous examples of good applications of archaeological method and theory, so it has been hard to choose among them. One school of thought urges the use of the latest examples from brand-new research. Another feels that one should balance male and female archaeologists equally in the examples, without, apparently, any concern for the significance of the site or the methods. We've chosen to mix three ingredients: important sites and case studies, many of them several generations old, which are still outstanding and well-known instances of archaeological research; examples from different parts of the world; and new discoveries. There are many familiar sites and discoveries (Olduvai Gorge, the tomb of Tutankhamun, and so on) that transcend the narrow interests of individual teachers and students. They are used without apology here. After all, the best-known and most spectacular sites are those that often stick in the mind, even if they were excavated several generations ago.

Then, there is the thorny issue of archaeological theory, the subject of Chapter 7. Archaeology has witnessed constant theoretical ferment over the decades, some of it inspired, some of it downright nonsense. The theoretical debates continue, most of them of little concern to the beginner. For this reason, this book espouses no particular theoretical bias because a wide range of instructors and students will use this book and also because individual teachers can easily use the general summaries given here and present their own perspectives on the tidal currents of archaeological theory.

The prehistory chapters (Chapters 8–16) attempt a simple, jargon-free account of humanity over the past 6 million years. Again, we've chosen a global perspective, for we believe that you cannot understand humanity or human diversity unless you examine what happened in all parts of the world. The prehistory of humankind viewed from the single perspective of, say, Egypt or the Andes, is meaningless, for the human experience in these regions is but a fragment of an infinitely larger jigsaw puzzle. We've told the story with a minimum of detail and with as few sites as possible, based on the argument that we're concerned here with the general outline of what happened in prehistory and why, not with minor details of local developments, which are covered in more detailed regional surveys. For the same reason, we've skated over the major theoretical debates that surround important issues such as the first settlement of the Americas, the origins of agriculture and animal domestication, and the beginnings of literate civilization. Instructors will discuss these controversies in class if they consider them relevant to the classwork.

Ancient Lives is a rapid-fire journey through the worlds of archaeology and prehistory. Inevitably, the discussions of many issues in these pages are cursory. We've erred on the side of overgeneralization, on the grounds that such excesses can easily be corrected in class or in later courses. It is best to get the point across and then qualify it, rather than wallowing in a mishmash of *probablys* or *perhapses*.

Ancient Lives is written for people who want to know more about archaeology and prehistory, not necessarily with a view to becoming professional archaeologists (although we explain how to do that in Chapter 17), but so that they can carry some knowledge of the remote past and how we study it with them in later life. The future of our past depends on responsible stewardship of the finite archives of archaeology for future generations by archaeologists and society as a whole.

We have a modest ambition for *Ancient Lives*. If this book leaves you with a lifetime interest in archaeology and prehistory, with enough background knowledge to understand the reasoning behind archaeological stories in popular journals such as *National Geographic*, and with respect for archaeologists and the achievements of our forebears, then its job is done.

Special Features and Changes in the Eighth Edition

The eighth edition reflects a combination of new discoveries and advances in archaeological methods and theoretical approaches.

Coverage

This book covers all aspects of archaeology and prehistory but pays particular attention to the following:

- Alternative perspectives on the past and on time (Chapters 1 and 3) and important issues for Native Americans and other indigenous peoples.

- Archaeological ethics, stewardship, and conservation of the past (Chapters 1, 2, and 17). Frequently neglected in beginning archaeology courses, these issues are fundamental to the survival of the discipline.
- The people of the past and the study of human diversity, including sex, gender, and ethnicity (Part 2).
- The study of ancient religious beliefs and other cultural intangibles, a fascinating and rapidly expanding direction in the field (Chapter 6).
- Career opportunities in archaeology and living with the past on a day-by-day basis (Chapter 17).
- A balanced, global perspective on human prehistory that emphasizes no one region at the expense of others.
- A jargon-free narrative focusing on four basic developments:
    - *Early human evolution:* Chapter 8 discusses the latest advances in the study of human origins, including recent fossil discoveries in Africa.
    - *Origins of modern humans:* Chapters 9 and 10 cover new research on the controversial issue of the earliest *Homo sapiens* and fresh perceptions of Neanderthal ancestry and behavior, as well as the diaspora of modern humans across the world.
    - *Origins of food production:* Chapter 11 describes the first farmers of the Old World, incorporating new dates and analysis for early agriculture obtained from accelerator mass spectrometry (AMS) radiocarbon technology and fine-grained genetic studies.
    - *Origins of states and civilization:* Chapters 12, 13, 15, and 16 offer an up-to-date description and analysis of the first complex urban societies in the Old World and the Americas.

Inevitably, we've made compromises in the subject matter. *Ancient Lives* does not provide extensive coverage of the history of archaeology (except in some boxes) nor of Cultural Resource Management (CRM), although we do explore CRM and its career possibilities. Nor is there much discussion of archaeological theory. All of these topics are more appropriately taught in greater detail in more advanced undergraduate courses. So are the minute details of archaeological survey, remote sensing, excavation, artifact analysis, and local archaeological sequences. The fact that something is not covered here does not mean that it's unimportant.

Changes

The eighth edition has been updated throughout, and includes the following changes:

- Detailed changes in method and theory chapters reflecting the latest advances.
- New coverage of human evolution, especially of recent DNA analysis.
- Discussion of the Neanderthals and the Denisovans of Siberia, who are slowly coming into sharper focus.
- New information on the first settlement of the Americas.
- Fresh insights into Maya civilization and into the beginnings of coastal Andean civilization.
- Revised critical thinking and further reading suggestions at the end of each chapter.

Special Features

- A jargon-free, easy-to-read writing style.
- Glossary explaining many terms used in the text. Some glossary terms appear in italics at first use, e.g. *public archaeology* on p. **534**. Only those that appear in the text boxes are in **bold**. Some terms appear in italics that are not in the glossary, e.g. *Egyptologist*, *Mayanist*, as their meanings are obvious.
- Unique, truly global coverage of archaeology and prehistory, reflected in a balanced treatment of many parts of the world.
- A comprehensive illustration program designed to amplify the text.

Feature Boxes

Three types of in-text feature boxes enhance the narrative:

- *"Doing Archaeology":* These boxes introduce key dating methods and other scientific approaches, such as radiocarbon and AMS dating, flotation for the recovery of seeds, and sourcing of obsidian (volcanic rock) traded over long distances in ancient times.
- *"Site":* Each of the first 16 chapters includes one or more boxes describing important sites and some aspect of them of unusual interest.
- *"Discovery":* Details of important archaeological discoveries are explored in these boxes.

Acknowledgments

Many colleagues, too numerous to list here, have advised us on this revision. We're deeply grateful for their encouragement and assistance. We thank our publisher, Matthew Gibbons, his assistant Manas Roy, and their other partners at Routledge. They have helped turn a complex manuscript into an attractive book and have done all they can to minimize unexpected difficulties. As always, we are most grateful for ciriticsms, comments, or details of new work, which can be sent by email to books@nadiadurrani.com.

Author Notes

This book divides roughly into two halves, the first devoted to the methods and theoretical approaches of archaeology, the second to a narrative of human prehistory. For consistency, we've adopted some basic conventions.

The narrative of prehistory in these pages is organized as linearly as possible, in chronological order. It is based on radiocarbon, potassium-argon, and tree-ring dates, as well as on historical documents. Although every effort has been made to ensure accuracy, many of these dates should be recognized for what they are—statistical approximations.

The following conventions for dates are used in this book:

Present	By scientific convention, the present is assumed to be A.D. 1950.
B.P.	Before the present. In general, years before 12,000 B.P. are given in years before present. Dates after 12,000 B.P. are expressed as B.C. or A.D., unless the context is obvious.
B.C. A.D.	To avoid confusion, we use B.C. and A.D. designations for dates. An alternative convention is B.C.E. and C.E. (i.e., Before the Common Era and Common Era), which is not used in this book.
Ma	Million years ago.
c.	Stands for *circa* ("about"), indicating an approximate date.

For clarity, all radiocarbon and potassium-argon dates are cited as specific numbers of years; however, readers should be aware that such estimates are subject to a "statistical error" of several percentage points in either direction.

All measurements are given in metric, the now-universal scientific convention, with mile, yard, foot, or inch equivalents provided.

The calibration of radiocarbon dates has reached a high degree of refinement as scientists develop ever more accurate time scales for the past 15,000 years, using tree-ring, coral, and ice-core data. Calibrated dates are quoted throughout this book where possible. It should be stressed that these calibrations are provisional, statistically based, and subject to modification, especially before 7000 B.C.

Site locations are shown on maps spaced at intervals in the text. The map of European sites in Figure 1.7 is placed in Chapter 1, as there are many instances throughout this book when the sites thereon are mentioned. Some sites are omitted from the maps for clarity. They can easily be located using Google Maps.

Nadia Durrani and
Brian M. Fagan

Author Notes

Part 1

Archaeology

Studying Ancient Times

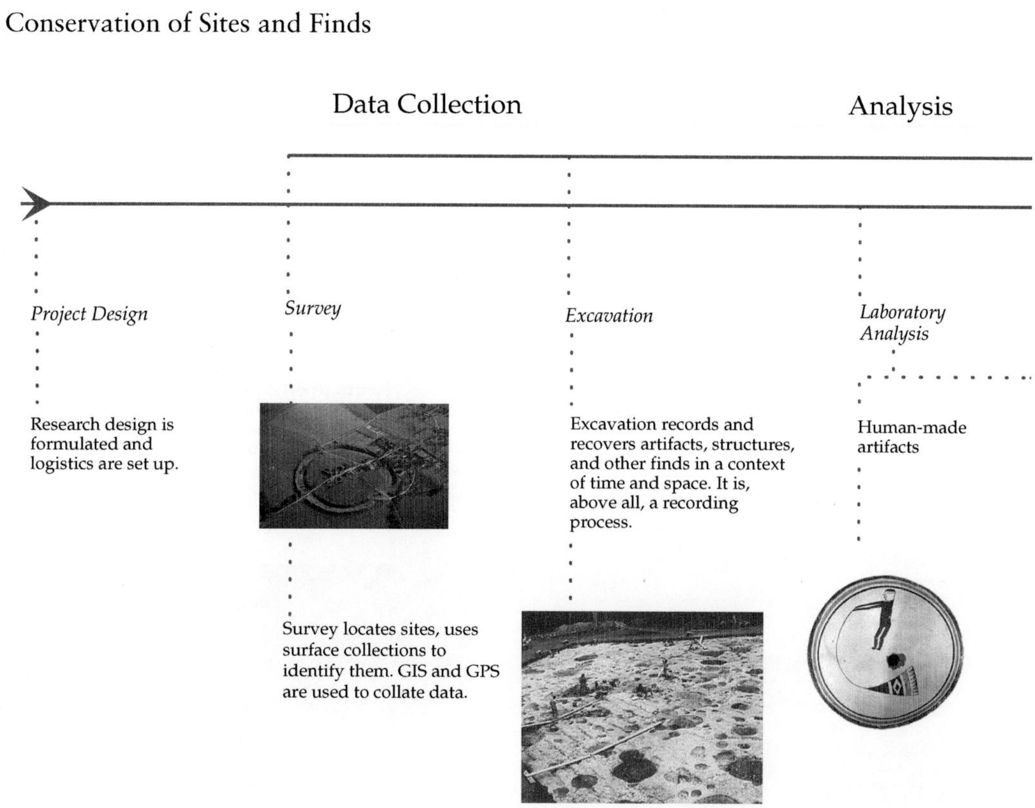

A flow chart shows the process of archaeological research from initial planning to final publication. Conservation is an important concern throughout the project.

Interpretation

Curation and Preservation

Food remains and so on.

Interpretation and Synthesis

Analyzed data are tested against research hypotheses and placed in theoretical context.

Publication

Formal report is prepared and published. Often includes recommendations for mitigating damage to the site.

Curation

Artifacts and other finds are stored in a permanent repository.

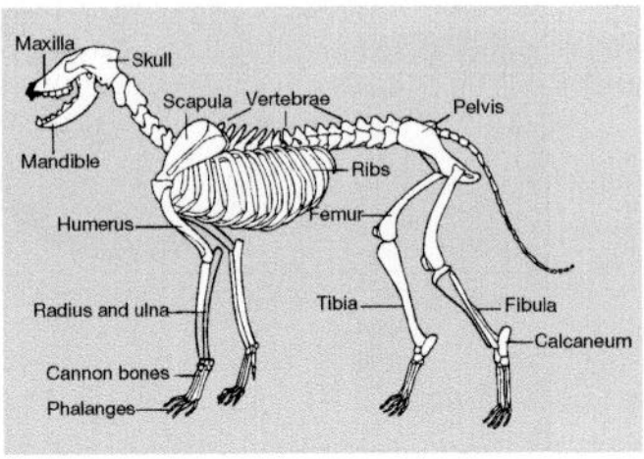

1 Introducing Archaeology and Prehistory

Chapter Outline

The Amphitheater at Epidauros, Greece, fourth century B.C.
Source: Thanos Karapanogiotis/Thinkstock.

Howard Carter and Lord Carnarvon paused before the doorway that bore the seals of the long-dead, little-known pharaoh, Tutankhamun. They had waited six long years, from 1917 to 1922, for this moment. Silently, Howard Carter pried a hole through the ancient

DOI: 10.4324/9781003592754-2

plaster. Hot air rushed out of the small cavity and massaged his face. He shone a flashlight through the hole and peered into the tomb. Gold objects swam in front of his eyes. Carter was struck dumb with amazement.

Lord Carnarvon moved impatiently behind him as Carter remained silent.

"What do you see?" he asked, hoarse with excitement.

"Wonderful things," whispered Carter as he stepped back from the doorway.

They soon broke down the door. In a daze of wonderment, Carter and Carnarvon wandered through the antechamber of Tutankhamun's tomb (see Figure 1.1). They fingered golden funerary beds, admired beautifully inlaid chests, and examined the pharaoh's chariots stacked against the wall. Gold was everywhere—on wooden statues, inlaid on thrones and boxes, in jewelry, even on children's stools. Soon, Tutankhamun was known as the golden pharaoh, and archaeology as the domain of buried treasure and royal sepulchers.

Archaeology is the stuff dreams are made of—buried treasure, gold-laden pharaohs, and the romance of long-lost civilizations. Many people think of archaeologists as romantic adventurers, like the film world's Indiana Jones. Cartoonists often depict us as eccentric scholars in sun hats digging up inscribed tablets in the shadow of great pyramids. Popular legend would have us be absent-minded professors, so deeply absorbed in ancient times that we care little for the realities of modern life.

Wrong! Archaeology has come a long way since then, turning from spectacular discoveries to slow-moving teamwork in often far from dramatic sites. But the complex detective work accomplished by today's archaeologists, which teases out minor details of

Figure 1.1 The antechamber of Tutankhamun's tomb on discovery.
Source: Heritage Image Partnership/Alamy.

Figure 1.2 A warrior from the terracotta regiment that guarded Chinese emperor Shihuangdi's tomb, 210 B.C.

Source: ImageBROKER/Alamy Stock Photo.

the past, still has a fascination that rivals that of Tutankhamun's tomb or Chinese emperor Shihuangdi's regiment of guards fashioned in terracotta that protected his tomb after his death in 210 B.C. (Figure 1.2) (see Box 13.1 on p. 424).

Chapter 1 introduces you to archaeology and describes how it began. We look at what archaeologists do and why this unique science is so important in today's world.

How Archaeology Began

How did it all begin? The roots of archaeology go back many centuries, to an era of adventurers and casual collectors. Seventeenth-century European nobles traveled on a Grand Tour of Italy, where they acquired statuary and other Roman artifacts for their collections. During the eighteenth century, the King of Naples employed miners to tunnel into the buried Roman city of **Pompeii,** in Italy, destroyed by an eruption of nearby Mt. Vesuvius in A.D. 79. By the early nineteenth century, British landowners were trenching into ancient burial mounds for funeral urns and skeletons (see Figure 1.3). They would celebrate their discoveries with fine dinners, toasting their friends with ancient clay vessels.

Pompeii, Italy Roman town buried by an eruption of Mt. Vesuvius in A.D. 79; layers of ash preserved evidence of life in the community intact.

Lost Civilizations

The Pompeii excavations and curiosity about Ancient Egyptian civilization led to a lively market in precious antiquities. Giovanni Battista Belzoni (1778–1822), a circus strongman

Figure 1.3 Chaotic excavation. Casual diggers uncover a bread oven at Pompeii during the 1880s. Source: North Wind Picture Archives/Alamy.

turned treasure hunter, ransacked tombs and temples along the Nile from 1816 to 1819. One of his specialties was collecting mummies. He scrambled into rocky clefts crammed with mummies, "surrounded by bodies, by heaps of mummies in all directions ... The Arabs with the candles or torches in their hands, naked and covered with dust, themselves resembled living mummies" (Belzoni 1820, 157). On one occasion, he sat on a mummy by mistake and sank down in a crushed mass of bones, dried skin, and bandages. Belzoni eventually fled Egypt under threat of death from his competitors. Those were the days when archaeologists settled their differences with guns.

The stakes were high a couple of centuries ago, when one could find a long-forgotten civilization in a month. Englishman Austen Henry Layard and Frenchman Paul-Émile Botta did just that in the 1840s. They dug into vast city mounds at **Khorsabad, Nimrud,** and **Nineveh** (see Figure 1.4) by the Tigris River in what is now Iraq, where they unearthed the shadowy Assyrian civilization mentioned in the Old Testament, a sensational discovery.

Khorsabad, Iraq Palace and capital of Assyrian King Sargon, dating to the eighth century B.C.

Nineveh, Iraq Capital of the Assyrian Empire under King Ashurbanipal, c. 630 B.C.

Nimrud, Iraq Capital of Assyrian kings Esarhaddon (680–669 B.C.) and Ashurbanipal (668–627 B.C.).

Figure 1.4 Englishman Austen Henry Layard supervises the removal of a winged bull from the Palace of Assyrian King Sennacherib at Nineveh, in what is now Iraq.

Source: Mary Evans Picture Library/Alamy.

We're lucky that many early archaeologists, including Layard, were fluent writers, which adds to the excitement. American travel writer John Lloyd Stephens and artist Frederick Catherwood revealed the spectacular Maya civilization of Mexico, Guatemala, and Honduras in 1839. They visited **Copán, Palenque, Uxmal,** and other forgotten ancient cities, captivating an enormous audience with their adventures in the rain forest and with their lyrical descriptions and pictures of an ancient society shrouded in tropical vegetation (see Figure 1.5 and Box 1.1). Stephens laid the foundation for all subsequent research on ancient Maya civilization by declaring that the cities he visited were built by the ancestors of the modern inhabitants of the region. Like Layard, he was a best-selling author whose books are still in print.

Copán, Honduras Major Maya center during the mid-first millennium A.D.

Palenque, Mexico Maya city and ceremonial center ruled by the Shield dynasty for many centuries and powerful in the seventh century A.D.

Uxmal, Mexico Maya city in the northern Yucatán that flourished c. A.D. 900.

But How Old Was Humanity?

Austen Henry Layard's discoveries of the Biblical Assyrian civilization coincided with an intense debate over human origins. For centuries, Christian teaching had proclaimed the story of the Creation in Chapter 1 of Genesis to be historical truth. Seventeenth-century

Figure 1.5 Frederick Catherwood's lithograph of the Governor's Palace, Uxmal, Mexico. Source: Artokoloro Quint Lox Ltd/Alamy.

Archbishop James Ussher of Armagh in Northern Ireland used the genealogies in the Old Testament to calculate the date of the Creation as 4004 B.C., allowing a mere 6,000 years for all of human existence. However, repeated discoveries of the bones of long-extinct animals in the same geological levels as human-made stone tools hinted at a much longer time span for human origins. The geologists also showed how the Earth had formed through natural geological processes such as rainfall, earthquakes, and wind action, not from a series of great floods triggered by Divine Wrath as the religious believed.

The debate over what was called the antiquity of humankind intensified during the 1840s, when Frenchman Jacques Boucher de Perthes announced the discovery of stone axes and the bones of long-extinct elephants in the gravels of the Somme River in northern France (Figure 1.6). British geologists dug into caves in southwestern England, where they also found extinct animals and human-made stone tools in the same levels.

Box 1.1 Rapturous Discovery
Stephens, Catherwood, and Maya Copán

Stephens and Catherwood traveled to the tiny village of Copán through heavy forest. They found themselves amid a complex of overgrown plazas, pyramids, and terraces. Richly decorated individual columns (stelae) depicted portraits of long-forgotten rulers. There were hieroglyphs carved into stucco (fine plaster) that adorned buildings. While Catherwood sketched in the rain, knee-deep in mud, Stephens wandered through Copán and realized at once that it was quite unlike Ancient Egyptian monuments along the Nile. He compared Copán to a shipwreck. "It lay before us like a shattered bark … her crew perished, and none to tell whence she came." The only sounds that disturbed the quiet of the ancient city "were the noise of monkeys moving among the top of the trees and the cracking of dry branches broken by their weight." The troops moved overhead "forty or fifty at a time." "They seemed like wandering spirits of the departed guarding the ruins of their former habitations."

Later, the two travelers explored the Maya ruins at Palenque in Mexico, where they described well-preserved buildings and more hieroglyphs. It was here that Stephens realized that he was gazing at great centers built not by foreigners like Ancient Egyptian colonists, but by ancient Native Americans, whose civilization had collapsed many centuries earlier. He drew what he called a "wonderful" conclusion. "It is the spectacle of a people skilled in architecture, sculpture, and drawing … originating and growing up here, without models or masters … like the plants and fruits of the soil indigenous."

On a later expedition in 1841–1842, the two men returned to the Yucatán and visited such now well-known sites as Chichén Itzá and Uxmal. Catherwood and Stephens were predominantly travelers, for, unlike Layard, they had no funds for excavation. But Stephens's two books about their adventures are classics of early archaeology.

Figure 1.6 Stone axes similar to those found in the Somme gravels. Source: Natural History Museum, London/Science Photo Library.

Matters came to a head in 1859, when the highly respected British archaeologist John Evans pulled a stone ax from the same level as an elephant bone in de Perthes's Somme gravels. He "could hardly believe it." Evans announced his find as biologist Charles Darwin published his *Origin of Species* in the same year. Darwin had developed a theoretical framework that provided an explanation for why extinct animals and humans coexisted far earlier than the 6,000 years put forth by the creationists. The scientific establishment rejected the biblical chronology and accepted the notion of a much earlier date for human origins.

The new chronology opened up a vast, blank landscape of the remote past that extended back far beyond Ancient Egypt and the other civilizations for tens of thousands of unexplored years (Figure 1.7). With the establishment of human antiquity, archaeology rapidly became a serious means of studying the past. Excavation methods improved, especially in the hands of German scholars working at Olympia in Greece, site of the Olympic Games, during the 1870s. Two English excavators, the eccentric General Augustus Lane Fox Pitt-Rivers, a firearms expert who excavated earthworks and burial mounds on his vast estate with great care, and Arthur Evans, who discovered the **Minoan civilization** of Crete, were among pioneer excavators, as was Leonard Woolley, who excavated the Royal Burials at **Ur** in southern Iraq during the 1920s and 1930s (Figure 1.8).

Minoan civilization Bronze Age kingdom centered on Crete that reached its height between 1900 and 1400 B.C.

Ur (Ur-of-the-Chaldees), Iraq Biblical Calah, a major city of the Sumerian civilization in the third millennium B.C.

Today's archaeology is very different from the old days at Copán or Ur. It is a finegrained discipline which, more often than not, focuses on everyday people and their sites—rather than on great pyramids or royal cemeteries. However, the information gleaned is every bit as fascinating.

A Pause for Definitions

At this point, let's put some definitions on the table.

Archaeology is the scientific study of human behavior based on the surviving material remains of the past. We, alone among all students of humanity, study human biological and cultural change over the entire stretch of human existence. Archaeologists use artifacts, food remains, and other objects to study human behavior from its beginnings in Africa millions of years ago, right up to modern times. Our insights into ancient behavior come from building theories and then applying scientific methods and theoretical concepts in studying the material remains of past human cultures.

Archaeologists do not study dinosaurs, as the general public sometimes believes. Instead, we focus entirely on evidence relating to humans. Our excavations and field surveys have discovered societies that flourished thousands, even hundreds of thousands, of years before Egyptian and Mesopotamian scribes developed writing systems some 5,000 years ago. However, the reconstructions and interpretations of the past come from surviving material things that resulted from ancient human behavior. As we shall see in Chapter 2,

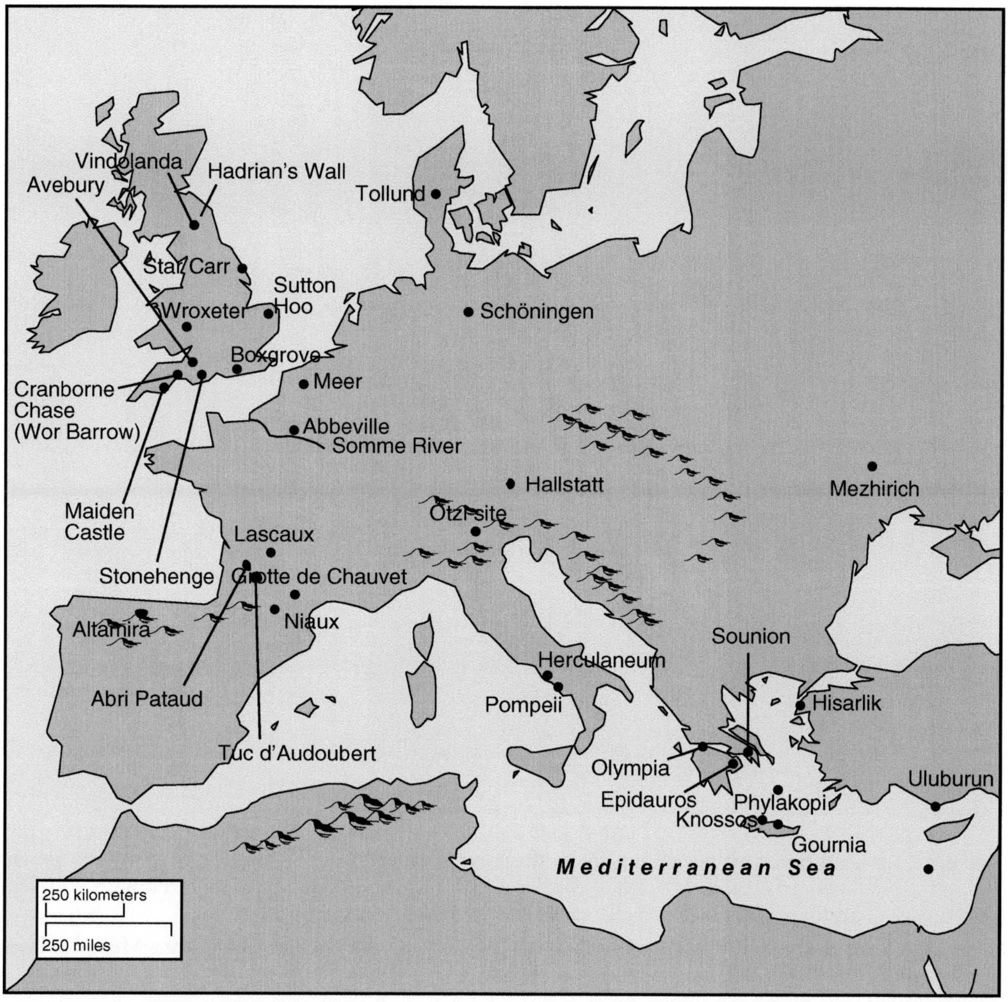

Figure 1.7 Major archaeological sites from Europe and the Mediterranean described in this book.

some materials last much longer than others. Stone and fired-clay vessels are nearly indestructible; wood, skin, metals, and bone are much more perishable. Thus, any picture of life in the remote past is likely to be very one-sided, often based on row after row of stone tools or painted pot fragments recovered from dated sites.

In many ways, the archaeologist is like a detective fitting together an incomplete collection of clues to give a general impression and explanation of ancient culture and society. Imagine for a moment taking two spark plugs, a fragment of a beer can, a needle, a bicycle chain, and a candleholder and trying to reconstruct the culture of the people who made those diverse objects on the basis of those objects alone!

Simply put, **archaeology** is the scientific study of material (or physical) evidence related to past human activity. While **history** tends to be written by the victors, archaeology has the potential to tell the story of everyone. This broad perspective on the past is vital if we hope to understand the present or attempt to look to the future. "Study the past, if you would define the future," asserted the Chinese philosopher Confucius five centuries before

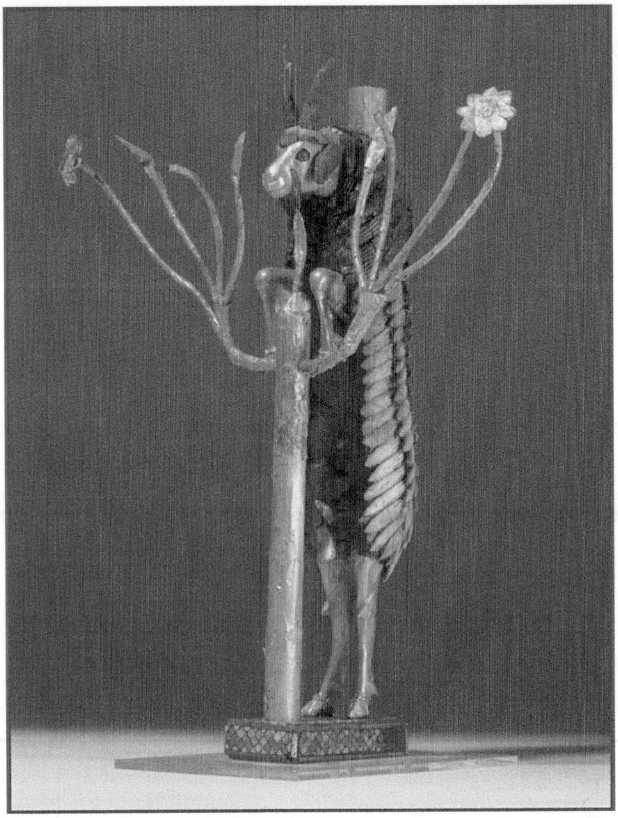

Figure 1.8 A famous ritual object from the royal cemetery at Ur, Iraq, called by excavator Leonard Woolley "Ram in the Thicket." The wood figure was covered with gold leaf and lapis lazuli. The belly was sheathed in silver, the fleece in shell.

Source: Ram in the Thicket. Accession d30-12–702. University of Pennsylvania Museum Neg. dT4-1000.

Christ. In 1948, Winston Churchill proclaimed that "those who fail to learn from history are doomed to repeat it." From climate change to governance, we cannot make informed decisions about the present and future without taking our past into account.

archaeology The study of the human past using the surviving material remains of human behavior.

Prehistorians, archaeologists concerned with **prehistory**, are searching for answers to fundamental questions about human origins. How can we account for the remarkable biological and cultural diversity of humankind? How did early humans settle the world and develop so many different societies at such different levels of complexity? Why did some societies cultivate the soil and herd cattle while others remained hunter-gatherers? Why did some peoples, such as the San foragers of southern Africa and the Shoshone hunter-gatherers of the Great Basin in North America, live in small family bands, while others, such as the Ancient Egyptians and the Aztecs of Mexico, develop highly elaborate civilizations? When did more complex human societies evolve and why? The answers to these questions are the concern of scientists studying **world prehistory**.

history The study of past human societies using written records.

prehistory The study of past human societies without writing.

prehistorians Individuals who study prehistory.

world prehistory The global study of human prehistory.

The development of today's scientific archaeology accelerated during the twentieth century. Much more refined excavation methods and broad theoretical frameworks using such concepts as cultural evolution and environmental adaptation coincided with a massive expansion of archaeology from a narrow focus on Europe, the Mediterranean, and parts of the Americas into a truly global enterprise. World prehistory came into being as a result of the development of radiocarbon (^{14}C) dating by University of Chicago physicists Willard Libby and J. R. Arnold in 1949 (see Box 10.1 on p. 317). For the first time, archaeologists had at their disposal a method of potential global application that enabled them not only to date sites in all parts of the world, but also to compare the date of the first agriculture in, for example, Southwest Asia with that in the Americas (see Box 10.1).

Today, there are thousands of archaeologists working in all parts of the world, from Australia and the Pacific Islands to China, Siberia, and tropical Africa. The study of prehistory is now a multidisciplinary enterprise that involves not only archaeologists, but also scientists from many other disciplines, including biologists, botanists, geographers, geologists, and zoologists, to mention only a few. Inevitably, today's archaeology is highly specialized, peopled by specialists in all kinds of ancient human societies and ways of studying them (see Box 1.2).

During our careers, we've worked with experts on very early humans, Egyptologists, historical archaeologists, and underwater archaeologists, to mention only a few relatively broad specialties. We've also collaborated with experts on Ancient Egyptian wine, Ice Age earthworms, southern African mice, eighteenth-century colonial American gardens, and World War I trench battle sites. All of these are apart from the many international, plus federal and state government, archaeologists, and private-sector specialists who have crossed our paths.

Many of these specialists are on the front lines of preserving the past for future generations. The material remains of the past are a finite resource. They may be a scatter of 100,000-year-old stone tools, an elaborate Maya ceremonial center of 1,500 years ago, or an architectural masterpiece like the Parthenon in Athens. Once disturbed, whether by agriculture, industrial activity, archaeological excavation, or looting for profit, the archive can never be replaced. This priceless record of the past is under catastrophic threat of destruction unless strenuous efforts are made to preserve it for future generations (see, for example, Figure 1.9). In the United States, thousands of sites are vanishing in the face of looters and industrial development, including plowing and mining. Since the 1960s, numerous federal and state laws have been enacted in the United States to protect sites and

Figure 1.9 An extreme example of site management. The façade of pharaoh Rameses II's temple at **Abu Simbel**, Egypt, after being moved to higher ground before the flooding of Lake Nasser as a result of the building of the Aswan Dam.

Source: Robertharding/Alamy Stock Photo.

artifacts on public lands. Equivalent legislation exists in all countries. In most countries, such protections extend to privately owned land, but not in the United States, where the Constitution defines private ownership differently.

In response, archaeology has changed from being a purely academic discipline into a profession, concerned with field and laboratory research aimed at assessing and preserving the past and mitigating the effects of construction and other activities. Such **cultural resource management (CRM)** is a type of archaeology concerned with the management and assessment of the significance of cultural resources such as archaeological sites. It is now the dominant activity in North American archaeology and in many other countries. In 2020, more than a third of all American archaeologists working for private consulting firms engaged in environmental monitoring and CRM, and the figure is climbing rapidly (see Box 17.1 on p. 533).

cultural resource management (CRM) Conservation and management of archaeological sites and artifacts as a means of protecting the past.

Increasingly, archaeologists are managers rather than professors, supervising a precious and rapidly vanishing resource: the human past. The pith-helmeted professor of yesteryear is the cultural resource manager of today.

Box 1.2 A Short Guide to Archaeologists

Prehistoric archaeologists (*prehistorians*) study human history before the advent of writing, from the earliest human ancestors to the threshold of recorded history. The numerous specialists within prehistoric archaeology include *paleolithic archaeologists*, experts on the culture and artifacts of early humans; they are authorities on stone technology, prehistoric art, and hunter-gatherers. Many prehistorians concentrate on the prehistory of specific regions—such as Africa, Europe, or the Americas—and often specialize even further, for example, by focusing on the American Southwest.

Classical archaeologists study the remains of the classical civilizations of Greece and Rome. While many classical archaeologists concentrate on art and architecture, others are concerned with the same kinds of economic, settlement, and social issues that interest prehistorians.

Biblical archaeologists are experts on a variety of ethnic groups living in what are now the countries of Israel, Lebanon, and Syria. They attempt to link accounts in biblical and Canaanite literature with archaeological data.

Egyptologists, Mayanists, and Assyriologists are among the many specialist archaeologists who work on specific civilizations or time periods. Such specialties require unusual skills, such as knowledge of Egyptian hieroglyphs.

Historical archaeologists work on archaeological sites and problems from periods for which written records exist. They excavate medieval cities such as Winchester and York, in England, or study colonial American settlements, Spanish missions, and nineteenth-century frontier forts in the American West. Many historical archaeologists are concerned mainly with the study of ancient material culture, for artifacts and technology tell us much about the diversity of ancient societies.

Underwater archaeologists study ancient sites and shipwrecks on the seabed and on lake beds and even under the rapids in Minnesota streams where fur traders once capsized and lost canoe loads of trade goods. Underwater archaeology uses diving technology, but its objectives are identical to those of archaeology on land—to reconstruct and interpret past cultures as well as ancient seafaring cultures. A famous example is the Bronze Age shipwreck off Uluburun, in southern Türkiye (see Chapter 5). The ship, wrecked in 1310 B.C., carried a cargo from ten different areas, a reflection of the diversity of trade in the eastern Mediterranean at the time.

Industrial archaeologists study buildings and other structures of the Industrial Revolution such as Victorian factories.

Archaeologists in many of these specialties are engaged in CRM, now the primary approach to archaeological research in North America and many other areas.

Apart from area specialists, there are experts in all manner of archaeological methods, including *paleoethnobotanists*, who study ancient food remains, *lithic technologists*, who are experts on stone technology, and *zooarchaeologists*, who specialize in ancient animal bones. We discuss their specialties in later chapters.

Written records of the past go back about 5,000 years in the Nile Valley and Mesopotamia, the land between the rivers Tigris and Euphrates of present-day Iraq. In archaeological terms, five millennia is merely a blink of an eye. Archaeology is unique because of its time scales. We think in millennia, in hundreds of thousands of years, and only rarely in centuries or smaller units of time. Archaeology is the study of the entire span of the human cultural past. Our archives include anything we left behind, including tools, food remains (whether animal bones or plant remains), human skeletal remains, inscriptions and other written records, art, and temples—the surviving remains of deserted human settlements.

Abu Simbel, Egypt Temple built overlooking the Nile by the pharaoh Rameses II to honor himself and the major deities of Egypt, c. 1240 B.C.

Prehistory and History

Prehistory (see Box 1.3) is what happened in the past, before the advent of literate civilizations. History is the study of the past using written records. The earliest written records, of 5,000 years ago, come from clay tablets in Mesopotamia and hieroglyphic texts on temple walls in Egypt, and later they come from papyrus reed documents. For many centuries, such records were very incomplete, many of them confined to business transactions or religious texts.

Writing came into use far later in many parts of the world, but, generally, is associated with complex, preindustrial civilizations like those of the Sumerians of Mesopotamia and the Egyptians. Written records were widespread in the eastern Mediterranean world by 2000 B.C., also in the Indus Valley of South Asia (though their code remains uncracked), and in China around 1500 B.C. The intricate hieroglyphs of the ancient Maya span about 2,000 years.

Box 1.3 Major Developments in World Prehistory

World prehistory is concerned with the broad sweep of the human past, but more specifically with four major developments (see Table 1.1).

Table 1.1 Major Developments in Human Prehistory

- The human (or hominin) lineage diverged from that of the chimpanzees by 6 million years ago. The oldest known material evidence for human behavior currently dates to around 3.3 million years ago, and is represented by crude stone tools from the site of Lomekwi 3 in Kenya.
- Many different hominin species coexisted in the past. Around 1.9 million years ago, *Homo erectus* (or upright human) emerged in Africa. This is the first hominin to show much more modern human traits, both physically and culturally. *Homo erectus* is thought to be our direct ancestor. The earliest fossil evidence for our species, *Homo sapiens*, is known from Morocco in North Africa and is dated to just before 300,000 years ago. From Africa, *Homo sapiens* moved into other areas and, despite some early "dead-end" ventures, ultimately permanently colonized the world. By 50,000 years ago, we had settled in Australia, and after around 50,000 years ago, we were permanently in Europe, and by 15,000 years ago, we were in the Americas.
- The origins of more complex forager societies and of agriculture and animal domestication, sometimes called food production, after about 12,000 years ago. Why did humans take up farming in the Near East, Europe, Asia, and the Americas?
- The origins of urbanized, literate civilization (state-organized societies) around 3100 B.C. in western Asia and the development of similar, complex societies in other parts of the world in later millennia.

Many parts of the world only acquired written records as recently as the European Age of Discovery after A.D. 1500—in tropical Africa and much of Amazonia as late as the nineteenth century. Historical time scales are much shorter, but often much more precise. Most of them, however, are concerned with the deeds of rulers and ritual beliefs. Only recently have a combination of archaeological excavation and work in historical archives helped document the lives of anonymous, nonliterate workers like farmers or fisherfolk living in the shadows of larger societies.

Before we move on, it is worth noting that to some, the word "prehistory" can evoke negative value judgments, with colonial overtones. Since prehistory begins with the prefix "pre," "before," the word could suggest that all prehistoric societies are on some initial inferior step before they develop into superior societies with full-blown written records. This is not the case. In time, perhaps better terms will evolve, but for now, we use the distinctions of prehistory and history since they are useful to the archaeologist.

There is, of course, an easy way out, for people who love fantasy adventures in their armchairs—what is often called pseudoarchaeology—and with good reason (see Box 1.4).

Box 1.4 Pseudoarchaeology, or You Too Can Be an Indiana Jones

Today's archaeology is slow moving, highly technical, and relies on data from a bewildering array of sources. A twenty-first-century excavation moves less earth in three months than a nineteenth-century excavator like Austen Henry Layard would have shifted in a few days. Yes, we tell a complex, and often fascinating, tale, but it's a far cry from the romantic adventures of Indiana Jones or the stirring dramas of the Mummy movies. Nor do we set out in search of fabled lands such as the Lost Continent of Atlantis or mythical items such as the Holy Grail.

However, in a world of instant gratification, archaeology, which requires infinite patience, is a bore for those who demand a healthy dose of adventure and intrigue in their daily lives. Who cares about the origins of wheat farming, or the finegrained genetic data for the dispersal of different human groups, when "alternative narratives" tell lively stories about super-advanced beings or secret organizations that once ruled the world? Small wonder that some people are enticed by alternative narratives about the past since they usually involve fast-paced, exotic journeys and mysterious, unknown civilizations, whose lavish histories are being suppressed by "the archaeological establishment." Welcome to the world of pseudoarchaeology.

The recipe changes but little over the years, even if outer space and computer models have become part of the story. Take a few intrepid adventurers in an ancient sailing vessel, some startlingly weird religious cult, a handful of pyramids, lots of gold, and exotic civilizations swirling in ever-roiling mists, and you have the irresistible ingredients for an epic "archaeological" tale. Pseudoarchaeologists are a clever bunch for they draw on real archaeology, particularly sites that are yet to be fully explained (or that have been poorly communicated to the general public by the experts)—from which they weave their own fun and fantastical tales. Their stories almost always evoke some higher consciousness, or ultra-advanced lost society, the existence of which the archaeologists (for unclear reasons) are trying to hide. The result can be highly profitable—for the author.

The literary formula, now expanded to TV series and online, is all the rage in a world where many people are fascinated by adventure, escapism, and science fiction. For instance, British journalist Graham Hancock has claimed that a great civilization flourished under Antarctic ice 12,000 years ago. (Of course, its magnificent cities are buried under deep ice sheets, so that—alas—we cannot excavate them.) Colonists spread to all parts of the world from this Antarctic home, colonizing such well-known sites as Tiwanaku in the Bolivian highlands (see Chapter 16) and building the Sphinx by the banks of the Nile. According to Hancock, humans crossed the Pacific and settled in North America some 130,000 years ago. A lost civilization created great monuments and a society with preindustrial technology that was wiped out by a comet at the end of the Ice Age. Lovely stuff for an escapist adventure story, but pure fiction.

Hancock weaves ingenious stories by piecing together all manner of controversial geological observations and isolated archaeological finds. He waves aside the obvious question of where traces of these ancient colonies and civilizations are to be found. Hancock fervently believes in his far-fetched theory. Being a vivid, popular writer, he has managed to piece together numerous best-selling books that read like "whodunits" written by an amateur sleuth. As for archaeologists, he tends to paint them as the enemy: pathetic figures, oppressed by dogma, who suppress the "truths" that he alone is revealing. He and his followers are hot on conspiracy theories in which archaeologists are the villains!

Perhaps the wildest theories of all involve ancient astronauts, who are said to have colonized the Earth from outer space, then founded ancient civilizations. These theories, popularized a generation ago by Swiss author Erich von Däniken in books like his best-selling *Chariots of the Gods*, published in 1968, claimed that Stonehenge and the Pyramids of Egypt were built by extraterrestrial beings. They still linger in the realm of pseudoarchaeology, but are complete scientific nonsense.

Pseudoarchaeology appeals to people who are impatient with the deliberate pace of science and like to believe in "faint possibilities." Some of the "cult archaeologies" show all the symptoms of becoming personality cults, even religious movements. The theories espoused by their leaders become articles of faith, the object of personal conversion. They are attempts to give meaning to being human and are often steeped in symbolism and religious activity.

We could write pages and pages on pseudoarchaeology, all of them at best poor fiction, but there's no point. If you choose to believe such narratives, it's up to you, but they are at best that: fantasies. This book describes the science of archaeology, which, ironically, can be more interesting than the best fantasy tales.

Why Is Archaeology Important?

Cave people, golden pharaohs, and lost civilizations grab the headlines. So do the occasional spectacular discoveries such as the perfectly preserved felt wall hangings from a frozen tomb in Siberia dating to 400 B.C. or the Moche lords of Sipán, Peru, found intact in an adobe platform where they were buried in the first millennium AD with all their gold and silver regalia (see Figure 16.7 on p. 509). Finds like Sipán or Ötzi the Iceman, a Bronze Age traveler of about 3300 B.C. found deep-frozen high in the Italian Alps, are fascinating, even romantic, discoveries (see Figure 5.2 on p. 156). Such scientific treasure troves appeal to the explorer and adventurer in all of us and bring the past to life in dramatic ways. But there are those who declare that archaeology is an expensive luxury in the twenty-first century. They argue that archaeology is irrelevant to contemporary society.

Such arguments are nonsense, for the past surrounds us on every side, offering guidance and precedents, warnings, and sometimes reassurance. We cannot, of course, use the past as a means of forecasting the future. The collapse of the Roman Empire, or of ancient Maya civilization, gives us no clues as to whether today's global civilizations will implode or survive. Archaeologists are not prophets. But they give humanity its past and help show us that we share many behavioral qualities with our diverse ancestors.

Identifying Our Similarities

Archaeology, with its long time perspective, reminds us that we *Homo sapiens* are all closely related, and all part of the same species. It reveals the many ways in which people lived, and what they thought about things in all kinds of ways. But how are such insights useful in today's world of short attention spans and instant gratification? Today, our societies are changing rapidly, so much so that long-term perspectives like those from the past, and long-term planning, appear not to make sense. But harsh reality reminds us that hard-won experience and such planning are the only ways of rising to such pressing challenges as global warming, rising population densities, ever-larger cities, and the expanding economic and social chasms between rich and poor.

Archaeology has the power to provide real insights into human behavior—in terms of not only our cultural diversity but also our fundamental similarities. While our societies certainly varied over time and space, we *Homo sapiens* are one species, all of us with the same analytical and cultural potential. In other words, if a certain group "failed" to do something (e.g., settle down and farm), it was simply that their world order did not require it, rather than because they were mentally inferior (as was once widely assumed).

Time and again, archaeology demonstrates our unity, if only by showing that each area of the world had many ways of doing things over time and space. This is of great relevance to the success of our increasingly globalized world whose success depends on us all coming together in work and life. Who you know and interconnectivity are essential for sparking new ideas. Of course, we now live in a world of bordered nation states, in which leaders wish to curtail movement and build walls to keep others out. The past tells us this is not the path to human innovation.

Identifying Our Diversity

Archaeology's unique ability lies in its capacity to reach back over the millennia, to reconstruct and explain the cultures and lifeways of ancient societies as they changed over many centuries and thousands of years. Why did some societies vanish without a trace while others developed agriculture or highly complex urban civilizations? Who first tamed fire or invented the plow? How did bronze and iron smelting change the course of human history? Archaeology enables us to study not only remote human origins, but also the ever-changing biological and cultural diversity of humankind.

We live in a complex world of almost bewildering human diversity. We can land people on the Moon, send space probes to Mars, determine our position within centimeters in the midst of a tropical rain forest, and build computers of mind-numbing speed and complexity. Yet, our collective understanding of human diversity and our ability to collaborate with others from different cultural backgrounds and cultural heritages remain at an elementary level. We tend to fear diversity—people who are different from us, who speak alien languages, or who look at the world with cultural perspectives that differ from our own. We fear diversity because of apprehension, sometimes bigotry, but all too often just plain ignorance. Archaeology is one of the major educational weapons in the fight against such ignorance.

The most important lesson about diversity that archaeology teaches us is that we are all descended from what Harvard University biologist Stephen J. Gould once called "a common African twig." Thanks to DNA studies and archaeological finds, we know that our own direct ancestors, *Homo sapiens*, originated in Africa and then spread out to the rest of the world, replacing other, older human species. Most important of all, both archaeology and DNA have shown that the relationships among all modern humans are closer than they are distant. Above all, we are all humans with identical abilities to conceptualize and shape our world, to make inventions, to love and hate, and to adapt to any environment on Earth. We just happen to do these things in different ways.

Archaeology studies diversity at its very beginnings, long before our intermingled industrial world was changed forever by the massive population movements of the nineteenth and twentieth centuries. We seek answers to fundamental questions. What makes us human? How did our societies develop? In what ways are today's societies similar or different, and why? What prompted some of us to permanently leave our African homeland and colonize the world roughly 50,000 years ago? This complex set of population movements and cultural changes was perhaps the seminal development of early human history. From it stemmed not only the brilliant biological and cultural diversity of modern humankind, but also art and religious life, agriculture and animal domestication, village life and urban civilization—the very roots of our own diverse and complex world.

Our job as archaeologists is to foster humanity's understanding of itself on a global scale. This is a far more important task than merely finding pharaohs and gold-laden burials—or invariably fictional lost civilizations.

Exploring Big Issues

Archaeology works to support arguments and solutions for big global issues, such as the ways in which humans have caused climate change, the history of social inequality, and uncovering unwritten history.

Climate Change

These days, no one, except committed ideologues, believes that climate shifts in our warming world are simply natural cycles, similar to those that have unfolded over millions of years. We live in a world that has ventured into uncharted climatic waters, where humans with our fossil fuels and environmental disruptions are the dominant agents. Thanks to the revolution in paleoclimatology, we now know a great deal about climatic shifts since the end of the Ice Age 15,000 years ago, and more every day about the climatic background to human existence over the past 6 million years. Today's multidisciplinary, team-based archaeology is a weapon in the debates about climate change, past and future.

A large number of archaeologists are now assessing the impacts of long- and short-term climatic change on human societies ranging from small bands to entire preindustrial cities. As the pace of research accelerates, we're acquiring a much more sophisticated understanding of climate as a significant player in major developments such as the first settlement of the Americas and the origins of agriculture. Above all, we're gaining insights into how different societies adapted to drought cycles, sea level rises, and such events as El Niños. We've discovered, for example, just how important ties of kin and links between ancient small-scale societies, even city neighborhoods, could be when hurricanes descended or flooding menaced farming villages. The same ties, often overlooked, are powerful tools for those surviving the major disasters of today, especially in poverty-stricken areas—and in an era of more frequent extreme weather events.

Social Inequality

Social inequality has a long history. The first preindustrial civilizations appeared around 5,000 years ago. All of them, as far as we can discern, depended on strongly centralized economic, political, and social organization, where the commoners labored to support a much smaller number of nobles, high officials, priests, and, at the pinnacle, a ruler who was often careful to claim some form of connection with the gods. Thousands of anonymous workers and vast amounts of animal power sustained them. In contemporary parlance, these were societies with haves and have-nots. Social inequality has been part of human society for a very long time and comes in many guises. Archaeology offers a unique perspective into how power relationships arise and change over time. Many complex societies promoted ideologies of divine rulership, for example, the demi-god Roman emperors, or the semi-divine pharaohs of Egypt, whose authority was that of the gods, so they had to be followed.

There's also the issue of social diversity. We tend to think of the past in simplistic terms, which means that we assume that more recent societies were much less socially diverse than they actually were. Ancient Rome was a remarkably cosmopolitan city. So were Teotihuacán and the Aztec Tenochtitlán in pre-Columbian highland Central America (see Figures 15.13 on p. 482 and 15.17 on p. 488). Here, again, archaeology excels, for our excavations yield a great deal of the commonplace and anonymous—the artifacts of slaves' quarters in Colonial America, Chinese laborers' encampments in the High Sierra of California, earthquake victims in a Roman town in Cyprus. Like the harshly treated laborers at pharaoh Akhenaten's capital by the Nile, they lived their lives in anonymity (see Box 1.5). Their only voices are their bodies, their artifacts, and sometimes whispers of the intangible in ritual objects and **oral traditions**.

oral traditions Historical data transmitted from one generation to the next by word of mouth.

Unfortunately, studying ancient diversity and inequality is very challenging, even with the increasingly vast data sets that archaeologists are gathering. Grave furniture has been used as a measure of wealth, which is obvious enough if you compare the tomb of Tutankhamun or a Lord of Sipán with the unadorned graves of commoners. There are other indicators, also, that separate the privileged from humble commoners, whether free or enslaved. Biological clues abound on the skeletons of people who engaged in manual labor, be it carrying building stone or grinding grain on one's knees. Bone health reflects nutrition; pathological conditions are barometers of years of harsh labor, witness the commoners interred in the cemeteries at the royal capital of the pharaoh Akhenaten at **El-Amarna** in Upper Egypt (see Box 1.5).

El-Amarna, Egypt Capital of the pharaoh Akhenaten, c. 1348 B.C.; occupied for only 17 years.

Box 1.5 Akhenaten's Laborers

The Egyptian pharaoh Akhenaten (1350–1334 B.C.) developed an obsession with the worship of Aten, the solar disk. He founded his own capital, Akhetaten, now known as El-Amarna, downstream of the traditional religious center at Thebes. There, he commissioned an imposing capital, dominated by an elaborate temple to Aten. Perhaps 10 percent of the 15,000–20,000 people who lived in the capital were privileged, lived in fine houses, and were buried in well-decorated tombs.

Meanwhile, an army of laborers worked on the growing city. Anonymous folk, they perished in large numbers. Many were buried in tightly packed cemeteries in what is called the South Tombs site. More than two hundred graves tell a sobering tale of backbreaking work and disease. Most of the dead were buried in rolled up mats with no decoration or grave goods. The skeletons of those between ages 3 and 25 display telltale signs of rickets, developed from a lack of vitamin D, which softens the bones of children, and scurvy. Many of the children's teeth are grooved, another clear sign of malnutrition. Those older than about eight-and-a-half years were seriously stunted, probably because of inadequate nutrition. Their bones display signs of constant muscle use, as if they were engaged in constant physical labor. The adults fared no better.

About three-quarters of adult skeletons displayed signs of arthritis in the limbs or spine, the result of very hard labor. Fractures and compressed vertebrae were commonplace, with no fewer than 67 percent of them showing signs of healing or healed fractures. These were people engaged in lifting and balancing heavy loads. The stone buildings at Amarna were constructed of standardized building blocks known as *talatats*, each weighing about 70 kilograms (155 pounds), apparently considered a suitable weight for a worker to carry. There is one inscription that shows a man balancing such a block on his shoulders. The researchers believe that such loads contributed to the high incidence of arthritis.

Figure 1.10 Happy harvesters. Workers harvesting grapes and making wine on the estate of Nakht, a prominent priest and scribe, c. 1380 B.C. A misleading portrait of reality.

Source: Heritage Image Partnership Ltd/Alamy.

Unlike modern cities, hardworking commoners were the infrastructure of Akhenaten's capital. Those in the South Tombs cemetery were apparently buried separately from their families and may have been brought to the city as forced labor. If they were, the move was effectively a death sentence at a young age. Nobles' tombs depict idyllic scenes of life on their estates, but behind them was a very different world (see Figure 1.10). The young age profile of the Akhetaten cemetery is both a striking barometer of social inequality and a reminder of the harsh realities that lay behind Ancient Egyptian life.

Writing Unwritten History

Archaeology has written vast chapters of history for societies all over the world, whose past was previously unwritten. With trowels, spades, radar, and more, it is recovering much of early sub-Saharan African history, developing and exploring new chapters of the Chinese past, and uncovering the colonization of Polynesia. Most importantly of all, it peers into bygone times that were not all statesmen and generals, palaces and royal achievements. It also gives us all a past that predates writing. In countries such as Britain, this means anything before the Romans (a "mere" 2,000 years ago—a drop in the ocean of archaeology's time). Meanwhile, for those settled in countries with no pre-colonial written history, it gives, at least in general terms, a historical identity.

But there are complications. To the archaeologist, the past is scientific data to be studied with all the rigor of modern science. To many indigenous peoples, the past is highly personalized and the property of the ancestors. Such perspectives are valid alternative versions of history that deserve respect and understanding, for they play a vital role in the creation and reaffirmation of cultural identity. Their perspectives on their forebears are based on oral histories, information passed from one generation to the next by word of mouth.

Furthermore, many non-Western societies do not perceive themselves as living in a changeless world. They make a fundamental distinction between the recent past, which lies within living memory, and the more remote past, which came before that. For instance, the Australian Aboriginal groups living in northeastern Queensland distinguish among *kuma*, the span of events witnessed by living people, *anthantnama*, a long time ago, and *yilamu*, the period of the Creation. Furthermore, many societies accept that there was cultural change in the past. In India, Hindu traditions of history speak of early people who lived without domesticated animals and plants.

Oral Traditions

Human histories take many forms, some with mythic creators of culture, usually primordial ancestors, deities, or animals establishing contemporary social customs and the familiar landscape; others with a more remote, discontinuous heroic era such as that of the Greeks, which allowed such writers as the playwright Aeschylus to evaluate contemporary behavior. Most human societies of the past were nonliterate, which means that they transmitted knowledge and history orally, by word of mouth. The Aztec oral histories, partially set down after the Spanish conquest in the sixteenth century A.D., are an excellent example. They were recited according to a well-defined narrative plot. This focused on great men, key events such as the dedication of the Sun God Huitzilopochtli's temple in the Aztec capital in 1487, and the histories of favored groups.

In these, as in other oral histories, the themes formed the central ingredients of a story and varied considerably from one speaker to the next, even if the essential content was the same. Many oral histories are mixtures of factual data and parables that communicate moral and political values. But to those who hear them, they are publicly sanctioned history, performed before a group and subject to the critical evaluation of an audience who may have heard the same stories before.

Oral traditions are hard to use scientifically, as their antiquity is difficult to establish. In some cases, there are instances of oral histories and archaeology coinciding in general terms. In Australia, for example, the traditions speak of the arrival of the first people from overseas, of flooding of coastal areas after the Ice Age, and of the hunting of giant marsupials (pouched animals like the kangaroo). So Australia's past can be said to come from two sources: archaeological data and oral traditions. In some instances, the archaeologists and indigenous people have shared interests and come together to identify sacred and historic places, often to ensure their preservation, even if the two groups disagree on the significance of a particular location (for instance, a site with no buildings or artifacts that the local people nevertheless consider sacred).

North American archaeologists are making efforts to work closely with Native American communities and tribes in attempts to reconcile differences between their findings and oral traditions. This requires highly sophisticated research that depends heavily on mutual respect between archaeologists and the communities they are studying. Some of the most forward-thinking work is being carried out in the Southwest (see Box 1.6).

We should never forget that alternative, and often compelling, accounts of ancient times exist. They play an important role in helping minority groups and others maintain their traditional heritage as it existed before the arrival of the Westerner.

Box 1.6 Journeys to the "Middle Place"

The Zuni people of the American Southwest have occupied their homeland for over a thousand years. They reside in a cultural landscape with places named by them to symbolize and recall the remote past. This past is projected into the contemporary world by defining and understanding the landscape.

The Zuni have a rich body of well-recorded oral tradition, including their "from the beginning talks," which describe their emergence and subsequent migration to Zuni Pueblo, the "Middle Place." *Telapnawe*, folktales or legends, are often recited to teach the young. Among them are "prayer talks," which are chants or prayers recited during ceremonies. They are often repetitions of fixed formulae performed with gestures and oral elaborations. Many such talks begin with the emergence from the lower world and the search for the Middle Place. Older men use various narratives to pass on the main outlines of Zuni history to the young in kivas on occasions such as the winter solstice. Other accounts are shared within families around the hearth during the winter.

From these spoken sources comes a summary that begins with the Zuni people emerging from the underworld at a place named Chimik'yana'kya dey'a, deep in a canyon along the Colorado River. Divine instruction taught them all manner of prayers, rituals, and sacred talks before their emergence. Once in the world, and guided by their religious societies, they migrated to what is now the Little Colorado River. Along the way, they stopped and occupied villages for "four days and four nights," a symbolic expression of a longer, unspecified time. At one of the springs

Figure 1.11 Zuni Pueblo, c. 1900.
Source: Niday Picture Library/Alamy.

on their journey, they assumed the appearance of humans. In the Lower Colorado River valley, the people were given a choice of colored eggs that led to them splitting into several groups. Those who chose bright blue ones split into several groups, the largest of which eventually settled at Halona Itiwana, the Middle Place, now Zuni Pueblo (Figure 1.11).

Research is ongoing to identify the places mentioned in the oral traditions, both the place of emergence and the various locations where the migrants paused and founded villages, also areas of symbolic and ritual importance. But can one take these historical accounts unduly literally? As Zuni interpreters of the oral traditions point out, the routes mentioned in chants and prayers do not describe exact routes. They tell us that ancestors of the modern-day Zuni traveled over a wide area of the Southwest, some of it outside the present homeland. The challenge for archaeologists, and for Zuni historians, is to reconcile different histories of the ancestors.

Experiencing the Past

The monuments of antiquity cast an irresistible spell. The jetliner and the package tour have made archaeological tourism big business. Package tours can take you to Egypt, to the Parthenon (see Figure 1.12), to the great city of **Teotihuacán**, Mexico (see Figure 3.8 on p. 83), and the stupendous ruins of **Angkor Wat** in Cambodia (see Box 13.2 on p. 428). The Great Pyramids of **Giza** in Egypt (see Figure 3.3 on p. 75), the ruins at the Maya city of **Tikal** bathed in the full Moon's light—as sights alone, they overwhelm the senses.

Figure 1.12 The Parthenon on the Acropolis at Athens, Greece.
Source: Medioimages/Photodisc/Thinkstock.

Some years ago, we traveled to the great classical amphitheater at **Epidauros**, Greece, on a spring evening as the setting sun turned the world a pale pink (see chapter opener on p. 3). As we sat high above the stage, a small group of German tourists gathered around their learned guide. He sent them to the stall seats, stood at center, and recited evocative stanzas from Euripides' play Ion. The ancient verses rolled and resonated through the still air. For a moment, we shut our eyes and imagined the theater crowded with a festive audience, incense wafting on the spring air, the stanzas gripping everyone's attention with electric tension, then pathos ... The guide's voice ceased. A deep silence fell, and the magic of Epidauros's acoustics faded.

Visiting ancient sites can be a deeply moving experience—the north wind blowing across **Hadrian's Wall** in northern England on a winter's day with a promise of snow, or a humid afternoon at **Moundville**, Alabama, when the air stands still and the thatched huts and imposing mounds of A.D. 1300 come alive in your mind with fresh color, with the smell of wood smoke, the cries of children, and the barking of dogs.

Teotihuacán, Mexico Major city in the Valley of Mexico that flourished from about 200 B.C. to A.D. 750.

Angkor Wat, Cambodia Royal capital and shrine built by the Khmer rulers of Cambodia between A.D. 1000 and 1200.

Giza, Egypt Major pyramid site of Old Kingdom Egypt, dating to c. 2600 B.C.

Tikal, Guatemala Classic Maya city that reached the height of its power in A.D. 200 to 600.

Epidauros, Greece Small Classical state, famous for its theater, dating to the fourth century B.C. and later.

Hadrian's Wall, England Frontier wall and forts across northern England built by the Roman emperor Hadrian to keep out Picts from the north in A.D. 122 to 130.

Moundville, Alabama Major Mississippian town and ceremonial center after A.D. 900.

You can get the same emotional connection the first time you see Tutankhamun's golden mask or a giant **Olmec** head with a snarling face from lowland Mexico (see Figure 15.2 on p. 467). Both lift you to a realm where achievement endures and perceptions seem of a higher order. Even humble artifacts such as a stone chopper or a finely made clay pot can evoke emotions of wonder and insight. A 2-million-year-old stone chopper whose flake scars reveal its maker was left-handed, a medieval pot shard marked by an errant child's thumb print, a rejected Roman roof tile spoilt by a dog's footprint: these are the whispers from the past that bond us with times long gone. These are the moments when the people of the past reach out to us, reminding us of our shared humanity. Whether amusing, comforting, encouraging, or upsetting, they offer precedent for human existence.

It's no coincidence that cultural tourism, which includes archaeological sites, is the fastest growing segment of global tourism.

Olmec Lowland Mesoamerican art style and series of cultures that formed one of the foundations of later civilizations in the region, c. 1500 to 500 B.C.

Who Needs the Past?

All societies have an interest in their past. It is always around them, haunting, mystifying, tantalizing, sometimes offering potential lessons for the present and future. The past is important because social life unfolds through time, embedded within a framework of cultural expectations and values. In the high Arctic, Inuit preserve their traditional attitudes, skills, and coping mechanisms in one of the harshest environments on Earth. They do this by incorporating the lessons of the past into the present. In many societies, the ancestors are the guardians of the land, which symbolizes present, past, and future.

Westerners have an intense scientific interest in the past, born partly of curiosity but also out of a need for historical identity. There are many reasons to attempt to preserve an accurate record of former times. None of us, least of all archaeologists, should assume that we are uniquely privileged in our interest. We have no monopoly on history (see Figures 1.13 and 1.14).

Figure 1.13 A bronze plaque from **Benin**, Nigeria, West Africa, showing a seated *oba* (king) with his attendants. These artifacts served as important historical records of royal reigns and genealogy and were stored in the royal palace.

Source: Adam Eastland/Alamy Stock Photo.

Figure 1.14 Ancient Maya history. Two monkey scribes sit on either side of a thick screen-fold book, discussing a page they have opened. The scribe on the left holds a writing instrument in his hand.

Source: Adam Eastland/Alamy Stock Photo.

Archaeology as a Political Tool

The past is often considered a political tool. Since civilization began, rulers and governments have always used it to justify the present. The Sumerians, who established the world's first urban civilization between the Euphrates and Tigris Rivers in southern Iraq, created a heroic past in the Epic of Gilgamesh, which was about a legendary ruler who reigned in the time before a mythic flood that frightened even the gods. When the flood waters subsided, the gods restored kingship to Earth at the city of **Kish**, where recorded history began.

The past has always served the present, for every society manufactures history. The Aztecs of highland Mexico were an obscure farming society in A.D. 1200. Only three centuries later, from a dazzling capital, **Tenochtitlán**, in the Valley of Mexico, they ruled over all of **Mesoamerica** (see Figure 15.17 on p. 488). In 1426, a powerful official named Tlacaelel became the right-hand man to a series of fifteenth-century Aztec rulers in highland Mexico. He prevailed upon his masters to burn all earlier historical records of other cities in the valley. In the place of these records, he concocted a convincing rags-to-riches story that recounted the Aztecs' mercurial rise from obscurity to the masters of Mexico, the chosen people of Huitzilopochtli, the Sun God himself. The new history was blatant political propaganda that justified a century of militant imperialism that made the Aztecs the rulers of a vast empire.

Kish, Iraq Early Sumerian city-state of about 2800 B.C. and later.

Tenochtitlán, Mexico Capital of the Aztec civilization from c. A.D. 1325 to 1521, estimated to have had a maximum population of about 250,000 people.

Mesoamerica The area of the Central American highlands and lowlands where state-organized societies (civilizations) developed.

An Objective Past?

Can we look at the past with entirely objective eyes? While archaeologists strive for empiricism, we all bring our individual cultural biases to the interpretation of history and archaeology, for we tend to look at ancient developments and events through the blinkered eyes of our own value system and society. Thus, any archaeological assessment of former times is a type of narrative that by the nature of its evidence is both a scientific and a political and literary enterprise. As part of this enterprise, **archaeological theory** aims to explain the past as well as describe it. Archaeology is peculiarly vulnerable to political misuse because it deals with ancient societies and events that are little known, even from archaeological sources.

archaeological theory A body of theoretical concepts providing both a framework and a means for archaeologists to look beyond the facts and material objects for explanations of events that took place in prehistory (see Chapter 7).

Most people who use the past for nationalistic or political ends are searching for a glorious past, a simple story that justifies their own political agenda. Before World War II, the Nazis unashamedly used archaeology to propagate notions of a pure "Nordic" race in ancient Europe. In the Balkans, the past has become a prize in endless political squabbles that span centuries. People manufacture a glorious past to sway public opinion, for the ownership of a real or imagined history and its monuments is a vital political resource. Such archaeologies, at best, stretch historical facts to the breaking point and promote bigotry, nationalism, and chicanery. Often, they resemble pseudoarchaeology at its worst.

Archaeology and Economic Development

One night, bone-chilling cold descended on the high plains around Lake Titicaca, Bolivia. White frost covered the dry hillsides where local farmers had planted their potatoes in thin soil. Many families watched all night as their growing potato plants withered and turned brown before their eyes. As dawn spread, they wandered through their ruined fields, glancing down at a thin white blanket of warm air covering some experimental plots on the plain below. They had watched suspiciously as archaeologists had dug across long-abandoned ancient fields in the lowlands, then had given one of their neighbors seed potatoes to plant in a replica of such a field. He had piled up layers of gravel, clay, and soil, and then had dug shallow irrigation canals alongside the raised fields. The green shoots of the new potatoes grew far higher than those on the arid slopes. As the temperature dropped below freezing, a white cloud of warm air formed above the raised fields, hiding them from view. Now the warming sun dispersed the white blanket, revealing lush, green potato plants, their leaves only slightly browned by frost.

After months of ground survey, excavation, and controlled farming experiments, archaeologists had rediscovered the forgotten genius of highland Andean farmers for the benefit of their descendants. The ancestors had used water to protect their crops against frost with such success that they supported the nearby city of Tiwanaku and its powerful kingdom for more than five centuries (see Figure 16.12 on p. 514). Today, more than 1,500 modern farmers have rediscovered the benefits of raised fields. Dozens of nearby communities clamor for training in ancient agriculture. Archaeology shows that the traditional system has many advantages—high crop yields, no need for fertilizer, and far less risk of frost or flood damage. Furthermore, high yields can be obtained with local labor and no expensive outside capital. At last count, nearly 860 hectares (2,125 acres) have been rehabilitated, and many more fields are planned.

The Lake Titicaca raised-field experiments have been so successful that archaeologists are now actively involved in several other such projects in the Americas, including the Amazon River Basin. Governments are now slowly discovering something that archaeologists have known for a long time. The ancients knew their environments intimately and exploited them efficiently without expensive technology.

Industrial-scale agriculture is not the universal answer to the world's food crisis, but studying ancient garbage disposal tells us much about economic life (see Box 1.7).

Community Archaeology and Stakeholders

All of us are stakeholders in the past, whether we live in a small Chinese village, on the Mongolian steppes, in New York, or on a Pacific island. Archaeologists are, of course, stakeholders, too, using scientific data to reconstruct ancient times with all the rigor of modern science. But so are the landowners where the sites lie, direct descendants of the former occupants of a prehistoric village, and local communities, also the broader cultural

Box 1.7 Garbology, or You Are What You Throw Away

Modern garbage offers insights into the more remote past. University of Arizona archaeologist William Rathje applied archaeological methods to the long-term study of modern garbage dumps in Tucson, Arizona, and other American cities. He found that bags of household garbage never lie. For example, empty beer cans and liquor bottles are more eloquent testimony to a family's drinking habits than any filled-out questionnaire that denies heavy alcohol consumption. Rathje's long-term research revealed fascinating differences between the wasteful discard habits of many lower-income families and the more careful consumption of leftovers by the wealthy.

Garbology (the term was coined by the writer and activist A. J. Weberman when he went through singer Bob Dylan's trash in 1971) is now widely used by local governments and commercial companies to study waste management at a time when the average U.S. citizen produces about 102 tons of garbage in their lifetime. The floating mass of plastic trash in the Pacific Ocean is also being studied for the same purpose. It is very easy to trivialize such research as being of more use to advertising executives than to archaeologists, but "garbology" has much to tell us about the discard habits of both ancient cultures and modern industrial society.

Benin, Nigeria West African forest kingdom, with a capital of the same name, which flourished from at least the fourteenth century A.D. until recent times.

groups of which they are part. All these stakeholders may have valid alternative versions of history that deserve respect and understanding, for they play a vital role in the creation and reaffirmation of cultural identity.

To local people, the past is often highly personalized and the property of the ancestors. There are also major issues over the excavation and reinterment of ancestral burials. Such questions raise fundamental questions such as those that lie behind many Native American objections to archaeological research. What do archaeologists have to offer a cultural group that already has a valid version of its own history? Why should archaeologists be permitted to dig up the burial sites of the ancestors or settlements and sacred places under the guise of studying what is, to the people, a known history? These are questions that archaeologists have barely begun to address.

These days, many fieldworkers are becoming closely involved in the communities where they work. Such community archaeology projects are based on collaboration with local stakeholders interested in preserving their cultural heritage for future generations. Preserving the past is an international, national, and local issue. People intimately involved in conservation and educating people about archaeology can be professional archaeologists or individuals from all walks of life. In recent years, much of the focus has been on local issues and stakeholders, whose active involvement in preservation issues affects what happens to archaeological finds, everything from saving threatened sites to ensuring that artifacts go to museums instead of private pockets.

Since 1973, the city of Alexandria, Virginia, close to Washington DC, has fostered an active archaeology program, where the city's archaeologists, volunteers, and students work closely with residents and developers to study and manage sites unearthed within the city boundaries. These include ships sunk along the old waterfront and the Lee Street site, which is the focus of the Alexandria Archaeology Museum. Local archaeologists uncovered a bakery, taverns, and residences that lay alongside the bustling waterfront. The same block became a hospital support facility for the Union Army during the American Civil War. This long-term program and museum opened up the city and the region's 13,000-year-old history to locals and visitors alike.

Much community archaeology develops on a much smaller scale, especially projects that work closely with small groups of stakeholders, who have deep roots in their region. A private organization, the Archaeological Conservancy, acquires and protects archaeological sites in the United States, working closely with local stakeholders. The Conservancy recently took over ownership of Amity Pueblo in the upper Little Colorado region of northeastern Arizona. This is an intensely significant ancestral village for the modern-day pueblo of Zuni, a rubble mound that may contain as many as 60 rooms. The pueblo lies in an area that connects Zuni Pueblo and its inhabitants with the people's traditional place of origin in the Grand Canyon. The action, taken in collaboration with federal and state agencies, the tribes, and the Arizona State Museum, among others, comes after years of neglect and destruction at the edge of the site. The Conservancy plans to develop a long-term management plan, consulting tribes, local property owners, and government agencies, which will include both monitoring the site and providing access to the land for the tribes, who regard this as a sacred place.

Summary

- Archaeology began over 150 years ago as a search for lost civilizations and artifacts. Since then, it has developed into a sophisticated, multidisciplinary way of studying past human behavior, using the material remains of the past.
- Archaeology is a unique way of studying culture change over long periods of time. It has an important role to play in the modern world, for it teaches important lessons about human diversity and gives us an appreciation of the common cultural heritage of humankind.
- Prehistoric archaeology is the study of prehistory, the period of the human past before the advent of written records.
- The study of world prehistory, which developed in the 1950s, is the study of human prehistory from a global perspective using archaeological data and other sources.
- All human societies are interested in the past, but they think of it in different ways and use it for different purposes. Archaeologists, Westerners generally, conceive of time in a linear way, while many traditional non-Western groups measure time by the cycles of the seasons and the movements of heavenly bodies. They use linear time only when it is of relevance to them.
- Archaeology is not the only way of approaching history, for many societies have oral histories, alternative perspectives on the past that are of vital importance in preserving traditional culture and values.
- Many stakeholders have a profound interest in the past and its preservation. Working closely with local communities has become an important part of archaeology.

Key Terms and Sites

Pompeii
Khorsabad
Nineveh
Nimrud
Copán

Palenque
Uxmal
Minoan civilization
Ur
archaeology
history
prehistory
prehistorians
world prehistory
Abu Simbel
paleoanthropologists
classical archaeologists
historical archaeologists
underwater archaeologists
cultural resource management (CRM)
oral traditions
El-Amarna
Teotihuacán
Angkor Wat
Giza
Tikal
Epidauros
Hadrian's Wall
Moundville
Olmec
Kish
Tenochtitlán
Mesoamerica
archaeological theory
Benin

Critical-Thinking Questions

1. Why is archaeology important in today's world? Is it because of the lure of exciting discovery, or is it significant to society for other reasons?
2. Do you think that scientific approaches to the study of the remote past are the only viable interpretations of early humanity? What other sources of information are available? Are they reliable?
3. Why is scientific archaeology more fascinating than pseudoarchaeology, with its talk of mysteries and lost civilizations? What are the differences in approaches between the two schools of thought?
4. What is the importance of community archaeology?

Further Reading

Several major college texts provide a comprehensive background on the method and theory of prehistoric archaeology. This text is a much-shortened version of N. Durrani and B. Fagan, *In the Beginning*, 15th ed. (Oxford: Routledge, 2025). The most comprehensive survey of archaeological methods available is C. Renfrew, P. Bahn, and E. DeMarrais, *Archaeology: Theories, Methods, and Practice*, 9th ed. (New York: Thames and Hudson, 2024). P. Bahn, ed., *The History of Archaeology:*

An Introduction (Oxford: Routledge, 2014) is a global history by experts. N. Durrani and B. Fagan *A Brief History of Archaeology*, 3rd ed. (Oxford: Routledge, 2021), is just that, for beginning students. B. Trigger's *A History of Archaeological Thought*, 2nd ed. (Cambridge: Cambridge University Press, 2006) is the definitive work on the subject. Indigenous archaeologies are discussed in J. Watkins, *Indigenous Archaeology: American Indian Values and Scientific Practice* (Walnut Creek, CA: AltaMira Press, 2001). See also M. Bruhac et al., eds., *Indigenous Archaeologies: A Reader in Decolonization* (Oxford: Routledge, 2016). For the role of archaeology in today's world, see L. Derry and M. Malloy, *Archaeologists and Local Communities: Partners in Exploring the Past* (Washington, DC: Society for American Archaeology, 2003); while B. Fagan and N. Durrani, *Bigger Than History: Why Archaeology Matters* (London: Thames and Hudson, 2019) surveys ongoing debates on this subject.

2 The Record of the Past

Chapter Outline

DOI: 10.4324/9781003592754-3

The Egyptian pharaoh Seti (c. 1280 B.C.) presents an offering to the god Horus.
Source: BasPhoto/Thinkstock.

Nine thousand years ago, a large village at **Çatalhöyük** in south-central Türkiye prospered off trade in volcanic glass, bartered over a wide area. The village grew into a crowded town covering 13 hectares (32 acres). As the population grew, the inhabitants intensified their farming of wheat, barley, and rye, and goat and sheep herding. A research team led by Clark Larsen of Ohio State University analyzed chemical signatures in burials, called stable carbon isotope ratios. They showed a diet heavy in grains and lower in animal proteins. The result was tooth decay, often called a "disease of civilization." Between 10 and 13 percent of dead adults' teeth displayed dental cavities.

As the community became more crowded, people had to work fields and use grazing grounds ever further from their home. This meant a great deal more walking, revealed by changes in the cross-sections of leg bones.

Everyone lived in crowded houses entered through their roofs. Trash pits and animal pens lay close to the dwellings. About a third of the dead showed signs of infections on their bones. Analysis of house walls and floors showed traces of animal and human fecal matter. The lack of sanitation must have contributed to the risk of infection.

Houses were crowded, so violence was commonplace. In a sample of 93 skulls, more than half were women, struck from behind on their heads. Twelve victims had been injured more than once, up to five times.

Çatalhöyük, one of the earliest towns, faced challenges such as infection and violence that are commonplace in today's cities. Working closely with biological anthropologists, archaeologists can peer into the lives of people in a troubled community.

Çatalhöyük, Türkiye Early farming town that prospered from the obsidian trade between about 7000 and 5000 B.C.

This chapter describes the goals of archaeology and the basic processes of archaeological research that lead to remarkable studies like that at Çatalhöyük and to the writing of the prehistory described in these pages. The chapter also defines the so-called archaeological record and discusses the all-important issue of archaeological context in time and space.

The Goals of Archaeology

The archaeologist has one primary and overriding priority: to preserve and conserve the material remains of the past for future generations. Archaeological sites and their contents are a unique record of our forebears in every part of the world. Unlike trees, this archive of the past, the archaeological record, is finite. Once disturbed or excavated, the record is gone forever. Conserving this priceless asset is our greatest responsibility to the past, whether we are professional archaeologists or laypeople.

(Ethics is all-important in archaeology. This is the first in a series of ethical statements in this chapter, all of which are set in italics.)

All archaeological research has three important goals, each of which builds on the others.

Constructing Culture History

culture history Descriptions of human cultures derived from archaeological evidence.

Culture history is an approach to archaeology that assumes that artifacts can be used to build up generalized pictures of human culture in time and space and that these can be interpreted. Culture history is the record of the human past described and classified in a context of time and space across the changing ancient landscape (see Box 2.1). In other words, it answers the fundamental question: What happened, where, and when?

Culture history relies on careful excavation, detailed classifications of finds of all kinds, and accurate sequences of human cultures defined through time and by spatial

Box 2.1 Discovery
The Folsom Bison Kill Site, New Mexico

One morning in August 1908, after a terrible flood that had killed 18 people, the African-American cowboy George McJunkin (1856–1922) rode slowly along the edge of a gully near the small town of **Folsom**, New Mexico. Stopping to attend to a damaged fence, he noticed some unusual bones projecting from the newly eroded soil. McJunkin pried at bones with his knife. A sharp stone fragment came loose in his hands, somewhat like the stone spear points he had seen lying on the ground on the ranch. The bones were much larger than those of a modern cow. McJunkin puzzled over his discovery and, recognizing the significance of the site, tried to interest archaeologists over the years, albeit with little success.

In 1925, a few years after his death, the material finally came to the attention of Jesse Figgins, director of the Colorado Museum of Natural History and one of the few paleontologists in the West. He identified the bones as those of a long-extinct bison that had roamed the plains at the end of the Ice Age. But the stone point was another matter. Was it associated with the extinct bison or a much later time? In 1926, Figgins dug into the Folsom arroyo and recovered more bison bones and stone tools, including a spear point directly associated with bison fragments (see Figure 2.1). He cut out the associated point and bone in a lump of soil to show his colleagues, but they were skeptical.

Figure 2.1 A Paleo-Indian Folsom projectile point from Folsom, New Mexico, lying next to two ribs of an extinct bison. This find proved that humans were contemporary with extinct animals in the Americas.

Few experts believed that people had lived in the Americas for more than a few thousand years. Figgins returned to Folsom a year later, inviting several colleagues to observe his excavations. Archaeologist Frank Roberts arrived just as Figgins was brushing the soil away from a projectile point still embedded between two ribs of a bison skeleton. He realized that this was a definitive proof of Native Americans living in North America perhaps as early as 10,000 years ago.

distribution. Until the 1950s, culture history dominated archaeological research. For example, during the 1930s, teams of archaeologists surveyed major river valleys in the southeastern United States in advance of dam construction. They found hundreds of archaeological sites, which they dated using sequences of stone tool and pottery forms. These now-classic surveys tell us a great deal about what happened in these river valleys, and when, but they tell us little about the ways in which the various river valley societies lived or why they became more complex and took up maize (corn) agriculture over the past 2,000 years.

Folsom, New Mexico Paleo-Indian kill site dating to c. 8000 B.C., a location providing the first definitive evidence of the association of humans with extinct animals in the Americas.

Culture history is the vital first stage of all archaeological research. You cannot examine more detailed questions until you have a clear idea about what happened in a region and when. In many parts of the world—Southeast Asia, for example—archaeological research has hardly begun. Many archaeologists working in Cambodia or Thailand still have a primary concern for culture history. This focus will change once the basic framework of the past is in place. The principles of culture history are discussed in Chapter 7.

Reconstructing Ancient Lifeways

potsherds Fragments of broken clay vessels.

Archaeology is also the study of ancient human behavior: of people, not their artifacts. Stone tools, **potsherds**, iron weapons, dwellings, and other material remains are indeed the raw materials for classifying the past, but we should never forget that they were made by people—men and women, adults and children, members of different households, communities, and societies. Logically, then, our second major goal is the reconstruction of how people made their living, the study of ancient lifeways.

The word *lifeways* covers many human activities, everything from hunting and gathering to agriculture, interactions between individuals and groups, social organization, and religious beliefs. Some of archaeology's most ingenious detective work reconstructs these activities, which, for convenience, can be grouped into broad categories.

Subsistence

subsistence Ways in which humans feed themselves.

How people make their living or acquire food is studied by using fragmentary animal bones, seeds, and other surviving evidence for ancient human diet and **subsistence** activities (see Chapter 4).

Environmental Modeling

Subsistence activities depend heavily on a society's relationship with the natural environment. This means that studying ancient subsistence goes hand in hand with reconstruction of changing prehistoric environments (see Chapter 4).

Human Interactions

People act out their lives at many levels: as individuals; as men, women, and children; as members of families, communities, and cultures. They may be divine rulers, merchants, artisans, common farmers, or slaves. Reconstructing lifeways means examining evidence for changing gender roles, assessing the importance of social ranking within societies, or reconstructing the complex mechanisms by which people exchanged exotic raw materials or precious artifacts over enormous distances.

Much cutting-edge research revolves around people questions, especially such issues as changing gender roles and the distinctive activities of inconspicuous and often historically anonymous minorities in large cities. We identify people from their artifacts, which are the products of cultural traditions handed down over many generations (see Chapter 6).

For instance, the great city of Teotihuacán in the Valley of Mexico attracted traders from every corner of the Mesoamerican world. The Teotihuacános ran a vast urban market where people came to trade everything from gold dust to tropical bird feathers. So lucrative and essential were some of these trading activities that the city authorities allowed foreigners from the distant Veracruz lowlands and the Valley of Oaxaca to live in their own compounds in Teotihuacán. We know this because the distinctive clay vessels characteristic of these two areas have come to light in several of the city's neighborhoods (see Chapter 15).

Social Organization and Religious Beliefs

Archaeologists are increasingly concerned with such intangibles as social organization and religious beliefs. Of course, we can never hope to capture the transitory events of the past, such as the ecstasy of a shaman's trance or a colorful dance performed in a plaza at Teotihuacán. However, artifacts, art styles, and even entire temples and cities are mirrors of the intangible, allowing us a fleeting glance into the social and spiritual worlds of ancient societies (see Chapter 6 and Box 2.2).

Explaining Cultural Change

Archaeology is a search for both facts and explanations. The third major objective of archaeology is to study and explain processes of cultural change (see Chapter 7). Such research addresses fundamental questions: After tens of thousands of years of hunting and gathering, why did people living in a huge area of southwestern Asia change over to agriculture around 10,000 B.C.? What caused Maya civilization in the southern Meso-american lowlands, with its huge cities and powerful lords, to collapse in A.D. 900? Why did no one settle the offshore islands of the Pacific until about 3,000 years ago?

Chavín de Huántar, Peru Ceremonial center in Peru's Andes foothills dating from as early as 1500 B.C. and thriving until between 900 and 600 B.C.; source of much Andean art in the distinctive style known as Chavín.

Chichén Itzá, Mexico Postclassic Maya center in the northern Yucatán, especially in the thirteenth century A.D.

cultural process The ways in which human cultures change over time.

Box 2.2 Discovery Sounds of the Past

The past comes down to us in silence—long-abandoned temples, city mounds, small farming villages, often mere scatters of stone tools or pot fragments. We often forget that these places were once alive with people—chants, dances, drumming, and all kinds of sounds would have filled the brightly colored shrines and palaces. Many of the world's most famous archaeological sites had potent acoustics, sound-bearing qualities that amplified human voices or created awe. These properties came from architecture, or from musical instruments. It's only in recent years that archaeologists have begun to study the importance of acoustics and sound in the past.

In 2001, archaeologists working at the ancient ceremonial center at **Chavín de Huántar** in the foothills of the Andes Mountains in Peru unearthed 20 complete conch-shell trumpets, *pututus*, dating to about 3,000 years ago (see Figures 16.5 and 16.6 on pp. 505 and 506). *Strombus galeatus* flourishes in shallow water off the Pacific coast of Ecuador, far from the shrine down steep mountain tracks, so every shell was imported. Polished, painted, and etched with symbols, the shells became trumpets with well-formed mouthpieces and V-shaped cuts that may have been intended for the player's thumb. The cuts would also allow the player to see ahead while playing.

Conch-shell trumpets were widely used in ancient societies and are still played at festivals in many parts of the world. The Greek fish-tailed sea god Triton was said to control the waves by blowing his conch trumpet. An ancient Hindu text, the *Bhagavad Gita*, a Song of God, describes how the Lord Krishna and the Prince Arjuna blew conch-shell horns as they rode into battle seated in a giant chariot pulled by white horses. The Maya considered conches sacred. Queen conch shells from shallow water bounding the Eastern Sea traveled far inland to Tikal and other Maya cities. The U.S. Coast Guard even lists conch horns as a legitimate sound-making device in its official *Navigation Rules*. However, at places like Chavín de Huántar, the conch was far more than a trumpet. It served an important acoustical role in subterranean rituals.

Chavín is a maze of subterranean passages and water channels, a shrine where rituals of transformation turned humans into animals such as the jaguar, transformations depicted on the temple walls (Figure 2.2). The shaman priests who conducted these rituals used hallucinogenic plants to induce deep trances. Such substances caused mucus to flow from the subject's nostrils, frequently depicted in Chavín and other Andean art. However, Chavín ritual also involved powerful acoustic effects produced by conch trumpets that echoed through narrow passageways, where the only light came from sunlight directed down air ducts. At Stanford University, a research group in computers and acoustics retained an expert musician to blow into a conch trumpet while using four tiny microphones, which were placed inside his mouth, the trumpet mouthpiece, the main body of the shell, and the large opening. A conch trumpet will only sound one or two tones, but, like a trumpet, if you place your hand into the large opening, the pitch changes.

The researchers then took the musician to the chamber where the trumpets were found. This time, they placed microphones around him, as he played in the stone chamber surrounded by twisting corridors and ventilator shafts. The results were startling. The trumpet's drone sounded as if it came from several directions simultaneously, an effect magnified by the dim lighting in the room. The effect was disorienting, confusing—a powerful sensory experience that may have been combined with the distorted, changing shadows of the participants projected on the surrounding walls by sunbeams from the air shafts.

Acoustic effects of all kinds were an important part of public rituals in many ancient societies. An acoustic engineer, David Lubman, spent 12 years studying the acoustics at the Maya city of **Chichén Itzá** (see Figure 2.3). He believes that the Maya used the acoustic effects of the steep stairway of the Kukulcán temple, where sound produces an eerie birdlike echo. Lubman compared the acoustic sound print

Figure 2.2 A Chavín de Huántar shaman transforms himself into a jaguar.
Source: Rafal Cichawa/Alamy.

Figure 2.3 The Great Ball Court at Chichén Itzá, Mexico.
Source: Yvonne Boyd/Alamy Stock Photo.

of the quetzal bird, much revered by the Maya, with that of the Kukulcán echo. They are identical. Here, as elsewhere in the ancient world, the natural and supernatural worlds, animals, humans, and mythic creatures, formed part of the cosmos, which was why reproducing evocative sounds was so important.

Today, rock bands use elaborate acoustic systems at their concerts with audiences of thousands; politicians rely on state-of-the-art public address systems. How did ancient priests control crowds and make themselves heard in front of large audiences? Again, it appears they relied on acoustics. The great Ball Court at Chichén Itzá has smooth stone walls carefully positioned to reflect sound, somewhat akin to today's band shells (Figure 2.3). Carefully designed galleries pushed sound waves down the court, somewhat like speaking through a long tube. These would have allowed a ruler to address crowds of up to 3,000 people without using a microphone, visitors to hear whispers from 140 meters (460 feet) away. Ball games were important rituals, so the sound effects on the court would have added an eerie dimension to the ceremony, perhaps compounded with hallucinogenic drugs. According to some sources, the sounds from the court were thought to have been the voices of the Lords of the Underworld. According to Lubman, a ball striking the court would have echoed four times a second, producing an effect somewhat like that of the rattles of a rattlesnake.

The study of ancient acoustics has hardly begun, but clearly our forebears were experts at producing exotic cavities, whether in the depths of late Ice Age painted caves in Europe, or in Greek and Roman amphitheaters like that at Epidauros, Greece, where soft voices travel long distances.

Studying **cultural process** is among the most challenging of all archaeological research. Chapter 7 describes some of the complex theoretical approaches that attempt to reconstruct such major developments as the origins of agriculture and the development of complex, urban civilizations. In recent years, archaeological theory has moved in new directions, away from the study of changing cultural systems to new perspectives in which researchers focus more and more on the role of people as agents of change.

Stewardship: Preserving the Past

The most fundamental objective of archaeology is to conserve, manage, and preserve the archaeological record of the past for future generations. This overriding objective has assumed major importance in recent years. Archaeological sites are precious, finite resources, and they are vanishing at a breathtaking speed. Already, most archaeological fieldwork around the world is devoted to salvage work and general management of the surviving archives of the past, often called cultural resource management (CRM). It is now the dominant paradigm in archaeology (see Box 17.1 on p. 533).[1]

The four main objectives of archaeology flow one into the other. A study of ancient lifeways depends on precise culture history, and an explanation of cultural processes requires large quantities of culture-historical, environmental, and lifeway data to be meaningful. And none of this research would be possible without responsible stewardship.

How, then, do archaeologists go about their work?

The Process of Archaeological Research

> *All archaeologists have an ethical responsibility to carry out their research according to established scientific procedures. Our research methods, however refined, destroy the archive of the past for future generations. This activity must include both full publication of the results of the work and proper conservation and storage of the finds.*

In other words, the ethics of archaeology demand a process of rigorous and well-planned research (see Figure 2.4) (for more on ethics, see Box 2.3).

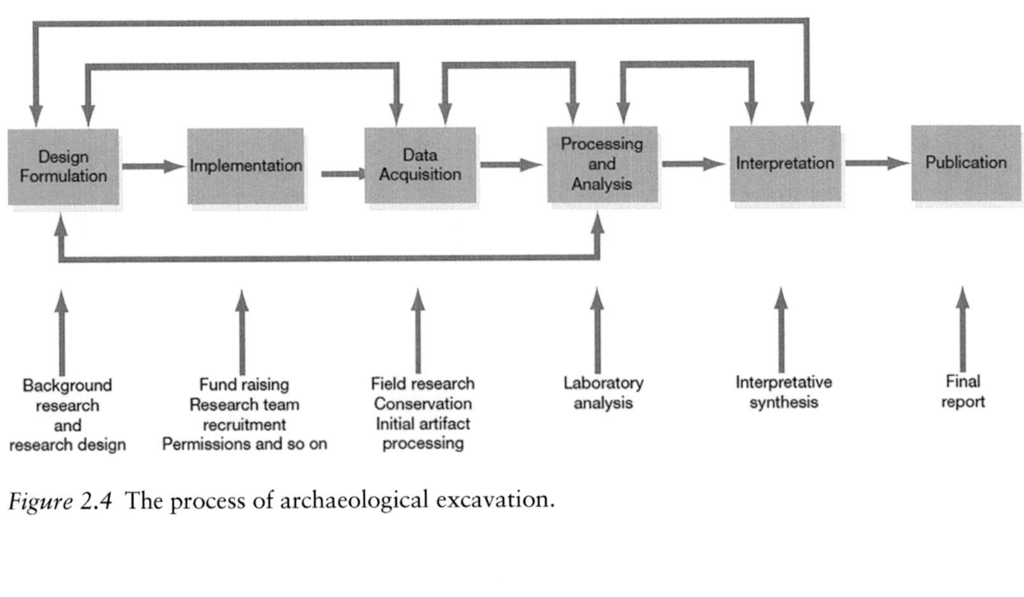

Figure 2.4 The process of archaeological excavation.

Box 2.3 Doing Archaeology
An Archaeologist's Ethical Responsibilities

Professional archaeologists live by multiple formal and informal codes of ethics that govern the ways in which they go about their business. The Society for American Archaeology's code is simple and to the point. It calls for professional archaeologists to do the following:

- Practice and promote the stewardship of the archaeological record for the benefit of all people.
- Consult effectively with all groups affected by their work.
- Avoid activities that enhance the commercial value of archaeological objects that are not readily available for scientific study or cared for in public institutions.
- Educate the public as to the importance of their findings and enhance public understanding of the past.
- Publish their findings in a widely accessible form.
- Preserve their collections, records, and reports properly, as part of a permanent record of the past for future generations. They must also allow other archaeologists access to their research materials without any legal or other compelling restrictions.
- Never undertake research without adequate training, experience, and facilities to complete the task at hand.

Brian's first solo excavation, on a 1,000-year-old farming village in Central Africa. His field training was rudimentary at best: a few digs in the United Kingdom, where you learned the basics as you worked as a student laborer. Now he was to dig on his own, a long way from anywhere, with six unskilled laborers and an occupation mound 400 meters (one-quarter mile) long and 3 meters (10 feet) deep in front of him (**Isamu Pati**, see Figure 2.5). The only advice he received was to dig into the highest point, on the grounds that it would yield the longest occupation sequence. He had no formal research plan or any idea of what he would find. In any event, his first trench did indeed find the deepest occupation in the village. But he made many mistakes and destroyed a lot of valuable artifacts and other finds before he found his scientific feet. Many years later, he would shudder at the casual way in which he first went digging. It was irresponsible and ethically wrong, both on his part and on the part of those who sent him into the field.

Isamu Pati, Zambia Village mound occupied by cattle herders and cereal farmers from c. A.D. 600 to 1200; major site of the Kalomo culture of southern Zambia.

Any time you disturb an archaeological site, you are effectively destroying it. Unlike in physics or chemistry, you cannot replicate your experiment again and again. As archaeologist Kent Flannery once remarked, we are the only scientists who murder our informants in the course of our research. As a result, every archaeological survey, every excavation, each laboratory project unfolds according to a carefully formulated but flexible research plan.

The process of archaeological research unfolds in five general stages, as follows.

Figure 2.5 General view of the excavations at the Isamu Pati mound in southern Zambia. Source: Brian Fagan.

Research Design

> *The ethics of archaeology require that you work closely with the people affected by your work, be they landowners, native peoples, or government agencies.*

research design A carefully formulated and systematic plan for conducting archaeological research.

The formulation of a **research design** is the most important part of any archaeological project, large or small. Such a design is the formal blueprint that lays out the goals of the inquiry, the steps to be taken, and the methods to be used to meet them. Preparing the design begins with the acquisition of as much background information as possible about the site or area to be investigated. What previous research has been done there? What collections and publications provide a starting point for you? What environmental and topographic data are on hand? You formulate initial questions that you hope to answer and develop general theoretical models that will frame the research. Your research design also spells out the strategies you will follow to test your hypotheses and meet the objectives of the research. Of course, these change as the fieldwork unfolds, but they provide a vital framework for the entire inquiry.

compliance In cultural resource management (CRM), the process of complying with federal and state laws affecting the archaeological record.

CRM projects are normally designed and carried out within tightly drawn boundaries, to ensure that they comply with legal requirements that the client, perhaps a developer or state roads department, has to fulfill; this is known as **compliance**. Some such projects have elaborate research designs.

In a sense, a research design is like a flowchart, for it is created both to monitor the validity of research results and to maximize efficient use of money, people, and time. For instance, when Brian Fagan first excavated an Iron Age village in Zambia, he read up on everything known about that kind of site (which turned out to be next to nothing). Then, he began to formulate the questions that the dig would investigate. He also raised funds for the excavation, acquired permission to dig from the landowner and relevant government agencies, and assembled the necessary equipment and staff to carry out the work.

Data Acquisition

Now it is time to go into the field for your survey or excavation, depending on the nature of your project. Data acquisition may take a few days, several weeks, months, or years, depending on the scope of the project. Dozens of archaeologists have collaborated on a long-term, multiyear investigation of the famous Maya city of Copán, Honduras (see Figure 15.8 on p. 475). The complex projects there include a major investigation of the main ceremonial complex, where tunnels have revealed that pyramids that were built by successive rulers between A.D. 400 and 800 were stacked one upon the other (see Chapter 15). Another large-scale project has surveyed the hinterland of the city and chronicled major changes in settlement in the Copán valley over many centuries (see Box 15.2 on p. 478).

At the other end of the spectrum, a single archaeologist may spend a day surveying and excavating a scatter of 5,000-year-old stone tools on a 0.4-hectare (1-acre) building site in the Chicago suburbs. As noted earlier, field survey is more important than excavation in contemporary archaeology as nonintrusive fieldwork designed to conserve the past becomes the norm.

Whether excavation or field survey, data acquisition is a process of observation and recording information in which meticulous records, combined with the finds, whether potsherds or animal bones or house foundations, provide the data sets for the next stage: **analysis**.

Analysis

analysis The process of classifying and describing archaeological finds.

Chumash Maritime and interior-adapted hunter-gatherers of the Santa Barbara Channel region of southern California, celebrated for their elaborate maritime culture.

Data analysis is the most fundamental of archaeological tasks, the classification and description of everything recovered from the field. The analysis of artifacts and food remains is described in Chapter 4. However, in these days, when many researchers try to excavate as little undisturbed archaeological deposit as possible, a great number of projects are purely laboratory undertakings. Often, modern experts work with notes left by their predecessors. For example, Smithsonian Institution anthropologist John Harrington spent a lifetime studying the customs and language of the few surviving **Chumash** Indians of southern California in the early 1920s. Harrington was a pack rat who assembled an extraordinary database on vanished Chumash culture—recorded on file cards, in notebooks, and on isolated slips of paper in Chumash, English, and Spanish. He died in 1961 without publishing any of them.

Harrington's unpublished notes lay in government offices all over the country at the time of his death. They constitute a priceless archive of a culture that effectively became extinct in the nineteenth century. Using Harrington's notes, anthropologists Thomas Blackburn and Travis Hudson succeeded in building a replica of a Chumash planked canoe. At the same time, they became archaeological sleuths in an attempt to track down hundreds of Chumash artifacts looted over a century earlier and now residing in collections scattered throughout the world. William Blackmore, a wealthy businessman, acquired many Chumash artifacts in the late nineteenth century. He donated his collections to the Salisbury Museum, a local organization in southern England. After his death in 1929, the museum disposed of the collection, with the archaeological finds going to the British Museum in London. Henry Beasley, a private collector, purchased the ethnographic artifacts. Upon his death, they ended up in museums in Cambridge, Liverpool, and London. Blackburn and Hudson tracked down Chumash baskets, stone tools, and weapons in Oxford, England; Edinburgh, Scotland; Ghent, Belgium; Göteborg and Stockholm, Sweden; Helsinki, Finland; and St. Petersburg, Russia. The two scholars documented an international archive of Chumash culture that amplified Harrington's firsthand observations and archaeological excavations.

Interpretation

interpretation Conclusions drawn from data collected in the context of an original theoretical model, developed and modified as a project proceeds.

At this important stage in the process, the researcher pulls together all the data and tests the propositions in the research design. The **interpretation** represents the conclusions drawn from the data in the context of the theoretical model developed and then modified as the project unfolded. In the case of his African village, Brian assembled all the chronological and stratigraphic information and the artifact analyses, with their information on changing pottery styles, and the subsistence data, and then wrote a detailed interpretation of the site. As part of the process of explanation, he argued that changes in pottery styles toward globular pots and a rapid increase in the percentage of cattle bones were signs of an economic shift toward cattle herding and milk consumption around A.D. 1000, at the very end of the site's occupation.

Publication and Curation

An archaeologist's primary responsibility is to publish a complete record of his or her research that is accessible to all.

Most important of all, the researcher publishes the results of the project in full. Many CRM excavations are covered by contracts and requirements dictated by legally mandated compliances. The completion of a formal report is part of that contract. However, whether academic- or contract-driven, full reporting in a form accessible to everyone is essential, for any excavation is destruction. Final publication, whether an elaborate monograph or a paper in a scientific journal, is the only permanent record of a now-vanished archive. As part of the publication process, the collections, basic data, photographs and drawings, and field notes should be archived in a proper curation facility, as they are part of the permanent record, to be consulted by future researchers.

Abu Hureyra, Syria Village site by the Euphrates River occupied first by foraging groups in about 11,500 B.C. and then by very early farmers; famous for its excellent botanical evidence for agricultural origins.

One of the great scandals of archaeology is the lax way in which some fieldworkers shrug off their ethical responsibilities to publish their results. Some of the world's most important and extensively excavated sites are virtually unpublished, often because their excavators have continued digging elsewhere instead of fulfilling their basic archaeological responsibilities. Unfortunately, it's a reality of archaeological life that we receive more credit for making interesting discoveries than for the responsible behavior of writing them up! A glowing example of full publication is the monograph on the **Abu Hureyra** farming village in Syria (see Chapter 11), written over many years by Andrew Moore and his research team.

What Is Culture?

hominins All living humans and all other species comprising the lineage that diverged from that of chimpanzees by 6 million years ago. Over 20 hominin species have been identified. Only some hominins are our ancestors, and many became extinct without giving rise to new species.

Archaeology is the study of ancient human behavior, of ancient cultures. The concept of culture is at the center of all archaeological inquiry.

On an intensely hot, windy day on the shores of Lake Turkana, East Africa, 2.5 million years ago, a small group of **hominins** (primate members of the family Hominidae, represented today by only one species, *Homo Sapiens*) runs up a dry streambed, carrying the bloody limbs of a recently killed antelope stolen from a lion kill. The females clasp their young to their bosoms and then set them on the ground under a shady thorn tree so they will be protected from the wind. They join the males in cutting up the fresh meat with sharp-edged stone tools, which were flakes struck from lumps of lava carried to this place weeks before. The small band eats quickly, always alert for lurking predators, breaking bones with stone lumps, sucking succulent marrow from the limb bones. They throw stones at hovering vultures and then drop the cleaned bones and stone tools as they move away to climb trees as the sun sets.

By 2.5 million years ago, the toolmaking hominins numbered but a few thousand, scattered over an enormous area of open grassland in eastern and southern Africa. These used a simple culture of manufactured stone and wood tools to butcher animals and dig up roots.

Though stone tool making had taken off by this time, earlier hominins had also used stone tools. Currently, the oldest recognizable stone tools come from the site of Lomekwi 3 in Kenya and date to 3.3 million years ago. The Lomekwi 3 tools, including large anvils and hammerstones, represent the oldest-known archaeological culture in the world.

culture The primary nonbiological means by which humans adapt to their natural environment.

Today, we are the only animals that use our **culture** as the primary means of adapting to our natural environment. Culture is our adaptive system. Biological evolution has protected the polar bear from arctic cold with dense fur and has given the duck webbed feet for swimming. Only humans make layered, tailored clothes and igloos in the Arctic and live with minimal clothing under light, thatched shelters in the tropics. We use our culture as a buffer between ourselves and the environment, a buffer that became more and more elaborate through the long millennia of the past. We are now so detached from our environment that removal of our cultural buffer would render us almost helpless and probably lead to our extinction in a short time.

anthropology The study of humankind in the widest possible sense.

Archaeologists, like anthropologists, study human cultures. Few concepts in **anthropology** have generated as much controversy as culture. The great Victorian anthropologist Sir Edward Tylor wrote one of the best definitions for this concept: "That complex whole which includes knowledge, belief, art, morals, law, custom, and any other capabilities and habits acquired by man as a member of society" (1871, 2). To Tylor's words archaeologists would add the statement that culture is our primary means of adapting to our environment. Tylor's definition and all other such formulations agree on one important point: culture and human behavior are shared ideas a group of people may hold.

Human cultures are made up of human behavior and its results, a mix of complex and constantly interacting variables. Human culture is never static and is always adjusting to both internal and external change, whether environmental, technological, or social.

Culture can be subdivided in all sorts of ways—into language, economics, technology, religion, political or social organizations, and art, to mention only a few categories. But human culture as a whole is a complex, structured amalgam in which all the categories shape one another. All cultures are made up of myriad tangible and intangible traits that result from complex adaptations to a wide range of ecological, social, and cultural factors.

We transmit much of human culture from generation to generation by sophisticated communication systems: by word of mouth and oral tradition, by practical example, and sometimes in writing. Culture's transmissibility allows us to forge ceaseless and complex adaptations to aid survival and help rapid cultural change take place, as happened, for example, when Western explorers and settlers came in contact with non-Western societies during the European Age of Discovery. Within two or three generations after the first European contacts in 1768 and 1769, Tahitian society changed rapidly as a result of connections with Western culture. At first, local chiefs tolerated missionaries, who were perceived as politically advantageous owing to their access to firearms. Within a half-century, Tahitian culture had been transformed by Christianity, and for the worse, as traditional customs and beliefs went underground and many people fell into grinding poverty.

hieroglyphs Pictographic or ideographic symbols used as a written record or language in Egypt, Mesoamerica, and elsewhere.

We all live within a culture of some kind, and every culture is qualified by a label, such as "middle-class American," "Aleut" or "Maya." The qualification conjures up characteristic attributes or behavior patterns typical of people associated with the cultural label. One attribute of a middle-class American might be the enjoyment of hamburgers or an enthusiasm for football; of the Aleut the kayak or skin boat; of the elite members of Maya society, elaborate cities and intricate **hieroglyphs**, an ancient writing featuring pictorial or ideographic symbols. Every culture has its individuality and recognizable style that shape its political and judicial institutions and its morals.

Unfortunately, cultural labels often become simplistic and sometimes demeaning stereotypes, such as that of the Native Americans as "feathered braves" or of the French as romantic, consummate lovers. Cultural reality is much more complex and often deeply challenging for an outsider to penetrate and comprehend.

For working purposes, archaeologists often think of culture as possessing three components:

cultural system The multifaceted mechanism that humans use to adapt to their physical and social environment.

- *The individual's own version of his or her culture:* the diversified individual behavior that makes up the myriad strains of a culture. Individual decisions play a vital role in changing even elaborate cultures.
- *Shared culture:* the elements of a culture shared by everyone. These can include cultural activities such as human sacrifice or warfare, as well as the body of rules and prescriptions that make up the sum of the culture. Language is critical to this sharing, and so is the cultural system.
- *The **cultural system:*** the system of behavior in which every individual participates. The individual not only shares the cultural system with other members of society but also takes an active part in it.

You can think of culture as either a blend of shared traits or a system that permits a society to interact with its environment. To do anything more than just study sequences of ancient human cultures, archaeologists have to view culture as a group of complex, interacting components. These components remain static unless you define the processes that operate the system.

Archaeologists are deeply involved with the study of cultural process—how ancient human societies changed through time (see Chapter 7).

The Archives of the Past: The Archaeological Record

The foragers came in early fall, just as the acorns and pistachios ripened. They camped on a small ridge close to the river, at the foot of a low cliff, with a fine view of the surrounding floodplain. While the men erected small brush shelters, the women collected wild grass seeds from the edges of a nearby swamp where a meander of the stream had left a shallow lake. They returned to camp with laden baskets, lit fires, and pounded the seeds for the evening meal. As the sun went down, some of the men stalked deer from the nearby forest as the timid animals came down to the water to drink. Dogs barked; children shouted and played; families sat by the fires in the gathering dark. The same daily routine unfolded for several weeks as each family spent its days in the forest gathering thousands of ripe acorns and nuts for the winter ahead. But as the days shortened and the leaves fell, the band moved on to a more permanent and better-sheltered winter camp upstream.

The abandoned shelters slowly collapsed under the weight of rain and winter snow. Small mudflows covered the hearths where families once sat. Within a few years, the small camp was invisible, the brush dwellings rotted away. The few discarded wooden artifacts had also vanished. Only a scatter of broken stone tools, some fractured deer bones, and thousands of minute seeds survived, buried under several inches of soil.

The soil weathered, centuries and millennia passed, and a dense woodland grew where the foragers once lived. Then European farmers came and cleared the trees, sinking their horse-drawn plows into the fertile soil. The plow blades cut through an ancient hearth, bringing some stone tools and charcoal to the surface of the plowed field. By chance, an archaeologist walked across the field, searching for artifacts and traces of human occupation. The ancient camp, once alive with people, became an archaeological site—part of the archives of the past.

archaeological data The materials recognized by the archaeologist as significant evidence, all of which are collected and recorded as part of research into the human past.

Archaeological data like these consist of any material remains of human activity. The archaeologist recognizes them as significant evidence. All are collected and recorded as part of the research. Data are different from facts, which are simply bits of observable information about objects, conditions, and so on.

band An egalitarian association of families knit together by close social ties.

archaeological record Artifacts, sites, and other human-manufactured features or results of ancient human behavior and their matrices, or the contexts in which they are found.

The data chronicling prehistory result from human activity. A hunter-gatherer **band** decides on a location for a temporary camp. The people gather building materials—sticks and grass, sod, mammoth bones—and then build dwellings and occupy them. Eventually, they abandon their houses, perhaps destroying them in the process. The archaeologist reconstructs the camp and the activities that unfolded there from the surviving material remains, discovered after centuries or millennia; this is what we call the **archaeological**

record, a generic name for traces of ancient human behavior, reflected by a more or less continuous distribution of artifacts over the Earth's surface, in highly variable densities.

transformation processes Processes (which can outlast a single phase and can occur over a wide area) that change an abandoned settlement into an archaeological site through the passage of time.

artifacts Objects **manufactured** or modified by humans.

artifact assemblage All the artifacts found at a site.

Human behavior is the first step in the formation of the archaeological record. But what happens when people abandon their camps, bury the dead, and move elsewhere? The collapsed brush shelters, a scatter of stone tools, the remains of a meal are of no further use to their owners. All manner of humanly caused (cultural) and natural (noncultural) **transformation processes** then come into play as time passes. Such transformation processes (sometimes called *site transformation processes*) are continuous, dynamic, and unique cultural or noncultural occurrences that affect archaeological sites after their abandonment (Figure 2.6). The bodies of the buried dead decay; toppled shelters rot away in the sun. Perhaps a nearby lake rises and covers the abandoned settlement with fine silt. Windblown sand may accumulate over stone **artifacts**, objects manufactured or modified by humans. Another completely different society may come and build a farming village on the same spot or simply pick up and reuse the stone artifacts left by their ancient predecessors. (A collection of artifacts found at a site is known as an **artifact assemblage**.)

Transformation processes vary from one location to another, for the archaeologist's data are always biased and incomplete, altered by a variety of such processes that can affect the state of preservation of artifacts and other finds. For example, World Wars I and II destroyed thousands of archaeological sites, whereas wet conditions in northern European swamps preserve even 3,000-year-old corpses in near-perfect condition.

ecofacts Archaeological finds that are of cultural significance but were not manufactured by humans, such as bones and vegetal remains; not a commonly used term.

Archaeological data resulting from human behavior and transformation processes make up the archaeological record. The archaeological record is a finite and precious chronicle of the human past, an archive of all our pasts, whether kings, queens, merchants, nobles, or commoners. Our archives are not dusty files, letters, or microfilms but archaeological sites, artifacts, and **ecofacts** (a term sometimes used to refer to food remains, such as animal bones, seeds, and other finds, that throw light on human activities)—all the material remains of ancient human behavior. A scatter of broken bones, a ruined house, a gold mask, a vast temple plaza—these are all part of the archaeological record. All the elements in this enormous archive, the common cultural heritage of all humankind, have a context in time and space. Once destroyed, an archaeological site can never be replaced. Once disturbed, the context of an artifact, or any form of human behavior, is gone forever. The archaeological record is perishable, irreplaceable, and vanishing daily.

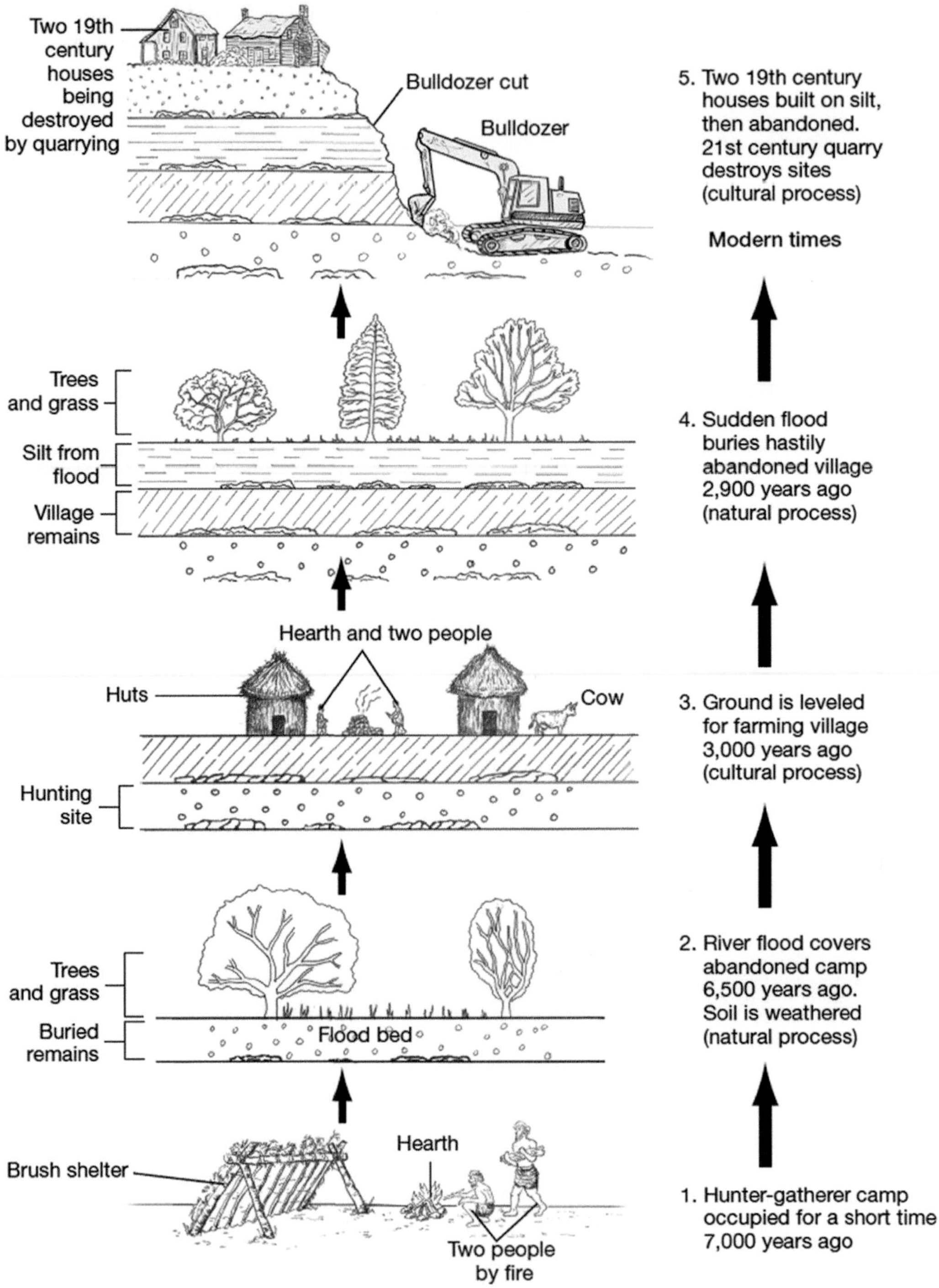

Figure 2.6 Site formation processes.

site Any place where ecofacts, features, or objects manufactured or modified by humans are found; may range from a living site to a quarry location, and can be defined in functional and other ways.

features Artifacts such as storage pits or postholes that cannot be removed from a site; usually only recorded.

The archaeological record can include unusually high densities of artifacts or other traces of human activity, which are subsumed under the term **site**—any place where objects, **features**, or other traces of human behavior are found. A site can range from a small camp to a city, from a quarry to a tiny scatter of stone artifacts. It can be defined by its function, such as a cemetery.

Such, then, are the finite archives of the past, which have come down to us in lamentably incomplete form. Fortunately, however, exceptional preservation conditions sometimes provide us with remarkably detailed portraits of ancient lives.

Preservation Conditions

Tollund Man Iron Age body of a man, a criminal or a sacrificial victim who was strangled with a cord, dating to some time between 375 and 210 B.C.

He lay on his left side in a crouched position, a serene expression on his face, his eyes tightly closed. He wore a pointed skin cap and a hide belt—nothing else except for a cord knotted tightly around his neck. He had eaten a gruel of barley, linseed, and several wild grasses and weeds 12–24 hours before his death. **Tollund Man** was choked or hanged about 2,000 years ago and then laid to rest in a Danish bog, where peat cutters found his well-preserved body in 1950 (Figure 2.7).

Figure 2.7 Tollund Man.
Source: Iconotec/Alamy.

The archives of the past come down to us in the form of a frustratingly incomplete archaeological record, consisting for the most part of an endless array of stone tools, potsherds, and more durable artifacts such as grindstones and lava hammers. The sharp edges of stone choppers fabricated more than 2 million years ago may be as sharp as on the day they were made, but such inorganic objects tell us little about their makers beyond details of their technology.

Just occasionally, though, the veil lifts when favorable preservation conditions bring us organic objects made of once-living substances, such as wood, leather, bone, or cotton. We know a great deal about Tollund Man, the manner of his death, his health, and his diet simply because his corpse survived under waterlogged conditions. Peat bogs, damp lakebeds, and other wet sites can preserve wood and plant remains in near-perfect condition. So can ultra-dry climates, such as that of Egypt: witness the well-preserved tomb of the pharaoh Tutankhamun. The preservative effects of both arctic cold, in which permafrost literally refrigerates archaeological sites, and volcanic ash provide us with opportunities to explore past societies. Let us look at four examples of truly exceptional preservation that demonstrate the potential for spectacular discoveries.

Must Farm, England Settlement site with exceptionally good preservation, dated to the Late Bronze Age (around 850 B.C.).

A Waterlogged Site: Must Farm, England

Very occasionally, archaeologists uncover a site that upends our perceptions of an entire era. Such is the case for **Must Farm** in eastern England, an extraordinarily well-preserved settlement dated to the Late Bronze Age (around 850 B.C.). The site lies in waterlogged marshland, where excavations in 2015–2016 revealed a small silted riverside settlement, including five Bronze Age roundhouses surrounded by a palisade and a walkway. Usually, all one finds are postholes or dark stains in the soil. But the Must Farm houses had collapsed into the marsh, complete with their contents, after a fire. The houses had originally been raised up on stilts, set over a sluggishly flowing watercourse, deep in the soggy Fenlands. As the fire raged from wooden house to wooden house, the timber platforms collapsed, plunging the dwellings and all their contents into the water. The riverbed was littered with scorched baskets, spindle whorls, exquisitely woven textiles, even a cart wheel—the largest and best-preserved Bronze Age wheel ever found in Britain (Figure 2.8), querns, pots, beads, metal spears and tools, and even uneaten vitrified servings of stew. These objects were then further sealed by the charred and waterlogged roof structures and silt.

Local archaeologists had previously accepted that groups who colonized such fenland environments would have relied on fish and foul, but we now know that the folk at Must Farm also ate cereals, mutton, pork, and beef. These were people who were plugged into a much wider economic and social network. The site contained objects from Spain, northwest France, and the Balkans. Must Farm is revealing how an assumed "isolated backwater" was, in reality, part of a widely connected and inter-dependent world.

Dry Sites: Huanchaquito-Les Llamas and Puruchucho-Huaquerones, Peru

Huanchaquito-Les Llamas, Peru Site of a mass sacrifice of children and juvenile llamas overlooking the Pacific near the city of Chan Chan, c. A.D. 1400–1450.

Figure 2.8 Archaeologists working at the c. 3,000-year-old site of Must Farm. The archaeologist is uncovering a wooden wheel: at 1 meter (3.2 feet) across with its hub still intact, it is the earliest complete example of a Bronze Age wheel ever found in Britain.

Source: Jada Images/Alamy Stock Photo.

Puruchucho-Huaquerones, Peru Inca cemetery on the outskirts of Lima (A.D. 1438–1532), famous for its mummy burials.

The Pacific coast of Peru is one of the driest landscapes on Earth. As we will see in Chapter 16, the coast was home to several important pre-Inca states, which became part of the empire during the fifteenth century A.D. Exceptionally dry conditions have preserved cordage, textiles, and other perishable objects. They are revealing details of ancient burial customs and rituals.

Between A.D. 1400 and 1450, more than 140 children and 200 young llamas were sacrificed and buried at **Huanchaquito-Les Llamas,** a low bluff overlooking the Pacific, less than 0.8 kilometers (0.5 miles) east of the city of Chan Chan, capital of the Chimu state (see Chapter 16). Most of the sacrificial victims were between 8 and 12, buried facing west, out to sea. Their bones show that their chests were opened, perhaps to remove their hearts. In contrast, the llamas, less than 18 months old, were interred facing the mountains to the east. An adult man and two women lay close by, all killed by blows to their heads. Perhaps they were part of the sacrifice event and were subsequently killed. Footprints preserved in a mud layer above the burials tell us that the animal and human victims were led to the site from both north and south. Some of the llamas left skid marks in the mud, as if they resisted. The efficient, fatal cuts make it likely that the victims died at the hands of trained operators.

Why this child sacrifice occurred remains a mystery. One clue is the mud layer above the graves, which may have resulted from a major El Niño, which would have brought heavy rains that destroyed local field systems and disrupted local fisheries. Whatever the cause, within a few decades, the Chimu were conquered by the Inca Empire.

The **Puruchucho-Huaquerones** cemetery, which dates a little later to Inca times (A.D. 1438–1532), lies under the Tupac Amaru shantytown on the outskirts of the city. Tupac Amaru came into being when fugitives from guerrilla activity in the highlands settled outside Lima in 1989. Almost at once, the squatters found ancient mummies; they burned many of them in fear that an archaeological investigation would hinder development of the town. The surge of urban development caused sewage and water to sink into the dry soil, decomposing the mummies underground. Guillermo Cock, of Peru's Institute of Culture, started work on the cemetery in 1999. In three seasons, he recovered more than 2,200 mummies of all social ranks, buried within 75 years of one another.

The mummy bundles survived virtually intact in the arid soil, buried in graves sealed with sand, rubble, and potsherds (Figure 2.9). Many bear false heads made of textiles and cotton. Magnificent woven garments adorn many mummies, some of which bear elaborate headdresses of bird feathers, with ear flaps and a long panel that drapes down the back of the neck. Sometimes as many as seven people lie in one bundle. Nearly half the burials in the cemetery were of children who had died of anemia.

One spectacular mummy bundle, wrapped with 130 kilograms (just under 300 pounds) of cotton, contained the body of a man and that of a baby, perhaps one of his children. He was buried with food and 170 exotic and everyday artifacts, together with a mace and sandals of a type worn by the elite. Exotic *spondylus* shells from distant Ecuadorian waters lay with the body, eloquent testimony to his social standing.

Figure 2.9 The Nevado Ampato mummy, Peru.
Source: Stephen Alvarez/National Geographic Creative.

Unfortunately, only a small fraction of the cemetery can be investigated. The thousands of mummies still underground are decomposing rapidly, owing to the shantytown above them. But once studied, the Puruchucho mummies will reveal many details of life in a province of the Inca domains. In particular, the mummies show how people living in the provinces of the empire copied Inca customs, adopting their costume and ornaments.

Cold Conditions: Nevado Ampato, Peru

Nevado Ampato, Peru Site of the discovery of a 14-year-old Inca girl who died in about A.D. 1480, killed as a sacrificial victim at an altitude of 6,210 meters (20,400 feet) in the Peruvian Andes.

Freezing conditions in an arctic environment or at high altitudes can literally dry out or refrigerate a corpse and preserve the finest of clothing. Anthropologist Johan Reinhard and his Peruvian assistant, Miguel Zarate, found the mummy bundle of a young girl at an altitude of 6,210 meters (20,400 feet) in the Peruvian Andes. The 14-year-old Inca girl died as a sacrificial victim five centuries ago and was buried on a summit ridge of the sacred **Nevado Ampato** mountain (see Figure 2.9). Her well-preserved body was wrapped in a rough outer garment and then a brown-and-white-striped cloth. Underneath, she had a finely woven dress and shawl fastened with a silver pin. Her feet wore leather moccasins, but her head was bare. She may originally have worn a fanlike feather headdress, which was dislodged when the summit ridge collapsed and her mummy bundle fell down a slope. Computerized tomography (CT) scans of her skull revealed fractures by the right eye. She died of a massive hemorrhage resulting from a swift blow to the head. Blood from the wound pushed her brain to one side of her skull.

Volcanic Ash: Cerén, El Salvador

Herculaneum, Italy Roman town buried by an eruption of Mt. Vesuvius in A.D. 79.

Pompeii, Italy Roman town buried by an eruption of Mt. Vesuvius in A.D. 79; layers of ash preserved evidence of life in the community intact.

Cerén, El Salvador Maya village destroyed by a volcanic eruption in the sixth century A.D.

Everyone has heard of **Herculaneum** and **Pompeii,** flourishing Roman towns buried by a massive eruption of Mount Vesuvius in A.D. 79. The smothering ash even preserved body casts of fleeing victims (see Figure 2.10). Similarly, in the sixth century A.D., at **Cerén** in El Salvador, a volcanic eruption buried a small Maya village without warning. The people had eaten their evening meal but had not yet gone to bed. Upon the eruption, they abandoned their homes and possessions and fled for their lives. Archaeologist Payson Sheets and a multidisciplinary research team have recovered entire buildings, outlying structures, and their contents exactly where they were dropped (see Box 2.4).

Figure 2.10 Victims smothered by volcanic ash at Pompeii, Italy.
Source: National Geographic Image Collection.

Box 2.4 Discovery Tragedy at Cerén, El Salvador

We would know little of the lives of commoners but for an ancient natural disaster. One August evening in the sixth century A.D., a sudden rumble shook a quiet Maya village at Cerén in El Salvador. An underground fissure less than a mile away had erupted without warning. A fast-moving cloud of ash darkened the twilight sky. The villagers fled for their lives, leaving everything behind. Minutes later, their houses lay under a thick layer of volcanic debris. Fifteen hundred years later, archaeologist Payson Sheets used **subsurface radar** to locate several houses buried deep under the ash. He then excavated the dwellings. Plotting every artifact, even individual wall fragments, seeds, and pieces of thatch, he discovered households where, just after their evening meal, the people had fled the cascading ash.

One household lived in a complex of four buildings—a kitchen, a workshop, a storehouse, and a residence—where the residents socialized, ate, and slept (see Figure 2.11). The residence had a front porch open on three sides. The main room covered 4 square meters (43 square feet), with storage pots against the back wall. One pot contained a spindle whorl for making cotton thread. A large adobe bench

Figure 2.11 A Maya house at Cerén, El Salvador.
Source: Dennis Cox/Alamy.

on the east side of the room served as a sleeping place. During the day, people rolled up their mats and stored them among the rafters. Even the sharp-edged obsidian knife blades, stored high in the roof for safety, still lay among the thatch.

A walkway linked the dwelling to a nearby storehouse, passing by a food-grinding area where a metate (grinding stone) still stood on forked sticks about 50 centimeters (20 inches) above the ground. The household owned a well-tended garden along the side of the storehouse with carefully spaced rows of three species of medicinal herbs about a meter (3.25 feet) apart, each plant standing in a small mound of soil. Just to the south, an ash-covered field contained ridges of young maize plants about 20–40 centimeters (8–16 inches) high, typical corn growth for August in this environment. Some of the maize plants were doubled over, the ears still attached to the stalk, a "storage" technique still used in parts of Central America today.

The Cerén excavations reveal Maya farmers going about their daily business, the men working in the fields and making obsidian tools, the women weaving cotton garments, making agave rope and twine, and fashioning clay vessels. Theirs was a life dictated by the passage of the seasons, by wet and dry months, by the cyclical demands of planting and harvest. By chance, the volcanic ash rained down just after supper, so their artifacts, including bowls smeared with food, preserve a chronicle of life at the end of a farmer's day.

Such well-preserved finds as those at Cerén (Box 2.4) or Ozette (see Box 4.3 on p. 118) are few and far between, but they show the enormous potential for minute reconstruction of the past from wet sites and other exceptional locations. For the most part, however, the archaeologist works with an archaeological record that is a thing of shreds and patches, where preservation conditions militate against detailed portraits of ancient cultures. Our knowledge of human prehistory depends not only on good preservation but also on careful observation of the contexts of artifacts, occupation layers, and archaeological sites in time and space.

Context

Archaeologists have an ethical responsibility not to collect artifacts or buy and sell them for profit. They are students of the past and, as such, have a responsibility to acquire information, not artifacts wrenched from their context in time and space.

subsurface radar Radar used to detect subsurface features such as houses and pits without or in advance of excavation.

Mimbres Regional variant of the Mogollon tradition of the southwestern United States, famous for its magnificent painted pottery, early to mid-first millennium A.D.

A superb **Mimbres** bowl (see Figure 2.12) depicted a man fishing and had clearly come from a grave. Unfortunately, an anonymous looter plundered the burial, scattered the bones, and carried away the bowl, which they sold to the highest bidder. One can admire the superb artistry of the painter, but the bowl was useless as archaeological data, for archaeologists had no information as to where it came from or about its precise age and cultural associations.

context In archaeology, the exact location of a site, artifact, or other archaeological find in time and space.

Figure 2.12 Mimbres painted bowl.
Source: Dr. Steven A. LeBlanc, Harvard University.

Ancient artifacts are not just objects to be displayed like paintings or sculpture. They come from precise contexts in time and space. Archaeological data do not consist of artifacts, features, structures, and ecofacts alone. They also include the **context**: the exact position of these finds in time and space.

Context is a vital element in any excavation. Brian always remembered how the thin line of a 1,000-year-old hut floor covered in cattle dung appeared in the bottom of a trench into an ancient Zambian village; it was a hard, semicircular patch of fire-baked clay lined on its outer side with the charred bases of wall posts. He removed the overlying ashy soil with slow care, using trowels and then paintbrushes. Three large boulders appeared in the soil. He brushed them off, exposing a patch of charcoal between them, as well as a broken ox jaw and the broken fragments of a small clay pot. The exposed floor was about 3 meters (10 feet) across, with the hearth set near the center of the house.

provenance Position of an archaeological find in time and space, recorded three-dimensionally.

Before he lifted the hearth, artifacts, and hut floor, he recorded the **provenance** by measuring the exact position of every find and feature three-dimensionally and tying the measurements into a site grid linked, in turn, to a map of the area. As he took up the boulders, in and of themselves, they were just three large stones; but, taken together, plotted in relationship to the charcoal and artifacts, they told a story of long-forgotten household behavior. The finds had a context.

However, context is far more than just a find spot, a position in time and space. How, for example, did the find get to its position (see, for example, Figure 2.13), and what had happened to it since its original users abandoned it? Three general factors can affect context:

- *The manufacture and use of the object, house, or other find by its original owners:* For instance, the builders may have oriented a dwelling to a southwestern exposure to achieve maximum warmth from the afternoon sun. Why is this important? Because archaeologists study not only houses but also the behavior that affected every aspect of their building and use.
- *Ancient human behavior:* Some discoveries, such as royal burials or caches of artifacts, were deliberately buried under the ground by ancient people; others vanished as a result of natural phenomena. Dilapidated houses that have been abandoned are slowly covered by blowing sand or rotting vegetation. Others vanish in natural disasters.
- *Later activity at the site:* Then there are questions about what happened to a find after its abandonment or use: For example, was a 2,000-year-old burial from a burial mound in the Midwest disturbed by later interments in the same mound?

primary context An undisturbed association, matrix, and provenance.

secondary context A context of an archaeological find that has been disturbed by subsequent human activity or natural phenomena; often applies to burials.

Figure 2.13 A vivid example of archaeological context and association. An iron arrow lodged in a man's spine, c. A.D. 43. From *Maiden Castle*, a large hill fort in southern England, where violence was commonplace.

Source: Society of Antiquaries, London.

To add to the complication, you can come across both **primary context** (the original context of an archaeological find, undisturbed by any factor, human or natural, since it was deposited by the people involved with it) and **secondary context** (the context of a find whose original position has been disturbed by later activity).

Secondary contexts can occur when a group allows a corpse to remain exposed until the corpse has decomposed, and then buries the bones in a bundle in a communal burial chamber, like a British Stone Age long barrow (a burial mound) or a Hopewell mound in the Ohio valley. Secondary context also refers to burials deposited in the same place at a later date. For example, in A.D. 500, a group of Chumash Indians camped by a rocky peninsula on the south side of Santa Cruz Island, off southern California. Their ancestors had collected shellfish and hunted sea mammals at this location for untold generations. They camped for several days, nursing a sick man. After the man died, they buried his body in the large shell heap downwind of their camp and moved away. Fifty years later, another group visited the same spot and buried two children in the same mound. As they dug their graves into a corner of the original sepulcher, they disturbed the bones of the long-forgotten ancestor. When archaeologists uncovered the burials centuries later, they referred to the later interments as secondary burials.

Secondary contexts are common occurrences. For example, the tomb robbers who entered the sepulcher of Egyptian pharaoh Tutankhamun, soon after his interment in 1342 B.C., searched frantically for gold and precious oils. They scattered other items of grave furniture into secondary contexts before being frightened away. In still other instances, finds can be shifted by the natural forces of wind and weather. Many of the Stone Age tools found in European river gravels have been transported by floodwaters to locations far from their original place of deposition. All of these disturbed finds are in secondary contexts.

Time and Space

Every human artifact has a provenance in time and space. The dimension of time can range from a radiocarbon date of 1400 ± 60 years B.P. for a Maya temple to a precise reading of A.D. 1623 for a historic building in a colonial village in Virginia. Frequently, it can simply be an exact position in an archaeological site whose general age is known. Provenance in space is based, finally, on associations between tools and other items that were results of human behavior in a culture. Provenance is determined by applying two fundamental archaeological principles: the laws of association and of superposition.

The Law of Association

The Han Dynasty ruled China from 206 B.C. to A.D. 220, a time of great wealth and prosperity, especially for emperors, their families, and the nobility. Their enormous wealth survives in a series of remarkable burials. Dou Wan, the wife of Prince Liu Sheng, elder brother of Emperor Wu-di, died about 103 B.C. She was buried in a tomb over 51 meters (170 feet) long, dug by hand by hundreds of laborers. She lay in a central chamber with wooden walls and tiled roof, once hung with finely embroidered curtains. Dou Wan lay in a magnificent jade suit sewn together with gold thread. Han emperors and their nobles believed in Taoist magical traditions, which taught that jade prevented body decay (Figure 2.14). All that remained was a jumble of jade plaques and gold thread. Her bones had vanished.

association The relationship between an artifact and other archaeological finds and a site level or another artifact, structure, or feature at the site.

Figure 2.14 The reconstructed jade suit of Dou Wan, c. 103 B.C.
Source: Xinhua/Alamy.

A gilt-bronze lamp modeled in the form of a young serving girl watched over the corpse. The serving girl was kneeling, a lamp in her hands. Both the lamp and its shade were adjustable so that the direction and intensity of its rays could be changed at will. The direct **association** between the corpse and the lamp made it certain that the lamp belonged to Dowager Dou, especially since it bore the inscription "Lamp of the Palace of Eternal Trust." The dowager's grandmother lived in a residence of that name, so Chinese archaeologists believe that the lamp may have been a wedding gift from the grandmother to her granddaughter.

The archaeological principle of association (see Figure 2.15) came into play in Dou Wan's sepulcher. This principle, sometimes called the law of association, is one of the foundations of all archaeological research. In 1859, association linked the bones of long-extinct animals in river gravels with human-made stone axes found in the same levels. This discovery provided indisputable evidence of a very ancient humanity. The association showed that humans and such beasts had lived on Earth at the same time, hundreds of thousands of years earlier than the mere 6,000 years suggested by the biblical Creation story. Association is a barometer of ancient human behavior, recorded in the intricate patterns of artifacts, food remains, and other finds in the soil.

The Law of Superposition

middens Accumulations of domestic garbage, shells, or other occupation debris.

Pecos Pueblo, New Mexico Important Pueblo settlement from about A.D. 1140 to 1540, the deposits of which yielded a long sequence of Pueblo culture that became a yardstick for a wide area; subsequently became a major Catholic mission center.

Archaeologist Alfred Kidder dug into the deep **middens** at **Pecos Pueblo**, New Mexico, in 1915. The pueblo had flourished centuries before, when the first Spanish conquistadors arrived in the Southwest in 1540. Kidder trenched into the historic levels and then dug through deep occupation horizons until he reached sterile bedrock. His huge trenches yielded over 750 burials in sealed graves with groups of pots and thousands of painted potsherds, whose designs changed considerably as he dug deeper into the ash and occupation debris. Kidder worked from the historic known back into the prehistoric unknown, using graves and potsherds to develop a long sequence of Pueblo culture, with the oldest at the base and the most recent at the top of the middens.

superposition Relationship between two objects, structures, or layers in the vertical plane.

Kidder used a fundamental principle of archaeology, the law of **superposition**, which comes from stratigraphic geology (see Figure 2.16). The principle of superposition states that the geological layers of the Earth are stratified one upon another, like the layers of a cake. Cliffs by the seashore and quarries are easily accessible examples. Obviously, any object found in the lowermost levels, whether a stone or something made by humans, was

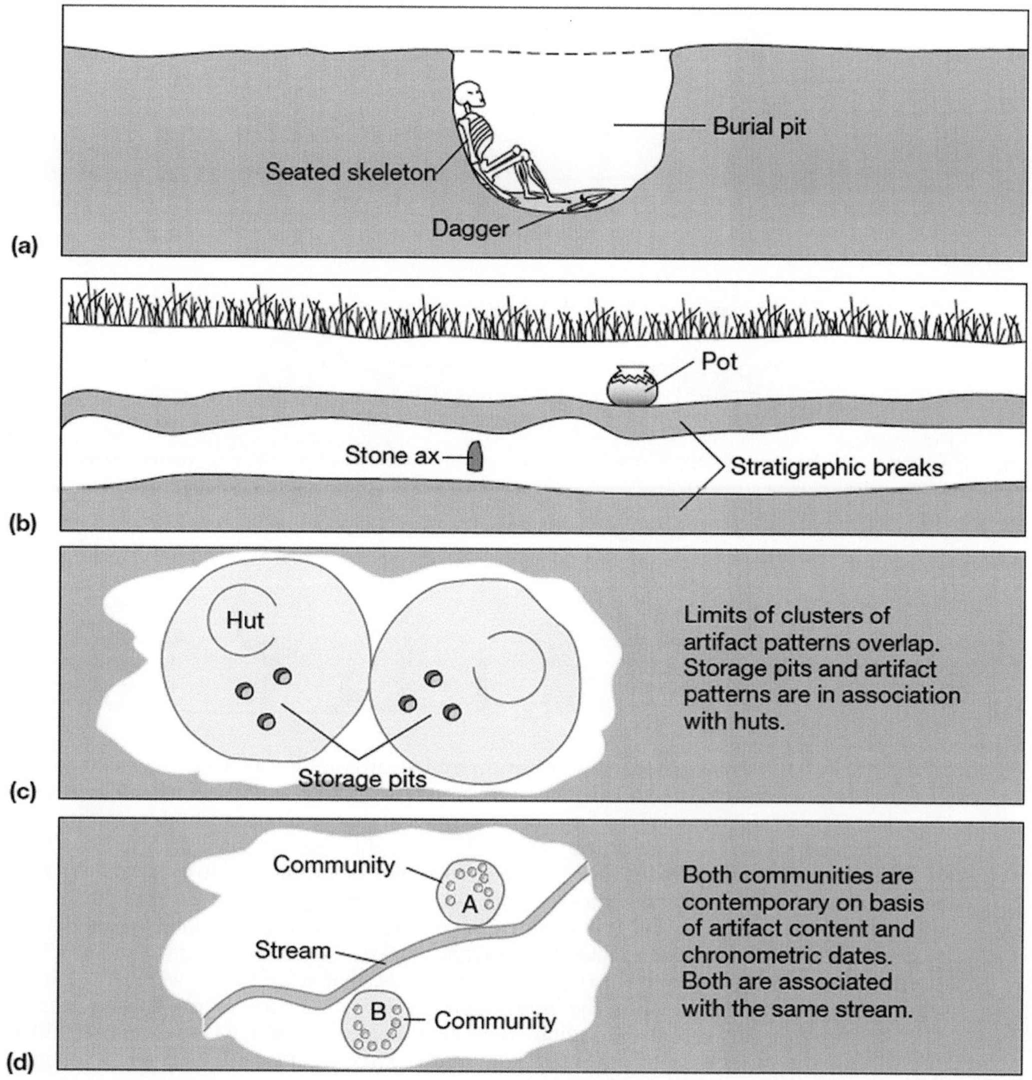

Figure 2.15 The law of association. Some archaeological associations: (a) The burial pit, dug from the uppermost layer, contains not only a skeleton but also a dagger that lies close to its foot. The dagger is associated with the skeleton, and both finds are associated with the burial pit and the layer from which the grave pit was cut into the subsoil. (b) In contrast, a pot and a stone ax are found in two different layers, separated by a sterile zone, a zone with no finds. The two objects are not in association. (c) Two different household clusters with associated pits and scatters of artifacts. These are in association with one another. (d) An association of two contemporary communities.

deposited there before the upper levels were accumulated. In other words, the lower strata are earlier than the upper strata. The same principle applies to archaeological sites. The order of deposition of tools, houses, and other finds in the layers of a site can be dated relative to the other layers by their association with the stratum in which they are found. But it should be noted that archaeological finds can become jumbled in archaeological layers for all manner of reasons, among them human activities.

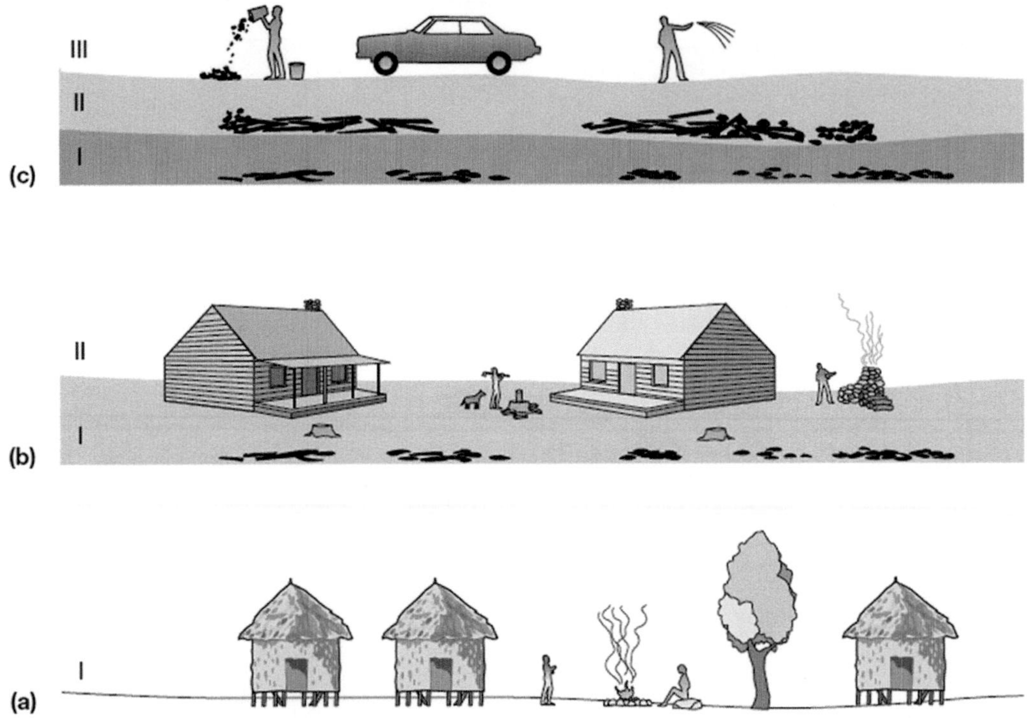

Figure 2.16 The law of superposition. Superposition and stratigraphy: (a) A farming village built on virgin subsoil. After a time, the village is abandoned and the huts fall into disrepair. Their ruins are covered by accumulating soil and vegetation. (b) After an interval, a second village is built on the same site, with different architectural styles. This is abandoned, in turn; the houses collapse into piles of rubble and are covered by accumulating soil. (c) Twentieth-century people park their cars on top of both village sites and drop litter and coins, which when uncovered reveal to the archaeologists that the top layer is modern. An archaeologist digging this site would find that the modern layer is underlain by two prehistoric occupation levels, that square huts were in use in the upper of the two, which is the later under the law of superposition. Round huts are strati-graphically earlier than square ones here. Therefore, village I is earlier than village II, but the exact date of either, or how many years separate village I from village II, cannot be known without further data.

stratigraphy Observation of the superimposed layers at an archaeological site.

The basis of all scientific archaeological excavation is the accurately observed and carefully recorded stratigraphic profile, or **stratigraphy**, which we discuss in Chapter 3.

Summary

- This chapter focused on the fundamental principles of archaeology.
- Archaeologists have a primary responsibility to conserve the past for future generations. Archaeology's other goals are to construct culture history, reconstruct ancient lifeways, and study processes of cultural change.

- The process of archaeological research begins with a research design and then proceeds to data collection, analysis, interpretation, and publication of the results.
- Archaeologists study past cultures, with culture being, in part, the shared ideas that human societies hold. Culture is also our primary way of adapting to our environment.
- Many archaeologists think of human cultures as cultural systems made up of numerous interacting subsystems, these cultures being part of much larger ecosystems.
- The study of cultural process involves interpreting the ways in which cultures change over long periods of time.
- The archaeological record consists of the material remains of human behavior, a finite archive of the past, which has a context in time and space.
- The chapter defined some of the components of the archaeological record and the widely differing preservation conditions that can affect our knowledge of the past.
- All archaeological finds have a context in time and space, defined by the laws of association and superposition.

Key Terms and Sites

Çatalhöyük
culture history
Folsom
potsherds
subsistence
Chavín de Huántar
Chichén Itzá
cultural process
Isamu Pati
research design
compliance
analysis
Chumash
interpretation
Abu Hureyra
hominins
culture
anthropology
hieroglyphs
cultural system
archaeological data
band
archaeological record
transformation processes
artifacts
artifact assemblage
ecofacts
site
features
Tollund Man
Must Farm
Huanchaquito-Les Llamas
Puruchucho-Huaquerones

Nevado Ampato
Herculaneum
Pompeii
Cerén
subsurface radar
Mimbres
context
provenance
primary context
secondary context
association
middens
Pecos Pueblo
superposition
stratigraphy

Critical-Thinking Questions

1. Why is the concept of culture so important in archaeology and what makes archaeology unique in studying cultural change?
2. Why do you think research design is central to the process of archaeological research? Use an example from the chapter to illustrate your points.
3. Archaeology has three major goals. Which of them, in your view, is the most important, or do they have equal significance?

Further Reading

The basic textbooks listed under Chapter 1 offer excellent summaries of the topics in this chapter. J. Deetz, *Invitation to Archaeology* (Garden City, NJ: Natural History Press, 1967) is a classic. See also M. Carver, *Archaeological Technique* (London: Routledge, 2008). G. Willey and P. Phillips, *Method and Theory in American Archaeology* (Chicago, IL: University of Chicago Press, 1958), is fundamental. So is V. G. Childe's insightful *Piecing Together the Past* (London: Routledge and Kegan Paul, 1956); an old book, but right on the money in many respects.

Note

1 Cultural Resource Management (CRM) is an enormous, complex part of archaeology. Space limitations make it impossible for us to describe this important aspect of archaeology in these pages, except for a brief account in Box 17.1 on p. 533.

3 Acquiring the Record

Chapter Outline

The Roman frontier fort at Housesteads, Hadrian's Wall, northern England. The fort dates to A.D. 122 and was occupied for four centuries.

Source: Commission Air/Alamy Stock Photo.

DOI: 10.4324/9781003592754-4

Avebury, England A stone circle complex dating to c. 2500 B.C. that lies at the heart of a Stone Age sacred landscape.

In 1649, a gentleman antiquarian named John Aubrey galloped into the middle of the village of **Avebury** in southern England while hunting foxes. He found himself surrounded by a deep ditch and mysterious, weathered stones erected in a circle inside the earthwork (see Figure 3.1). Aubrey said he was "wonderfully surprized *(sic)* at the sight of these vast stones, of which [he] had never heard before," and he returned later to sketch and explore (Malone 1989, 21). Today, the Avebury stone circles are among the most famous archaeological sites in Europe.

Aubrey made the first survey of one of Great Britain's most remarkable sacred monuments. He speculated that it was built by ancient Britons, "who were ... two or three degrees less savage than the Americans."

Avebury was well known to local farmers in Aubrey's day, but he was the first person to draw the site to the attention of a wider scientific community (see also Box 3.1). Earthworks like Avebury, burial mounds, and entire cities are relatively easy to find, for they form an easily identified part of the modern landscape. But how do archaeologists locate inconspicuous Stone Age foraging camps, tiny early farming villages, and sites that appear to leave no traces whatsoever on the surface? This chapter describes how archaeologists find and excavate sites, recover the record of the past, and date it.

Figure 3.1 Avebury stone circle in southern England, from the air.
Source: Loop Images Ltd/Alamy Stock Photo.

Box 3.1 Discovery
Recording the Behistun Inscription, Iran

Sometimes discovery is not hard but recording it is a nightmare. Here is the story of the Great Rock at **Behistun,** Iran, a key to the decipherment of ancient cuneiform script.

Persian King Darius (548–486 B.C.) was a bombastic adventurer who liked to boast of his conquests. Fortunately for archaeology, Darius commemorated his victory over five rebel chiefs with a trilingual inscription set on a virtually inaccessible cliff face, up on the Great Rock of Behistun in the Iranian highlands. The inscription, in Old Persian, Elamite, and Babylonian cuneiform, was the Rosetta Stone of Mesopotamia, for it provided clues for the decipherment of the wedge-shaped script, the major diplomatic writing of its day (see Figure 3.2).

English cavalry officer Henry Rawlinson was both a globe-trotter and an expert in Asian languages. He was posted to Kurdistan, near the Great Rock, in 1833 and spent ten years gradually recording the inscriptions, climbing high above the ground without scaffolding. He copied the more accessible script by hanging on one hand from a ladder while holding a notebook. But the cuneiform inscription was said by the local hills people to be unreachable. Rawlinson could copy the script with a powerful telescope, but he wanted to make paper casts of the individual

Figure 3.2 The Great Rock at Behistun, commemorating the victory of Darius I over rebel monarchs in 522 B.C. The ruler has placed his foot on the neck of the rebel Gautama. The god Ahura Mazda hovers overhead in the winged disk.

Source: Design Pics Inc/Alamy Stock Photo.

impressions. Eventually, he persuaded a "wild Kurdish boy" to scale the slope. The boy swung himself across with wooden pegs and seemingly insecure footholds until he could pass a rope across the cliff. Then, he formed a swinging seat like a window cleaner's cradle and made paper casts under Rawlinson's supervision. This was a simple process, involving the hammering of wet sheets of paper into the crevices with a stout brush. When dry, the sheets provided an accurate cast of the inscription.

The Behistun inscription helped unlock the secrets of cuneiform. As for the casts, once finished with, they moldered in the British Museum and were eaten by mice.

Behistun, Iran Carved and polished rock face that commemorates a victory by the Persian King Darius over rebel leaders in 522 B.C.

cuneiform (from the Greek word cuneus, "wedge") Mesopotamian script made by stamping clay tablets with a wedge-shaped stylus, long used as an international diplomatic script in the ancient eastern Mediterranean world.

As witnessed in Chapter 2, all archaeological research goes through the same general process—design and implementation, data acquisition, processing and analysis, interpretation, and publication (see Figure 2.4 on p. 44). This disciplined process, carried out at thousands of archaeological sites large and small, has provided the narrative of world prehistory in the second half of this book. Entire libraries of books and periodicals cover archaeological methodology and theory, a literature of daunting complexity laden with obscure jargon. Here we are concerned only with the basic principles and, inevitably, gloss over many controversies and interesting byways of archaeological methods.

As we have seen, the stereotypical images of Indiana Jones rummaging through pyramids and burial chambers bear no resemblance to the realities of modern scientific archaeology, which is slow moving, disciplined, and focused on keeping meticulous records of the contexts of one's finds.

This chapter discusses three basic questions regarding the data acquisition process in archaeology: (1) How do you find sites? (2) How do you know where and how to dig? (3) How old is it?

How Do You Find Archaeological Sites?

The first time Brian Fagan went out in the field looking for Stone Age sites, back in 1959 as a 22 year old, he and a companion were walking through a dry river valley where river gravels showed through the stunted dry-season grass. His experienced companion walked with his eyes glued to the ground, picking up Stone Age scrapers without apparent effort. Brian moved at half his speed, puzzling over every piece, for he had not done this before. After half an hour, they had hundreds of 100,000-year-old artifacts, collected from acres of gravel that had been sorted again and again by floodwaters. Artifacts from dozens of campsites had been mingled together in a hodgepodge of brown-colored artifacts and waste flakes. Suddenly, his companion bent down and picked up a broken flake. "That's the other half of a flake I collected in 1938," he declared. "Impossible!" Brian replied. But he was right. When they got back to the museum, they opened the 1938 collection, and the two pieces fitted together perfectly. It was a sobering lesson in the power and precision of an experienced archaeological eye.

How do you know where to dig? How do you find sites? Many people are amazed at archaeologists' seemingly uncanny ability to choose the right place for their excavations. Part of this ability is having a good eye for landscape, a penchant for putting yourself in the shoes of the people you are seeking, and plain old-fashioned common sense. However, formal survey methods play an important role in archaeological fieldwork, especially today, when many projects are carried out under fast-moving Cultural Resource Management (CRM) programs.

Accidental Discoveries

Some archaeological sites are so conspicuous that people have always known of their existence. The Pyramids of Giza in Egypt have withstood the onslaught of tourists, treasure hunters, and quarriers for thousands of years (see Figure 3.3). The Pyramid of the Sun at Teotihuacán, Mexico, is another easily visible archaeological site (see Figure 3.8). Most archaeological sites are far less conspicuous. They may consist of little more than a scatter of pottery fragments or a few stone tools lying on the surface of the ground. Other settlements may be buried under several feet of soil, leaving few surface traces except when exposed by moving water, wind erosion, or burrowing animals. Finding archaeological sites depends on locating such telltale traces of human settlement.

Lascaux Cave, France Major site of Magdalenian cave painting in southwestern France, dating to about 17,000 years ago.

Figure 3.3 Pyramids of Giza, Egypt.
Source: Volker Kreinacke/iStockphoto.

Figure 3.4 A wild ox from Lascaux Cave, France, c. 17,000 years ago.
Source: Ancient Art & Architecture Collection Ltd/Alamy.

Many sites come to light by accident. Some boys out hunting rabbits in 1940 found the magnificent late Ice Age paintings in **Lascaux Cave** in southwestern France when their dog became trapped in an underground chamber entered through a rabbit hole. Their flashlights shone on giant wild bulls cavorting over the cave walls (see Figure 3.4). A perfectly preserved Maya village of about A.D. 580 came to light at Cerén, El Salvador, when a bulldozer operator exposed a long-buried house covered with several meters of volcanic ash (see Figure 2.11 on p. 61).

Modern industrial development such as road construction, deep plowing, and dam-building frequently uncovers important archaeological sites. Mexico City lies atop the ruins of the Aztec capital, Tenochtitlán. Over 40 tons of pottery and a small temple came to light during the construction of the city's subway system. Even more dramatic was the accidental rediscovery of the great Templo Mayor in the heart of Mexico City. Construction activity revealed the most sacred shrine of Aztec Tenochtitlán, the temples of the gods Huitzilopochtli and Tlaloc. Mexican archaeologist Eduardo Matos Moctezuma's excavations subsequently unearthed at least five successive temples and many rebuildings going back to at least A.D. 1390. The temple, visited by Spanish conquistador Hernán Cortés, had 114 steps and a drum so loud it could be heard 10 kilometers (6 miles) away. The conquistadors pulled it down to build a cathedral nearby. The abandoned shrines were forgotten until the 1970s (see Box 15.4 on p. 490).

Olduvai Gorge, Tanzania Site where stratified early hominin archaeological sites are associated with long-dried-up Lower and Middle Pleistocene lakes dated to between 1.75 million and 100,000 years ago.

Nature itself sometimes uncovers sites for us; such sites are then found by a sharp-eyed archaeologist looking for natural exposures of likely geological strata. **Olduvai Gorge** is a great gash in the Serengeti Plain of northern Tanzania. An ancient earthquake eroded a deep gorge, exposing hundreds of meters of lakebeds that had been buried long before. These buried lake deposits have yielded early tool and bone concentrations dating back at least 1.75 million years. They would never have been found without the assistance of an earthquake and subsequent erosion (see Figure 8.12, on p. 265).

European fields have yielded many caches of buried weapons, coins, smith's tools, and sacrificial objects: valued treasures that were buried in times of stress by their owners. For whatever reason, the owners never returned to recover their valuables. Thousands of years later, a farmer may come across the hoard and, if he is a responsible citizen, report the find to archaeological authorities. If such valuables are never recovered—or are not reported when they are found—yet another valuable fragment of the past is lost to science.

Remote Sensing: Google Earth and Other Developments

Deliberate archaeological survey often begins with satellite imagery and other **remote sensing** data, with platforms such as Google Earth (GE). GE is a widely used platform that allows archaeologists to examine high-resolution imagery of much of the world. Basically a highly detailed, high-resolution map, you can use a geographic information system (GIS) client (easily installed on your machine) to add labels known as "placemarkers" to the maps, to mark the locations of sites and other archaeological data—to say nothing of restaurants and other attractions. Once your placemarkers are located, you can share them with others using GIS or GE. Your markers can be simply location points, or you can add all kinds of data to suit your needs.

One of the longest-running remote-sensing projects is in the Arroux valley area of Burgundy in France, where a team of scientists from many disciplines are studying the complex and changing interactions between different societies and the physical environment. Researcher Scott Madry alongside others, has identified over 150 previously unrecorded archaeological sites in France using GE and other satellite imagery platforms. This method of site discovery has expanded significantly in recent years, with advances in both satellite technology and AI-driven analysis, leading to even more precise mapping and identification.

Other research initiatives have used satellite imagery to document earthworks in Ohio, map the Inca Trail through the Andes, and explore ancient southwestern pueblos. Archaeologists worldwide continue to leverage tools like GE and other remote-sensing technologies—especially for CRM projects, which require extensive surveys across large or remote areas that are hard to access by traditional means. While on-the-ground survey remains irreplaceable, these technologies have proven invaluable in identifying areas that may warrant further investigation and in offering a virtual "first look" at distant sites, from ancient Rome to the temples of Angkor Wat in Cambodia.

The *GlobalXplorer* program, developed by Sarah Parcak and her team, is an online platform, which involves thousands of participants globally, and has helped identify thousands of potential archaeological features and sites, with notable finds in Egypt, Peru, and parts of Southeast Asia. The project's latest focus has shifted to India, where satellite imagery is being used to map ancient settlements and potential archaeological sites in under-explored regions. With continued growth in both the number of participants and the sophistication of satellite data, the potential for global archaeological exploration has expanded exponentially.

Much of today's archaeology is concerned with large-scale surveys, often as part of CRM projects. These require sophisticated sampling methods, and also the use of GE and other remote-sensing methods—the use of such devices as aerial photographs and satellite imagery, as well as ground-penetrating radar and even small drones, such as were recently used to find an Anglo-Saxon fish trap of the seventh century A.D., which only appears in the Stour River estuary at very low tides. The drone, armed with a camera, hovered over the fish trap while the archaeologists on dry land viewed the trap from various altitudes. The primary purposes of many remote-sensing surveys are to map concentrations of sites and, on larger projects, to identify where maximal efforts in ground surveying and excavation should be concentrated. Such surveys are also invaluable for placing sites within environmental zones. Aerial photography gives an overhead view of the past, revealing sites such as plowed-down burial mounds and earthworks that leave no trace on the surface (see Figure 3.5). Systematic aerial reconnaissance can save weeks of ground time, for one can often pinpoint sites before going into the field.

remote sensing The detection and recording of archaeological features using aerial, satellite, or other sensor data without direct contact with the ground.

Today's archaeologists use multispectral and infrared imaging to track shallow, subsurface water sources once used by ancient peoples, and use side-looking airborne radar, and increasingly, satellite imagery, to locate sites and study entire ancient landscapes (see Figure 3.7). One important method is LiDAR (Light Detection and Ranging), the optical

Figure 3.5 Crop marks reveal ancient agricultural activity and other features.
Source: fotolincs/Alamy.

equivalent of radar. It uses a laser rangefinder to measure height, which can yield accurate and dense digital models of topography, even the vertical structures of buildings and trees, from the air. LiDAR provides astonishingly precise images of everything from standing ruins like pueblos to abandoned house depressions and European medieval towns.

The space shuttle *Columbia* used an imaging radar system to bounce radar signals off the surfaces of the world's major deserts in 1981. This experiment was designed to study the history of the Earth's aridity, not archaeology, but it identified ancient river courses in the limestone bedrock 1.5 meters (5 feet) or more below the Sahara's surface. Remote sensing is useless unless checked on the ground, so a team of geologists, including archaeologist C. Vance Haynes of the University of Arizona, journeyed far into the desert to investigate the long-hidden watercourses. About the only people to have worked this terrain were the World War II British Army and present-day Egyptian oil companies, the latter of which kindly arranged for a skip loader to be transported into the desert. To Haynes's astonishment, the skip loader trenches yielded some 200,000-year-old stone axes, dramatic and unexpected proof that early Stone Age hunter-gatherers had lived in the heart of the Sahara when the landscape was more hospitable than today. The Haynes find is of cardinal importance, for African archaeologists now believe that the Sahara was a vital catalyst in early human history that effectively sealed off archaic humans from the rest of the Old World (see Chapters 9 and 10). In later times, sub-Saharan Africa was isolated from the Mediterranean world until camel caravans opened up the desert in the first millennium A.D.

Back to (Real) Earth: Ground Survey

Survey from space and the heavens is no substitute for verifying your findings on the ground. Archaeological survey means walking the landscape, often along carefully laid-out transects and recording observations with GPS and digital mapping tools. A large-scale survey means lots of it, day after day, week after week, on carefully laid-out transects that cross hill and dale. We always enjoy survey, for you develop a sense of the local landscape, meet all kinds of people, and get a unique impression of a place. And there is always the prospect of an important discovery. The authors once spent a month looking for Stone Age rock shelters in southwestern England and found no traces of human occupation whatsoever. Whereas we returned from a week in southern Zambia with records of over 30 large mound villages, and over six millennia of diverse occupation evidence following a fortnight of ground surveying on the Red Sea coast of Yemen. Survey is fascinating because no two days are alike, and the rewards can be immense.

An archaeological survey can vary from spending an afternoon searching a city lot for traces of historical structures to a large-scale survey over several years of an entire river basin or drainage area. In all cases, the theoretical ideal is easily stated: to record all traces of ancient settlement in the area. But this ideal is impossible to achieve. Many sites leave no traces above the ground. And no survey, however thorough, will ever achieve the impossible dream of total coverage. The key to effective archaeological survey lies in carefully designing the research before one sets out and in using techniques to estimate the probable density of archaeological sites in the region.

A great deal depends on the thoroughness of the field survey. The most effective surveys are carried out on foot, where the archaeologist can locate the traces of artifacts: the gray organic soil eroding from a long-abandoned settlement, and the subtle colors of rich vegetation that reveal long-buried houses. Plowed fields may display revealing traces of ash, artifacts, or hut foundations. Scatters of broken bones, stone implements, potsherds, or other traces of prehistoric occupation are easily located in such furrowed soil. Observation is the key to finding archaeological sites and to studying the subtle relationships between prehistoric settlements and the landscape on which they flourished.

Archaeologists have numerous inconspicuous signs to guide them. Gray soil from a rodent burrow, a handful of human-fractured stones in the walls of a desert arroyo, a blurred mark in a plowed field, a potsherd—these are the signs they seek. After a few days, you learn to spot the telltale gray earth sent up by burrowing animals from village sites from some distance off. And often local landowners can provide information on possible sites, for they have an intimate knowledge of their own acreage.

In the early days, archaeologists concentrated on conspicuous, easily found sites. Now, with so many sites endangered by all kinds of industrial development, they hurry to find as many prehistoric locations as possible. Often a survey is designed to make an inventory of archaeological sites in a specific area. When an area is to be deep-plowed or covered with houses, proof that archaeological sites do or do not exist in the endangered zone is the responsibility of the archaeologists. Time is often short and funds limited. The only way the archaeologists can estimate the extent of the site resource base is to survey selected areas in great detail, using formal sampling methods to provide a statistically reliable basis of archaeological data from which to make generalizations about the wider area.

Settlement Patterns and Settlement Archaeology

cultural landscape A landscape as defined by a culture that dwells in it.

Every archaeological site once flourished within a local landscape, so it follows that archaeologists are very concerned with settlement patterns. These are the result of relationships among people who decided for economic, social, and political reasons to place their houses, settlements, and religious structures where they did. They created a **cultural landscape**, with its own associations and memories—"landscapes of memory," if you will. A landscape is like a piece of sculpture, which changes as it is molded by the artist's hands. In archaeological terms, the landscape around a Maya city or the stone circles at Avebury in southern England have been changing ever since humans settled in both areas. Both landscapes have changed radically within the past century, in ways unrelated to their functions in previous centuries and millennia of use. Our challenge is to reconstruct the landscape as its various users saw it—their landscape of memory.

settlement archaeology The study of changing ancient settlement patterns in the context of their environments.

Angkor Wat, Cambodia Royal capital and shrine built by the Khmer rulers of Cambodia between A.D. 1000 and 1200.

A half-century ago, excavation of archaeological sites was all-important. Today, **settlement archaeology**, the archaeology of landscape and settlement, is much more commonplace in an era when the study of ancient environments is assuming ever-greater importance. Settlement archaeology allows us to examine relationships among different communities and trading networks, and to examine the ways in which people exploited their environments, as well as changing social and political conditions. Studies of entire landscapes can sometimes throw light on a society's view of the world or the cosmos. For example, ancient Maya cities were symbolic replicas of the complex spiritual world of their builders, with sacred mountains (pyramids), temples (doorways to the other world), and columns (trees symbolizing kingship) (see Figure 3.6). **Angkor Wat** in Cambodia, a flamboyant Khmer palace and temple, was a replica in stone and stucco of the Hindu world with its lakes and sacred mountains, and was revealed by surface photography and LiDAR (see Figure 3.7) (for details of a major city-mapping project, see Box 3.2).

geographic information system (GIS) A system for mapping archaeological and other data in digitized form, thereby allowing the data to be manipulated for research purposes.

GIS technology takes all these data and provides integrated views of ancient landscapes. A GIS is a computer-aided system for the collection, storage, retrieval, analysis, and presentation of spatial data of all kinds. GIS incorporates computer-aided mapping, computerized databases, and statistical packages, and is best thought of as a computer database with mapping capabilities. It also has the ability to generate new information based on the data within it.

Figure 3.6 The central precinct of the Maya city at Tikal, Guatemala, which is a symbolic representation of sacred mountains, forests, and trees. The city center is a model of the Maya cosmos.

Source: Simon Dannhauer/Thinkstock.

(a)

(b)

Figure 3.7 (a) Angkor Wat, Cambodia: The central precincts. (b) Mahendraparvata is another large settlement area—a city of the Khmer Empire in Cambodia, where the first Khmer ruler, Jayavarman II, was consecrated in A.D. 802. It lies about 40 kilometers (25 miles) north of the temple at Angkor Wat (see Figure 3.7a). Much of the city lies under thick vegetation and earth. In 2013, a team of archaeologists led by Damian Evans and Jean-Baptiste Chevance used helicopter-mounted LiDAR starting from an earlier, limited ground survey. They located 30 hitherto unidentified temples, a grid-like network of roads, dikes, and ponds that defined the city, which once stood on deforested land. LiDAR has revealed the much greater extent of the Angkor urban landscape, and has been used to study the Maya city of Caracol in Belize. After years of laborious ground research, the LiDAR revealed more than 200 square kilometers of agricultural terraces, buildings arranged around squares, waterways and numerous reservoirs, as well as caves. These are but two exciting applications of a technology that is already revolutionizing our knowledge of archaeological sites large and small, and entire landscapes. But, despite its success, there is ultimately no substitute for on-the-ground investigation, which is the follow-up stage of LiDAR research.

Source: Olga Anourina/Thinkstock.

Box 3.2 Site
Teotihuacán, Mexico

Site surveys are complex, and their complexity increases with the size of the area under study. Perhaps the largest site survey project ever undertaken was the Teotihuacán Mapping Project, directed by George Cowgill and René Millon. Teotihuacán lies northeast of Mexico City and is one of the great tourist attractions of the Americas (see Figure 3.8). This great pre-Columbian city flourished from about 200 B.C. until A.D. 750. Up to 150,000 people lived in Teotihuacán at the peak of its prosperity. Huge pyramids and temples, giant plazas, and an enormous market formed the core of the well-organized and neatly planned city. The houses of the priests and nobles lay along the main avenues; the artisans and common people lived in crowded compounds of apartments and courtyards.

Cowgill and Millon realized that the only effective way to study the city was to make a comprehensive map of all of the precincts; without it, they would never have been able to study how Teotihuacán grew to be so huge. Fortunately, the streets

Figure 3.8 Teotihuacán, Mexico. The Avenue of the Dead with the Pyramids of the Sun at right, the Pyramid of the Moon at the far end.

Source: David South/Alamy Stock Photo.

and buildings lay close to the surface, unlike the vast city mounds in the Near East, where only deep excavation yields settlement information.

The mapping project began with a detailed ground survey, conducted with the aid of aerial photographs and large-scale survey maps. The field data were collected on 147 map data sheets of 500-meter (1,640-foot) squares at a scale of 1:2,000. Intensive mapping and surface surveys, including surface collections of artifacts, were then conducted systematically within the 20-square-kilometer (8-square-mile) limits of the ancient city defined by the preliminary survey. Ultimately, the architectural interpretations of the surface features within each 500-meter square were overprinted on the base map of the site. These architectural interpretations were based on graphic data and surface data collected on special forms and through artifact collections, photographs, and drawings. Extensive use of sophisticated sampling techniques and quantitative methods was essential for successful completion of the map.

By the end of the project, researchers had recorded more than 5,000 structures and activity areas within the city limits. The Teotihuacán maps do not, of course, convey to us the incredible majesty of this remarkable city, but they do provide, for the first time, a comprehensive view of a teeming, multifaceted community with vast public buildings, plazas, and avenues; thousands of small apartments and courtyards, which formed individual households; and pottery, figurine, and obsidian workshops, among the many diverse structures in the city. The survey also revealed that the city had been expanded over the centuries according to a comprehensive master plan (for more on Teotihuacán, see Chapter 15).

We always think of GIS in terms of layers, the basic layer being the topographic map, to which you add layer after layer of information such as vegetation, water sources, archaeological sites, and so on—preparing a map that can display all kinds of different information, and which can be changed at will. The metaphor is a base map, upon which you pile layers of tracing paper or transparent plastic that display different kinds of data. You use a database, where all the data, be it about soils or sites, is recorded using the same mapping system. Each data point has its own database, where information such as artifact frequencies, unusual finds, and so on is displayed, to say nothing of architectural features, storage pits, or contour lines.

In short, the past is at your fingertips, and in such a format that you can ask questions of your map. How far away from a specific village were acorn-rich oaks to be found? What food resources and toolmaking materials lay within 5 kilometers (3 miles) of the settlement? How far did people have to walk to reach the best soils for cultivating maize? You can even bring up the landscape in such a way that you can see the same view as the ancient inhabitants saw, an important strategic concern when you are afraid of raiders or surprise attacks from the sea. GIS does what archaeologists have done for generations—that is, look at sites in the context of their environment—but it does it in a fraction of the time that it used to take, and with far greater sophistication and precision once the databases are constructed: an extremely lengthy process but one that makes sense when you are concerned with the inventorying of sites and predictive surveys.

Wroxeter, England Major Roman city in west-central England that assumed great importance in the second century A.D.

Stonehenge, England Circular stone complex with associated sacred landscape first established before 3000 B.C.; its heyday was c. 1800 B.C.

From the archaeological perspective, GIS has the advantage that it allows the manipulation of large amounts of data, especially useful for solving complex settlement analysis problems at places like the Roman towns of Pompeii, Italy, and **Wroxeter**, England. You can model different landscape scenarios by manipulating the data, and compare changing settlement patterns with natural environmental changes. British archaeologist Vincent Gaffney has produced a remarkable "virtual landscape" of the Bronze Age stone circles of **Stonehenge** in southern England at the various stages of construction, which allows one to "walk" the landscape and to reconstruct the sight lines from various features to the stone circles (Figure 3.9). He has also reconstructed the now submerged land surfaces of the North Sea when they were dry land at the end of the Ice Age. In 2010, the Stonehenge Hidden Landscapes Project used a state-of-the-art magnetometer and geo-radar system to produce three-dimensional images and map 14 square kilometers (5.4 square miles) of the landscape around the monument. Among other important finds, they located a "henge-like" monument with stone uprights just 900 meters (984 yards) northwest of the iconic stone circle. This nonintrusive archaeological project will help us learn what the landscape really looked like when Stonehenge was built and used. No site can be understood without reference to its surrounding landscape, least of all a major sacred site like Stonehenge.

Figure 3.9 Stonehenge, England.
Source: Creatas Images/Thinkstock.

How Do You Dig Up the Past?

Excavation: The very word conjures up images of magnificent pyramids and mysterious cities revealed by the spade. Reality is very different, for modern-day excavation is a deliberate, usually slow-moving process of observation and recording, a search for information rather than spectacular discoveries. Nevertheless, archaeological excavation exercises a peculiar fascination, perhaps because of the lure of unexpected discoveries and sometimes spectacular finds.

Until a couple of generations ago, excavation was considered a primary objective of archaeological fieldwork. However, the destruction of the archaeological record has reached such epidemic proportions that excavation has now become a strategy of last resort. Every archaeologist knows that the record is finite, that once disturbed, archaeological context is gone forever. We are all aware that every excavation destroys part of the archaeological record.

nonintrusive archaeology Archaeological field research conducted without excavation and without disturbing the archaeological record.

Nonintrusive archaeology, archaeology without excavation, has become increasingly important in recent years as regional studies have replaced site-oriented investigations as a primary thrust in archaeology. At the same time, excavation has become increasingly selective, both because of its high cost and because of a desire to leave part of a site intact for future generations to investigate.

The Ethical Responsibilities of the Excavator

Excavators shoulder a heavy responsibility, for they destroy the past on the one hand even as they record it in meticulous detail on the other. An archaeologist's excavation is only as good as the notes, computer records, photographs, and plans that reconstruct the dig when it is complete.

Every excavator has vital ethical responsibilities:

- To excavate only within the context of a specific research design.
- To record the archaeological context of the finds and to make a complete record of the excavation.
- To respect the feelings of local people and to work closely with them, especially if human remains come to light. (The issue of reburial and repatriation of skeletal remains is extremely complex and sensitive. Owing to space considerations, it is not discussed here.)
- To publish a permanent record of the results and to ensure that the notes, drawings, maps, plans, artifacts, and other finds are deposited in a facility that will preserve them permanently.
- To conserve and curate artifacts and other finds, as part of taking responsibility for stewardship.

Excavation is the culminating step in the investigation of an archaeological site. It recovers data from the Earth that is not obtainable in any other way. Like historical archives, the soil of an archaeological site is a document whose pages must be deciphered, translated, and interpreted before they can be used to write an accurate account of the past.

Excavation is destruction—the archaeological deposits so carefully dissected during any dig are destroyed forever and their contents are removed. Here, again, there is a radical difference between archaeology and both history and other sciences. A physical scientist can readily re-create the conditions for a basic experiment; an historian can return to the archives to reevaluate the complex events in, say, a politician's life. But all that we have after an excavation are the finds from the trenches, the untouched portions of the site, and the photographs, notes, and drawings that record the excavator's observations for posterity. Therefore, accurate recording and observation are vital in the day-to-day work of archaeologists, not only for the sake of accuracy in their own research, but also because they are creating an archive of archaeological information that may be consulted by others.

Research Design and Problem-Oriented Excavation

Archaeological sites are nonrenewable resources. Unfocused excavation is therefore useless, for the manageable and significant observations are buried in a mass of irrelevant trivia. Any excavation must be conducted from a sound research design intended to solve specific and well-defined problems.

There was a time when archaeologists selected a site for excavation because it "looked good" or because dense concentrations of surface finds suggested that promising discoveries lay below the surface. Excavations are traditionally conducted on larger sites, on sites that look more productive, on sites threatened by development, or on sites nearest to roads. These criteria bear no resemblance to the goal that is actually required, which is acquiring representative and unbiased data to answer a particular question—a problem whose limits are ultimately defined by available money and time. Unbiased data, which do not reflect the investigator's idiosyncrasies, can properly yield statistical estimates of the culture from which the samples were drawn. This kind of information requires explicit sampling procedures to select a few sites from an area to excavate and to control reliability of the information by using probability and statistics.

Excavation costs are so great that problem-oriented digging is now the rule rather than the exception, with the laboratory work forming part of the continuing evaluation of the research problem. The large piles of finds and records accumulated at the end of even a small field season contain a bewildering array of interconnected facts that the researcher must evaluate and reevaluate as inquiry proceeds—by constantly arranging propositions and hypotheses, correlating observations, and reevaluating interpretations of the archaeological evidence. Finds and plans are the basis of the researcher's strategy and affect fieldwork plans for the future, the basis for constant reevaluation of research objectives.

Let's take three brief examples of well-planned excavation:

Koster, Illinois Stratified site in the Illinois River valley of the North American Midwest inhabited from about 7500 B.C. to A.D. 1200 by foragers and then maize farmers.

Koster, Illinois

Koster lies in the Illinois River valley, a deep accumulation of 26 ancient occupation layers extending from about 10,000 years ago to around A.D. 1100 to 1200. The wealth of material at Koster first came to light in 1968 and was the subject of extremely large-scale excavations during the 1970s, resulting in a classic example of sound North American excavation. The dig involved collaboration by three archaeologists and six specialists from other disciplines such as zoology and botany, as well as the use of a computer laboratory.

Archaeologists James Brown and Stuart Struever faced a number of formidable difficulties. Thirteen of the Koster cultural horizons are isolated from their neighbors by a zone of sterile slopewash soil, which makes it possible to treat each as a separate problem in excavation and analysis—as if it were an individual site—although, in fact, the 13 are stratified one above another. Large-scale excavations were needed to uncover each living surface so that the excavators could not only understand what the living zones within each occupation were like but also, after studying in detail the sequence of differences in activities, make statements about the processes of cultural change.

From the large scale of the excavations, Brown and Struever saw the need for immediate feedback from the data flow from the site during the excavation. Changes in the excavation method would no doubt be needed during the season's fieldwork to ensure that maximum information was obtained. To accomplish this flexibility, both excavation and data-gathering activities were combined into a data-flow system to ensure feedback to the excavators that would be as close to instantaneous as possible. The categories of data—animal bones, artifacts, vegetable remains—were processed in the field, and the information from the analyses was then fed to a computer in Evanston, Illinois, many kilometers away. Pollen and soil samples were sent directly to specialist laboratories for analysis (see Figure 3.10).

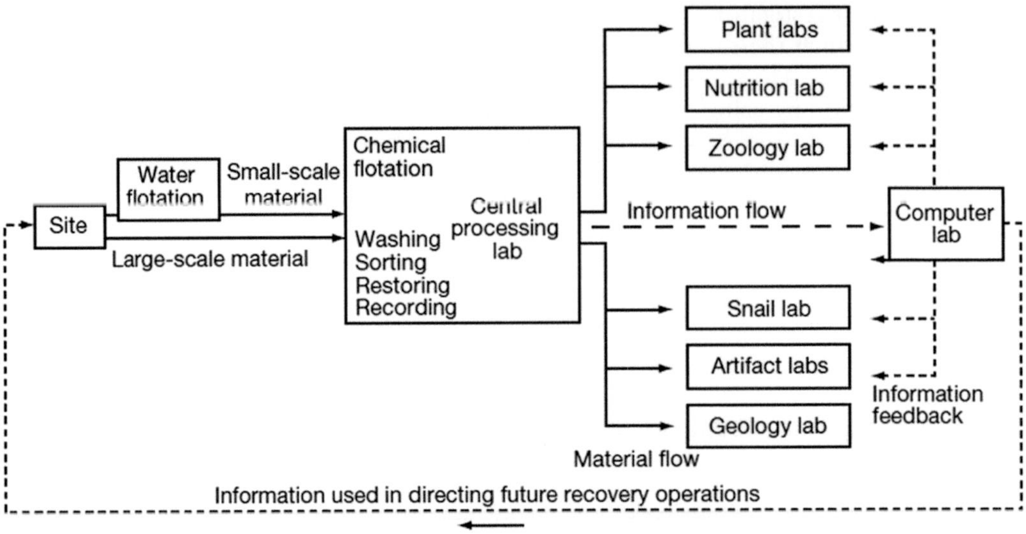

Figure 3.10 The data-flow system at the Koster excavations, a version of which is common to many excavations and other field projects. The Internet now plays an important part in data management and sharing.

Shiloh Mound A, Tennessee Mississippian earthworks occupied about A.D. 1000.

Shiloh Mound Complex, Tennessee A Mississippian center on the Tennessee River, dating from c. A.D. 1000 to 1350.

Shiloh Mound A, Southwestern Tennessee

When the U.S. National Park Service decided to excavate and stabilize **Mound A**—a 1,000-year-old Mississippian earthwork once surrounded by a wooden palisade in the **Shiloh Mound Complex** on the Tennessee River—the excavator, David Anderson, had to balance investigation of the mound and its complex internal structure, revealed by remote sensing, with the need to protect it against the encroaching Tennessee River, which was eroding the archaeological deposits. The research design included a program of dispersed test pits and the excavation of a 2-meter (6.5-foot) wide step trench into two sides and across the top of the mound (see Figure 3.11). At the same time, a stabilizing program was put into place, which made assumptions about the amount of loss to be expected over the next half-century. The research design, which involved the work of scientists from a wide array of disciplines, posed a number of specific questions to be investigated, most of them revolving around the construction of Mound A, as well as information on the cultural changes, possibly including maize agriculture, that took place over the site's history. Finally, the plan outlined the stages of fieldwork to be undertaken, as well as access and safety measures to be implemented. Plans were also laid for consultations with the local Chickasaw Nation as excavation proceeded.

Dust Cave, Alabama Cave site occupied between about 8000 and 1600 B.C., with evidence of extensive plant exploitation and fishing activity.

Figure 3.11 Shiloh Mound A, Tennessee. A meticulously excavated trench forms a cross-section of the mound, which is being eroded by the Tennessee River. The excavation included measures to stabilize the site.

Source: Dennis K. Johnson/Alamy Stock Photo.

Dust Cave, Alabama

Dust Cave lies in a limestone bluff on the Middle Tennessee River in northwestern Alabama. Extensive Paleo-Indian and Archaic occupations, dating between about 8000 and 1600 B.C., reach a depth of 5 meters (16.4 feet). Excellent preservation conditions conserved animal bones and plant materials, also features such as hearths, pits, and clay floors. Archaeologists from the University of Alabama sunk 2-meter by 2-meter (6.5-foot by 6.5-foot) test pits into the cave floor. When they located stone artifacts, they excavated a large 2-meter by 12-meter (6.5-foot by 39-foot) cutting down to sterile bedrock. The excavators dug the cave using the stratified layers of human occupation as their guide, each being dissected meticulously. All the occupation deposits were passed through a 6-millimeter (0.25-inch) mesh screen, while large samples were processed through water to obtain seeds and other minute plant remains, a technique known as flotation (see Chapter 4). They identified the different human occupation stages by using highly diagnostic stone projectile points that changed significantly over time. This elaborate vertical excavation is a classic example of scientific cave excavation.

Data-flow systems like that pioneered at Koster are highly beneficial. The routine analysis of artifacts and food residues is completed on the site, and the data are available to the excavators in the field after a few days instead of months later, as is usual. The research design can be modified in the field at short notice, with ready consultation among the team members in the field. Today, many excavators, especially on CRM projects, make use of the Internet to record and transmit data. Laptop computers and digital measuring devices have also made data recording on-site an easy task.

In many projects, excavation is only part of the overall research design. As a method, it should be used sparingly, for the end result is always destruction of the site.

Types of Excavation

How do you dissect a stratified archaeological site? Obviously, there is no one standardized way of excavating them, for they vary infinitely in their size, preservation conditions, and complexity.

geometric excavation Excavation in arbitrary levels.

In the **geometric excavation** method, the excavator lays out a rectangular trench, then levels the surface within before taking the deposits down in thin spits, or arbitrary layers, up to 10 centimeters (4 inches) thick. As the excavation proceeds, the exposed walls display the stratigraphic profile. The horizontal surface consists of the same layers truncated and seen from the top. By recording both sets of layers, the researcher obtains a three-dimensional picture of the entire deposit from top to bottom. This is an efficient way of excavating and recording a site, but it has the disadvantage that one never looks at the layers for what they actually are—the record can be called somewhat inhuman in terms of recording ancient human behavior. Brian has used this method extensively to excavate mounded farming villages, where the stratigraphic layers were very hard to see and where he was working with unskilled workers (see Figure 2.5 on p. 46).

sampling excavation Excavation using sampling methods to place trenches, usually random sampling.

Figure 3.12 Mortimer Wheeler-style excavation using baulks and boxes at the **Jingsha** site near Chengdu, China, c. 1000 B.C. (excavation displayed in the site museum).

Source: Best View Stock/Alamy.

Sampling excavation is a variant on the geometric method, which gives you multiple views of the stratigraphic sequence at different points. The great British excavator Sir Mortimer Wheeler put his boxes in shallow sites in formal grids covering a considerable area, allowing him to monitor the stratified layers in the "baulks" between the boxes. Once excavation and recording was complete, he would then remove the baulks, knowing that he had tight control over the stratigraphy (Figure 3.12). North American excavators commonly use random sampling to place their boxes—expanding, joining, or linking them if this is judged necessary. This approach has the advantage of being faster and providing a quick impression of a site. It is most successful with relatively homogeneous sites like shell middens, but has the disadvantage that different activities take place at different locations within a site and you may miss some of them.

Jingsha, China Important center of the Shu kingdom, c. 1000 B.C.

stratigraphic excavation Excavation that involves exposing individual layers.

Stratigraphic excavation is the hardest form of dissection, for it involves exposing each of the layers, one by one, and as they lie in the ground. If you have well-colored, sharp layers, stratigraphic excavation, while challenging, is relatively straightforward. If the layers have decayed or are less well-defined, then difficulties proliferate. With stratigraphic excavation, you record as you go along, following a sequence of defining the layer—which can be a feature, a posthole, an occupation horizon—then recording, removing, and recording it again, perhaps in a broader context of other features exposed nearby.

Stratigraphic excavation is notoriously difficult in caves and rock shelters that have been visited repeatedly over long periods of time. Almost invariably, you are working in a restricted space, which means your trenches will be vertical cuts into the stratified deposits. In many places, where stratigraphic excavation is the norm, researchers tend to expose large, continuous areas—horizontal excavations—that reveal large numbers of individually recorded components. The advantage is that you expose the entire area of a single deposit, like the central precincts of a small farming village, but the approach places heavy responsibility on those who record individual features. It is hard, too, to obtain an overall check on the stratigraphy.

Vertical and Horizontal Excavation

vertical excavation Excavation undertaken to establish a chronological sequence, normally covering a limited area.

Many archaeologists make a distinction between vertical and horizontal excavation. **Vertical excavation** is selective digging, uncovering a limited area on a site for the purpose of recovering specific information. Most vertical excavations are probes of deep archaeological deposits, their real objective being to reveal the chronological sequence at a site (Figure 3.13).

test pits Cuttings of limited size sunk into archaeological sites for sampling purposes, to establish stratigraphy or to define the limits of a site.

Figure 3.13 A classic example of vertical excavation from the Iron Age hill fort at Maiden Castle, England, where Sir Mortimer Wheeler used the approach to investigate the dates of earthen ramparts before World War II. The white posts are for measurement purposes. This excavation was conducted almost a century ago and has set standards ever since, which is why we illustrate it here.

Source: Society of Antiquaries, London.

Test pits, sometimes referred to by the French term *sondages* or even as "telephone booths," are a frequently used form of vertical excavation. They consist of small trenches just large enough to accommodate one or two diggers and are designed to penetrate to the lower strata of a site to establish the extent of archaeological deposits (Figure 3.14). This method maybe supplemented by augers or borers.

As we saw at Dust Cave, test pits are a preliminary to large-scale excavation, for the information they reveal is limited at best. Carefully placed test pits can provide valuable insights into the stratigraphy and artifact content of a site before larger-scale excavation begins. Test pits are also used to obtain samples from different areas of sites, such as shell middens, where dense concentrations of artifacts are found throughout the deposits. In such cases, test pits are excavated on a grid pattern, with the positioning of the pits being determined by statistical sampling or by a regular pattern such as alternate squares (for different archaeological sites, see Box 3.3).

Full-scale vertical trenches are much larger, deeper cuttings used to establish such phenomena as sequences of building operations, histories of complex earthworks, and long cultural sequences in deep caves. Such cuttings are widely used to excavate early village sites such as Abu Hureyra in southwestern Asia. They may also be used to obtain a cross-section of a site threatened by destruction or to examine outlying structures near a

Figure 3.14 Test trenches at Quiriguá, Guatemala.
Source: University of Pennsylvania Museum, Image 07458.

village or a cemetery that has been dug on a large scale. Vertical excavations of this kind are almost always dug in the expectation that the most important information to come from them will be the record of layers in the walls of the trenches and the finds from them. But clearly, the amount of information to be obtained from such cuttings is of limited value compared with that from a larger excavation.

Horizontal or area digs are commonly associated with stratigraphic excavation, exposing large areas of a site to uncover house plans or settlement layouts. As a general rule, the only sites that are completely excavated are very small hunter-gatherer camps, isolated structures, and burial mounds. With larger settlements, all one can do is excavate several portions of the site in order to sample areas representative of the entire settlement. Again, modern archaeological ethics require minimal horizontal excavation consistent with the carefully controlled objectives of the investigation.

horizontal excavation Excavation of a large horizontal area, designed to uncover large areas of a site, especially houses and settlement layouts. Also known as *area excavation* or *block excavation*.

Horizontal excavation is highly effective with small hunter-gatherer sites, such as the artifact and bone scatters at Olduvai Gorge and other early human sites in East Africa, where the position of every stone flake and animal bone is recorded in place. Such an approach also works well with complex structures like Iroquois longhouses, which survive as complexes of decayed wooden postholes buried under a few inches of topsoil (see Figure 3.15). Such structures were often expanded, rebuilt, or sited on top of another structure, resulting in a jigsaw of posthole patterns that can only be deciphered with a large area excavation.

An excellent example of horizontal excavation exposed the Grewe site, a Hohokam farming village in the modern-day Phoenix area (Figure 3.16). Here, the excavators

Figure 3.15 Reconstruction of an Iroquois longhouse based on archaeological excavation.
Source: Stock Montage, Inc./Alamy.

Figure 3.16 Pithouses and courtyard groups exposed by area excavation at the Grewe site, Arizona.
Source: Courtesy of the Arizona State Department of Transportation and Northland Research, Inc.

exposed about two dozen courtyard groups: complexes of semisubterranean pithouses that shared central courtyards and food-roasting pits. The groups, in turn, surrounded a large central plaza. The largest courtyard group contained 26 houses and covered more than 604 square meters (6,500 square feet). Careful excavation revealed that only a few houses in each group were occupied at one time, most of the households comprising no more than about ten people. Furthermore, the courtyard groups were occupied for varied lengths of time: some for centuries, others for a few generations. This may show that ownership of houses and compounds passed from one generation to the next, sometimes over long periods of time.

ziggurat Mesopotamian temple mound.

Kanesh, Türkiye Hittite settlement founded in the seventeenth century B.C., famous in later centuries for its Assyrian trading quarter.

Ceremonial sites are those devoted primarily to religious and ritual observances. Some formed part of much larger communities. The Mesopotamian **ziggurat** (temple mound) of 3000 B.C. dominated its mother city (see Figure 3.18). Mesoamerican cities such as Teotihuacán boasted imposing pyramid temples and open plazas surrounded by acres of crowded urban apartment compounds (see Figure 3.8). Other famous ceremonial sites, like Stonehenge in England (see Figure 3.9), are isolated monuments. Ceremonial artifacts, such as stingray spines used in mutilation rituals, and statuary may be associated with sacred sites.

Box 3.3 Archaeological Sites

Archaeological sites can be classified by their artifact content and by the patterning of such finds within them. Here are the most common categories.

Living or habitation sites are the most important sites, for they are the places where people have lived and carried out a multitude of activities (Figure 3.16). The artifacts in living sites and in midden heaps reflect domestic activities, such as food preparation and toolmaking (Figure 3.17). Dwellings are normally present. The temporary camps of California fisherfolk are living sites, as are Stone Age rock shelters, American Southwestern pueblos, and Mesopotamian city mounds. Such structures—houses, granaries, temples, and other buildings—can be identified from standing remains, patterns of postholes, and other features in the ground. Habitation sites of any complexity are associated with other sites that reflect specialized needs, such as agricultural systems, cemeteries, and temporary camps. Often, these sites contain many features, artifacts, and artifact associations, such as postholes and ditches that cannot be removed intact from the ground.

Kill sites are places where prehistoric people killed game and camped around the carcasses while butchering the meat. They are relatively common on the American Great Plains. For example, archaeologist Joe Ben Wheat excavated the Olsen-Chubbock bison kill site of about 6000 B.C. He was even able to determine the direction of the wind on the day of the game drive (see Box 14.1 on p. 438).

Figure 3.17 Australian Aboriginal shell mound, Tarkine coast, Tasmania.
Source: Rob Blakers/Getty Images.

Figure 3.18 Reconstruction of a Sumerian ziggurat temple from Eridu, Iraq, one of the earliest cities in the world.

Burial sites include both cemeteries and isolated tombs. We have been burying our dead since at least 50,000 years ago and have often taken enormous pains to prepare the bodies for the afterlife. Perhaps the most famous burial sites of all are the Pyramids of Giza in Egypt (see Figure 3.3). Royal sepulchers, such as that of the Egyptian pharaoh Tutankhamun, absorbed the energies of hundreds of people in their preparation (see Figure 12.17 on p. 408). Many burials are associated with special grave furniture, jewelry, and ornaments of rank.

Trading and quarry sites are locations where specialized activities took place. The special tools needed for mining obsidian, copper, and other metals identify quarry sites. Trading sites are identified by large quantities of exotic trade objects and by their strategic position near major cities. The Assyrian market that flourished outside the Hittite city of **Kanesh**, Türkiye, in 1900 B.C. is one of these.

Art sites, which abound in southwestern France, southern Africa, Australia, California, and other areas, are identified by engravings and paintings on the walls of caves and rock shelters.

The arbitrary subdivision between vertical and horizontal excavation has some merit, and is commonly used. However, it disguises a much more flexible reality. What matters is to use the appropriate methods for the site and problem at hand. Excavating a site with ill-defined layers, or the backfilling of a ditch or large burial pit, may be best achieved by the geometric methods. Stratigraphic excavation works best for sites with easily distinguishable layers. What matters is establishing how things actually were in the past. As Martin Carver remarks: "An archaeological deposit is a three-dimensional artifact, only seen once and never seen whole. It deserves an analytical approach that is special to itself, not just to be dissected and recorded, but to be studied" (Carver 2009, 123). A good excavation is as creative an activity as writing a book—and is redesigned every time you put a spade into the ground.

Excavation as Recording

Archaeological excavation is an extremely precise recording process that provides the context of prehistoric societies in time and space. Philip Barker, an English archaeologist and expert excavator, advocates a combined horizontal and vertical excavation for recording archaeological stratigraphy. He points out that a vertical profile gives a view of stratigraphy in the vertical plane only. Many important features appear in the section as a fine line and are decipherable only in the horizontal plane. The principal purpose of a stratigraphic profile is to record the information for posterity so that later observers have an accurate impression of how the layers of the profile were formed. Because stratigraphy demonstrates relationships—among sites and structures, artifacts, and natural layers—Barker advocates cumulative recording of stratigraphy as excavation is under way, which enables the archaeologist to record layers three-dimensionally. Such recording requires extremely skillful excavation. Various modifications of this technique are used in both Europe and North America.

total data station An electronic and optical theodolite integrated with an electronic distance meter to read slope distances and other archaeological data.

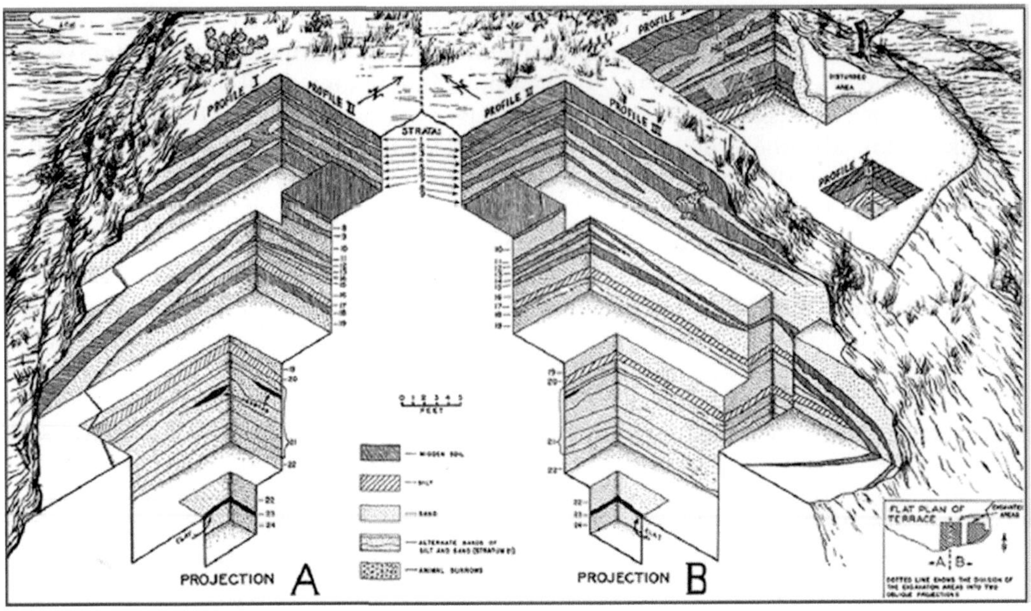

Figure 3.19 An exemplary stratigraphic diagram of the Devil's Mouth site, Amistad Reservoir, Texas. The diagram shows three-dimensional stratigraphy and correlates layers in different trenches with one another.

Source: Department of Anthropology, University of Texas, Austin.

All archaeological stratigraphy is three-dimensional; that is to say, it involves observations in both the vertical and horizontal planes. The ultimate objective of archaeological excavation is to record the three-dimensional relationships throughout a site, for these are the relationships that provide the context of each find. Large open-area excavations require accurate recording over considerable distances, made much easier when the position of houses and finds can be recorded with a **total data station**, an electronic device that measures distance and angles with high precision, allows archaeologists to capture detailed spatial data, which is then transferred to a laptop or cloud-based system for further analysis. A superb example of an accurate section drawing appears in Figure 3.19.

The process of archaeological excavation itself ends with filling in the trenches and transporting the finds and site records to the laboratory. The archaeologist leaves the field with a complete record of the excavations and with the data needed to test the hypotheses that were formulated before going into the field. But with this step, the job is far from finished; in fact, the work has hardly begun. The next stage in the research process is analyzing the finds, a topic covered in Chapters 4 and 5. Once the analysis is completed, interpretation of the site can begin.

Even in these days of tree-ring dating and radiocarbon samples, a primary concern of the excavator is stratigraphy and chronology, which brings us to the fundamental question: How old is it?

How Old Is It?

Time—our lives depend on it. We live from day to day according to tight schedules: class times, doctors' appointments, flight departures, and tax deadlines. The hours of the day are the framework of our daily lives, our jobs, and our leisure. Not for us the broad sweep of changing seasons or days measured by sunrise and sunset. We depend on the clock to guide us through the day, to regulate our lives. Let's say I wrote these words at precisely 10:16 A.M., then I could have obtained a reading for the exact moment when I wrote the numeral 10 if I wished. Modern Westerners are obsessed with the passage and measurement of time. Archaeologists are even more concerned with it than anyone. How do we know that humans originated over 6 million years ago?

Archaeologists refer to two types of chronology:

- **Relative chronology**, which establishes chronological relationships between sites and cultures.
- **Chronometric dating**, which refers to dates in years.

relative chronology Time scale developed by the law of superposition or artifact ordering.

chronometric dating Dating in calendar years before the present, often called absolute dating.

Relative Chronology

My black-and-white cat has just come into the study. His tummy bulging with breakfast, he gives me a plaintive meow and looks for a patch of sunlight on the carpet. He spots one, just where I have put down a pile of important papers. Thump! With a sigh, he settles right on top of the documents and passes out blissfully as I write. Time passes, and I realize that I need one of the articles in the pile under the faithful beast. I debate whether to have a cup of coffee and procrastinate or to disturb him, fearing that there will be angry claws. In the end, writing deadlines prevail. I gently elevate the cat and slip the papers out from under him. The beast protests halfheartedly and settles down again as I congratulate myself on escaping grievous injury (see Figure 3.20).

The case of the cat and the papers is a classic example of stratigraphy in action. Let's consider the sequence of events. I sit at his computer, consult some documents, and lay them to the side on the floor. This is the first event in the sequence. Sometime later, the second event takes place: the cat settles on the papers and goes to sleep. More time passes. I need an article from the pile, so I lift the cat and remove the papers. This third event is followed by the final act of this stirring drama as the cat settles down again. An outside observer could use the law of superposition (see Chapter 2) to reconstruct the sequence of events from the earliest (the putting of papers on the floor) to the latest (the cat settling down again). However, although the observer can establish the sequence of events relative to one another in time, he or she cannot tell how long a span of time passed between each one. Nor can he or she know the age of the various objects in the pile. For instance, a document compiled in 2026 might lie in a folder beneath another one containing a letter written ten years earlier.

Relative chronology is a foundation of all archaeological research, a time scale established either by stratigraphic observation or by placing artifacts in chronological order. As we saw in Chapter 2, stratigraphic observation is based on the law of superposition, which states that in general, the earliest layers lie below later ones. Many ancient settlements,

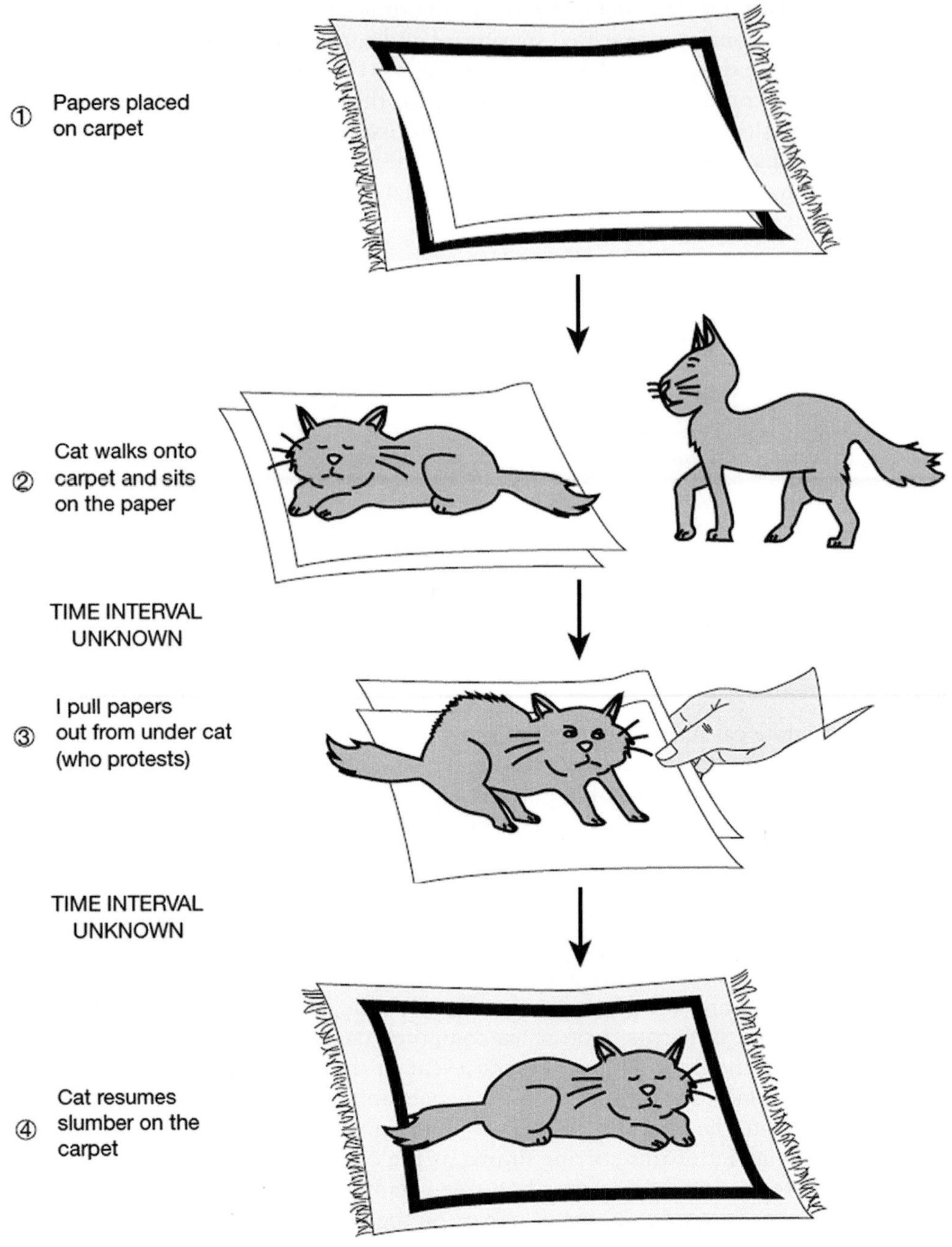

Figure 3.20 A case of feline chronology.

such as long-occupied caves and rock shelters or huge city mounds in southwestern Asia, can contain literally dozens of occupation levels, sometimes separated by layers of sterile soil. People lived in houses for a generation or more and then knocked them down and rebuilt on the same spot. They lost beads and ornaments, trampling them into the earth. They laid new floors, a layer of tile, or a few centimeters of liquid cattle dung over earlier living surfaces. Buildings crumbled, floods may have demolished structures, or fires may have consumed entire city blocks. People dug graves and storage pits, resurfaced streets, enlarged temples and open plazas. The archaeologist's relative chronology comes from deciphering these kinds of chronological jigsaw puzzles. Brian once spent two weeks excavating a 0.6-meter (2-foot) section cut through a Stone Age campsite where at least five temporary occupations could be seen in the wall of the trench. Unfortunately, none of the excavators could separate them, or their artifacts, horizontally.

The law of association also comes into play, for the artifacts, food remains, and other finds that come from different occupation layers are as vital as the stratigraphy itself. Each layer in a settlement, however massive or however thin, has its associated artifacts, the objects that archaeologists use as chronological indicators and evidence of cultural change. Stratigraphic observation is rarely straightforward. Some key questions are never far from the observer's mind: Was the site occupied continuously? Was the sequence interrupted by a natural catastrophe such as a flood, or was it abandoned and then reoccupied generations later? Far more is involved than merely observing different layers. Basically, the excavator has to reconstruct both the natural and the cultural processes that have affected the site since it was abandoned.

Artifacts are valuable tools in establishing relative chronology, for different styles come into fashion and then fall out of favor again (see Figure 3.21). Unfortunately, we do not have the space to explore this subject in detail here.

Figure 3.21 Relative chronology. Placing artifacts in relative chronological order involves tracing changes in style through time. Gravestones from around the time of the American Revolution from Shirley, Massachusetts, showing the cherub motif, which was most popular between 1780 and 1789. Stylistic changes on New England tombstones have provided a classic example of artifact seriation.

Source: Inga Spence/Alamy.

Chronometric Dating

"The first question is about dinosaurs; the second asks how old it is." An old archaeologist friend welcomes visitors to his excavations but finds their questions repetitive, especially in a society fascinated by dinosaurs. "Why are we so obsessed with dates?" he asks, and with good reason. Perhaps it comes from the fascination of handling artifacts that were used hundreds or thousands of years ago. We will never forget the first time we handled a Neanderthal skull from a cave in southwestern France. The feeling of holding the head of someone who had lived in the Ice Age gives you an evocative sensation that you shall always remember.

Many of our most fundamental questions about the past involve chronology. How old is this stone ax? Are these villages contemporary? When was this woman buried? More effort has gone into inventing methods of dating the past than into almost any other aspect of archaeology.

The landscape of the human experience stretches back many millions of years. Relative dating has serious limitations. It allows us to people this landscape with myriad long- and short-lived human cultures, ordered in local, regional, and continent-wide sequences. The relatively dated past is like a branching tree, but a tree whose branches and limbs have never grown evenly or sprouted at the same time. Relative dating allows us to erect the tree and plot its boughs and twigs in reasonably accurate order. We have a sense of a changing landscape but no perspective of passing years.

Without chronometric dates, we do not know when humanity originated, when specific cultures began and ended, or how fast they changed. Nor do we have any inkling of when different major developments, such as the changeover from hunting and gathering to farming, took place in the Americas as opposed to in southwestern Asia, or in China relative to tropical Africa. Chronometric dating is essential if we are to measure the rates of cultural change over long and short periods of time.

Dates in calendar years are the force that causes the stationary body of the past to come alive in the archaeologist's hands. Extremely precise tree-ring dates from the American Southwest tell the story of a prolonged drought cycle that affected the Ancestral Pueblo in the twelfth century, perhaps causing the residents to disperse from large pueblos to small villages. Radiocarbon dates calibrated with tree rings from Abu Hureyra, Syria, tell us that people switched from foraging to farming within a remarkably short time, perhaps a few generations. We now know that urban civilizations developed first in Egypt and Mesopotamia in about 3100 B.C., before 2000 B.C. in northern China, and in Central and South America shortly thereafter.

The time scale of the human past is hard to imagine. We are separated by 15,000 years from the end of the Ice Age, when great ice sheets covered much of Europe and North America. At least 300,000 years have passed since the first *Homo sapiens* appeared in Africa. At that time, fewer than a million pre-modern humans lived in Africa, Asia, and Europe, while the Americas were uninhabited. Two million years ago, the only pre-modern humans on Earth lived in tropical Africa. Some idea of the scale of prehistoric time can be gained by piling up 100 quarters. If the whole pile represents the entire time that humans and their culture have been on Earth, then the length of time covered by historical records would equal considerably less than the thickness of one quarter.

How, then, do archaeologists date the past? The chronology of world prehistory is based both on stratigraphic observations and on a variety of chronometric dating methods (see Box 3.4 and Table 3.1) that take us far back into the past, long before the earliest historical records appear in western Asia, in about 3100 B.C. Ninety-nine percent of all human existence lies in prehistoric times and can be measured only in millennia or, occasionally, centuries.

Table 3.1 Chronological Methods for Dating Prehistory

Date		*Method*	*Major developments*
Modern times (after A.D. 1)	↕	Historical documents, dendrochronology, imported objects	Columbus in the New World; Roman Empire
2500 B.C.			Origins of cities
			Origins of food production
c. 500–50,000 B.P.	↕	Radiocarbon dating (organic materials)	Colonization of New World
			Colonization of Australia
c. 1,000–500,000 B.P.	↓	Uranium series dating	*Homo sapiens*
Over 250,000 B.P.	↕	Potassium-argon dating (volcanic materials)	Early humans

Box 3.4 Dating the Past

dendrochronology Tree-ring dating.

radiocarbon (^{14}C) dating Radiometric dating method based on the decay rates of radiocarbon isotopes; highly effective for dating developments over the past 40,000 years.

potassium-argon dating Radiometric dating method that establishes the ages of geological strata and early archaeological sites from volcanic rocks; used to date prehistory from the earliest times up to about 100,000 years ago.

King lists and other documents of known historical age can be used to date the past only as far back as the beginnings of writing and written records, which first appeared in western Asia in about 3100 B.C. and much later in other parts of the world.

Dendrochronology (Tree-Ring Chronology) (Present Day to c. 8000 B.C.)

The annual growth rings of long-lived trees such as sequoias, bristlecone pines, and European oaks, used for beams, posts, and other purposes by ancient peoples, can be used to date sites in some areas such as the American Southwest, the Mediterranean, and western Europe. Originally used on Southwestern pueblos, **dendrochronology** (tree-ring dating), using sequences of growth rings, is also used to calibrate radiocarbon dates (see Box 14.2 on p. 447). In addition, tree rings are a useful barometer of long-and short-term climatic change.

Radiocarbon Dating (c. A.D. 1500 to 40,000 Years Ago)

The **radiocarbon (^{14}C) dating** method is based on the measurement of the decay rates of carbon-14 atoms in organic samples like charcoal, shells, wood, or hair. When combined with accelerator mass spectrometry, it can produce dates from tiny samples, which are then calibrated, if possible, against tree-ring dates to provide a date in calendar years. Radiocarbon chronologies date most of prehistory after about 40,000 years ago, well after modern humans appeared in Africa for the first time (see Box 10.1 on p. 317).

Potassium-argon Dating (250,000 Years Ago to the Origins of Life)

This method is used to date early prehistory by measuring the decay rate of potassium-40 atoms in volcanic rocks (see Box 8.1 on p. 252). **Potassium-argon dating** is an excellent way of dating East African hominin fossils, many of which are found in volcanic levels.

Other commonly used dating methods include paleomagnetic dating, thermoluminescence, and uranium-thorium dating. However, none of these can be universally applied.

We acquire much of the data about prehistory from surveys and excavations, from stratigraphic observations and the ordering of artifacts, and from a variety of dating methods. But how do we turn this raw material of the past into a chronicle of vibrant, interacting people and societies? These issues are the focus of the chapters in Part II.

Summary

- This chapter described how archaeologists find, excavate, and date sites.
- Archaeological survey allows not only the discovery of sites, but also the study of human settlement in a region.
- Archaeological sites manifest themselves in many ways, such as in the form of mounds, middens, caves, and rock shelters. Many more are much less conspicuous and are located only by chance or via soil discolorations or surface finds.
- Ground survey ranges from general surveys leading to the location of only the largest sites down to precise foot surveys aimed at covering an entire area in detail.
- In most cases, total survey is impracticable, and so archaeologists rely on sampling methods to obtain unbiased samples of the research area.
- A battery of survey techniques involves aerial photography and remote sensing, including side-scan aerial radar and scanner imagery.
- Geographic Information System (GIS) technology offers a great way of mapping archaeological data and analyzing them in a wider environmental context.
- Excavation is a primary way in which archaeologists acquire subsurface data about the past. Modern archaeologists tend to do as little excavation as possible, however, because digging archaeological sites destroys the archaeological record.
- Sites can be excavated totally or, as is more common, selectively. Vertical excavation is used to test stratigraphy and to make deep probes of archaeological deposits. Test pits, often combined with various sampling methods, are dug to give an overall impression of an unexcavated site before major digging begins.
- Vertical excavation investigates stratigraphic sequences, earthworks, and other features without opening large areas. Horizontal or area excavation is used to uncover far wider areas and especially to excavate site layouts and buildings.
- Careful stratigraphic observation in three dimensions is the basis of all good excavation and is used to demonstrate relationships among layers and between layers and artifacts.

- Excavation is followed by analysis and interpretation and, finally, publication of the finds to provide a permanent record of the work carried out.
- The chapter also discussed the dating of the past. A distinction was made between cyclical and linear time, as well as between absolute and relative chronology.
- Relative chronology is based on the law of superposition and provides a relative framework for the past. Such chronologies come from the observation of stratified layers in archaeological sites or from artifact ordering.
- Chronometric (absolute) dating methods assign specific dates or ranges of dates to sites and artifacts. Archaeologists use four major chronological methods to date the past in calendar years. Objects of known age come from historic times, which include the past 5,000 years in some parts of the world. Prehistory is dated with tree-ring chronologies and by radiocarbon and potassium-argon dating methods. Other absolute dating methods are still under development.

Key Terms and Sites

Avebury
Behistun
cuneiform
Lascaux Cave
Olduvai Gorge
remote sensing
cultural landscape
settlement archaeology
Angkor Wat
geographic information system (GIS)
Wroxeter
Stonehenge
nonintrusive archaeology
Koster
Shiloh Mound A
Shiloh Mound Complex
Dust Cave
geometric excavation
sampling excavation
Jingsha
stratigraphic excavation
vertical excavation
test pits
horizontal excavation
ziggurat
Kanesh
total data station
relative chronology
chronometric dating
dendrochronology
radiocarbon (^{14}C) dating
potassium-argon dating

Critical-Thinking Questions

1. Preservation conditions are all-important in archaeology. What kinds of evidence are preserved when conditions are very good, and what dimensions does such evidence add to our understanding of ancient societies? Think of examples for discussion.
2. You hear a lot of talk about context in archaeology. Why is this concept so important, and what are its critical dimensions?
3. Why do you think ethics are so important to archaeologists? Can you name the most important ethical principles in archaeology?

Further Reading

A wonderful set of small paperbacks summarize the process of archaeological research. L. J. Zimmerman and W. Green, *Archaeologist's Toolkit* (Walnut Creek, CA: AltaMira Press, 2003) is a set of seven short volumes that cover the essentials of doing archaeology in the field and laboratory. The volumes in the series are written by real dirt archaeologists of considerable experience. Each volume has a strong ethics orientation and is concerned as much with CRM archaeology as it is with academic research. Any serious student should buy the whole series. Stephen L. Black and Kevin Jolly, Archaeology by Design, the first volume in the series, offers a wonderful summary of the basics of research design. The second volume, James M. Collins and Brian Leigh Molyneaux, Archaeological Survey, does the same for survey, with a strong emphasis on nonintrusive methods. M. Carver and M. Hummler, *Archaeological Investigation* (London: Routledge, 2024) is a comprehensive account of excavation and archaeological survey. See also G. G. White and T. F. King, *The Archaeological Survey Manual* (Walnut Creek, CA: Left Coast Press, 2007). For an American-oriented manual, see T. R. Hester, H. J. Shafer, and K. L. Feder, *Field Methods in Archaeology*, 7th ed. (New York: Thames and Hudson, 2016).

4 How Did People Live?

Chapter Outline

A Moche bottle from coastal Peru depicting a fisherman paddling a reed canoe.
Source: Werner Forman Archive/Getty Images.

A multitude of artifacts, in clay, metal, stone, wood, and other raw materials, defines the prehistory of humankind. Today, we can land an astronaut on the Moon, transplant human hearts, and build sophisticated computers. Yet our contemporary tool kits, for all their sophistication and diversity, have evolved from the first simple tools made by the earliest human beings. In a real sense, technology defines prehistory, for it formed the basis for the many artifacts used by our forebears to adapt to, and extend their use of, their natural environments.

DOI: 10.4324/9781003592754-5

Technologies of the Ancients

The first part of this chapter summarizes the major technologies used by the ancients. You will find some discussion of the analysis of artifacts in the boxes in this section (for classification of artifacts, see Box 4.1).

Box 4.1 Doing Archaeology
Classifying Artifact Types

The classification of artifacts is a basic archaeological skill that is largely irrelevant to the story in this book except in the sense that human prehistory is based, in large part, on artifact studies (see Figure 4.1). Central to this is an exercise known as **typology**, artifact classification. A huge literature surrounds typology and what are known as **archaeological types**: different ways of classifying artifact forms. Archaeologists tend to use three "types of types." These are summarized briefly here.

Descriptive types are based solely on the form of the artifact—physical or external properties. The descriptive type is employed when the use or cultural significance of the object or practice is unknown. Descriptive types are commonly used for artifacts from early prehistory, when functional interpretations are much harder to reach.

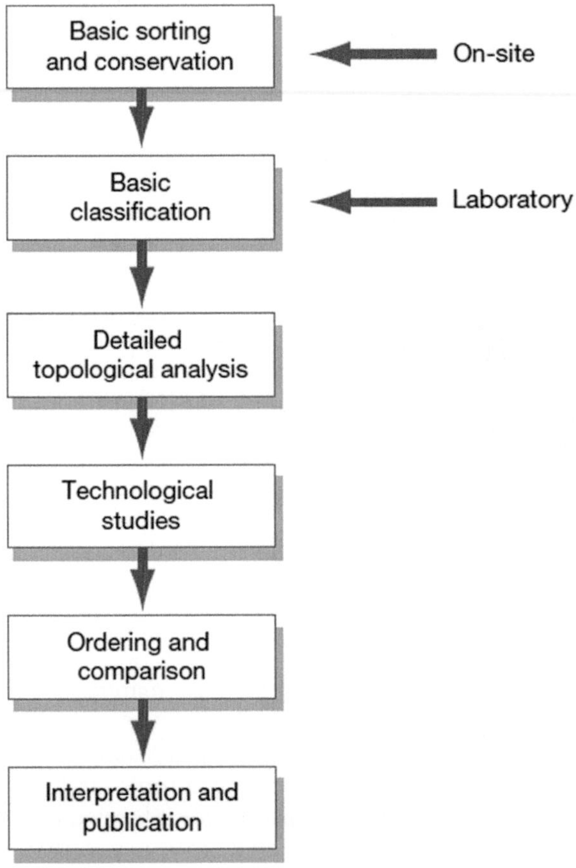

Figure 4.1 The process of artifact analysis.

Chronological types are defined by decoration or form but are time markers. They are types with chronological significance. Chronological types are defined in terms of attributes that show change over time. For example, on the Great Plains of North America, Clovis and Folsom points were used for short periods of prehistoric time, Clovis for several centuries from about 13,050 to 12,750 years ago (see Figure 2.1 on p. 38). Projectile points have long been used as chronological markers in North American archaeology.

Functional types are based on cultural use or the role in their user's culture rather than on outward form or chronological position—"weapons," "clothing," "food preparation," and so on (see Figure 4.2). Although in some cases obvious functional roles, such as that of an arrowhead for hunting or warfare or of a pot for carrying water, can be correctly established in the laboratory, functional classifications are necessarily restricted and limited (see the iron arrowhead in Figure 2.13 on p. 64).

Figure 4.2 The difficulties of artifact classification are well demonstrated by this Pomo Indian basketry tray from northern California. The design was formed in the maker's mind by several factors, most important of which is the tremendous reservoir of cultural experiences learned by the Pomo, generation by generation. The basket designs are learned and relate to a feeling that a particular form and color are "correct" and traditionally acceptable. But there are more practical reasons, too, including the circular, bowl-like shape that enables the user to winnow wild seeds by tossing them gently. The problem for the archaeologist is to measure the variations in human artifacts, to establish the causes behind the directions of change, and to find what these variations can be used to measure. This fine tray serves as a warning that variations in human artifacts are both complex and subtle. The Pomo occupied a stretch of the northern California coast and interior north of the San Francisco Bay area. There were about 12,000 of them at European contact, living in small bands. They enjoyed a complex ritual and social life.

Source: Inga Spence/Alamy.

typology Classification of archaeological types.

archaeological types Groupings of artifacts created for comparison with other groups, based on tool types, which may or may not reflect the use of the tool as intended by the original manufacturers.

descriptive types Types based on the physical or external properties of an artifact.

chronological types Types defined by form that are time markers.

functional types Types based on cultural use or function of artifacts rather than on outward form or chronological position.

Stone

Watching an expert stoneworker (or "lithic technologist," as they prefer to be called, from the Greek *lithos*, "stone") is a true pleasure. With seemingly effortless skill, a rough lump of fine-grained stone is changed into an elegant projectile point or a replica of a delicate, straight-edged hand ax fashioned by a Stone Age forager over 100,000 years ago. Some archaeologists have become experts at ancient stone technology. They have learned to feel and "read" the subtle textures and contours of toolmaking stone to the point where they can make a hand ax in less than two minutes or replicate the finest products of Ancient Egyptian or Maya stone artisans. These skills enable them to decipher the technology of long-vanished societies and provide fascinating detail, such as information about lefthanded stoneworkers.

The prehistory of humankind is literally wrought in stone, for this most durable of all toolmaking materials provides the framework for thousands of years of gradually evolving human technology, since the first hominin put stone cobble to stone cobble more than 3 million years ago. The evolution of stoneworking over the millions of years during which it has been practiced has been infinitely slow. Nonetheless, people eventually exploited almost every possibility afforded by suitable rocks for making implements.

reductive (subtractive) technology Stoneworking technique in which stone is shaped by removing flakes until a desired form is attained.

core In archaeology, a lump of stone from which humanly struck flakes have been removed.

flakes Stone fragments removed from cores, often used as blanks for finished artifacts.

The manufacture of stone tools is what is called a **reductive (subtractive) technology**, for stone is gathered and then shaped by removing flakes until the desired form is achieved. Obviously, the more complex the artifact, the more reduction is required. Basically, the process of tool manufacture is linear. The stoneworker acquires the raw material, prepares a **core** of stone (the lump of stone from which **flakes** or blades are removed), and carries out the initial reduction by removing a series of flakes. These flakes are then trimmed and shaped further, depending on the artifact required. Core tools are those made from the core; flake tools are those made from flakes removed from a core. Later, after use, a tool may be resharpened or modified for further use.

Generally, Stone Age people and other makers of stone tools chose flint, obsidian, and other hard, homogeneous rocks from which to fashion their artifacts. All these rocks break in a systematic or predictable way, like glass (see Figure 4.3). The effect is similar to that of a hole in a window produced by a BB gun. A sharp blow by percussion or pressure directed vertically at a point on the surface of a suitable stone dislodges a flake, with its apex at the point where the hammer hit the stone.

Figure 4.4 shows some of the major stone-flaking methods ancient peoples used. The simplest and earliest was direct fracturing of the stone with a hammerstone (Figure 4.4a). After thousands of years, people began to make tools flaked on both surfaces, such as Acheulean hand axes (Figure 4.4b). As time went on, the stoneworkers began to use bone, "soft" antler, or wood hammers to trim the edges of their tools. The hand ax of 150,000 years ago had a symmetrical shape, sharp and tough working edges, and a beautiful finish.

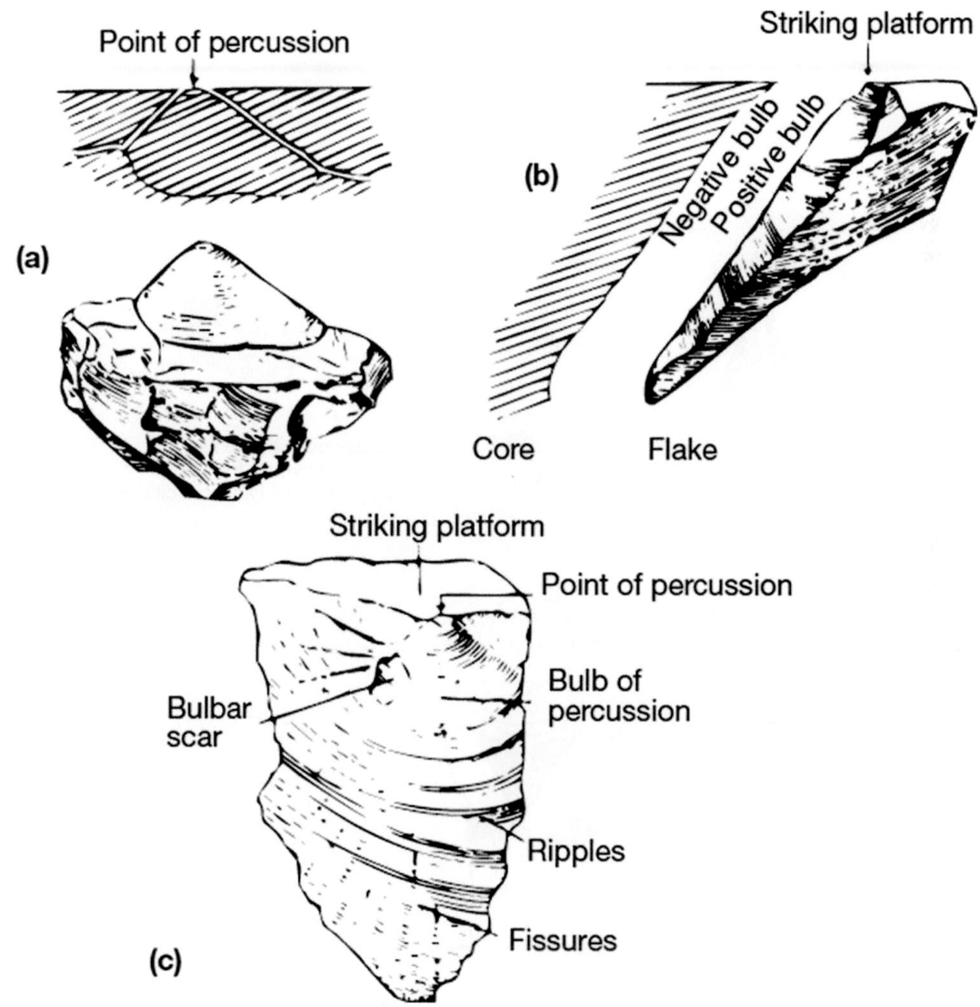

Figure 4.3 Making a stone tool: The **conchoidal fracture** forms when a blow is struck on homogeneous types of rock. (a) When a blow is struck, a cone of percussion is formed by the shock waves rippling through the stone, known as a conchoidal fracture. (b) A flake is formed when the block (or core) is hit at the edge and the stone fractures along the edge of the ripple. (c) The struck flake exhibits a number of standard features.

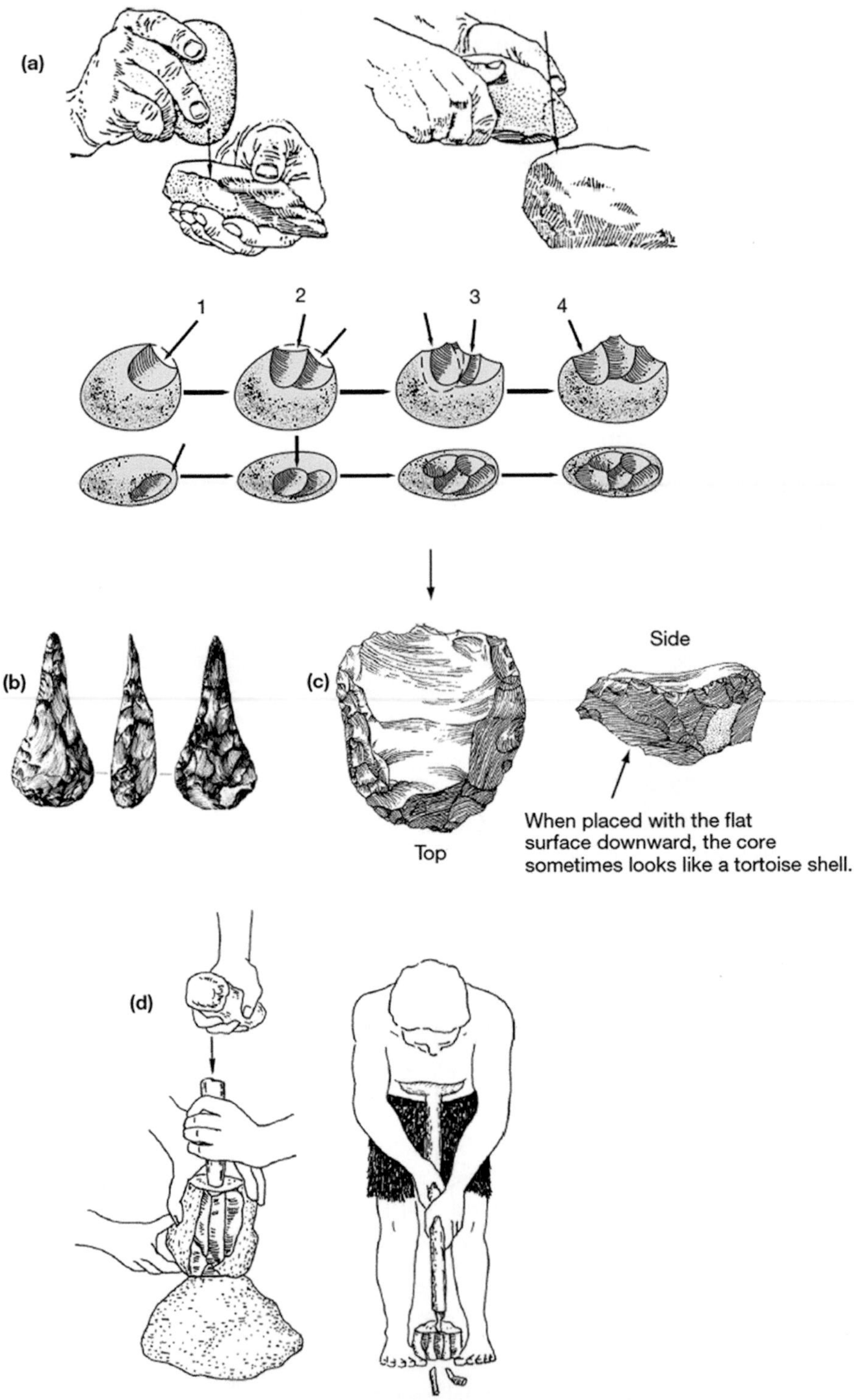

Figure 4.4 Stone-flaking techniques: (a) direct fracturing of a stone with a hammerstone; (b) a hand ax with fine edges made by using a bone hammer in what is known as **Acheulean stone technology**; (c) a carefully prepared core designed to produce standard-sized flakes; (d) blade technology using a punch.

As people such as the hunter-gatherers of about 100,000 years ago became more skillful, they developed stone technologies to produce artifacts for highly specific purposes. They shaped special cores that were carefully prepared to provide one flake or two of a standard size and shape (Figure 4.4c). About 40,000 years ago, some stoneworkers developed a new technology based on preparing cylindrical cores. Indirect percussion removed parallel-sided blades with a punch and hammerstone (Figure 4.4d). These regular blanks were then trimmed into knives, scraping tools, and other specialized artifacts. In later times, stoneworkers used a small billet of wood or antler pressed against the working edge to exert pressure in a limited direction and remove a fine, thin, parallel-sided flake. This formed one of many flake scars that eventually covered most of the implement's surfaces. Such pressure flaking facilitated the production of many standardized tools with extremely effective working edges in a comparatively short time, such as projectile points (see Figure 2.1 on p. 38).

conchoidal fracture The fracturing tendency of igneous rocks that allows the manufacture of flakes, blades, and hence stone artifacts.

Acheulean stone technology A technology (named after the town of St. Acheul in northern France) based on hand axes, cleavers, and flake artifacts that flourished in Africa, Europe, southwestern Asia, and parts of Southeast Asia between about 1.7 million and 200,000 years ago.

Later Stone Age peoples ground and polished stone when they needed a sharp and highly durable blade. They shaped the edges by rough flaking and then laboriously polished and ground them against a coarser rock, such as sandstone, to produce a sharp, tough, working edge. Modern experiments have demonstrated the greater effectiveness of polished stone axes in felling forest trees, the toughened working edge taking longer to blunt than that of a flaked ax. Polished stone axes became important in many early farming societies, especially in Europe, Asia, Central America, and parts of temperate North America. They were used in New Guinea as early as 28,000 years ago and in Melanesia and Polynesia for the manufacture of canoes, which were essential for fishing and trade.

Expert stoneworkers still fashion artifacts to this day, especially gunflints for use in flintlock muskets. Gunflint manufacture was a flourishing industry in Great Britain and France into the twentieth century and is still practiced in Angola, Africa, where flintlock muskets are in regular use for hunting.

lithic analysis Analysis of ancient stone technologies.

Lithic analysis, the study of stone tool technology, involves far more than merely classifying different stone artifact types, as was the practice half a century ago. Today, astoundingly minute details of long-forgotten human behavior come from combining several powerful analytical approaches (see Box 4.2).

Box 4.2 Doing Archaeology
Lithic Analysis

It is all too easy to think of stone artifacts as merely lifeless objects when, in fact, they once had a life of their own. Today's lithic analysis is as much concerned with processes of manufacture and tool use as it is with complete artifacts. A combination of sophisticated methods reveals valuable information about human behavior.

Debitage analysis involves reconstructing the "reduction sequence" that the original toolmaker used to create a finished artifact. Most steps in stone tool manufacture can be recognized by studying finished artifacts, cores, and the debris, often called **debitage** (French for "discarded waste"), left behind by the stoneworker. By close examination of debitage, an expert lithic technologist can separate the primary flakes that resulted from the rough blocking-out of the core from the finer flakes that were removed as the artisan prepared the striking platform on the top or sides of the core. Then, there are the flakes that all this preparatory work was aimed at—the artifact blanks struck from the core. Finally, there are the fine retouching flakes that turn the blank into the finished projectile point, scraper, or whatever other implement was needed.

Refitting (sometimes called *retrofitting*) is the reconstruction of ancient stone tool manufacture by fitting flakes back on to the core. Watch someone making stone tools, and you will find him (or her) sitting in the middle of a pile of ever-accumulating debris—chips, flakes, abandoned cores, and discarded hammerstones. Prehistoric stoneworkers produced the same sort of debris—hundreds, if not thousands, of small waste fragments, by-products of toolmaking that are buried on archaeological sites of all ages. Vital information on prehistoric lithic technology comes from careful excavation of all the debitage from a place where a prehistoric artisan worked and then trying to fit the pieces together one by one to reconstruct the procedures used.

Refitting requires great patience but can provide valuable information about stone tool manufacture. You can sometimes trace the movement of individual fragments or cores horizontally across a site, a process that requires even more patience than simple refitting. This procedure is of great value in reconstructing the functions of different locations in, say, a rock shelter site, where a stoneworker might make tools in one place and then carry a core to a nearby hearth and fashion another blade for a different purpose.

Archaeologists have experimented with the making of stone tools since the midnineteenth century. Today, many archaeological laboratories ring to the sound of people trying to make stone tools and replicate ancient technology—and cutting their fingers in the process.

Modern experimenters have drawn on both experimentation and ethnographic observation to work out ancient techniques. Recent research has focused on reconstructing reduction sequences and also on quarry sites as part of efforts to reconstruct prehistoric trade in obsidian and other rocks, which can be traced back to their source, and to achieve closer understanding of the relationships between human behavior and lithic technology.

Use-wear (edge-wear) analysis involves microscopic examination of artifact working edges and actual experiments using stone tools in an effort to interpret telltale scratches and edge luster resulting from their use. Many researchers have experimented with both low- and high-power magnification and are now able to distinguish with considerable confidence among the wear polishes associated with different materials such as wood, bone, and hide. The approach is now reliable enough to allow one to state whether a tool was used to slice wood, cut up vegetables, or strip meat from bones, but relatively few archaeologists are trained in the use of the microscopes and photographic techniques required for analyzing wear. Another approach studies organic residues, the trace elements of debris from use that adhere to tool edges.

Petrological analysis has been applied with great success to the rocks from which stone tools are made, especially ground stone axes in Europe. **Petrology** is the study of rocks (in Greek, *petros* means "stone"). A thin section of the ax is prepared and examined under a microscope. The minerals in the rock can then be identified and compared with samples from ancient quarry sites. British archaeologists have had remarkable success with this approach and have identified more than 20 sources of ax-blade stone in Great Britain alone.

Spectrographic analysis of distinctive trace elements in **obsidian** has yielded remarkable results in southwestern Asia and Mesoamerica, where this distinctive volcanic rock was traded widely from several quarry centers.

debitage analysis The study of debitage as a way of examining ancient stone technologies.

debitage Waste by-products produced while working stone.

refitting The reconstruction of ancient stone technologies by refitting flakes and blades to cores; also known as *retrofitting*.

use-wear (edge-wear) analysis Microscopic analysis of artifacts to detect signs of wear on their working edges.

petrological analysis The study of the mineral contents of stone or stone tools.

petrology The study of rocks; in archaeology, analysis of trace elements and other characteristics of rocks used to make such artifacts as ax blades, which were traded over long distances.

obsidian Volcanic glass.

Bone, Antler, and Ivory

Bone and antler were probably used from the beginnings of human history. The earliest artifacts apparently consisted of little more than fragments of fractured animal bone used for purposes that could not be fulfilled by wood or stone implements. The earliest standardized bone tools date from about 100,000 years ago, but they assumed much greater levels of sophistication during the late Ice Age, when *Homo sapiens* used sharp-edged stone chisels to cut long splinters from antlers and turn them into spear points, harpoons, and fishing spears, as well as to make many specialized tools for foraging, fishing, and ceremonial purposes. They also used antler and bone as palettes for fine carvings and engravings of animals and geometric designs. The humble bone or ivory needle appeared at least 25,000 years ago; it was a revolutionary artifact because it enabled humans to manufacture layered, tailored clothing, essential for colonizing the bitterly cold, open plains of Europe and Eurasia with their nine-month winters.

Figure 4.5 An ivory mask of the Ipiutak culture. The mask once had a wooden backing. It was found at a burial site in Point Hope, Alaska.

Source: Werner Forman Archive/American Museum of Natural History, New York.

Bone and ivory technology achieved great sophistication in the Bering Strait area of the northern Pacific, where a highly specialized tool kit for hunting sea mammals came into use over 2,000 years ago. Elaborate studies have been made of the stylistic and functional changes in diverse items such as harpoons and the winged ivory objects fastened to harpoon butts. Other artifacts include picks made of walrus tusk and snow shovels and wedges of ivory and bone, as well as drills and domestic utensils (see Figure 4.5).

Wood

Schöningen, Germany Stone Age archaeological site that yielded the earliest known wooden spears, which are dated to around 300,000 years ago.

Like bone, wood was used for human artifacts from the earliest times. Yet only occasionally do such artifacts survive, the earliest being a series of long wooden throwing spears from **Schöningen, Germany**, which have been dated to around 300,000 years ago, and would have been lethal against large game. The bogs and marshes of northern Europe have preserved entire wooden tool kits made by foraging families, perhaps as early as early as 7000 B.C. Items include dugout canoes, fishing spears, traps, and spear points, and also wooden trackways across waterlogged ground. The dry conditions of western North America have yielded rich finds of such artifacts as throwing sticks and even duck decoys used to pursue waterfowl. Delicately made furniture survives in the pharaoh Tutankhamun's tomb.

Ozette, Washington A Makah Indian village dating to the past 1,000 years.

The manufacture of wood tools involves such well-understood mechanical processes as cutting, whittling, scraping, planing, carving, and polishing. Fire was often used to harden sharpened spear points. Oil and paint made from red ocher, charcoal, and other raw materials imparted a fine sheen to all kinds of wood artifacts. Even more revealing are wood fragments from abandoned buildings, fortifications, and track walkways. Microscopic analysis of wood fragments and charcoal can provide information on the wood types used to build houses, canoes, and other such objects. On very rare occasions, stone projectile heads and axes have been recovered in both waterlogged and dry conditions in which their wood handles and shafts have survived together with the thongs used to bind stone to wood. The Ozette excavations (see Box 4.3) yielded complete house planks and even some wood boxes that had been assembled by the skillful grooving and bending of planks.

ground stone Technique used for manufacturing artifacts by pecking the surface and edges with a stone and then grinding them smooth to form sharp working edges; often used to make axes and adzes employed for felling trees and woodworking.

Wood was probably the most important raw material available to our ancestors. The thousands upon thousands of **ground stone** axes in the archaeological record all once had wooden handles. Wood was used for housebuilding, fortifications, fuel, canoes, and containers. Most skilled woodworking societies used the simplest technology to produce both utilitarian and ceremonial objects. They used fire and the ringing of bark to fell trees, stone wedges to split logs, and shells and stones to scrape spear shafts.

Clay (Ceramics)

Fired-clay objects are among the most imperishable of all archaeological finds, but pottery is a relatively recent innovation. The oldest-known ceramic items are the clay objects crafted by people of the Gravettian culture of around 31,000–27,000 years ago, such as the "Venus of Dolní Věstonice" figurine found in the Czech Republic. The oldest-known pottery vessels were made some 18,000 years ago, in southern China, and somewhat later in southwestern Asia.

From the very earliest times, people used animal skins, bark trays, ostrich eggshells, and gourds for carrying loads beyond the immediate surroundings of their settlements. Such informal vessels were ideal for hunter-gatherers, who were constantly on the move. The invention of pottery seems to have coincided with the beginnings of more lasting settlement. Fired-clay receptacles have the advantage of being both durable and long-lived. We can assume that the first clay vessels were used for domestic purposes: cooking, carrying water, and storing food. They soon assumed more specialized roles in salt making, in ceremonial activities, and as oil lamps and burial urns. Broken ceramic vessels are among the most common archaeological finds.

Modern industrial potters turn out dinnerware pieces by the millions, using mass-production methods and automated technology. Prehistoric artisans created each piece individually, using the simplest of technology but attaining astonishing skill in shaping and adorning their vessels.

temper Coarse material such as sand or shell added to fine potting clay to make it bond during firing.

The clay used in pot making was selected with the utmost care; often it was even traded over considerable distances. The consistency of the clay is critical; it is pounded meticulously and mixed with water to make it entirely even in texture. By careful kneading, the potter removes the air bubbles and makes the clay as plastic as possible, allowing it to be molded into shape as the pot is built up. When the clay is fired, it loses its water content and can crack, so the potter adds a **temper** to the clay, a substance that helps reduce shrinkage and cracking and also ensures even firing and cooling. Although some pot clays contain a suitable temper in their natural state, pot makers commonly added other materials, such as fine sand, powdered shell, or even mica, as artificial temper.

Box 4.3 Site
Ozette, Washington

For more than 2,500 years, the ancestors of modern-day Makah Indians hunted whales and other sea mammals from a village at **Ozette**, on Washington's Olympic peninsula. About 200 years ago, a sudden mudslide buried much of the village of cedar plank houses. Liquid mud cascaded over the dwellings, preserving their contents as the inhabitants abandoned them. Archaeologist Richard Daugherty of Washington State University used high-pressure hoses and fine sprays to tease the still-waterlogged soil from the remains of four perfectly preserved cedar log houses.

Figure 4.6 Example of superb preservation in a wet site. This whale fin carved from cedar wood and inlaid with more than 700 sea-otter teeth was excavated from the mud at Ozette, Washington. The teeth at the base are set in the design of a mythical bird with a whale in its talons.

Source: Courtesy of the Makah Museum, Neah Bay, WA.

The wet muck that had engulfed the houses had mantled them in a dense, wet blanket that preserved everything except flesh, feathers, and skins. One house was 21 meters long and 14 meters wide (69 feet by 46 feet). There were separate hearths and cooking platforms. Low walls and hanging mats served as partitions. More than 40,000 artifacts came from the excavations, including conical rain hats made of spruce root fibers, baskets, wooden boxes, wooden bowls still impregnated with seal oil, mats, fishhooks, bows and arrows, and fragments of looms (see Figure 4.6).

The Ozette site is a classic example of how much can be recovered from a waterlogged archaeological site. Ozette is important in other ways, too, for the ancestors of the Makah Indians who lived there flourished along the coast for more than 2,500 years. Archaeology extended their known cultural heritage far into the remote past.

ceramics Vessels and other objects made of clay.

Pot making (**ceramics**) is a highly skilled art, with three major methods used:

1. *Coil:* The vessel is built up from a clay lump or with long coils or wedges of clay that are shaped and joined together with a mixture of clay and water (see Figure 4.7). Such hand methods were common wherever pot making was a part-time activity satisfying local needs.
2. *Mold:* The vessel is made from a lump of clay that is either pressed into a concave mold or placed over the top of a convex shape. Molding techniques were used to make large numbers of vessels of the same size and shape, as well as figurines, fishing net weights, and spindle whorls. Sometimes several molds were used to make the different parts of a vessel.
3. *Potter's wheel:* Wheel-made pots came into wide use after the invention of the potter's wheel in Mesopotamia about 5,000 years ago. The vessel is formed from a lump of clay rotating on a platform turned by the potter's hands or feet. The wheel method has the advantage of speed and standardization and was used to mass-produce thousands of similar vessels, such as the bright red Samian ware found throughout the Roman Empire.

slip A fine, wet finish applied to a clay vessel before it is decorated and fired.

Surface finishes provided a pleasing appearance and also improved the durability of the vessel in day-to-day use. Exterior burnishing and glazing with a tough surface-coating made vessels watertight, or nearly so. Often a wet clay solution, known as a **slip**, was applied to the smooth surface. Brightly colored slips were often used and formed painted decorations on the vessel (see Figure 2.12, on p. 62). When a slip was not applied, the vessel was allowed to dry slowly until the external surface was almost leatherlike. Many utilitarian vessels were decorated with incised or stamped decorations, using shells, combs, stamps, and other tools. Some ceremonial pots were even modeled into human effigies (see Figure 4.8) or decorated with motifs imitating the cords used to suspend the pot from the roof.

Figure 4.7 A Hopi woman making pottery with clay coils, Oraibi Pueblo, Arizona, 1903. Source: Corbis.

Figure 4.8 A Moche portrait vase. These may be actual portraits of specific individuals. Source: Prisma Archivo/Alamy Stock Photo.

Most early pottery was fired over open hearths. The vessels were covered with fast-burning wood whose ash would fall around the vessels and bake them evenly over a few hours. Far higher temperatures were attained in special ovens, known as *kilns*, which would not only bake the clay and remove its plasticity, but also dissolve carbon and iron compounds. Once fired, the pots were allowed to cool slowly, and small cracks were repaired before the pots were put into use (for information on ceramic analysis, see Box 4.4).

Box 4.4 Doing Archaeology
Ceramic Analysis

An enormous expenditure of archaeological energy has gone into **ceramic analysis**. As with stone technology, the emphasis has shifted in recent years from pure classification to broader-based research into the behavior of pot makers and the role of their products in society. Some analytical approaches are the following:

- *Analogy and experiment:* Controlled experiments to replicate prehistoric ceramic technology provide data on firing temperatures, properties of tempers, and glazing techniques. Ethnographic analogy has been a fruitful source of basic information on potters and their techniques.
- *Form and function analysis:* Two features of prehistoric pottery are immediately obvious when we examine a collection of vessels: **form** (shape) and decoration. Functional analysis depends on the common assumption that the shape of a vessel directly reflects its **function**—bowls were used for cooking and eating, portrait head pots were ceremonial vessels, large pots were used for water storage, and so on. Such functional classifications bristle with obvious difficulties when one is separated from the pot makers by many centuries or millennia, so form analysis is a more viable option. Form analysis is based on careful classification of clusters of different vessel shapes. These shapes can be derived from complete vessels or from potsherds that preserve the rim and shoulder profiles of the vessel. It is possible to reconstruct the pot form from these pieces by projecting measurements of diameter and vessel height. Such analyses produce broad categories of vessel form that are capable of considerable refinement.
- *Stylistic analysis:* Stylistic analysis is much more commonly used, for it concentrates not only on the form and function of the vessel, but also on the decorative styles used by the potters. These are assumed to be somewhat independent of functional considerations. In such regions as the American Southwest, pottery styles have been used to trace cultural variations over thousands of years. Most stylistic analyses use small numbers of distinctive **attributes**, which appear in associated sets of features that provide the basis for erecting types and varieties of pottery styles. These are assumed to represent the social system behind the pots studied. However, can one really assume that pottery styles reflect social behavior? We do not yet know.
- *Technological analysis:* The more elaborate, computer-generated classifications of today reveal that many of the archaeologist's classificatory cornerstones, such as pottery temper, are in fact subject to complex behavioral and environmental factors rather than being the simple barometers of human behavior that they were once thought to be. Technological analyses of pottery focus on the fabric and paste in potting clays and relate ceramic vessels to locally available resources. These also provide useful, statistically based yardsticks for interpreting

variation among different pottery forms. Numerous procedures yield valuable information on ancient ceramics, including X-ray diffraction studies and ceramic petrology. These approaches can be used in combination to study what can be called *ceramic ecology*: the interaction of resources, local knowledge, and style that ultimately lead to a finished clay vessel. Even the sediment found inside ancient pots can be examined spectrographically and sometimes identified, as was the case with a wine storage jar from Iran dating to 4000 B.C.

Metals and Metallurgy

"Hough!" "Hough!" A goatskin bellows emits a steady puffing noise as the African smith raises and lowers the bag with his hands, singing along the way. Every 20 minutes, another member of the team takes over as the master smith keeps a close eye on the clay furnace loaded with iron ore and charcoal. He adds charcoal, then more ore, then charcoal again. The smelt continues for seven hours until the master is satisfied. Then, he rakes out the white-hot charcoal and recovers a lump of slag and smelted iron from the fire. All the preparation time and the seven hours of arduous bellows-work produced just enough iron to make one small hoe. In these days of mass-produced steel and all kinds of exotic metals, we forget just how much labor went into producing even a single iron tool. The development of metallurgy is one of humanity's great innovations, but it was certainly not a labor-saving invention.

Metals first became familiar to people in the form of rocks in their environment. Properties of metal-bearing rocks—color, luster, and weight—made them attractive for use in the natural state. Eventually, people realized that heat made such stone as flint and chert easier to work with. When this knowledge was applied to metallic rocks, stone-workers discovered that native copper and other metals could be formed into tools by a sequence of hammering and heating. Of the seventy or so metallic elements on Earth, only eight—iron, copper, arsenic, tin, silver, gold, lead, and mercury—were worked before the eighteenth century A.D. Some of the properties of these metals that were important to ancient metalworkers were color, luster, reflecting abilities (for mirrors), acoustic quality, ease of casting and welding, and degrees of hardness, strength, and malleability. Metal that was easily recycled had obvious advantages.

ceramic analysis The study of pottery (ceramics).

form The physical characteristics—size and shape or composition—of any archaeological find; an essential part of attribute analysis.

function The way in which an artifact was used in the past.

attributes Individual features of artifacts.

Copper

The earliest metal tools were made by cold-hammering copper into simple artifacts. Such objects were fairly common in Near Eastern villages by 6000 B.C. Eventually, some people began to melt the copper. They may have achieved sufficiently high temperatures with established methods used to fire pottery in clay kilns. The copper was usually melted or smelted into shapes and ingots within the furnace hearth itself. Copper metallurgy was widespread in the eastern Mediterranean by about 4000 B.C. European smiths were working copper in the Balkans as early as 3500 B.C. In the Americas, copper working achieved a high degree of refinement in coastal Peru among the Moche and Chimu, also in western Mesoamerica. The Archaic peoples of Lake Superior exploited the native deposits of copper ore on the southern shores of the lake, and the metal was widely traded across eastern North America and cold-hammered into artifacts from Archaic to Woodlands times.

Bronze

The real explosion in copper metallurgy took place midway through the fourth millennium B.C., when southwest Asian smiths discovered that they could improve the properties of copper by alloying it with a second metal such as arsenic, lead, or tin. Perhaps, the first alloys came about when smiths tried to produce different colors and textures in ornaments. But they soon realized the advantages of alloys that led to stronger, harder, and more easily worked artifacts. Most early bronzes contain about 5–10 percent alloy material (10 percent is the optimum for hardness). An explosion in metallurgical technology occurred during the third millennium B.C., perhaps in part resulting from the spread of writing. The use of tin alloying may have stimulated much trading activity, for the metal is relatively rare, especially in the eastern Mediterranean region. Bronze working was developed to a high pitch in northern China after 2000 B.C. (see Figure 4.9).

Figure 4.9 A Shang Dynasty *yeou* vase (a ritual grain alcohol container), twelfth century B.C.
Source: The Art Archive/Alamy.

Gold

Gold played a vital part in prestige and ornament in many ancient societies. The pharaoh Tutankhamun is sometimes called the "Golden Pharaoh"; his grave was rich in spectacular gold objects. The burials of the Moche lords around A.D. 400 at Sipán, on the northern coast of Peru, revealed the remarkable wealth of this desert civilization. One shroud-wrapped warrior-priest wore a pair of gold eyes, a gold nose, and a gold chin-and-neck visor; his head was lying on a gold, saucerlike headrest; hundreds of minute gold and turquoise beads adorned this lord of Sipán, who wore 16 gold disks as large as silver dollars on his chest (see Figure 16.7 on p. 509). There were gold-and-feather headdresses and intricate ear ornaments, one of a warrior with a movable club.

The Aztecs and the Inca also were talented goldsmiths whose magnificent products were shipped off to Europe and melted down for royal treasuries in the sixteenth century. Spanish conquistadors marveled at the Coricancha, the temple of the Sun God Inti in the Inca capital at Cuzco, high in the Andes. The outside of the beautifully built stone temple was gilded with gold and silver, while inside lay a garden with golden clods of earth, golden maize, and golden herdsmen guarding golden llamas (see Figure 4.10).

Gold is a metal that rarely forms compounds in its natural state. It was collected in this form or in grains gathered by crushing quartz and concentrating the fine gold by washing. The melting point of gold is about the same as that of copper, so no elaborate technology was needed. Gold is easily hammered into thin sheets without annealing—heating and cooling of metal to make it less brittle. Prehistoric smiths frequently used such sheets to sheath wooden objects such as statuettes. They also cast gold and used appliqué techniques, as well as alloying it with silver and other ores. Gold was worked in the Near East almost as early as copper, and it soon became associated with royal prestige. The metal was widely traded in dust, ornament, and bead form in many parts of the world.

Figure 4.10 Inca silverwork. A maize cob.
Source: Heritage Image Partnership Ltd/Alamy.

Iron

Bronze Age smiths certainly knew about iron. It was a curiosity, of little apparent use. They knew where to find the ore and how to fashion iron objects by hammering and heating. But the crucial process in iron production is carburization, in which iron is converted into steel. The result is a much harder object, far tougher than bronze tools. When an iron object is carburized, it is heated in close contact with charcoal for a considerable period of time. The solubility of carbon in iron is very low at room temperature, but increases dramatically at temperatures above 910°C (1,670°F), which could easily be achieved with charcoal and good Bronze Age bellows. It was this technological development that led to the widespread adoption of iron technologies in the eastern Mediterranean area at least by 1000 B.C.

> **Hallstatt culture, Austria** An Iron Age culture widespread over central and western Europe, c. 750 B.C.

Iron tools are found occasionally in some sites as early as 3000 B.C., but such artifacts were rare until around 1200 B.C., when the first iron weapons in eastern Mediterranean tombs appeared. The new metal was slow to catch on, partly because of the difficulty of smelting it. Its widespread adoption may coincide with a period of disruption in eastern Mediterranean trade routes as a result of the collapse of several major kingdoms, including that of the Hittites, after 1200 B.C. Deprived of tin, the smiths turned to a much more readily available substitute—iron. It was soon in use even for utilitarian tools and was first established on a large scale in continental Europe in the seventh century B.C. by people of the **Hallstatt culture**.

Iron ore is much more abundant in the natural state than copper ore. It is readily obtainable from surface outcrops and bog deposits. Once its potential was realized, it became much more widely used, and stone and bronze were relegated to subsidiary, often ornamental, uses. The influence of iron was immense, for it made available abundant supplies of tough cutting edges for agriculture. With iron tools, clearing forests became easier, and people achieved even greater mastery over their environment. Ironworking profoundly influenced the development of literate civilizations, but the pre-Columbian Americans never developed iron metallurgy.

Metal Technologies

Copper technology began with the cold-hammering of the ore into simple artifacts. Copper smelting may have originated by the accidental melting of some copper ore in a domestic hearth or oven. In smelting, the ore is melted at a high temperature in a small kiln and the molten metal is allowed to trickle down through the charcoal fuel into a vessel at the base of the furnace. The copper is further reduced at a high temperature and then cooled slowly and hammered into shape. This annealing adds strength to the metal. Molten copper was poured into molds and cast into widely varied shapes.

Copper ores were obtained from weathered surface outcrops, but the best material came from subsurface ores, which were mined by expert diggers. Many early copper workings have been found in southern Africa, where the miners followed surface lodes under the ground (see Figure 4.11).

Figure 4.11 Excavation in an ancient copper mine at Kansanshi, Zambia, Central Africa. The miners followed copper ore outcrops deep into the ground with narrow shafts, the earth fillings of which have yielded both radiocarbon samples and artifacts abandoned by the miners.

Source: Courtesy Professor Michael Bisson.

Some of the most sophisticated bronze working was created by smiths in China, who cast elaborate legged cauldrons and smaller vessels with distinctive shapes and decorations in clay molds (see Figure 4.9).

Ironworking is a much more complex technology that requires a melting temperature of at least 1,537°C (about 2,800°F). Prehistoric smiths normally used an elaborate furnace filled with alternating layers of charcoal and iron ore, which was maintained at a high temperature for many hours with a bellows. A single firing often yielded only a spongy lump of iron, called a *bloom*, which then had to be forged and hammered into artifacts. It took some time for the metallurgists to learn that they could strengthen working edges by quenching the tool in cold water. This process gave greater strength, but it also made the tool brittle. The tempering process, reheating the blade to a temperature below 727°C (1,340°F), restored the strength. Iron technology was so slow in developing that it remained basically unchanged from about 600 B.C. until medieval times.

Africa is the only region where a handful of village smiths still use ancient methods to smelt iron or, more often, to recycle modern metals. Peter Schmidt of the University of Florida has spent many years studying traditional iron smelting in the Great Lakes area of East Africa, where he has found that such activities unfold within a rich fabric of history, myth, and ritual. Over many centuries, the East African ironworkers have innovated continually in response to ever-changing circumstances, such as changing ritual identities and new economic opportunities among neighboring groups. Ironworking was sometimes organized around competitive family or clan groups that produced high-phosphorus iron, steel, and cast iron, using such innovations as larger ore fragments, closely packed furnace pits, and reflecting bellows pipes to create higher temperatures inside the fire. All ancient metallurgy was labor-intensive and very time-consuming.

Basketry and Textiles

Basket production is one of the oldest crafts. Basketry includes such items as containers, matting, bags, and a wide range of fiber objects. Textiles are found in many dry sites, and they are well preserved along the Peruvian coast. Some scholars believe that basketry and textiles are among the most sensitive artifacts for the archaeologist to work with, culturally speaking, on the grounds that people lived in much more intimate association with baskets and textiles than with clay vessels, stone tools, or houses. Furthermore, even small fragments of basketry and textiles display remarkable idiosyncrasies of individual manufacture. When preserved, baskets are amenable to the same kinds of functional and stylistic analyses as other artifacts.

Patricia Anawalt was a textile expert who spent many years studying pre-Columbian garments depicted on Mexican Indian codices. This research has enabled her to work out some of the complicated sumptuary rules that governed military uniforms and other clothing. For example, the lengths, materials, and decorations of Aztec men's cloaks were regulated precisely by the state. Even the type of knot used to fasten capes was specified (see Figure 4.12).

Paracas, Peru Coastal cemetery near the modern city of Pisco, famous for its mummies and fine textiles, dating to over 2,000 years ago.

The dry climate of the central Peruvian coast has preserved the wardrobes of **Paracas** nobles buried between 600 and 150 B.C. Paracas rulers wore mantles, tunics, ponchos, skirts, loincloths, and headpieces. These garments were embroidered with rows of brightly colored anthropomorphic, zoomorphic, and composite figures (see Figure 4.13). Interpreting the iconographic patterns that appear on these ancient garments tells us something of Paracas religious and social customs. Many of the rulers' garments were adorned with shaman figures, showing that the wearer had a special relationship with the supernatural (see the chapter-opening photo for Chapter 16). From this, we might conclude that one of the important functions of a Paracas ruler was to mediate between people and the supernatural forces that influenced and determined life's events.

People have accused archaeologists of being obsessed with the minute details of artifacts and technology to the exclusion of almost anything else. Doubtless there are such obsessives among us, but most researchers know that priceless information about people and human behavior lies behind even simple artifacts. We have only begun to tap into the potential of multidisciplinary research into ancient technologies (see Box 4.5).

Abydos, Egypt Ancient Egyptian town, famous for its cemeteries and shrines, thought to be the site of an entrance to the underworld, c. 3000 B.C. and later.

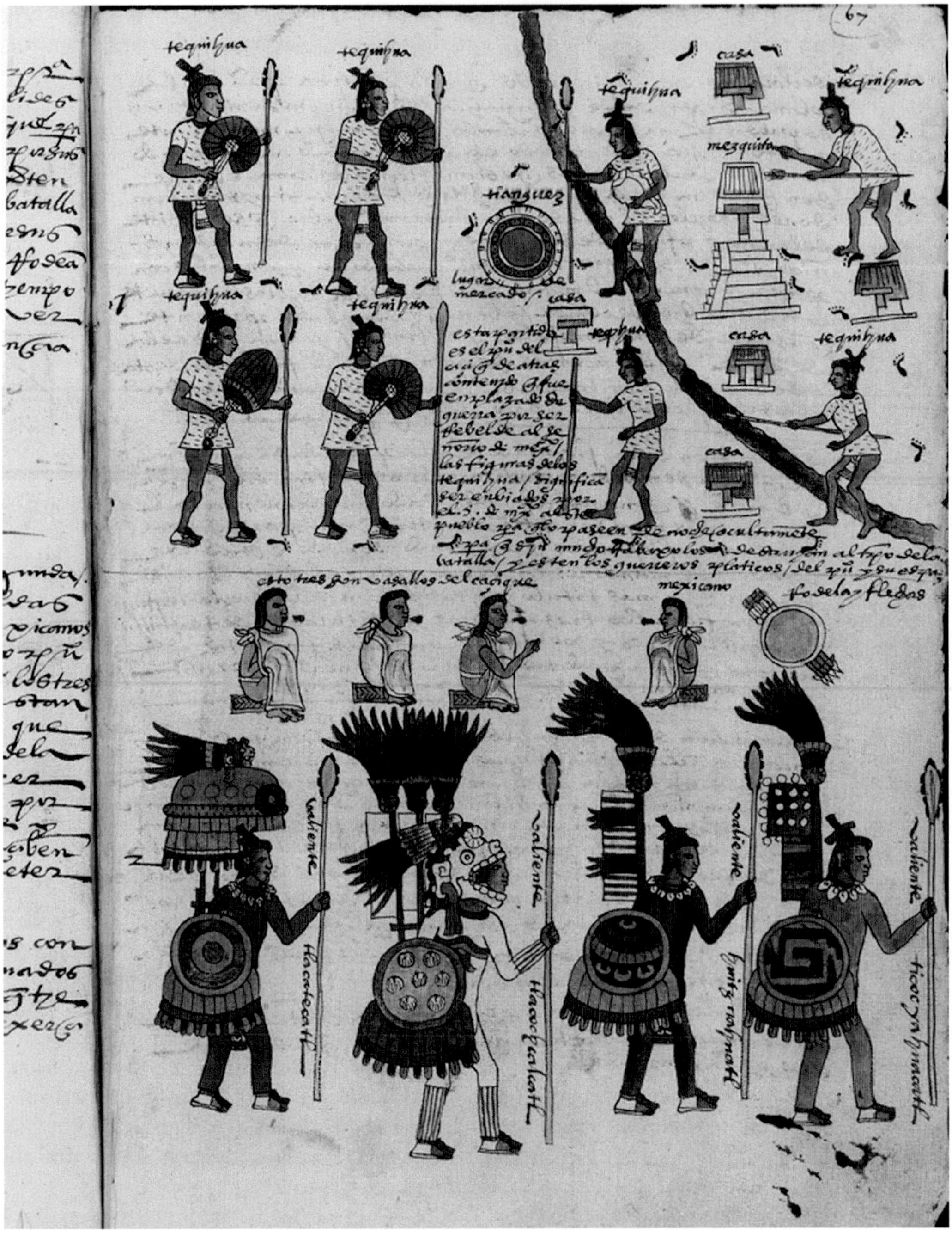

Figure 4.12 Aztec warriors dressed in their capes according to grade. From the *Codex Mendoza*. Source: The Art Archive/Bodleian Libraries, University of Oxford.

Figure 4.13 A cotton funerary textile from the Paracas peninsula, Peru, dating to c. 300 B.C. Source: J. Enrique Molina/Alamy.

Box 4.5 Site
Ancient Wine at Abydos, Egypt

Some of the most remarkable ceramic research involves not the vessels themselves but their contents. In 1988, German Egyptologist Günter Dreyer excavated the tomb of one of Egypt's first leaders at **Abydos**, midway down the Nile. Scorpion I lived at about 3150 B.C. His elaborate tomb contained four rooms stocked with at least 700 jars that held about 4,550 liters (1,200 gallons) of wine. Forty-seven of the jars contained grape seeds, together with remains of sliced figs that were once suspended on strings in the wine, probably to sweeten it. The crusty residues adhering to the insides of the pots were analyzed using infrared spectrometer and liquid chromatography, which revealed the remains of tartaric acids (found naturally in grapes) and also of terebinth resin, which ancient vintners used to prevent wine from turning into vinegar. Neutron activation analysis of the jar clay yielded trace-element clusters that were compared with a large database of samples from Egypt and the eastern Mediterranean. The database pointed to the southern hill-country of Israel and Transjordan as the source of the vessels, an area where vine growing was well established in 3100 B.C. The wine probably traveled the Nile across an ancient trade route, "the Way of Horus," that linked southern Israel with Egypt via the Sinai. By 3000 B.C., wine growing was firmly established in the Nile Delta in northern Egypt, the source of the wines of pharaoh Tutankhamun, nearly 1,500 years later.

Subsistence: Making a Living

The prehistory of how we have fed ourselves is as complex as the history of technology. For all but a mere 12,000 years of human existence, people everywhere survived by hunting and gathering, subsisting off animals large and small and a broad range of wild plant foods. After about 40,000 years ago, hunting methods became more effective and weapons more sophisticated; people hunted certain animals, like reindeer, more intensively. As the Ice Age ended some 15,000 years ago, plant gathering intensified. Fishing and fowling (bird hunting) became important activities in many areas, and mollusks became a popular food. By 12,000 years ago, some communities in the Near East were cultivating wild cereal grasses and, soon after, domesticating wild sheep and goats.

We know all this, and much more, from the study of animal bones, ancient plant remains, and other sources (see Box 4.6). Ancient subsistence—obtaining and eating food—is an intricate archaeological jigsaw puzzle that can be summed up in a few words. Take the forelimb of a deer, a handful of wild grass seeds, a maize cob, and a few grinding implements. Study them closely in a laboratory and come up with a reconstruction of the diet of the people who lived at the site where you found these few food remains. This is basically what archaeologists attempt to do when they study the subsistence practices of ancient societies.

Box 4.6 Doing Archaeology
Studying Ancient Subsistence

Archaeologists reconstruct ancient lifeways from the surviving material remains of subsistence activities, which come in many forms. Like every other form of archaeological research, the perspective is multidisciplinary, for we rely on the expertise of scientists from many other fields, among them botanists, ecologists, and zoologists.

- *Environmental data:* Background data on the natural environment are essential for studying subsistence. Such data can include information on phenomena that include animal distributions, ancient and modern flora, and soils—the range of potential resources to be exploited.
- *Animal bones (faunal remains):* Animal bones are a major source of information on hunting practices and domestic animals.
- *Plant remains:* Plant remains can include both wild and domestic species, obtained using flotation methods and from actual seeds found in dry sites or carbonized by fire.
- *Human bones:* Stable carbon isotopes of skeletal collagen from human bones provide vital information on ancient diets (see p. 143). Bones also give evidence of anatomical anomalies, ancient diseases, and dietary stress.
- *Feces (coprolites):* Feces yield vital evidence for reconstructing prehistoric diet in animals and, in our context, humans.
- *Artifacts:* The picture of human subsistence yielded by artifacts can be limited because of poor preservation, but implements such as plow blades can be useful sources of evidence.
- *Rock art:* Occasionally, rock art depicts scenes of the chase, fishing, and food gathering, and can provide useful information on subsistence activities.

Most reconstructions of ancient lifeways rely on evidence from several of these sources.

feces Body waste.

Animal Bones

zooarchaeology The study of ancient animal bones found at archaeological sites.

The Old Testament prophet Ezekiel unwittingly defined the task of the zooarchaeologist:

> And I prophesied as I was commanded; and as I prophesied, there was a noise, and behold, a rattling; and the bones came together, bone to its bone. And as I looked, there were sinews on them, and flesh had come upon them, and skin had covered them.
>
> (Ezekiel 37:10)

Zooarchaeologists put the flesh on long-dead animals, reconstructing the environment and behavior of ancient peoples to the extent that animal remains allow. **Zooarchaeology** is a specialized expertise; it requires a background in paleontology or zoology.

Paleontologists studying dinosaurs and ancient mammals have it easy compared with zooarchaeologists, for they deal with relatively complete bones. Almost invariably, the bones found in occupation sites have been broken to splinters. Every piece of usable meat was stripped from the bones, sinews were made into thongs, and the skin was formed into clothing, containers, or sometimes housing materials. Even the entrails were eaten. Limb bones were split for their delicious marrow; some bones were made into such tools as harpoon heads, arrow tips, or mattocks.

Animal bones in archaeological sites come from dismembered carcasses butchered either on-site or out in open country. Small deer might be taken back whole, slung over the shoulder. Hunter-gatherers sometimes camped at the site of a kill of a large animal, where they ate parts of the carcass and then dried parts for later use. The Paleo-Indian and bison hunters of the North American Great Plains drove entire herds of bison over cliffs and into narrow gullies, rendering them helpless and then killing them. Hundreds of animals perished in these occasional hunts. The hunters butchered them where they lay (see Figure 4.14; see also Box 14.1 on p. 438).

Head-Smashed-In, Canada Major bison kill site on the plains of Alberta, used as early as 5,500 years ago.

Quite apart from human modification of bones, many other processes operate on organic remains such as bone after the organism dies (see Figure 4.15). Predators such as hyenas or lions can disarticulate and mangle hunters' kills. Detecting such activity requires meticulous research. For example, experiments with captive hyenas have shown that they choose to eat backbones and hip bones first, which they usually destroy completely. Then, limb-bone ends are often chewed off, but shafts are frequently left intact. This seems like esoteric research, perhaps, until you realize that the patterns of bone fractures tell us that the 1.75-million-year-old hominin bone caches at Olduvai Gorge, Tanzania, were picked over by hyenas after the site's human owners had departed (see Chapter 8). Humans

Figure 4.14 An artist's reconstruction of a bison drive at **Head-Smashed-In**, Alberta, Canada, where hunters preyed on bison as early as 5,500 years ago.

Source: Alberta Historic Sites.

butchered and disarticulated animals with tools long before the carcasses were dispersed by natural phenomena or by carnivores, so the study of such systematic activities is at least a baseline for examining patterns of damage on ancient bones.

You cannot assume that the fragmentary bones found in an archaeological deposit will give you either an accurate count of the number of animals killed by the inhabitants or precise insights into the environment at the time of occupation. The "archaeological animal" consists of a scatter of broken bones that have been shattered by a butcher, then subjected to hundreds or thousands of years of gradual deterioration in the soil, something very different from a once-living animal that was butchered, its abandoned bones scattered on the ground.

Many cultural factors can affect animal-bone counts in a settlement. For example, people may carry in some game from far away yet kill all of their goats at the village. Also, we have no means of knowing what spiritual role some animals played in ancient societies or of studying taboos and other prohibitions that may have caused certain animals to be hunted and others to be ignored. Nor do we know precisely what the relative frequencies of different animal species were in the ancient environment.

faunal analysis The study of animal bones.

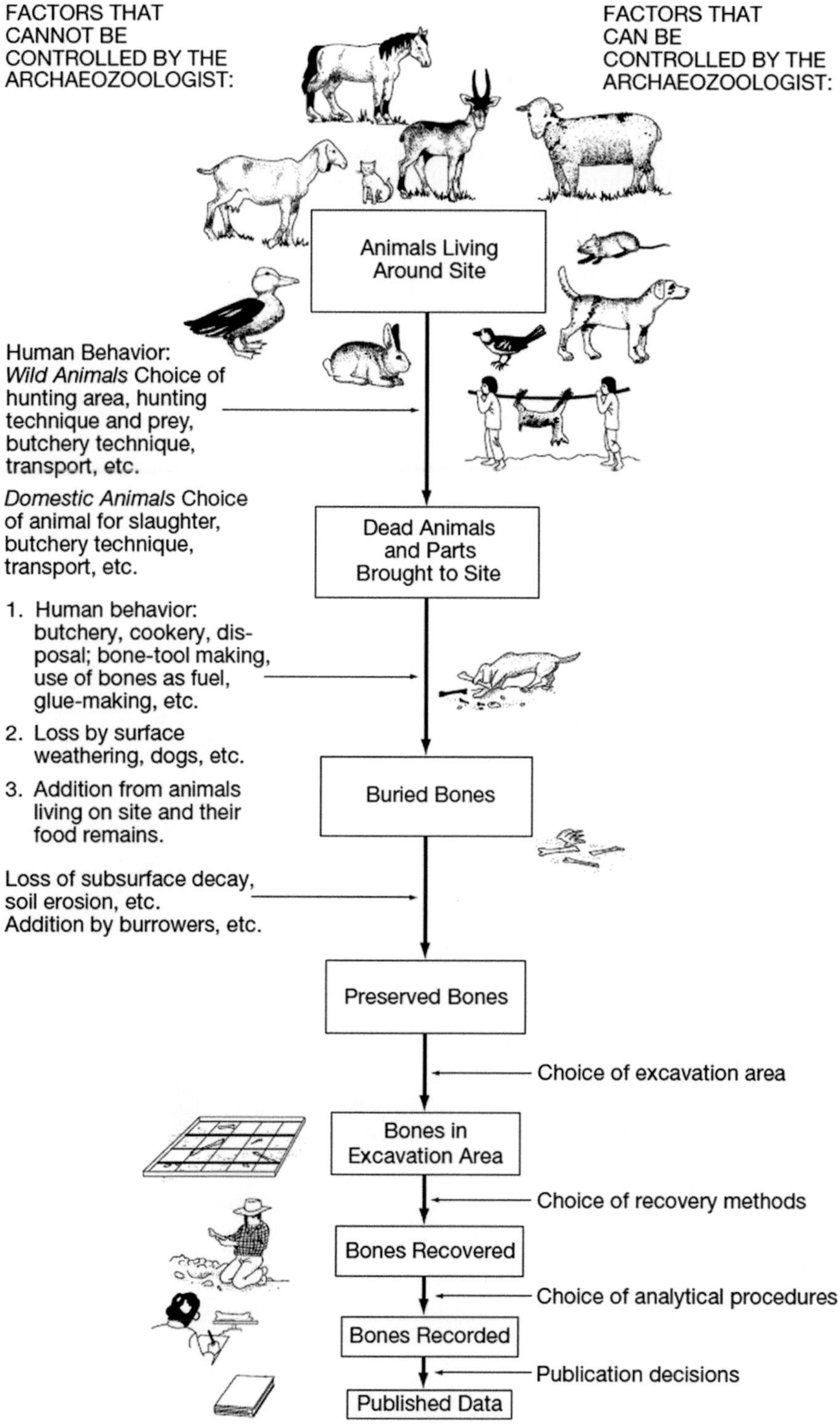

Figure 4.15 Analysis of bone from the archaeological record. This figure shows some of the factors that affect faunal data. Factors that the archaeologist cannot control are on the left; those that the researcher can control are on the right.

Bone Identification

Most bone identification (**faunal analysis**) is done by direct comparison with bones of known species. It is a fairly simple procedure and easily learned by anyone with sharp eyes (see Figures 4.16 and 4.17).

The identification stage of bone analysis is the most important, for several fundamental questions need answering: Are domestic and wild species present? If so, what are the proportions of each group? What types of domestic stock did the inhabitants keep? Did they have any hunting preferences that are reflected in the proportions of game animals found in the occupation levels? Are any wild species characteristic of, say, cooler or warmer climatic conditions in the region?

Olsen-Chubbock, Colorado Paleo-Indian kill site dating to c. 6000 B.C., the location of a mass bison kill involving more than 150 beasts.

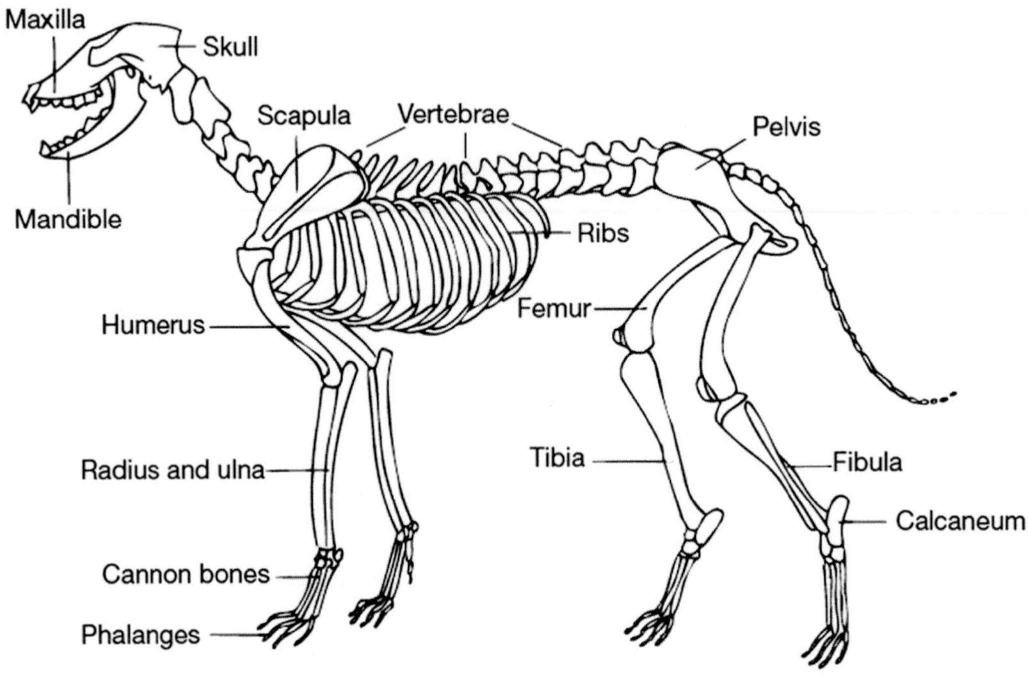

Figure 4.16 The skeleton of a dog, a typical mammalian skeleton, showing the most important bones from a zooarchaeological standpoint. Upper and lower jaws and their dentition, individual teeth, the bony cores of horns, and sometimes the articular surfaces of long bones are easy to identify. In some parts of the world, the articular ends of long bones can be used as well, especially in such regions as southwestern Asia or parts of North America, where the indigenous mammalian fauna is somewhat restricted. But in other areas, such as tropical Africa, the indigenous fauna is so rich and varied, with such small variations in skeletal anatomy, that only horn cores or teeth can help distinguish among species of antelope and separate domestic stock from game animals. Experts disagree as to what constitutes identifiability of bone, so it is best to think in terms of levels of identifiability rather than simply to reject many fragments out of hand. For example, you can sometimes identify a fragment as coming from a medium-sized carnivore even if you have no way of telling whether it is from a wolf or a dog.

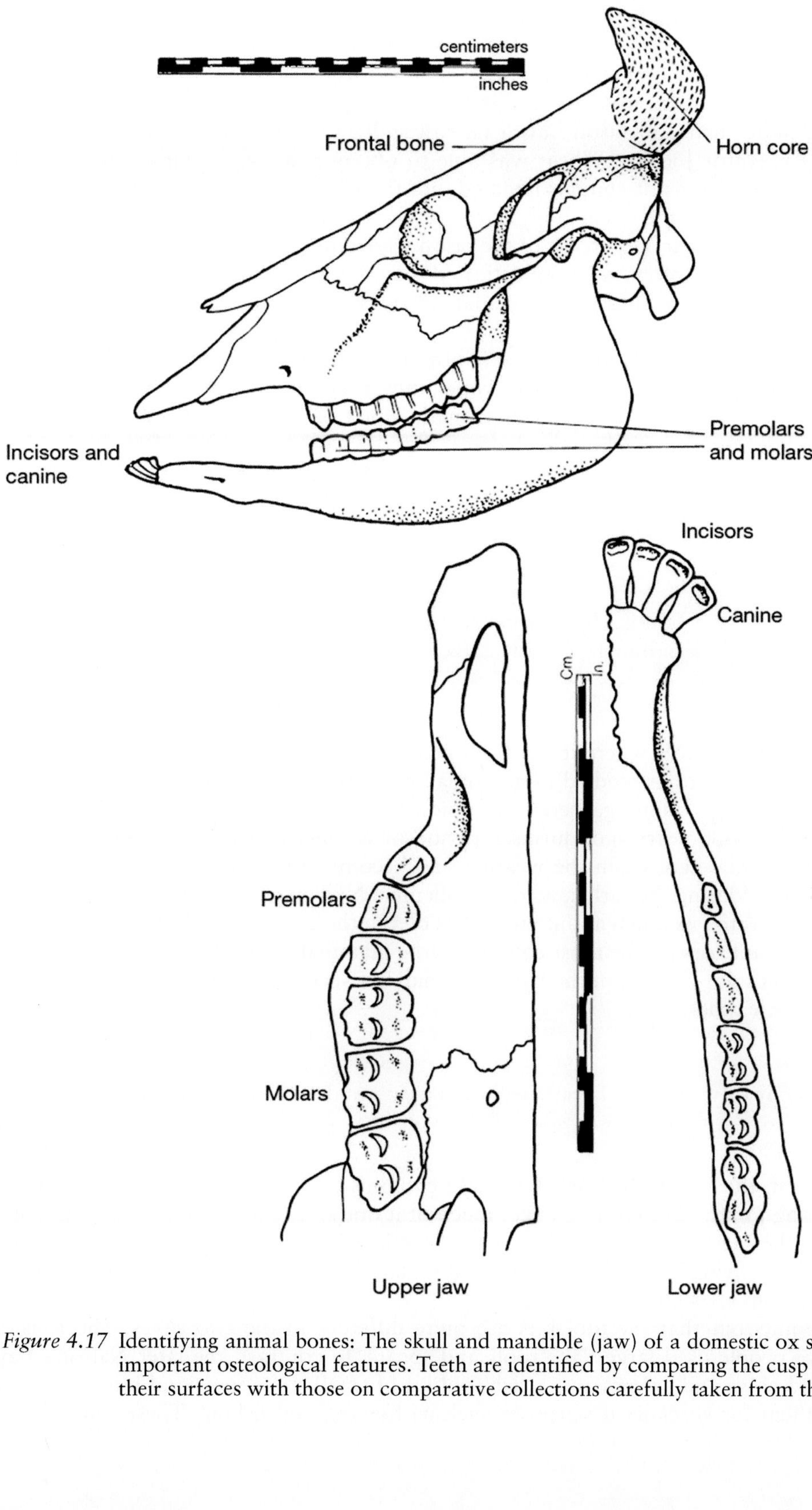

Figure 4.17 Identifying animal bones: The skull and mandible (jaw) of a domestic ox showing the important osteological features. Teeth are identified by comparing the cusp patterns on their surfaces with those on comparative collections carefully taken from the site area.

Establishing the number of animals killed or eaten at a site is virtually impossible, except by counting the number of individual body parts. One of the best ways of obtaining an accurate kill count is on game drive sites, such as those on the North American plains. The **Olsen-Chubbock** site in Colorado preserves a single kill, when a group of hunters stampeded more than 150 bison into a narrow gully. Of those, 110 were females and 80 males. Excavator Joe Ben Wheat was able to obtain relatively accurate counts both from complete skeletons of animals jammed into the lowermost levels of the arroyo and from partial skeletons and other body parts butchered systematically after the hunt. He could even establish that 57 percent of the bison were adults (see Box 14.1, p. 438).

Zooarchaeologists often use sophisticated computer programs to compare bone collections from different sites and to estimate the number of animals in different occupation layers and sites.

Identifying the number of animals present in a site is relatively straightforward compared with the problem of explaining why the proportions of different animals change from one layer to another. Was this the result of climatic shifts or the consequence of changing hunting preferences? While climatic changes, like the global warm-up after the Ice Age 15,000 years ago, caused massive extinctions of cold-loving animals like the mammoth, the arctic elephant, and the wooly rhinoceros of northern latitudes, some extinctions do reflect human activity—changes in the ways in which people exploited other animals.

Klasies River Cave, South Africa Stone Age cave, c. 100,000 years ago, where some of the earliest modern human remains have been found.

One of the few places where it has been possible to document such changes is South Africa. Richard Klein has studied large faunal samples from two coastal caves in Cape Province. Stone Age hunter-gatherers occupied the **Klasies River Cave** between about 130,000 and 95,000 years ago, during a period of warmer climate, and thereafter until about 70,000 years ago, when the weather had become much cooler. The seashore was close to the cave during the earlier, warmer millennia. Numerous mollusks, seal bones, and penguin remains tell us much about Stone Age diet in the cave. Seabirds and fish are rare. Eland, a large antelope, is the most common large mammal, more than twice as common as the Cape buffalo. The rest of the land mammals are species common in the area during modern historic times.

Nelson's Bay Cave, South Africa Late Stone Age coastal cave dating to after 8000 B.C.

In contrast, the nearby **Nelson's Bay Cave** contains evidence of later Stone Age occupation dating to after 20,000 years ago, much of it during a time when the sea was some miles from the cave during the coldest part of the last Ice Age glaciation with its low sea levels. Bones of flying seabirds and fish are abundant in this cave, whereas eland are only a third as common as buffalo.

Klein points out that the tool kits are quite different in the two caves. The Klasies River Cave people used large flake tools and spears. In contrast, the later Nelson's Bay hunters had bows and arrows and a rich tool kit of small stone tools and bone artifacts, many of them for specialized purposes such as fowling and fishing. These innovations allowed them to kill dangerous or more elusive species with greater frequency. Thus, the reason that the Klasies River people took more eland was not that such animals were more abundant in earlier times, but that more elusive creatures were captured less frequently. There is every indication that the Klasies people were less sophisticated behaviorally. Klein combines some other faunal evidence with his mammalian and climatic data. The Klasies River site contains larger tortoise and limpet remains, as if these creatures were permitted to grow to a larger size than in later times. This implies less pressure on the tortoise and shellfish populations from a smaller human population before technologically more advanced people arrived.

Examples of specialized hunting are common, even if the reasons for the attention given to one or more species are rarely explained. The specialized buffalo-hunting economies of the North American Plains Indians are well known. The long-term exploitation of a single, often slow-breeding animal can result in overhunting or the gradual extinction of a favorite species. One well-known example is *Bos primigenius* (see Figure 4.18), the European aurochs, or wild ox, which was a major quarry of late Ice Age hunters in western Europe and was still hunted until medieval times. The last aurochs died in a Polish park in A.D. 1627. Modern efforts to reconstitute the aurochs have produced fierce, lively animals with long horns.

Nearly all domestic animals originated from a wild species with an inclination to be sociable, facilitating an association with humans (see Chapter 11). Domestic animals did not all originate in the same part of the world; they were domesticated in their natural area of distribution in the wild. Domestication everywhere seems to begin when a growing population needs a more regular food supply to feed larger groups of people; domestication is dependent on such conditions and is a prerequisite for further population growth.

Figure 4.18 The aurochs, *Bos primigenius*, illustrated by Sigmund von Herberstain, who observed one in the flesh in 1549. We know from illustrations and contemporary descriptions what these massive animals looked like. The bulls were large, up to 2 meters (6.5 feet) at the shoulder, and often had very long horns. The male coat was black with a white stripe along the back and white curly hair between the horns. Through careful, long-term breeding and selecting for the physical features of the aurochs, German and Polish biologists have "reconstituted" these beasts successfully. Reconstituted aurochsen are fierce, temperamental, and extremely agile if allowed to run wild. The biological experiments have provided a far more convincing reconstruction of a most formidable Pleistocene mammal than any number of skeletal reconstructions or artists' impressions could.

Wild animals lack many characteristics that are valuable in their domestic counterparts. Thus, wild sheep have thick coats, but their wool is not the type produced by domestic sheep, which is suitable for spinning; aurochs, ancestors of the domestic ox, and wild goats produce sufficient milk for their young, but not in the quantities so important to humans. Considerable changes take place during domestication as people develop characteristics in their animals that often render the animals unfit for survival in the wild.

The history of domesticated species is based on fragmentary animal bones found in the deposits of innumerable caves, rock shelters, and open sites. A number of sites have produced evidence of gradual change in skeletal anatomy toward domesticated animals. If the bones of the wild species of some prehistoric domesticated animals are compared with those of the domestic animals throughout time, the range of size variations first increases, and eventually selection in favor of smaller animals and less variation in size appears. This transition is fluid, however, and with the human eye alone, it is difficult to identify wild or domestic individuals from single bones or small collections.

However, science marches on, and in the twenty-first century, particularly since the 2010s, our understanding of the domestication process of a range of animals, including goats, pigs, dogs and cattle, has been greatly enhanced by advances in DNA analysis. The genetic analysis of ancient and modern animal remains has provided insights that were previously inaccessible, revealing patterns of genetic variation that align with shifts in domesticated traits like size, temperament, and behavior. DNA analysis has also helped clarify the timeline of domestication events with much more precision.

epiphyses The articular ends of limb bones that fuse at adulthood in animals and humans.

Killing Patterns

How old were these cattle when they were slaughtered? Did the inhabitants concentrate on immature wild goats rather than on fully grown ones? These are the kinds of questions that are important at many sites. To answer them, researchers must establish the age at death of the animals in the bone sample. The skeletal parts most commonly used to determine the age of an animal at death are teeth and the fused or unfused **epiphyses** at the ends of limb bones.

Teeth and upper or lower jaws provide the most accurate way of establishing animal age. Teeth are an almost continuous guide to the age of an individual from birth to old age. Complete upper and lower jaws allow us to study immature and mature teeth as they erupt from the bone. Thus, we can identify the proportion of young animals and very old animals as well.

If you have a large enough sample of jaws, or even of individual teeth, you can sometimes identify one of two distinctive age profiles:

catastrophic age profile Distribution of ages at death of animals in a population that died of natural causes.

attritional age profile Distribution of ages at death of animals in a population that were killed by selective hunting or predation.

- The **catastrophic age profile** is stable in size and structure and has progressively fewer older individuals. This is the normal distribution for living ungulate populations (see the left side of Figure 4.19) and is normally found in mass game kills that entailed driving herds into swamps or over cliffs.
- The **attritional age profile** (see the right side of Figure 4.19) shows an under representation of prime-age animals relative to their abundance in living populations and an overrepresentation of young and old. This profile is thought to result from scavenging or simple spear hunting.

In South Africa, zooarchaeologist Richard Klein found that the age distributions of Cape buffalo from the Klasies River and Nelson's Bay sites were close to those observed for modern buffalo killed by lions, where both young and old males are vulnerable to attack because they are isolated from the large herds of formidable prime animals. Thus, he argued, the Stone Age hunters at both caves enjoyed a lasting, stable relationship with their prey populations of buffalo. The distributions for eland and bastard hartebeest (smaller, gregarious antelopes) were much more similar to the catastrophic profile. Klein speculates that they were similar because these species were hunted in large game drives, like the bison on the Great Plains. Thus entire populations would be killed at one time.

Hunting and slaughter patterns are subject to all manner of subtle variables. While studying hunting practices among the Nunamiut of Alaska, Lewis Binford found that the hunters butchered animals as part of a much broader subsistence strategy. The Nunamiut rely heavily on stored meat for most of the year and thus orient their hunting practices toward storage objectives, as well as many other considerations. In the fall, they may hunt caribou calves to obtain skins for winter clothing, and the heads and tongues of these animals provide the meat for the people who process the skins. Binford stressed that it is difficult to interpret slaughter patterns without closely understanding the cultural systems of which hunting was a part.

Domestic animals are a controllable meat supply and subject to very different selection criteria. In more advanced agricultural societies, cattle or horses might have been kept until old age for draft purposes, surplus males being castrated and females being retained until they stopped lactating or were of no further use for breeding or plowing. Even if riding or work animals were not kept, the problem of surplus males persisted. This surplus was an abundant source of prime meat, and these animals were often slaughtered in early adulthood. Cattle stood for wealth in many traditional societies, as they do in some today, and they were slaughtered for special occasions such as funerals or weddings. The herd surplus was consumed in this manner, and the owner's social obligations were satisfied.

With all animal-bone collections, the problem is to establish the meaning of archaeological distributions in terms of human behavior. Just how complicated this is in the context of butchery can be appreciated from Binford's observation that the Nunamiuts' criteria for selecting meat for consumption are the amount of usable meat, the time required to process it, and the quality of the flesh. So anyone interpreting butchery, or any other hunting or herding activities for that matter, must take into account everything known about the culture as a whole.

Plant Remains

Animal bones tell only part of the subsistence story. Throughout human history, people have relied heavily on plant foods of all kinds. For the past 12,000 years, they have grown them as well. In many societies, game meat formed far fewer meals than vegetable foods, which are often completely invisible in archaeological sites. For example, the !Kung San,

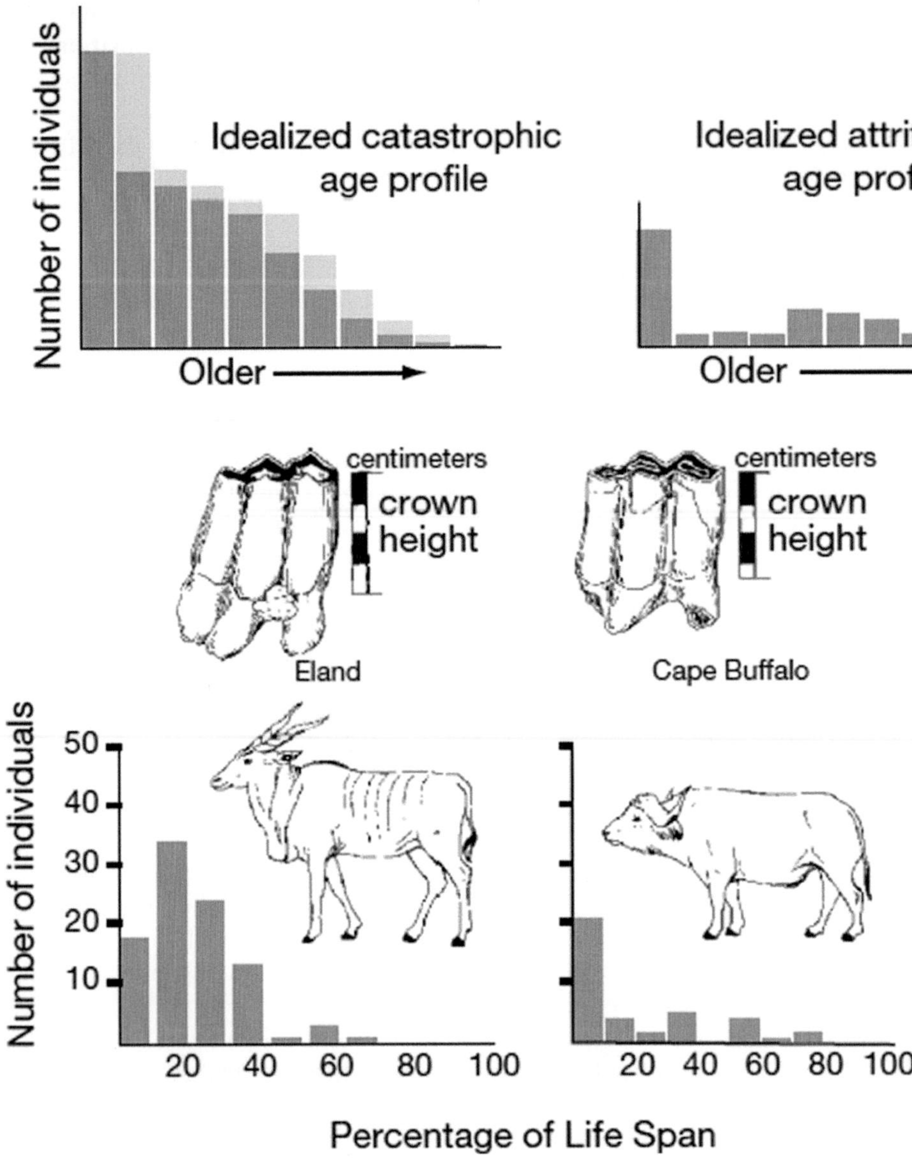

Figure 4.19 Determining killing patterns: Two common South African game animals, the eland and the Cape buffalo, provide mortality data based on the molar crowns, idealized catastrophic age profile (left) and idealized attritional age profile (right).

present-day inhabitants of the Kalahari Desert in southern Africa, know of at least 85 edible seeds and roots. Most of the time they eat only eight of these. The rest of the vegetable resource base provides a reliable cushion for this foraging population in times when key vegetable foods are scarce. Such people have a buffer against famine that many farmers with their cleared lands, much higher population densities, and crops that rely on regular rainfall rarely enjoy. The San's lifeway raises a question: Is a farming life really to be preferred? A few studies of the skeletons of early farming populations show how malnutrition due to food shortages was commonplace in many areas.

In the twentieth century, most evidence for plant remains came from sites in very dry environments—Hogup and Gatecliff in the Great Basin of the arid west are two examples, with much of the former's deposits consisting very largely of chaff, seeds, and other botanical remains. In Mexico's Tehuacán valley, Richard MacNeish assembled a continuous sequence of human occupation for the period from 10,000 years ago to the Spanish conquest. He dug more than a dozen open sites and caves, all so dry that they yielded 80,000 wild plant remains and 25,000 specimens of domestic corn. MacNeish was able to identify diminutive maize cobs in several caves, which have been AMS-dated to about 2700 B.C. These early maize cobs were no more than 2 centimeters (0.78 inches) long, but later ones were far larger. During his research, MacNeish was unfortunately unable to identify the original wild ancestor of Tehuacán maize, which we now known to be a native grass still growing in Mexico today—teosinte.

Into the twenty-first century, and advances in DNA analysis have revolutionized our understanding of plant domestication, offering new insights into how crops were developed and spread across the world. Ancient DNA extracted from archaeological remains—such as seeds, pollen, and plant fibers—has enabled researchers to pinpoint the genetic changes associated with domestication, such as size increases, changes in reproductive cycles, and adaptation to human cultivation.

One of the key breakthroughs has been the sequencing of ancient plant genomes, which allows scientists to track the genetic transition from wild ancestors to domesticated forms. For example, the latest studies on maize (corn) have used genetic data to show that teosinte, the wild grass mentioned above, was domesticated in southern Mexico about 9,000 years ago. The comparison of genetic sequences from ancient maize remains with modern crops has highlighted the small genetic changes that led to the larger, more productive maize plants we know today.

DNA analysis has also contributed to our understanding the spread of domesticated plants. By comparing the genetic diversity of ancient crops across different regions, researchers can track the routes of trade and migration, showing how crops like rice spread from Southeast Asia to other parts of the world. For instance, rice domestication is now known to have occurred in at least two regions: the Yangtze River Valley in China and the Ganges River Valley in India, with genetic evidence confirming independent domestication events in these areas.

macrobotanical remains Easily recognizable plant remains such as pine nuts, maize cobs, charred nuts, or seeds.

But how do archaeologists access ancient plant samples? Under less than ideal preservation conditions elsewhere, the only plant remains that survived are **macrobotanical remains**—easily recognizable items such as pine nuts, maize cobs, charred nuts or seeds preserved in a hearth or charcoal, but very rarely remains of cooked meals. Grain impressions preserved in wet clay pot-walls occasionally provide information. For example, Maya farmers in northern Belize cultivated raised fields in wetlands. The waterlogged soils contained avocado, maize, and other domesticated grass seeds. At Dust Cave in Alabama, already described in Chapter 3, the inhabitants processed large quantities of hickory nuts and acorns, also black walnuts, hackberry, and hazelnuts. But hickories were the dominant nut, the discarded shells being used as fuel, for they have a high fat content and burn hot. Acorns were an important staple throughout the west and elsewhere. They have the disadvantage that they require quite lengthy processing to leach out toxins, but provide protein-rich food and also have the priceless quality of being easily stored for months, an important consideration for people living in arid environments with only seasonal nut harvests.

paleoethnobotanist A scientist who studies ancient plant remains and their relationships with ancient peoples.

In recent years, **paleoethnobotanists**—scientists who recover, identify, and study ancient vegetable remains and assess the relationships between people and plants—have made major strides in the study of plant remains, using a variety of methods and lines of evidence that were unimaginable in earlier years. Some important methods of recovering and studying plant remains are now routine:

flotation A method of recovering plant remains by passing them through screens and water.

palynology (pollen analysis) The study of ancient vegetation by using minute pollens preserved in organic deposits.

opal phytoliths Minute silica particles from plant cells.

coprolite Human (or animal) feces.

- **Flotation** recovers tiny seeds and other botanical finds by passing soil samples through water or chemicals (see Figure 4.20). Flotation methods have revolutionized the study of ancient plants, for they provide large seed samples that can be studied with statistical methods. At the Ali Kosh mound in Iran, Kent Flannery and Frank Hole thought that plant remains were scarce. Then, they used flotation methods and recovered 40,000 seeds from the trenches. In recent years, botanists have obtained literally pints of seed samples from the early farming village at Abu Hureyra in Syria—samples so complete that botanist Gordon Hillman has been able to chronicle major shifts in plant-gathering preferences over more than 3,000 years. When Abu Hureyra was a small foraging settlement before 10,000 B.C., the people relied heavily on acorns and other nut crops in nearby forests. But as the forests retreated in the face of dry conditions, the people turned to wild cereal grasses, which they soon domesticated to provide extra food supplies.
- **Palynology (pollen analysis)**, described in Chapter 7, provides a wealth of information not only about ancient environments, but also about human activities. Domesticated plants have characteristic pollen spores. So do cultivation weeds, like *Plantago lanceolata*, which appear when land is cleared for cultivation. Pollens are minute and can travel long distances, which means that samples from an archaeological site provide but a generalized impression of what people might have found to eat in the vicinity. Such impressions can be invaluable. For example, the Paiute and Shoshone Indians of the Great Basin relied heavily on upland plants such as piñon nuts, whereas the people living near the Stillwater Marsh in the Carson Desert, Nevada,

about a thousand years ago, appear to have relied almost entirely on plant foods from nearby wetlands. They seem not to have walked 20 kilometers (12 miles) to obtain piñons from higher ground.

- **Opal phytoliths** (minute particles of silica from plant cells absorbed through a plant's roots) take the form of the cells of the plants in which they are deposited. They have been used to identify early maize use in Central America and the Andes, but are of most use for identifying the abundance of different grasses in occupation deposits.
- **Coprolites** (desiccated human feces) are sometimes recovered from dry caves in the American West and elsewhere. They provide unique information on ancient diets. For instance, coprolites from Hidden Cave near Stillwater Marsh contained fragments of bird, fish, and plant remains, among them bulrush millet and cattail pollen. Small waterfowl feathers and the bones of the minnow-sized tui chub abounded, as did insects and snails. The people who stopped at Hidden Cave ate a varied diet from an environment where a wide range of foods was available.
- Bone chemistry methods look at stable isotopes, described earlier in the chapter, which provide valuable information on diet at a general level. For instance, the bone chemistry of the inhabitants of Pecos Pueblo in the American Southwest shows that they ate predominantly maize and very little meat. Northwest Coast populations tended to have diets that relied heavily on maritime foods, as one would expect.

These are but a few of the methods that are now used to study ancient plant remains. These inconspicuous, and hitherto often neglected, finds can offer valuable information on important questions. Samples from flotation analysis can provide enough seeds to record differences in seasonal occupation. For instance, a spring visit in search of one form of edible grass that ripens in spring, and is overwhelmingly abundant in the sample, is clear evidence for seasonal occupation. But a word of caution: ancient environments differed, often dramatically, from those of today, so any study of plant use cannot be divorced from a parallel understanding of the surrounding environment at the time. Plants had, and still have, important symbolic and ritual associations in many societies, among them hallucinogenic mushrooms, peyote. Many ancient societies had encyclopedic knowledge of medicinal and poisonous plants—for curing all manner of diseases and for such esoterica as toxic arrowhead poisons—and substances like aconite, smeared by Native Americans in Alaska on their whaling harpoons and lances.

paleoethnobotany The study of ancient botanical remains.

Wild vegetable foods were a staple of the prehistoric world from the earliest times until people first began to cultivate the soil some 12,000 years ago. They are still important in many farmers' diets. **Paleoethnobotany** is the study of ancient plant remains. Unfortunately, seeds, fruits, grasses, leaves, and roots are among the most fragile of organic materials and do not survive long unless they are carbonized, preserved under very wet or arid conditions, or impressed into the walls of clay vessels before they are fired brick-hard.

Hogup Cave, Utah Long-occupied cave in the Great Basin, with levels extending back to at least 7000 B.C.

Carbonized and unburned seeds are normally found in cooking pots, as impressions in the wet pot clay, in midden deposits, or among the ashes of hearths, where they were dropped by accident. The extremely dry conditions of the western North American desert and of the Peruvian coast have preserved thousands of seeds, as well as human coprolites, which contain a wealth of vegetal material. **Hogup Cave** in Utah was occupied as early as 7000 B.C. From about 6400 to 1200 B.C., the inhabitants relied so heavily on pickleweed seeds in their diet that the early deposits are literally golden with the chaff threshed from them. After 1200 B.C., deposits of pickleweed and the milling stones used to process them decline rapidly. An abrupt rise in the nearby Great Salt Lake may have drowned the marsh where the seed was collected, so the cave was only visited by hunting parties thereafter. Dry caves in Mexico's Tehuacán valley have yielded small, very early maize cobs (see Chapter 14).

The study of plant remains requires much larger samples than those obtained from occasional dry caves or carbonized remains. Flotation methods pass large samples of occupation deposits through water and fine screens and can preserve large quantities of seeds for botanists to study (see Box 4.7). Andrew Moore used flotation with great efficiency on the Stone Age farming village at Abu Hureyra on the Euphrates River in Syria (see Chapter 11). He acquired 712 seed samples from soil deposits that made up a bulk of more than 500 liters (132 gallons). Each sample contained as many as 500 seeds from over 150 plant taxa, with many of them edible. By dissecting these large samples, botanist Gordon Hillman was able to document the retreat of oak forests in the region and the changes in plant gathering that accompanied environmental change. He showed that Abu Hureyra was in the grip of a prolonged drought at about 9000 B.C. At first, the people turned to drought-resistant small-seeded grasses; then they deliberately cultivated them to expand their food supplies, an example of the earliest farming activity.

The intensive exploitation of plant remains is, above all, a phenomenon of human subsistence since the end of the Ice Age some 15,000 years ago, when people turned increasingly from big game to smaller animals and to edible plants, many of which they eventually domesticated (see Chapters 11 and 14). At the same time, they exploited salmon runs and migrating waterfowl, further widening the food quest. Human societies everywhere developed more specialized hunter-gatherer economies in which birds, fish, and shellfish, as well as plant foods, assumed ever-greater importance.

Fishing and Fowling

The systematic pursuit of fish and birds generated new and distinctive technologies: lightweight stone-barbed arrows, bone fishhooks, and barbed fishing spears. Such artifacts and easily identifiable bird and fish bones provide information not only on such activities, but also on seasonal hunting. For example, farming communities in the Mississippi valley killed and dried thousands of waterfowl each spring and fall 2,000 years ago, for the valley lies on a major flyway for migrating birds (see Chapter 14). Sometimes one can discern seasonal activities from bird bones. A large 1,000-year-old shell mound at Emeryville, California, yielded numerous immature cormorant bones from young birds taken from nearby rookeries. Measurements showed that most of the cormorant bones equaled those of adult birds in size, but the ossification was less complete and equivalent to that in modern birds of about five to six weeks old. Modern rookery records from the San Francisco area place birds as being that old on about June 28, the prime date for rookery raids.

Fishing was of vital economic importance to many later hunter-gatherer and farming societies, for fish provided a relatively reliable food source throughout the year. Prehistoric

Box 4.7 Doing Archaeology
Flotation Methods

Early excavators recovered seeds from hearths and dry storage pits and obtained but a tiny fraction of what lay in the deposits. Flotation uses water or chemicals to free the seeds, which are often of microscopic size, from the fine earth or occupation residue that masks them; the vegetal remains usually float and the residue sinks. Although this technique enables researchers to recover seeds from many sites where it was impossible before, by no means can it be applied universally because its effectiveness depends on soil conditions. The methods used are being refined as more experience is gained under varied field conditions.

At first, researchers simply used converted oil drums and processed samples laboriously through a series of screens, but the pace of sample processing was too slow. A number of ingenious machines have been developed to carry out large-scale flotation (Figure 4.20). The sample of earth is poured into the screened container and agitated by the water pouring into the screen. The light plant remains and other fine materials float on the water and are carried out of the container by a sluiceway that leads to fine mesh screens. There the finds are caught, wrapped in fine cloth, and preserved for study. The heavy sludge, in the meantime, sinks to the bottom of the container inside the oil drum.

The advantage of flotation is obvious. It provides much larger samples of plant remains that can reflect not only human consumption and exploitation of edible plants, but also the surrounding natural vegetation. In eastern North America, for example, regular use of flotation has yielded thousands of tiny seeds and a slowly emerging story of a gradual shift from foraging of wild plant foods to subsistence patterns that relied heavily on the deliberate cultivation of native plants, long before maize and beans arrived in the region. Flotation comes into its own when studying the contents of storage pits, where seed crops and other foods were kept for many months. It has also been used to study the contents of historic privies and the fills of individual rooms in southwestern pueblos.

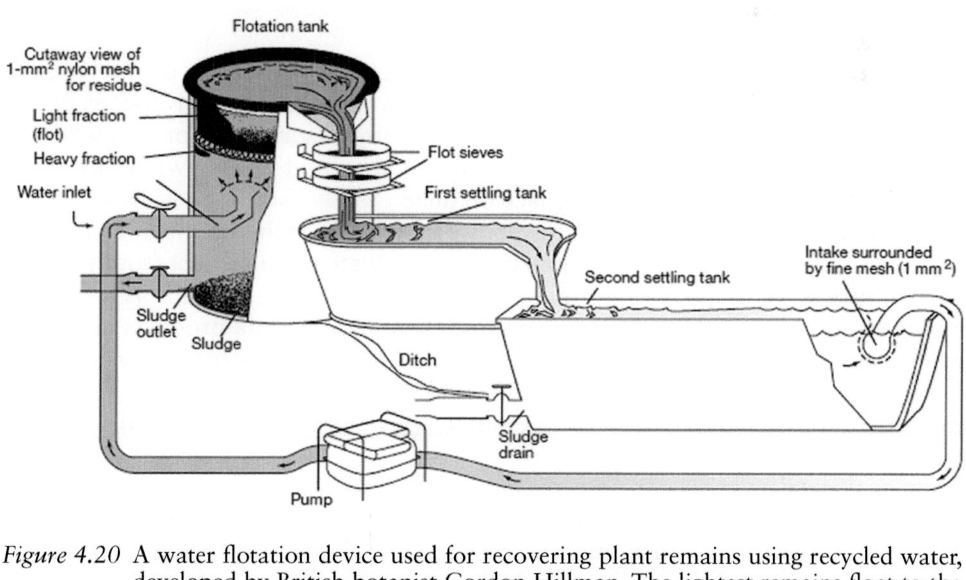

Figure 4.20 A water flotation device used for recovering plant remains using recycled water, developed by British botanist Gordon Hillman. The lightest remains float to the surface and are caught in the float screens. The heavier material sinks and is caught in light nylon mesh.

societies along the Klamath River of northwestern California subsisted almost entirely off seasonal salmon runs, where the harvest was limited only by the ability of the people to process hundreds of large fish a day for drying or smoking. Offshore fishing required seaworthy watercraft, like the famous *tomol* of the Chumash Indians of southern California. Fish bones are easily identified and provide reliable evidence of inshore or offshore fishing, as well as information on the ages and weights of fish taken. Swordfish, for example, are taken in deep water, while leopard shark and halibut can be taken inshore in Chumash waters. Far inland, lakeside groups in the Great Basin took hundreds of small fish such as the tui chub, a staple for many centuries.

Shellfish from seashores, lakes, and rivers were a reliable food source and often of overwhelming importance during the lean months of the year. From the very earliest times, they were a staple for coastal people in central California and in parts of the eastern coast of the United States. Huge shell middens, accumulations of abandoned shells, are commonplace in many parts of the world, such as the shores of the Baltic Sea in Scandinavia, the California coast, and the shores of South Africa's Cape region. The changing proportions of shell species in different levels of a midden can tell us much about changing dietary habits over the centuries or about environmental changes. For example, the 6,000-year-old levels of shell middens on the shores of Los Batiquitos Lagoon north of San Diego yielded numerous oysters, denizens of a rocky shoreline. By 4600 B.C., the lagoon had silted so much that oysters vanished, to be replaced by other forms of shellfish.

Both freshwater shells and seashells became valued ornaments or ritual objects, like the *spondylus* shell, which was sacred high in the Andes. Perhaps the most extreme example was the Indian Ocean *Conus* shell, a highly prized symbol of chiefly prestige in Africa's far interior. Nineteenth-century missionary and explorer David Livingstone records that on his visit to Chief Shinte in western Zambia in 1855, the going price for two *Conus* shells at that time was a slave; for five, a tusk of elephant ivory. Such shells occasionally came from ancient village sites far from the coast dating to the past 2,000 years.

Reconstructing Ancient Diet

Food remains tell us much about ancient subsistence but do not, in themselves, reconstruct the actual diet. What proportion of the diet was meat? How diverse were dietary sources? Did the principal sources of diet change from season to season? To what extent did the people rely on food from neighboring areas? Was food stored? What limitations or restrictions did technology or society place on diet?

Diet (what is eaten) and nutrition (the ability of a diet to maintain the body in its environment) must be studied in close conjunction, for they are quite distinct from subsistence, the actual process of obtaining resources. Despite such recovery methods as flotation, it is still impossible to assess the intake of vitamins, minerals, and milk products in prehistoric diets. Nor do we have adequate data on the waste of food during preparation and storage, or on the effects of different cooking techniques. Archaeological data can only indicate some of the foods eaten by prehistoric communities and show, at least qualitatively, how important some of them were generally.

Human skeletal remains can sometimes provide evidence of ancient malnutrition and other dietary conditions. For example, the bones of the Iceman, who perished in the Italian Alps in about 3200 B.C., reveal episodes of serious malnutrition during his lifetime (see Chapter 5).

carbon isotope analysis Analysis of isotopic ratios in human bones to discern ancient diet.

We can identify the general categories of plant foods eaten by individuals during their lifetimes by **carbon isotope analysis** of prehistoric bone and hair. Carbon isotope analysis not only chronicles when people took up farming, but also indicates their degree of reliance on marine foods. By using the ratio between two stable carbon isotopes—carbon-12 and carbon-13 in animal tissue—researchers can establish how much maize was consumed or how much marine food was eaten as opposed to terrestrial resources. Research on controlled animal populations has shown that as carbon is passed along the food chain, the carbon composition of animals continues to reflect the relative isotopic composition of their diet. Carbon is metabolized in plants through three major pathways: C3, C4, and crassulacean acid metabolism (an addition to the normal carbon dioxide fixation, mainly found in succulents). The plants that make up the diet of animals have distinct carbon-13 values. Maize, for example, is a C4 plant. In contrast, most indigenous temperate flora in North America are composed of C3 varieties. Thus, a population that shifts its diet from wild vegetable foods to maize will also experience a shift in dietary isotopic values. Because carbon-13 and carbon-12 values are stable and do not change after death, researchers can study archaeological carbon from food remains, soil humus, and skeletal remains to gain insight into ancient diet.

Concentrations of strontium, a stable mineral component of bone, as opposed to calcium, can be used to measure the contribution of plants to diet. For instance, it has been shown that prehistoric people in the eastern Mediterranean ate similar proportions of meat and plant foods from 100,000 years ago up to the end of the Ice Age. Then, there was a significant shift toward the consumption of plant foods. At Chalcatzingo, an Olmec site in Mexico, strontium analysis has shown that the elite, buried with valuable jade ornaments, had a lower strontium level, for they ate more meat, compared with commoners, who consumed very little.

Stomach contents and feces provide unrivaled insights into meals eaten by individual members of a prehistoric society at specific times in the year. Dietary reconstructions based on these sources, however, suffer from the disadvantage that they are rare and represent but one person's food intake. Furthermore, some foods are more rapidly digested than others. But even these insights are better than no data at all. The stomach of Tollund Man, who was executed in Denmark some time between 375 and 210 B.C., contained the remains of a finely ground meal made from barley, linseed, and several wild grasses; no meat was found in the stomach contents.

Technology and subsistence went hand in hand throughout prehistory. By studying both of them, we acquire a framework for the human past: simple stone technologies, then more sophisticated tools and weaponry, followed by metallurgy; and hunting and gathering acquiring greater complexity, then being replaced rapidly by agriculture and animal husbandry on an ever more intensive scale. But what can we discover about the people who created these technologies and of their interactions with one another, which pitted individual against individual, group against group? What can we discern of the beliefs and other intangibles that sustained human life and society? These questions, and the ways in which archaeologists explain the past, form the subject of the three chapters in Part II.

Summary

- This chapter described the principal technologies used by ancient human societies and the ways in which archaeologists study ancient subsistence.
- One of the main inorganic materials used by prehistoric people was stone, especially hard, homogeneous rock, which fractures according to the conchoidal principle. They used these basic techniques for manufacturing stone tools.
- Lithic experimentation and ethnoarchaeology have leading roles in the study of stone technologies; use-wear analysis and sourcing studies throw light on the trade in raw materials and the uses to which tools were put.
- Ceramics (clay objects) are a major preoccupation of archaeologists, and such artifacts largely date to the past 10,000 years. This chapter describes the process of pottery manufacture, the various methods used, and the surface finishes employed. Ceramic analysis proceeds by typology, analogy, and experiment.
- Metallurgy began with copper artifacts, then alloys involving copper, lead, or tin to make bronze. Gold was made into ornaments at least 6,000 years ago. Iron technology developed in the second millennium B.C.
- Archaeologists rely on many sources to reconstruct prehistoric subsistence. These include environmental data, animal bones, vegetal remains, human bones and feces, stable isotopes, artifacts, and prehistoric art.
- Zooarchaeology involves the study of animal bones. Bone identification is carried out by direct comparison between modern and ancient bones. Game animal remains can give insights into prehistoric hunting practices. The proportions of animals present can be affected by cultural taboos, the relative meat yields of different species, hunting preferences, and the effects of domestication. Early domesticated animals are very difficult to distinguish from their wild ancestors based on skeletal evidence alone; though DNA analysis has greatly improved our ability to identify domesticated species. In terms of skeletal changes, domestication alters both the characteristics of an animal and its bone structure. Slaughtering and butchery practices can be derived from the frequency and distribution of animal bones in the ground. Hunting and slaughter patterns are subject to all manner of subtle variables, including convenience and season of the year.
- DNA analysis has become a crucial tool in understanding the domestication of plants and animals. By sequencing ancient genomes, scientists can trace genetic changes over time, revealing how domesticated species evolved through human selection. These insights have helped refine timelines and geographic locations for the domestication of key species, enhancing our understanding of how early humans interacted with their environment and food sources.
- Carbonized and unburned vegetable remains, studied by paleoethnobotanists, are recovered from hearths and pits, often using a flotation method to separate seeds from the matrix around them.
- Bird bones provide valuable information on seasonal occupation; fish remains reflect specialized coastal adaptations that became common in later prehistoric times.
- Freshwater and saltwater mollusks were both consumed as food and traded over enormous distances as prestigious luxuries or ornaments.
- Prehistoric diet and nutrition must be studied together, for they are distinct from subsistence, which is the actual process of obtaining food. Human skeletal remains, stomach contents, and feces are the few direct sources available to us for information on prehistoric diet. Carbon isotope analysis offers promise as a way of studying dietary changes through time and among social classes.

Key Terms and Sites

typology
archaeological types
descriptive types
chronological types
functional types
reductive (subtractive) technology
core
flakes
conchoidal fracture
Acheulean stone technology
lithic analysis
debitage analysis
debitage
refitting
use-wear (edge-wear) analysis
petrological analysis
petrology
obsidian
Schöningen
Ozette
ground stone
temper
ceramics
slip
ceramic analysis
form
function
attributes
Hallstatt culture
Paracas
Abydos
feces
zooarchaeology
Head-Smashed-In
faunal analysis
Olsen-Chubbock
Klasies River Cave
Nelson's Bay Cave
epiphyses
catastrophic age profile
attritional age profile
macrobotanical remains
paleoethnobotanist
flotation
palynology (pollen analysis)
opal phytoliths
coprolite
paleoethnobotany

Hogup Cave
carbon isotope analysis

Critical-Thinking Questions

1. Stone tools are among the most common of all prehistoric artifacts. What information can you glean from them, and what methods give you this information?
2. What are the uses and limitations of animal bones and plant remains for studying ancient diet? Do they give you a balanced picture of what people ate in the past?
3. What uses did metals have in ancient times? What were the special properties of bronze, gold, and iron, and what was the critical point at which metal artifacts became commonplace in societies with metallurgy?

Further Reading

A general account of artifact analysis for beginners can be found in C. R. Ewen, *Artifacts* (Walnut Creek, CA: AltaMira Press, 2003), the fourth volume in the *Archaeologist's Toolkit* series. This should be read in conjunction with L. P. Sullivan and S. T. Childs, *Curating Archaeological Collections* (Walnut Creek, CA: AltaMira Press, 2003), the sixth volume in the same series. G. Willey and P. Phillips, *Method and Theory in American Archaeology* (Chicago, IL: University of Chicago Press, 1958), describes some of the archaeological units used in the Americas. For animal bones, see S. J. M. Davis, *The Archaeology of Animals* (London: Batsford, 1987) and T. O'Connor's, *The Archaeology of Animal Bones* (Texas: Texas A&M University Anthropology, 2008). See also E. J. Reitz and E. S. Wing, *Zooarchaeology*, 2nd ed. (Cambridge: Cambridge University Press, 2008). R. Klein and K. Cruz-Uribe, *The Analysis of Animal Bones from Archaeological Sites* (Chicago, IL: University of Chicago Press, 1984), and D. Grayson, *Quantitative Zooarchaeology* (New York: Academic Press, 1984), are more advanced essays. *Identifying and Interpreting Animal Bones* (Texas: Texas A&M University Press, 2013) by April M. Beisaw is a field-tested analytical manual for identifying faunal remains. Fishing: B. Fagan, *Fishing: How the Sea Fed Civilization* (New Haven, CT: Yale University Press, 2017) is a popular summary. For plants, D. Pearsall, *Paleoethnobotany: A Handbook of Procedures*, 2nd ed. (San Diego, CA: Academic Press, 2009), is an excellent starting point. See also E. N. Anderson et al., eds., *Ethnobiology* (New York: Wiley-Blackwell, 2011).

Part 2

Ancient Interactions

5 Individuals and Interactions

Chapter Outline

A Maori man from New Zealand wearing a flax cloak with a bone toggle. His face is heavily tattooed. Drawn by eighteenth-century artist Sydney Parkinson.

Source: INTERFOTO/Alamy.

DOI: 10.4324/9781003592754-7

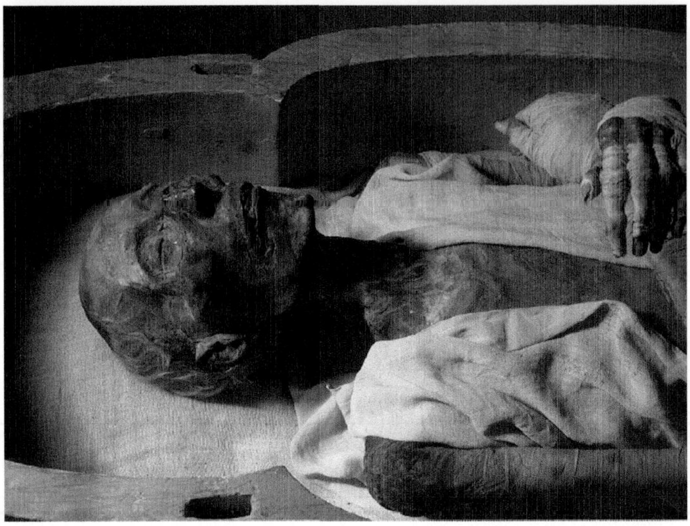

Figure 5.1 The mummy of Egyptian pharaoh Rameses II (1279–1212 B.C.).
Source: The Art Archive/Alamy.

Egyptian pharaoh, Maya lord, Pueblo farmer, or Ice Age forager—all are equal in the face of death and modern archaeological and medical science. Human skeletons, frozen corpses, and mummies are the medical records of the past, one of the few ways we can study actual individuals from ancient societies. Some famous people from the past are known to us by name. The Egyptian King Rameses II's mummy reveals that he stood 1.74 meters (5 feet 8 inches) tall and that he suffered from arthritis, dental abscesses, and poor circulation (see Figure 5.1). Maya Lord Pacal lay in a magnificent stone sarcophagus adorned with his genealogy under the Temple of the Inscriptions at Palenque, Mexico. The glyphs on the sarcophagus lid reveal the dates of his reign (A.D. 615–683). Most individuals from the past, though, survive as nameless corpses or skeletons, members of long-forgotten communities far from royal courts and magnificent temples. For all their anonymity, their bodies yield priceless information about their lives.

This chapter turns from artifacts and subsistence to the actual peoples of the past and their interactions—as men and women, as small groups within diverse societies, and as communities trading with one another.

An Individual: Ötzi the Iceman

Only rarely do archaeologists have the chance to study a well-preserved individual from the remote past. When they do, the full array of modern medical sciences comes into play.

In September 1991, German mountaineers Helmut and Erika Simon made their way around a narrow gully at 3,210 meters (10,530 feet) near Hauslabjoch in the Italian Alps. Erika suddenly spotted a brown object projecting from the ice and glacial meltwater in the bottom of the gully. At first, she thought it was merely a doll, but she soon identified the skull, back, and shoulders of a man with his face lying in water. She had stumbled across a casualty of a 5,000-year-old mountain incident.

The first police on the scene assumed that the man was a climbing victim. A unique archaeological find became corpse 91/619 on the local coroner's dissection table. Within days, the authorities realized that the body was very old and called in archaeologist Konrad Spindler of the University of Innsbruck, Austria. Local archaeologists organized a dig at the site, which was already under 0.6 meter (2 feet) of snow. They used a steam blower and a hair drier to recover parts of a grass cloak, leaves, tufts of grass, and wood fragments. By the end of the excavation, they had established that the man, now nicknamed "Ötzi the Iceman," had deposited his ax, bow, and backpack on a sheltered ledge. He had lain down on his left side, his head on a boulder, perhaps taking shelter from rapidly deteriorating weather in the small gully. Judging from his relaxed limbs, the man had gone to sleep and frozen to death a few hours later. For 5,000 years, Ötzi's body lay in the gully, which protected his corpse as a glacier flowed overhead.

The university research team called on the latest archaeological and medical science to conserve and study the body of the c. 45-year-old man, the age established by careful examination of his anatomy and teeth. Within a few weeks, five AMS radiocarbon tests dated Ötzi's body to between 3350 and 3150 B.C. Biological anthropologists estimated his height at about 1.6 meters (5 feet 3 inches) and took DNA samples, which showed that his genetic makeup was similar to that of late Europeans (see Box 9.2 on p. 301). Ötzi's stomach was empty, so he was probably weak and hungry at the time of his death. He also suffered from parasites. Smoke inhaled while living in small dwellings with open hearths had blackened his lungs as much as those of a modern-day smoker. Ötzi had endured prolonged malnutrition in his ninth, fifteenth, and sixteenth years, identified from telltale marks on his bones. His hands and fingernails were scarred from constant manual labor. He had groups of tattoos—mostly parallel vertical lines—on his lower back, left calf, and right ankle.

On his last day alive, Ötzi wore a leather belt that held up a loincloth. Suspenders led from the belt to a pair of fur leggings. He wore an outer coat of alternating stripes of black and brown animal skin and also an outer cape of twisted grass, just like those worn in the Alps a century ago (see Figure 5.2). Ötzi's bearskin cap was fastened below his chin with a snap. On his feet he wore bearskin and deerskin shoes filled with grass held in place by a string "sock."

Ötzi was a self-sufficient man on the move. He carried a leather backpack on a wooden frame, a flint dagger, a copper-bladed ax with wooden handle, and a yew longbow and skin quiver filled with 14 arrows. His equipment included dry fungus and iron pyrite (for fire lighting) and spare arrowheads.

Today, Ötzi lives in a special freezer that replicates glacial conditions. Scientists are still puzzling over why he was so high in the mountains. A few wheat seeds lodged in his fur garments tell us that he had recently been in a farming village. Some of the wild seeds came from a valley south of the Alps, as if he had climbed from the Italian side. Was he a shepherd caught out at high altitude? Had he fled to the mountains to escape a family feud, or was he simply hunting wild goats? We know that he died violently, for a stone arrowhead lies deep in his left shoulder and the tendons of his left hand were severed by a dagger wound. He may have escaped his assailants, collapsed in a sheltered ravine, and frozen to death. The mystery of his death remains unresolved.

Ötzi the Iceman is the earliest European to survive as an identifiable individual, one of the few people of the past to come down to us so well preserved that we know more about his physical condition than he knew himself—his injuries, his diseases, his parasites. This remarkable discovery comes as something of a jolt, because we come face to face with a once-living person who laughed, fought, worked, played, and interacted with others.

Figure 5.2 Reconstruction of Ötzi the Iceman in his grass cloak.
Source: MARKA/Alamy.

Social Ranking

Social inequality has been a feature of human life at least since the first appearance of farming some 12,000 years ago, and it had become institutionalized in civilization by 3000 B.C.

social ranking In ancient human societies, evidence of differences in social status, usually detected in burial ornamentation.

ethnicity In archaeology, the study of different ethnic groups within a society.

Social ranking—social distinctions among individuals, communities, and other units of society—exists in several forms: as social differences among individuals (often reflected in graves); as relationships among individuals, communities, and the wider society (discerned from the study of architecture, settlement patterns, and distributions of luxury goods such as gold ornaments); and as social diversity (**ethnicity**), which is social distinctions reflected in the relationships among groups within society.

social stratification In archaeology, evidence of different social classes, usually arranged hierarchically.

All early civilizations flourished for the benefit of a tiny minority at the pinnacle of society. With the possible exception of the still not fully fathomed Indus Valley Civilization of the Asian subcontinent, a vast social chasm separated rulers and nobles from commoners, who were at the bottom of the social pyramid. Ancient Egyptian pharaohs ruled over a long-lived, socially stratified civilization along the Nile River. Their civilization was broken down into distinct social classes. **Social stratification** is a term commonly used in archaeology to refer to the structure of state-organized societies, where groups (classes) have unequal access to the means of production. The pharaohs and their high officials commanded the loyalty of several million commoners, who supported the state with their labor and products. Such highly centralized societies as those of the Egyptians or the Aztecs controlled every aspect of life, with all wealth and secular or religious power concentrated in the hands of a few (see Box 5.1).

Babylon, Iraq Major early city-state and later capital of the Babylonian Empire under King Nebuchadnezzar in the sixth century B.C.

Box 5.1 Doing Archaeology
The Law Code of Hammurabi of Babylon, 1760 B.C.

Occasionally, individuals had a great influence on the course of history. One example is the Babylonian King Hammurabi, who ruled over **Babylon** in what is now Iraq from 1792 to 1750 B.C. He was a conqueror and a diplomat, mainly remembered for developing the first written law code. His laws survive on a stela (column) from Susa in southwestern Iran, where it had been carried by the Elamites as a trophy (see Figure 5.3). He claimed that he received his laws from Shamash, Sun God and god of justice. The laws themselves are not a comprehensive code, but they cover a wide variety of subjects, from ransom of prisoners of war to pledges of land in payment for debts and punishment for adultery. The provisions make clear that Babylonian society was based on social inequality, divided into aristocrats, commoners, and slaves. Women held a subordinate position, although they were allowed to own property and could divorce their husbands for maltreatment, provided that they themselves were of good character. Here are some laws from the code:

- If fire broke out in a man's house and a man who went to extinguish it cast his eye on the goods of the owner of the house and has appropriated the goods of the owner of the house that man shall be thrown into the fire (§25).
- If outlaws have congregated in the establishment of a woman wine-seller and she has not arrested those outlaws and did not take them to the palace, that wine-seller shall be put to death (§109).
- If a physician performed a major operation on a man with a bronze lancet and has caused the man's death, or he opened up the eye-socket of a man and has destroyed the man's eye, they shall cut off his hand (§219) (Scarre and Fagan 2016, 187).

Figure 5.3 The Law Code of Hammurabi lies on a black basalt stela carved with 282 lines in cuneiform script. The scene shown here at the top of the stela features Hammurabi standing in prayer before the Sun God Shamash, the Babylonian god who was also the god of justice, 1792–1750 B.C.

Source: Ivy Close Images/Alamy.

Powerful religious beliefs unified these increasingly complex societies. Usually, their rulers reigned as living gods. For generations, archaeologists have speculated about the origins of the early civilizations in which social ranking was pronounced and supreme power was expressed by enormous public works such as the Great Pyramids of Giza or the Pyramid of the Sun at Teotihuacán (see Figures 3.3 on p. 75 and 3.8 on p. 83). Elaborate paintings, sculpted reliefs, and public inscriptions reinforced divine messages, the social inequality sanctioned by gods and goddesses. These large-scale manifestations of social ranking, however, reveal less than burials, which were part of the ritual of passage from life to the afterworld.

The expectation that life will continue uninterrupted after death is a powerful force in human society and has been for thousands of years. As early as the late Ice Age, more than 25,000 years ago, some human societies blurred the distinction between the living world and the spiritual world, from where the ancestors watched over the interests of their descendants. The Egyptians believed that the souls of well-behaved people enjoyed immortality in the afterlife. Maya lords communicated with the ancestors, those who had gone before. In many ancient societies, the dead set out on their journey to the next world adorned in all their finery and accompanied by their finest possessions (see Box 5.2). These

Box 5.2 Site
The Sepulcher of the Maya Lord Pacal, Palenque, Mexico

Palenque is a Maya city, famous both for its architecture and for a long dynasty of talented lords, starting with Chan-Bahlum (Snake-Jaguar), who ascended the throne on March 11, A.D. 431. The dynasty flourished for just under 400 years, achieving the height of its power under the rule of Pacal (Shield) and his son in the seventh century. Pacal ruled for 63 years and turned Palenque into a major political force in the Maya lowlands. When he died, he was buried in an underground sepulcher beneath a pyramid and the celebrated Temple of the Inscriptions, built over a period of 15 years.

In 1949, Mexican archaeologist Alberto Ruz, convinced that a royal tomb lay beneath the pyramid, lifted a flagstone in the floor of the temple and cleared a rubble-filled stairway leading into the heart of the artificial mountain. Five months of backbreaking work over two seasons cleared a stairway with 45 steps, then a sharp U-turn, which led to another short 21-step staircase and a corridor at the same level as the foot of the pyramid. After removing a stone and lime obstruction, Ruz came to a triangular doorway slab, guarded by six young sacrificial victims. He moved the stone enough to slip into an enormous rock-cut crypt with a procession of priests in stucco around the walls. A huge stone slab bearing intricate hieroglyphs filled the floor of the chamber (see Figure 15.7 on p. 474). To lift the 5-ton stone, Ruz's workers felled a hardwood tree, lowered four sections of the trunk down the stairway, and levered up the sarcophagus lid with car jacks and the timbers. Inside the sepulcher lay a tall man wearing jade and mother-of-pearl ornaments. He wore a jade mosaic mask with eyes of shell, each iris of obsidian (see Figure 5.4).

At the time of the excavation, no one could read Maya glyphs, so the identity of the ruler remained unknown. We now know it was Pacal. His carved sarcophagus lid commemorates his divine ancestry.

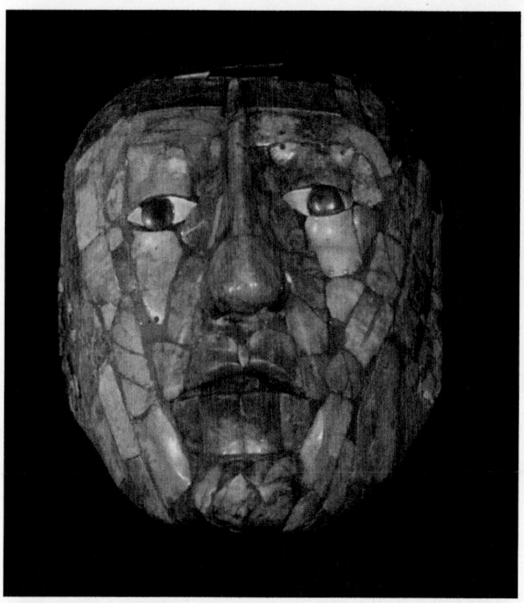

Figure 5.4 The jade mask of the Maya Lord Pacal.
Source: Mireille Vautier/Alamy.

artifacts might be a meager necklace of shell beads or the enormous wealth of a Moche warrior-priest (see Figure 16.7 on p. 509), but they are a barometer of social ranking, of the power and prestige that set one individual or class of individuals apart from another.

Palenque, Mexico Maya city and ceremonial center ruled by the Shield dynasty for many centuries and powerful in the seventh century A.D.

Khok Phanom Di, Thailand Pottery-making community famous for its fine burials, c. 2000 to 1400 B.C.

A remarkable example of social ranking came from the **Khok Phanom Di** mound, near Bangkok, Thailand. The 7-meter (23-foot) mound lies on a river floodplain; it was occupied between about 2000 and 1400 B.C. Khok Phanom Di was both village and burial ground, with clusters of graves separated by occupation debris and perhaps

Figure 5.5 The woman of Khok Phanom Di, Thailand.
Source: Charles Higham.

wooden barricades. Archaeologists Charles Higham and Rachanie Thosarat unearthed a raised platform containing the burial of a woman interred with several elaborately decorated pots, thousands of shell beads, and a clay anvil she once used to fashion pots (see Figure 5.5). She wore shell disks on each shoulder and an exotic shell bangle on her left wrist. Alongside her lay the skeleton of a child, presumably her daughter, whose head rested on a shell disk.

The Khok Phanom Di burials were a mirror of a community that produced fine pottery for export, with potting skills conferring high status on the best practitioners, such as the woman buried on the special platform. Higham and Thoserat believe that prestige and status came from personal achievement in a community dominated by women potters, who held most of the wealth. So many clusters of burials came from the mound that they could trace the rising and declining fortunes of generations of different families by the richness of the artifacts deposited with successive women.

This important excavation reveals the great complexities behind the study of social ranking. In affluent societies, the differences between, say, rulers, merchants, and commoners are easy to discern from grave furniture. But what about humbler, more egalitarian societies where differences in rank and status were more muted? Many variables, such as age, sex, personal ability, personality, and even circumstances of death, affected the way in which people were buried. Even the position of the grave may have depended on kin relationships or social status. As a general rule, the greater and more secure a ruler's authority, the more effort and wealth were expended on his or her burial. Thoroughly and carefully studied, an ancient cemetery can provide invaluable information on social ranking.

Mississippian societies Maize- and bean-farming cultures in the midwestern and southeastern United States dating from A.D. 900 to 1500, remarkable for their large ceremonial centers, elaborate religious beliefs, and powerful chiefdoms.

A thousand years ago, a series of powerful chiefdoms ruled over major river valleys in the North American Southeast (see Chapter 14). Their rulers enjoyed exceptional supernatural powers and special relationships with the supernatural world. Only a small number of people governed these **Mississippian societies**, which were like social pyramids, known to us from contemporary cemeteries. The Mississippian center at Moundville, Alabama, was in its heyday in the thirteenth and fourteenth centuries A.D., about two centuries before European contact. More than 20 mounds topped by earthworks and the residences of nobility lay inside a wooden palisade covering 150 hectares (370 acres) on the banks of the Black Warrior River. The highest-ranking people with the richest graves were buried in or near the earthen mounds at the hub of the site (see Figure 5.6). A second group had fewer grave goods and were not buried in mounds, and the lowest-ranking people lay in almost undecorated graves at the edge of the site.

The Moundville study and other such cemetery researches are often more concerned with general patterns of social organization than with the complex interactions between people as individuals and groups as they vie for authority and prestige. Such "horizontal" interactions between men and women, between factions within a nobility, or among religious and ethnic groups have been largely ignored until recent years.

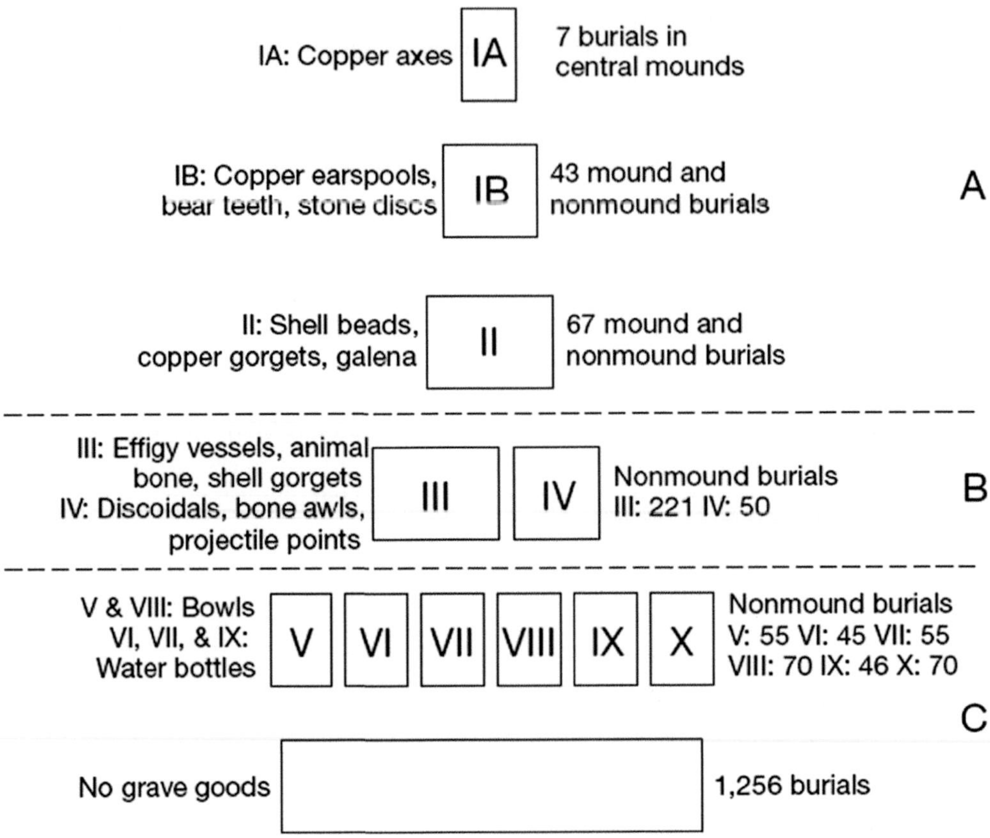

Figure 5.6 The pyramid-like social hierarchy of Moundville burials based on the analysis of more than 2,000 graves. Artifacts listed against individual skeletons are grave goods found with them.

Gender Roles

Archaeologists have long studied people and households, but have also examined the complex issues of gender and gender relations.

Gender is not the same as *sex*, which refers to being *biologically* male or female or, on occasion, intersex. *Gender* refers to *behaviors* that are socially and culturally associated with being male or female or indeed intersex. Gender roles and relations evolve and change in culturally and historically meaningful ways. This means that gender is a vital and dynamic part of human social relations and a central issue in the study of ancient human societies.

The expression of gender varies and has always varied from society to society and through time. Some archaeologists, such as Margaret Conkey and Joan Gero, write of "engendering archaeology," an attempt to reclaim men and women in nonsexist ways in the past. This goes much further than simply trying to identify women's activities in the archaeological record, or demonstrating the activities linked to each sex by a given society. The archaeology of gender deals with the ideology of gender and gender relations—the ways in which gender intersects with all aspects of human social life. How are roles and social relationships constructed? What contributions did men and women make to ancient societies? An engendered archaeology uses a wide diversity of archaeological methods and approaches to find out how gender operated in ancient societies and to unravel its cultural meanings.

Grinding Grain at Abu Hureyra, Syria

Farmers' bones reveal telling information about male and female roles. The Abu Hureyra farming village in Syria, described in Chapter 11, is the earliest known agricultural settlement in the world. In about 9000 B.C., the inhabitants switched from hunting and foraging to growing cereal crops. A thousand years later, they founded a close-knit community of rectangular, one-story mud-brick houses, separated by narrow alleyways and courtyards, set in the midst of their fields. For hours on end, the Abu Hureyra women would labor on their knees, grinding grain for the evening meal, as the monotonous scraping sound of grinding corn echoed through the settlement. Thanks to some exciting detective work by biological anthropologist Theya Molleson, we can be certain that women rather than men ground grain.

Molleson is an expert on human anatomy and pathological conditions in bones caused by stress and disease. She studied the many skeletons found under the Abu Hureyra houses and found that the people were remarkably healthy except for bone deformities caused by arduous and repetitive tasks. Then, she noticed that some adolescents had enlarged portions on their neck vertebrae, the result of carrying heavy loads. She also identified many knee bones with bone extensions on their articular surfaces, the result of repeated kneeling for long periods of time. Many people also had stressed lower-back vertebrae, enlarged toe joints, and gross arthritic conditions of the big toe (see Figure 5.7).

Molleson was puzzled by these deformities until one of her colleagues visited Egypt and noticed that kneeling supplicants on the walls of ancient temples always had their toes curled forward. The only activity at Abu Hureyra that could produce the same effect was kneeling in front of the stonegrinding querns set into the house floors. Intrigued, Molleson reconstructed the grinding process. The grinder put grain on the quern and gripped the grinding stone with both hands. The person then knelt with the toes bent, pushing the stone forward, arms turning inward as the stone reached the end of the quern. At the end of the stroke, the upper body was almost parallel to the floor. Repeated every day, such to-and-fro movement would cause backbone damage identical to that on the skeletons, would also place bending stress on the knee and hip joints, and would eventually cause arthritic conditions in the toes—all conditions found in the Abu Hureyra bones.

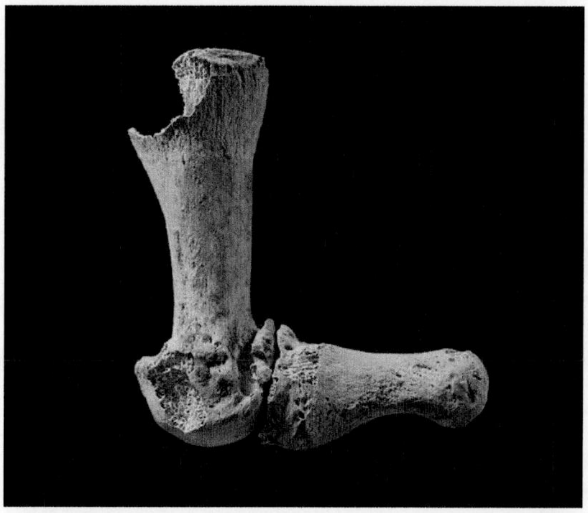

Figure 5.7 A woman's deformed toe bone from Abu Hureyra, Syria.
Source: The Trustees of the Natural History Museum, London.

Next, Molleson asked who had done the grinding. She measured the first metatarsal bone of the foot. The larger male bones showed little wear, whereas the shorter female metatarsals displayed signs of heavy wear. Theya Molleson is virtually certain that women and girls suffered repetitive-stress injuries because they shouldered the laborious task of preparing food.

Abu Hureyra is one of the few instances in which we have clear archaeological evidence for the division of labor between men and women in the past.

The Engendered Past

To engender the past means to focus not only on major material achievements such as metallurgy or pot making, or on ancient environments, but also on interpersonal relations and the social dynamics of everyday activities. These are the activities that take up most of people's daily lives—hunting, gardening, preparing meals, building houses, and so on. But gender also has an effect on trade, craft specialization, state formation, religion, and ritual—to mention only a few major human activities.

Gender research in archaeology is concerned not just with studying women, but with people as individuals and their contributions to society. Archaeologist Elizabeth Brumfiel has studied Aztec women, who were expert weavers; indeed, weaving was a fundamental skill for an Aztec noblewoman (see Figure 5.8). However, Brumfiel points out that to characterize Aztec women merely as weavers ignores the vital links between weaving, child rearing, and cooking (to mention only a few women's tasks) and the wider society in which the women lived. The population of the Valley of Mexico rose tenfold during the four centuries before the Spanish conquest, a striking testimony to the success of the Aztec household economy. Women wove textiles and the capes that were the badges of social status in Aztec society. Their woven products were vital to the enormous tribute system on which Aztec civilization depended. Cotton mantles even served as a form of currency. Cloth was a primary way of organizing the ebb and flow of goods and services that sustained the state.

Figure 5.8 An Aztec woman teaching her daughter how to weave.

Brumfiel shows that the Aztec household and the roles of women were much more varied than those attributed to them by early Spanish observers. Furthermore, the skills of cooking and weaving were important political tools, ways of maintaining social and political control. Thus, she argues, the idealization of these skills in both Aztec folklore and schooling developed because women were makers both of valuable goods and of people. It was they who ensured the continuity of Aztec kin groups. More simplistic views of Aztec life mask the dynamic and highly adaptive role that women played in this remarkable civilization.

What, then, is an "engendered past"? Scientific reporting tends to obliterate the individuals whose deeds created the past. An engendered archaeology ventures into new territory, using innovative approaches to present the multiple voices of the past in order to report both data and stories of the past. Such research requires exceptionally complete data and meticulously excavated sites.

Losing the Gender Baggage

While archaeologists have been seeking to write women into the past, they have also been reviewing our gender biases and assumptions. Some have noted that there may have been other factors, beyond one's sex (biology) or gender (expression of self), that might have been more important to the way people organized themselves in the past.

Such was the realization made by Prof. Rosemary Joyce when she revisited the 1940s excavation report of Tlatilco, an agricultural village on the outskirts of Mexico City that flourished from around 1200 to 200 B.C. The original excavators recorded over 200 burials, and on cataloguing these burials, they assumed that any differences in the grave goods corresponded with the sex of the dead person. Yet, Joyce found that "nothing I tested ended up being securely correlated with variations between men and women" (Joyce 2009). Instead, she noticed that the main differences between the graves were based on the ages of the deceased, and not on their sex, with the highest number of objects and the most unusual things routinely found in the graves of young adults. By contrast, older men and women tended to be buried with clay rattle balls and more varied body ornaments. Could it be, she speculated, that (our own) male–female divide did not dominate this society, but that its people organized themselves according to age? Such research makes us aware of our own potential bias when looking at the past, and makes us reassess our assumption that one's sex was necessarily always the major divider in society.

Ongoing research is also looking at how archaeologists have loaded their own gender expectations onto the past. For example, in male-dominated societies (including our own), maleness is generally associated with dynamism, aggression, domination; femaleness with passivism, gentleness, submission, and attraction. But how valid are these assumptions?

In the 1880s, a team uncovered a Viking warrior burial in Birka, Sweden. The Viking was buried with a cache of military items, including a long-bladed sword, a spear, and two sacrificed horses. Gaming pieces lay on the body's lap, suggesting the warrior had died while planning tactics. Given our own associations between men and war, the Birka Warrior was assumed to be a man—until a 2017 DNA analysis of "his" bones confirmed beyond doubt that the grave actually belonged to a woman. In the opposite vein, in 1823, when a geologist digging in Wales (UK) found a skeleton daubed in red ocher and surrounded with bone jewelry and shell necklaces, he named his find the "Red Lady of Paviland." The geologist assumed the lady had been a Roman prostitute or perhaps a witch—to his Victorian mind, these were the only roles for a (literally) scarlet woman. In fact, subsequent analysis has shown that the bones belonged to a young male who lived around 33,000 years ago. These are powerful examples of how our own gender assumptions used to imbue archaeological thinking, but also how we are now moving beyond these blinkered ways of seeing the past.

Ethnicity and Inequality

For the most part, archaeologists have focused their attention on two broad topics: culture change and relationships between human societies and their environments. In recent years, however, an increasing number of scholars have used archaeology's unique perspective to study ethnic diversity and what is sometimes called the archaeology of inequality: the ways in which people have exercised economic and social power over others. This is a reaction against approaches that minimize the importance of social power and assume that ancient societies enjoyed a high degree of cultural uniformity.

In fact, many archaeological studies have shown that cultural change can occur very rapidly, sometimes at a speed that is well within the limits of human memory, as it does in our society. Nor should one minimize the importance of social power in the appearance of early states, such as that of the Maya or Aztecs. Despite a few studies that are now focusing on the importance of social ranking and the political power of kings and nobles, almost no archaeologists have studied the phenomenon of resistance to overwhelming social and political power and the archaeology of ethnic minorities.

Ideologies of Domination

ideologies of domination Overarching philosophies or religious beliefs used by rulers or entire civilizations to focus their power and ensure conformity among their subjects.

Elites have used many tactics to exercise power over others, everything from gentle persuasion to divine kingship, precedent, economic monopolies, and naked force. Perhaps most important of all are the **ideologies of domination**. The ancient Maya lords built great ceremonial centers with towering pyramids and vast plazas that were symbolic models of the sacred landscape, of the Maya universe. Their pyramids were sacred mountains, the sites of sacred openings that were the threshold to the spiritual world of the ancestors. It was here that the ruler went into a shamanistic trance, communicating with the gods and ancestors in opulent public ceremonies. Everything validated the complex relationship between the living and the dead and between the ruler and the commoner, displayed in lavish, pointed metaphors that confirmed the divine power of the supreme lords (see Chapter 12). By the same token, Ancient Egyptian pharaohs carefully choreographed their public appearances as spectacles commemorating and validating their wealth and spiritual power.

Artifacts, Social Inequality, and Resistance

Political and social powers are extremely heterogeneous phenomena that are exercised in many forms. From the archaeologist's point of view, it is fascinating that one can use material objects such as pottery to study how people negotiated their social positions and resisted the submergence of their own culture. Artifacts offer a unique way of examining the history of the many communities that kept no written records, but expressed their diverse feelings and cultures through the specific artifacts and commodities that they purchased and used. Our examples come from historic sites in North America, but research into similar topics is now extending back into prehistoric times.

Garrison Plantation, Maryland Plantation of the eighteenth century A.D. where the excavated slave quarters are famous for their artifacts of African inspiration.

Kingsmill Plantation, Virginia Plantation of the eighteenth century A.D. famous for artifacts excavated from its slave quarters.

The earliest Africans to reach North America brought their own notions of religion, ritual, and supernatural power to their new homes. They even maintained small shrines in their living quarters. Historical records rarely refer to such shrines, but archaeologists have found blue beads and other charms at many slave sites in the North American Southeast. At the **Garrison Plantation** in Maryland and the **Kingsmill Plantation** in Virginia, engraved pewter spoons bear motifs remarkably similar to those executed by African Americans living in Suriname in South America. Bakongo-style marks like those made in Central Africa have come from bowls found in other American southern sites. Archaeology reveals that these people arrived in North America with cultural values and a worldview radically different from those of their masters.

Slave plantations were part of very complex, much wider networks that linked planters to other planters, planters to slaves, and slaves to slaves on other plantations. Slaves within these harsh, oppressive, and racist environments were able to maintain important elements of their own culture. Despite such conditions, African Americans held on to their own beliefs and culture, which they melded over the generations with new ideas and material innovations from their new environment. They believed that their culture, their way of living—everything from cuisine to belief systems—was the best way. African spiritual beliefs in all their variety were highly flexible and were often responses to outside influences, whether political, religious, or economic. Consequently, prevailing spiritual beliefs adapted readily to the new American environment, with the people adopting new artifacts or modifying existing ones over the generations. For example, archaeologists working at Thomas Jefferson's Monticello estate have recovered crystals, pierced coins, and other ritual artifacts from Mulberry Row, where his slaves resided.

Many slaves were unable to avoid accepting the inferior social status imposed on them by whites on a day-to-day basis, but they ignored European American culture in favor of their own and rejected any ideology that rationalized their enslavement.

Another fascinating chronicle of ethnic resistance comes from an archaeological investigation of the route taken by a small group of Northern Cheyenne when they broke out of Fort Robinson, Nebraska, on January 9, 1879. They fought a running battle with the garrison, across the White River, up some bluffs, and into open country, where it took the military 11 days to capture them. This much is beyond controversy, but the route that the Cheyenne took out of the river valley is disputed. According to military accounts, the escaping party moved up an exposed sandstone ridge to reach the bluffs. This exposed route was illogical, indeed foolhardy, for there was a full moon. Cheyenne oral traditions insist on another route to the bluffs through a well-protected drainage that would have offered excellent cover from pursuing riflemen.

Researchers from the University of South Dakota Archaeology Laboratory investigated the escape routes with the collaboration of local Cheyenne representatives. They used random shovel testing and metal detectors to search for spent bullets in three areas—two drainages and the exposed ridge mentioned in military accounts. The survey recovered no bullets from the exposed ridge but did find them in the drainages, thereby confirming the oral account of the Cheyenne outbreak.

This may seem like a footnote to modern history, but it is important to remember that the outbreak has become a classic story of the American West from the white perspective, immortalized by John Ford's movie *Cheyenne Autumn*. This film tells the story from the victors' point of view and is a form of moral tall tale of the Old West. Now oral tradition and archaeology have shattered part of the myth, telling the story from the Native American perspective in circumstances where science has helped fashion a mosaic of the recent past that is the historical truth rather than myth.

As so often happens, methods developed on historical sites will ultimately be applied to prehistoric situations. What, for example, was the social position of Oaxacan merchants living in Teotihuacán, Mexico, in A.D. 600? Were they treated differently from citizens of the city? Does their material culture reflect carefully orchestrated responses to the dominant culture around them? What was the lifeway of slaves and workers in Egypt? How did their relationships with their noble masters change over the centuries as the kingdom became more militaristic?

Artifacts tell powerful stories about the lowly and the anonymous, the men and women who labored in the shadow of great states and mighty rulers. The lives of ordinary folk are as compelling in the tales they tell as those recorded on papyri, in government archives, or on clay tablets (see Box 5.3).

Thebes, Egypt Capital of Middle and New Kingdom Egypt after 1520 B.C. and a major center of the worship of the Sun God Amun; called Wa-set by the Egyptians.

Archaeology, with its rich potential for studying the mundane and the trivial, the minutest details of daily life, is an unrivaled tool for the dispassionate study of social inequality and ethnicity. It also studies broader interactions among people and groups through artifacts passed along exchange and trade routes.

Trade and Exchange

Many Americans drive Japanese cars. French teenagers like the taste of American hamburgers. Pacific Islanders buy Mexican-made television sets. We live in an international world where economic ties link nations many thousands of miles apart. Over the past 2,000 years, and especially during the European Age of Discovery after A.D. 1500, human societies throughout the world have become part of a vast web of economic interconnectedness. But the ultimate roots of our modern-day global economic system date back more than 5,000 years, to the dramatic growth of long-distance trade that preceded the appearance of the world's first civilizations in Egypt, Mesopotamia, and the Indus Valley.

exchange systems for exchanging goods and services between individuals and communities.

Box 5.3 Discovery
War Casualties at Thebes, Egypt

Few tales of ordinary people are as vivid as a remarkable discovery made at **Thebes** in 1911 by Egyptologist Herbert Winlock in a sepulcher close to the tomb of the Middle Kingdom pharaoh Mentuhotep (2061–2010 B.C.). Sixty soldiers killed in battle were stacked in the tomb dressed in linen shrouds. All the soldiers were young men in the prime of life, each with a thick mop of hair bobbed off square at the nape of the neck. Their dried-out bodies were so well preserved that they began to decay when removed from the tomb. Winlock used biological and archaeological data to reconstruct their last battle: all had perished in an attack on a fort, for their wounds came from arrows shot from above or from the crushing blows of stones thrown down from a fortification.

Contemporary pictures show the attackers sheltering themselves under thin shields as they attempted to breach the defenses under a rain of missiles.

In this case, the fire was too fierce, so the men had run out of range. A shower of arrows overtook some of them. At least one was hit in the back with an arrow that came out on the other side of his chest. He pitched forward and the slender reed shaft broke off as he fell and bled to death. The defenders of the fort then sallied forth and mercilessly clubbed to death at least a dozen of the wounded attackers with heavy blows. Then waiting vultures and ravens descended on the corpses and worried away the flesh with their beaks. A second attack was successful, and the torn bodies were recovered and buried with honor in a special tomb next to their pharaoh. We do not know where the battle took place, but it was somewhere in Egypt, for the arrows that killed the attackers were of Egyptian design. Few discoveries make such a powerful statement about the lives of the anonymous players of the past as this one.

Exchange systems were part of human life long before the Sumerians and Ancient Egyptians. Shells from the Black Sea appear in late Ice Age hunting encampments deep in Ukraine from at least 18,000 years ago. The Paleo-Indians of the Great Plains exchanged fine-grained toolmaking stone over long distances as early as 9000 B.C. Few human societies were completely self-sufficient, for they depended on others for resources outside their own territories. And as the need for raw materials or for prestigious ornaments increased, so did the tentacles of exchange and trade among neighbors near and far. This trade often had powerful political or symbolic overtones, conducted under the guise of formal gift giving or as part of complex exchange rituals.

People make trade connections and set up the exchange systems that handle trade goods when they need to acquire goods and services that are not available to them within their own local area. The movement of goods need not be over any great distance, and it can operate internally, within a society, or externally, across cultural boundaries within interaction spheres. Both exchange and trade always involve two elements: the goods and commodities being exchanged and the people doing the exchanging. Thus, any form of trading activity implies procurement and handling of tools and raw materials, and some form of social system that provides the people-to-people relationships within which the trade flourishes. We must never forget that not only raw materials and finished objects, but also ideas and information passed along trade routes.

We study trade and exchange by using objects that are found in archaeological sites yet are alien to the material culture or economy of the host society. For instance, glass was never manufactured in sub-Saharan Africa, yet imported glass beads are widespread there in archaeological sites of the first millennium A.D. Until recently, imported objects were recognized almost entirely on the basis of style and design—the appearance of distinctive pottery forms far from their known points of origin, and so on. Sometimes exotics such as gold, amber, turquoise, or marine shells, commodities whose general area of origin was known, provided evidence of long-distance exchanges. Between 5,000 and 2,000 years ago, Late Archaic and Woodland peoples in the North American Southeast used native copper from outcrops near Lake Superior and conch shells from the Gulf Coast, both commodities of known origin.

In the early days of archaeology, such exotica were deemed sufficient to identify trade, even what were loosely called "influences" or "invasions." The assumptions made about the nature of human interactions were very limited and never precise. Today, however, studies of prehistoric exchange are far more sophisticated, owing to two major developments. The first is a new focus throughout archaeology on regional studies. The second is the development of a wide range of scientific techniques that are capable of describing the composition of certain types of raw material and even of identifying their sources with great precision.

Types of Exchange and Trade

Exchange can be internal, within a society, or external, with other groups. Internal distribution of artifacts and commodities is commonplace even in the least complex societies.

kula ring Ceremonial shell-ornament exchange system in the southwestern Pacific involving gifts of shell necklaces between important individuals.

gift exchanges of goods and commodities between two parties, marked by the ceremonial giving of gifts that signify a special relationship between the individuals involved.

Gift Exchange

Much internal exchange is gift giving. Perhaps the most famous example is that of the **kula ring** of Melanesia in the southwestern Pacific. An elaborate network of **gift exchanges** passes shell necklaces in one direction, arm shells in the other. They are passed as ceremonial gifts from one individual to another in gift partnerships that endure for decades. These gift exchanges enjoy great prestige yet serve as a framework for the regular exchange of foodstuffs and other more day-to-day commodities. With all gift exchange, much depends on the types of commodities being exchanged. In the case of the kula ring, precious sea-shell ornaments pass between individuals of higher status; foodstuffs are a more common form of transaction involving many individuals and families. And of course, not only objects but also information can be exchanged, which may lead to technological innovation or social change.

Gift giving is a common medium of exchange and trade in societies that are relatively self-supporting. The exchange of gifts is designed primarily to reinforce a social relationship between individuals and groups. The gifts serve as gestures that place obligations on both parties. This form of exchange is common in New Guinea and the Pacific and was widespread in Africa during the past 2,000 years, as well as in the ancient Americas. Gift giving and bartering formed a basic trading mechanism for millennia, a simple means of exchanging basic commodities. But this sporadic interaction between individuals and communities reduced people's self-sufficiency and eventually made them part of a larger society whose members were no longer able to provide everything they needed by themselves and so came to depend on one another for basic commodities and also for social purposes.

reciprocity Obligations between individuals or fellow kin members or groups, involving the expectation that the other party will respond when called on to do so.

Reciprocity is the mutual exchange of goods between two individuals or groups; it is at the heart of much gift giving and barter trade. It can happen year after year at the same place, which can be as humble as someone's home. Such central places become the focus of gift giving and trade. When a village becomes involved in both the production of trade goods and their exchange with other communities, it will probably become an even more important center, a place to which people will travel to trade.

redistribution The passing out of foodstuffs, goods, or commodities by a central authority such as a chief, thereby ensuring even distribution throughout a community or wider group; often used to refer to the redistribution of exotic goods traded from afar.

Redistribution, the dissemination of goods or commodities received by an individual throughout a community, group, or culture, requires some form of organization to ensure that it is equitable. A chief, a religious leader, or some form of management organization may control the redistribution of such items throughout the society. Such an individual or organization might oversee production of copper ornaments or simply handle distribution and delivery of trade objects.

The collection, storage, and redistribution of grain and other commodities require social organization. The chief, whose position is perhaps reinforced by religious power, has a serious responsibility to his community that can extend over several villages as his lines of redistribution stretch out through people of lesser rank to individual villagers. A chief will negotiate exchanges with other chiefs, substituting the regulatory elements of reciprocal trading for a redistributive economy in which individual households do less trading of exotic objects.

Prehistoric exchange was an important variable that developed in conjunction with sociopolitical organization. In many areas, external trade proceeded from simple reciprocal exchange to the more complex redistribution of goods under a redistributor. In other words, trading is closely tied to growing social and political complexity, although it does not necessarily imply the special production of exotic artifacts specifically for exchange.

market A permanent place where trading or exchange takes place; usually centered in a large village, town, or city.

Markets

The term **market** covers both places and particular styles of trading. The administration and organization encourage people to set aside one place for trading and to establish relatively stable prices for staple commodities. This stability does not mean regulated prices, but some regulation is needed in a network of markets within which commodities from an area of abundant supplies are sold to one with strong demand for the same materials. The mechanisms of the exchange relationship, particularly, require some regulation.

Markets are normally associated with more complex societies. No literate civilization ever developed without strong central places where trading activities were regulated and monopolies developed over both sources of materials and trade routes themselves. Successful market trading required predictable supplies of basic commodities and adequate policing of trade routes. For example, most early Mesopotamian and Egyptian trade took place on rivers, where policing was easier. When the great caravan routes opened, the political and military issues—tribute, control of trade routes, and tolls—became paramount. The caravan, which predated the great empires, was a form of organized trading that kept to carefully defined routes set up and maintained by state authorities. The travelers moved along these set routes, looking neither left nor right, bent only on delivering and exchanging imports and exports. These caravans were a far cry from the huge economic complex that accompanied Alexander the Great's army across Asia or, in India, the Grand Mogul's annual summer progress from the heat in Delhi to the mountains, which moved a half million people, including the entire Delhi bazaar.

Sourcing

sourcing The study of the sources of traded commodities, such as obsidian, using spectrographic analysis and other scientific approaches.

Studying long-distance trade involves far more sophisticated inquiry than merely plotting the distributions of distinctive artifacts hundreds of miles away from their place of manufacture. Fortunately, modern scientific technology allows us to trace the sources of many important trade materials, a procedure known as **sourcing**. By far the most significant of these materials is obsidian, volcanic glass that is ideal for fabricating stone tools, ornaments, and, in Mesoamerica, highly polished mirrors (see Figure 5.9). The first sourcing studies focused on the Mediterranean and southwestern Asia, where obsidian was a major trade commodity for many thousands of years (see Box 5.4).

Many scholars have attempted to trace the trade routes in Mesoamerica over which obsidian traveled from highlands to lowlands. The use of source data enables researchers to conceive of exchange on a regional basis, an approach used with success at the Maya city of Copán, combined with obsidian hydration dating to trace changes in obsidian trade networks over many centuries. Nowadays, the ultimate research goal is to identify the exchange mechanisms that distributed the obsidian within each exchange zone. Thus, the data requirements have changed. No longer is it sufficient to know the approximate source of a raw material or an artifact. Sources must be pinpointed accurately, and distributions of traded goods or commodities must be quantified precisely. Such data provide the groundwork for studies of trade. However, it remains to translate these distributions and the source data into characterizations of human behavior, which requires use of comparison with available historical sources.

Figure 5.9 Obsidian mirror from Mesoamerica.
Source: American Museum of Natural History.

Ancient quarries, such as those in Greece, Mesoamerica, and Australia, are potentially valuable sources of information on the exchange of exotic materials. Archaeologist Robin Torrence studied the Aegean Sea obsidian trade, in the Mediterranean, and found that the exchange was noncommercial and noncompetitive. The prehistoric stoneworkers visited quarries and prepared material for exchange with minimal concern for economical use of the raw material. On the island of Melos, for example, the visitors simply quarried what they wanted and left. There is no evidence of specialized production. During early farming times, obsidian mining may have been a seasonal activity, but after 2000 B.C. it became a specialized occupation requiring specific voyages to Melos and other quarries. The reason for the shift is unknown, but perhaps it was connected to a rising demand that outstripped the yield from seasonal visits.

characterization studies of sources of raw materials used to make artifacts.

Sourcing researches are sometimes called **characterization studies** because they involve petrology and other approaches for identifying the characteristic properties of the distinctive raw materials used to fashion, say, stone axes. One should stress the word *distinctive*, for the essence of these methods is that they enable one to identify the specific source with great accuracy. For example, obsidian from Lipari Island off Sicily, traded over a wide area of the central Mediterranean, has highly specific characteristics that show it came from Lipari and nowhere else.

Isotopic chemistry has been highly effective in studying metal sources. For example, the isotopic composition of lead depends on the geological age of the ore source. Lead mines were few and far between in antiquity. Provided their location is known, it is possible to study lead sources in bronze artifacts and also those of silver, for the latter is extracted from lead ores. This technique has been used to distinguish between classical Greek silver coins made from mainland ore and those manufactured with metal from the Aegean island of Siphnos and other locations.

Box 5.4 Doing Archaeology
Obsidian Sourcing

Scientists studied the sources of toolmaking stone long before the advent of spectrographic analysis, relying on both petrology and distinctive rocks, such as the butter-colored and easily recognized Grand Pressigny flint, widely used in France by Stone Age farmers. High-tech analytical methods have revolutionized sourcing since the 1960s, when British archaeologist Colin Renfrew and others used spectrographic analysis to identify no fewer than 12 early farming villages that had obtained obsidian from the Ciftlik area of central Türkiye. This pioneering study showed that 80 percent of the chipped stone in villages within 300 kilometers (186 miles) of Ciftlik was obsidian. Outside this "supply zone," the percentages of obsidian dropped away sharply with distance, to 5 percent in a Syrian village and 0.1 percent in the Jordan valley. If these calculations were correct, each village was passing about half its imported obsidian farther down the line (see Figure 5.10). Renfrew and his colleagues identified no fewer than nine obsidian "interaction zones" between Sardinia and Mesopotamia, each of them linked to well-defined sources of supply and each yielding obsidian with its own distinctive trace elements identifiable spectrographically.

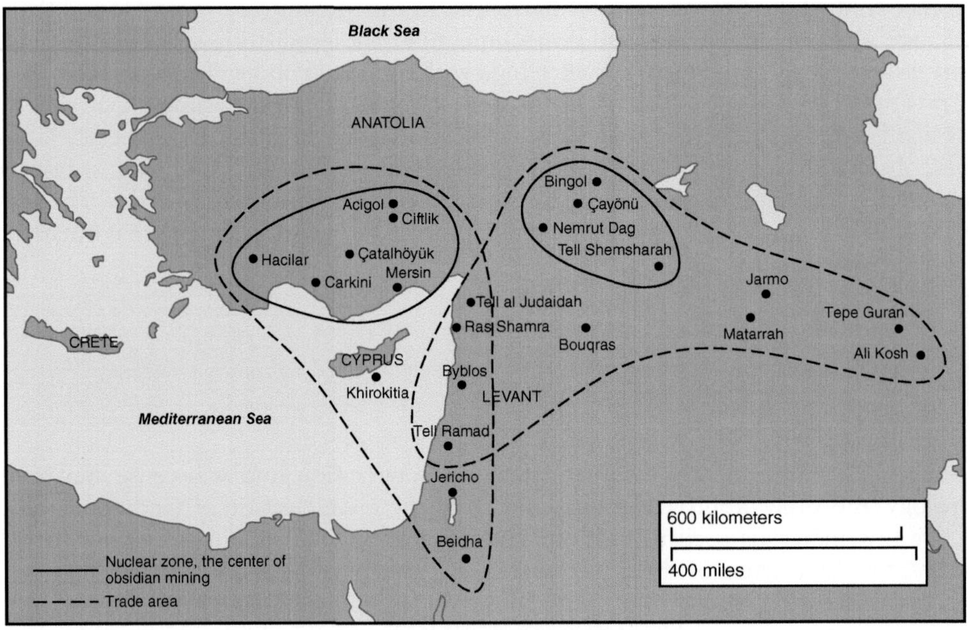

Figure 5.10 Obsidian sourcing in the eastern Mediterranean region. Sourcing studies reveal that early farming communities in Cyprus, Anatolia, and the Levant obtained their obsidian from two sources in central Anatolia. Meanwhile, villages far to the southeast relied on sources in Armenia. Settlements such as Çatalhöyük, in Anatolia were so close to obsidian sources that they probably collected their own supplies. More than 80 percent of their stone artifacts are made of the material, while obsidian tools are much rarer down the line the farther one travels from the source.

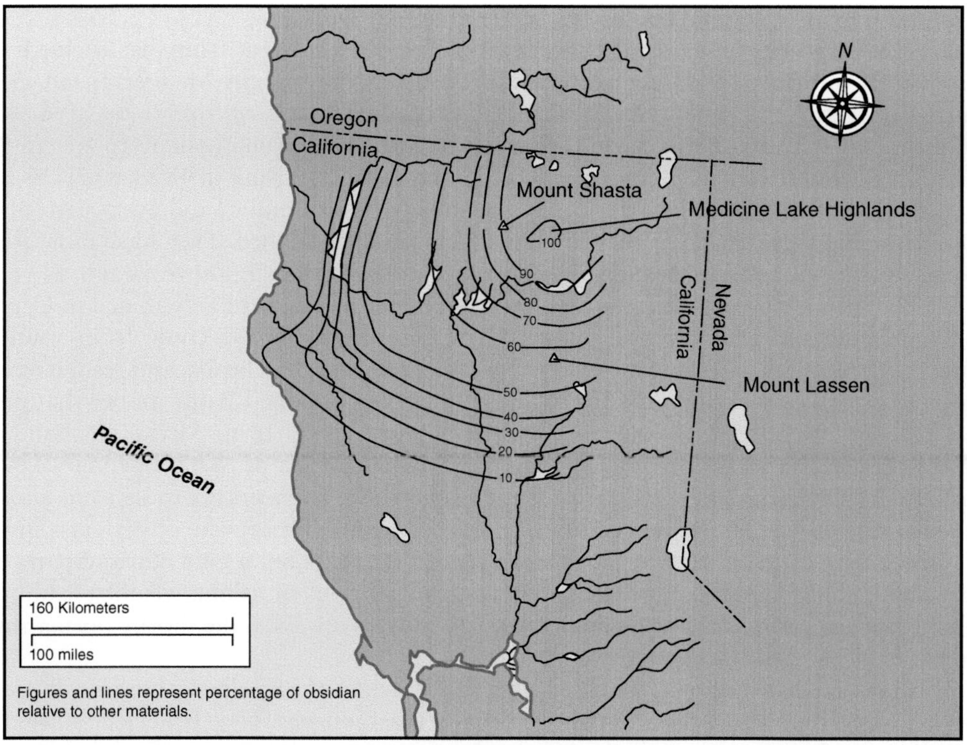

Figure 5.11 Obsidian sourcing in North America. Medicine Lake Highlands obsidian in northern California exhibits a pattern similar to that found in the Mediterranean, with usage declining sharply as one moves away from the source.

In recent years, obsidian sourcing has expanded to many areas of the world. In California, for example, archaeologists have used hundreds of samples to show how obsidian from the Medicine Lake Highlands region of northern California was used over an enormous area, up to 160 kilometers (100 miles) from the source. Their trade map indicates how use declined sharply according to distance from source (see Figure 5.11).

A Unique Portrait of Ancient Trade: The Uluburun Ship

Merely studying the distribution of artifacts gives a grossly inadequate picture of ancient trade, for such factors as the logistics of transportation, as well as local political and economic conditions, affected every aspect of trade and exchange.

Uluburun, Türkiye Bronze Age shipwreck site off southern Türkiye, dating to the fourteenth century B.C.

Few archaeological finds rival the extraordinary cargo found aboard a Bronze Age ship wrecked off the rugged **Uluburun** cliffs in southern Türkiye. Shipwrecks like this offer unique opportunities to study ancient trade, for each ship on the seabed is a sealed capsule, it holds a mirror of trading conditions at the time.

George Bass and Cemal Pulak's excavation of the Uluburun ship has yielded vast amounts of information on the commercial world of the eastern Mediterranean in the fourteenth century B.C. The heavily laden ship was sailing westward from the eastern Mediterranean when it was shattered on the jagged rocks of Uluburun about 1316 B.C. (a date determined from tree rings in firewood found in the wreck). It sank in 48 meters (157 feet) of water. Bass and Pulak plotted the exact position of every timber and every item of the ship's equipment and cargo as they lifted artifacts from the seabed. They have recovered a unique portrait of eastern Mediterranean trade from more than 3,000 years ago.

The Uluburun ship was laden with 6 tons of copper ingots, probably mined in Cyprus, and tin ingots and artifacts (see Figure 5.12). The tin may have come from southern Türkiye. Canaanite jars from Palestine or Syria held olives, glass beads, and resin from the terebinth tree, used in religious rituals. The ship's hold contained Baltic amber that probably reached the Mediterranean overland, ebony-like wood from Africa, elephant and hippopotamus ivory, and ostrich eggshells from North Africa or Syria. Egyptian, Levantine, and Mycenaean daggers, swords, spearheads, and woodworking tools were aboard, and also sets of weights, some fashioned in animal forms. There were costly glass ingots, Mesopotamian cylinder seals, a Mycenaean seal stone, and even a gold cup and parts of a tortoiseshell lute. The ship carried Egyptian scarabs, dozens of fishing weights, fishhooks, and 23 stone anchors, vital when anchoring in windy coves. Even the thorny burnet shrub used to pack the cargo was preserved.

By using find distributions from land sites and a variety of sourcing techniques, Bass and Pulak have reconstructed the anonymous skipper's last journey. They believe he started his voyage on the Levant coast, sailed north up the coast, crossed to Cyprus, and then coasted along the southern Turkish shore. The ship called at ports large and small on its way west, along a well-traveled route that took advantage of changing seasonal winds, to Crete, some Aegean islands, and perhaps to the Greek mainland. The skipper had traversed this

Figure 5.12 Excavating copper ingots from the Uluburun shipwreck, Türkiye.
Source: Institute of Nautical Archaeology, Texas A&M University.

route many times, but, on this occasion, his luck ran out and he lost his ship, the cargo, and perhaps his life on Uluburun's pitiless rocks.

From the archaeological perspective, the Uluburun shipwreck is a godsend, for it allows researchers to fill in many details of an elaborate trade network that linked the eastern Mediterranean with Egypt, the Aegean, and Greece more than 3,300 years ago. Bass and Pulak suspect that the Uluburun ship may have been carrying an unusually valuable cargo, but the owners remain a mystery.

The study of ancient trade is a vital source of information on social organization and the ways in which societies became more complex. Trade itself developed great complexity, in both goods traded and the interactions of people involved. Colin Renfrew identified no fewer than ten types of interactions between people that can result from exchange and trading, ranging from simple contact between individuals to trading by professional traders, such as the *pochteca* (professional traders) of the Aztecs, who sometimes acted as spies.

Summary

- A new generation of archaeological research is turning away from impersonal cultural processes toward the study of people and small groups. Such research marries modern archaeological data recovery methods with new interpretive approaches that consider the archaeologist an "active mediator" of the archaeological record of the past.
- Discoveries of actual individuals from the past, like the Iceman discovery in the European Alps, allow us to make detailed studies of the health, diet, and activities of individual people.
- Social ranking is difficult to study from archaeological evidence. It can be studied in the archaeological record by using burials and associated grave furniture, as at Ur in Mesopotamia, and by using structures or artifact patterns.
- The archaeology of gender is assuming increasing importance as a means of identifying changing male and female roles in the past and of studying individuals in prehistory. These researches involve detailed studies of grave furniture; studies of female pathology, which reflects such activities as constant grain grinding; and extrapolations of material data into hypothetical scenarios of changing gender relations.
- Archaeologists working with African-American sites and other sites in North America have studied ethnicity and social inequality. Such researches involve identifying distinctive artifacts that reflect African religious beliefs and material signs of silent resistance to the dominant culture.
- Trade and exchange were important means of human interaction from the earliest times. Much early trade probably took the form of gift exchanges and the bartering of food and other commodities among neighboring settlements.
- Trade is normally recognized in the archaeological record by the discovery of objects far from their places of origin. Prehistoric trade networks are studied by examining the distributions of such objects and the sources of raw materials used to make artifacts. One example is the Uluburun shipwreck off southern Türkiye, which revealed the complexity of eastern Mediterranean trading in the fourteenth century B.C.

Key Terms and Sites

social ranking
ethnicity
social stratification

Babylon
Palenque
Khok Phanom Di
Mississippian societies
ideologies of domination
Garrison Plantation
Kingsmill Plantation
Thebes
exchange systems
kula ring
gift exchanges
reciprocity
redistribution
market
sourcing
characterization studies
Uluburun

Critical-Thinking Questions

1. Why is the study of gender important in archaeology? Discuss some of the ways in which archaeologists examine male and female roles in ancient society.
2. Trade and exchange have been important in human life since the late Ice Age. Discuss some of the reasons why such activities have been such a major part of human life. How do you distinguish between trade and exchange?
3. Equality and inequality are features of ancient societies. Discuss the ways in which archaeologists distinguish between egalitarian and socially stratified societies. Why do you think inequality became so prevalent in human society over time?

Further Reading

On bioarchaeology: J. Buikstra and L. Beck, *Bioarchaeology: The Contextual Analysis of Human Remains* (San Diego, CA: Academic Press, 2006). The Iceman is well described by K. Spindler, *The Man in the Ice* (London: Weidenfeld and Nicholson, 1994). E. Service, *Primitive Social Organization* (New York: Random House, 1973) is a (now outdated) classic that discusses socioeconomic classification of human societies. L. Ferguson, *Uncommon Ground* (Washington, DC: Smithsonian Institution Press, 1991) is a fascinating essay on African-American archaeology that reveals some of the potential of this approach to historical archaeology. See also S. Jones, *The Archaeology of Ethnicity: Constructing Identities in the Past and Present* (London: Routledge, 1997). Gender: J. Gero and M. Conkey, eds., *Engendering Archaeology* (Oxford: Blackwell, 1991) is still a definitive starting point. R. A. Joyce, *Ancient Bodies, Ancient Lives: Sex, Gender, and Archaeology* (London: Thames and Hudson, 2008) is a very readable title that explores gender and sexuality through time. For those who wish to delve deeply into the subject, see S. Stryker and D. McCarthy Blackstone, eds., *The Transgender Studies Remix* (New York: Routledge, 2022), while Fagan and Durrani provide an accessible overview on gender roles in *Bigger Than History* (London: Thames and Hudson, 2019). E. Brumfiel and T. K. Earle, eds., *Specialization, Exchange, and Complex Societies* (Cambridge: Cambridge University Press, 1987) discusses long-distance exchange.

6 Studying the Intangible

Chapter outline

A painting of the Aztec Sun God, Tonatiuh. He wears an elaborate feathered headdress while dancing and waving a snake scepter.

Source: American Museum of Natural History. Neg. 332105. Logan, Dept. of Library Services.

DOI: 10.4324/9781003592754-8

If you ever visit the great city of Teotihuacán in highland Mexico, you will be haunted by the past. Looking down from the summit of the Pyramid of the Sun, at the tiny human figures dwarfed by the massive artificial mountain, you'll be mesmerized by the scale of a city built by thousands of people working in the service of divine lords and powerful gods. Down in the plaza, at the foot of the pyramid, you can almost feel the overwhelming weight of political authority and supernatural power that the builders wished to convey. Teotihuacán is a powerful statement, but so much is lost. The pyramid was once the setting for dazzling spectacles, a stage where masked lords appeared in trance, where brilliantly colored dancers performed, where chants and incense rose into the evening sky. The colors have long faded. No banners fly over temples; the stories told by narrators and priests have vanished on the wind. Teotihuacán is now an empty stage, devoid of the spirit that once brought the cosmos to life. All that is left are the material remains of the spiritual and the sacred—mirrors of the intangible. This chapter describes how archaeologists wrestle with the toughest problem of all: reconstructing the intangible religious beliefs, ideologies, and social relationships of the past.

A Framework of Common Belief?

As modern humans, we are capable of subtlety, and of passing on knowledge and ideas through the medium of language. We have consciousness and self-awareness and are capable of foresight. We can express ourselves and show emotions. DNA researchers trace the roots of modern humans back to Africa, with the earliest fossil examples of our species, *Homo sapiens*, known from North Africa and dated to over 300,000 years ago (see Chapter 9). However, the skulls of these very earliest *Homo sapiens* show a mix of "archaic" and "modern" elements. It was only after about 160,000 years ago that *Homo sapiens* become physically—and presumably, mentally—indistinguishable from any of us today. These are the "fully anatomically modern humans" or "*Homo sapiens sapiens*" to give them (and us) our precise scientific label.

Archaeology tells us that *Homo sapiens* settled permanently in western Asia over 50,000 years ago, and permanently in western Europe by 45,000 years ago. According to the archaeological record, *Homo sapiens* displayed a remarkable capacity for sophisticated symbolic and spiritual thought, for defining the boundaries of existence and the relationships of the individual, the group, and the cosmos. Late Ice Age cave art tells of our blossoming creativity. Yet judging from the very early *Homo sapiens*' art found at the Blombos Cave in South Africa, it is very likely that our ancestors melded the living and spiritual worlds by at least 70,000 years ago—if not long before that.

Yet we must exercise caution. Only written documents can give us clear insights into how, or what, people thought. Moreover, no given culture is set in stone: beliefs are ever changing. We also tend to approach the past—and indeed other living cultures—with our own cultural assumptions and "baggage." Nonetheless, as some archaeologists and anthropologists argue, perhaps it's possible to extrapolate a basic framework of common human beliefs.

First, drawing on basic observations of the natural world, a great many cultures believe that we belong to a multilayered cosmos, with the heavens stretching above, an underworld below, and sometimes comprising primordial waters. God/s, goddesses, spirit beings, and the dead inhabit the supernatural layers of this cosmos. This universe often began as a dark sea of primordial waters or, as Genesis puts it, a world "without form."

Second, a vertical axis, perhaps a symbolic tree or a symbolic support for the bowl of heaven, typically links these various cosmic layers. Mircea Eliade, one of the great religious historians of the twentieth century, stressed the importance of this *axis mundi* (axis of the world), which joined the living and spiritual worlds at a mythic center, a sacred place:

either a natural feature such as a cave or mountain or a human-made structure such as a pyramid. Such sacred places, and the mythic landscapes associated with them, certainly appear to have played vital roles in all societies with recorded records. Eliade called them "instruments of orthogenetic transformation," settings for the rituals that ensured the continuity of cultural traditions, and a place where the word of the gods rang out in familiar chants passed from one generation to the next. Sacred mountains such as the Hindus' Mount Meru, the Lakota Indians' Black Hills, or the Greeks' Olympus often served as the cosmic axis (see Figure 6.1). The Egyptian pharaohs erected pyramids as sacred mountains linking the domain of the Sun to the realm of Earth. Maya lords built great ceremonial centers as symbolic representations of their world of sacred mountains, caves, trees, and lakes. To demolish a sacred place was to destroy the essence of human existence itself. In A.D. 1521, Spanish conquistador Hernán Cortés razed the Aztec capital Tenochtitlán in the Valley of Mexico in full knowledge that its temples and plazas replicated the cherished and all-encompassing supernatural world of the Aztec people.

Third, many people believe that the material and spiritual worlds form a continuum, with no boundary between them. An "external" landscape on Earth is also an "internal" landscape of the mind, or "landscape of memory," where colors, jagged peaks, streams, groves of trees, cardinal directions, and other phenomena have spiritual associations and their places in local mythology. Usually, ancestors, those who had gone before, are the intermediaries between the living and the supernatural worlds. They look after the welfare of the living and, particularly among settled communities, are the guardians of the land—giving their living descendants apparent rights over the land.

Fourth, individuals with unusual supernatural powers—whether shamans, spirit mediums, or priests—are believed to have the ability to pass effortlessly into altered states of consciousness. They move between the material and spiritual realms using ritual

Figure 6.1 Mount Olympus, Greece, home of Zeus.
Source: Jupiterimages/Thinkstock.

activities: perhaps prayers, music, chanting, dance, or hallucinogens. Such men and women "of power" are believed to have direct and personal links to the supernatural world, and an ability to change the living world. Shamans, for example, move easily into the spiritual world. There, they "dream," going through visionary experiences where they see dots, lines, spirit animals, gods, and ancestors. From their dream journeys, they acquire the wisdom to keep their worlds in balance with the sacred and the power to influence events in the natural world. Shamans are healers, the people who can bring rain and good fortune, but who can also be sorcerers and cause disease, factional strife, or even war. A shaman, like many of our own religious leaders in the modern West, is a spiritual person who functions as an intermediary to the ancestors and the spiritual world (see Box 6.1).

Shang civilization Early civilization centered on the Huang He River of northern China, dating from c. 1766 to 1122 B.C.

Anyang, China Central core region of the Shang civilization of northern China between 1400 and 1122 B.C.

Box 6.1 Discovery
Shang Oracle Bones, China

The earliest civilizations of northern China were the stuff of legend—Xia, Shang, and Zhou, three dynasties of legendary rulers. The first of them is said to have been Huang Di, who founded civilization in the north in 2698 B.C. This famed warlord set the tone for centuries of oppressive government that was the hallmark of early Chinese civilization. In about 2200 B.C., a Xia ruler named Yu the Great is said to have gained power through his military abilities and knowledge of flood control, by which he could protect his river valley people from inundations. Huang Di, Yu, and the three dynasties remained mere legend until the discovery of Shang oracle bones in curio shops and drugstores, where they were ground up for medicine.

The first inscribed bone came from a curio shop—it was part of an ox shoulder blade that seemed out of place among precious jade and porcelain bowls. Archaeologist Tung Tso-pin was intrigued and wondered if the weathered bone was connected to the ancient legendary **Shang civilization**. The Shang people had lived on the banks of the Huang He, their capital said to be near the town of **Anyang**. Even as early as the eleventh century A.D., local scholars had collected exotic bronze vessels from the flat farmland where Shang kings once lived. Tung Tso-pin had visited Anyang in the late 1920s, just after the river had changed course nearby, exposing rich cultural debris—including more ox shoulder blades—in the banks. He dug several deep pits that contained carefully packed "archives" of oracle bones—ox shinbones and scapulae—and tortoiseshells, marked with inscriptions that gave historians a list of the Shang kings until their capital was destroyed by catastrophic floods.

When archaeologists dug into a walled site named Chengziyai by the Huang He in Shandong province in 1930–1931, they found not only the remains of a farming village, but also dozens of cracked ox shoulder blades that they identified as oracle bones used in divination ceremonies (see Figure 6.2). The cracks were made by applying hot metal to the bone and then were interpreted as messages from the ancestors. When Chinese archaeologists dug into the ancient Shang capital at

Figure 6.2 A Shang oracle bone with signs burned into it. Cracks were produced in the surface of the ox bone by applying heat to it, and priests interpreted the cracks as messages from the ancestors, sacred divinations.

Source: President and Fellows of Harvard College, Peabody Museum of Archaeology and Ethnology, PM# 35–79-60/2539 (digital file# 60743310).

Anyang farther upstream, they found hundreds of shoulder blades in pits. Many of them bore inscriptions as well as divination cracks. They are a mine of information about the origins of Chinese civilization, a unique written archive of official deliberations by the very first kings of northern China.

As early as 2500 B.C., divination rituals were a vital part of village government. All official divinations were addressed to the royal ancestors, who acted as intermediaries between the living and the ultimate ancestor and supreme being, the ruler of heaven and the creator, Shang Di. This deity served as the ancestor not only of the royal line, but also of the "multitude of the people." The king was the head of all family lines, which radiated from his person to the nobility and then to the common people. These actual and imputed kinship ties were the core of early Chinese civilization, for they obligated the peasants to provide food and labor for their rulers.

In addition to shoulder blades from oxen and water buffalo, the diviners used tortoiseshells for their ceremonies. The term *scapulimancy*, meaning "shoulder blade divination," refers to the bones used most frequently in the ceremonies. The bones and shells were smoothed and cleaned, and perhaps soaked in liquid to be softened. Rows of hollows were then produced on the underside to make the substance thinner and the surface more susceptible to being cracked. When a question was posed, the diviner would apply a metal point to the base of the hollow, causing the surface to crack. The response of the ancestors was "read" from the fissures. A skillful diviner could control the extent and direction of the cracks. Thus, divination provided an authoritative priest with a useful and highly effective way of giving advice. A leader could regard disagreement as treason.

Last, human life was governed by the cycles of the seasons, the times of planting, growth, and harvest, identified by movements of the heavenly bodies. Notions of fertility, procreation, life, and death lay at the core of such a cyclical human existence. Myth and ritual played an important part in defining this world order. They allowed the material and spiritual worlds to pass one into the other as a single constellation of belief. Through poetry, music, dance, and evocative surroundings, a deep sense of sacred order emerged.

The intangible assumed many forms, but these commonalities, observed by anthropologists and religious historians in many human societies throughout the world, may provide a viable framework for scientific investigation of ancient sacred places, the settings for mythic performance. The stone circles at Avebury and Stonehenge in Britain, the Maya pyramids, and the Palace of Minos in Crete (c. 1900–1100 B.C.) all tell us much of long-vanished religious beliefs (see Figure 6.3).

Many archaeologists throw up their hands in despair when confronted with ancient religion. One anonymous researcher described religion as "the last resort of cynical excavators." In the mid-1980s onward, a small group of scholars challenged their colleagues to move beyond artifacts and food remains. They asked, why should we interpret the past in terms of purely ecological, technological, and other material factors? They grappled with a scientific methodology for studying human consciousness, especially religion and belief. The resultant "archaeology of mind" was a marriage of cultural systems theory, settlement archaeology, environmental reconstruction, ethnographic analogy, and, where available, the decipherment of written records. Critics of this approach argue that, without written records, it is impossible to understand "the intangible," since

Figure 6.3 The Throne Room in the Palace of Minos, Knossos, Crete. Part palace, part administrative center, and part shrine, Knossos was an important cult center. Palm trees and two griffins flank the throne. The griffins guard the goddess, represented ceremonially by a priestess, who sat on the throne.

Source: imageBROKER/Alamy.

one can never get inside the minds of the ancients. However, let's attempt to approach this complex, contentious, subject with specific examples.

Ethnographic Analogy and Rock Art

The late Ice Age rock paintings of southwestern France and northern Spain are justly famous for their brilliant depictions of long-extinct game animals, painted between 15,000 and potentially 37,000 years ago (see Figures 10.6 to 10.8, pp. 324 to 327). For generations, scholars have grappled with the meaning of the paintings, for they realized that they were far more than merely art for art's sake. In an era when AMS radiocarbon dating allows researchers to date individual paintings and chemical analyses are deciphering the composition of the ancient paints, we can reasonably hope that we can achieve a greater understanding of the meaning of the art. This greater comprehension will result, in part, from research in southern Africa (see Box 6.2).

Altamira, Spain Magdalenian painted cave dating to about 15,000 years ago; famous for its polychrome bison paintings.

Box 6.2 Doing Archaeology
Copying South African Rock Paintings

All research into the meaning of rock art starts with accurate copies. Scientists have striven for a high degree of accuracy ever since the early twentieth century, when color photography was unknown. The French priest and archaeologist Abbé Henri Breuil was a gifted artist whose copies of late Ice Age paintings at such sites as **Altamira** in northern Spain are justly famous. He spent weeks on end lying on his back tracing paintings on to translucent rice paper by the light of a flickering acetylene lantern. He taped the paper to the rock or had an assistant hold it in place. The artist roundly cursed his helper every time he fidgeted. Many times he made a sketch first and then finished it later. Breuil had inadequate lighting and materials, but he achieved miracles of improvisation.

Today's rock art specialists have an arsenal of superior materials and technological methods at their disposal. Laser scanning to capture precise copies of the art is proving to be particularly effective. However, more traditional techniques can also be effective. For example, hand-drawn copies are still made, in which archaeological artists set up sheets in front of a wall to avoid direct contact with the painting; they then trace the paintings, checking their drawings against photographs and measurements. Color photography allows accurate recording without harming the images. Infrared film or light makes red ochers transparent, so the observer can see other pigments under red figures. Ultraviolet light sources cause calcite and living organisms on cave walls to fluoresce, which allows assessment of damage caused by wall growths. Such recording processes go hand in hand with other dating methods, such as AMS radiocarbon dating using tiny flecks of charcoal and other paints. However, the uranium-thorium method may be the future standard method of rock art dating. It dates stalactites overlying art to produce minimum ages, requires minuscule samples, and unlike radiocarbon, does not damage the art itself.

As in Europe, scholars in southern Africa have experimented with various rock art copying methods. In the 1940s, Abbé Breuil made color reproductions of South African rock art, using butcher's paper. Another early scholar, Walter Battiss, painted in watercolors. The beginnings of a revolution in San culture rock art studies came with the development of affordable color photography in the 1950s. A South African rock art expert, Alex Willcox, photographed thousands of paintings, especially in the Drakensberg Mountains, where some of the finest cave paintings in Africa are to be found. Willcox was something of a romantic. Captivated by the beauty and variety of the paintings, he waxed lyrical about the leisurely, prosperous life of the ancient San. He wrote of expert artists who took great joy in their depictions of animals and people. This, he said, was "art for art's sake." In reality, the paintings were a rich source of information about ancient San life and hunting practices.

Patricia Vinnecombe also worked in the Drakensberg region and compiled a remarkable statistical record with drawings and color photography. A 1970s scholar, Harold Pager, photographed the paintings in black and white, measured the drawings, and then returned to the site to color in the photographs. Another photographer, Neil Lee, used color film, shooting the art from an overall perspective, then moving closer and closer to take detailed close-up photographs. This approach allowed him to study the painter's technique, the draftsmanship, the types of brushes used, and the different paint types.

Today's sophisticated theories about San rock art are based on a growing database of carefully recorded paintings. To accumulate such a database is an urgent priority, for many paintings are vanishing rapidly due to natural causes, excess tourism, or vandalism.

The rock paintings painted by Stone Age artists in southern Africa are also justly famous, but are very different from those of late Ice Age Europe. While most European paintings and engravings depict animals, human hands, and numerous signs, the southern African art commemorates not only animals, but also scenes of the hunt, women gathering, people in camp, and elaborate ceremonies (see Figure 6.4). We have no idea of the meaning of these paintings, though archaeologist David Lewis-Williams has developed some interesting suggestions based upon the long-forgotten research notebooks of a German linguist named Wilhelm Bleek.

Bleek made a lifetime's study of African languages. In 1870, he discovered that there were 28 San convicts working on the breakwaters of Cape Town harbor; he arranged for them to be released into his supervision, and used them as informants. Bleek and his sister-in-law, Lucy Lloyd, recorded an enormous body of San mythology and folklore over a period of nearly 20 years. Their work lay neglected in the University of Cape Town Library until Lewis-Williams discovered it in the 1970s.

The Bleek archive contains numerous accounts of rainmaking and other rituals recounted by men who had practiced them themselves. Bleek himself was familiar with a few rock paintings, and his informants were able to explain scenes of men charming a mythic rainmaking animal with sweet-smelling grasses. Lewis-Williams argued that the paintings were the result of thought patterns that reflected shared beliefs and behavior over large areas where the paintings were to be found. He talked to San hunter-gatherers in the Kalahari Desert and showed them pictures of paintings. His informants were able to identify antelope of different sexes, and groupings of them painted at different times of year.

Figure 6.4 A San hunter from the Drakensburg, South Africa with his bow and arrows. Source: Africa Media Online/Alamy.

Lewis-Williams became particularly interested in the eland, a large, fat antelope that is so slow that a hunter can run it down on foot. A single eland can feed a small band for days, which meant that the animals assumed great importance in environments where food supplies could be irregular. Bleek's informants had recited myths that associated the scent of recently killed eland with honey. Lewis-Williams has examined hundreds of eland paintings in the Drakensberg Mountains and elsewhere, including scenes of eland staggering in their death throes as dancers cavort around them. White dots depict the sweat dripping from a dancer who is "dying" in trance. Lewis-Williams believes that these dancers were acquiring the potency released by the death of the eland, a process shown by the antelope heads, feet, and hair on the dancers. He realized that painting after painting linked society with the supernatural. The medium responsible for this linking was a shaman, who induced trance by intense concentration, prolonged rhythmic dancing, and hyperventilation.

Today, the !Kung San of the Kalahari still dance next to the carcass of a freshly killed eland as a shaman enters trance. By combining careful observations from ethnographic data with archaeological observations, Lewis-Williams believes he can "read" some of the rock paintings as meaningful scenes. Dance, miming, and sounds made the dead eland "appear" real before the participants. As the shaman danced, he hallucinated and "saw" the eland standing in the darkness beyond the glow of the fire. As the dance continued, the dancers became as one with the eland spirit, and the transfiguration was complete. Afterward, the shaman-artists remembered their trance experiences and painted their hallucinations on the walls of rock shelters (see Figure 6.5). Painted, the visions of the unconscious were then transferred to the world of the conscious. Lewis-Williams points out that many of the hallucinogenic experiences of Stone Age artists were very similar to those induced in modern times by LSD, peyote, or other hallucinogens.

These paintings may reflect a belief that an underground world takes a shaman to the spiritual world. An informant showed Lewis-Williams how the San once danced in the painted rock shelter to which she took him. They raised their hands during the dance and

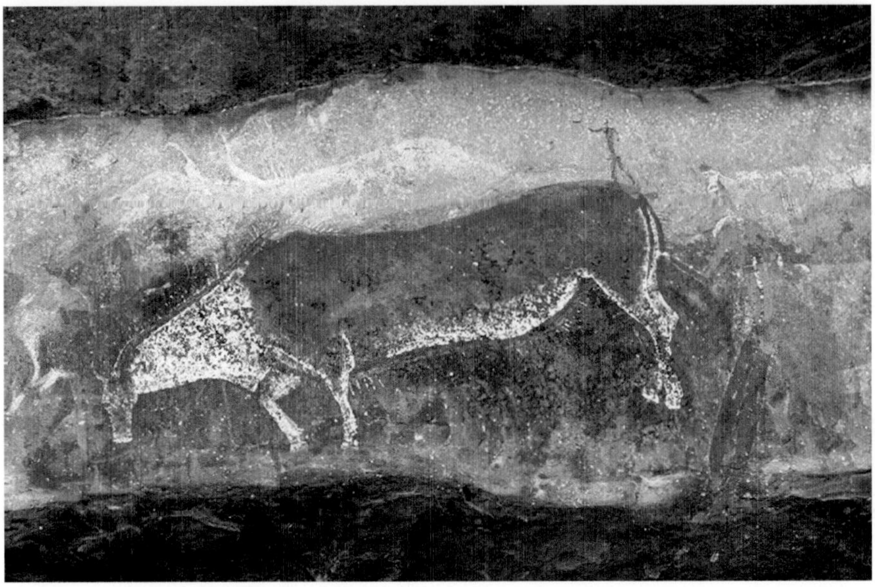

Figure 6.5 Dancing San surrounding a dying eland in a rock painting from Natal, South Africa. This scene has deep symbolic meaning, which defies modern interpretation, but the human figures are elongated in a way that may depict an altered state of consciousness.

Source: blickwinkel/Alamy.

turned to the paintings to identify their potency. Thus, the paintings began to affect the flow of mental images that entered the dancers' minds as they moved, clapped, and sang. The people may have visited the same locations again and again, which would account for the jumble of paintings at some presumably potent locations.

Yet we must remember that ethnography gives only general clues to the past. Critics of Lewis-Williams' shamanistic interpretation for the rock art observe that modern/historical-era San art cannot be used to draw firm conclusions on art traditions of 20,000 years ago. What's more, various researchers are now questioning the validity of a shamanistic interpretation of rock art, historical San or otherwise.

Among the critics is Anne Solomon, who revisited the nineteenth-century ethnographies used by Lewis-Williams to provide evidence for trance dancing and shamanist healing. Solomon argues that the original ethnographies conflate two separate traditions of the southern San and the Kalahari San to provide a single narrative that obscure important differences, concluding that there is no evidence that dances or trance states were connected with healing in San society. These confusions, she argues, undermine key aspects of the shamistic interpretation of rock art.

Just as we cannot use the (supposed) San experience and ethnography to definitely interpret the prehistoric local rock art, so we cannot use San behavior to work out what was going on in the Ice Age European art. Yet, it is interesting to note that there are some general similarities between the prehistoric art of both Europe and Africa. Recurring themes include the placement of animal images in dark caves, the occasional presence of human-animal figures, and a combination of naturalistic and geometric images that could indeed carry an undertone of altered consciousness. One scene in the Grotte de Chauvet in southeastern France depicts a man in a bison skin as part of an animal frieze; he is facing the entrance of the chamber, as if awaiting his audience.

So how do we explain prehistoric art? Is it all primarily spiritual, supernatural, shamanistic? Or is it practical information? Or something else? Or all of the above? Perhaps that is the point. Cultures are dynamic, ever changing. Art has many meanings even within a given society. As to ethnographic analogy, ultimately it can only go so far. It can provide fascinating perspectives and highlight new ways of seeing the world, but we cannot use the present to draw solid conclusions about the prehistoric past.

The Archaeology of Death

Sutton Hoo, England Site of the ship burial of the Anglo-Saxon king Raedwald, who died c. A.D. 625.

Sutton Hoo, eastern England, A.D. 625: The mourners dragged the 27-meter (88-foot) ship nearly a kilometer (about 1,000 yards) from a nearby river to its final resting place under a burial mound (Figure 6.6a). They built a timber burial chamber amidships, laying out the body of the deceased Anglo-Saxon ruler Raedwald inside. He lay in all his splendor, wearing a decorative helmet (Figure 6.6b) of Swedish style, his robe gathered by a belt with a magnificent golden buckle inlaid with animal designs. His sword and shield were beside him. Gold coins from France and silver vessels from distant Byzantium, together with many weapons and other ornaments, accompanied the wealthy and powerful king.

All the details of this spectacular burial came from days of meticulous excavation in the sandy layers of the great burial mound that covered the king and his ship. Archaeologist Charles Phillips and team used small coal shovels to slice away the sand in thin layers, exposing discolorations in the soil. They were able to trace the outline not only of the burial chamber but also of the ship's planks. The timbers had rotted away, but the iron nails that had once secured them were still in position. So precise was the excavation that Phillips was able to establish that the ship had been repaired several times. Thanks to these careful excavations, a half-size modern replica of Raedwald's ship has been constructed. It is said to sail well and to be fast under oars.

(a)

(b)

Figure 6.6 (a) The burial complex at Sutton Ho. (b) The helmet of the Anglo-Saxon ruler Raedwald. Source: The National Trust Photolibrary/Alamy and Simon Balston/Alamy.

The symbolism of death and burial is an important source of information on ancient religious beliefs as well as social ranking, most notably in the regalia and artifacts deposited with the deceased. For Egyptian pharaohs, the actual disposal of the corpse was really a minimal part of the sequence of mortuary practice in that society. Funerary rites are a ritual of passage and are usually reflected not only in the position of the body in the grave, but also in the ornaments and grave furniture that accompany it. For instance, the Egyptian pharaoh Khufu expended vast resources on building his pyramid and mortuary temple at Giza in 2550 B.C. (see Figure 3.3 on p. 75). Thousands of laborers moved more than 2.3 million limestone blocks weighing between 1.5 and 2.5 tons each to build his pyramid during his 23-year reign. The royal tomb was looted within a few centuries, but the pyramid shape endures as a powerful statement of Egyptian kingship. Egyptian pharaohs were considered to be the living embodiment of the Sun God Ra and joined him in the skies upon their death. The pyramids were symbolic sun rays, like the sun bursting through clouds overhead, a type of ladder to heaven for their owners.

Hopewell tradition Religious and burial cult centered in Illinois and the eastern United States that flourished from around 100 B.C.–A.D. 500.

Some Native American groups, notably the people of the **Hopewell tradition** of eastern North America, buried magnificent ceremonial artifacts with prominent individuals. Such artifacts as soapstone pipes, copper sheet portraits, and masks reflected not only the status of the owner, but also the person's clan affiliation and importance as a shaman or priest (see Chapter 14).

Artifacts: The Importance of Context

In 1953, British archaeologist Kathleen Kenyon unearthed a cache of plastered human skulls in a pit under a house floor at Jericho in the Jordan valley. Each head was a naturalistic, individual portrait, with nose, mouth, and ears modeled with remarkable delicacy (see Figure 6.7).

Likely, the heads were portraits of ancestors. The cowrie-shell eyes of the ancients glare unblinkingly at the beholder, giving an impression of inner wisdom. We will never know what ritual surrounded these ancestor portraits, but their context, buried under a hut

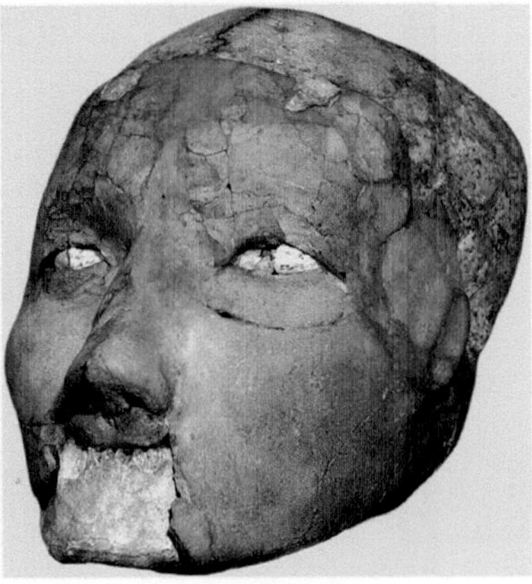

Figure 6.7 Plaster portrait head from Jericho, on the West Bank of the Jordan River.
Source: www.BibleLandPictures.com/Alamy.

floor, speaks volumes about the close relationship between living households and their ancestors. Plastered human heads may be considered the ultimate artifacts, but they—like other art objects and tools of all kinds—can also give us insights into ancient beliefs. Very often, their contexts within sites are as important as the objects themselves. Nowhere is this context more important than in the controversies surrounding the existence of an ancient Mother Goddess in Mediterranean lands.

The cycle of birth, death, and rebirth—fecundity, childbearing, the planting and harvesting of grain—lies at the heart of ancient thinking about Creation. In many farming societies, the Earth is considered female, the source of life and rich harvests. When archaeologists with classical educations found clay female figurines in early farming villages throughout western Asia, the Aegean islands, and southeastern Europe, they remembered their Homer, espousing the notion of an age-old, universal Earth Mother, the primordial Mother Goddess. From the earliest days of farming, and perhaps much earlier, the myth of the primordial Mother Goddess flourished when less rigorous scientific interpretations allowed the archaeologist to speculate. The creator goddess became a universal Great Earth Mother long before archaeological evidence gave such a goddess validity. It made sense that farming and fertility went together. So it seemed logical to add an Earth Mother, a Mother Goddess, to the equation.

The credibility of the Mother Goddess cult depends on archaeological context, not mere stylistic resemblances. Archaeologists have found hundreds of human figurines in western Asia over the past century: figures with no signs of divinity from Mesopotamia; anthropomorphic male and female depictions from 6,000-year-old Egyptian villages; figures of a female deity at the village of Çatalhöyük in central Türkiye; and a range of figurines of both sexes and without sex from all over the rest of Türkiye, the Aegean islands, and Greece. British archaeologist Peter Ucko studied every known early female figurine from the eastern Mediterranean region in 1968 and found that few of them had precise cultural contexts. Many were thrown out of houses with the domestic garbage. Some were children's toys, others trade objects, mourning figures in tombs, ancestral spirit figures, or tokens to encourage pregnancy.

Despite Ucko's rigorous, critical analysis from over half a century ago, archaeologists and others have persisted in writing about universal Mother Goddess cults. In a study of painted figurine fragments found in early Greek farming villages, Lauren Talalay showed that 18 widely scattered fragments were not goddess figurines, as they had once been labeled, but perhaps trading tokens, split into two halves by parties to an exchange transaction (see Figure 6.8).

Despite the figurine controversy, the occurrence of distinctive artifacts and ritual buildings in a site or a society may be significant. In Mexico's Valley of Oaxaca, public buildings appear between 1400 and 1150 B.C., many of them oriented 8 degrees west of north and built on adobe and earth platforms. Rare conch-shell trumpets and turtle-shell drums traded from the coastal lowlands were apparently used in public ceremonies in such buildings. Clay figurines of dancers wearing costumes and masks that make them look like fantastic creatures and animals, as well as pottery masks, are also signs of communal ritual (see Figure 15.11 on p. 480).

The personal ritual of self-mutilation by bloodletting was widespread in early Mesoamerica (see Figure 6.9). The Spanish described how the Aztec nobles would gash themselves with knives or with fish or stingray spines in acts of mutilation that were penances before the gods, imposed by religion. A few stingray spines have come from early Oaxacan villages, probably traded far into the interior for the specific use of community leaders. Archaeologist Kent Flannery suggests that fish spines for bloodletting were kept and used at home and that they were also used in public buildings. The ritual artifacts in the Oaxacan villages enabled Flannery and his colleagues to identify three levels of religious ceremony: personal bloodletting; dances run by kin groups, which cut across household lines; and public rituals in ceremonial buildings, involving a region wider than one village. The Bronze Age shrine at Phylakopi on the island of Melos in the Aegean Sea is an excellent example of archaeological context in action (see Box 6.3).

Phylakopi, Greece Mycenaean town famous for its shrine, 1390–1090 B.C.

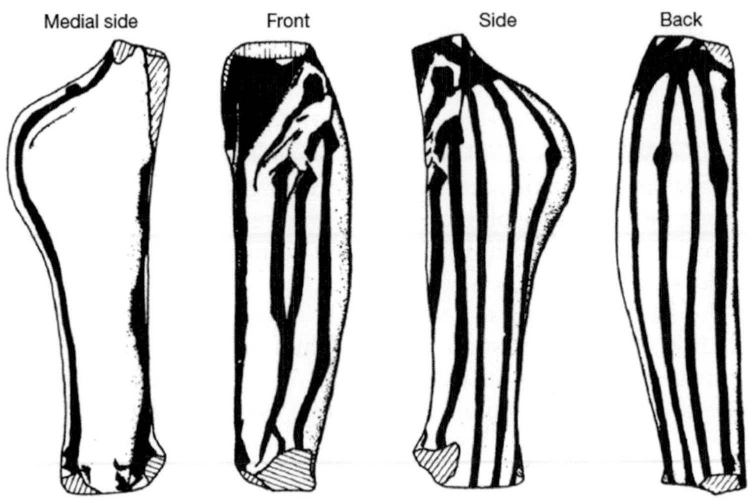

Figure 6.8 Fragment of a clay human leg from Franchthi Cave, southern Greece, shown at one-half full size. The leg is thought to have been split in half for use as tokens by two parties involved in exchanges of goods or commodities.

Figure 6.9 Ancient bloodletting ritual. Maya Lady Balam-ix pulls a rope through her tongue while kneeling next to Lord Bird Jaguar, who is about to pierce his penis in a similar ritual.

Source: charistoone-photo/Alamy.

Box 6.3 Site
The Shrine at Phylakopi, Greece

The small Mycenaean town of **Phylakopi**, on the island of Melos in the Aegean Sea, was home to an estimated 1,400 to 2,100 people between 1390 and 1090 B.C. The settlement was a maze of small stone houses, narrow alleyways, and courtyards. Colin Renfrew excavated the settlement, using a 10-meter (33-foot) grid that allowed him to record architectural changes and stratigraphy with great precision. This excavation method, combined with meticulous studies of Mycenaean pottery, provided very precise contexts for the finds and enabled Renfrew to identify an important shrine in the town. He first suspected a shrine when he recovered broken animal and human figurines in his trenches. Slow-moving excavation over the floors of the putative shrine rooms revealed stone platforms and exotic objects like seal stones. But the evidence for religious activity was modest at best until the excavators uncovered a side chamber and a wall niche in the westernmost shrine room (see Figure 6.10). This contained a pedestaled vase, the fragments of an oxlike figure, other figurines, and a remarkable female figurine, which stood upright in the room. "The Lady of Phylakopi," as Renfrew named her, had a conical stem painted like a long skirt, a bulbous body with small breasts, a painted brown chin, staring eyes, and eyebrows and hair outlined in brown. Another complete female figurine stood to one side.

The figurines could have come from a storeroom, so Renfrew studied the design of the chambers. He found that the builders had laid them out in such a way that the symmetrically placed platforms were the focus of attention. The objects displayed on them would have caught attention at once. Furthermore, the "shrines" yielded conch-shell trumpets identical to those blown by priestesses depicted on seals from Crete. Perforated tortoiseshell fragments were the remains of lyre bodies. The fine pottery found inside the two shrines was of much better quality than that from elsewhere on the site.

The precise contexts of these finds allowed Renfrew to conclude that he had found the town shrine, which is duplicated, at least superficially, at other sites on Crete and the Greek mainland.

Figure 6.10 The Mycenaean site of Phylakopi, Melos, Aegean Sea, Greece.
Source: CM Dixon/Heritage Image Partnership.

Artifacts and Art Styles

> **ideology** The knowledge or beliefs developed by human societies as part of their cultural adaptation.

Ideology is a product of society and politics, a body of doctrine, myth, and symbolism associated with a social movement, institution, class, or group of individuals, often with reference to some political or cultural plan, along with the strategies for putting the doctrine into operation.

Writing is power, especially in societies where only a tiny proportion of the population is literate. For most people, knowledge of all kinds—hunting expertise, farming know-how, weaving skills, and religious beliefs—is passed from one generation to the next by word of mouth, through chants, rituals, and many other means. Art and architecture are powerful ways of propagating religious beliefs and ideologies, especially in highly centralized societies where the entire fabric of society depends on social conformity.

Strong ideologies drove all preindustrial civilizations. The Egyptian pharaohs were seen as living personifications of the Sun God Ra. Maya lords had divine ancestry and unique abilities to communicate with the supernatural world. The supreme Inca ruler epitomized the Sun. The ideologies that reinforced these beliefs surrounded everyone and were depicted with familiar motifs on textiles and pottery, and on temple walls and carvings. Artifacts and buildings were often expressions of widely held religious beliefs. Such ideologies come down to us in highly attenuated form. We see them on the snarling faces of Olmec portrait heads, axes, and altars from lowland Mesoamerica, where lords and jaguars had close associations and where human shamans transformed themselves in trance into fierce beasts. Decoding such messages is extremely difficult, especially when there are no ethnographic or historical accounts to guide the researcher.

> **Moche state, Peru** Coastal Peruvian civilization centered on the Chicama and Moche valleys, dating from around A.D. 1–800.

The **Moche state** on the north coast of Peru enjoyed a flamboyant ideology and set of religious beliefs that are known to us only from the magnificent burials of the lords of Sipán (see Figure 16.7 on p. 509) and from detailed studies of sculpted and painted clay vessels crafted by Moche artisans. Archaeologist Christopher Donnan has attempted to decode the iconography behind the pottery, but has succeeded in doing so only in the most general terms. For example, he has identified a complex ceremony involving human sacrifice that was performed before warrior-priests wearing regalia precisely the same as that worn by the lords of Sipán. The Sipán regalia reflect an ancient Andean duality between Sun and Moon, day and night, but to go into more detail without written sources is well-nigh impossible (see Figure 6.11; see also Box 16.1 on p. 509). Fortunately, some exceptional studies of native South American religions, ancient and modern, give insights into such institutions as shamanism and ancestor worship in earlier times.

Research like Donnan's requires exceptional rigor, for it is all too easy to rely on intuition and aesthetic sense rather than demanding analysis. Another scholar, Olga Linares, has studied the ideology behind high-status cemeteries in central Panama. Using sixteenth-century Spanish eyewitness accounts of local Panamanian chiefdoms engaged in

Figure 6.11 An ear ornament worn by a Moche lord of Sipán, c. A.D. 400.
Source: Frans Lemmens/Alamy.

constant warfare and raiding, and detailed information on local animal species, Linares studied graves and the associated flamboyant polychrome vessels found in them. They were open pots designed to be seen from above, where mourners could see the animal motifs painted on them. Sometimes, apparently, the pots were so valuable that they were exhumed from one grave and put in another.

ethnohistory The study of history using oral and other traditional sources.

Accounts based on **ethnohistory** mention that the highly competitive chiefs vied constantly for leadership and prestige, painting and tattooing their bodies with badges of rank and bravery. Each group of warriors wore different symbols that associated them with their leader. They went to their graves with helmets, weapons, other military paraphernalia, and painted pottery. Linares noticed that the art styles rarely depicted plants, but featured numerous animal species, motifs that commemorated qualities of aggression and bravery. Crocodiles, large felines, sharks, stingrays, scorpions, and even poisonous snakes were the animals that were dangerous and therefore, symbols of bravery. They often appeared on clay vessels, and sometimes parts of the animals' bodies, such as sharks' teeth and stingray spines, were buried with the dead. In contrast, prey species and animals with soft parts like, say, monkeys, were largely ignored by the artists. Thus, the Panamanian chiefdoms used carefully selected animals to communicate the qualities most admired in chiefs and warriors.

Most of what we know about ancient religion comes from literate societies, where documents and inscriptions amplify the archaeological record in dramatic ways. We know a great deal about Mesopotamian and Ancient Egyptian religion, but the most dramatic advances of recent years have come with the decipherment of Maya glyphs (see Box 6.4). Linda Schele and David Freidel studied Maya images and hieroglyphs and used changes in them to trace changes in the meaning of symbols associated with political power. For

Box 6.4 Doing Archaeology
The Ancient Maya World through Glyphs

The decipherment of Maya glyphs was a magnificent scientific triumph that resulted from inspired teamwork among epigraphers living in many countries. The process of decipherment continues to this day, to the point that we now have a rudimentary understanding of the intricate cosmology and religious beliefs of the ancient Maya, even if many details remain controversial. The glyphs give us a new understanding of the complex, multilayered Maya world. The layouts of great cities such as Copán, Palenque, and Tikal depicted the geography of the sacred world. Maya glyphs tell us that the world was alive and imbued with a sacredness that was concentrated at sacred points such as caves and mountains. The gods created these spots when they created the cosmos. Living people built cities and communities within the matrix of the sacred landscape, which merged with divinely created patterns in caves and at the summits of humanly raised pyramids. At the same time, the world of human beings was connected to the otherworld along the axis of a World Tree, which ran through the center of existence. This axis moved constantly, but could be materialized through powerful rituals at any point in the natural and human-made landscapes.

Glyphs tell us that Maya lords went into hallucinogenic trances atop pyramid-mountains. They gashed their penises with stingray spines, a bloodletting ritual that brought the World Tree into existence through the middle of the temple atop the pyramid. The temple doorway became a sacred entrance to the otherworld. Here the ruler would mediate between the people and the gods and ancestors. Clouds of incense rose high above the temple as the ritual unfolded. This was the Vision Serpent, whose twisting coils symbolized the path of communication that linked the living and supernatural worlds.

Maya artists depicted the cosmos on special tripod plates designed to catch the blood that helped open the door to the otherworld. A great bearded serpent with gaping jaws emits the pure, life-bearing waters of the Earth. Below flow the dark waters of the underworld, with the World Tree emerging from the head of the evening star god as he rises from primordial black waters.

A new generation of Maya research combines glyphs with archaeology in efforts to decipher royal genealogies, to identify the builders of temples and pyramids, and to untangle the complex political history of a flamboyant and volatile civilization.

example, they theorize that the religious symbolism of the late Preclassic era 2,000 years ago was based on the passage of Venus as morning and evening star with the rising and setting of the Sun. The people of any Maya community could identify and verify their cosmos simply by observing the sky (Maya civilization is described in Chapter 15).

As time went on, Maya cosmology was expanded and elaborated. The names of late Preclassic rulers were not recorded publicly. Perhaps such permanent verification on public monuments was not yet deemed necessary. Classic rulers followed a quite different strategy. They legitimized their rule through genealogies, public ceremonies, and monuments—much Classic Maya art was created as part of this process of legitimizing rulers, who claimed identity with gods in the Maya cosmos. Schele and Freidel believe that the metaphor of the twin ancestors—Venus and the Sun—provided a potent image for lateral blood ties between lineages, communities, and everyone who believed in the same myths. Just as twins are of the same womb and blood, the Maya are all of common ancestry and blood.

Research on Maya glyphs and archaeological sites shows that archaeologists can never think of religion and ritual in isolation, but rather as integral to social organization, economic life, and political systems. The ideas and beliefs, the core of all religions, are reflected in many aspects of human life, especially in art and architecture. Every society has its own model of how the world is put together, its own ultimate beliefs. These sacred propositions are interpreted for the faithful through a body of theology and rituals associated with it. The rituals are more or less standardized, religious acts often repeated at regular times of the year—harvests, plantings, and other key events. Others are performed when needed: marriages, funerals, and the like. Some societies, such as those of the Ancient Egyptians and the Maya, made regular calendars to time religious events and astronomical cycles. These regular ceremonies performed important functions not only in integrating society, but also in such activities as redistributing food, controlling population through infanticide, and dispersing surplus male cattle in the form of ritually accumulated wealth.

Religious experiences are predominantly emotional, often supernatural and aweinspiring. Each aspect of religion—sacred propositions, ritual, experience—supports the others. A religion will operate through sanctified attitudes, values, and messages, an ethic that adds a sacred blessing, derived from the ultimate sacred propositions of the society, to elicit predictable responses from the people. Such predictability, sparked by directives from some central religious authority, ensures orderly operation of society. In time, as in Mesopotamia, that authority can become secular as well. The institutions and individuals associated with these messages can become sanctified, for they are associated with the sacred propositions that lie at the heart of the society's beliefs.

As societies became more complex, so did the need for a stable framework to administer the needs of the many increasingly specialized subgroups that made up society as a whole. Architecture and sacred places played a central role in this ideological framework.

Sacred Places

The cathedral of Notre Dame in Chartres, France, constructed in a mere quarter century and completed in A.D. 1195, was the sixth church built on the same site, a masterpiece where the infinite was a miracle in stone and glass (see Figure 6.12). The cathedral was all windows, the great rose window of the western front symbolizing the Virgin Mary herself. Stained-glass windows were a major element in Gothic architecture—ethereal settings among soaring beams and graceful arches. At Chartres, they became a form of new language, bringing together ancient principles of Christianity, many of them derived from even older cosmic beliefs. The rose was a powerful symbol, evoking the soul, eternity, the wheel, the Sun, and the cosmos. The rose was sacred to the Egyptian goddess Isis, to the Greek Aphrodite, and to Venus as a symbol of human love transcending passion, which signified the Virgin Mary in Christianity. The major rose windows at Chartres depict the Virgin and Child (north), martyrs who spread the Word and the New Testament (south), and the wounded Christ at the center of the Last Judgment (west). Each uses the same vocabulary of color, form, geometry, and symbol. The gemlike transmutation of the light shining through the windows created transcendental effects that could heal and revivify worshippers crowded in the nave. The pictures in the windows communicated the message of God for the illiterate who came to pray.

Like Ancient Egyptian artists, medieval artisans followed a standard vocabulary of forms as far as the disposition of figures and backgrounds was concerned. They made use of unique geometrical compositions to structure the motifs of the windows, often with

Figure 6.12 The cathedral of Notre Dame in Chartres, France.
Source: Gautier Willaume/Shutterstock.

close ties to astrological and cosmological images as well as zodiacal symbolism. Like the Aztec great temple at Tenochtitlán, Mexico, the Egyptian pyramids, and Maya centers, the Chartres cathedral's windows were an integral part of a setting that brought heaven to Earth and joined the secular and the spiritual.

Chartres served the same purpose as much older sacred places. The cathedral was a magnet. The permanent population of medieval Chartres may have been no more than 1,500 people, but the cathedral regularly attracted 10,000 worshippers, an offering to God as powerful as the human sacrifices of the Aztecs and the propitiating killing of children for Minoan deities. The cathedral provided a way of connecting the divine to the living world, for all things emanated from the Kingdom of God. Requiring enormous expenditures of human labor and sometimes extreme deprivation, Gothic cathedrals were expensive outpourings of love for the Lord and also metaphorical sacrifices in stone and material goods offered in the expectation of divine favors in return. Chartres was the setting for dazzling spectacles. Sung Masses and mystery plays depicting the life of Jesus or episodes in the lives of saints brought forth intense emotional reactions among the faithful. The great cathedral bells tolled at times of joy and at moments of mourning. They sounded warnings and rang out in exultation and in crisis. Great preachers attracted huge crowds. Baptisms, marriages, funerals and prayers for the dead, ordinations and excommunications, victory celebrations, and public meetings—the cathedral was the focus of human life.

Like Mesoamerican Indians, medieval Christians worried about the fertility of the land, the continuity of life itself. Every Easter Eve, a "new light" was kindled, celebrating the Resurrection and the year's start. A thousand candles were lit and carried from town to village, village to household, as life renewed. Fall harvest festivals saw churches decorated with the fruits of the soil, commemorating the bounty of the soil, like the green corn ceremonies of eastern North American groups. Seven centuries ago, the medieval cathedral was the Bible of the poor, an image of the cross and of the body of Christ, a corner of God's Kingdom.

Sacred places were among ancient humanity's greatest achievements, often mirrors of the spiritual world. Great Maya cities such as Copán and Tikal were vast replicas of the spiritual world wrought in stone and stucco, with sacred mountains (pyramids), carved stelae (trees), and reservoirs (lakes). They were oriented with the heavenly bodies and were settings for elaborate ceremonies when powerful lords in trance would appear before their subjects. Angkor Wat in Cambodia is one of the masterpieces of the ancient world (see Figure 3.7a on p. 82). Khmer king Suryavarman II erected Angkor Wat as an observatory, shrine, and mausoleum in the early twelfth century A.D. The temple honors Vishnu, ruler of the western quarter of the compass. The five multitiered towers of the temple depict Mount Meru, home of the Hindu gods and center of the universe. Celestial maidens twist and cavort in endless dances on Angkor's walls, depicting the pleasures of paradise. More than a dozen Khmer princes built their shrines near this sacred place.

The great temple or ceremonial center was the focus of human life, the sanctified terrain where scheduled rituals guaranteed the seasonal renewal of cyclic time and where the splendor, potency, and wealth of rulers symbolized the well-being of the whole community. Such centers ensured the continuity of cultural traditions; the religious and moral models of society were laid down in sacred canons recited in temples in reassuring chants passed from generation to generation.

Sacred places lay at the heart of much wider cultural landscapes, defined by generations of experience with supernatural qualities. They were the focus of much wider worlds, which is why settlement archaeology plays such an important role in the study of ancient religions. For instance, the celebrated stone circles at Avebury in southern Britain formed part of a much larger sacred landscape, defined not only by natural landmarks but also by burial mounds, sacred avenues delineated by stone uprights, and structures where the bodies of the dead were exposed before burial in communal tombs (see Figure 3.1 on p. 72; Figure 6.13). In recent years, teams of archaeologists have been gradually reconstructing this long-vanished, fragmentary Stone Age landscape with survey and excavation that reveal its gradual evolution over many centuries.

Cahokia and Ancient Cosmology

> **Cahokia, Illinois** Major ceremonial center of the Mississippian culture built after A.D. 900.

Cahokia, the great Mississippian center, lies in the heart of a pocket of extremely fertile bottomland on the Mississippi floodplain, near modern-day St. Louis, known as the American Bottom (see Chapter 14 and Figure 14.14 on p. 457). At the height of its powers, between A.D. 1050 and 1250, Cahokia covered an area of more than 13 square kilometers (5 square miles), about the size of Teotihuacán in the Valley of Mexico. Several thousand people lived in pole-and-thatch houses that covered about 800 hectares (2,000 acres) of ground and were clustered on either side of a central east–west ridge. More than 100 earthen mounds of various sizes, shapes, and functions dot the Cahokia landscape,

Figure 6.13 The West Kennet long barrow, part of the Avebury sacred landscape. This communal burial place stands on a ridge and may also have served as a territorial marker, built after 3600 B.C.

Source: Richard Melichar/Thinkstock.

most grouped around open plazas. The largest, Monk's Mound, dominates the site and the surrounding landscape. Monk's Mound rises in four terraces to a height of 31 meters (100 feet) and covers 6.4 hectares (16 acres): a slightly larger area than Egypt's Great Pyramid. Fortunately for science, the ancient cosmology and religious beliefs behind Cahokia can be pieced together, at least partially, from a combination of archaeology in the American Bottom and ethnohistory derived from historic Southeastern Indian groups.

The layout of Cahokia reflects a traditional Southeastern cosmos with four opposed sides, reflected in the layout of the platform mounds, great mounds, and imposing plazas. By A.D. 1050, the rectangular plaza surrounded by mounds replicated the ancient quadripartite pattern of the cosmos seen in much earlier settlements along the Mississippi. Four-sided Mississippian platform mounds may portray the cosmos as "earth islands," just as modern-day Muskogean Indians once thought of the world as flat-topped and four-sided. Archaeologist John Douglas uses ethnographic and archaeological data to argue that the four-sided cosmos had a primary axis, which ran northwest to southeast, with an opposite axis dividing the world into four diamond-shaped quarters. Cahokia is oriented along a slightly different north–south axis, but it certainly perpetuates the notion of spiritual links between opposites and a cosmos divided into quarters. Researchers believe that the orientation reflects observations of the Sun rather than the Moon. Astroarchaeologist Anthony Aveni thinks that Cahokia's rulers used the Sun to schedule the annual rituals that commemorated the cycles of the agricultural year.

Southeastern cosmology revolved around dualities. In the case of Cahokia, these may have included the upper and lower worlds, also a powerful and pervasive fertility cult linked to commoners and the elite. These dualities were carried through to the smallest ritual centers. Changing settlement layouts imply that, at first, local communities and kin groups controlled fertility rituals in dispersed households divided into symbolic quarters, with ceremonial structures facing a central square. Later, centers display more formal layouts, with central plazas, elaborate sacred buildings, and storage and ritual pits filled with offerings made during fertility and world-renewal ceremonies. By this time, experts believe, power was passing from local kin leaders to an elite based at Cahokia—a shift reflected in increasingly elaborate ceremonial architecture, residences for local leaders at local centers, and special mortuary complexes. Their carefully laid-out centers brought together two central ritual themes: the spiritual realm of fertility and life and the validation of living rulers, who were intermediaries between the supernatural realm and that of the living. Cahokia and other Mississippian centers reflect an ancient cosmology in a symbolic language intelligible to noble and commoner alike.

Astroarchaeology and Stonehenge

> **astroarchaeology** The study of ancient astronomical knowledge using archaeological methods.

Astroarchaeology is the study of ancient astronomical observances. The movements of the Sun and Moon and other heavenly bodies played an important role in many ancient societies, among them the Egyptian, Maya, and many Andean cultures. Astroarchaeology is an important source of information about ancient religious beliefs and cosmologies.

Astroarchaeology is a far cry from the crazy theories of cultists, who claim that Egypt's Great Pyramids of Giza were giant, highly sophisticated astronomical observatory complexes run with computers. (For this book, any correspondence from such "theorists" is buried in a file named "Pyramidiots.") Modern research into ancient astronomy uses computer software to examine the sky over the Maya homeland on specific dates and makes highly accurate observations of astronomical alignments at Stonehenge, the Hopewell monuments in Ohio, and other sites known to have astronomical associations.

More nonsense has been written about the stone circles at Stonehenge, England (see Figure 3.9 on p. 85) than about almost any other archaeological site in the world. After more than three centuries of sporadic research, scientists are still deeply divided about the significance of this extraordinary monument, the prehistoric equivalent of a Norman cathedral, used and modified from about 2950 to 1600 B.C. Was it the center of some long-forgotten religious cult, or was it an observatory, a sophisticated place of dialogue with the Sun and stars?

In the 1960s, Boston astronomer Gerald Hawkins used an IBM mainframe computer to plot the positions of 165 key points: stones, stone holes, earthworks, and other fixed points. He found "total correlation" with a network of 13 solar and 11 lunar alignments, all of them based on features of early rather than later Stonehenge, where the alignments were less precise. Hawkins called Stonehenge a "Neolithic computer" used for predicting lunar eclipses. From the archaeologist's point of view, the fatal flaw in Hawkins's reasoning was his assumption that any alignments he saw, as a twentieth-century astronomer, were also known to the original builders. Hawkins was familiar with obscure astronomical data. Could one assume that Stone Age or Bronze Age farmers had the same expertise, especially since they had to cope with the cloudy and unpredictable sighting conditions of the British heavens? Hawkins's astronomy was little more than an anecdotal way of explaining Stonehenge. A decade later, retired engineering professor Alexander Thom announced that Stonehenge's stone circles were a central "backsight" for observing heavenly bodies, used with no fewer than eight "foresights," mostly earthworks identified on the visible horizon. Unfortunately, Thom failed to reconcile the archaeological and astronomical evidence. Nearly all his "foresight" earthworks are of later date than the stone circles of the "backsight."

Was Stonehenge an observatory? One cannot speak of it in the same breath as sophisticated Maya observatories or of the builders as astronomers on a par with Babylonian priests. We have known since the seventeenth century that Stonehenge was aligned on the axis of the midsummer Sun. But the stone circles were never an elaborate device for predicting eclipses or measuring the sky (see Figure 6.14). Rather, Stonehenge reflects a distinctive *idea* of time that revolved around the cyclical movements of Sun, Moon, and stars across the heavens, as indicators of the passing seasons. Also, it was not a stand-alone

Figure 6.14 Stonehenge trilithons. The lintels are so large that an eighteenth-century antiquarian was able to dine on top of one with friends.

Source: Maisna/Thinkstock.

shrine, but part of an extensive sacred landscape of burial mounds, avenues, and other sacred circles, which is only now being deciphered with the aid of new excavations, surveys, and remote sensing.

The farmers who built the later Stonehenge lived in a demanding environment where the passage of the seasons governed their lives. Every year, the eternal cycles of planting, growth, and harvest, of symbolic life and death, repeated themselves in endless successions of good and bad harvests, of drought and flood, of famine or plenty. We know that the people placed great store in death rituals, in reverence of the ancestors, the guardians of the land.

They devoted enormous resources to the great stone circles in the midst of their sacred landscape, where their priests and shamans used the stone uprights and stone alignments to observe the passage of the seasons. At midsummer sunrise and, perhaps, on the shortest day of the year, about December 21, the priests stood at the open side of the horseshoes to observe sunrise or sunset. In winter, the setting of the winter Sun at the solstice signaled the beginning of lengthening days and the certainty that the cycle of the seasons would begin anew.

We have great difficulty envisaging Stonehenge in its heyday, sitting as it does in its twenty-first-century landscape of mown fields and a large road running by. Our only impressions can come from our physical perceptions of what it was like to move around both outside and inside the monument. These perceptions must be fundamentally similar to those of the ancients, for the stone uprights still tower overhead and restrict the view, as they did 4,500 years ago. With the exercise of ritual power, setting is everything. Stonehenge was such a setting.

The lesson of Stonehenge lies in the continuities of farming life rather than changes. Chieftains lived and died, achieved great power and supernatural authority, and in time became ancestors. As villages prospered and more people crowded the densely farmed landscape, always at the center of this busy world lay a set of ancient values and beliefs epitomized by the weathered stone circles of Stonehenge. The seasons came and went, and so did human life itself, while Stonehenge remained an idea of time, a place where relationships between the living, the dead, and the supernatural were commemorated in stone.

Southwestern Astronomy and Chaco Canyon

Agriculture and religion intersected the lives of the ancient Pueblo Indians of the Southwest, living as they did in a region of unpredictable rainfall, where the timing of harvest and planting was everything. The Pueblo world was one of close interdependence between farming and religious observance and between isolated communities large and small. The major ceremonies of the summer and winter solstices brought people together in implicit recognition of this interdependence.

The Pueblo tied their world to the horizon and the heavens by making a calendar out of the environment around them. The Hopi oriented themselves to the points on the horizon that mark the places of sunrise and sunset at the summer and winter solstices. The Pueblo anchored time, and their ritual cycles, to these events—especially to the winter solstice, when the Sun is at its southernmost point. They believed that if the Sun did not turn around, it would fall off into the underworld. Some groups observed a period of "staying still" to keep the Sun in its winter house. Winter solstice ceremonies guided the Sun in the correct direction. The sun priests set the days for these ceremonies, as well as the lesser celebrations in the annual calendar, starting their prayers and observations about 28 days before the winter solstice and 29 days before the summer solstice. They used a chosen spot in the village for their work, tracking the Sun's seasonal position with the aid of horizon markers, which showed up clearly at sunrise. Sometimes they employed windows in buildings to manipulate light and shadow.

Sun watching required much more than observation of solstices and other events. The sun priest had to make anticipatory observations over three weeks *before* an event such as a solstice celebration to allow for preparations to be made. He also required lengthy training so that he could predict events even during times of bad weather. This is why he had to know the position of sunrise relative to horizon markers several weeks before the event. At the solstice, the Sun stands still on the horizon for four days, making the observation of the actual solstice day impossible beforehand. So the sun priest had to make his observations at a time when the Sun was still moving perceptibly, in human-eye terms, about ten minutes of arc (arcmins) a day. He could have predicted the day of the solstice by making the observation and then keeping a tally of days on a notched stick. This approach solved the problem of cloud cover and bad weather. By using any clear day well ahead of time, the observer could have used his notched stick to calculate the correct day of solstice even if the sky was overcast. The predictions of the summer solstice were remarkably accurate, almost invariably to within a day and a half. Such accuracy was essential. A major disaster would transpire if the ceremonies took place and the Sun had already turned or was still moving toward its turning point, as if it were about to fall off the Earth. Accurate predictions reinforced priestly power and strengthened bonds within the community, in addition to validating the worldview.

Ecological time served the Pueblo Indians well. They lived a well-regulated life attuned to the solstices and to the realities of their arid environment. The yearly cycle repeated itself endlessly. As one year ended, another began, measured in the passage of moons and days. Fortunately for science, pre-Columbian astronomers used buildings, pictographs, and other humanly manufactured objects for their observations, enabling us to trace Pueblo astronomy back to the Ancestral Pueblo, whose primordial roots extend back as far as 2,500 years ago (for more background on the North American Southwest, see Chapter 14).

Hovenweep, Colorado Ancestral Pueblo and observatory of the late twelfth to mid-thirteenth century A.D.

The best archaeological evidence for Pueblo astronomy comes from **Hovenweep** pueblo in Colorado, erected by Ancestral Pueblo people related to nearby Mesa Verde communities between the late twelfth and mid-thirteenth centuries. The pueblo includes round, square, and D-shaped towers (see Figure 6.15). At least one, Hovenweep Castle, has special sun-sighting ports aligned with the summer and winter solstices. Nearby, Holly House contains petroglyph panels with symbols that may represent the Sun and other heavenly bodies.

Chaco Phenomenon Generic name given to the Ancestral Pueblo sites and associated phenomena of Chaco Canyon, New Mexico, in the eleventh and twelfth centuries A.D.

Figure 6.15 Towers at Hovenweep Pueblo, Colorado.
Source: zrfphoto/iStock.

The first farmers of the Southwest dwelt in small communities of pit houses. By A.D. 900, southwestern farming populations had increased considerably. Many Ancestral Pueblo communities moved into large, well-constructed towns, epitomized by the great pueblos of Chaco Canyon. For two-and-a-half centuries, the Chaco Canyon pueblos flourished, during a time of constant climatic change. By 1050, the **Chaco Phenomenon** (an archaeological term) was in full swing. The phenomenon expanded from its canyon homeland to encompass an area of more than 65,000 square kilometers (25,000 square miles) of the surrounding San Juan Basin and adjacent uplands. Roads and visual communication systems linked outlying communities with the canyon. Great pueblos such as semicircular Pueblo Bonito housed hundreds of people (see Figure 6.16). The population of Chaco Canyon rose from a few hundred to perhaps as many as 5,500 inhabitants, with many more people visiting for major ceremonies and trading activities.

During the 1970s and 1980s, aerial photographs and side-scan radar placed Chaco at the center of a vast ancient landscape. A web of over 650 kilometers (400 miles) of unpaved ancient roadways links Chaco with more than 30 outlying settlements. The Ancestral Pueblo had no carts or draft animals, but the people built shallow trackways up to 12 meters (40 feet) wide, cut a few inches into the underlying soil or demarcated by low banks or stone walls. Each highway runs straight for long distances, some for as much as 95 kilometers (60 miles), and each is linked to a major pueblo at the canyon itself. The people approached the canyon along straight walkways, descending to the pueblos down stone-cut steps in the cliffs (see Figure 6.17).

The Chacoan "roads" are a mystery. Were they used for travel or for transport of vital commodities? For years, archaeologists have argued for some form of integrating Chacoan

Figure 6.16 Pueblo Bonito, Chaco Canyon, New Mexico.
Source: Daniel Fiverson/Thinkstock.

Figure 6.17 The Jackson Stairway (named after the nineteenth-century photographer who first rediscovered it) carved into a sandstone mesa near Casa Rinconada in Chaco Canyon, New Mexico, part of the canyon's road system.
Source: Buddy Mays/Alamy.

cultural system, which would have unified a large area of the Southwest a thousand years ago. One authority, archaeologist James Judge, believes that the San Juan Basin's harsh and unpredictable climate, with its frequent droughts, caused isolated Ancestral Pueblo communities to form loosely structured alliances for exchanging food and other vital commodities. Chaco lay at the hub of the exchange system and also served as the ritual center for major rainmaking ceremonies and festivals. The canyon's great houses were the homes of privileged families who were able to predict the movements of heavenly bodies and control ritual activity.

In Judge's scenario, the roads were pilgrimage and trading walkways. However, archaeologist John Roney, of the U.S. Bureau of Land Management, points out that there are no signs of domestic rubbish or encampments along the roads. On the ground, he has followed many of the fuzzy lines on air photographs, verifying more than 60 road segments, many of them short and without specific destination. Roney is certain that major north and south tracks radiated from Chaco, but he is cautious about joining segments into long lines uniting distant places on the map. He is sure of a mere 250 kilometers (155 miles) of roads and believes that the Chacoans constructed the walkways as monuments, as a ritual gesture, not to be used.

Do roads have to lead to a destination, as we Westerners always believe? The answer to the Chaco road mystery may lie not in the archaeological record, but in Pueblo Indian cosmology. The so-called Great North Road is a case in point. Several roadways from the "great houses" of Pueblo Bonito and Chetro Ketl ascend Chaco's north wall to converge on Pueblo Alto, a pueblo above the canyon. From there, the Great North Road travels 13 degrees east of north for about 3 kilometers (2 miles) before heading due north for nearly 50 kilometers (30 miles) across open country to Kutz Canyon, where it vanishes. North is the primary direction in the mythology of modern-day Keresan-speaking Pueblo peoples, who may have ancestry among Chaco communities. North led to the place of origin, the place where the spirits of the dead went. Chaco's Great North Road may have been an umbilical cord to the underworld, a conduit of spiritual power. Another Pueblo concept, that of the Middle Place, was the point where the four cardinal directions converged. Pueblo Bonito, with its cardinal layout, may have been the Middle Place.

The great houses and trackways of Chaco Canyon may have formed a sacred landscape, a symbolic stage where the Ancestral Pueblo acted out their beliefs and commemorated the passage of seasons. Fortunately, new scientific technologies such as geographic information systems are combining multispectrum imagery, color infrared photographs, and 1930s halftone images. By enhancing different light, heat, and vegetational conditions, fieldworkers can go into the field with information on hitherto invisible features, locating themselves on the ground with the satellite-driven Global Positioning System, which can fix their position within a meter or two. New survey work is establishing the true extent of Chacoan roads and placing them in a precise topographical context.

It is hard for us to reconstruct the intangible religious beliefs of the remote past, separated as we are from them by many centuries. Just how hard can be imagined by listening to modern-day storytellers as they recite well-known tales to an audience that has heard them over and over, but never tires of the stories and their morals. Brian has heard Pueblo Indian storytellers recite from memory, face to face with their audiences, often for as long as an hour at a time, holding their listeners spellbound with tales that bind living people to the world of the Sun and Moon, of humanlike animals and plants. The plots twist and turn, with heroes, terrifying hazards, and tests of skill and wisdom. Almost invariably, the tales involve deeply felt religious beliefs and the spiritual world. Only a fraction of these tales survive into modern times, lovingly transcribed, edited, and translated as a permanent record of a vanishing world. Many tell of the Sun, whose powers of warmth and light sustained life itself. One Hopi tale recounts how a young man was conceived by the Sun and journeyed to visit his father. After many adventures, including a journey across the heavens, he returned happy: "I saw for myself how he attends to our needs every single day of our lives. Therefore we must live out our lives in a good manner, and he will never forsake us" (Swann 1994, 678).

Fortunately, a new generation of archaeological research is beginning to study the fascinating and complex world of the intangible.

Summary

- Archaeologists study the religious beliefs of ancient societies by using material remains and information from a variety of sources.
- Many ancient religions shared common features: a multilayered cosmos, a cyclical existence, important locations that were axes of the world, and a concern with ancestors and shamanism.
- Ethnographic analogy plays an important role in studying ancient rock art, thanks to anthropological research among the San of southern Africa a century ago.
- Richly adorned burials can provide information on religious beliefs as well as social ranking, but the major source of such information comes from art and artifacts. The context of artifacts in time and space is of vital importance, as context can often reveal more information than the objects themselves.
- Rigorous studies of art styles, such as that of the Moche of Peru or the Maya, can yield valuable information on ancient ideologies, especially if combined with ethnographic or written records.
- Sacred places such as Cahokia in Illinois, medieval cathedrals, or Maya cities were vital catalysts for religious beliefs, for they were the settings for rituals of validation and other ceremonies.
- Settlement archaeology plays an important role in studying such locations in the context of their wider landscape. So does astroarchaeology, the study of ancient astronomy, notably successful in the American Southwest, at Stonehenge in England, and with the Maya civilization.

Key Terms and Sites

Shang civilization
Anyang
Altamira
Sutton Hoo
Hopewell tradition
Phylakopi
ideology
Moche state
ethnohistory
Cahokia
astroarchaeology
Hovenweep
Chaco Phenomenon

Critical-Thinking Questions

1. "Shamans and shamanistic rituals played an important role in ancient societies." Discuss what you know about shamanism, and assess whether you agree with the statement in quotes.
2. Discuss what is meant by a "sacred place." What sacred places do you have firsthand experience of, and how do they differ from places like Stonehenge or Chaco Canyon?
3. Why do you think that the commemoration of death is so important to human societies? Are there differences between how we handle death and how the ancients dealt with it? What and how do we know about such practices?

Further Reading

The ancient intangible: B. Fagan, *From Black Land to Fifth Sun* (Reading, MA: Perseus, 1998). L. Schele and D. Friedel, *A Forest of Kings* (New York: William Morrow, 1991) is a popular if sometimes controversial account of Maya civilization that covers religion, iconography, and social ranking. The same authors' *Maya Cosmos* (New York: William Morrow, 1993) is an informative sequel. The best set of essays on the whole area of the intangible appears under the title "What Is Cognitive Archaeology?" in the *Cambridge Archaeological Journal* 3 (2) (1993): 247–270. Several archaeologists are now questioning the notion of shamanism as a sort of primordial religion, or as an explanation for the prehistoric rock art, see for example, D. Gheorghiu et al., eds., *Archaeological Approaches to Shamanism* (Newcastle Upon Tyne: Cambridge Scholars Publishing, 2017) or see Anne Solomon, "The Death of Trance: Recent Perspectives on San Ethnographies and Rock Art" in *Antiquity* 87 (338) (2013): 1208–1213. Thomas Wynn and Frederick L. Coolidge have also written *An Introduction to Evolutionary Cognitive Archaeology* (Oxford: Routledge, 2022), a very readable primer on hominin cognitive evolution.

7 Explaining the Past

Chapter Outline

King Ashurbanipal of Assyria rides out on a lion hunt in his chariot, as depicted in a bas-relief from Nineveh, Iraq, dating to the seventh century B.C. His attendants fend off an attacking lion.
Source: World History Archive/Alamy Stock Photo.

Brian once excavated a deep, 1,000-year-old Central African village that had occupied the same site for more than 400 years. The inhabitants had settled on a low ridge overlooking rolling woodland and open clearings, where their cattle had grazed. After four centuries of occupation, the settlement lay atop a mound of occupation debris more than 90 meters (295 feet) across and 3 meters (10 feet) deep. Brian and his team dug through

DOI: 10.4324/9781003592754-9

stratified hearths and collapsed houses and collected thousands of decorated potsherds and animal-bone fragments. As far as they could tell from the stratigraphy, the village—a cluster of thatched huts and cattle enclosures surrounded by a thorn fence to keep out lions, which had abounded in the area until modern times—had been occupied more or less continuously.

The portrait of the village seemed simple until Brian unpacked the pottery and animal bones back in the laboratory. After sorting the artifacts and recording the undecorated pot fragments, he laid out the decorated pieces from each layer on a large table. Startling differences caught his attention at once. The earliest inhabitants had used well-made, thick-walled pots adorned with coarse, stamped decoration. However, as time went on, the village potters changed their style. Over three centuries, their vessels became rounder and thinner, with decoration confined to a single cord-like band just below the lip. A thousand years ago, there was another change: everyone started using bag-like pots with out-turned rims, which could only have been used for carrying liquids.

While he puzzled over these remarkable changes, Brian turned his attention to the animal bones. Again, dramatic differences emerged over the centuries. The earliest villagers kept cattle and goats but relied heavily on game meat. They hunted small antelope, which still flourish near the site, and occasionally larger animals such as the kudu. However, as the centuries passed, the people began to rely more and more on cattle and goats, to the point that hunting became unimportant. Interestingly, the bag-like pots of the upper layers coincided with a sudden increase in cattle bones.

A straightforward, long-occupied settlement turned out to be much more complex than Brian had imagined. How could he explain the changes in pottery styles and cattle herding over four centuries? Had different cultural groups settled at the site one after the other? Or did the sequence merely reflect a process of gradual cultural change among people who had lived in the same region for many generations and relied more and more on cattle? The jury remains out, and it is still unclear why the village's culture changed so profoundly over the course of four centuries.

So far, we have discussed the ways in which archaeologists recover and analyze sites and artifacts—the archaeological record. This chapter describes some of the ways by which people try to explain prehistory. This is a particularly important chapter because it provides theoretical background for the narrative of human prehistory, which begins in Chapter 8.

Culture History

descriptive (inductive) research methods The development of generalizations about a research problem based on numerous specific observations on artifacts and other finds.

normative view of culture A view of human culture arguing that one can identify the abstract rules regulating a particular culture; a commonly used basis for studying archaeological cultures through time.

As was discussed in Chapter 2, culture history describes human cultures in the past and is based on the chronological and spatial ordering of archaeological data. Culture history depends on scientific observations of the archaeological record in time and space—on artifacts and other data from one or many sites. Culture history is based on two fundamental principles: **descriptive (inductive) research methods**, which involve the development of generalizations about a research problem based on numerous specific observations, and a **normative view of culture**, an assumption that abstract rules govern what human societies consider normal behavior. The normative view assumes that surviving artifacts display stylistic and other changes that reflect evolving norms of human behavior over time. It also assumes considerable uniformity within a culture at any time.

The interpretation of culture-historical data depends on analogies from historical and ethnographic data. For instance, when excavating his African village, Brian found some heavily worn iron blades with short tangs. By comparing them with modern equivalents from the same area, he was able to show that they were hoes used to turn the soil before planting.

Most archaeological interpretation begins with the culture-historical approach, for this provides the basic framework in time and space for studying cultural change and explaining the past. In the final analysis, our knowledge of prehistory comes from thousands of local cultural sequences reconstructed in time and space using descriptive and normative approaches. The result is an ever-changing and accumulating synthesis of what happened in the human past that leads to generalizations based on the available data.

Constructing Culture History

Culture-historical construction proceeds in four broad steps that build one on the other to produce a synthesis of a segment of the past in time and space:

1. *Identification of a research area and site survey:* A preliminary stage in which the researcher identifies as many sites as possible and develops a provisional chronology based on the ordering of surface artifacts.
2. *Excavation:* Carefully selected excavations designed to test the validity of the sequence and to refine and expand it as well. The digs may proceed at several sites and recover houses or even complete settlement layouts, but their primary focus is always on stratigraphic observation and recording of occupation layers and developing relative and absolute chronologies.
3. *Artifact analysis:* Laboratory analysis and classification of the database of artifacts and structures to refine preliminary classifications and chronologies that were put together before digging began.
4. *Synthesis:* Comparing and contrasting the cultural sequences from different sites into a broader synthesis, using such methods as artifact ordering and cross-dating (see Chapter 3).

Synthesis

The basis of all culture-historical reconstruction is a precise and carefully described site chronology. The synthesis of such chronologies beyond the narrow confines of a single site or local area involves repeating the same descriptive process at other sites and also constantly refining the cultural sequence from the original excavations. The resulting synthesis is cumulative, for some new excavations may yield cultural materials that are not represented in the early digs. This is, of course, an entirely descriptive process that yields no explanations whatsoever.

In the case of the aforementioned African village, Brian discovered about a dozen similar settlements within a 50-kilometer (30-mile) radius. Were they all occupied at the same time? Did similar cultural changes unfold at all of them? Were some abandoned before others came into use? Unfortunately, his team did not have the funds or the time to survey or excavate all the sites, but a colleague had excavated what appeared to be a similar but smaller settlement about 16 kilometers (10 miles) away. So Brian sank a small trench into this site to obtain larger pottery samples and seriated the two cultural sequences. Both radiocarbon dates and a "fit" between the two pottery series showed that the smaller site had been abandoned about a century before the inhabitants of the original site had developed a fashion for bag-shaped vessels and had relied almost entirely on cattle for meat. If a team were to return to the area, they would certainly be able to develop a highly detailed cultural sequence for this locale. However, this sequence would tell absolutely nothing about the reasons why individual villages were occupied or abandoned, or why the cultures that lived there changed so much.

A Hierarchy of Archaeological Units

The database from the archaeological record consists of artifacts, structures, food remains, and other information. Artifacts and structures are the objects of primary interest to a culture historian, for they provide often sensitive barometers for correlating cultural sequences from many sites. All culture history depends on artifact classifications and on the grouping of artifact complexes into increasingly larger units that transcend space and time. It is a site-oriented procedure, an exercise of classification in time and space.

Archaeologists use a series of arbitrary time-space units to help in the process of culture-historical construction. This hierarchy of archaeological units developed in a somewhat haphazard fashion in the early days of archaeology, but was standardized in its present general form for the Americas by archaeologists Gordon Willey and Philip Phillips in 1958. Such units represent the combining of the formal contents of one or more sites with their distribution in time and space. For instance, a deep cave in Missouri contains six occupation levels, each with its own distinctive artifact assemblages, which have been sorted into different types (for a discussion of types, see Chapter 4). A dozen nearby sites have yielded examples of these comparable six layers. What arbitrary units can we use to compare these various sites and occupation levels with their different contents? The hierarchy of archaeological units proceeds from artifacts and artifact assemblages (defined in Chapter 2) to components and phases and then to regions and culture areas (see Figure 7.1 and Box 7.1).

components All the artifacts from one occupation level at a site.

phases Archaeological units defined by characteristic groupings of cultural traits that can be identified precisely in time and space, that last for a relatively short time and are found at one or more sites in a locality or region, and that have cultural traits that are clear enough to distinguish one phase from other phases.

La Madeleine, France Rock shelter near Les Eyzies, Dordogne, where early traces of the Magdalenian culture were discovered.

regions Areas defined by natural geographic boundaries that display some cultural homogeneity.

culture areas Arbitrary geographic or research areas in which general cultural homogeneity is found.

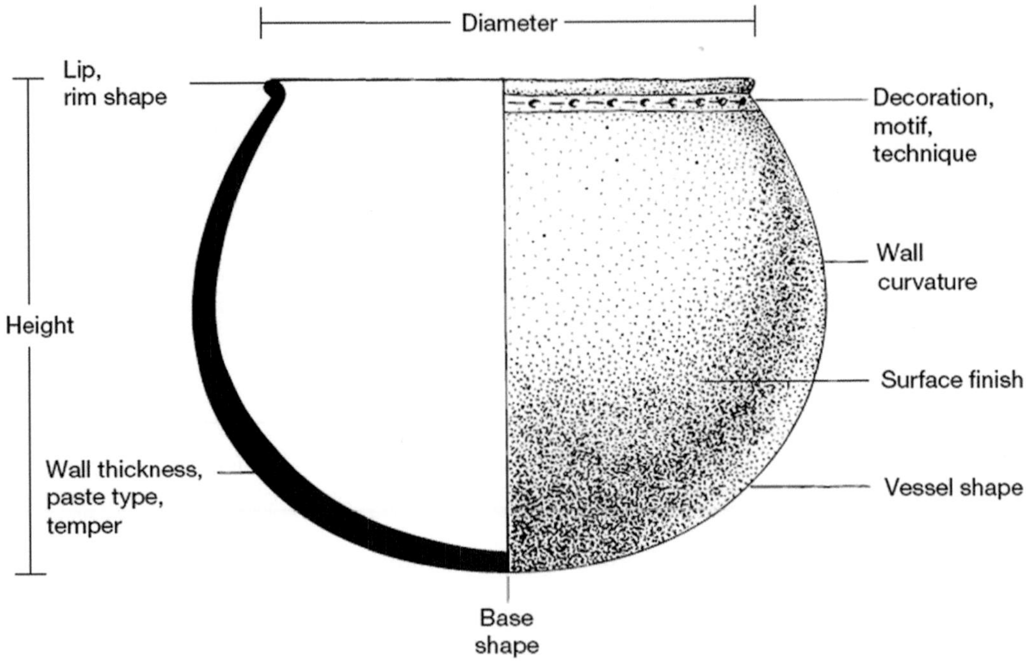

Figure 7.1 A pot from the Isamu Pati mound, Zambia, showing its major attributes. Figure 7.2 Thor Heyerdahl's Kon-Tiki raft in 1947, in which he sailed from Peru to Polynesia. His theories are now rejected.

horizons Widely distributed sets of culture traits and artifact assemblages whose distribution and chronology allow researchers to assume that they spread rapidly; often formed of artifacts that were associated with widespread, distinctive religious beliefs.

traditions Persistent technological or cultural patterns identified by characteristic artifact forms that outlast a single phase and occur over a wide area.

Clovis tradition Widespread Paleo-Indian tradition associated with very early settlement throughout North America, dating to 13,050–12,750 years ago.

Descriptive Models of Cultural Change

Back at his African mound village, Brian completed the classification and analysis of thousands of potsherds, iron tools, and animal-bone fragments. Four hundred years of significant cultural change measured by these finds lay in front of him on the laboratory table. The pottery styles changed from relatively coarse vessels to much finer wares, culminating in the globular vessels that accompanied a dramatic increase in cattle bones. Now the question of questions: How did these changes come about? Was it from continuous cultural change among people who settled in the same general area for four centuries? Or had successive groups arrived from outside and settled on an abandoned village site where nitrogen-rich soils yielded nice crops? At this point, he turned to two widely used descriptive models of cultural change—inevitable variation and cultural selection; and to three classic processes of change—invention, diffusion, and migration.

Box 7.1 Doing Archaeology
A Hierarchy of Archaeological Entities

Components occur at one location, the physically bounded portions of a site that contain a distinct assemblage, which serves to distinguish the culture of the inhabitants of a particular land. For example, many rock shelters in southwestern France contain multiple occupation levels separated by sterile layers, which can be distinguished one from another by their artifact content.

Phases are cultural units represented by similar components at different sites or at separate levels of the same site, although always within a well-defined chronological span. The assemblages of artifacts characteristic of a phase may be found over hundreds of square kilometers within the area covered by a local sequence. Phases can endure for a few years or centuries and include numerous subphases or components, each dated to short periods of time with its own characteristic artifacts.

Many archaeologists use the term culture in the same sense as phase. Phases or cultures are usually named after a key site where characteristic artifacts are found. For example, the late Ice Age Magdalenian culture of 16,000 years ago is named after the southwestern French rock shelter of **La Madeleine,** where the antler harpoons and other artifacts so characteristic of this culture were found (see Chapter 10).

Archaeological **regions** are normally defined by natural geographic boundaries and display some cultural homogeneity: for example, the Ohio valley or southern Mesopotamia.

Archaeological **culture areas** define much larger areas of land and often coincide with broad ethnographic culture areas identified by early anthropologists. The North American Southwest is a classic example of a culture area, defined by a century of research and by cultural and environmental associations that endured for more than 2,000 years.

Two other terms that follow are in common use in the Americas.

Horizons link a number of phases in neighboring areas that have general cultural patterns in common. For instance, an all-embracing religious cult may transcend cultural boundaries and spread over enormous areas. The distinctive Chavín art style and its associated religious beliefs spread widely over the highland and lowland Andean region between 900 and 200 B.C.—hence the term Early Horizon in Peruvian prehistory (see Chapter 16).

Traditions define artifact types, assemblages of tools, architectural styles, economic practices, or art styles that last much longer than one phase or even the duration of a horizon. For instance, the celebrated **Clovis tradition** of North America originated over 13,000 years ago. The tools were so effective that they were used across a wide area.

Inevitable Variation

As people learn the basic behavioral patterns of their societies, inevitably some minor differences in learned behavior appear from generation to generation. Although minor in themselves, these differences accumulate over a long period of time in a snowball effect called **inevitable variation**. For instance, after 1.8 million years ago, ancient humans in Africa developed a form of stone hand ax, with rough edges and a crude point, for butchering game and other uses (see Figure 9.6 on p. 289). This highly effective multipurpose tool spread over much of Africa, Europe, and southern Asia over the next million years. Hundreds of small, isolated forager bands used the same tool and developed hand axes to a high degree of refinement. By 150,000 to 100,000 years ago, inevitable variation among isolated populations produced great variations in hand-ax design in Europe and Africa.

Inevitable variation Cumulative culture change due to minor differences in learned behavior over time.

cultural selection Process that leads to the acceptance of some culture traits and innovations that make a culture more adaptive to its environment; somewhat akin to natural selection in biological evolution.

Cultural Selection

Cultural selection is somewhat akin to the well-known process of natural selection in biological evolution. Human societies accept and reject new ideas, whether technological, economic, or intangible, on the basis of whether they are advantageous to society as a whole. Like inevitable variation, cultural selection leads to cumulative cultural change and operates within the prevailing values of the society in general. For instance, the great civilizations of Mesopotamia and Mexico resulted from centuries of gradual social evolution, throughout which centralized political organization seemed advantageous.

invention New ideas that originate in a human culture by accident or design.

Invention

We live in a world that honors inventors, people who think up truly new ideas that can change our lives. The electric light bulb, the transistor, and the computer are three examples. An **invention** implies either the modification of an old idea or series of ideas or the creation of a completely new concept either by accident or by intentional research. The atom was split after long and deliberate experimentation aimed at such an objective. Fire was probably tamed over 1.5 million years ago by accident. Inventions spread, and if they are sufficiently important, as the plow certainly was, they spread rapidly and widely.

Over a century ago, Victorian scientists believed that farming, metallurgy, and other major innovations were invented in only one place and then spread all over the world. But now that we understand the great importance of environment in the past, we realize that many inventions were not the work of solitary geniuses, but the result of complex, interacting pressures such as climate change, rising population densities, and fundamental social change that occurred in many places. For instance, agriculture was developed independently in southwestern Asia, southern China, Mesoamerica, and the Andes.

diffusion The spread of ideas over short or long distances.

Diffusion

Inventions and ideas spread. **Diffusion** is the process by which new ideas or cultural traits spread from one person or group to another, often over long distances. Back in the early twentieth century, British anatomist and amateur Egyptologist Elliot Grafton Smith, famous for his pioneering X-rays of Egyptian mummies, became obsessed with Sun worship along the Nile. He wrote a series of widely read books in which he proclaimed that Egyptian "children of the Sun" voyaged all over the world from their Nile homeland, carrying the arts of civilization, pyramid building, and Sun worship with them. Smith's simplistic theories and others of this ilk are long discredited, for the vast quantities of archaeological data from all parts of the world show his ideas to be ludicrous. However, diffusion is an important mechanism of cultural change that is hard to identify from archaeological remains.

Had Brian wished to invoke diffusion as a factor in "his" mound village, he would have had to identify, say, a distinctive pottery type that suddenly appeared at a highly specific moment in the 400-year sequence. This would be just the first step. He would then have had to identify similar potsherds in neighboring sites and those at a greater distance, and then have had to study the site distribution and date each occurrence of the fragments so that he could identify not only the moment the vessels appeared at each site, but also a chronological gradient for diffusion from a place of origin. In any event, there were no clay vessel forms that were distinctive enough to warrant such an inquiry, and it is questionable whether he would have been able to identify the process of diffusion.

We know that ideas and technologies spread by word of mouth and from hand to hand, but this process is very hard to identify in the archaeological record.

Migration

In 1947, Norwegian explorer and archaeologist Thor Heyerdahl electrified the world with a courageous voyage across the eastern Pacific from Peru to Polynesia in the balsa raft *Kon-Tiki*, a replica of an ancient Andean raft. Heyerdahl undertook his passage to prove that Peruvians colonized Polynesia in prehistoric times. His successful ocean journey showed that a balsa raft could reach Polynesia on the wings of the prevailing trade winds, but it certainly did not prove that ancient Peruvians migrated by sea to the heart of the Pacific. Seventy years of research since the voyage have not revealed a single Peruvian artifact anywhere in Polynesia. Few people accept Heyerdahl's theory today (Figure 7.2).

migration The deliberate movement of people from one area to another.

Migration, however, is the process of deliberate settlement, when entire populations, large or small, decide to move into a new area. Migration can be peaceful or the result of military invasion and conquest. For migration to be identified in the archaeological record, an archaeologist needs to find local sequences in which the phases show a complete disruption of earlier cultural patterns by an intrusive new phase with a completely new tool kit or lifeway, even if some earlier culture traits survived and were integrated into the new culture.

Classic examples of migration in prehistory abound, among them the first settlement of the Americas and Australia. Perhaps the best known is the colonization of Polynesia, not from the east but from the west, by open-water voyagers in double-hulled canoes, starting about 3,000 years ago. The voyagers who colonized Tahiti, remote Easter Island

Figure 7.2 Thor Heyerdahl's *Kon-Tiki* raft in 1947, in which he sailed from Peru to Polynesia. His theories are now rejected.
Source: 914 collection/Alamy.

(Rapa Nui), and Hawaii did so as acts of deliberate exploration and set out with intentions of returning (see Figure 7.3; see also Chapter 11). In this case, carefully excavated sites and radiocarbon dates document a process of colonization that proceeded over many centuries, identified by pottery styles with close relationships to those used on the western Pacific islands.

Nguni people, South Africa Offshoot of the Zulu people of South Africa, who spread widely northward into Zimbabwe and eastern Zambia in the early nineteenth century A.D.

There are other types of migration, too. For instance, the Mexican city of Teotihuacán accepted entire colonies of merchants from the Valley of Oaxaca and other distant places because they were of economic advantage to the metropolis. Artisans and slaves wandered as unorganized migrants, as did seamen, accounting for the great and often unsuspected diversity of many early cities, among them imperial Rome. Finally, there were the great warrior migrations of the past, such as those of eastern nomads in Europe and of the warlike **Nguni people** of South Africa, who raided and settled as far north as eastern Zambia.

Construction of culture history is a complex descriptive process that needs large quantities of well-dated finds to be effective. In the end, the changes in the cultural sequence at

Figure 7.3 Tahitian war canoes depicted by John Webber, artist on Captain James Cook's first expedition, 1769.

Source: Granger Collection.

"Brian's" African mound left him somewhat challenged. He concluded that the pottery style and economic changes were the result of cultural selection among people living in an environment ideal for cattle herding and subsistence agriculture. But he never took his investigation further, for the explanation of cultural process requires far more complex models based on quite different approaches to archaeology—models that were not in existence when he published his excavations.

Analogy

analogy A process of reasoning whereby two entities that share some similarities are assumed to share many others.

The very first models of prehistoric times came from the work of nineteenth-century anthropologists such as the Englishman Edward Tylor and the American Lewis Morgan. Fervent believers in evolutionary doctrines, they thought of ancient and living human societies as involved continually in the process of acquiring ever-greater complexity. They and their disciples felt comfortable making direct comparisons between living societies such as the Eskimo of the Arctic and late Ice Age peoples who lived in France 16,000 years ago, on the grounds that these groups were at the same stage of development and thus enjoyed close cultural similarities. Such comparisons, or analogies, to use the common archaeological term, have long been abandoned, as they are far too simplistic. Nevertheless, **analogy** plays a vital role in archaeology, for it infers that the relationships among various traces of human activity found in the archaeological record are like those of similar phenomena found among modern "primitive" cultures.

Archaeologists use analogy in several ways, but they are always aware that the past cannot be explained simply with reference to the present, for to do so is to assume that nothing new has been learned by generations of people and that the past was the same as, or not much different from, the present.

Martin's Hundred, Virginia Colonial settlement of the early 1620s on the shore of the Chesapeake Bay.

Historical analogies work from the known to the unknown, from living peoples with written records to their ancestors for whom we have no written records. A classic example comes from **Martin's Hundred,** a tiny settlement in colonial Virginia (see Box 7.2).

Historical records also provide valuable analogies when they describe the customs and societies of nonliterate cultures with which they came into contact. The Roman general Julius Caesar, who conquered Gaul (present-day France), left valuable accounts of

Box 7.2 Classic Archaeological Detective Work Martin's Hundred, Virginia

Historical archaeology sometimes fills in long-forgotten details of the past, when used in conjunction with often sparse written records. Ivor Noël Hume was a brilliant excavator and archaeological detective, who used both archaeological and often obscure historical records to reconstruct the life and death of Wolstenholme Towne, a tiny colonial settlement near Williamsburg, Virginia. The inhabitants had built a palisaded fort for protection against the local Indians and also the Spaniards. On March 22, 1622, a surprise Indian attack destroyed the village and most of the outlying farms. From 1976 to 1981, Noël Hume and his excavators in a now-classic excavation unraveled a jigsaw puzzle of postholes, graves, and garbage pits. There were few written records of the fort itself, but the team consulted sources such as Virginia court archives to interpret their finds. The Martin's Hundred houses were defined by posthole patterns and large pits. Noël Hume came across a description of housing from the Dutch city of New Amsterdam, now New York, which revealed that poor farmers dwelt in pit houses with the roof eaves resting on the ground. Such was apparently the case at Martin's Hundred.

The excavators found some short strands of gold and silver wire in the earth-fill of one of the houses. Each was as thick as a sewing thread, the kind of wire used in the early seventeenth century for decorating clothing. Noël Hume turned to historical records for analogies. He found European paintings showing military captains wearing clothes adorned with gold and silver wire. He also located a resolution of the Virginia governor and his council in 1621 forbidding "any but ye Council and heads of hundreds to wear gold in their cloaths (*sic*)" (Noël Hume 1982, 216).

William Harwood, the head administrator of Martin's Hundred, had signed the resolution, so the property could have been his. When a cannon ball came to light in the house, the identification was conclusive, for Harwood was shown in a 1625 document to be the only person owning "a piece of Ordnance."

The Martin's Hundred excavations reconstructed a vanished settlement from a network of supporting evidence—centuries-old artwork, museum pieces, and even items from shipwreck. For example, at Graz in Austria, Noël Hume found helmets identical to fragmentary examples at Martin's Hundred. The Austrians had used them against the Ottoman Turks. The colonists at Martin's Hundred found them too cumbersome for protection against nimble Indian attackers. Even a grisly English murder in 1979 helped, when a skull of a Wolstenholme victim bore marks identical to those on a modern victim killed by his wife with a garden spade.

the warlike Gauls in his *Commentaries*. British navigator Captain James Cook's accounts of Tahitian society are a valuable source of information about Polynesian culture at the time of European contact. The scripts of early civilizations like those of the Egyptians and the Maya provide critical information about the identities of rulers or even about religious practices (see Box 7.3).

Waka, a Guatemalan Maya center, was founded in c. 500 B.C. and was at the height of its importance between A.D. 400 and 800.

stelae (sing., stela) Commemorative columns or uprights.

Box 7.3 Discovery
A Tale of Three Maya Superwomen: Waka, Guatemala

Guatemalan archaeologist Héctor Escobedo and his American colleague David Freidel are excavating and conserving an important Maya center known as **Waka** (modern El Péru), 60 kilometers (37 miles) west of the great city of Tikal in northern Guatemala. Waka was once an important economic and political center of the Maya world, with 672 monumental structures and numerous dwellings. The site was founded as early as 500 B.C. and reached its peak between A.D. 400 and 800. At least 22 kings ruled over the city during its long existence. More than 40 carved **stelae** record the rulers, their conquests, and their deaths.

The excavations have studied the large ceremonial complex in the southeastern part of the city and investigated numerous ritual sites. The main palace compound, where the rulers once lived, also served as a royal burial place. In 2004, archaeologist David Lee uncovered a royal burial chamber containing the burial of a female ruler or queen surrounded by 2,400 artifacts. She was interred in a vaulted burial chamber built inside the shell of an existing building between A.D. 650 and 750. She lay with greenstone artifacts, shell ornaments, and obsidian. A series of greenstone plaques formed a war helmet of a type associated with supreme Maya warlords. She wore a carved royal jade or *huunal* that may once have been part of this headdress. Stingray spines traditionally used in royal bloodletting rites lay on her pelvis.

In 2005, Michelle Rich and Jennifer Piehl excavated into a stone shrine midway up the face of a pyramid. They broke into a vaulted chamber where two elite-status women lay. The women were in excellent health and between 25 and 35 years of age. Buried at the same time, they lay one on top of the other, as if they were sacrificial victims, perhaps the attendants of an important royal personage. Seven fine pots associated with the women date to about A.D. 350, one with a lid bearing three royal crowns. Escobedo and Freidel believe the victims were sacrificed as part of the dedication of a stairway shrine or during the accession ceremonies of a new ruler. In some Maya art, two nude women are shown assisting the resurrection of the maize god. Freidel believes the two stacked bodies may represent the helpers of the maize god.

Ongoing excavations at Waka revealed yet a third important woman. Thus in 2012, David Freidel found the late seventh-century A.D. body of a Maya queen, likely Lady K'abel who governed the Wak kingdom for her family. She was buried with an array of grave goods, including ceramic vessels, stone figurines, and jade jewelry.

However, the effectiveness of direct historical analogies such as these diminishes rapidly the further back in time you venture, for human cultures everywhere change constantly in response to many factors.

Many archaeological analogies are at a simple level. For example, researchers working on the North American plains have inferred that small, pointed pieces of stone were projectile points because there are ethnographic records of people making small, pointed pieces of stone for spear and arrow tips. Such objects have also been found embedded in the bones of both animals and people, so the general analogy is secure. Such analogies are obvious enough, but they are a far cry from claiming that both the ancient and modern societies used the projectile point in exactly the same way.

functionalism The notion that a social institution within a society has a function in fulfilling all the needs of a social organism.

Functionalism is an important school of thought in anthropology. It argues that cultures are not made up of random selections of culture traits, but that such traits are integrated in various ways and influence each other in fairly predictable ways. This line of thinking appeals to archaeologists, who think of cultures as systems of interacting subsystems, in turn, interacting with the ecosystem. Six thousand years ago, Great Basin peoples used nicely made fiber sandals and moccasins, which survive in dry cave deposits. The same footwear was also popular among other historical groups (see Figure 7.4).

However, the functionalist approach fosters other questions, such as the following: Were sandals made by men or women? Were they made by individuals on their own initiative or by people working in groups? We turn to the ethnographic literature and find that Australian Aborigines and the !Kung of the Kalahari Desert use sandals, which are usually made by women working alone or with one or two helpers. On this basis, we might argue that Great Basin sandal making was a domestic task carried out by women. But Pueblo men in the American Southwest weave in special ceremonial rooms, and because much ritual performed there reflects very ancient Pueblo Indian practices, we might infer that Great Basin peoples

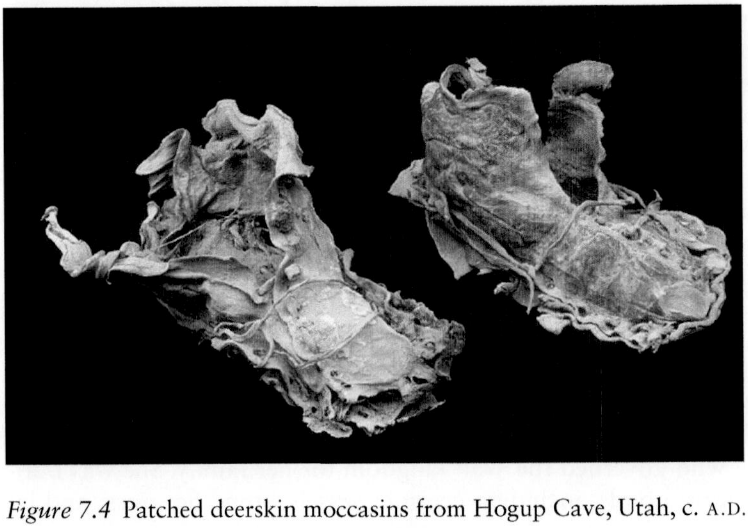

Figure 7.4 Patched deerskin moccasins from Hogup Cave, Utah, c. A.D. 500.
Source: Francois Gohier/Photo Researchers.

did not regard weaving as a domestic task 6,000 years ago, so it must have been carried out by men. No matter which alternative we choose, we cannot have much confidence in our choice. That is, we have not directly evaluated the data at hand.

ethnographic analogy Analysis of living societies to aid in understanding and interpreting the archaeological record.

Ethnographic analogy is only the first step in the inquiry. In the case of the Great Basin sandals, archaeologists would take the two conflicting analogies back to the field. They would develop implications to be tested against the archaeological data:

- If sandal making were a domestic task carried out by women, one would expect to find the raw materials for sandal manufacture associated with tools that may represent women's work, such as grinding stones for food preparation.
- If men made the sandals as a ritual activity, one would anticipate finding the same raw materials in different settings, perhaps in a special area of the settlement associated with known ceremonial artifacts such as dance rattles.

Such testing requires large quantities of data, sophisticated excavation and recording, and advanced analytical tools, including statistical tests. Nonetheless, ethnographic analogy often provides the raw material for letting the present serve the past.

Archaeology by Observation and Experiment

The present is alive and dynamic; the archaeological record of the past is static and has been so since it ceased to be part of the culture that created it. To understand and explain the past, we must comprehend the relationship between static, material properties common to both past and present and the long-extinct dynamic properties of the past.

Ethnoarchaeology

ethnoarchaeology The study of living societies to aid in the interpretation of ancient ones.

Ethnoarchaeology is the study of living societies to aid in understanding and interpreting the archaeological record. By living in, say, an Australian Aborigine camp and watching the activities of its occupants, the archaeologist hopes to record archaeologically observable patterns, knowing what activities brought them into existence. Ethnoarchaeology goes far beyond simple observations of artifact scatters or the surveying of recently excavated !Kung San campsites in the Kalahari Desert to record tool and animal-bone patterns as a basis for interpreting far earlier sites. In fact, such research deals with the dynamic processes of human behavior in the modern world.

Hadza people, Tanzania East African group who still live by hunting and plant gathering.

Since 1984, James O'Connell of the University of Utah and his colleagues have recorded more than 70 incidents of large-mammal butchery by hunter-gatherers among the **Hadza people** in East Africa (see Figure 7.5). The Hadza hunt animals when they encounter them and also ambush their prey from specially constructed blinds near waterholes in the late dry season. They are determined hunters, tracking wounded quarry for hours, even days. They also scavenge meat from predator kills at every opportunity. O'Connell records kill rates for a single camp: 70–80 large animals a year, or about 1 animal killed for every 40 to 60 days of hunting, with scavenging accounting for about 10–15 percent of the total. The researchers were mainly interested in time allocation, food choice, and food-sharing activities, so they routinely recorded site location, distance from residential bases, method of acquiring the prey, carcass condition, details of the butchery, and the sexes and ages of the people involved. In addition, they collected comprehensive "archaeological" data from each location, when possible, including the positions of broken bones and abandoned artifacts.

The Hadza research casts serious doubt on many of the assumptions made by archaeologists about ancient hunter-gatherer kill sites. O'Connell's team found that 75–80 percent of the Hadza's large-mammal prey were underrepresented in their bone samples, by virtue of the people's hunting and butchering practices. Most prehistoric kill sites have been excavated on a small scale, whereas many Hadza butchery sites occupy a large area, through which the hunters scatter the bones, often in the process of finding shade in which to work. Furthermore, the disarticulation of bones follows a similar pattern whether carnivores or humans are at work—the limbs first, then the backbone, with differences being more the result of individual animal anatomy than deliberate cultural choice.

Figure 7.5 Ethnoarchaeology in action: Recording details of a modern hunter's kill among the Hadza of Tanzania, East Africa, can shed light on the actions of past hunter-gatherers in the region.

Source: Travel Africa/Alamy Stock Photo.

Nunamiut people, Alaska Modern Alaskan hunters who prey on seasonal migrations of caribou.

In another famous ethnoarchaeological study, Lewis Binford studied caribou hunting among the **Nunamiut people** of Alaska in a research project that involved meticulous recording of butchery procedures and archaeological sites. He found that the hunters behaved absolutely rationally in their exploitation of caribou in spring and fall, taking full account of the vagaries of the local environment and logistical considerations. They had an encyclopedic knowledge of caribou anatomy and were utterly pragmatic in their approach to hunting. All these factors resulted in a great variety of archaeological sites and profound differences in artifact frequencies among them.

In other words, archaeology is about ancient human behavior, not changing percentages of artifacts and animal bones!

Experimental Archaeology

Controlled experiments with precise replicas of prehistoric artifacts and with ancient technologies offer fruitful sources of data for studying cultural dynamics. Such research began in the eighteenth century, when people tried to blow the spectacular bronze horns unearthed from peat bogs in Scandinavia and Britain. One ardent experimenter, Robert Ball of Dublin, Ireland, blew an Irish horn so hard that he was able to produce a deep bass note that resembled a bull's bellow. Sadly, a later experiment with a trumpet caused him to burst a blood vessel, and he died several days later. Ball is the only recorded casualty of experimental archaeology, which has become an important part of interpretation by analogy.

experimental archaeology Conducting controlled experiments with ancient technologies and other methods to provide a basis for interpreting ancient human behavior.

Most **experimental archaeology** is confined to replicating ancient technologies, such as stone toolmaking, pot-making techniques, or traditional metallurgies. Louis Leakey, the archaeologist of Olduvai Gorge fame, trained himself to become an expert fabricator of stone axes and other Stone Age tools. Another lithic expert, rancher Don Crabtree of Idaho, spent 40 years experimenting with the manufacture of North American Paleo-Indian projectile points. He managed to replicate the distinctive "flute" or thinning flake at the base of the well-known Paleo-Indian Clovis and Folsom points (see Figure 2.1 on p. 38). Crabtree also learned of descriptions by early Spanish friars of how Native American stoneworkers used chest punches to remove dozens of thin, parallel-sided blades from cylindrical pieces of obsidian (volcanic glass). When Crabtree had to have eye surgery, he made obsidian blades, which he specified should be used in the surgery; these blades were sharper than the finest surgical steel.

Does the production of an exact replica mean, in fact, that modern experimentation has recovered the original technique? We can never be certain, but lithic experimentation is quite valuable if combined with other analytical approaches, such as refitting flakes on to their original cores or edge-wear analysis (see Chapter 4). Experimental archaeology can rarely give conclusive answers. It can merely provide material for careful analogies or insights into the methods and techniques possibly used in prehistory, for in many cases, such as prehistoric agriculture, many of the behaviors involved have left few traces in the archaeological record. All experimentation is undertaken under controlled conditions, using precisely the same raw materials and the same manufacturing techniques. For instance, there would be no use in conducting an experiment with a carefully replicated prehistoric plow without using plow-trained oxen. The loss of efficiency would be enormous.

Butser, England Modern replica of an Iron Age settlement used to experiment with prehistoric farming methods and technology.

Archaeology by experiment covers a wide range of activities, everything from controlled experiments on forest clearance with stone axes to burning down replicas of ancient dwellings to duplicate foundations for comparison with ancient remains. At **Butser** in southern England, archaeologists have built an Iron Age village as part of a long-term experiment that explores every aspect of Iron Age life. The researchers grow prehistoric cereals using Iron Age technology, keep a selection of livestock that resembles prehistoric breeds, and even store grain underground in sealed pits for long periods without the grain rotting (see Figure 7.6).

Such types of long-term controlled experiments will give archaeologists the objective data they need to understand the static archaeological record as studied in the dynamic present. They will help us to evaluate our ideas about the past and to answer the question of questions: not "what happened?" but "why?"

Figure 7.6 The reconstructed Iron Age village at Butser, England.
Source: AA World Travel Library/Alamy.

Explaining Cultural Change

Culture history and the mechanisms of cultural change give us a global framework for the human past, defined in time and space. Ethnographic analogy and controlled experimentation give us insights into many details of ancient lives. But how do archaeologists explain cultural change in prehistoric times or, for that matter, the lack of change over centuries, even millennia? Why did hunter-gatherers in Syria's Euphrates valley change over from foraging to agriculture 12,000 years ago? What caused widely separated human societies in different parts of the world to make the same changeover in later millennia? Why did some human societies develop into highly complex civilizations while others flourished as simple village societies? These and many other questions about cultural processes have baffled archaeologists for generations. Today's complex theoretical models for explaining such developments as the origins of agriculture stem from more than a century of often passionate debate about theories of cultural change. They also result from an explosion of new scientific methods and from the now routine use of computers to manipulate enormous amounts of raw archaeological data.

Archaeologists have long abandoned models of simple, linear human progress. Instead, they envisage change in the past in terms of increasing complexity. For example, the development of fully articulate speech and the development of logical reasoning were obvious turning points in human prehistory that involved not only changes in the brain, but also complex interactions at the point where the brain and human culture interacted. If ever there was a nonlinear model for change in the past, this is it. British archaeologist Clive Gamble rightly stresses that much change in the past is "the unintended consequence of the complex interaction of biology and culture with which we are all involved" (Gamble 2001, 179). This applies as much to the origins of agriculture as it does to the appearance of language.

Gamble quotes the work of biologist C. H. Waddington, who wrote of how natural selection will tend to replace flexible, adaptive responses to environmental challenges with genetic predispositions. Thus, behavior becomes fixed, giving a degree of stability to a living system. In contrast, humans often create artificial systems with their own checks and balances designed to preserve stability. These include powerful ideologies, careful control of agricultural production and grain storage, and institutions designed to preserve law and order.

What models can we then use to explain the increasing complexity of ancient human societies and such major developments as the beginnings of agriculture and the development of states?

Cultural Systems and Cultural Processes

The modern era of archaeological explanation began during the early 1960s, when Lewis Binford, a young archaeologist trained at the University of Michigan, wrote a series of papers about archaeological theory that sent archaeology along a new theoretical track. Binford stressed the close links between archaeology and ethnography. He pointed out that science was a disciplined and carefully ordered search for knowledge, carried out in a systematic manner. For decades, Binford said, archaeologists had made inferences about archaeological data by simple inductive reasoning, using ethnographic knowledge of modern societies and experiments with such technologies as stone toolmaking as interpretive guides. Binford acknowledged that these methods worked quite well much of the time, but advocated a more explicitly scientific approach, based on deductive reasoning (see Box 7.4).

Box 7.4 Doing Archaeology
Deductive and Inductive Reasoning

Science establishes facts about the natural world by observing objects, events, and phenomena. Archaeologists proceed by using both inductive and deductive reasoning in making their observations.

Inductive reasoning is a relatively simple process that takes specific observations and makes a generalization from them. For example, Brian once found nearly 10,000 wild plant fragments in a 4,000-year-old Stone Age hunter-gatherer camp in Central Africa. More than 42 percent of them were from the bauhinia shrub. The bauhinia flowers from October to February. He learned from an anthropologist colleague that modern-day !Kung San foragers of southern Africa's Kalahari Desert region, a few hundred kilometers away from his site, still eat bauhinia fruit and roots. From these observations, he used the process of induction to hypothesize that the bauhinia was a preferred seasonal food in Central Africa for thousands of years.

Deductive reasoning, by contrast, is based on developing specific hypotheses using induction and then testing them against archaeological data. Archaeologists form specific implications from the hypotheses. For example, anthropologist Julian Steward studied the **Shoshone people**, foragers of the Great Basin in the western United States, in the 1920s and 1930s. He formulated general hypotheses about the ways the Shoshone moved their settlements throughout the year. In the late 1960s, archaeologist David Hurst Thomas asked, "If the late prehistoric Shoshoneans behaved in the fashion suggested by Steward, how would the artifacts they used have fallen on the ground?" Thomas constructed more than 100 predictions based on Steward's original hypotheses. Next, he devised tests to verify or invalidate his predictions. He expected to find specific forms of artifacts associated with particular activities such as hunting or plant collecting in seasonal archaeological sites where different activities were important. Then, he collected the archaeological data needed for his tests in the field. Finally, Thomas tested each of his predictions against the field data and rejected about 25 percent of his original ones. The same data supported the remaining predictions and refined Steward's original hypotheses. Thus each generation of fieldwork fine-tunes earlier hypotheses and provides more data to test them further.

inductive reasoning Using specific observations to form general conclusions.

deductive reasoning Forming specific implications from a generalized hypothesis.

Shoshone people, Nevada Hunter-gatherer peoples of the Great Basin, famous for their mobility.

scientific method Method of inquiry based on the formal testing of hypotheses, cumulative research, and replicable experiments.

The **scientific method** advances archaeological knowledge not by proof but by disproof, proposing the most adequate explanations for the moment. Every scientist knows that new and better explanations will come in the future. The key to the scientific method is the continuous self-correction that goes with the process of researching the past.

Binford also challenged the assumption that because the archaeological record is incomplete, reliable interpretation of such intangibles as religious beliefs or perishable components of ancient society and culture is impossible. He argued that the artifacts found in an archaeological site functioned at one time within a particular culture and society; thus, they occur in meaningful patterns that are systematically related to economies, kinship systems, and other contexts in which they were used. The archaeologist's task is to devise methods for extracting this information from the archaeological record.

Binford combined a cry for more scientific rigor with a synthesis of several converging lines of thought, including systems theory, cultural ecology, and multilinear evolution. The result was the now widely used approach known as processual archaeology.

Processual Archaeology

processual archaeology Studying the process of culture change using a systems or environmental approach.

Processual archaeology, the study of the processes by which human societies changed in the past, combines three elements: (1) general systems theory, (2) cultural ecology, and (3) multilinear cultural evolution.

general systems theory The notion that any organism or organization can be studied as a system broken down into many interacting subsystems or parts; sometimes called *cybernetics*.

General Systems Theory

During the late 1950s, scientists developed **general systems theory**, a body of theoretical constructs that provides a way to look for "general relationships" in the empirical world of science. From this perspective, a system is a whole that functions by virtue of the interdependence of its parts. Thus any organization, however simple or complex, can be studied as a system of interrelated concepts. Systems theory has obvious appeal to archaeologists, who study cultures made up of many interacting elements such as technology, social organization, and religious beliefs. Today, they often talk of cultural systems made up of dozens of interacting subsystems: an economic subsystem, a political subsystem, a social subsystem, and so on.

The systems perspective provides a conceptual framework for looking at sites and ancient landscapes. For example, in Syria's Euphrates valley, the people of the small settlement now called Abu Hureyra lived on the borders of several environmental zones: the river floodplain, oak forests, and open grassland. For thousands of years, they exploited both fall nut harvests and the spring and fall migrations of gazelles, small desert antelopes (see Chapter 11). About 9500 B.C., a severe drought cycle caused local nut-bearing forests to shrink and retreat far from the site. The people responded by foraging for wild grasses, then by planting their own cereals. Eventually, the foragers became farmers. The effect of the changeover from foraging to agriculture rippled through the entire cultural system, affecting architecture, social organization, technology, religious beliefs, and the entire human relationship to the natural environment. All the many and interacting components of the cultural system adjusted to changes in one another and in the ecosystem.

Cultural Ecology

Between the 1930s and 1950s, two scientific discoveries changed the way archaeologists looked at the past. The first was aerial photography, which became highly refined in World War II and provided an overhead view of changing ancient landscapes (see Chapter 2). The second was the work of Swedish botanist Lennart von Post, who used minute fossil tree pollens preserved in Scandinavian bogs to reconstruct the dramatic changes in northern European vegetation after the Ice Age (see Chapter 11). Subsequently, archaeologists used these advances in innovative field research that changed the face of archaeology forever.

Settlement archaeology was another important innovation, one of the most significant of the latter half of the twentieth century. Harvard University archaeologist Gordon Willey spent several field seasons in the coastal Virú River valley of Peru during the late 1940s. Using aerial photographs and maps, he walked most of the valley, recording hundreds of archaeological sites and studying the dramatic changes in human settlement as ever more complex farming societies developed in the region. The Virú valley project established settlement archaeology as a highly effective approach to studying the past.

Star Carr, England Mesolithic hunter-gatherer site of 11,000 years ago, famous for its wooden artifacts.

palynology (pollen analysis) The study of ancient vegetation by using minute pollens preserved in organic deposits.

In 1949, Cambridge University archaeologist Grahame Clark excavated a tiny, 11,000-year-old Stone Age hunter-gatherer site at **Star Carr** in northeastern England. Star Carr lies on the edge of a long-dried-up glacial lake close to the North Sea. From the beginning of the excavation, Clark and a team of carefully selected scientists from other disciplines deliberately studied the tiny site in the context of its ecosystem. Star Carr featured a tiny platform of birch trees set in the midst of lakeside reeds (see Figure 7.7). **Palynology (pollen analysis)** showed that the birch forest came close to the water's edge, where the Star Carr people hunted red deer and elk. Radiocarbon dates on the birch wood in the site dated to about 8500 B.C., a time when world sea levels were much lower than today and much of the nearby North Sea was dry land. The wet deposits preserved not only the birch platforms, but also a canoe paddle, bark rolls, and red deer antler spearheads used for hunting and shallow-water fishing. By studying the many red deer antlers among the animal bones, Clark was able to show that Star Carr was visited on several occasions in late spring and early summer.

The Star Carr excavations were a sensation when they were published in 1954, causing archaeologists all over the world to realize the importance of studying sites within their natural settings. Recent researches have confirmed the essential correctness of Clark's conclusions, even if refined AMS radiocarbon dates and tree-ring chronologies have now dated the founding of Star Carr to before 9000 B.C., uncovered a dwelling, and have even identified isolated brief, single visits to the site.

cultural ecology The study of the ways in which human societies adapt to and transform their environments.

Figure 7.7 Artist's reconstruction of the Star Carr site.
Source: Art by Dominic Andrews, Star Carr Archives Project.

Just as the Star Carr project ended in 1954, anthropologist Julian Steward of the University of Illinois developed the concept of **cultural ecology**. This approach, revolutionary at the time, argued that similar human adaptations may be found in widely separated cultures in similar environments. For example, the African !Kung, the Australian Aborigines, and the Fuegian Indians of South America lived in small bands with kinship descent passing through the father. Their environments differed dramatically, from desert to cold and rainy plains, yet the practical requirements of their hunter-gatherer lifeway and general adaptations were very similar. Steward also pointed out that no culture has ever achieved an adaptation that remained unchanged over any length of time, for environments change constantly. Cultural ecology views human cultures as subsystems interacting with other subsystems, all forming a total ecosystem with three major subsystems: human culture, the biotic community, and the physical environment. Clark, Steward, and Willey each helped establish one of the foundations of modern archaeological theory. Archaeologists cannot study cultural change without studying ancient cultures within the contexts of their changing environments.

Multilinear Cultural Evolution

During the 1950s, anthropologists Julian Steward and Leslie White were responsible for far more sophisticated formulations of human cultural evolution. They developed a new multilinear (many-tracked) model of cultural evolution that recognized the existence of many evolutionary tracks, from simple to complex, with the differences resulting from the adaptations made by individual societies to widely differing environments.

multilinear cultural evolution Cultural evolution along many diverse tracks.

Multilinear cultural evolution is best thought of as a bush with many branches and clusters of twigs expanding from a single trunk. This loosely formulated model is of vital importance because it brings together the notion of cultural systems and cultural ecology into a closely knit, highly flexible way of studying the processes of cultural change (see Figure 7.8).

Processual archaeology has enjoyed considerable success, largely because it allows the study of complex relationships among cultural change, subsistence, and environmental shifts. The combination of a systems and ecological approach allows us to examine the ways in which cultural systems function both internally and in relation to external factors such as the natural environment. Intricate in its development and application, the processual approach frees us from simplistic explanations of such phenomena as the origins of the first civilizations. No longer can we claim that a single agent of change—for example, irrigation or diffusion—was responsible for, say, Maya civilization. With cultural ecology and cultural systems at its core, the processual approach has emphasized environmental change, subsistence, and settlement: critical parts of the story of human prehistory (for a classic example, see Box 7.5).

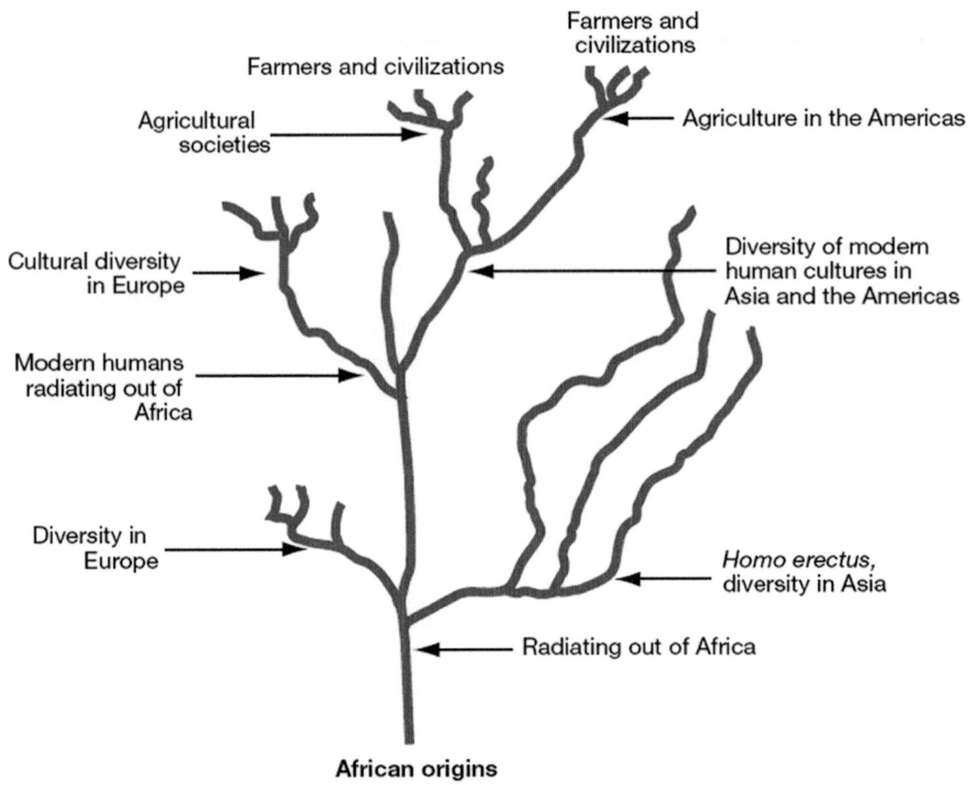

Figure 7.8 Multilinear cultural evolution is a bush-like concept. This grossly simplified diagram shows how many of the major developments in prehistory can be modeled as a bush-like development, with the main trunk originating in Africa, where humans evolved.

Box 7.5 Site
Guilá Naquitz Cave

Guilá Naquitz Cave in Mexico's Valley of Oaxaca was occupied sporadically by a tiny band of hunter-gatherers over a span of a few thousand years after 8750 B.C. Kent Flannery excavated the site in a classic instance of sophisticated processual archaeology. Searching for evidence of early maize and bean agriculture, he used the unspectacular finds of stone artifacts, animal bones, and seeds from the cave to reconstruct a portrait of changing adaptations in a high-risk environment. Flannery asked two questions: (1) What was the strategy that led to the choice of the wild plants eaten by the inhabitants? (2) How did this strategy change when they began planting?

Archaeologist Robert Reynolds developed a computer model to approach these questions, starting with a hypothetical and totally ignorant band of five people who settled in the area. Over a long period of trial and error, they "learned" how to schedule the gathering of 11 major food plants over the year, in an environment with highly unpredictable rainfall. Experience passed from one generation to the next was vital, for this was the basis on which they developed survival strategies that enabled them to endure hungry years. After many generations, the people developed strategies that ranked plant foods in order of size of harvest. The band became so efficient that it achieved a stable performance level.

The plant food mix from the cave matched the simulated mix very well, showing that a wide range of plant foods was used in wet years while a much narrower spectrum of higher-yielding species was used in dry years. At first, the people deliberately planted wild beans in rare wet years, when they could afford the risk, in an attempt to extend the distributions of existing food plants. The strategy had so many advantages that they extended it to dry years as well. The simulation suggests that bean cultivation near the cave allowed the people to collect more food and travel less. As the group gained experience with planting, yields rose, and they placed ever more emphasis on cultivation as opposed to foraging. Eventually, their descendants became full-time farmers. When Reynolds added climate change and population growth to his simulation, he found that unpredictable climatic fluctuations and population shifts were major factors that led to the shift to food production.

The computer simulation helped Flannery use an ecosystem model to interpret the Guilá Naquitz excavations. This model allows for people's responses to changes in their ecosystem in several ways—for example, by reducing the search area for wild plants and then growing protein-rich beans.

Guilá Naquitz Cave, Mexico Cave occupied by a small band of foragers between 7350 and 6670 B.C.; important for the study of early bean and squash cultivation.

People, Not Systems

Inevitably, there has been a reaction against processual archaeology, general systems theory, cultural ecology, and multilinear cultural evolution. Many critics of these approaches claim that they have dehumanized the past in a quest for anonymous, broad cultural processes. They ask: What about people? How did the constant interactions among the individuals, households, communities, and diverse groups that made up ancient human societies affect cultural change? What about religious beliefs, symbolism, ideology, and social organization?

These criticisms come from the context of a boisterous late twentieth-century and early twenty-first-century world. We live in fractious times, in societies riven by factional disputes, special-interest groups, accusations of racism, and calls for political correctness. Inevitably, today's archaeologists look at the past with new, more individualistic eyes, peering beyond anonymous cultural processes to a past made up of people following widely diverse and often controversial agendas.

postprocessual archaeology Approaching the past by examining ideology, motives, and nonenvironmental aspects of culture change.

Postprocessual archaeology is a loosely defined term describing various, and often shortlived, schools of archaeological thought involving social theory that focuses on the roles of people and their involvement in cultural change. Archaeologists of this general persuasion argue that we can no longer interpret the past purely in terms of ecological, technological, and other material considerations. As we saw in Chapter 2, culture is interactive, created by people as actors who interpret, manipulate, and remake the world they live in. We are doing this ourselves in the rapidly changing industrial societies of today, where ethnic identity, gender roles, and social equality are constant issues in daily life. Surely, the postprocessual-minded point out, the same kinds of behavior marked the diverse societies of the past and played a major role in the creation of civilizations and myriad societies large and small, simple and complex.

Processual archaeology uses multilinear cultural evolution theories with the widely held assumption that all human societies change, over the long term, from the simple to the more complex. Postprocessual, or social, schools of thought are more "horizontal" in their thinking. The thinking shifts constantly, but in general such approaches are more concerned with the *meaning* of ancient cultures and the diversity within them than with general, more "vertical" models of increasing cultural complexity, which emphasize individual power and social ranking.

Social approaches to complexity contribute two important elements to our study of the past and are based on the long-held assumption that culture is interactive, the result of people's actions, as individuals, groups, and entire societies. Such approaches argue that one cannot interpret cultural change without examining the hitherto neglected perspectives of those who have been called "the people without history," including women, ethnic minorities, and innumerable illiterate commoners.

Furthermore, these perspectives assume that archaeologists, whatever their cultural or political affiliations, bring their own cultural biases to their interpretations of the past. In other words, there is no such thing as a totally dispassionate take on ancient societies. Many Westerners believe that science offers the broadest perspective on human history. Others consider the Old Testament the literal historical truth. Native Americans often discount scientific archaeology and prefer their own worldview. All archaeologists can do is be active mediators of the past.

cognitive archaeology The "archaeology of mind," using archaeological methods to study human motives, ideologies, and intangibles.

Researchers working with social theory grapple with a fundamental question: Can we study the development of human consciousness, religious beliefs, and the whole spectrum of human behavior—human cognition—from the material remains of the past? The dictionary defines *cognition* as "the action or process of knowing in its broadest sense, including sensation, perception, memory, and judgment." Clearly, we ignore "human knowing," the "archaeology of mind" (**cognitive archaeology**), at our peril. Some archaeologists are trying to bring together the best of the scientific processual approaches with the more all-embracing, sometimes instinctual, methods of postprocessualists—the archaeology of mind.

Cognitive-Processual Archaeology

The archaeology of mind includes all forms of archaeology that combine the scientific rigor of processual archaeology with data from many sources to study intangible human behavior.

cognitive-processual archaeology An approach to archaeology that combines the methods of processual and postprocessual researchers.

Archaeologists Kent Flannery and Joyce Marcus (1993, 260, 265) consider the archaeology of mind to be the "study of all those aspects of ancient culture that are the product of the ancient mind." This includes cosmology, religion, ideology, iconography, and all forms of human intellectual and symbolic behavior. They believe that this form of **cognitive-processual archaeology** offers great promise when rigorous methods are applied to large data sets. To do otherwise, they write, causes archaeology to become "little more than speculation, a kind of bungee jump into the Land of Fantasy."

Monte Albán, Mexico Major city and state in the Valley of Oaxaca during the first millennium A.D.

Flannery and Marcus applied a rigorous cognitive-processual approach in the Valley of Oaxaca, Mexico, where they used ethnographic data, historical records, and archaeological finds to trace the appearance of a distinctive ideology that rationalized social inequality. An ideology is a product of society and politics, a body of doctrine, myth, and symbolism associated with a social movement, a class, or a group of individuals, often with reference to some political or cultural plan, along with the strategies for putting the doctrine into place. Flannery and Marcus excavated simple village communities dating between 1400 and 1150 B.C. in which there was no apparent social ranking. Between 1150 and 850 B.C., the first depictions of supernatural ancestors appeared, some representing the Earth, others the sky in the form of lightning or a fire serpent. The new art appeared at a time when the first signs of hereditary social rank appeared in Oaxaca villages, identified from exotic artifacts clustered in some households. Then, the great city of **Monte Albán** rose to power, ruled by a powerful Zapotec nobility (see Figure 7.9). The art the rulers commissioned to commemorate their power depicts sky and lightning, while earth and earthquake symbols fade into obscurity. Thus careful analysis of artistic motifs and other finds chronicles a vital ideological shift that rationalized social inequality throughout Zapotec domains.

Figure 7.9 The city of Monte Albán, Valley of Oaxaca, Mexico.
Source: Dmitry Rukhlenko/Thinkstock.

The archaeology of mind is at its most powerful when archaeologists can work with both historical documents and archaeological data. For instance, a half-century ago, archaeologists of Maya civilization (Mayanists) believed that Maya lords were peaceful astronomer-priests who had a preoccupation with calendars. In one of the great triumphs of twentieth-century science, a group of scholars succeeded in deciphering the intricate Maya script. This decipherment revealed a far more complex Maya world: one of constant diplomatic activity, intense competition among different kingdoms, and endemic warfare (see Box 6.4 on p. 196). It seems that the Maya lords were not peace-loving priests but ambitious, power-hungry leaders obsessed with gaining prestige and authority. The intricate Maya glyphs, with their tales of conquest and genealogical chronicles, are a sobering reminder that we can never hope to unravel the full complexity of even the seemingly simplest ancient societies without the help of written records. However, by combining the rigor of processual archaeology with the more people-oriented approaches of the archaeology of mind, we can sometimes achieve remarkable insights into the intangible forces that once drove human culture change.

Explanation in archaeology is never easy. The coward takes the easy way out—uses the methods of culture history and then relies on the assumption that change is inherent to the system. Processual archaeologists prefer scientific methods and embrace the power of broad cultural processes. In other words, the system is more important than the individual. Others espouse neo-Darwinism and consider natural selection a powerful instrument of cultural change. A growing number of archaeologists draw on social theory, considering people, both individuals and interacting groups, more important than the institutions of which they are part. All of this raises a question: Do individuals and groups shape a society, or do the institutions into which they are born mold it? All of us have networks of people with whom we interact constantly—a few close friends and family members, then a widening circle of individuals and groups with whom we have regular or sporadic dealings. This constantly changing network involves interaction and negotiation, and by its very nature ensures consequences of all kinds and ultimately shifts and changes in society, all of which can have long-term consequences.

The Issue of Complexity

One of the great debates about human prehistory surrounds the growing complexity of human societies over time. How can we measure complexity so as to compare one society with another? Here there is little agreement. Archaeologist Kent Flannery, a systems advocate, stresses the centralization of control in more complex societies and the increasing distinctions among different segments of society. In contrast, Randall McGuire, a scholar of Marxist persuasion, measures complexity by the degree of access people have to resources of all kinds (inequality) and the number of different human players in the society, both independent variables in the complexity equation. The debate continues, with no resolution in sight.

Change and No Change

The issues of change and no change (stasis) are of critical importance to our understanding of prehistory. Not surprisingly, we are much preoccupied with change in prehistory. But we must also consider stasis, the state of little or no change, a much more common condition of humankind. For example, about 1.9 million years ago, simple stone axes, flaked on both surfaces, appeared in tropical Africa (see Chapter 9). The same basic technology, and the simple hunter-gatherer lifeway associated with it, spread into Asia and Europe and remained basically unchanged for over a million years. People living along the Thames River in Great Britain used the same artifacts and obtained food in much the same way as their contemporaries in Africa and India.

Stasis continued to be the rule in later times. For example, human societies throughout the world in the 20,000-to 5,000-year-old time bracket had a life span of between 2,000 and 5,000 years. Many ancient Native American societies in North America flourished for 10 to 20 generations, some 200 to 400 years. Contrast these longer life spans with the volatility of preindustrial civilizations. The Maya are famous for the cyclical rise and fall of their city-states (see Chapter 15). For all the seemingly even tenor of the Classic period (A.D. 300–900), there were constant cycles of growth and collapse as one state conquered another and then was itself eclipsed as a neighboring city rose to dominance. The landscape of Maya civilization was never stable; it was always in a state of change. Only recently have archaeologists turned their attention to stasis, which is just as important as change.

Explaining prehistory will never be an easy undertaking. Pursuing the people of the past and their intangible behavior requires large data sets, excellent preservation, and sophisticated theoretical models. The pursuit is often frustrating and relies on a broad array of scientific methods from dozens of scientific disciplines, among them botany, nuclear physics, and zoology. Australian historian Inga Clendinnen, an expert on the Aztec civilization, cites *Moby Dick* when she likens archaeologists to the following:

> Ahabs pursuing our great white whale ... We will never catch him ... It is our limitations of thought, of understandings, of imagination we test as we quarter these

> strange waters. And then we think we see a darkening in the deeper water, a sudden surge, the roll of a fluke—and then the heart-lifting glimpse of the great white shape, its whiteness throwing back its own particular light, there on the glimmering horizon.
> (Clendinnen 1991, 275)

The seven chapters in Parts 1 and 2 have taken us on a lightning tour of archaeology, the study of the human past, discussing the basic principles of archaeological research, the ways we find, recover, analyze, and interpret the past. In the next chapter, we begin our journey through the long millennia of prehistory, a narrative encompassing more than 6 million years. The stage is set, and the actors are in the wings. Let the play begin!

Summary

- This chapter examined the ways in which archaeologists describe and explain the past.
- Culture history describes ancient human cultures in a context of time and space and is based on the normative view of culture and descriptive research methods.
- As part of this descriptive process, archaeologists use a hierarchy of arbitrary archaeological units, which proceed from artifacts and assemblages to components, phases, regions, and cultural areas.
- Syntheses of culture history rely on descriptive models of cultural change: inevitable variation, cultural selection, invention, diffusion, and migration.
- Culture-historical interpretation relies on analogy from historical and ethnographic sources, tested against archaeological data, with the aid of ethnoarchaeological and experimental research.
- Explaining cultural change involves both processual and postprocessual approaches. Processual archaeology is a combination of general systems theory, cultural ecology, and multilinear cultural evolution. Such approaches have been criticized for being too impersonal.
- Postprocessual approaches have focused on the study of people and intangibles such as religious beliefs using cognitive approaches that combine ethnographic and historical records with scientifically acquired archaeological data.
- Much research surrounding explanation is concerned with two basic issues of prehistory—the reasons why human societies became more complex or why they remained in a state of stasis for hundreds, often thousands, of years.

Key Terms and Sites

descriptive (inductive) research methods
normative view of culture
components
phases
La Madeleine
regions
culture areas
horizons
traditions
Clovis tradition
inevitable variation
cultural selection
invention

diffusion
migration
Nguni people
analogy
Martin's Hundred
Waka
stelae
functionalism
ethnographic analogy
ethnoarchaeology
Hadza people
Nunamiut people
experimental archaeology
Butser
inductive reasoning
deductive reasoning
Shoshone people
scientific method
processual archaeology
general systems theory
Star Carr
palynology (pollen analysis)
cultural ecology
multilinear cultural evolution
Guilá Naquitz Cave
postprocessual archaeology
cognitive archaeology
cognitive-processual archaeology
Monte Albán

Critical-Thinking Questions

1. Discuss the difference between descriptive models of cultural change and models that seek to explain cultural process. Use examples in your discussion.
2. Why are analogy, experimentation, and ethnoarchaeology important to archaeologists? How do they bear on the study of cultural change?
3. "People, Not Systems" is an important subheading in this chapter. How do people as individuals and groups affect culture change, and how should we study them? Cite examples from the chapter in your discussion.

Further Reading

L. R. Binford, *In Pursuit of the Past*, rev. ed. (London: Thames and Hudson, 2001) summarizes this remarkable archaeologist's thinking. M. Johnson, *Archaeological Theory*, 3rd ed. (New York: Wiley-Blackwell, 2019) and R. Chapmans', *Archaeological Theory: The Basics* (London and New York: Routledge, 2022) are excellent summaries. B. G. Trigger, *A History of Archaeological Thought*, 2nd ed. (Cambridge: Cambridge University Press, 2006) is a must for serious students.

Part 3

The World of the First Humans

Part 3 begins the narrative of human prehistory, the second half of this book. The narrative is divided into four parts—a play, as it were, in four acts. In this section of two chapters, we discuss human origins over 6 million years ago (Ma) and the spread of early hominins out of their original homeland in tropical Africa after 2 million years ago. We describe the famous Neanderthals of Europe and Eurasia, who survived until perhaps 40,000 years ago. Finally, we analyze competing theories surrounding the origins of modern humans, *Homo sapiens* (us). Part 4 consists of a single chapter devoted to the subsequent permanent diaspora (spread) of modern humans out of Africa, a process that was underway by 50,000 years ago until soon after the end of the Ice Age, about 15,000 years ago. Part 5 continues the story in the Old World, with the rapid environmental changes after the Ice Age, the beginnings and spread of farming, and the appearance of state-organized societies (civilizations) in Egypt, Mesopotamia, and Asia. Finally, Part 6 surveys developments in the Americas after first settlement and the development of sophisticated, indigenous chiefdoms and states in the New World.

8 Human Origins

Chapter Outline

DOI: 10.4324/9781003592754-11

Two hominins walking on volcanic ash at Laetoli, Tanzania, around 3.7 million years ago. Source: Raul Martin/MSF/Science Photo Library.

It was a blazingly hot day at Olduvai Gorge, East Africa, in 1959. Back in camp, Louis Leakey lay in his tent, suffering from a bout of influenza. Meanwhile, his wife, Mary Leakey, sheltered by a beach umbrella, was excavating a small scatter of broken bones and crude artifacts deep in the gorge. Hour after hour, she brushed and pried away dry soil. Suddenly, she unearthed part of an upper jaw with teeth so humanlike that she took a closer look. Moments later, she jumped into her Land Rover and sped up the track to camp. "Louis, Louis," she cried as she burst into their tent. "I've found Dear Boy at last." Louis leapt out of bed, his flu forgotten. Together, they excavated the fragmentary remains of a magnificent, robust hominin skull. The Leakeys named it *Zinjanthropus boisei* ("African human of Boise"), a Mr. Boise being one of their benefactors. With this dramatic discovery, they changed the study of human evolution from a part-time science into an international detective story.

Biologist Thomas Huxley called it "the question of questions," the nature of the exact relationship between humans and their closest living relatives such as the chimpanzee and the gorilla—the question of human origins. Ever since his day, scientists have been locked in controversy as they trace the complex evolutionary history of humanity back to its very beginnings. At first, they thought in terms of simple, ladderlike evolutionary schemes. These theories have now given way to highly tentative studies of early human evolution completed by reconstructing precise evolutionary relationships from fossil specimens, a process fraught with difficulty when bone fragments are the raw materials. Experts in this field rely on precise bone measurements, small anatomical details revealed in highly fragmentary fossil bones, and careful study of the stratigraphy and chronology of the place where they were found.

In this chapter, we examine some of the controversies that surround the biological and cultural evolution of humankind and describe what we know about the behaviors and lifeways of our earliest ancestors.

Quaternary The geological epoch also known as the *Pleistocene*.

Pleistocene The last geological epoch, sometimes called the Ice Age or Quaternary epoch.

The story of humanity begins deep in geological time, during the later part of the Cenozoic era, the age of mammals. For most of geological time, the world's climate was warmer than it is today. During the Oligocene epoch, some 35 million years ago (Ma), the first signs of glacial cooling appeared with the formation of a belt of pack ice around Antarctica. A major drop in world temperatures between 14 and 11 Ma followed. As temperatures fell, large ice sheets formed on high ground in high latitudes. About 3.2 Ma, large ice sheets formed on the northern continents. Then, some 2.5 Ma, glaciation intensified even more, and the Earth entered its present period of constantly fluctuating climate. These changes culminated during the **Quaternary** period or **Pleistocene** epoch, the most recent interval of Earth history, which began at about that time. This period is sometimes called the Age of Humanity, for it was during this epoch, the Great Ice Age (c. 2.5 million to 15,000 years ago), that various human species first peopled most of the globe. The major climatic and environmental changes of the Ice Age form the backdrop for some of the most important stages of evolution.

The term *Ice Age* conjures up a vision of icebound landscapes and frigid temperatures that gripped the Earth in a prolonged deep freeze. In fact, the Pleistocene witnessed constant fluctuations between warm and intensely cold global climates. Deep-sea cores lifted from the depths of the world's oceans have produced a complex picture of the Ice Age climate.

These cores have shown that climatic fluctuations between warm and cold were relatively minor until about 800,000 years ago. Since then, periods of intense cold have recurred about every 90,000 years, with minor oscillations about 20,000 and 40,000 years apart. Many scientists believe that these changes are triggered by long-term astronomical cycles, especially that of the Earth's orbit around the Sun, which affect the seasonal and north–south variations of solar radiation received by the Earth.

There were at least nine glacial periods that mantled northern Europe and North America with great ice sheets, the last one retreating only some 15,000 years ago. Interglacial periods, with climates as warm as or warmer than those of today, occurred infrequently, and the constant changes displaced plants and animals, including humans, from their original habitats. During colder cycles, plants and animals generally fared better at lower altitudes and in warmer latitudes. Populations of animals spread slowly toward more hospitable areas, mixing with populations that already lived there and creating new communities with new combinations of organisms. For example, paleontologist Björn Kurtén has estimated that no fewer than 113 of the mammalian species living in Europe and adjacent Asia evolved during the past 3 million years. This repeated mixing surely affected human evolution in many ways.

Some of the early chapters of human evolution unfolded during a period of relatively minor climatic change. Between 4 million and 2 million years ago, the world's climate was somewhat warmer and more stable than it was in later times. The African savanna and woodland landscapes, the probable cradle of humankind, contained many species of mammals large and small, including a great variety of the order of primates, of which we humans are a part.

Early Primate Evolution and Adaptation

The Primate Order

primates Mammals belonging to the order that includes tree-living placental mammals.

anthropoids Members of the taxonomic suborder of apes, humans, and monkeys.

prosimians Members of the taxonomic suborder of primates that includes lemurs, tarsiers, and other so-called premonkeys.

pongids Members of the family of nonhuman primates closest to humans.

All of us are members of the order of **primates**, which includes most tree-loving placental mammals. There are two suborders: **anthropoids** (apes, humans, and monkeys) and **prosimians** (lemurs, tarsiers, and other so-called premonkeys). The many similarities in behavior and physical characteristics between the hominins (primates of the family Hominidae, which includes modern humans, earlier human subspecies, and their direct ancestors) and the **pongids** (our closest living nonhuman primate relatives) can be explained by identical characteristics that each group inherited millions of years ago from a common ancestor. In other words, humans and our closest nonhuman primate relatives evolved along parallel lines from a common ancestor.

When did humankind separate from the nonhuman primates? Experts disagree violently about the answer. It was in Africa that humans and apes diverged from monkeys, but no one knows when this divergence took place. Several species of apes were flourishing in Africa at the beginning of the Miocene epoch, some 24 Ma. The basic anatomical pattern of the large hominins appears in the Middle Miocene, 18–12 Ma. A second radiation began in the Late Miocene, between 8 and 5 Ma. This radiation eventually produced four lineages, at least one of which, human beings, is known to have been considerably modified. It is interesting to note that a similar evolutionary pattern occurs among herbivores such as elephants. In both cases, the patterns reflect changing climates and habitats—from warmer, less seasonal, more forested regimens to colder, more seasonal, and less forested conditions. They also mirror changes in the configuration of continents, mountain systems, and Antarctic ice.

hominoids Members of the primate superfamily that includes apes and hominins.

For the hominins, the critical period was between 10 million and 5 million years ago, when the African lineage radiated to produce gorillas, chimpanzees, and hominins. Unfortunately, this 5-million-year period is largely a black hole in our knowledge of early human evolution. We can only guess at the nature of most of the apelike **hominoids** that flourished in Africa during these millennia. Paleoanthropologist David Pilbeam theorizes that these animals were mostly tree-living, with long arms and legs and a broad chest. They would have used all four limbs in the trees, occasionally scrambling on the ground and even standing on their rear limbs at times. About 5 Ma, Pilbeam believes, the hominoid lineage divided into western and eastern parts. The western segment, the chimpanzee lineage, remained dependent on fruit and other tree foods, scattered resources that required a flexible social organization. Intense controversy surrounds the relationships among humans, chimpanzees, and gorillas, but many biologists agree that chimpanzees are humans' closest relatives. Using molecular time clocks, they calculate that these primate lineages last shared a common ancestor about 6 million to 7 million years ago.

"Coming Down from the Trees"

Over the period of human evolution covered in this chapter, there was a long-term trend toward a cooler and drier global climate. A deep-sea core from the Arabian Sea has probed deep into nearly 1,000 feet of seabed deposits. It reveals swings from wetter to drier conditions and back about every 23,000 years. These were responses to changes in monsoon climates attributable to wobbles in the Earth's orbit. Superimposed on these oscillations was a long-term trend toward dry, open grasslands, the first patches expanding in East Africa about 8 Ma. We know of these changes from studies of carbon isotopes from soils and rocks that show a rapid expansion of grassland, while forests receded. East African grasslands may have expanded by 50 percent or so between 3 and 2 Ma. As the grasslands spread, so grazing animals became more common. Just like hominins, they experienced comprehensive extinction, speciation, and adaptation.

About 5 Ma, many mammalian species inhabited the African savanna, with its patches of forest and extensive grassland plains. So did specialized tree-dwellers and other primates. Some of these were flourishing in small bands, probably walking upright and conceivably making tools out of stone and wood. This was when hominins with a four-footed gait had to move out of the trees and experiment with life on the ground. Such a move would have required an ape capable of standing upright, of balancing its trunk and legs, and supporting its upper-body weight through its arms and shoulders. This move did not accelerate evolution among the diverse populations of hominins, which remained modest in brain size, with archaic long arms and short legs.

bipedal Walking upright on two feet.

Coming down from the trees created three immediate problems. First was the difficulty of getting around in open country. Hominins adopted a **bipedal** posture as a way of doing so by at least 4 Ma. Our ancestors became bipedal (walking on two feet) over a long period of time, perhaps as a result of spending more and more time feeding on food resources on the ground. Bipedalism is a posture that is configured for endurance rather than power or speed. An upright posture and bipedal gait are the most characteristic hominin physical features.

knuckle walking Specialized way of getting around on four limbs, using the backs of the hands for supporting body weight.

Upright posture is vital because it frees the hands for other actions, like toolmaking. It contrasts with **knuckle walking**, which provides an excellent power thrust for jumping into a tree or a short sprint (think of a football lineman). It is a specialized way of moving around in which the backs of the fingers are placed on the ground and act as weightbearing surfaces. Knuckle walking was adaptive in the forest because long arms and hands, as well as grasping feet, were still vital for climbing (see Figure 8.1). Human arms are too short for us to be comfortable with this posture. Bipedalism favors endurance and the covering of long distances which are important considerations in open country. It was a critical antecedent of hunting, gathering, and toolmaking.

Furthermore, the savanna abounded in predators, making it hard for primates to sleep safely. Large hominins made home bases, where they sheltered from the hot Sun and slept in safety. What form these home bases took is a matter of great debate.

Last of all, high-quality plant foods, abundant in the forests, were widely dispersed over the savanna. It is striking that later foragers subsisted off a broad range of game and plant foods. As part of human evolution, their hominin ancestors expanded their food range to include more meat, perhaps during long periods of plant scarcity. Among mammals, these characteristics are associated with a trend toward larger brain size. And as brain size increased, the lifeways of evolving hominins gradually became less apelike and closer to those of human foragers, a process that took hundreds of thousands of years to unfold.

Early hominins faced three major adaptive problems: (1) they were large mammals, (2) they were terrestrial (living on the ground) primates, and (3) they had to deal with an open, tropical savanna environment. Human beings are large and have greater food requirements than apes due to higher metabolic rates. This means that each hominin had to range efficiently over a larger area to obtain food. Larger mammals are more mobile than their smaller relatives. They cover more ground, which enables them to subsist off resources that are unevenly distributed not only in space, but also at different seasons. Mobility allows larger mammals like humans to incorporate unpredictable, often seasonal resources in their diets. They can tolerate extremes of heat and cold, a capacity that may have contributed to the spread of humans out of the tropics later in prehistory. Bipedal humans have sweat glands and are heavily dependent on water supplies. These glands are a direct adjunct to bipedalism, for they enhance endurance for long-distance foraging.

These and several other factors, such as increased longevity and brain enlargement, created adaptive problems for emerging humans. These problems had a number of solutions, among them wider territorial ranges, the scheduling of food gathering, the use of technology, a broadening of diet, a high degree of mobility, and much greater behavioral flexibility. This flexibility included enhanced intelligence and learning capacity, parental care, and new levels of social interaction. Major landscape changes had profound

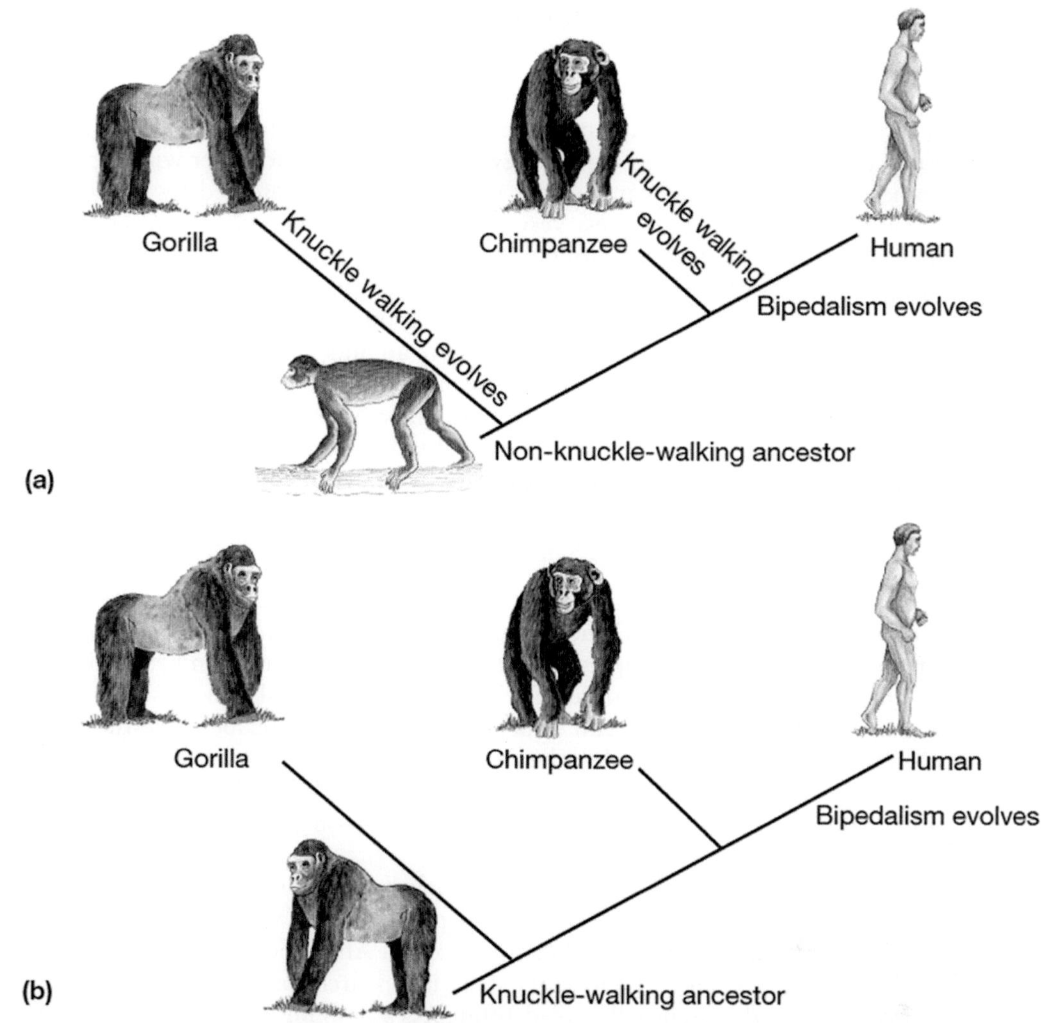

Figure 8.1 Bipedalism and four-footed posture. Two major theories account for the evolution of bipedalism: (a) If the last common ancestor of chimpanzees, gorillas, and humans was not a knuckle walker (the body's center of gravity lies in the middle of the area bounded by legs and arms), then knuckle walking would have evolved independently in both chimpanzees and gorillas. Under this theory, the ancestral locomotion for humans was not knuckle walking. (b) If the last common ancestor for chimpanzees, gorillas, and humans was a knuckle walker, then the ancestral condition for humans is knuckle walking. Humans are bipedal; the body's center of gravity is displaced much less, making walking much more efficient.

effects on hominins as they did on animals—which is revealed not by soils and rocks, but by teeth. By examining the fossils from the Lake Turkana region in Kenya, Thure Cerling and others have shown that early *Homo* sought diverse foods from increasingly uniform landscapes, as opposed to robust australopithecines, who lived in a narrow dietary niche and perhaps inevitably became extinct. Perhaps the more elaborate, albeit still simple, tool kits used by *Homo* over tens of thousands of years resulted from their owners having to exploit more varied food resources scattered over considerable distances.

The Fossil Evidence for Human Evolution (c. 6 Million to 1.5 Million Years Ago)

Studying the extremely thin fossil record between 6 and 1.5 million years ago is a matter of fine and careful judgment, the weighing of anatomical details, the weighting of different characteristics, and the assessment of chronology and stratigraphy, together with the application of other scientific techniques. Most of the fossils are represented by single teeth found in fossil-rich South African caves. Very few are skull fragments or jaws, the most valuable of all fossil finds. During this long period, our ancestors went through dramatic transformations, visible only through an incomplete paleontological lens. We know that many hominin forms flourished in tropical Africa during this period. Which of them, however, were direct human ancestors? We can only achieve an understanding of human evolution by getting to know as many species as we can, and this task has hardly begun.

Indeed, we currently know of more than 20 hominin species, and at least half of these species are based on fossils unearthed in the last 30 years alone. The summary of fossil hominin species that follows is certain to be outdated within a few years.

The Earliest Known Hominin: Toumaï, Sahelanthropus tchadensis

The Toro-Menalla region of the Djurab Desert in Chad, Central Africa, is a brutal place for paleoanthropological research. But French scholars Michel Brunet, Patrick Vignaud, and their colleagues have found the chimpanzee-sized skull of a likely hominin between 6 and 7 million years old. The cranium is confusing. From the back, the skull looks like that of a chimpanzee. From the front, the facial structure and tooth layout look like those of a hominin of about 1.75 Ma, an australopithecine (see the section that follows). The point at the base of the skull where the neck muscles attach suggests that this creature walked upright. Brunet and his team have named this remarkable fossil *S. tchadensis* (hominin of the Sahel, of Chad).

S. tchadensis confirms what many people have long believed: Hominin evolution was much more complicated than we suspected. In all probability, a wide variety of apelike primates—some with larger brains—flourished in tropical Africa between 8 and 5 Ma, of which the Chad find is but one. At this early stage in research, paleoanthropologists are uncertain whether *S. tchadensis*, usually called Toumaï, is a hominin or not. Though its position on the human evolutionary tree is far from secure, many believe it may be a very early hominin, perhaps even an ancestor of *Ardipithecus ramidus*, a hominin known from Ethiopia after 5 Ma. Whatever the ultimate status of Toumaï, the new find shows that very early human evolution took many branches and was not a matter of simple linear development.

Many paleoanthropologists believe that East Africa was the main crucible of early human evolution, largely because this is the area that has yielded the greatest diversity of primordial hominins. Between about 5 and 4 Ma, the now desert regions of Ethiopia and northern Kenya were open savanna grassland teeming with herds of antelope and other mammals that were hunted by both predators and our remote hominin ancestors. And it is here that some of the earliest known hominins have been found, many of them australopithecines (see Figure 8.2 for a map of archaeological sites).

What Is *Australopithecus*?

Taung, South Africa Quarry in which the first *Australopithecus africanus* fossil was found in 1924.

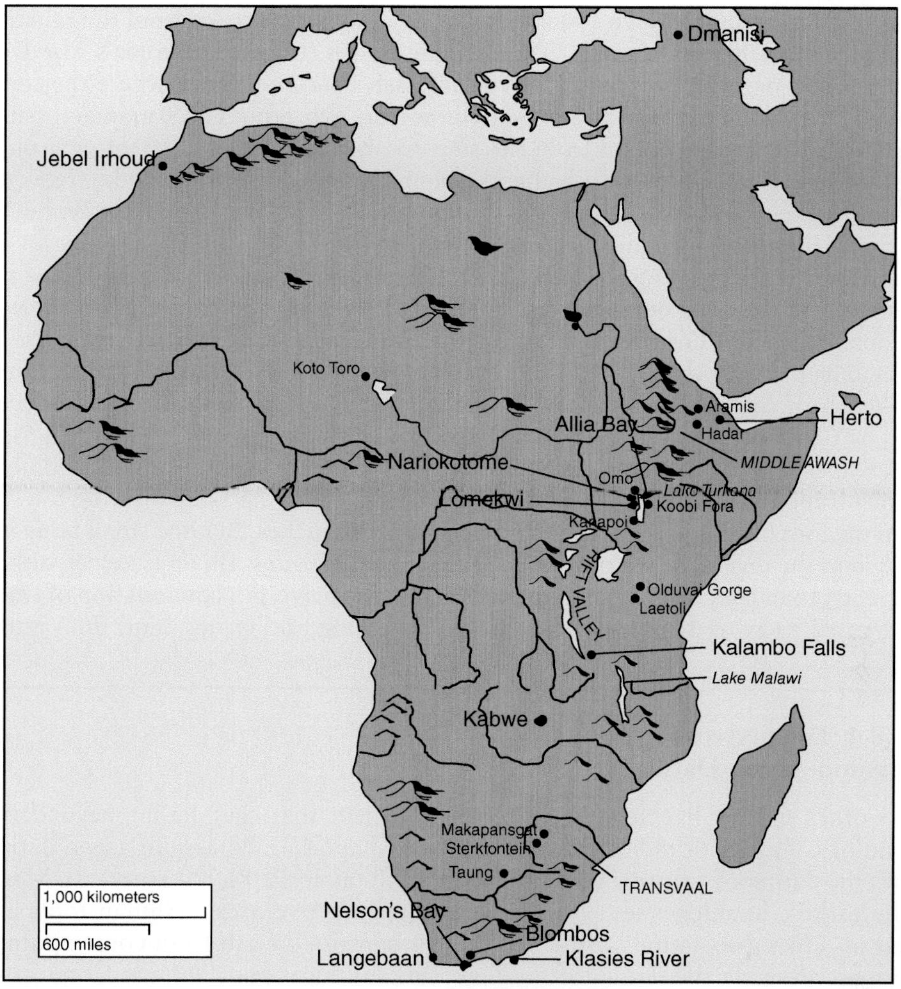

Figure 8.2 Archaeological sites described in this chapter. Some sites are omitted for clarity.

Australopithecus (Latin for "southern ape") was first identified by anatomist Raymond Dart at the **Taung** site in South Africa in 1924. Dart described a small, gracile primate that displayed both human and apelike features. He named his find *A. africanus*, a much lighter creature than another, more robust form of australopithecine that subsequently turned up at other South African sites and, later, in East Africa. The latter is known as *Australopithecus robustus*, a squat, massively built primate with a crested skull (see Figure 8.7).

For years, paleoanthropologists thought that *A. africanus* was the original ancestor of humankind. More recent finds from East Africa have refined the picture and revealed far earlier primates on the human line.

Ardipithecus ramidus

Aramis, Ethiopia Site on the Awash River where *A. ramidus* was discovered and dated to 4.4 Ma.

A. ramidus is the earliest known fossil ancestor of humanity, known from the remains of over 36 individuals found at **Aramis** in the Middle Awash region of Ethiopia's Afar Desert. Potassium-argon dates of two layers of volcanic ash over and above where the remains were found date *Ardipithecus* to about 4.4 million years ago. Some 6,000 animal fossils and other environmental information from the sites reconstruct a very different environment from the present desert—a moist woodland, abounding in edible plant foods—reflected in the isotopic makeup and wear patterns in *Ardipithecus*'s teeth (for dating, see Box 8.1).

The first *Ardipithecus* fragments came to light in 1992; decades of work by an international team were required to conserve and study the badly preserved fossils. The bones were removed in their surrounding rock, then carefully extracted from the matrix with a microscope and needles. From the rock emerged 125 fragments of a female *Ardipithecus* skeleton, including pieces of the crushed skull, much of the feet and—a rarity with early human fossils—much of the hands. The skull fragments were CT-scanned, then fitted together digitally, by Gen Suwa, a paleoanthropologist at the University of Tokyo (Figure 8.3).

Unlike other later bipedal hominins, *Ardipithecus* walked on the ground bipedally, but with a quadruped gait when moving in the trees. The surviving skeleton's big toe splays out from the foot like an ape's, the better for grasping branches. But one small bone inside a tendon kept the divergent toe more rigid, which helped it to walk on two feet, although less efficiently than later human ancestors. Similarly, the pelvis is a combination of features that prevented swaying from side to side while walking and strong hind limb muscles,

Box 8.1 Doing Archaeology
Potassium-Argon Dating

The world's first archaeological sites are so ancient that they lie far beyond the chronological range of radiocarbon dating (see Chapter 3). Potassium-argon dating allows the dating of volcanic rocks between 2 billion and 100,000 years old. Many of the earliest hominin sites occur in volcanically active areas. Human tools are found in direct association with cooled lava fragments or ash from contemporary eruptions, allowing the dating of the East Turkana locations, Olduvai Gorge, and other famous early sites. Potassium (K), an abundant element in the Earth's crust, is present in nearly every mineral. In its natural form, potassium contains only a small proportion of radioactive potassium-40 (^{40}K) atoms. For every 100 ^{40}K atoms that decay, 11 percent become argon-40 (^{40}Ar), an inert gas that can easily escape from its material by diffusion when lava and other igneous rocks are formed. As volcanic rock forms by crystallization, the ^{40}Ar concentration drops to almost nothing, but the process of ^{40}K decay continues, and 11 percent of every 100 ^{40}K atoms will become ^{40}Ar. Thus, it is possible, using a spectrometer, to measure the concentration of ^{40}Ar that has accumulated since the volcanic rock formed.

Recent advances in potassium-argon dating involve computerized laser fusion, a variant of the method that uses a laser beam to analyze irradiated grains of volcanic ash that give off a gas; that gas is purified, and its constituent argon atoms are measured in a spectrometer. The new method draws on crystals of volcanic materials from layers associated with hominin fossils to produce much more accurate dates, like readings of about 3.18 million years for Lucy, *Australopithecus afarensis*.

Potassium-argon dating has provided the first relatively reliable method of establishing the chronology of the earliest stages of human evolution and of the first human cultures on Earth.

Figure 8.3 Artist's reconstruction of *Ardipithecus ramidus*.
Source: J. H. Matternes.

essential for tree climbing. However, *Ardipithecus* was nothing like a modern ape, with highly flexible wrists and fingers, which meant that she walked on her palms while in the trees. The limb anatomy is quite unlike that of modern chimpanzees and gorillas, which are well adapted to climbing up trees and hanging from branches.

What, then, is *A. ramidus*? Is it the hominin who evolved into *Australopithecus* forms, described below? Or is it a relic that possessed a mosaic of both primitive and more advanced traits that eventually became extinct? Paleoanthropologist Tim White, one of the leaders of the team, believes that he has seen nothing that excludes *Ardipithecus* from being an ancestor of modern humans, but he, like everyone else, points out that many more fossil discoveries are needed to resolve the question of ancestry. At this point, the weight of the evidence favors some sort of ancestral relationship with two later East African hominins.

Australopithecus anamensis *and* Australopithecus afarensis

Allia Bay, Kenya Site near Lake Turkana that yielded *A. anamensis*, c. 4 Ma.

Kanapoi, Kenya Site near Lake Turkana that yielded *A. anamensis*, c. 4 Ma.

About 4 million years ago, another form of upright-walking hominin flourished at **Allia Bay** and **Kanapoi**, on the shores of Lake Turkana, northern Kenya. The fossil fragments, found by Meave Leakey and Alan Walker and named *A. anamensis* (*anam* means "lake" in Turkana), come from a hominin with large teeth and a mosaic of what appear to be apelike and more evolved features. The hind limbs are thick enough to support the extra weight of walking on two feet, but *A. anamensis* was not as efficient a walker as modern humans.

Measurements of the hind limb suggest that the hominin weighed between 47 and 55 kilograms (104–121 pounds). The anatomical relationships between the Aramis fossils and this later find still remain highly uncertain.

Hadar, Ethiopia Location where *A. afarensis* has been found, dating to about 3 Ma.

A. ramidus and *A. anamensis* were the ancestors of a much better known and somewhat later australopithecine found at **Hadar,** about 72 kilometers (45 miles) north of Aramis, also on the Middle Awash River. It was at Hadar, in northern Ethiopia, that Maurice Taieb and Donald Johanson discovered a remarkably complete skeleton of a small primate (the famous "Lucy"), together with fragments of at least 13 males, females, and children. Lucy, who dates to about 3.2 million years ago, stood just under 1.2 meters (4 feet) tall and was 19 to 21 years old (see Figure 8.4). She was a powerful, heavily muscled primate, fully bipedal, with arms slightly longer for her size than those of humans. Lucy and her contemporaries had humanlike hands and brains about the size of those of chimpanzees. Johanson and Tim White have classified Lucy as *A. afarensis*, implying that the Hadar hominins were direct ancestors of later australopithecines. Undoubtedly, they are correct.

A nearly intact *A. afarensis* skull and arm bones from several other males have come from another Awash location about 1.6 kilometers (1 mile) upstream and date to about 3 Ma, some 200,000 years later than Lucy. This important find confirms that all the *A. afarensis* fragments found over the past 20 years are from a single australopithecine species. It also confirms that *A. afarensis* displays considerable size variation. Some individuals stood 1.5 meters (5 feet) tall and probably weighed approximately 68 kilograms (150 pounds), a far cry from the comparatively small and slender Lucy.

arboreal Living in trees.

These early australopithecines were powerful, heavily muscled individuals, thought to be as strong as chimpanzees. Like *A. ramidus*, *A. afarensis* was an anatomical mosaic, bipedal from the waist down, **arboreal** in the upper part of the body. All were fully bipedal, with the robust, curved arms associated with tree climbers. The arms were slightly longer for their size than the arms of modern humans.

Laetoli, Tanzania Site where hominin footprints were preserved in hardened volcanic ash 3.7 Ma.

Figure 8.4 Reconstruction of *Australopithecus afarensis* (Lucy).
Source: Universal Images Group Limited/Alamy.

Even more remarkable evidence of bipedalism comes from fossil-bearing beds at **Laetoli** in Tanzania, where Mary Leakey uncovered not only hominin fossils like those at Hadar, but also the actual 3.7-million-year-old footprints of big game and some fairly large bipedal primates (see Figure 8.5). The footsteps are those of an adult male and female, the latter carrying a child. "The tracks indicate a rolling and probably slow-moving gait, with the hips swiveling at each step, as opposed to the freestanding gait of modern man," Mary Leakey wrote (Leakey and Harris 1990, 49). Some scientists believe that the Laetoli prints are from *A. afarensis*, flourishing about 1,600 kilometers (1,000 miles) south of Hadar.

Koto Toro, Chad *A. afarensis* site south of the central Sahara dating to about 3.0 to 3.5 Ma.

The Hadar and Laetoli finds confirm that the fundamental human adaptation of bipedalism predates the first evidence of toolmaking and the expansion of the brain

Figure 8.5 Hominin footprints from Laetoli, Tanzania.
Source: John Reader/Photo Researchers/Science Source.

beyond the level found in our nearest living relatives, the African apes. Bipedalism also implies that later hominins were preadapted (had evolved sufficiently) to use their hands for toolmaking.

Originally, experts thought *A. afarensis* was confined to East Africa. French paleontologist Michel Brunet has discovered a 3–3.5-million-year-old fossilized *A. afarensis* jaw with seven teeth at **Koto Toro** in Chad, in the southern reaches of the Sahara Desert. The Chad hominin flourished in a savanna-woodland environment, much wetter than the arid landscape of today. Koto Toro is the first australopithecine find west of East Africa's Rift Valley and debunks a long-held theory that the great valley formed a barrier separating ape populations and causing those in more open country to move from the trees on to the ground. The evolutionary picture was much more complex than that.

Many scientists consider *A. afarensis* a primitive form of the australopithecine that displayed considerable anatomical variation yet was hard enough to adapt to harsh, changing savanna environments and survive for nearly a million years. Without question, there were several as yet largely unknown hominin forms in eastern Africa before 3 million years ago.

About 3 million years ago, the descendants of *A. afarensis* split into different lines. At this point, the evolutionary plot really thickens. One line comprises the more gracile

A. africanus, first identified by Raymond Dart in 1925 and known entirely from South Africa, far from the putative East African cradle of humankind. The second line held at least three species of robustly built australopithecines, somewhat later than *A. africanus*, which became extinct by 1 million years ago. There are certainly other, still undescribed lines. With this diversification, we emerge into a more complex chapter in human evolution, marked by geographic and biological diversification and many competing theories. As British biological anthropologist Chris Stringer once put it, "The field is littered with abandoned ancestors and the theories that went with them" (1984, 52). Here follows an overview of the australopithecines who existed from around 3.5 Ma to 2 Ma.

Gracile Australopithecines: **Australopithecus africanus**

A. africanus (3.3–2.1 Ma) was a gracile, highly mobile hominin, marked in fossil form by a small, almost delicate skull and prognathous (jutting-out) face (see Figure 8.6). Found exclusively in South Africa, *A. africanus* is an evolutionary mystery, for no one has yet found this form in East Africa, where *A. afarensis* (3.9–2.9 Ma) flourished, despite the belief that *A. africanus* was related to this widely distributed ancestor. It could have been an evolutionary experiment that went nowhere or may even have been among the first of a doomed line of robust hominins.

Robust Australopithecines: **A. aethiopicus, A. boisei,** *and* **A. robustus**

The robust australopithecines, known by several taxonomic labels, lived between around 3 million to 1 million years ago. Found in both eastern and southern Africa, they are remarkable for their heavy build. These hominins had small brains and large teeth that were specialized for the chewing of coarse, fibrous plant foods (see Figure 8.7). As a group, these squat, heavily built hominins were very diverse.

Australopithecus garhi

Working the arid wastes of Ethiopia's Awash Desert, a team of 40 researchers from 13 countries recently unearthed teeth and skull fragments from yet another hominin form,

Figure 8.6 Australopithecus africanus skull.
Source: Javier Trueba/MSF/Science Photo Library.

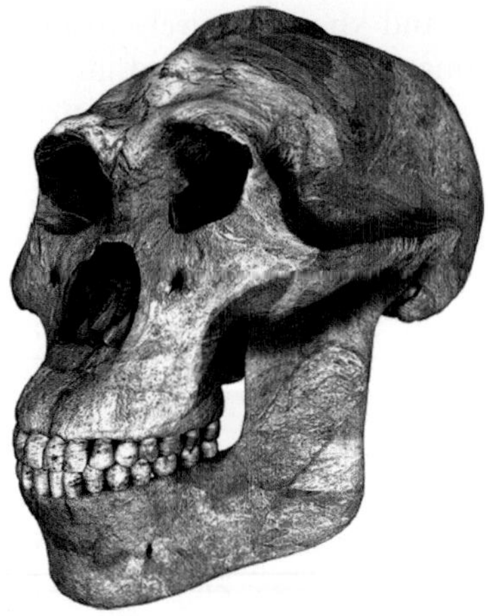

Figure 8.7 Australopithecus robustus skull.
Source: Friedrich Saurer/Science Photo Library.

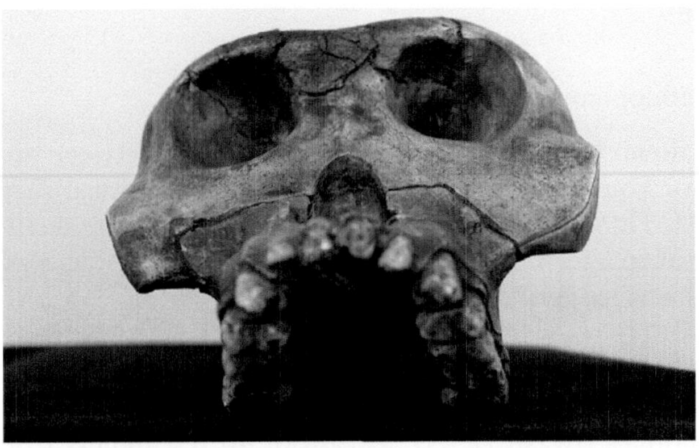

Figure 8.8 Australopithecus garhi.
Source: Hemis/Superstock.

dating to around 2.6 Ma to 2.5 Ma. The new hominin, named *Australopithecus garhi* (*garhi* means "surprise" in the local dialect), stood about 1.46 meters (4 feet 10 inches) tall and had protruding features, much like those of a chimpanzee (see Figure 8.8). The lower molars were three times the size of those of modern humans, the canines almost as large. *A. garhi*'s brain was only a third of the size of a modern human brain. The legs were long and humanlike, while the arms were long and more like an ape's. This hominin was an efficient scavenger. Bones of antelope and other large animals found only a few feet away display cut marks from stone tools, the earliest known instance of hominin butchering of animals. Unfortunately, no stone tools were found close to the fossil remains, but surface finds of crude stone flakes and cobbles have come from a nearby lakebed level have been associated with it.

That this hominin was eating meat suggests that a switch to a high-energy, high-fat meat diet was under way. This may, in turn, have led to an increase in brain size among some hominins, which occurred only a few hundred thousand years later. With its apparent tool-making and meat-eating propensities, *A. garhi* could conceivably be the exclusive ancestor of the *Homo* family tree and technically the first member of our genus. No one, least of all Tim White, the leading expert on *A. garhi*, is prepared to make such a claim on so little fossil evidence. What we do know is that a far-from-robust australopithecine derived from *A. afarensis* survived until at least 2.5 Ma. But whether this form participated in a rapid evolutionary transition or in a series of transitions into an early form of *Homo* remains a complete mystery. However, we do know that major changes to the hominin skull and face occurred after 2.5 Ma, many of them as a direct consequence of brain enlargement. New behavior patterns connected with obtaining more meat and marrow using stone tools may have played an important role during what may have been a short and crucial period of human evolution.

Early *Homo*: *Homo habilis* (c. 2.5 Million to 1.6 Million Years Ago)

Koobi Fora, Kenya Location of some of the earliest traces of stone manufacture in the world, c. 2.5 Ma.

East Turkana, Kenya Location where fossil hominins and their sites date to c. 2.5–1.6 Ma.

Louis and Mary Leakey were the first to identify a hominin that was classified as early *Homo* at Olduvai Gorge in Tanzania in 1960. They named their fragmentary discovery *H. habilis* ("handy person"), a label that commemorated the assumed toolmaking abilities of these hominins. Then, Richard Leakey found the famous Skull 1470 at **Koobi Fora** in **East Turkana**, a large-brained, round-headed cranium that confirmed the existence of *H. habilis* in no uncertain terms (see Figure 8.9).

If you had encountered *H. habilis* 2 million years ago, you would have seen little to distinguish the new hominin from *Australopithecus*. Both were of similar height and weight, about 1.3 meters (4 feet 3 inches) tall and about 40 kilograms (88 pounds). Both were bipedal, but *H. habilis* would have looked less apelike around the face and skull. The head was higher and rounder, the faceless protruding, and the jaw smaller. Some of the most significant anatomical differences involved the more even and less specialized teeth. The molars were narrower, the premolars smaller, and the incisors larger and more spade-like, as if they were used for slicing. However, microscopic wear studies of the teeth have shown that both *Australopithecus* and *H. habilis* were primarily fruit eaters, so there does not seem to have been a major shift in diet between the two. *H. habilis* had a larger brain, with a cranial capacity between 600 and 700 cubic centimeters (37–43 cubic inches), in contrast to that of australopithecines, which ranged between 400 and 500 cubic centimeters (24–31 cubic inches).

Thigh and limb bones from Koobi Fora and from Olduvai confirm that *H. habilis* walked upright. The hand bones are somewhat more curved and robust than those of modern humans. This was a powerful grasping hand, more like that of chimpanzees and gorillas than of humans, a hand ideal for climbing trees. An opposable thumb allowed both powerful gripping and the precise manipulation of fine objects. With the latter capacity, *H. habilis* could have made complex tools. There was probably a considerable difference in size between males and females.

H. habilis's skeletal anatomy gives a mosaic picture of both primitive and more advanced features, of a hominin that both walked bipedally and retained the generalized

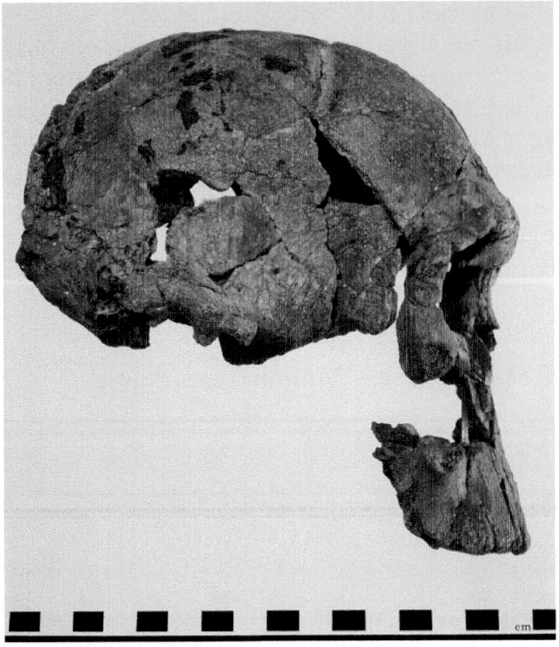

Figure 8.9 Skull 1470 from East Turkana, northern Kenya, a specimen of early *Homo* known as *Homo habilis*.

Source: John Reader/Science Photo Library.

hominoid ability to climb trees. A telling clue comes from one of the Olduvai specimen's upper arm bones, which, like Lucy's, are within 95 percent of the length of the thigh bone. The chimpanzee has upper arm and upper leg bones of almost equal length, whereas modern human upper arms are only 70 percent of the length of the upper leg bones. Almost certainly *H. habilis* spent a great deal of time climbing trees, an adaptation that would make it much less human in behavior, and presumably in social structure, than had been assumed even a few years ago.

H. habilis, like many taxonomic labels, accommodates what may actually be two or more early human species. The resulting proliferation of hominin names reflects a concern with documenting an anatomical variation that far exceeded possible differences between males and females. For example, *H. habilis* may have lived alongside another East African form, *Homo rudolfensis*. For clarity, we retain the generic term early *Homo* here but stress that it disguises considerable morphological variation, especially after 2 Ma, when new human forms were evolving in Africa and perhaps in Asia, too.

A Burst of Rapid Change?

Our scientific predecessors thought of evolution as a gradual and progressive mechanism. The early East African fossils suggest a very different scenario, coinciding with that of the current view of evolution as "punctuated equilibrium"—long periods of relative stability, followed by bursts of rapid change caused by new, selective pressures resulting from altered conditions, perhaps environmental change or changes in the organism itself.

Such a burst of rapid change could have taken hold during the years that separate *A. garhi* from *H. habilis*. Regardless of who was the first toolmaker, the development of stone tool technology gave its inventors a major advantage over other hominin species. Stone hammers and flakes let them exploit predator kills and thus shift to an energy-rich, high-fat diet, which could lead to all manner of evolutionary consequences. During the millennia that separated early *Homo* (*H. habilis*) from *H. erectus*, who appeared in East Africa about 1.9 Ma, brain size increased. While *H. habilis*'s brain size ranged from 600 to 700 cubic centimeters (or 36–43 cubic inches), the brain size of the African *H. erectus* ranged from 600 to 910 cubic centimeters (or 37–56 cubic inches). As to the *H. erectus* specimens found in Asia, their brain sizes ranged yet larger: from 750 to 1,300 cubic centimeters (or 46–79 cubic inches). There were further modifications in hips and limbs for bipedal locomotion and a reduction in sexual dimorphism (size difference due to sex). The primitive body form and sexual dimorphism characteristic of earlier hominins vanished only with the emergence of the much more advanced *H. erectus*. But what caused this change of evolutionary pace remains a mystery, although climate change, especially cooler temperatures, played a role.

Defining *Homo*

A couple of generations ago, human evolution was thought of as a ladder through time, with an apelike ancestor at the base and modern humans at the top. These creatures were thought to become human at the moment when toolmaking began. This was the reasoning that caused the great controversies of the 1960s as to who was the earliest toolmaker. Was it *Australopithecus* or some closely related hominin form, like the hopefully named *Homo habilis*? As the pace of discovery accelerated, it became apparent that there were several hominin forms around at the time when toolmaking began, making identification of the first "human" an even more challenging task. In recent years, four criteria have generally been used to assign a fossil to the genus *Homo*:

- An absolute brain size of 600 cubic centimeters (37 cubic inches) or more.
- The possession of some language, identified from casts of the brain patterns on the inside of the braincase.
- The possession of a modern, humanlike precision grip and an opposable thumb.
- The ability to manufacture stone tools.

There are serious problems with all of these criteria. Absolute brain capacity is of dubious biological importance. We now know that evidence of language cannot be inferred from a braincase. Furthermore, we still do not know much about the range of precision grips found among the earliest hominins. Stone tools are an inconclusive criterion to use, simply because at 2.6 Ma, both early *Homo* and robust australopithecines flourished in the same area where some of the earliest artifacts are found, while the very earliest known stone tools (as detailed later in this chapter) date to 3.3 Ma—quite a stretch in time before *Homo*.

adaptive radiation A burst of evolution, when a single species fills a number of ecological niches, the result being several new forms.

cladistics A method of analyzing evolutionary relationships that stresses diversity.

Hominin evolution involves a far greater level of species diversity than was previously thought. Human evolution can be seen as one or more instances of **adaptive radiation** (a burst of evolution in which a single species diverges to fill a number of ecological niches, the result being a variety of new forms) rather than a simple, one-track evolution of successive species. This view stems from **cladistics,** an analytical system for reconstructing evolutionary relationships, first proposed in the 1950s. Classical evolutionary analysis is based on morphological similarities between organisms. So is cladistics, but with a difference: cladistic analysis concentrates not only on features that identify common ancestry, but also on those that are derived independently and are unique to specific lineages. Inevitably, cladistics tends to emphasize diversity over homogeneity.

monophyletic Descended from a single ancestor.

A cladistic definition considers the human genus a group of species that are more closely related to one another than to species assigned to another genus. This interpretation insists that the human genus is **monophyletic,** that is, with all its members ultimately descended from a common ancestor. Bernard Wood and Mark Collard define the human genus as "a species, or monophylum, whose members occupy a single adaptive zone" (1999, 66). Using this definition, they carried out a cladistic analysis of all the known fossil *Homo* species and devised a scheme that separates all the australopithecine forms; and *H. habilis* into one genus; and later humans, starting with *Homo erectus* (or *Homo ergaster* as the African form of *erectus* is sometimes known), into another (see Figure 8.10). Their intricate statistical analyses suggest that enough is known of body size and shape, locomotion, development, and relative size of chewing apparatus to divide fossil hominins' adaptive strategies into two broad groups:

- The australopithecines and *H. habilis* (and variants) belong in a group of hominins with a reasonably low body mass, a body shape better suited to a relatively closed environment, and a postcranial skeleton that combines terrestrial bipedalism with expert climbing. The teeth and jaws of these hominins are well adapted to chewing and biting a varied and mechanically demanding diet. Studies of *Australopithecus* teeth and upper leg bones show that the rate of development (and dependence) of young hominins in this group was closer to that of modern African apes. The tooth

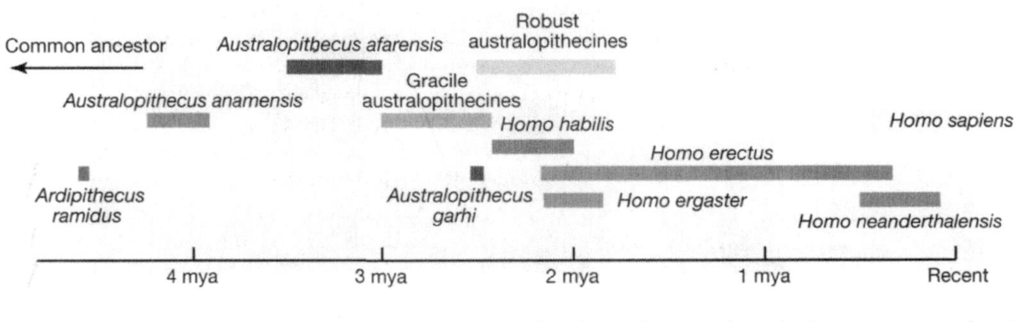

Figure 8.10 A highly simplified diagram showing the chronology and evolutionary status of early hominins and humans.

development of *H. habilis* and other early *Homo* forms also appears to have been closer to that of African apes, as if their development period was also shorter than that of modern humans.

- *Homo erectus*, and contemporary and later human forms belong in a second group, marked by a larger body mass, a modern, humanlike physique that was adaptive in more open terrain, and a postcranial skeleton consistent with terrestrial bipedalism. The ability to move around in trees was very limited, and teeth and jaws had mechanical properties similar to those of modern humans.

This definition of *Homo* makes a clear distinction between the hominins of earlier than 1.9 Ma and *H. erectus* and its successors who evolved after that date. It implies that a behavioral and evolutionary chasm separates true humans from the many other hominins who flourished in Africa before 2 Ma. Just what caused this adaptive shift in human evolution is unknown. Did it correspond with significant climatic and environmental changes, with equivalent evolutionary changes in other large mammal groups, or with specific changes in hominin culture? The answers will have to come from a new generation of research.

Hominin evolution can be thought of as a series of adaptive radiations that unfolded over at least 6 million years. The first radiation was of bipedal apes, which lived, for the most part, in the drier parts of Africa. Two later radiations gave rise to what is still called early *Homo* and the robust australopithecines, each with their own adaptive theme. In the case of early *Homo*, expanded brain size played a key role, while the robust australopithecines developed specialized teeth. Although the latter varied greatly in morphological terms, later humans radiated not so much morphologically as ecologically, spreading from Africa and creating distinct geographic populations. This flowering of hominin types is exactly what evolution is about: "an endless production of novel ways of doing things, exploring alternatives, trying out new strategies as conditions themselves shift and change all driven by natural selection" (Foley 1995, 103). Hominins were no different than other mammals, which began as a slim stem and radiated into distinct branches. We still do not know much about the relationships between such branches.

This same pattern of adaptive radiation may have continued much later in prehistory, during the long millennia when *H. erectus* flourished in Africa, Asia, and Europe. Only a small part of this evolutionary process resulted in modern humans, *Homo sapiens*, in Africa.

The Earliest Human Technology

"Humans the toolmakers"—this phrase has served to distinguish the earliest toolmaking humans from all other primates of the day, hailing their ability to manufacture tools as a clear sign of that uniquely human attribute, culture (see Chapter 1). Other animals like chimpanzees make tools to dig for grubs or other specific purposes, but only people manufacture artifacts regularly and habitually as well as in a much more complex fashion. We have gone much further in the toolmaking direction than other primates. One reason is that our brains allow us to plan our actions much more in advance.

The earliest human tools may well have been made of perishable wood, perhaps rudimentary clubs, digging sticks, or spears, but they have not survived. Animal bones from Dikika in Ethiopia, dating to 3.4 Ma, have signs of cut marks that were quite likely made by stone tools that remain undiscovered. Indeed, the oldest known stone tools are those from the site of **Lomekwi 3** in West Turkana, Kenya, and were probably the work of local hominins, perhaps a relatively small-brained species known as *Kenyanthropus platyops*.

Despite their crude appearance, the Lomekwi 3 tools are enormously significant to us, as archaeologists, for they provide the start date for the origin of all human material culture.

Prior to their discovery in the 2010s, the oldest known tools were dated to 2.6 Ma and are those from the Olduvai Gorge, in East Africa. Known generically as Oldowan technology, such tools occur in large numbers throughout eastern and southern Africa and are associated with broken animal bones in the East Turkana region (see Figure 8.11) and at Olduvai Gorge (see Box 8.2). They were made from convenient pebbles, some perhaps converted into simple choppers by removing one or two flakes.

Lomekwi 3, Kenya Site in West Turkana, Kenya; home of earliest known, crudely chopped, stone tools, dated to 3.3 Ma.

Oldowan Earliest known widespread human stone tool technology, based on simple flakes and choppers, which appeared about 2.6 Ma and remained in use for nearly a million years; named after Olduvai Gorge.

tuff Volcanic bedrock.

Stone tool expert Nicholas Toth has shown that the most important artifacts were not pebbles or even crude choppers, but the sharp-edged flakes removed from them (see Figure 8.13). Angular flakes and lumps of lava made weapons, scrapers, and cutting tools, used to cut meat, butcher animals, and perhaps shape wood. There are few formal tools, but Toth's controlled experiments show that the first toolmakers had a clear understanding

Figure 8.11 The arid landscape of East Turkana, where many early human fossils have been found. Source: christophe_cerisier/iStock via Getty Images.

Box 8.2 Site
Olduvai Gorge, Tanzania

Olduvai Gorge is a vast gash in the game-rich Serengeti Plain of northern Tanzania, formed by an earthquake more than 100,000 years ago and called a miniature Grand Canyon by many visitors (see Figure 8.12). The Earth movement exposed a long series of ancient lakebeds extending back as far as 2 Ma, stratified in the walls of the gorge. Geologists have identified four major series of lakebeds, labeled Bed I (at the base) to Bed IV, which formed in a semiarid environment much like that of today.

Olduvai was discovered by German butterfly hunter Wilhelm Kattwinkel before World War I and was investigated by paleontologist Hans Reck in the 1920s. Reck found numerous fossil animal bones, including a long-extinct elephant that he named after himself. Today, more than 150 species of extinct animals, ranging in size from elephants to birds and rodents, are known from Olduvai. But the gorge will always be associated with Louis and Mary Leakey, who realized the great potential of Olduvai for documenting early human evolution. Louis Leakey first found stone axes in the gorge in 1931. Between 1935 and 1959, the Leakeys surveyed and excavated numerous sites and published an important monograph on the Olduvai stone tools in which they traced the evolution of stone artifacts from a simple technology based on lava lumps—an approach they named the **Oldowan**—to progressively more complex and better-made hand axes and flake tools (the Acheulian). In 1959, they discovered *Z. boisei* and changed the chronicle of human evolution forever. Subsequently, large-scale excavations by the Leakeys unearthed other hominin fossils, including *H. habilis*, whom they considered the first toolmaker. Don Johanson of Lucy fame has also worked in the gorge and recovered further *H. habilis* fragments.

Figure 8.12 Olduvai Gorge, Tanzania.
Source: Steven Allan/iStock via Getty Images.

The most important Olduvai hominin fossils come from Beds I and II. Bed I lies on a volcanic bedrock, known as a **tuff**, which has been potassium-argon dated to about 2 Ma, an excellent baseline for the lakebed sequence above. The beds themselves were close to the shore of an extensive shallow lake that expanded and contracted from one season to the next. The waters covered places where hominins had paused to process and eat animal parts they had scavenged from nearby predator kills, preserving both stone tool fragments and broken animal bones, as well as the occasional hominin fossil in situ.

Excavating these land surfaces requires great patience and skill. Once a location is identified, the investigators sift the ground surrounding the original find through fine screens, looking for significant fossils. Then, they excavate into the lakebed to establish the stratigraphic relationship of the ancient land surface to the surrounding lakebed layers before exposing the scatter of artifacts and bones in the horizontal plane. This process is slow moving and calls for meticulous excavation and recording, with each fragment, even those as small as snake fangs, being exposed in place and then its precise location being recorded before removal. The end product after months of work is a precise three-dimensional plan of the artifact and bone scatter so that the relationships between stone fragments and other finds, including any hominin fossils, are established with the greatest possible precision.

The pioneer excavation methods used by the Leakeys at Olduvai have been adopted and refined in both the Lake Turkana and Hadar regions, where archaeologists work alongside human paleontologists, geologists, geomorphologists, and other specialists in a multidisciplinary investigation of the earliest human behavior.

of the potential of stone as the basis for a simple, highly effective technology that grew more complex over time. Eventually, the simple choppers evolved into crude ax-like tools, flaked on both surfaces—the hand axes used widely over a million years ago.

Nicholas Toth has replicated thousands of Oldowan artifacts and has shown by experiment that sharp-edged flakes are highly effective for slitting skin and butchering game animals. By studying the working edges of the tools under microscopes, he has detected wear from three possible uses: (1) butchering and meat cutting, (2) sawing and scraping wood, and (3) cutting soft plant matter. Toth believes our earliest ancestors had a good sense of the mechanics of stone tool manufacture. They were able to find the correct acute angle for removing flakes by percussion. Not even modern beginners have this capacity; it takes hours of intensive practice to acquire the skill.

Unlike chimpanzees, who rarely tote the sticks and stones they use more than a few yards, early Homo carried flakes and pebbles over considerable distances, up to 14 kilometers (9 miles). This behavior represents a simple form of curation, retaining tools for future use rather than just utilizing convenient stones, as chimpanzees do.

Toth hypothesizes that the hominins tested materials in streambeds and other locations, transported the best pieces to activity areas, and sometimes dropped them there, carrying the rest off with them. He also points out that they must have relied heavily on other raw materials, like wood and bone, and that stone artifacts do not necessarily give an accurate picture of early hominin cognitive abilities.

What does the Oldowan mean? Did the early toolmakers possess a form of "protohuman culture," with its simple stone artifacts a first step on the long evolutionary trail

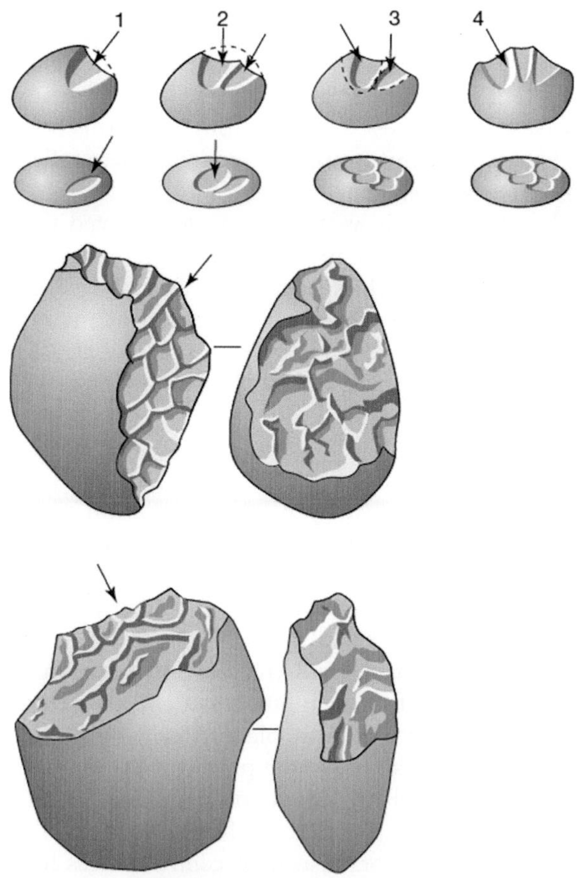

Figure 8.13 The earliest widespread human technology is the Oldowan industry, named after Olduvai Gorge (note that the 3.3 million-year-old Lomekwi 3 tools from Kenya vastly predate this broad industry). Many cobbles at Koobi Fora and Olduvai were used as cores to produce sharp-edged flakes. First, sharp blows were struck near the natural edge of a pebble to remove flakes. The pebble was then turned over, and more blows were struck on the ridges formed by the scars of the earlier flakes. A core with a jagged edge, perhaps used as a chopper, resulted. Many cores were "mined" for as many flakes as possible before being discarded. The figure shows Oldowan cores from Olduvai Gorge. Arrows show flake edges. Front and side views are shown 40 percent of actual size.

to modern humanity? Or were the Oldowan hominins, and certainly those at Lomekwi 3, simply at an apelike grade of behavior? After all, the conceptual abilities and perceptions needed to manufacture Lomekwi 3 or Oldowan tools also appear in ape-manufactured tools like termite-fishing tools and sleeping platforms. Furthermore, not only Oldowan hominins, but also chimpanzees scavenged and hunted for game—chasing down small animals, carrying meat over considerable distances, and using convenient objects to break open animal bones and nuts.

Chimpanzees, like early hominins, use the same places again and again, pounding nuts at the same locations and carrying food to their favorite eating sites. Even if the specifics vary in some instances and the natural environments are different, the behavioral pattern of Lomekwi 3 or Oldowan hominins is generally similar to that of apes. There are, however, two behavioral differences between apes and early hominins. First, hominins were at an advantage in that they were bipedal, a posture that is far more efficient for carrying objects than walking on four limbs. Second, Lomekwi 3 and the Oldowan humans were adapted to savanna living, where they had to organize and cover far larger territories in open country than their primate relatives in the forest. Over the long term, this may have resulted in new concepts of space and spatial organization, concepts that were reflected in more complex stone tool forms a million or so years ago.

Early hominins with their larger brains probably would not have behaved the same way as modern apes. We can be certain that there were significant differences between nonhuman primates and hominins 2 Ma, but these changes may not be reflected in stone artifacts. Without question, our ancestors became more and more dependent on technology. The opportunistic nature of primeval stone technology is in sharp contrast to the better-designed, much more standardized stone artifacts of later humans.

Hunters or Scavengers?

Studying early hominin behavior is complicated both by poor preservation conditions and by the vast time chasm that separates us from our remotest ancestors. Two sources of information on very early human behavior survive in East Africa. The first is manufactured artifacts; the second is scatters of tools and food remains found at a few locations like Koobi Fora and Olduvai.

Concentrations of broken animal bones and stone tools in these two regions and a few others have been excavated and studied with meticulous care. The concentrations are usually only some 6 to 9 meters (20 to 30 feet) across, places that were visited and used by hominins either once or on several occasions. Later prehistoric foragers made habitual use of central places where they returned to sleep, cook food, and engage in a wide variety of social activities. Are we, then, to assume that the Koobi Fora and Olduvai concentrations are evidence that our earliest ancestors also used central places like their successors did? Did they hunt and kill big-game animals, or did they merely scavenge flesh from abandoned predator kills?

At Koobi Fora, a group of hominins found the carcass of a hippopotamus in a streambed about 1.8 Ma. They gathered around and removed bones and meat from the dead animal with small stone flakes. The sandy deposits in which the artifacts lay are so fine that we can be certain that every stone cobble was carried in to make tools at the carcass, some of them from as far as 14 kilometers (9 miles) away. The site contains abundant evidence of butchering and of tool manufacture, but we do not know if the hominins actually killed the animal.

Site FxJj50, at Koobi Fora as well, is also in an ancient watercourse, a place where the hominins could find shade from the blazing Sun, located close to water and abundant toolmaking stone (see Figure 8.11). The site is a cluster of stone artifacts and fragments, including sharp flakes, choppers, and scraping tools. More than 2,000 bones from at least 17 mammalian species, mostly antelope, are associated with the tools, some of which have been chewed by hyenas and other carnivores. There are clear signs that the bones were smashed and cut by hominins, for reconstructed fragments show traces of hammer blows and fine linear grooves that may have resulted only from cutting bone with stone flakes. Many of the FxJj50 bones had their articular ends chewed off by carnivores, a characteristic of bone accumulations resulting from carnivore kills. Perhaps the hominins simply chased away lions and other predators and moved in on a fresh kill; we cannot be sure.

At Olduvai Gorge, Mary Leakey plotted artifact and bone scatters in the lowest levels of the ancient lakebed. Many artifacts and bones were concentrated in areas about 4.6 meters (15 feet) across. At one site, a pile of shattered bones and rocks lay a short distance away, the bones perhaps piled in heaps as the marrow was extracted from them. Microscopic studies of the Olduvai scatters have shown that many of the bones were heavily weathered. They had lain on the surface for considerable periods of time, some for perhaps as long as a decade. The bones of many different animals come from the scatters, parts of carcasses from a very ecologically diverse set of animals. Limb bones predominate, as if these body parts were repeatedly carried to the sites.

At both Koobi Fora and Olduvai, meat- and marrow-rich bones occur concentrated in small areas with stone tools. The percentage of carnivore bones is somewhat higher than in the natural environment, as if there was intense competition between hominins and other carnivores. Perhaps, the presence of such predators restricted the activities of hominins at Olduvai. They may have grabbed meat from fresh carnivore kills and then taken their booty to a place where they had a collection of stone tools near water or other predictable food supplies. There they would hastily cut off meat and extract the marrow before abandoning the fresh bones to the carnivores hovering nearby. Without fire or domesticated animals, scientists believe that *H. habilis* probably had to rely on opportunistic foraging for game meat, it being unsafe to camp near open watercourses or on lakeshores. It is worth noting that one hominin bone found at Olduvai Gorge had been gnawed by carnivores.

Most of the bones from the Olduvai accumulations are of smaller animals that could be run down and thrown to the ground with ease. This is more of an apelike form of behavior, although apes have been observed scavenging meat. Microscopic studies of the Olduvai bones show that the hominins rarely butchered and disarticulated large animals and carried their bones back to base. They seem to have obtained meat without cutting up too many carcasses, as if they scavenged it from already dismembered predator kills. In some cases, human cutting marks overlay predator tooth marks, as if the hominins had scavenged bones from carcasses that had already been killed by other animals. In others, predators have chewed bones abandoned by *Homo*.

Archaeologist Robert Blumenschine spent several field seasons studying animal predators on the game-rich Serengeti Plain of northern Tanzania. Semiarid grassland crossed by occasional streams lined with trees—this was the kind of environment that early hominins shared with other predators like lions and hyenas. Blumenschine observed dozens of predator kills, studying the abandoned shattered bones and comparing them with the archaeological finds at Olduvai Gorge.

As a result of these observations, Blumenschine concluded that the hominins could take unique advantage of two scavenging opportunities. The first was near streams, because lions kill close to water in the dry season. Sometimes more than a day would elapse before hyenas moved in: ample time, Blumenschine believes, for hominins to seize their share. It is here, too, that leopards hide small antelope kills in trees, high above the ground but not out of reach of humans. Scavenging would have been most common in the dry months, when game (and predators) stayed near permanent water supplies and plant foods were in short supply. During the rains, both antelope and predators would range far over the plains, where it was easy for hyenas to find lion kills. But these were the months when hominins relied on plant foods and fruit in more wooded environments. Blumenschine argues that scavenging and plant gathering went hand in hand, each complementing the other at different times of year. Opportunism has always been an important quality of humankind, from the earliest times. Undoubtedly, however, plants and all kinds of vegetable foods made up a major part, if not the largest part, of the very early human diet. The Blumenschine theory is somewhat controversial, with other experts arguing that the earliest humans hunted animals as well as doing some scavenging. The debate continues.

Plant Foraging and Grandmothering

Beyond some microscopic wear traces from plant tissues on early stone artifacts, there is as yet no archaeological evidence that plant foods were consumed by early hominins because such data do not preserve well. There is no question, however, that Lower Pleistocene hominins had diets very similar to those of modern nonhuman primates. *H. habilis* limb bones reveal an unexpected inconsistency, for their anatomy was far more arboreal than that of a terrestrial bipedal primate of 2 Ma. Such adept tree climbers are certain to have relied on fruit and other plant foods, perhaps enjoying a diet closer to that of modern apes than to that of hunter-gatherers.

A new generation of research is causing some rethinking of the long-held assumption that the earliest humans transported meat and bones from animals of all sizes back to sites for processing. More fieldwork among modern tropical foragers has shown that hunting, with its irregular success, though sometimes productive, is not a reliable strategy for feeding a family.

The old hunting arguments assumed that men hunted and women gathered plant foods—behavior said to be typical of hunter-gatherers, but not found among the great apes. This behavior pattern, it was argued, developed as a result of a long-term trend toward a cooler, drier climate 2 Ma that reduced the availability of plant foods while favoring the spread of game-rich savannas. According to this argument, males added large animals to the diet, a potentially sharable resource. Females paired with the hunters, which gave them access to the new food and enabled them to reduce their foraging activities. The nuclear family, sexual division of labor, and provisioning by the father came into being; female fertility and the survival of offspring increased; long dependence on parents by children, larger brain size, increased learning, and much greater behavioral flexibility resulted. The new hominins were successful in evolutionary terms because they possessed a great ability to cope with environmental diversity and could range over much larger territories.

Today, we are a little more self-aware. Anyone can see how this model simply reflected our own twentieth-century Western assumptions of what a family unit should look like (not least the idea that humans pair into a nuclear—or two parent—family headed by the active father). Moreover, we now know a great deal more about both nonhuman primates and hunter-gatherer life. For instance, male primates such as chimpanzees hunt frequently and share the meat with others but without any use of central places. Fieldwork among modern tropical hunter-gatherers shows that men do indeed hunt larger game, but the supply of such prey is unpredictable and is insufficient for the feeding of entire families and bands. It often serves social ends as much as it does dietary needs. It's also worth remembering that all modern hunter-gatherers live marginal lives, usually pushed into tough environments, which would not necessarily have been the case in deep prehistory when they could, relatively speaking, move where they wished. As we outlined in Chapter 6, modern lives cannot be assumed windows onto the past.

Moreover, current opinion holds that early hominins were not so much hunters as scavengers. It seems that they scavenged meat from predator kills, but even if the scavenging was aggressive, the meat supply could never have been sufficient to satisfy the daily nutritional requirements of adults and also of the young. Nor is there solid archaeological evidence that the scavengers transported meat to central places rather than consuming it close to where they scavenged meat and bones. As archaeologist James O'Connell and others point out, these observations transform and challenge many long-held assumptions about the behavior of early hominins—the notion that there was division of labor between males (hunting) and females (plant gathering) and the theory that there were nuclear families this early in human history.

O'Connell and his colleagues also developed a "grandmother hypothesis," based on ecological theory and field observations of modern-day tropical hunter-gatherers, specifically the Hadza people of Tanzania in East Africa. Everyone except the very old and very young are active, productive foragers. Very often, older women in their sixties and seventies are more efficient foragers than their younger female kin of reproductive age. By the age of 5, Hadza children can supply as much as half their daily nutritional requirements by their own efforts. Both mothers and grandmothers deliberately target easy-to-acquire foods, such as fruit during the rainy season that children can also take in large numbers. Foraging opportunities for children largely determine adult female strategies, especially during the rainy season. Then, when foods easily exploited by the young are unavailable, the adults provision them with other foods—in the case of the Hadza, the woody rootstock, a plant that favors deep, stony soils and requires considerable upper-body strength and endurance to acquire, as well as the use of fire to process it into food. Children under 8 ignore woody rootstock, but adults can acquire as much as 2,000 calories per hour from this plant in all seasons of the year. Thus, the Hadza can live in habitats that would be precluded if their young had to forage for themselves, as is the case with nonhuman primates.

Another factor comes into play as well. When a mother bears a child and is nursing, her foraging time declines. Now the grandmother steps in and takes up the slack, feeding the weaned children of her kin. The O'Connell team notes that childbearing careers are of similar length in apes and humans, but humans survive far longer after menopause. Weaned children depended on food from adults; ancestral human grandmothers would have had a chance to affect their fitness in ways other apes could not. The result was a selection against rapid aging, lower adult mortality rates, and lengthening adult life spans.

There are other effects, too. Instead of a reduced fecundity that accompanies aging, the assistance of grandmothers would pay off in higher fertility, allowing mothers to have babies more frequently. Not only do humans have longer life spans than our nonhuman relatives, but our ancestors began to mature later and to produce offspring at a higher rate. Again, while we may not be able to blindly fling this model onto the past, it does provide an interesting perspective.

Imagine an ancestral hominin group with a life history and foraging patterns similar to those of modern-day chimpanzees. The members reached maturity at about 10–12 years, with only moderate fecundity. Life expectancy was at most about 50 years, while juveniles for the most part foraged for themselves, albeit with some (probably minor) assistance from mothers and older siblings. Imagine, then, a scenario in which food supplies accessible to the same juveniles became scarcer—perhaps due to more arid conditions. The groups might adjust their foraging ranges, even abandoning some areas. Alternatively, they could invest more in provisioning, that is to say, the acquisition of food resources that had been ignored before because they were inaccessible to the young. Such resources would have to be predictable, constantly available, and in sufficient quantity to feed not only the collector, but also others over long periods of time. Without such qualities, the new supplies would be of limited use to the growing young.

As provisioning became a routine practice, so the role of older females, still active but no longer fertile, could have become more important as they helped in feeding the young. The result would be closer-spaced births and a higher survival rate for immature members of the group. After some time, the delayed mortality, a longer period of growth, larger adult body size, and later age of maturity would result.

Such hypothetical ancestral hominin populations would have enjoyed reduced juvenile mortality because of provisioning, which removed the pressures of competition for food among the young. If this occurred in areas with abundant food resources, larger foraging groups could have come into being, a situation in which grandmothers and other older kin would stay close to daughters and grandchildren to support them. This, in turn, would result in the exploitation of much larger foraging territories, where members of the band were not restrained by the foraging capabilities of the young. Inevitably, this would have led to more efficient ways of foraging, including new technologies such as stone tools.

The Earliest Human Mind

By 2 Ma, there were probably several species of early *Homo*, but for convenience, we can group them under a single toolmaking species, *H. habilis* or early *Homo*. What, if anything, were the specialized mental processes found in these earliest humans as opposed to much earlier hominins?

Some clues lie in stone tool manufacture. Chimpanzees shape termite twigs with their teeth from convenient wood fragments, removing leaves so they can poke the artifact down a small hole (see Figure 8.14). They are also said to use crude wooden spears. The making of stone tools requires good hand-eye coordination, the ability to recognize acute angles in stone, and the mental processes necessary to shape one tool by using another. But the hominin stoneworkers were carrying out simple tasks: shaping stones so they could hold

Figure 8.14 A chimpanzee using a stick to eat and grub for insects.
Source: jeryltan/iStock via Getty Images.

them in one hand to crack bones and striking off sharp-edged flakes. Their artifacts defy precise classification in the way that one can subdivide later stone tools into forms such as choppers, scrapers, and knives. Their lumps and flakes display continuous variability, an understanding of basic fracture mechanics, not the ability to impose standardized forms or to choose easily worked raw materials. Could chimpanzees have made such tools, as has been suggested? When Nicholas Toth tried to train a pygmy chimpanzee named Kanzi to make Oldowan-style tools, he found that Kanzi could make sharp flakes, but he never mastered the art of recognizing acute angles in stone or other flaking. Archaeologist Steven Mithen argues for two possibilities: either a more general intelligence had evolved, or some mental processes for basic stone working had appeared—intuitive physics in the mind of early *Homo*.

Early stone tools were mainly used to process animal carcasses, for skinning, cutting joints and meat, and breaking open bones. But how did early *Homo* interact with the natural world? One obvious and significant difference between early *Homo* and chimpanzees appears in the archaeological record of 2 Ma: a dramatic rise in meat consumption. In practice, early *Homo* was probably a behaviorally flexible, nonspecialized forager whose lifeway was marked by diversity and by shifts between hunting and scavenging and between food sharing and feeding on the move. The larger brain of early *Homo* would have required the consumption of more energy and a higher quality of diet. The stable basal metabolic rate was maintained by a reduction in the size of the gut, which could only become reduced as a result of a higher-meat diet, as a high-fiber diet requires more intestinal action.

Mithen argued that this need for more meat required a cognitive ability not needed for toolmaking—being able to use one's knowledge of the environment to develop ideas about where to find predator kills and high densities of animals. He argues that the presence of toolmaking stone up to 10 kilometers (6 miles) from its source is a sign that early *Homo* was moving not only stone, but also meat to different, sometimes third, ever-changing locations. Such ability suggests a relatively sophisticated interaction with the environment when compared with chimpanzees, which only transport "tools" to fixed locations.

Early *Homo* was so far confined to tropical Africa, to a relatively narrow range of savanna and grassland environments, in contrast with later humans, who adapted to every climate imaginable. Many groups lived close to permanent water, tethered, as it were, to places like the shallow lake at Olduvai, where sites are "stacked" one above another over considerable periods of time. Many animal species appear in the Olduvai caches, as if our ancestors ranged widely over the surrounding landscape, but they may have transported much of their food to well-defined locations.

Early *Homo* shared the ability of its earlier ancestors to "map" resources over wide areas. But it may also have possessed additional cognitive abilities: to develop ideas about where food might be found and to use telltale signs such as animal droppings to find it, within a relatively narrow environmental setting. At the same time, its general intelligence was supplemented by some specialized abilities in artifact manufacture, which were to be an important foundation for environmental intelligence in later millennia.

Social intelligence may have evolved significantly. Anthropologist Robin Dunbar has studied living primates and discovered evidence for larger brain size in individuals living in larger groups, developing an equation for relating brain size to group size. He then estimated the brain size of *H. habilis* and applied his figures to the chimpanzee equation. Chimpanzees lived in predicted group sizes of about 60 individuals. In contrast, he predicted that australopithecines lived in groups with a mean size of about 67 individuals, whereas early *Homo* flourished in larger groups of about 81. Group living was an essential for early *Homo*, which lived in an environment teeming with carnivores, often competing with them for meat with only the simplest of weapons for protection. Large-group living has dramatic advantages for hominins in environments where resources come in large "parcels" that are irregularly distributed across the landscape. Members of a group can search for food individually or in pairs and then share it with others, allowing the group as a whole to cover a much larger area. Mithen believes that the larger brain of the first humans allowed for greater social intelligence and for coping with the complexities of living in closer juxtaposition to others, where assuming that others know things is of vital importance.

The Development of Language and Speech

Cooperation, the ability to get together to solve problems of both subsistence and potential conflict, is a vital quality in human beings. We are unique in having a spoken, symbolic language that enables us to communicate our most intimate feelings to one another. But at what point did hominins acquire the ability to speak?

Our closest living relatives, the chimpanzees, communicate with gestures and many voice sounds in the wild, whereas other apes use sounds only to convey territorial information. However, chimpanzees cannot talk to us because they do not have the vocal apparatus to do so. Articulate speech was an important threshold in human evolution because it opened up whole new vistas of cooperative behavior and unlimited potential for the enrichment of life. When did hominins abandon grunts for speech? We cannot infer speech from the simple artifacts made by early *Homo*, but there are two potential lines of research open.

Both comparative anatomy and actual fossils can be used to study differences between apes and humans. Biological anthropologist Jeffrey Laitman and others studied the position of the larynx in a wide variety of mammals, including humans. They found that all mammals except adult humans have a larynx high in the neck, a position that enables the larynx to lock into the air space at the back of the nasal cavity. Although this position allows animals like monkeys and cats to breathe and swallow at the same time, it limits the sounds they can produce. The pharynx—the air cavity part of the food pathway—can produce sounds, but animals use their mouths to modify sounds because they are anatomically incapable of producing the range of sounds needed for articulate speech.

Until they are about 18 months to 2 years old, human children have their larynx situated high in the neck. Then, the larynx begins to descend, ending up between the fourth and seventh neck vertebrae. How and why are still a mystery, but the change completely alters the way the infant breathes, speaks, and swallows. Adult humans cannot breathe and swallow simultaneously, so they can suffocate when food lodges in an airway. However, an enlarged pharyngeal chamber above the vocal cords enables them to modify the sounds they emit in an infinite variety of ways, which is the key to human speech.

In fact, it's not just about speech: when studying human verbal communication, physical anthropologists and linguists draw a very clear distinction between "language" (the mental process of communication) and "speech" (the externalization of it). Both speech and language must have been vital to human evolution since they open up whole vistas of cooperative behavior and unlimited potential for the enrichment of life. While we can assume that the first humans had more to communicate with than the gestures and grunts of nonhuman primates, it appears that articulate speech and language was a more recent development.

In terms of the ability to speak, the fossils are revealing clues: using sophisticated statistical analyses, Laitman and his colleagues ran tests on as many complete fossil skulls as possible. They found that the australopithecines of 4 million to 1 million years ago had a flat skull base and a high larynx, whereas those of *H. erectus*, dating to about 1.9 million years and later, show somewhat more curvature, suggesting that the larynx was beginning to descend to its modern position. This spells a move toward a human capacity for speech. Without wishing to jump ahead in time too much, by 400,000 years ago, it seems that humans may have already been capable of speech. Genetic research indicates that our Neanderthal cousins (see Chapter 9) had the same FOXP2 gene for speech as us, and very similar hyoid bones to ours (the neck bone that helps govern speech), signifying that the Neanderthals had the potential to produce the same range of sounds as us.

But how about language? When did more sophisticated language appear? One interesting line of research lies in the tools themselves. It used to be assumed that one could not possibly infer language from artifacts. However, scientists have recently been demonstrating how the areas of the brain used in language processing and generation "light up" when novices try to knap stone tools—especially Acheulean tools. In this way, they argue that stone tools could even provide evidence for the development of grammar before 700,000 years ago.

The Earliest Social Organization

The few early sites that have been excavated show that the first phase of human evolution involved shifts in the basic patterns of subsistence and locomotion as well as new ingredients—food sharing and toolmaking. These led to enhanced communication, information exchange, and economic and social insight, as well as cunning and restraint. Human anatomy was augmented with tools. Culture became an inseparable part of humanity, and social life acquired a new and as yet little understood complexity.

What sort of social organization did early *Homo* enjoy? However much we look at contemporary nonhuman primates, we cannot be sure. Most primates are intensely social and live in groups in which the mother–infant relationship forms a central bond. The period of infants' dependency on mothers found in, say, chimpanzees was probably lengthened considerably with early *Homo*. The larger brain size would mean that infants were born with much smaller heads than adults, at an earlier stage of mental maturity. This biological reality would have had a major impact on social organization and daily habits.

Chimpanzees have flexible, matriarchal social groups. They occupy a relatively small territory, one with sufficient vegetable resources to support a considerable population density; this pattern contrasts sharply with the average hunter-gatherer band, typically a close-knit group of about 25 people of several families. The kind of systematic hunting such people engage in requires much larger territories and permits much lower densities per square mile. The few sites that have been excavated suggest that early *Homo* tended to live in bands that were somewhat more akin to those of modern hunter-gatherers. But in all probability, their social organization resembled more closely that of chimpanzees and baboons, which is very different from that of humans.

The world of early *Homo* was much less predictable and more demanding than that of even *Australopithecus*. What was it that was more complex? Why do we have to be so intelligent? It is not for hunting animals or gathering food but for our interactions with other people. The increased complexity of our social interactions is likely to have been a powerful force in the evolution of the human brain. For early *Homo*, the adoption of a wider-based diet with a food-sharing social group would have placed more acute demands on the ability to cope with the complex and the unpredictable. And the brilliant technological, artistic, and expressive skills of humankind may well be a consequence of the fact that our early ancestors had to become more and more socially adept.

Summary

- The story of human evolution begins with the separation of the chimpanzee and human lines from a common ancestor by 6 million years ago (Ma) at the latest.
- Over 20 hominin species are known from the past 6 million years, though the relationships between these hominins are complex and often unresolved. Only some of them are our ancestors, and many became extinct without giving rise to new species.
- The earliest possible hominin is the possibly bipedal *Sahelanthropus tchadensis*, it is known from Chad, and dates to between 7 and 6 Ma.
- The first hominins were at least partly arboreal (tree-dwellers), with long arms and legs and broad chests. With time, they adapted to more open country in Africa, which resulted from global cooling over 4 Ma, by broadening their diet to include more meat and by achieving great mobility and behavioral flexibility.
- The small hominin named *Aridipithecus ramidus* is the earliest known hominin to have definitely walked on two feet; it flourished 4.5 Ma in Ethiopia.
- A later hominin, *Australopithecus afarensis*, was ancestral to later hominins and flourished after 3.8 million years ago.
- By 3 Ma, the hominin line had radiated into many forms, among them robust and more gracile australopithecines and the larger-brained early *Homo*, a forager who scavenged game meat and perhaps hunted. These hominins used a simple stone technology, had some ability to communicate, and had a very rudimentary social organization.
- Recent definitions of the genus *Homo* make a major distinction between the more ape-like hominins of this chapter, which flourished before 2 million years ago, and the true humans, beginning with *H. erectus* which evolved no more than 1.9 million years ago.

Key Terms and Sites

Quaternary
Pleistocene
primates
anthropoids
prosimians
pongids
hominoids
bipedal
knuckle walking
Taung
Aramis
Allia Bay
Kanapoi
Hadar
arboreal
Laetoli
Koto Toro
Koobi Fora
East Turkana
adaptive radiation
cladistics
monophyletic

Lomekwi 3
Oldowan
tuff

Critical-Thinking Questions

1. Why was bipedal posture so important to early human evolution? Is there any truth in the old saying that humans "came down from the trees"?
2. Discuss the major differences between *Australopithecus africanus* and early *Homo*. Why did early *Homo* give rise to the modern human line, while the australopithecines became extinct?
3. What does archaeology contribute to the study of human origins? Use Lomekwi 3, Koobi Fora and Olduvai Gorge as reference points for your examples.

Further Reading

Research into human evolution moves swiftly. On a yearly basis, finds are made that transform our understanding of the past. As a result, we recommend you turn first to current journals and digest the latest scientific papers (you might start with the journal *Nature* or the on-line peer-reviewed site *Plos One*). For books, stay with those published in the five or last ten years. For a richly illustrated book full of past human forms, see A. Roberts's, *Human Evolution: The Human Story*, 2nd ed. (London: Dorling Kindersley, 2023). For a short overview see M. Kissel's *Bioanthropology: the basics* (New York: Routledge, 2026), or B. Wood's, *Human Evolution: A Very Short Introduction*, 2nd ed. (New York: Oxford University Press, 2019), while *Human Origins: 7 Million Years and Counting* (London: New Scientist Instant Expert, 2018) is also a good—and readable—way into this subject. Note that you will sometimes find contradictions in the literature as different researchers hold different stances, or simply because the research has moved on.

9 African Exodus

Chapter Outline

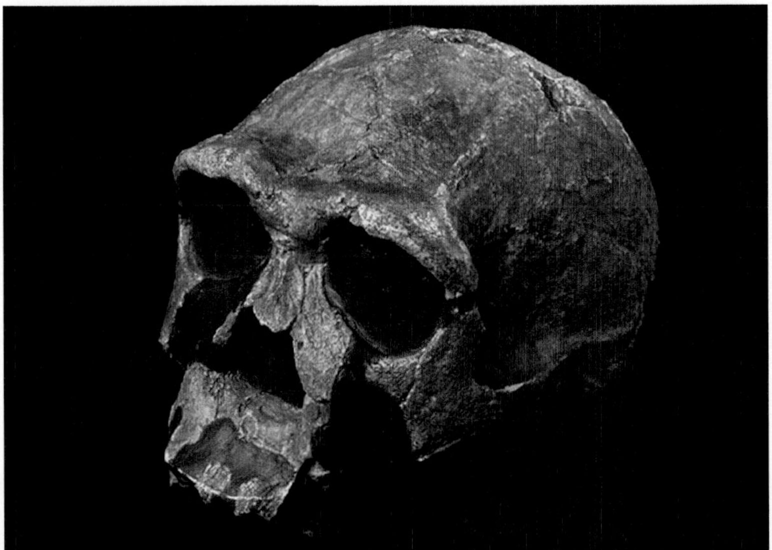

Skull of *Homo erectus* from Nariokotome, Kenya.
Source: Pascal Goetgheluck/Science Photo Library.

DOI: 10.4324/9781003592754-12

Trinil, Java, Indonesia Gravel deposits up to 1.8 million years old that have yielded the fossil remains of *Homo erectus*.

Eugene Dubois was a Dutchman obsessed with the "missing link," the mythical being that was the evolutionary connection between apes and modern people. A surgeon by profession, young Dubois wangled a posting as an army physician to distant Sumatra in Southeast Asia in 1887, where he was convinced that the missing link would be found. Incredible though it may seem, Dubois actually found what he claimed was such an ancestor on nearby Java in 1891. Digging into fossil-rich ash and river sediments at **Trinil** on the Solo River in northeastern Java, he found not only the bones of extinct animals but also a human tooth, a thick-walled skull, and a human thigh bone.

Dubois was ecstatic and named his fossil *Pithecanthropus erectus*, "ape-human which stood upright." This, he claimed, was the missing link between apes and humans, a very primitive human being. On his return to Europe in 1895, he was greeted with skepticism and then scorn. Dubois's reaction was to withdraw from the scientific arena. He is said to have kept his fossils under his bed. Modern science has vindicated Eugene Dubois, for he was the first to discover what is now known as *H. erectus*, a direct ancestor of modern humanity. Despite this assertion, don't fall into the trap of thinking human evolution looks like a ladder, with just one human type morphing into the next. Rather, be aware that at any one time, many human forms coexisted. It is only today that *Homo sapiens* is the only hominin around (unless we count the chimp as a hominin, which a minority of researchers do). With that in mind, let's now wind back the clock to the emergence of *H. erectus* in Africa some 1.9 million years ago.

These humans were, as far as we can tell, capable of far more complex and varied lifeways than any previous or contemporary hominins (such as the handy *Homo habilis* who persisted until 1.6 Ma). *H. erectus* were the first humans to tame fire and the first to settle outside the tropical savannas of Africa. They did so at the beginning of the last geological epoch, the Pleistocene, sometimes called the Ice Age. This chapter describes *H. erectus* and the humans who joined them and came after them, and their typically increasingly sophisticated adaptations to constant climatic change during the early Ice Age.

Ice Age Background

The Pleistocene began about 2.5 million years ago, after an intensification of glaciation worldwide. By this time, great mountain chains had formed in the Alps, the Himalayas, and elsewhere. Landmasses had been uplifted; the connection between these higher latitudes and southern areas was reduced, lessening their heat exchange and causing greater temperature differences between them. Northern latitudes became progressively cooler after 3 Ma, but climatic fluctuations between warmer and colder climatic regimens were still relatively minor during the first million years of the Ice Age. This was a critically important time when a more advanced human form evolved in Africa and moved out of the tropics into Asia and Europe.

Matuyama–Brunhes boundary Moment of reversal of the Earth's magnetic field, c. 780,000 years ago.

About 780,000 years ago, the Earth's magnetic field changed abruptly from the reversed state it had adopted about 2.5 Ma to the normal one. This **Matuyama–Brunhes boundary**, named

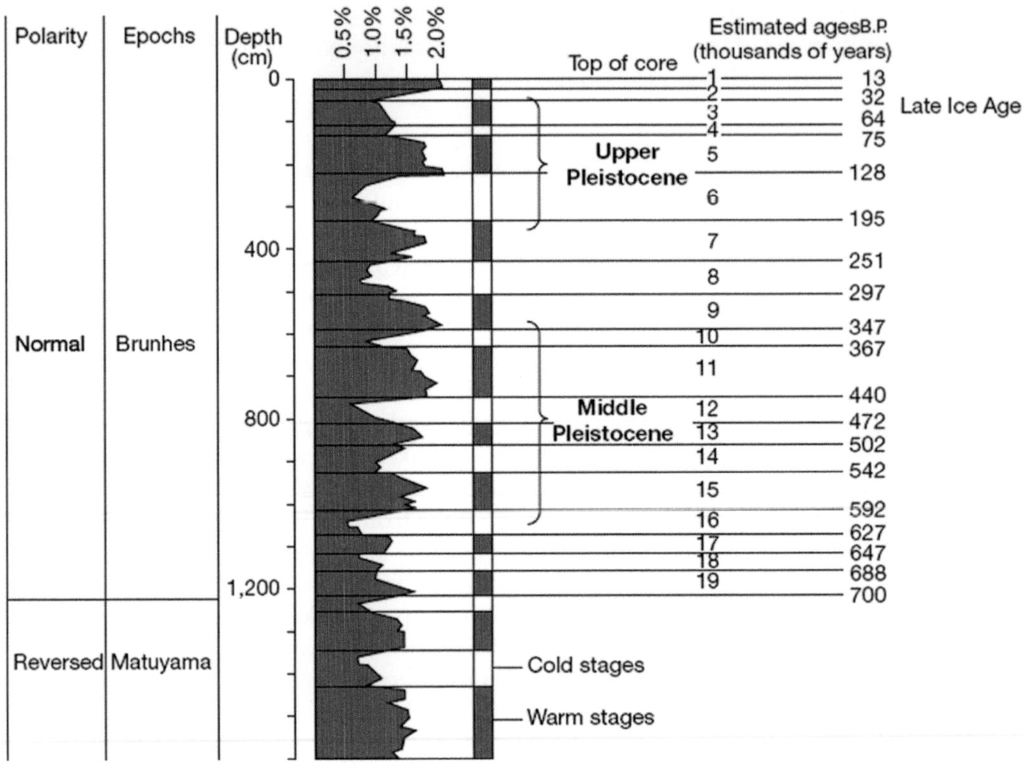

Figure 9.1 Stratigraphic record of the climatic events of the Pleistocene, from deep-sea core V28 238, Solomon Plateau, Pacific Ocean. The Matuyama–Brunhes boundary occurred about 780,000 years ago, at a depth of 11.9 meters (39 feet). Above it, a sawtooth-like curve records the relative size of the world's oceans and ice caps, and identifies eight complete glacial and interglacial cycles, a more complete record of the Middle and Upper Pleistocene than comes from land sediments.

Source: Based on Shackleton and Opdyke, 1983.

after the geologists who first discovered it, marks the beginning of constant climatic change for the remainder of the Ice Age. Deep-sea cores give a record of changing sea temperatures. They tell us that ice sheets formed gradually but deglaciation and global warming trends took place with great rapidity (see Figure 9.1). These coincided with major rises in sea level that flooded low-lying coastal areas. During glacial maxima, ice sheets covered a full third of the Earth's surface, mantling Scandinavia and the Alps in Europe, as well as much of northern North America (see Figure 10.2 on p. 316). As a result, sea levels fell dramatically, hundreds of meters below modern levels. The glaciers were about as extensive as they are today during warmer periods, the so-called interglacials, when sea levels were close to present shorelines. Much less is known about changes in tropical regions, although it is thought that the southern fringes of Africa's Sahara expanded dramatically during cold periods.

Both *H. erectus* and the hominins who came after it, including *H. sapiens*, evolved during a long period of constant climatic transition between warmer and colder regimens in northern latitudes. Experts believe that the world's climate has been in transition from one extreme to the other for more than 75 percent of the past 780,000 years, with a predominance of colder climate over the period. There were at least nine glacial episodes, a major one about 525,000 years ago, when there was ice as far south as Seattle, St. Louis, and New York City in North America, and sea levels were as much as 200 meters (650 feet) below modern levels. In contrast, there were periods of more temperate conditions between 515,000 and 315,000 years ago. This was the time when early hominin settlement outside Africa expanded as small bands of foragers exploited the rich animal and plant resources of European and Asian river valleys and forests.

Another intensely cold cycle lasted from about 180,000 to 128,000 years ago, a cycle that coincided in general terms with the period when *H. sapiens*, modern humans, were becoming fully anatomically modern (so that by around 120,000 years ago, their skeletons fully resemble any of ours). From our African homeland, we made early forays out of Africa; however, the period between roughly 50,000 and 15,000 years ago, i.e. the last Ice Age glaciation, saw the permanent spread of *H. sapiens* throughout the Old World and into the Americas. These constant climatic changes played an important role in the spread of early human beings throughout temperate and tropical latitudes.

Homo erectus in Africa

Early hominin evolution forms a complex pattern of constant diversification, with several species of hominin coexisting at any one time. As we saw in Chapter 8, true humans, in the sense of members of the genus *Homo*, may only have appeared about 1.9 Ma, with the evolution of *H. erectus* in eastern Africa—a powerfully built human with massive brow ridges, a large face, and a long, low skull to accommodate a much larger brain—which flourished from about 1.8 Ma to 600,000 years ago. Note that some researchers prefer to categorize the African version of *H. erectus* as *Homo ergaster*. Whether we define it as *H. ergaster* or *H. erectus*, this entire set of humans was larger than previous hominins and with overall skeletal proportions much like those of modern humans.

The earliest known African specimens come from the Lake Turkana region of northern Kenya, where current estimates place their appearance at about 1.9 Ma. Skull KNM-ER 3733 from East Turkana dates to between 1.6 and 1.5 Ma. This fossil, with its massive brow ridges, enlarged brain size, and high forehead, is morphologically very close to examples of *H. erectus* dating to a million years ago and earlier.

> **Nariokotome, Kenya** Site on the west shore of Lake Turkana, and findspot of "Turkana boy," an almost complete specimen of *H. erectus* (or *H. ergaster*), dated to around 1.5 Ma.

Richard Leakey and anatomist Alan Walker discovered the virtually complete skeleton of a young *H. erectus* boy at **Nariokotome** on the western shores of Lake Turkana dating to about 1.5 million years ago (see Figure 9.2 and chapter opener). The footprints of hippopotamuses and other animals nearby suggest that the decomposing corpse was trampled to pieces. From the neck down, the boy's bones are remarkably modern-looking. The skull and jawbone are more primitive, with brow ridges and a brain capacity perhaps as much as 700–800 cubic centimeters (43–49 cubic inches), about half the modern size. The skeleton shows that the boy stood about 1.6 meters (5 feet 2 inches) tall. Despite his height, Turkana boy was still a boy: a child who perished before his body had fully matured. The ends of the long bones in his arms and legs retain evidence of cartilage growth plates that only disappear with adulthood; the platelike bones of his skull are not fully fused; and his teeth are not quite fully adult. These elements indicate that he was somewhere between 7 and 11 years old when he died, though recent estimates place him at the younger end of this age range, suggesting the pattern of his growth and development was somewhat different from (and quicker than) that of modern humans. His near-complete skeleton is

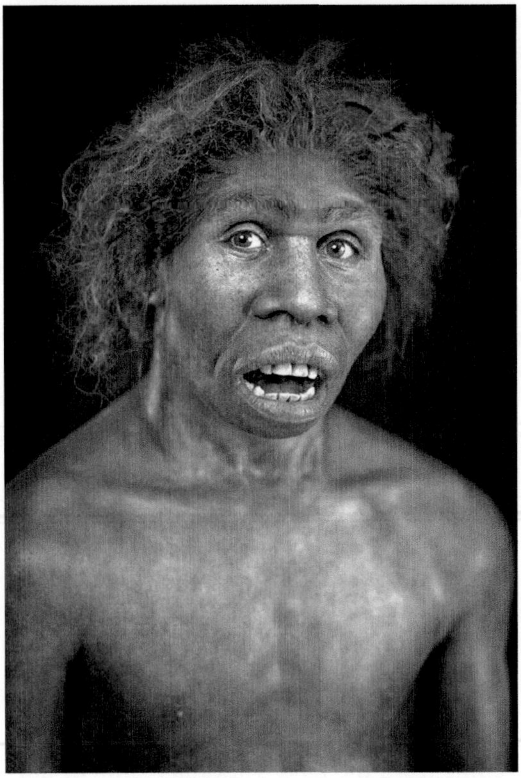

Figure 9.2 Reconstruction of a young *Homo erectus* boy who died in a small lagoon on the western shores of Lake Turkana, East Africa, about 1.5 million years ago.

Source: S. Entressangle/E. Daynes/Science Photo Library.

(apart from the skull) very similar to a modern human's, with its slender body frame and relatively shorter arms and longer legs than any earlier hominin species. This change in limb and body proportions shows that this species was, like us, fully terrestrially bipedal. It may also have been the first hominin to run fast, a crucial ability for hunting and scavenging over long distances. The more constricted pelvis would have reduced the amount of brain growth before birth, which led to a longer infant dependence on caregivers, something that is a hallmark of modern humans.

However, the brains were certainly not yet fully modern. Some of the African *H. erectus* specimens have crania with modest brain sizes of 508–580 cubic centimeters (31–35 cubic inches), while others are larger, ranging between 508 and 909 cubic centimeters (31–55 cubic inches)—but still considerably smaller than those of modern humans, which range between 1,000 and 2,000 cubic centimeters (61–122 cubic inches). Those specimens with smaller brains have vertical upper faces and large, projecting upper jaws, while those with bigger brains tend to have stronger brow ridges, wide nasal opening, and projecting mid-faces. Culturally, they developed new tool forms, but they, their contemporaries, and their descendants made few changes to their simple technology over hundreds of thousands of years.

Homo erectus Outside Africa (c. 1.8 Million to at Least 250,000 Years Ago)

H. erectus was the first hominin species to be identified outside of Europe, by Eugene Dubois, whom we met earlier in this book. While everyone now accepts that this is an early hominin, the status of *erectus* remains shrouded in controversy. Debates rage over the precise evolutionary relationship between the African *H. erectus* (categorized by some as *H. ergaster*) and the bulk of *erectus* specimens, which are known from China, Java, and Indonesia. Part of the issue is that the fossil record of *H. erectus* from East and Southeast Asia is dominated by skulls, teeth, and jaws, with only fragmented remains from other parts of the body. Nonetheless, it appears that the Asian *H. erectus* was large-bodied with fully modern bipedalism. With a cranial capacity ranging from 750 to 1,300 cubic centimeters (46–79 cubic inches), it had a relatively large brain. Like those hominins that went before it, *H. erectus* could adapt to a variety of climates and habitats. Both *Australopithecus* and early *Homo* had adjusted to plunging global temperatures during a glacial episode between about 2.7 and 2.5 Ma. The colder conditions turned much of Africa's moist woodland into much drier, open savanna. The hominins thrived in these conditions as tree-dwelling primates yielded to bipedal forms better able to survive in the open. This adaptability let hominins move into new environments, where their mixed diet of meat and plant foods caused them to cover large home territories. *H. erectus* was just as adaptable and mobile, but also was the first human to use fire, fashion more elaborate tools, and leave Africa.

Radiating Out of Africa

If potassium-argon dates for *H. erectus* fossils in Indonesia are to be believed, these new humans, who had emerged in Africa at around 1.9 Ma, were in the Southeast Asian rainforest by 1.8 Ma. But, ask some, would a radiation of human populations from Africa into Asia occur within such a "short" time frame as 100,000 years? While 100,000 years seems to be a sprint against a backdrop of 6 million years of human evolution, this is in reality an enormous stretch of time, representing thousands of generations of people, so the movement seems eminently possible.

With *H. erectus* covering large, open territories where food resources were scattered unevenly over the landscape, even an expansion of about 30–50 kilometers (20–30 miles) per year soon translates to hundreds and then thousands of kilometers within a few generations. Unfortunately, accurately tracing movements is hard since the archaeological and fossil evidence for this extraordinary radiation is still tantalizingly incomplete and often poorly dated.

The climate probably played a role in all this: at around 2 Ma, hominins were adjusting to cyclical alterations among savanna, forest, and desert as the Ice Age began. Humans now ranged over much greater distances, in part due to greater flexibility in their behavior in the face of short-term environmental changes, increased sociality, and relatively high rates of reproduction. They did so by migrating with changing vegetational zones, as many mammals did, or by adapting to new environments, changing their dietary emphasis from meat to plant foods. Finally, they could move out of tropical latitudes altogether, into habitats that human beings had never occupied before.

Very likely *H. erectus* adapted to changing circumstances in all these ways, radiating out of Africa by way of the Sahara, when the desert was capable of supporting human life. Geologist Neil Roberts has likened the Sahara to a pump, sucking in population during wetter savanna phases and forcing foragers out northward to the margins of the desert during drier cycles. In radiating out of Africa, *H. erectus* behaved just like other mammals in its ecological community.

H. erectus was a meat and plant eater and thus linked ecologically with other predators. There was widespread interchange of mammals between Africa and more temperate latitudes during the Pliocene and Lower Pleistocene. For example, a major change in the mammalian populations of Europe took place about 700,000 years ago. Hippopotamuses, forest elephants, and other herbivores and carnivores like the lion, leopard, and spotted hyena seem to have migrated northward from Africa at this time. Migrations by the lion, leopard, and hyena—the animals with which hominins shared many ecological characteristics—were in the same direction as that taken earlier by *H. erectus*. That the first successful human settlement of tropical Asia and temperate Europe coincided with radiations of mammalian communities out of Africa seems plausible. It may also have coincided with the taming of fire.

Gesher Benot Ya'aqov, Israel 800,000-year-old site that has yielded the first evidence for the controlled use of fire.

The earliest known controlled use of fire comes from an 800,000-year-old settlement at **Gesher Benot Ya'aqov** in Israel, but humans are thought to have tamed it much earlier. Early humans would have been familiar with the great grass and brush fires that swept across the African savanna during the dry months. Fire offered protection from predators (even insects and rodents flee from a line of flames) and an easy way of hunting game. Perhaps *H. erectus* developed the habit of conserving fire, taking advantage of long-smoldering tree stumps ignited by lightning strikes and other natural causes to kindle flames in order to light dry brush or simply to scare off predators. Fire may have been a truly revolutionary innovation for humanity, for it enabled people to cook food for the first time.

Dmanisi, Georgia Site dating to c. 1.8 Ma that has yielded crania of *H. erectus*-like people, the earliest hominins known in Europe and Eurasia.

It may be no coincidence that the radiation of *H. erectus* out of tropical Africa into temperate environments in Asia and Europe occurred during a period of accelerated climatic change. While most experts agree that Asia was settled from around 1.8 Ma, the evidence for first settlement in southwestern Asia and Europe is more uncertain. To judge from the Southeast Asian dates, *H. erectus* moved rapidly eastward out of Africa, but settling the more northerly latitudes of Europe and Eurasia may have presented a more formidable challenge, especially during glacial cycles. The earliest hominins found in Europe are represented by a collection of fossils—belonging to women, men, and children—from a single site in Georgia, that of **Dmanisi**, southwest of Tbilisi (see Figure 9.3). Perhaps some of the first hominins to leave Africa, archaeologists found these *erectus*-like individuals in association with crudely shaped choppers and flakes. Dated to about 1.8 million years ago, these people had relatively small brains (610–775 cubic centimeters, or 37–47 cubic inches), were of smaller stature than most later hominins, but had limb proportions similar to modern humans (and the earliest African *Homo*), and were fully bipedal. These finds show that after 2 Ma, humans foraged widely in search of food, their movements driven perhaps as much by hunger as by superior technology.

But who were these mysterious "first Europeans"? Were they really *H. erectus*, or something else? They are currently formally classified as *H. erectus*, but their status is controversial. Many researchers prefer to categorize them as *Homo georgicus* (a unique species to Georgia), while others point out that at least one skull (D2700) looks more like *H. habilis*.

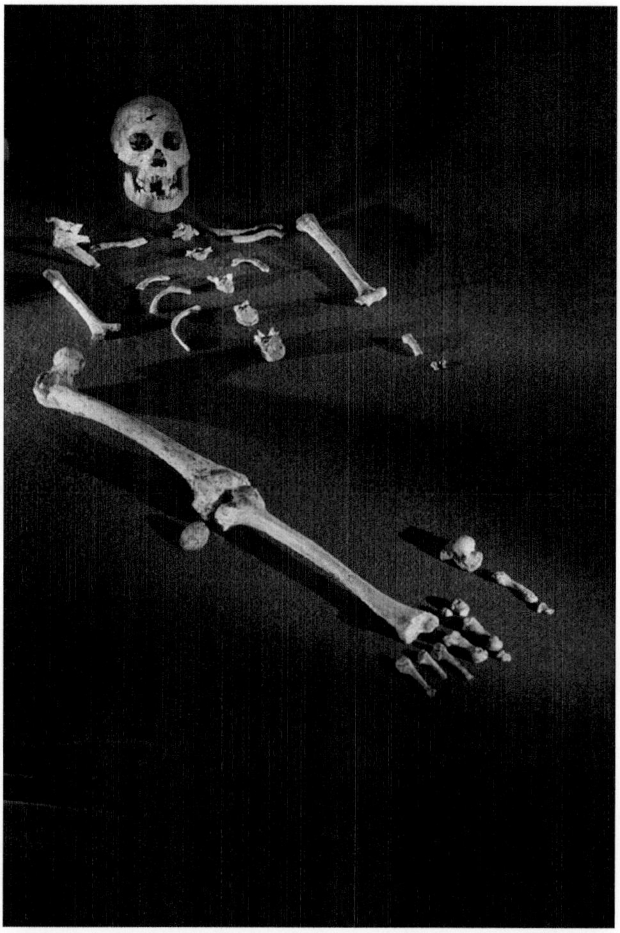

Figure 9.3 Skeletal remains of a 1.8 Ma Dmanisi individual, likely a subadult female. Her body shows a mix of modern and archaic traits, but she was clearly bipedal.

Source: Danita Delimont/Alamy.

Homo erectus in Asia

The classic *H. erectus* fossils come from Asia, from the Trinil area of Java, where they date to between 1.8 million and 600,000 years ago, and from northern and southern China, potentially dating to between 600,000 and 100,000 years ago, perhaps considerably earlier. These well-preserved specimens show that these archaic humans had a brain capacity between 775 and 1,300 cubic centimeters (47–79 cubic inches), indicating much variation. It is probable that their vision was excellent and that they were capable of extensive reasoning. The *H. erectus* skull is more rounded than that of earlier hominins. It also has conspicuous brow ridges and a sloping forehead. *H. erectus* had limbs and hips fully adapted to an upright posture. Adults ranged from 1.6 to 1.8 meters (5 feet 2 inches to 5 feet 9 inches) and had hands fully capable of precision gripping and toolmaking.

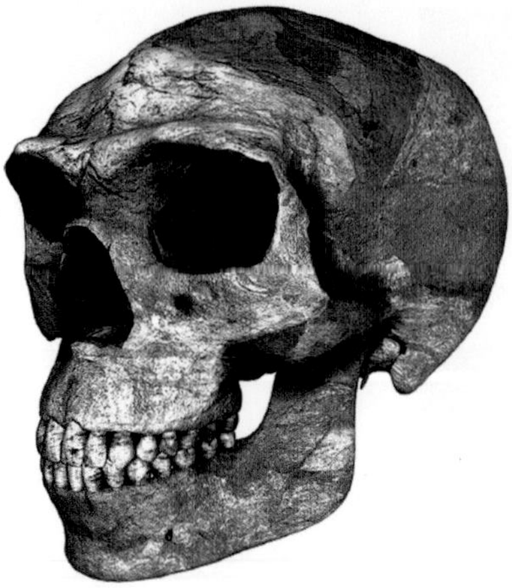

Figure 9.4 A *Homo erectus* skull from Zhoukoudian, China.
Source: Friedrich Saurer/Alamy.

Zhoukoudian, China Cave site famous for its *H. erectus* fossils dating to as early as 600,000 years ago.

During *H. erectus*'s long history, humanity adapted to a far wider range of environments, from tropical savannas in East Africa to forested Javanese valleys, temperate climates in North Africa and Europe, and the harsh winters of northern China and central Europe. They were certainly capable of a far more complex and varied lifeway than previous hominins. With such a wide distribution, it is hardly surprising that some variations in population occurred. For example, Chinese scholars claim that the *H. erectus* fossils from the famous **Zhoukoudian** cave near Beijing display a gradual increase in brain capacity from about 900 cubic centimeters (55 cubic inches) 600,000 years ago to about 1,100 cubic centimeters (67 cubic inches) in more recent individuals (Figure 9.4). In any case, *H. erectus* was far more human than *H. habilis*, and was a habitual biped who had probably lost the thick hair covering that is characteristic of nonhuman primates.

The Lifeway of *Homo erectus*

We still know little of the world of *H. erectus* beyond a certainty that between 1.8 million and half a million years ago, humans had radiated far beyond their tropical African homeland (see Figure 9.5). Nowhere were human beings abundant, and the global population of archaic humans was undoubtedly minuscule. As far as is known, *H. erectus* did not settle in extreme arctic latitudes, in what is now northern Eurasia and Siberia, nor did they cross into the Americas, nor did they develop the watercraft needed to cross from the islands of Southeast Asia to New Guinea and Australia, landmasses that remained isolated by the ocean until the late Ice Age.

Throughout this enormous area of the Old World, *H. erectus* populations developed a great variety of lifeways and local tool kits that reflected different needs. The hominins were part of a vast animal community, and their long-term success resulted from their ability to adapt to the cyclical changes in the Ice Age environment: from temperate to much colder, then to full glacial conditions, and then even more rapidly to warmer

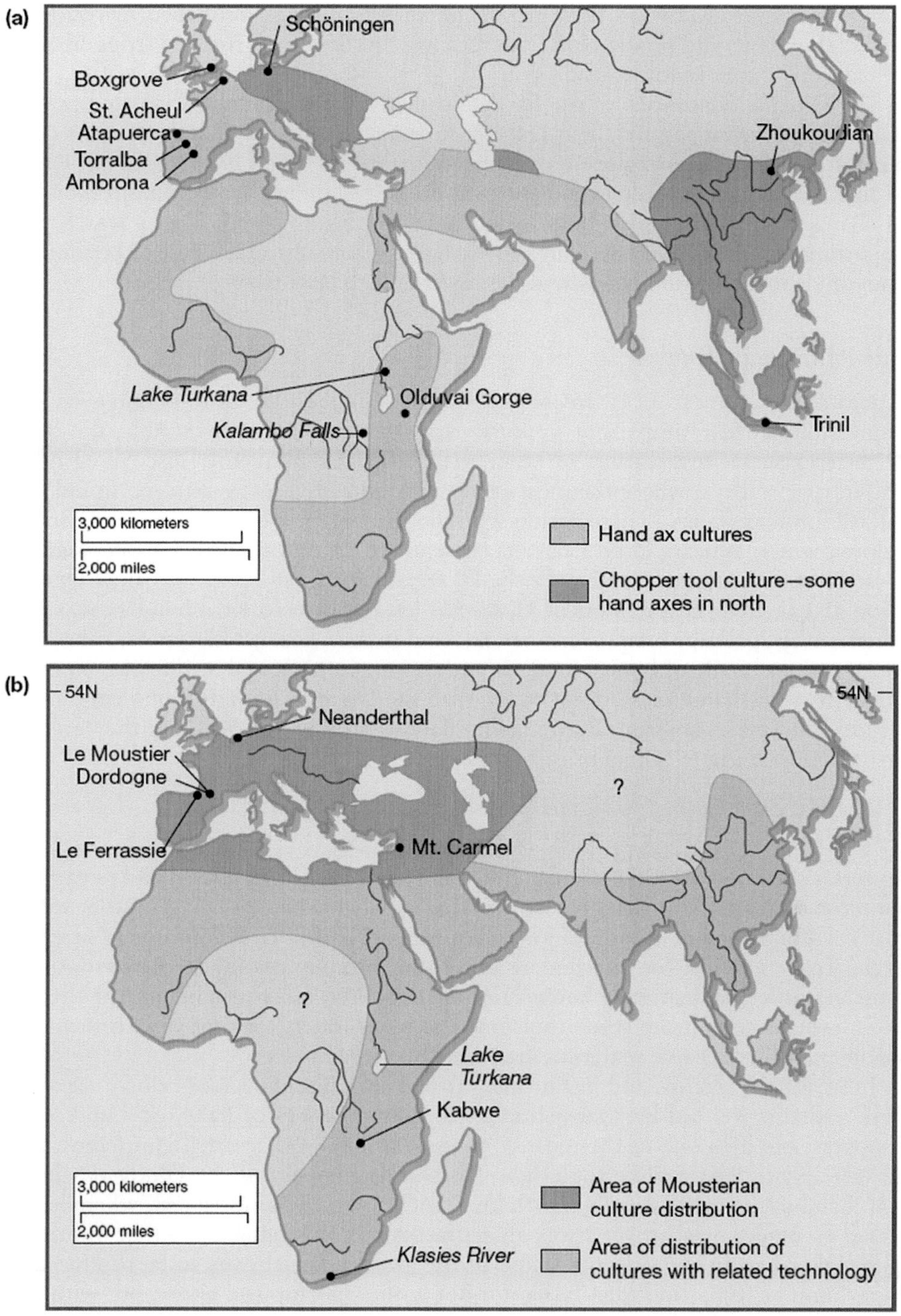

Figure 9.5 The distribution of (a) *Homo erectus* and contemporary species and (b) Neanderthals.

conditions again. Many of these early human populations flourished in regions where dense, abundant, and predictable resources were to be found, isolated from other regions where similar conditions existed.

The climatic conditions of the Ice Age sometimes brought these isolated populations together and then separated them again, ensuring gene flow and genetic drift and continued biological and cultural evolution over the millennia. As it had been for *H. habilis*, the key to adapting to temperate environments was mobility. Human bands could respond quickly to changes in resource distribution by moving into new areas. Theirs was a primarily opportunistic adaptation based on knowledge of where resources were to be found, rather than on deliberate planning, as was the case in much later times.

Hand Axes and Choppers

Separated as we are from *H. erectus* by time, it is difficult for us to obtain even a general impression of their simple but opportunistic lifeway. Almost invariably, the only signs of their existence are scatters of stone artifacts, most frequently discovered near lakes and in river valleys, where the most plentiful food resources were to be found. A major innovation that occurs in association with the African *H. erectus* is the large hand ax (see below), which appears after 1.65 Ma, first in Africa and then in Europe. Significantly, these hand axes do not occur with the *H. erectus* fossils in Asia. Why not? One explanation may be that the ancestors of *H. erectus* left Africa before the hand ax was invented. Alternatively, perhaps hand axes were rejected in Asia because choppers, flakes, or other tools, perhaps made of bone, wood, or antler, were more suited to the local environment. Likewise, these hand axes do not occur with the Dmanisi hominins of Georgia (the only *erectus*-like specimens from Europe, who date to around 1.8 Ma), but they are found in association with later hominins in Europe.

Hand Axes

To zero in on hand axes, the simple Oldowan technology of *H. habilis* had remained in use for more than a million years before evolving slowly into a more diverse stone technology that itself remained in use for half a million years. Neither *H. habilis* nor *H. erectus* relied exclusively on stone, for our remote ancestors certainly made use of wood, one of the most versatile raw materials known to humanity. Yet, most insights into the technology of *H. sapiens* come from stone tools and the by-products associated with them, because wood and other organic materials are rarely preserved.

In Africa, *H. erectus*, and in Europe, various later hominins (see below) are associated with a distinctive tool kit that includes not only a variety of flake tools and sometimes choppers, but also one of the most common exhibits in the world's museums, the hand ax (see Figure 9.6). Unlike the crude flakes and choppers of the Oldowan, the Acheulean hand ax (named after the northern French town of Saint-Acheul, where it was first found by modern researchers) was an artifact with converging edges that met at a point. The maker had to envision the shape of the artifact, which was to be produced from a mere lump of stone, and then fashion it not with opportunistic blows, but with carefully directed hammer strokes.

Acheulean hand axes come in every size, from elegant oval types 7–8 centimeters (3 inches) long to heavy axes more than 30 centimeters (12 inches) long and weighing 2.3 kilograms (5 pounds) or more. They were multipurpose tools, used for woodworking, scraping skins, and the skinning and butchering of animals. The hand ax and its near relative the cleaver, with a straight end, were ideal for butchering because the artifact

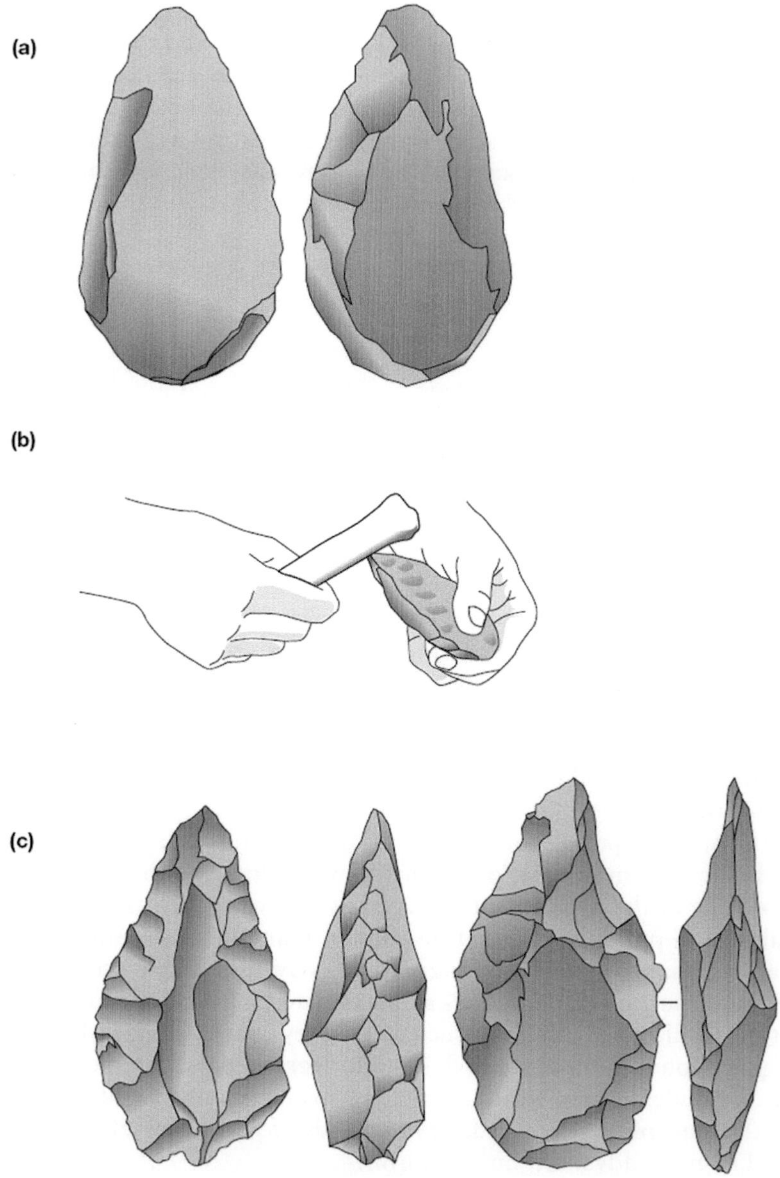

Figure 9.6 The long-lasting Acheulean technology, pioneered by *Homo erectus*: (a) Hand axes were multipurpose artifacts shaped symmetrically around a long axis. (b) A stone-worker thins the edge of a hand ax with a bone hammer. (c) On the left is an Acheulean hand ax from **Swanscombe**, England, and on the right, a cleaver from **Kalambo Falls,** Zambia.

could be sharpened again and again. When it became a useless lump of stone, it could be recycled into flake tools. But one can achieve effective butchering with simple flakes as well. A number of researchers have wondered whether the hand ax was not used for other purposes such as throwing at game or digging for roots. Hand axes and related artifacts occur over an enormous area of the Old World and underwent considerable refinement during the million years or so that they were in use. But what do we know of the behavior of their makers? Without question, *H. erectus* hunted and foraged for food, probably in far more effective ways than early *Homo*. Time and time again, hand axes and other butchering artifacts have been found in association with the bones of large game animals. But did the hunters actually kill such formidable herbivores as the elephant and the rhinoceros? To do so would require social mechanisms to foster cooperation and communication abilities far beyond those of their predecessors.

Swanscombe, England Thames valley site that yielded Acheulean hand axes and a skull of an archaic hominin, c. 400,000 years old.

Kalambo Falls, Zambia Lakebed site where Acheulean occupation levels over 200,000 years old were found.

Bamboo and Choppers

The eastern portions of the archaic human world lay in Asia, in an enormous region of woodland and forest with great environmental diversity. The tropical forests of East Asia are rich in animal and plant foods, but these food resources are widely dispersed over the landscape. People were therefore constantly on the move, carrying tools with them. Under these circumstances, it was logical for them to make use of bamboo, wood, and other fibrous materials—the most convenient materials at hand. There was no need for the specialized, often more complicated artifacts used in the open country of the west either for spear points or for the butchering tools used on large animals.

As archaeologist Geoffrey Pope has pointed out, the distribution of the simple choppers and flakes used by many eastern populations coincides very closely with the natural distribution of bamboo, one of the most versatile materials known to humankind. Bamboo was efficient, durable, and portable. It could be used to manufacture containers, sharp knives, spears, weapon tips, ropes, and dwellings. To this day, it is widely used in Asia as scaffolding for building skyscrapers. Bamboo is an ideal material for people subsisting not on large game, but on smaller forest animals such as monkeys, rats, squirrels, lizards, and snakes, as well as plant foods. Simple stone flakes and jagged-edged choppers, the only artifacts to survive the millennia, would be ideal for working bamboo and may indeed have been used for this purpose for hundreds of thousands of years, long after *H. erectus* had been superseded by more advanced human forms.

As far as we can tell, *H. erectus* groups were eclectic and flexible hunter-gatherers who relied on hunting, scavenging, and plant foods. They may have understood the telltale signs of the passage of seasons, the meanings of cloud formations, the timing of game and bird migrations, and the geography of their territories. But they never exploited small game, birds, fish, or sea mammals on any significant scale, as modern humans did almost at once.

H. erectus probably lived in relatively large groups at times, both to reduce the danger from carnivores and to improve the chance of finding food, especially larger animals. At other times, band size may have been much smaller, especially when plant foods were more abundant and easily obtained by individuals. All of this argues for considerable social flexibility and intelligence on the part of *H. erectus*, reflected in these hominins' larger brain size. However, they may have been unable to integrate their social intelligence—their ability to share food and cooperate in the hunt—with other aspects of human intelligence.

H. erectus had a large brain with a well-developed Broca's area which is the zone associated with speaking ability. Its vocal tracts were more modern, suggesting considerable potential for articulate speech. Language and speech no doubt evolved as a way to handle increasingly complex social information. As group sizes increased, so did a capacity for language, used primarily to talk about social relations.

After, and Alongside, *Homo erectus*

H. erectus used to be considered the single human form to have lived on Earth, before evolving ladder-like into *H. sapiens*. However, we now know that this was not the case. This broad, false, all-embracing classification, dates from the days when we thought of human evolution in linear terms. It linked anatomically primitive features such as heavy brow ridges and bun-shaped skullcaps, which are indeed common to the various *H. erectus* fossils from Africa, Asia, and Europe. Specialized features, such as the massive faces found on Asian individuals, may in fact be evidence for geographically defined forms, only one of which evolved into *H. sapiens*, us. This branching view sees *H. erectus* as an adaptive radiation of hominins after 1.9 Ma, with only a small part of this evolution resulting in the emergence of *H. sapiens*. In the following sections, we will highlight some of the hominins that appeared after the emergence of *H. erectus*, but whose relationship, whether to *H. erectus* or to us (*H. sapiens*) or indeed the other hominin forms that once coexisted, is not always clear. To reiterate: today are we the only hominin left standing. Before around 40,000 years ago various hominin species used to coexist at any given time, and there was no simple ladder of human evolution.

Homo antecessor (1.2 Million to c. 800,000 Years Ago)

Earlier in this chapter, we wrote of the hominins found from Dmanisi in Georgia, which are dated to around 1.8 Ma. These are the oldest known hominins in Europe and are currently categorized as *H. erectus* (though their status is contentious, and many prefer to refer to them as *H. georgicus*). They arrived in Europe before the "invention" of the hand ax in Africa (put at around 1.6 Ma). Though there is no other skeletal evidence for *H. erectus* in Europe, *erectus*-like hand axes, and indeed Oldowan-style tools, show up at various sites throughout Europe—but in association with various other hominins.

Thus, the earliest hominin fossils to be found in western European (potentially) belong to *Homo antecessor* ("Pioneer Man"). However, this species is again controversial, since it shares many features with other species particularly *Homo heidelbergensis* (see below). Moreover, *H. antecessor* is known only from one site: the Gran Dolina cave, *Atapuerca*, in northern Spain. There, excavators have found the partial remains of between 8 and 14 individuals, which date from around 1.2 Ma to 800,000 years ago. The fossils suggest *H. antecessor* would have been fully bipedal, fairly modern in appearance, both in terms of its face and body, with a cranial capacity of about 1,000 cubic centimeters (61 cubic inches). Researchers have also uncovered several hundred stone tools in association with these people, including hammerstones, small flakes, and cores, that are rather similar to the Oldowan technology from Africa.

Homo heidelbergensis (600,000 to 300,000 Years Ago)

H. heidelbergensis (600,000–300,000 years ago) is sometimes thought to be the last common ancestor of Neanderthals in Europe, and modern humans in Africa. However, recent genetic evidence suggests that the Neanderthal and modern human lineages may have diverged earlier than previously thought, raising the possibility that their common ancestor actually belonged to an earlier, still poorly known population. Whatever the case, *H. heidelbergensis* (or Human from Heidelberg, Germany, where it was first found) seems to have lived across a wide area, ranging from southern Africa to northern Europe.

Significant material is known from the site of **Kabwe** in Zambia. The so-called Kabwe Skull is one of the most robust crania assigned to *H. heidelbergensis* and has a massive brow ridge and thickened bone at the rear that once supported strong neck muscles. Brain size varied from around 1,100 to 1,400 cubic centimeters (67–85 cubic inches), which is within the range of modern humans, and slightly smaller than in Neanderthals. Its body shows a mix of Neanderthal and modern human traits. For example, the upper vertebrae that once supported its head are shallow and wide, similar to those found in the Neanderthals, while its bone proportions and degree of robusticity are comparable to modern humans.

Kabwe (Broken Hill), Zambia Site in Central Africa where a robust form of early *H. sapiens* was discovered, exact age unknown.

We know of several skulls from Europe and Africa that appear to be *H. heidelbergensis* (see Figure 9.7), while good evidence for the rest of its body is known from the "Pit of Bones" (Suma de los Huesos) site in Spain. There, researchers have found the remains of at least 30 individuals. It seems the adult males of this species were relatively tall, averaging around 1.75 meters (5 feet 9 inches). Some skeletons show evidence for disease, perhaps indicating the harsh conditions of Pleistocene Europe, and of healed injuries hinting that these were a "humane" people who cared for their sick.

Ambrona, Spain Acheulean butchering site dating to between 200,000 and 400,000 years ago.

No question, *H. heidelbergensis* and its contemporaries were expert big-game hunters. **Ambrona**, a site in a swampy valley in central Spain, yielded the remains of between 30 and 35 dismembered elephants, butchered between 200,000 and 400,000 years ago.

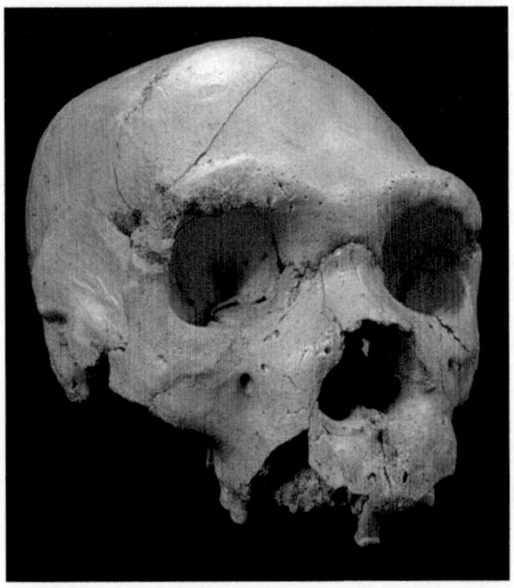

Figure 9.7 Homo heidelbergensis skull from the Pit of Bones, Atapuerca, Spain.
Source: Javier Trueba/Science Photo Library.

Concentrations of broken bones lay all over the site, and the skulls of the elephants had been broken open to get at the brains. In one place, elephant bones had been laid out in a line, perhaps to form stepping stones in the swamp where the animals had been killed. Ambrona, and the nearby **Torralba** site, where the left side of an elephant had been cut to pieces, were littered with hand axes, cleavers, scrapers, and cutting tools.

Boxgrove, England Hunting site in southern England used by *H. heidelbergensis* some 500,000 years ago.

Similar evidence for hunting comes from the 500,000-year-old tidal site of **Boxgrove** in southern England. This site contains the earliest known hominin fossils in Britain: two lower incisors and a gnawed shinbone belonging to *H. heidelbergensis*. The people at Boxgrove left a rich cultural record of occupation, including finely knapped Acheulean hand axes. Alongside the tools were the remains of rhinoceros, bison, deer, horses, and bears. Much of the prey was butchered near a waterhole where the animals gathered, suggesting that the hunters lay in wait for game at the same location over many generations. How many people were involved is unknown, but at least six butchering sites have been excavated near a single horse skeleton. The meat yields from the larger animals were enormous, if the marrow and entrails are included. A rhinoceros would yield 700 kilograms (nearly 1,550 pounds) of meat alone. The butchering was thorough, with much of the meat and skin removed for later use, as if considerable amounts of flesh were dried in the sun. One hand ax bears the distinctive wear patterns associated with scraping hide. A horse shoulder blade at Boxgrove displayed a hole made by a wooden spear. Even more dramatic evidence for the hunting prowess of *H. heidelbergensis,* or perhaps more likely the Neanderthals, comes from **Schöningen**, Germany, where complete wooden spears came to light (see Box 9.1).

Schöningen, Germany Stone Age archaeological site that yielded the earliest known wooden spears, dated to around 300,000 years ago.

The Neanderthals (At Least 400,000 to c. 40,000 Years Ago)

In 1856, workers in the Feldhofer cave in the Neander valley, Germany, discovered a partial skeleton that would later be described as *Homo Neanderthalensis* ("Human from the Neander valley"). Since that time, thousands of Neanderthal fossil specimens have been excavated from hundreds of sites across Europe and into Siberia and Southwest Asia. The record includes everything from premature fetuses to the very elderly.

The Neanderthals are still a subject of great controversy. Most date to after around 350,000 years ago, though the oldest potential Neanderthal bones are dated to around 430,000 years ago. Likewise, the Neanderthals' relationship to us and the reason for their extinction remains unclear. Moreover, there are widespread misunderstandings over the potential intelligence of these hominins.

The general public typically uses the word *Neanderthal* as an insult to describe dim-witted, brutish, apelike people. This stereotype, like that of the shambling cave people so beloved by cartoonists, comes from mistaken studies of Neanderthal skeletons in the early years of the twentieth century. In fact, the Neanderthals were strong, robustly built humans with large brains (1,200–1,750 cubic centimeters, or 73–107 cubic inches). There is every reason to believe that they were expert hunters and beings capable of considerable

Box 9.1 Site
A Hunt, Around 300,000 Years Ago, at Schöningen, Germany

Since 1983, Harmut Thieme has investigated a 6-square-kilometer (2.31-square-mile) area within an open-cast coal mine at Schöningen, northern Germany, where mining operations cut deep into massive Pleistocene deposits. He has uncovered important lakeshore sites at which pre-modern hominins once camped. At the location known as Schöningen 12, a campsite by a lake, the inhabitants butchered elephants and other animals, and also caught birds and fish. Here Thieme recovered four worked branches from silver fir trees, each with a diagonal groove cut into one end, perhaps to hold sharp stone flakes or flint tools. The wood was carefully selected—the hard, intact roots of the boughs of rotted fir trunks.

About 10 meters (33 feet) below the modern ground surface at another location, Schöningen 13 II–4, a hunt had taken place on the shores of a shallow, elongated lake. Because the area was dry and treeless, the hunters could watch their prey. Here a hunting band stalked, intercepted, killed, and butchered a complete herd of wild horses.

Thieme and his colleagues excavated more than 3,200 square meters (34,445 square feet) of an organic mud where the artifacts lay. Pollens from the mud revealed a meadow and forest landscape that thrived in a cool, temperate climate. The inhabitants of the site butchered at least 20 wild horses, whose remains represent more than 90 percent of the 25,000 bone fragments at Schöningen 13. The hunters carried stone scrapers and points manufactured elsewhere and resharpened or reworked on-site; there was no toolmaking debris, just refinishing flakes. Three spectacular wooden spears came to light in 1995.

Since then, more than a half-dozen additional weapons have been found. Most of the spears are made of spruce, between 1.82 and 2.5 meters (6 and 8.2 feet) long, each made from an individual tree that was felled, the branches and bark stripped off, with tips made from the hardest wood at the foot of the tree. The points are carefully shaped and symmetrical, the tails pointed and tapering toward the proximal end. The hunters smoothed and shaped the surfaces of their weapons with great care so that the maximum thickness and weight lay a third of the way from the tip. Thieme remarked that the spears resembled modern hunting javelins. A replica spear tested under controlled conditions displayed excellent ballistic qualities and a range of about 60 meters (198 feet) with good penetrating power.

The first wooden tool from the site, found in 1994, was a spruce stick with carefully sharpened ends, 0.78 meters (2.6 feet) long made from the trunk of a small tree. Thieme believes that this was a throwing stick, its shape and size like those used by Australian Aborigines to hunt birds in flight. It would have been very effective against the geese that lived in the reeds around the lake and whose bones appear in the site.

Numerous other worked wood fragments came from this large hunting camp, among them a carefully shaped and charred stick that may have been used to cook meat over a fire. Hearths lie along the western edge of the main concentration of finds, about a meter (3 feet) apart. The nearby finds include large bison bones whose flat surfaces show traces of repeated cut marks, as if people were slicing meat into strips for drying. Thieme points out that the hearths lay on dry ground, so they were probably used in late summer or fall when water levels were low and rainfall sparse. Then, in late fall, the first snow covered the bones and abandoned tools with a thick layer of decaying reeds before rising waters in spring preserved the site for posterity.

intellectual reasoning. And in evolutionary terms, their skeletons are very similar to ours, though they tend to be slightly shorter and more robust, which may be adaptations to the cold environments of Ice Age Europe (see Figure 9.9).

But when were they made and by whom? The spears were initially dated to around 400,000 years ago, but have recently been redated to around 337,000 to 300,000 years old. Though no hominin remains have been found associated with the tools, they were most likely made by *H. heidelbergensis* or Neanderthals. The spears provide some of the earliest surviving physical evidence of the importance of wood as a material for tools; they also indicate that human ancestors were closer to us in their technical ability and social structure than previously thought

Their skulls were bun-shaped, with retreating foreheads, forward-projecting faces, and sometimes heavy eyebrow ridges. They had large nasal openings and probably prominent and fleshy noses, again potentially adaptations to the cold, with big jaws and front teeth that are larger than modern humans (see Figure 9.8).

mitochondrial DNA inherited through the female line, used to trace the origins of modern humans and major population movements in prehistory.

DNA analysis has helped us to understand more about the status of the Neanderthals and indeed their relationship to us. In a first tranche of research, specialists at the University of Munich, Germany, and at Pennsylvania State University were able to extract deoxyribonucleic acid (DNA) from the fossil from the Neander valley. The scientists pulverized a small amount of arm bone and were able to extract several small fragments of **mitochondrial DNA** (mtDNA). MtDNA is only inherited through the maternal (mother) line and their work indicated that there is no Neanderthal DNA in modern humans.

However, in 2013 scientists sequenced the entire Neanderthal genome—that is the DNA inherited from both parents. This, together with a 2010 project, revealed previously unexpected evidence for admixture between Neanderthals and *H. sapiens*. The 2010 team concluded that all modern humans outside sub-Saharan Africa (where Neanderthals never ventured) have 1–4 percent Neanderthal inherited genetic material. This estimation has since been refined to 1.5–2.1 percent. How to explain this? It seems that after some *H. sapiens* left Africa (roughly 50,000 years ago), a few must have mated with Neanderthals, so carrying the Neanderthals' genetic material onward to the rest of the world, and into

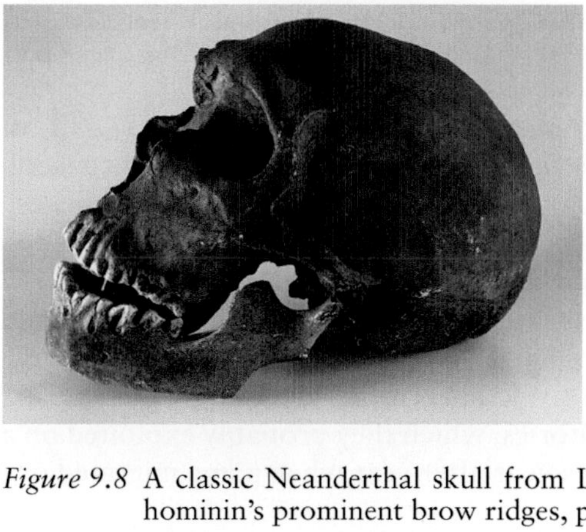

Figure 9.8 A classic Neanderthal skull from La Ferrassie, southwestern France, showing the hominin's prominent brow ridges, prognathous face, and massive jaw.

Source: The Art Archive/Alamy.

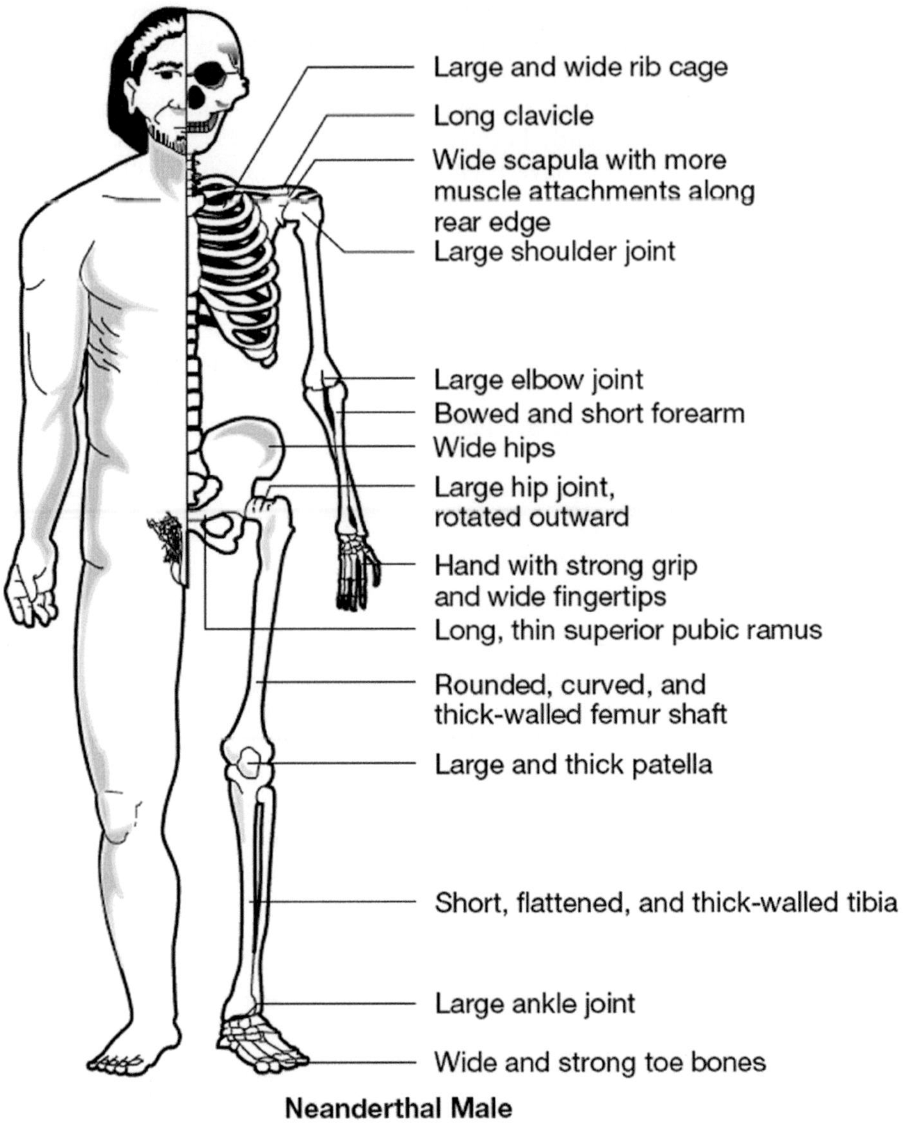

Figure 9.9 The skeleton of a male Neanderthal, showing major anatomical features.

most of us. However, while most of us carry a small amount of Neanderthal DNA, we are still a separate and distinct species to the Neanderthals. Indeed, a 2016 study suggests that Neanderthal males may not have had viable male offspring with *H. sapiens* females. This could explain why no modern man has yet been found with a Neanderthal Y chromosome.

In terms of Neanderthal culture, their technology was far more complex and sophisticated than those of their Acheulean predecessors. Many of their artifacts were not multipurpose tools but were made for specific uses, such as stone spear points mounted on wooden spears or curved scrapers for treating pegged-out hides (see Figure 9.10). Like their predecessors, they occupied large territories, which they probably exploited on a seasonal round, returning to the same locations year after year when game migrated or plant foods came into season.

Mousterian Name applied to a stone tool technology associated with Neanderthal peoples of Europe, Eurasia, and the Near East after about 160,000 years ago, based on carefully prepared disk cores; named after the French village of Le Moustier.

composite tools Artifacts with more than one component, such as a stone spear point and wooden shaft.

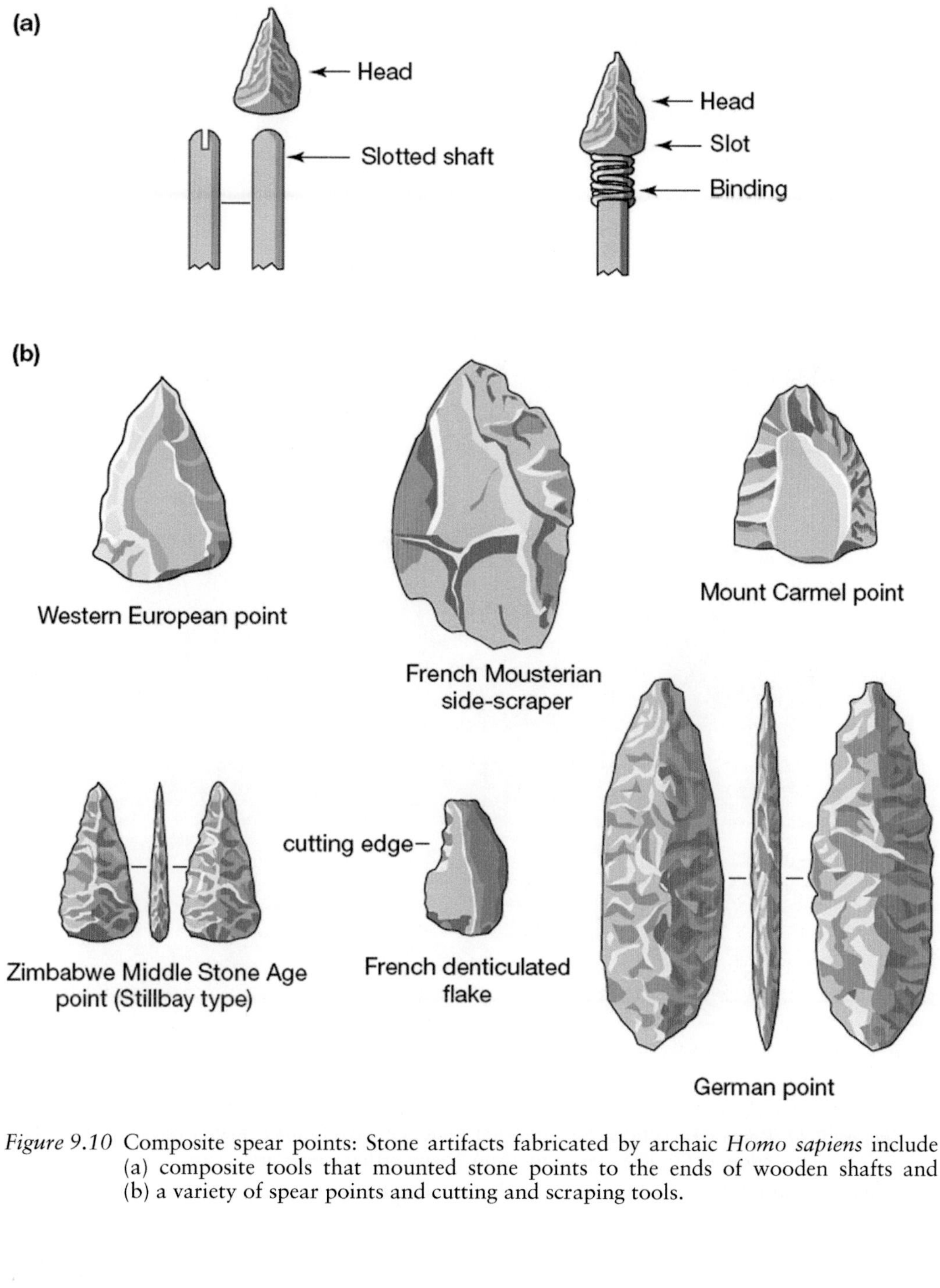

Figure 9.10 Composite spear points: Stone artifacts fabricated by archaic *Homo sapiens* include (a) composite tools that mounted stone points to the ends of wooden shafts and (b) a variety of spear points and cutting and scraping tools.

The Neanderthals were skilled hunters, especially when one realizes that they had to attack game at close quarters with spears and clubs rather than with bows and arrows (see Figure 9.11a). They were not afraid to tackle such formidable animals as mammoths, bison, or wild horses. Many western European bands lived in caves and rock shelters during much of the year as a protection against arctic cold. During the brief summer

(a)

(b)

Figure 9.11 Reconstruction of Neanderthal lifeways: (a) Hunters during the early last glaciation, c. 80,000 years ago. (b) A Neanderthal camp site.

Source: Natural History Museum, London/Science Photo Library and Jose Antonio Penas/Science Photo Library.

months, they may have fanned out over the open plains, living in temporary tented encampments, also exploiting plant foods (see Figure 9.11b). There can be little doubt that the Neanderthals knew their local environments intimately or that they planned their lives around migration seasons and such factors as herd size and the predictability of animal movements. By this time, too, humans had learned how to store food for the lean months, maximizing the meat taken from seasonally migrating herds of reindeer and other animals. The resulting cultural variability is reflected in the diverse **Mousterian** tool kits of Neanderthal groups (named after the site of Le Moustier in southwestern France). Unlike the hand-ax makers, the Neanderthals made most of their artifacts of flakes, the most common being scraping tools and spear points. Some of their weapons were **composite tools**, artifacts made of more than one component—for example, a point, a shaft, and the binding that secured the head to the shaft, making a spear. Their technology was simple, highly variable, and a logical development of earlier technologies developed over hundreds of thousands of years.

Neanderthal sites in France have yielded a great diversity of tool kits. Some levels include hand axes, others, notched flakes, perhaps used for stripping meat for drying or pressing fibrous plants. Such wide variation in Mousterian tool kits is found not only in France, but also at other Neanderthal sites throughout Europe and southwestern Asia, and in North Africa, where other archaic *H. sapiens* made similar tools. No one knows exactly what all these variations in tool kits mean, but they reflect the ability of the Neanderthals and other archaic *H. sapiens* to develop tools for different, highly specific activities, perhaps at a time of rising human populations and slightly enhanced social complexity.

La Ferrassie, France Rock shelter near Les Eyzies, Dordogne, where evidence of Neanderthal burials was found.

The Neanderthals, just like their *H. sapiens* and other contemporaries elsewhere, were foragers, and the world's population was still small, but life was gradually becoming more complex, including the first signs of religious ideology, of a preoccupation with the hereafter. Some Neanderthal bands buried their dead. Neanderthal burials have been recovered from caves and rock shelters and from open campsites. One rock shelter, **La Ferrassie**, near Les Eyzies in southwestern France, yielded the remains of two adult Neanderthals and four children buried close together in a campsite. Group sepulchers occur at other sites, too, signs that the Neanderthals, like later foragers, believed in life after death.

We find in the Neanderthals and their increasingly sophisticated culture some hints of our own complicated beliefs, societies, and religious sense. But the Neanderthals, like other contemporary hominins such as the Denisovans, are no more. By 30,000 years ago we were the only hominins to still walk the Earth. It was we who created a late Ice Age world unimaginably different from that of earlier prehistory.

Early *Homo sapiens* (c. 300,000 to 120,000 Years Ago)

H. sapiens means "wise person." We are the clever people, capable of subtlety, of manipulation, and of self-understanding. Among our skills, which may indeed have been shared by other hominin contemporaries, including the big-brained Neanderthals, is our ability to speak fluently and articulately. We communicate, we tell stories, and we pass on knowledge and ideas, all through the medium of language. Consciousness, cognition, self-awareness, foresight, and the ability to express oneself and one's emotions—these are direct consequences of fluent speech. They can be linked with another attribute of the fully fledged human psyche: the capacity for symbolic and spiritual thought, concerned not only with subsistence and technology, but also with the boundaries of existence and the relationships among the individual, the group, and the universe.

Fluent speech, the full flowering of human creativity expressed in art and religion, and expert toolmaking are some of the key traits of *H. sapiens*. With these abilities, humans eventually colonized not just temperate and tropical environments, but the entire globe. The controversies surrounding the origins of modern humanity have been among the most vigorous in archaeology.

Continuity or Replacement?

If you read any human evolution books published before about the year 2010, you will find two major, and diametrically opposed, hypotheses to explain the origins of modern humans:

- The *multiregional* (or *candelabra*) *model* hypothesized that *H. erectus* populations throughout the Old World evolved independently, first to archaic *H. sapiens* and then to fully modern humans. This continuity model argued for multiple origins of *H. sapiens* and no migrations later than those of *H. erectus*. It therefore held that modern geographic populations have been separated from one another for a long time, perhaps 2 million years. Under this scenario, continuous gene flow within the group meant that highly adaptive, novel anatomical features spread rapidly, thereby keeping all human populations on the same fundamental evolutionary path toward anatomically modern people, even if some evolved into fully modern humans before others.
- The *out-of-Africa* (or *Noah's ark*) *model* took the diametrically opposite view. According to this model, *H. sapiens* evolved in one place and then spread to all other parts of the Old World. This model, which assumes population movement from a single point of origin, implies that modern geographic populations have shallow roots and derived from a single source in relatively recent times.

These two models represent extremes, which pits advocates of anatomical continuity against those who favor rapid replacement of archaic populations. Until the early 1990s, most anthropologists favored the multiregional model. Thereafter, consensus swung toward the out-of-Africa model, owing to overwhelming evidence from the genetic, molecular and the fossil records. However, fine-grained DNA research in the current century has moved the debate yet further. We now know that the out-of-Africa model requires refinement. Thus, while there is wide agreement that modern humans first developed in Africa, by 300,000 years ago, we now think that there was some minor hybridization outside Africa—between *H. sapiens* and now-extinct hominins (including the Neanderthals and the Denisovans).

Molecular Biology and Homo sapiens

Molecular biology has played a significant role in dating earlier human evolution and is now yielding important clues to the origins of *H. sapiens* (see Box 9.2).

Box 9.2 Doing Archaeology
DNA and Human Origins

Ever since the identification of the ABO blood system in the early twentieth century, genetics has had a profound effect on the study of human evolutionary history. Modern molecular biological techniques have made it much easier to detect and analyze new polymorphic genes (genes present in slightly different forms in different people) that might have medical or anthropological interest. All humans carry in their genes the record of their past history. Studies of mtDNA present outside the cell nuclei in small structures called mitochondria have attracted particular attention. This DNA is inherited through the female line and is passed from mothers to offspring virtually unaltered except for rare changes caused by mutation.

Large-scale studies of human mtDNA in present-day populations from all parts of the world have shown relatively little mtDNA variation throughout the globe, suggesting that there was a relatively recent branching out of human populations. The African mtDNAs were the most variable, having had more time to accumulate genetic changes, consistent with the theory that the African human lineages were the oldest ones. Molecular biologists Rebecca Cann, Mark Stoneking, and Alan Wilson proposed that all modern humanity is descended from a single *H. sapiens* who lived in tropical Africa about 200,000 years ago. This hypothesis has been widely criticized and refined, and indeed we now know of humans in North West Africa by 300,000 years ago. However, it is almost universally agreed that *H. sapiens* evolved in Africa and then spread into other parts of the Old World and eventually to the Americas. mtDNA research on Native American populations links them to Siberian ancestors, as one might expect.

The first ancient DNA sequences were reported by Swedish scientist Svante Pääbo, who extracted and characterized DNA from the skin of a predynastic Egyptian of about 4000 B.C. in 1985. Since then, DNA has been extracted from bones, teeth, and plant remains using a technique called the polymerase chain reaction (PCR). Pääbo used this technique on a human brain of 3000 B.C. from a hunter-gatherer site at **Windover**, Florida, and identified an mtDNA strain not previously observed in North America. In recent years, scientists have succeeded in extracting DNA from a Neanderthal bone over 50,000 years old and have shown that these archaic Europeans were genetically distinct from the modern humans who succeeded them. mtDNA analysis of ancient human skeletons from Easter Island in the Pacific has also shown that the ultimate origins of the Easter Islanders lie in Polynesia, for this remote landmass was colonized by people from the Society Islands (the Tahiti region) by A.D. 500. Molecular biology is playing an increasingly important role in the study of ancient human populations and population movements.

The picture from the mtDNA has been massively enhanced in recent years, thanks to yet more extraordinary work by Svante Pääbo and others. Perhaps the most stunning achievement has been the 2013 reading of the entire nuclear Neanderthal genome (that is the DNA inherited from both the mother and the father). This work, together with other fine-grained nuclear DNA research since 2010, has revealed a new picture of human connections that was not apparent from the mtDNA alone.

Consequently, we now know that there was minor admixture between *H. sapiens* and other hominin forms. To explain further: once *H. sapiens* permanently left Africa (roughly around 50,000 years ago), some mated with local hominins outside sub-Saharan Africa, including the Neanderthals and the Denisovans (another contemporary hominin species known from very limited fossil information); while those *H. sapiens* who remained in Africa appear to have mated with another still unknown hominin. The DNA contribution of these other hominins is minor and often displayed today as negative health blips. However, the picture of evolutionary connections, as revealed by the entire DNA record, is clearly much more complicated than people once envisaged. Of final interest to unraveling the secrets of human origins is the so-called "molecular clock" (a method to time events based on apparently regularly occurring DNA mutations). The speed at which this clock ticked is open to question, but current estimates suggest that modern humans and the Neanderthals split with a common ancestor somewhere between 750,000 and 400,000 years ago.

Windover, Florida Archaic hunter-gatherer site of c. 3000 B.C., remarkable for the preservation of human remains.

Researchers have zeroed in on mtDNA, a useful tool for calibrating mutation rates because it accumulates mutations much faster than nuclear DNA. mtDNA is inherited only through the maternal line; it does not mix and become diluted with paternal DNA. Thus, it provides a potentially reliable link with ancestral populations. When genetic researchers analyzed the mtDNA of 147 women from Africa, Asia, Europe, Australia, and New Guinea, they found that the differences among them were very small. Therefore, they argued, the five populations were all of comparatively recent origin. There were some differences, sufficient to separate two groups within the sample—a set of African individuals and another comprising individuals from all groups. The biologists concluded that all modern humans derive from a 200,000-year-old African population, from which populations migrated to the rest of the Old World with little or no interbreeding with existing, more archaic human groups.

Moreover, the mtDNA provides evidence that indigenous Africans display more diverse types of mtDNA than other present-day populations elsewhere in the world, a finding that suggests they had more time to develop such mutations. Studies of the entire (nuclear) DNA and of its products (blood groups and enzymes) further display a hierarchy of clusters. This indicates that there was a primary split between Africans and non-Africans, then a later one between Eurasians and Southeast Asians. These findings also imply that modern humans originated in Africa, then dispersed from there to split again in Asia.

Using careful modeling and sophisticated statistical approaches, the mtDNA further indicates that the process of origin and spread was more complex than originally thought. Geneticist Max Ingman and his colleagues have shown that the three deepest branches of the African tree were exclusively African. The next deepest was a mixture of Africans and non-Africans. They believe this pattern arose from the evolution of DNA lineages in Africa for some time, followed by an out-migration by a few people. This resulted in a population bottleneck, followed by a rapid expansion. Their estimate for the start of the process is 171,500 ± 50,000 years. The first clade with both African and non-African members dates to an estimated 52,000 ± 27,500 years. This also means that, assuming a constant rate of genetic diversification, all human variation could have arisen in the past 150,000 years or so.

Currently, scientists are beginning to extract yet more information from the aforementioned nuclear DNA (where genetic information comes from both parents, not just the mother as in the mtDNA). Based on the genome-wide data from both extinct hominins and living people, DNA researchers suggest an exodus out of Africa somewhere between as early as 100,000 and 50,000 years ago, and then at least three to five admixture (interbreeding) events with four distinct hominin species, including the Neanderthals and the Denisovans.

While the details remain far from crystal clear, the archaeological and fossil evidence confirms an early appearance of modern humans in Africa. But where in Africa? Before 2017, all the earliest *H. sapiens* fossils were known exclusively from sub-Saharan Africa (and we list these below). Then, in 2017, new data hit the headlines as researchers identified the presence of very early *H. sapiens* in Morocco, northwest Africa. This material not only pushes back the earliest known evidence for *H. sapiens* to over 300,000 years ago but also forces us to revise the notion that East Africa was the "cradle" of *H. sapiens*.

Jebel Irhoud, Morocco Site of the earliest known *H. sapiens* in the world.

The Moroccan fossils, representing five individuals, together with stone tools, come from the site of **Jebel Irhoud**. Most of the material was found in the early 1960s and the individuals were originally labeled "African Neanderthals" and estimated to be around 40,000 years old. Subsequent researchers realized that these people were in fact early *H. sapiens*, and proposed a date of around 190,000–90,000 years old.

In 2017, the current team announced that they had found more human fossils and more tools. But the real bombshell came with the dating. Using improved dating techniques, particularly in luminescence dating, the team has concluded that the fossils come from a layer dating to about 350,000–280,000 years old (giving the tools and fossils a weighted average date of 315,000, give or take about 34,000 years). With such a shockingly early date (roughly twice as old as previously thought) the team then investigated the status of the hominins—were they really *H. sapiens*? Using shape-analysis techniques to compare the fossils with hominins dated to between 1.8 Ma and 150,000 years ago, the results showed that all of the Jebel Irhoud specimens are most comparable to modern *H. sapiens*—albeit with some more archaic traits. Thus, the lower jaw is much like ours, if a little larger; while other traits such as the elongated braincase are rather primitive. These hominins therefore appear to represent an intermediate form between more archaic and fully anatomically modern *H. sapiens*—which is to be expected given their antiquity.

How do we explain their presence in North Africa? Researchers widely acknowledge that Africa is a dramatically understudied continent. The fact that all other early African *H. sapiens* come from East Africa may simply be archaeological bias, since there are virtually no excavations in other regions. Nonetheless, East Africa does seem to be a hominin hot spot, and until the last few years, the rest of the early *sapiens* corpus has hailed from this region, as we shall now outline.

Herto, Ethiopia Site of three 160,000-year-old *H. sapiens* skulls.

At **Herto**, about 225 kilometers (140 miles) northeast of Addis Ababa, Ethiopian paleo-anthropologist Y. Haile-Selassie and his colleagues unearthed three 160,000-year-old skulls, one of them a child, as well as other human fragments, from a location where people had caught numerous fish and killed or scavenged hippopotamuses. The skulls are clearly from anatomically modern people, although there are minor differences that mark them as more primitive, sufficient for them to be labeled *Homo sapiens idaltu* (after the local Afar name for "elder"). The adult male skull is long and rugged, with heavily worn teeth, also slightly larger than modern crania. Interestingly, there are signs that the skulls were defleshed with stone tools after death, and the child's skull displays a polish resulting from repeated handling. Judging from modern-day practices in New Guinea and elsewhere, the people may have preserved heads as part of some ancestor cult—the earliest evidence of any form of death ritual from the past.

The Herto finds show that the anatomical developments that led to the emergence of *H. sapiens* had been completed in Africa as early as 160,000 years ago, far earlier than any equivalent developments in Europe or Southwest Asia. At this time, the evolution of the classic and late Neanderthals had run its course in those areas. In evolutionary terms, the transition from *H. erectus* to archaic *H. sapiens* seems to have occurred not quickly, but relatively slowly and continuously. It is difficult to draw a line between the two species. In contrast, the "modernization" of the human skull into its present configuration took place considerably faster, sometime at the very end of the Middle Pleistocene or the beginning of the Upper Pleistocene, by 120,000 years ago.

Langebaan Lagoon, South Africa Site where 117,000-year-old footprints of a *H. sapiens* are preserved in a fossilized sand dune.

Some well-preserved footprints of a *H. sapiens* survive in a fossilized sand dune at **Langebaan Lagoon** near Cape Town, South Africa, dating to at least 117,000 years ago. The Klasies River Cave on the southeastern coast, mentioned in Chapter 4, has yielded modern human remains dating to about 100,000 years ago.

However, there is yet more to the story. Over the past few years, researchers have begun to identify (not always without controversy) some surprisingly early *H. sapiens* fossils far outside Africa. These finds do not cause us to question an African origin for our species, but they do make us consider whether there were earlier (albeit likely "deadend") *sapiens* migrations out of Africa, rather than just one big modern human exodus by around 50,000 years ago (as discussed further in Chapter 10).

Thus, in 2018, an upper jawbone with several teeth belonging to an early *H. sapiens* was found in a cave in Misliya, Israel, and dated to a little under 200,000 years ago. This date was almost twice as old as any previous *H. sapiens* remains discovered outside Africa (the oldest fossils previously discovered, near Misliya, date to 80,000–120,000 years ago). Then, in 2019, some skull fragments found in the Apidima Cave on the Mani peninsula of Greece were dated to an even earlier 210,000 years ago. The latter claim remains unverified, but if correct, this Greek fossil would indeed be the oldest known *H. sapiens* in Europe.

While such evidence supports the idea that some *H. sapiens* had journeyed out of Africa at a very early date, these ancient exits appear to have been "unsuccessful" or "failed"—i.e. impermanent in the great scheme of things. The Misliya lineage, for example, contributed little, if any, DNA to modern-day people. Instead, the genetic data show that these folk likely went extinct or were genetically swamped by a more extensive *sapiens* dispersal from Africa by around 50,000 years ago.

In short, the latest genetic and archaeological research points to an African homeland for *H. sapiens*, with some early (deadend) dispersals out of Africa, and a main (successful/enduring) exodus by very much later.

Ecology and Homo sapiens

Ecological anthropologist Robert Foley points out that the savanna woodland of Africa 100,000 years ago was an ideal environment for promoting the speciation of modern humans. He has studied monkey evolution in Africa and found that the widely dispersed populations had diverged; they did not continue on a single evolutionary course. Africa experienced considerable habitat fragmentation and reformation during the cold and warm cycles of the Ice Age, fluctuations that enhanced the prospects of speciation among the continent's animals and plants. For example, says Foley, one monkey genus alone radiated into 16 species at about the same time as modern humans may have evolved in Africa.

Foley's monkey studies have convinced him that modern humans evolved in just such a fragmented mosaic of tropical environments, developing distinctive characteristics that separated them from their archaic predecessors. There were areas where food resources were predictable and of high quality. In response to such regions, some human populations may have developed wide-ranging behavior, lived in larger social groups with considerable kin-based substructure, and been highly selective in their diet.

As part of these responses, some groups may have developed exceptional hunting skills, using a technology so effective that they could prey on animals from a distance with projectiles. With more efficient weapons, more advance planning, and better organization of foraging, our ancestors could have reduced the unpredictability of the environment in dramatic ways. Few archaeologists would be so bold as to associate ancient technologies with specific fossil forms, but we do know that tens of thousands of years later, *H. sapiens* relied on much more sophisticated tool technology than its predecessors. The new tool kits were based on antler, bone, wood, and parallel-sided stone blade manufacture. This technology was far more advanced than anything seen so far and took many millennia to develop. There is no question that it would have conferred a major advantage on its users, in terms of both hunting efficiency and energy

Interestingly enough, there are signs of technological change throughout eastern and southern Africa between 200,000 and 130,000 years ago, as age-old hand-ax technology gave way to lighter tool kits that combined sharp stone flakes with wooden spear shafts and to other more specialized artifacts used for woodworking and butchering. Such simple artifacts, made from medium-sized flakes, could have been the archaic prototypes of far more efficient tools and weapons developed by modern humans after 100,000 years ago (see Figure 9.12). Some spear points were made with pressure-flaking techniques and achieved remarkable sophistication that may have required enhanced cognitive abilities. Interestingly, after around 120,000 *H. sapiens* appears to have become fully anatomically modern. These *H. sapiens* were physically, and presumably mentally, identical to us today—with the same intellectual and physical potential of any living human.

Blombos Cave, South Africa Cave site with evidence of art and *H. sapiens*-style artifacts dating to as early as 100,000 years ago.

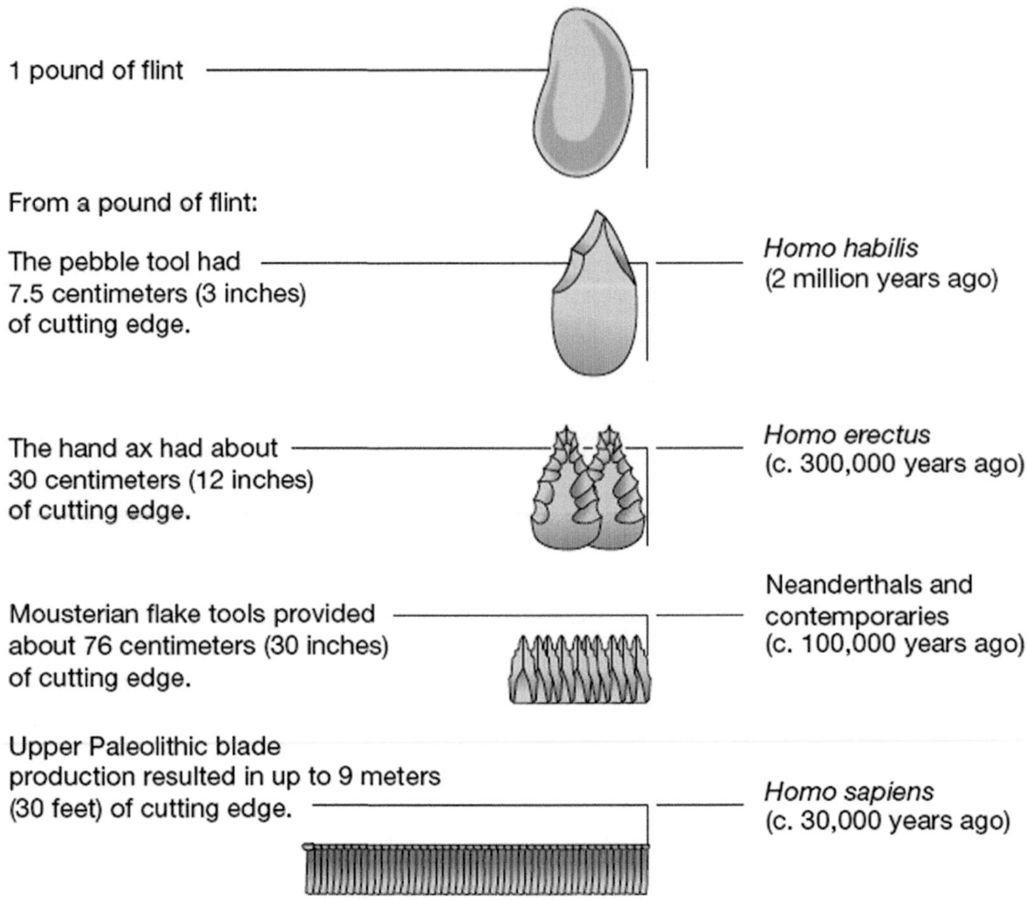

Figure 9.12 The growing efficiency of stone technology, shown by the ability of ancient stoneworkers to produce ever-larger numbers of cutting edges from a unit of stone or other fine-grained rock. The Neanderthals were far more efficient stone artisans than their predecessors. By the same token, *Homo sapiens* used blade and other technologies that produced up to 9 meters from c. 450 grams (1 pound) of rock.

A number of elements of clearly modern human behavior find their first known expression in sub-Saharan Africa. Blombos Cave, near the southern tip of South Africa, has yielded extensive occupation deposits dating to at least 70,000 years ago, containing numerous finely trimmed blade tools, spear points, and possible bone points. The occupants ate a broad range of foods, including fish, shellfish, game of different sizes, and plants. Numerous fragments of red ocher came to light. One of them has edges worn by grinding and scraping and bears crosshatched lines (see Figure 9.13). Other finds, from earlier levels as much as 75,000 years old, include perforated seashells and 41 estuarine tick shells perforated for suspension. The possibility that these shells were probably strung together to form a necklace suggests a very modern way of thinking, in terms both of personal ornamentation and of the rituals associated with burial. In 2011, the excavation team also found receptacles that may have contained paints along with other art supplies dating to around 100,000 years ago. Of course, the "paint" may have had other uses, including hafting, skin protection against insects or medicine, but nonetheless, it opens up the possibility that humans were making art

Figure 9.13 A red ocher "crayon" from Blombos Cave, South Africa, bearing crisscross scratches. Source: Anna Zieminski/AFP/Getty Images.

far earlier than we once imagined. Alas, no contemporary skeletal remains have been found in the cave, so while we can't definitely say that the material was the work of *H. sapiens*, the stone tools are all of the type used by *H. sapiens*.

Out of Africa

With all data pointing to Africa as the cradle of modern humans, how and why did *H. sapiens* spread permanently into Europe and Asia? The critical period, based on the genetic and archaeological data, was between 100,000 and 45,000 years ago, the date by which modern humans were certainly living in southwestern Asia. The only major barrier to population movement between tropical Africa and the Mediterranean Basin is the Sahara, today some of the driest territory on Earth. Bitterly cold glacial conditions in the north brought a cooler and wetter climate to the desert from before 100,000 until about 40,000 years ago. For long periods, the country between East Africa and the Mediterranean was passable, supporting scattered game herds and open grassland. The Nile valley was always habitable, even during periods of great aridity in the desert. Thus, small groups of modern people could have hunted and foraged across the Sahara into the Nile valley and southwestern Asia as early as 100,000 years ago. Very recently, signs of human occupation dating to before 100,000 years ago have come from the Persian Gulf region, which was then lush coastal marshlands, but investigations have hardly begun.

From there, their successors may have moved into southern and southeastern Asia at a still unknown date, but perhaps between 70,000 and 50,000 years ago, following a massive volcanic eruption in Sumatra that covered much of southern and southeastern Asia with ash. As southwestern Asia became increasingly dry and less productive around 50,000 years ago, small numbers of modern people may have responded to population pressure and food shortages by moving across the wide land bridge that joined Türkiye to southeastern Europe at the time, spreading into the homeland of the European Neanderthals within a few millennia.

With these still little-known population movements, the permanent radiation of modern humans throughout the Old World ended, perhaps by about 40,000 years ago. As we shall see in Chapter 10, the next 30,000 years saw the greatest human diaspora take our ancestors to island Southeast Asia, New Guinea, Australia, Siberia, and ultimately the Americas.

Summary

- The climatic events of the Great Ice Age (the Pleistocene) between about 2.5 million and 15,000 years ago saw complex fluctuations between glacial maxima and much shorter interglacial periods that were the backdrop to the evolution not only of *H. erectus*, but also of many other hominins, including modern humans—*H. sapiens*.
- *H. erectus* had evolved in tropical Africa by 1.9 million years ago, at about the same time that fire was tamed; this erect human then radiated into Europe and Asia as part of a general migration of mammalian species soon afterward.
- *H. erectus* used a simple technology based on hand axes and basic flake technology in the west, relying heavily on bamboo and other forest products in Southeast Asia.
- Various hominins with enlarged cranial capacities evolved thereafter, such as *H. antecessor*, who had reached Western Europe by 780,000 years ago; also *H. heidelbergensis* (c. 600,000–300,000 years ago), sometimes thought to be the last common ancestor of Neanderthals in Europe and modern humans in Africa.
- By 400,000 years ago, the Neanderthals of Europe and Asia emerged. They had sophisticated tools, were adept hunters and foragers, and buried some of their dead.
- The oldest known *H. sapiens* are those from Jebel Irhoud in Morocco and they date to around 300,000 years ago. Other early *H. sapiens* are known from eastern Africa.
- Two competing theories used to account for the appearance of *H. sapiens*. The now discredited multiregional hypothesis had it that modern humans developed independently in Africa, Europe, and Asia and that the biological diversity of contemporary humankind has very deep roots in prehistory. With the appearance of modern humans, the long prehistory of the archaic world ends. Pitted against this was the out-of-Africa hypothesis, which argues that modern humans evolved much more recently in Africa and then spread permanently into other parts of the world. Scientific consensus now holds that Africa was our homeland, though genetic analysis points to very minor admixture with other hominin forms in various places (notably with the Neanderthals and the Denisovans after some *H. sapiens* left Africa).
- Important insights into human evolution have come from recent genetic analysis since 2010, including the reading of the entire Neanderthal genome.

Key Terms and Sites

Trinil
Matuyama–Brunhes boundary
Nariokotome
Gesher Benot Ya'aqov
Dmanisi
Zhoukoudian
Swanscombe
Kalambo Falls
Kabwe
Ambrona
Torralba
Boxgrove
Schöningen
Atapuerca
mitochondrial DNA
Mousterian

composite tools
La Ferrassie
Windover
Jebel Irhoud
Herto
Langebaan Lagoon
Blombos Cave

Critical-Thinking Questions

1. Why do you think hunting was important to pre-modern humans? How did *H. erectus* differ from earlier hominins as far as hunting was concerned?
2. Why do you think people used to think of human evolution in a linear fashion? Why do we now think about evolution as a far more complex process?
3. How has recent genetic work helped us to understand what we know about the evolutionary relationships between *H. sapiens* and other hominins such as the Neanderthals?

Further Reading

There are now a few general summaries of the long millennia covered by this chapter. I. Tattersall, *Masters of the Planet: The Search for Our Human Origins* (New York: St. Martins Griffin, 2015) is one of many popular titles on the origin of modern humans, as is the highly recommended *Our Human Story* (London: Natural History Museum, 2018) by Louise Humphrey and Chris Stringer. On human genetics, D. Reich's, *Who We Are and How We Got Here* (Oxford: Oxford University Press, 2018) is aimed at the general public. Finally, T. Higham's, *The World Before Us: The New Science Behind Our Human Origins* (New Haven, CT: Yale University Press, 2023) is a very readable book about the links between us, the Neanderthals, mysterious Denisovans, and more.

Part 4

Modern Humans Settle the World

10 The Great Diaspora

Chapter Outline

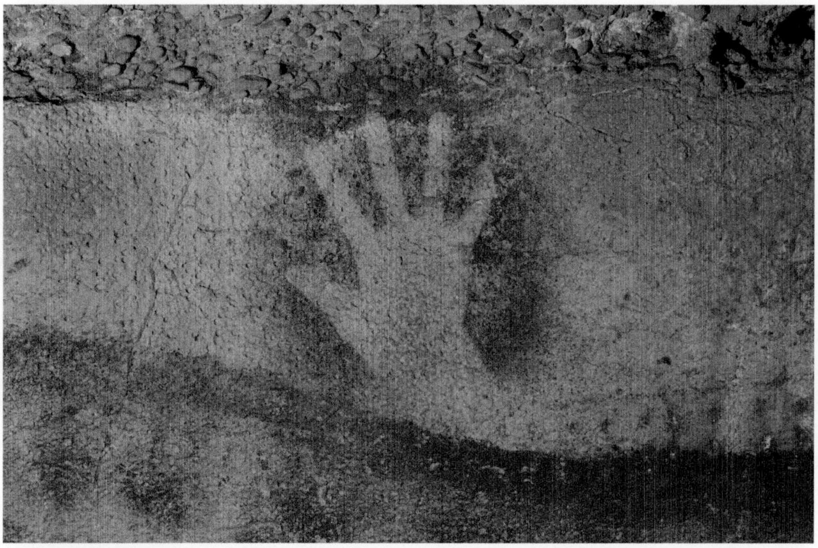

Handprint made on a cave wall by a Cro-Magnon individual.
Source: Patrick Cabrol/Centre de Préhistoire du Pech Merle/akg-images.

Spanish landowner Marcellino de Sautuola had a casual interest in archaeology. He had visited an exhibit in Paris of some of the fine stone tools from French caves. In 1875, he decided to dig for some artifacts of his own in the caverns of Altamira on his estate. Sautuola's five-year-old daughter, Maria, begged for the chance to dig with him, so he good-naturedly agreed. Maria soon tired of the muddy work and wandered off with a flickering lantern

DOI: 10.4324/9781003592754-14

into a low side-chamber of the cave. Suddenly, he heard cries of *Toros, toros*! ("Bulls, bulls!"). Maria pointed excitedly at brightly painted figures of bison and a charging boar on the low ceiling. Daughter and father marveled at the fresh paintings, arranged so cleverly around bulges in the rock that they seemed to move in the flickering light.

Sautuola was convinced that the paintings had been executed by the same people who had dropped stone tools in the cave. But the experts laughed at him and accused him of smuggling an artist into Altamira to forge the bison. It was not until 1904 that the long-dead Spaniard was vindicated, when some paintings with strong stylistic links to Altamira came to light in a French cave that had been sealed since the prehistoric artists had worked there. Clearly, whoever had painted on the cave walls at Altamira was a far cry from earlier prehistoric people.

Between about 60,000 to 50,000 years ago, the pace of human life, of cultural evolution, accelerated rapidly. Some scientists have called these changes a "cultural explosion," but a better term is probably a series of "sparks," where there was rapid cultural change in one area but not in others. One such spark was the settlement of Australia, by 50,000 years ago, another was the development of new stone technologies in southwestern Asia by 50,000 years ago, and a third was the appearance of art in Europe after 40,000 years ago. Only after about 30,000 years ago, during the late Ice Age, did rapid cultural change take hold in all parts of the world.

This chapter describes the rapidly changing late Ice Age world of about 50,000 to 15,000 years ago. The chapter shows how humans first adapted to extreme Arctic climates and developed highly specialized forager cultures that subsisted off cold-loving animals such as the mammoth and steppe bison. It also discusses the permanent radiation of *Homo sapiens* throughout the Old World and then turns to one of the most controversial subjects in modern archaeology, the first settlement of the Americas.

The Late Ice Age World (50,000 to 15,000 Years Ago)

For most of the past 50,000 years, the world was very different from that of today. At the height of the last Ice Age glaciation, some 18,000 years ago, vast ice sheets mantled Scandinavia and the Alps, leaving a chilly corridor of open tundra between them. Sea levels were more than 90 meters (300 feet) lower than today. Great Britain was joined to the European continent, the North Sea was under ice, and the Baltic Sea did not exist. Vast, treeless plains stretched north and east from central Europe to the frontiers of Siberia and beyond, a landscape of rolling scrub country dissected by occasional broad river valleys (see Figure 10.1). The only signs of life were occasional herds of big-game animals like the mammoth, bison, and reindeer, and they were often confined to river valleys. For humans to survive in these exposed landscapes required not only effective hunting methods and weaponry, but also well-insulated winter dwellings and layered, tailored clothing that could keep people warm in subfreezing temperatures.

Sunda Continental shelf of Southeast Asia during the late Ice Age.

Wallacea Sulawesi and Timor, Southeast Asia, during the late Ice Age.

Sahul The landmass consisting of Australia, New Guinea, and the surrounding continental shelf during the late Ice Age.

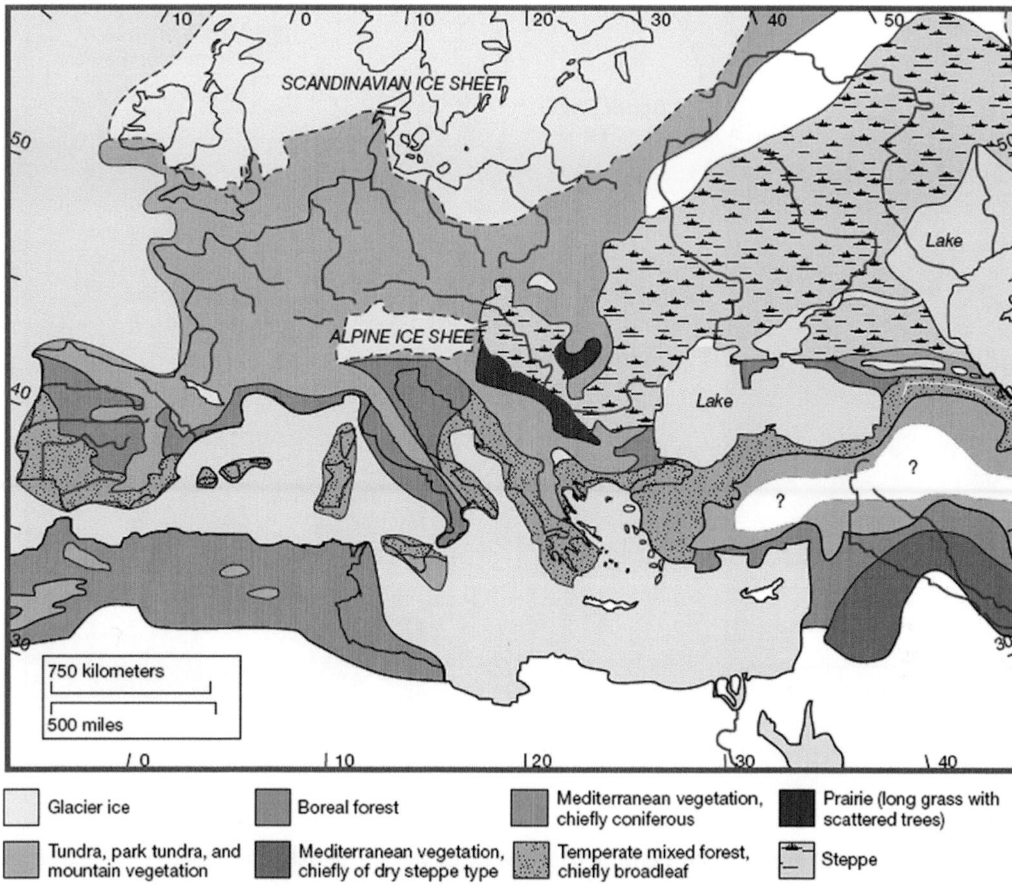

Figure 10.1 Generalized vegetation of Europe during the late Ice Age.

In more temperate and tropical latitudes, the effects of the last glaciation are harder to detect in geological strata. Tropical regions were often drier, many rainforests shrank, and there were more open grasslands and woodlands. In Africa, the Sahara was as dry as it is today, if not drier, as cold polar air flowed south of the Mediterranean. Much lower sea levels exposed enormous areas of continental shelf in Southeast Asia. Many offshore islands became part of the Asian mainland. Great rivers meandered over what were then exposed coastal plains, across another sunken Ice Age continent known to scholars as **Sunda**. Offshore lay two large landmasses—**Wallacea,** made up of the present-day islands of Sulawesi and Timor, and **Sahul**, a combination of New Guinea, Australia, and the low-lying and now flooded shelf between them (see Figure 10.2).

Let us now look at how late Ice Age humans peopled this diverse and often harsh world. Our knowledge of this long diaspora relies heavily on radiocarbon dating (see Box 10.1).

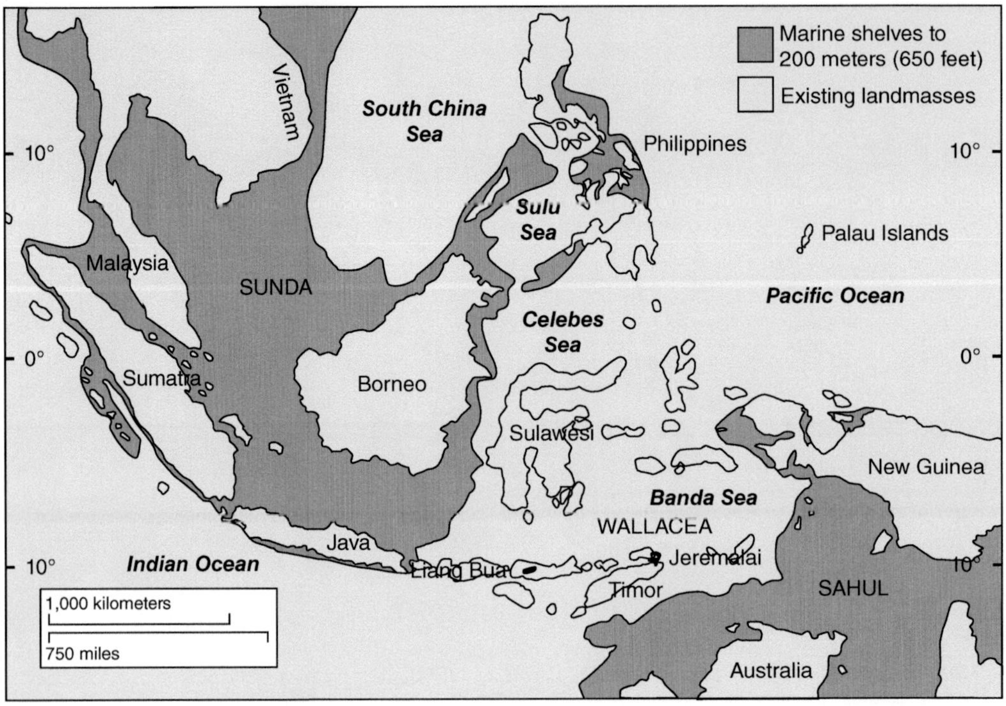

Figure 10.2 Sunda and Sahul during the late Ice Age.

Homo sapiens in Southeast Asia and Australia (by 50,000 Years Ago)

Liang Bua Cave, Flores Site that yielded a series of diminutive human skeletons, *Homo floresiensis*, dating to between 100,000 and 60,000 years ago.

H. sapiens had appeared in Southeast Asia, including Indonesia and the Philippines, by at least 50,000 years ago. At the time, sea levels were much lower than today, so human settlement on Sunda, the exposed continental shelf, may have been concentrated in river valleys, along lakeshores, and on the coasts. Our forebears were soon venturing offshore, as far as Flores Island, which had long been settled by other hominins: first *Homo erectus*—perhaps as early as 1 Ma, though the dates remain controversial—and later by a diminutive hominin nicknamed "the hobbit," who seems to have gone extinct at around 50,000 years ago. Whether the intrepid *H. sapiens* ever met the hobbit, let alone "wiped them out" (as some might guess from the dates), remains unknown.

Evidence for the hobbit, or rather *Homo floresiensis* to give them their proper name, came to light during excavations begun in 2004 in **Liang Bua Cave.** A team, led by Michael Morwood, revealed a remarkable series of diminutive hominin skeletons, associated with stone flakes and other artifacts, as well as the bones of a now-extinct elephant-like animal known as a stegodon. The hominins stood at about a meter (3.2 feet) and their bones displayed a unique mixture of primitive and more advanced characteristics. Their brains were the same size as those of chimpanzees, the skull displaying prominent brow ridges

Box 10.1 Doing Archaeology
Radiocarbon Dating

Radiocarbon dating is the primary method used to date the archaeological record from about 40,000 years ago to the past 2,000 years. The method is based on the knowledge that living organisms build up their own organic matter by photosynthesis and by using atmospheric carbon dioxide. The percentage of radiocarbon in the organism is equal to that in the atmosphere. When the organism dies, the carbon-14 (^{14}C) atoms disintegrate at a known rate, with a half-life of 5,730 years. It is possible then to calculate the date of an organic object by measuring the amount of ^{14}C left in the sample. The initial quantity in the sample is low; therefore, the limit of detectability is soon reached, so the oldest reliable radiocarbon dates are about 40,000 years old.

Radiocarbon dates can be obtained from many types of organic material, including charcoal, shell, wood, and hair. The beta particle decay rate is conventionally measured with a proportional counter, but the use of accelerator mass spectrometry has refined the procedure dramatically. Every radiocarbon date arrives with a statistical error, a standard deviation. For example, a date of 2,200 ± 200 years means that the date has a probable range of 200 years, with a two-out-of-three chance that the date lies between the span of one standard deviation (2,400 and 2,000 years). Unfortunately, the concentration of radiocarbon in the atmosphere has varied considerably over time, as a result of changes in solar activity and in the strength of the Earth's magnetic field. It is possible to correct dates by calibrating them against accurate dates from tree rings—via radiocarbon dating rings—and developing a mastercorrection curve. Dates as far back as nearly 9000 B.C. can be calibrated with tree rings, earlier dates with coral growth rings from tropical seas (see Box 11.2 on p. 353).

and a low braincase. However, their faces were small and delicate like those of modern humans, being tucked under the brain, like those of *H. sapiens*. Their teeth also were entirely modern, whereas their legs were slight and their hips were like those of an australopithecine (see Figure 10.3). Originally dated to between about 38,000 and 13,000 years ago, subsequent excavations between 2007 and 2014 indicated that their stone tools actually went out of use around 50,000 years ago, while their skeletal remains have been re-dated to between about 100,000 and 60,000 years ago.

Their evolutionary status is a puzzle. Were these tiny hominins a remnant *Homo erectus* population? Did they develop their unique anatomical characteristics and small stature as a result of isolation that led, among other things, to endemic dwarfing? Or were they related to some other, as yet unidentified earlier hominin?

As to their culture, they used stone tools and there is evidence that they used fire. If there were technological changes associated with *H. sapiens*, they probably involved more efficient ways of exploiting the rich and highly varied environments of the mainland and offshore islands. The coastlines that faced offshore were relatively benign waters that probably offered a bounty of fish and shellfish to supplement game and wild plant foods. *H. sapiens* may also have been the first to make paintings on cave walls, some of which may be as early as 45,500 years old, and include depictions of animals. Perhaps, coastal peoples constructed simple rafts for fishing in shallows or used rudimentary dugout canoes for bottom fishing. At some point, some of these people crossed open water to Wallacea and Sahul.

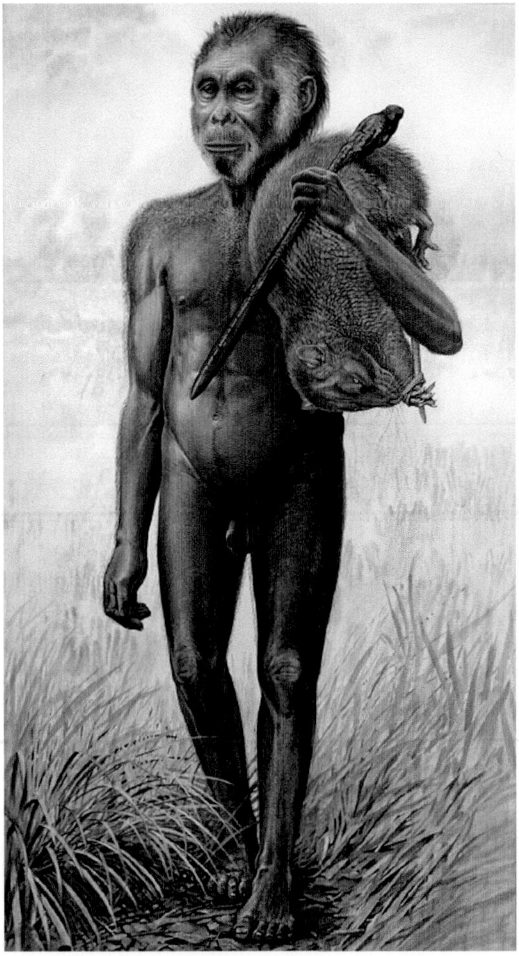

Figure 10.3 An artist's reconstruction of *Homo floresiensis*.
Source: Agefotostock/Alamy Stock Photo.

Jeremalai Cave, East Timor A cave visited by tuna fishers at least 42,000 years ago, early evidence for the human occupation of Wallacea off Southeast Asia.

Sahul was a landscape of dramatic contrasts, of rugged mountain chains and highland valleys in the north and rolling semiarid lowlands over much of what is now Australia. Colonizing Sahul meant an open-water downwind passage of at least 98 kilometers (61 miles), an entirely feasible proposition in simple watercraft in warm tropical waters and smooth seas. Tuna fishers were visiting **Jeremalai Cave** on East Timor by at least 42,000 years ago.

Huon Peninsula, New Guinea Site where 40,000-year-old ground stone axes offer early evidence of human settlement on the island.

The earliest documented archaeological human settlement of New Guinea comes from the highlands and dates to about 50,000 years ago, while newly extracted genetic data may push this date back to 55,000 years ago. Some 40,000-year-old ground stone axes have come to light on the **Huon Peninsula** in the southeastern corner of the island. The Huon Peninsula faces New Britain Island, 48 kilometers (30 miles) offshore. Fisherfolk were living in caves on the island by at least 32,000 years ago. Some 4,000 years later, people had sailed between 130 and 180 kilometers (81 and 112 miles) to settle on Buka Island in the northern Solomons to the south. From Buka, it would have been easy to colonize the remainder of the Solomon chain, for the islands are separated by short distances. All these data point to a rapid spread of late Ice Age foragers through Sahul by at least 40,000 years ago, using some form of effective watercraft.

Willandra Lakes, Australia Shell middens and campsites dating from 37,000 to about 26,000 years ago.

Human occupation in what is now Australia is well documented by 35,000 years ago, but ongoing work at the Warratyi Rock Shelter in Southern Australia is suggesting dates as early as 49,000 years ago—which feeds into the genetic data that suggest Australia may, in fact, have been occupied around 55,000 years ago. Moreover, ongoing excavations at Madjedbebe, a rock shelter in Kakadu National Park, suggest human occupation at around 65,000 years ago, and potentially as far back as 80,000 years ago, though these dates remain controversial. Recent research from the possible midden (trash) site of Moyjil in Victoria has returned dates as early as 120,000 years ago, but definitive proof of human occupation is lacking.

The **Willandra Lakes** region has yielded shell middens and campsites dating from perhaps as early as 37,000 to about 26,000 years ago. They include the skulls and limb bones of robustly built, anatomically modern people, the earliest human remains found in Australia. By 33,000 years ago, human beings had crossed the low-lying strait that joined the island of Tasmania to the Australian mainland in the far south to colonize the most southerly region of the Earth settled by Ice Age people. At the height of the glacial maximum, people lived in the rugged landscape of the Tasmanian interior, hunting red wallabies and ranging over a wide area for many centuries.

The ancient Australians adapted to a variety of late Ice Age environments, as did people living in northern China, in Japan, and on coastlines bordering chilly Ice Age seas. All of the diverse societies of the late Ice Age world will not be discussed here, but on the other side of the globe from Australia, the hunter-gatherer societies of Europe and Eurasia offer insights into the remarkable adaptive and opportunistic skills of the inhabitants of this long-vanished world.

Homo sapiens in Late Ice Age Europe (c. 50,000 to 15,000 Years Ago)

Cro-Magnon, France Rock shelter near Les Eyzies in southwestern France where remains of the first late Ice Age people (Upper Paleolithic people of western and central Europe, traditionally called Cro-Magnons) were found in 1868.

The first permanently settled *H. sapiens* in European are sometimes known as the Cro-Magnons after the **Cro-Magnon** rock shelter near the village of Les Eyzies in southwestern France. Like all *H. sapiens*, they were colonists from Africa and geneticists note that their skin would have been black/dark, and they developed a versatile stone-tool kit, which we describe below. They are first known from France's Rhône Valley by 50,000 years ago, and perhaps as early as 56,800 years ago. By at least 40,000 years ago they were in southeast and central Europe. How our ancestors interacted (or not) with the local Neanderthals has long been the source of great debate—with some claiming that we wiped them out, and others arguing that they were already on their way out and we had no hand in their demise. Whatever the case, the genetic analyses indicate that, even though we were separate species, some of our ancestors certainly mated with Neanderthals and with other contemporary species such as the Denisovans. Yet by 40,000 years ago, the Neanderthals and the Denosovans had vanished.

After 6 million years of human evolution, only our species *H. sapiens* remained. The density of our settlement now intensified considerably, and the rest of this book is exclusively about us, and what we did next.

Subsistence

Modern humans permanently entered Europe during a brief period of more temperate climate. Even then, climatic conditions and seasonal contrasts may have been such as to require new artifacts and much more sophisticated hunting and foraging skills. These adaptations developed rapidly, indeed spectacularly, after 30,000 years ago. It was during these millennia that our direct ancestors finally mastered winter, for it was in northern latitudes that modern human ingenuity and endurance were tested to the fullest. The people of western and central Europe developed elaborate and sophisticated hunting cultures during this period. Their cultures were marked not only by many technological innovations, but also by a flowering of religious and social life, reflected in one of the earliest art traditions in the world.

The center of these activities was away from the open plains, in the river valleys of southwestern France and northern Spain and in parts of central Europe like the Danube Basin. Here, deep valleys supported lush summer meadows and a mix of open steppe and forest where cold-tolerant animals ranging in size from the mammoth and bison to the wild horse and boar flourished. High cliffs often provided caves and rock shelters warmed by the winter sun. The area lay astride reindeer migration routes in spring and fall, while salmon swam the length of fast-running rivers. We may have migrated to open country during the short summer months, concentrating in more sheltered river valleys from fall through spring. They hunted not only big game but also smaller animals such as the Arctic fox, beavers, rabbits, wolves, and birds; in addition, they gathered plant foods. After about 16,000 years ago, people also fished for salmon, trout, perch, and eels from rivers and streams.

Our modern human ancestors survived in a harsh and unpredictable environment not only because they were expert hunters and foragers, but also because they had effective ways of keeping warm outside in the depth of winter and the ability to store large amounts of meat and other foods to tide them over during lean periods. Above all, anyone living in late Ice Age Europe had to be adaptable, capable of cooperating with others, and ready to grab opportunities to obtain food when they arose. Survival depended on diversification, on never concentrating on one or two animals to the exclusion of others.

For most of the year, people lived in small groups, subsisting off a wide range of game and stored foods. The times when they came together in larger groups may have been in spring, summer, and early fall, when reindeer and later salmon were abundant. This period of coming together was an important annual occasion, when social life was at its most intense. It was then that people arranged marriages, conducted initiation rites, and bartered raw materials, artifacts, and other commodities with one another. Then, as winter closed in, the groups would disperse through the sheltered river valleys, returning to their stored foods and the small herds of game animals that also took refuge from the bitter winds.

Abri Pataud, France Rock shelter used by Upper Paleolithic foragers in southwestern France during the late Ice Age; famous for its evidence of reindeer hunting.

Reindeer were vital to survival. At the **Abri Pataud** rock shelter near Les Eyzies in France's Dordogne region (see Figure 10.4), reindeer constituted up to 30 percent of all prey for more than 10,000 years. The hunters located their camps close to shallow river crossings where they knew migrating reindeer were likely to pass. This complex rhythm of reindeer hunting was a part of a constant pattern of group movements that persisted over many thousands of years. It survived from at least 32,000 years ago right up to the end of the Ice Age, when the glaciers finally melted and dense forest spread over the open plains and deep valleys of central and western Europe. This is not to say that life stayed exactly the same through these many millennia, for climatic conditions changed constantly. The people had an efficient and highly versatile Cro-Magnon tool kit and a wide range of food resources to choose from, so they could readily adjust to changing circumstances.

Figure 10.4 Excavations at the Abri Pataud rock shelter, Les Eyzies, France.

Source: Gift of the Carnegie Institution of Washington. © President and Fellows of Harvard College, Peabody Museum of Archaeology and Ethnology, Harvard University, PM# 58-34-20/38653 (digital file# CI732212).

Cro-Magnon Technology

Cro-Magnon technology was versatile yet fundamentally very simple. It depended on four interrelated foundations:

burin Chisel like stone tool made on a blade used for grooving stone, antler, bone, and wood and for making rock engravings.

groove-and-splinter technique Longitudinal grooving of antler and bone to produce long, parallel-sided grooves for making spear points, harpoons, and other artifacts; used by Upper Paleolithic and Mesolithic peoples.

- Careful selection of fine-grained rock such as chert, flint, or obsidian for blade cores.
- The production of relatively standardized, parallel-sided artifact blanks from these cores that could be used to make more specialized cutting, piercing, and scraping tools.
- The refinement of the **burin** (engraving tool), which enabled people to work antler and bone efficiently.
- The use of the so-called **groove-and-splinter technique** for working antler and bone.

These technological innovations had a profound impact on the future course of human prehistory, for they were the material means by which humans adapted to the climatic extremes of Eurasia and Siberia.

blades Long, parallel-sided flakes produced from preshaped cores with the aid of a punch; characteristic of many Upper Paleolithic peoples.

Late Ice Age stoneworkers everywhere were highly selective in their use of flint and other fine-grained rock. Their primary objective was to produce **blades**, long, parallel-sided artifact blanks that could then be turned into a wide spectrum of specialized artifacts for hunting, for butchering and processing skins, for woodworking and clothing manufacture, and for the production of the raw materials needed to create specialized antler and bone tools in treeless environments. So great was their concern for good toolmaking stone that they bartered it with neighbors over considerable distances. Once procured, the precious raw materials were turned into carefully prepared blade cores that were carried around from one camp to the next. The cores were a kind of savings bank, an account of toolmaking stone used to produce blanks whenever they were needed. This allowed people to respond at a moment's notice to an opportunity to butcher an animal or to cut long slivers from fresh reindeer antlers.

The closest analogies in our own technology are the Leatherman and Swiss Army knives (or "snap-on" mechanics' tools) (see Figure 10.5). Both are multipurpose artifacts built on a strong chassis with a special spring system that enables the user to call on a wide variety of tools, from scissors to pliers. The late Ice Age equivalents were the cores and the blades that came from them.

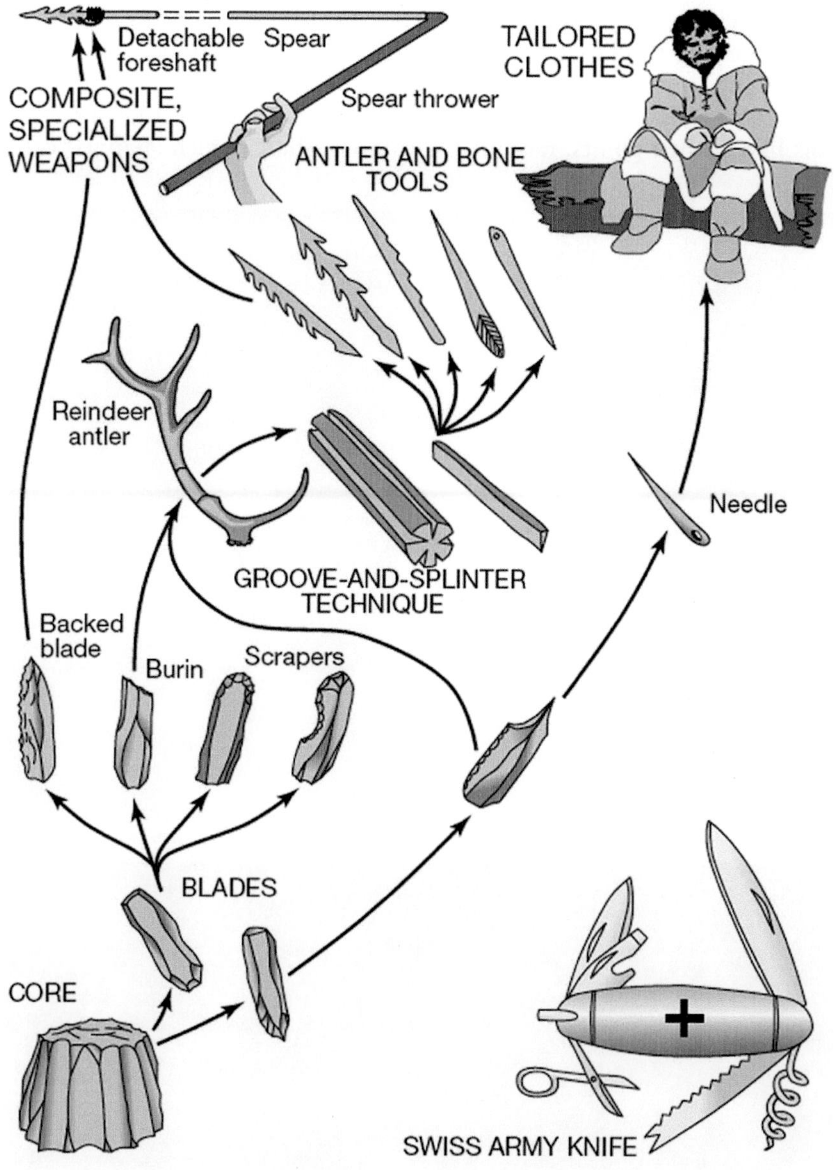

Figure 10.5 Blade core technology serves the same purpose as a Swiss Army knife, producing blanks for making many specialized artifacts for working antler and bone.

foreshaft A short staff on which a projectile point or harpoon was mounted, the foreshaft then hafted to a long stave. (When the weapon hit its quarry, the foreshaft would break off in the wound, allowing the hunter to rearm his weapon, as well as causing a more serious injury to the quarry.)

spear thrower A hooked and sometimes weighted stick or equivalent device used for hurling spears.

The burin was a vital Cro-Magnon artifact, a delicate chisel for carving fine lines. Burins were woodworking tools, used for cutting grooves in animal hides, for engraving designs on antler, bone, and cave walls, and especially for cutting the long antler blanks for making artifacts of antler, bone, and ivory (see Figure 10.6). Many of these were specialized tools like barbed points, mounted with a **foreshaft**, which snapped off when

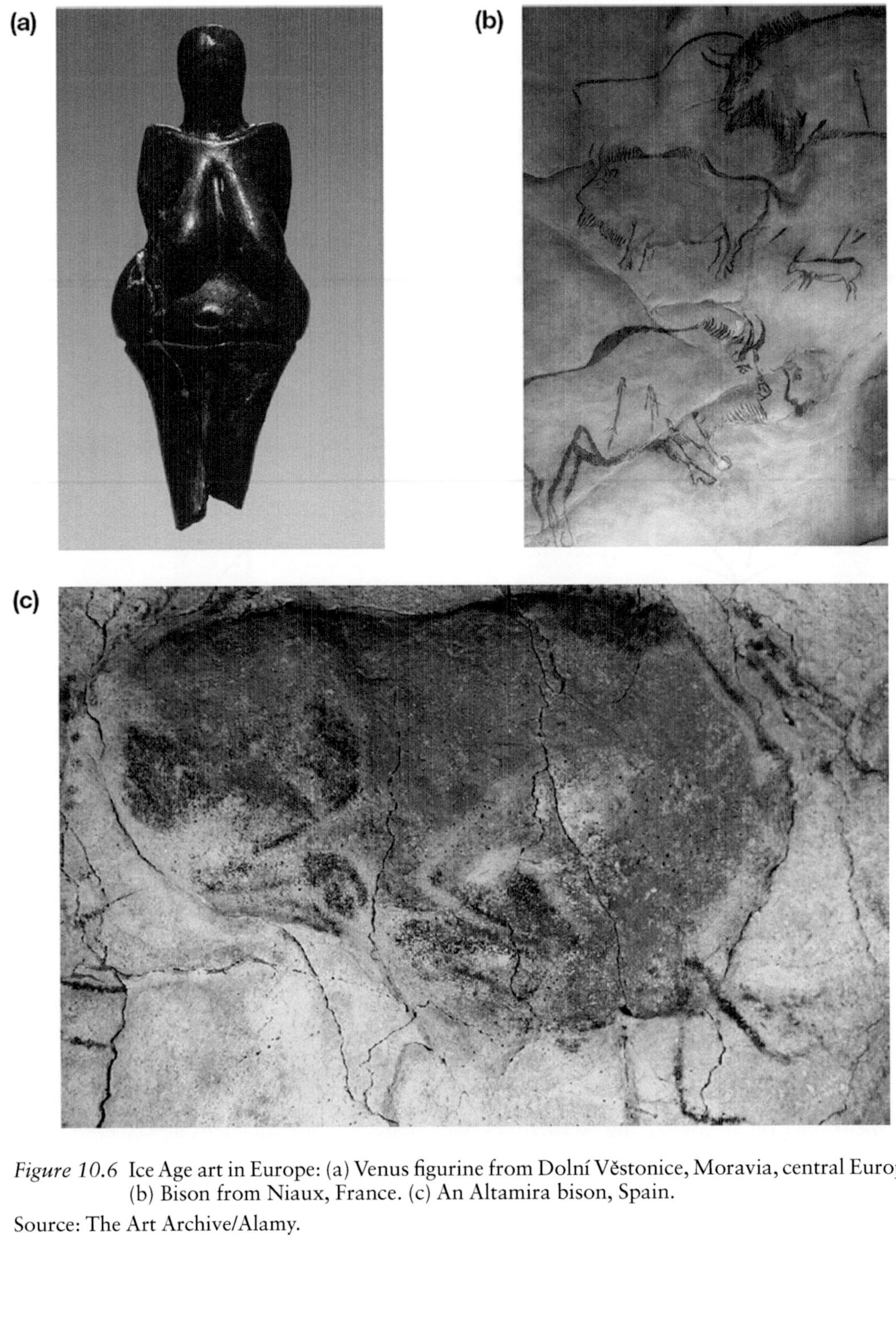

Figure 10.6 Ice Age art in Europe: (a) Venus figurine from Dolní Věstonice, Moravia, central Europe. (b) Bison from Niaux, France. (c) An Altamira bison, Spain.

Source: The Art Archive/Alamy.

the spear entered its quarry. Some were important innovations, especially the eyed needle, essential for making tailored winter clothes, and the **spear thrower**, a hooked and sometimes weighted device that extended the range and accuracy of hunting weapons (see Figure 10.5). The same technology of fine-barbed antler head spears and stone-barbed weapons could be used for hunting big game, as well as for taking salmon in shallow water, for dispatching rabbits, even for developing bows and arrows, which appeared sometime during the late Ice Age.

Magdalenian culture Late Ice Age culture (named after La Madeleine) with sophisticated technology and art tradition found in southwestern France, parts of central Europe, and northern Spain; flourished between 15,000 and 12,000 years ago.

The archaeological record reflects many refinements in Cro-Magnon technology over more than 15,000 years. In the early years of the twentieth century, French archaeologist Henri Breuil classified the late Ice Age cultures of southwestern France into four basic cultural traditions that culminated in the celebrated **Magdalenian culture** of about 18,000 to 12,000 years ago. The Magdalenian, named after the La Madeleine rock shelter on the Vezère River, was not only a technologically sophisticated culture, but also one with a new concern for artistic expression and body ornamentation.

Late Ice Age Art in Europe

Our modern human ancestors are known to have been painting in southern Africa, southeast Asia, and Australia at around the same time that they were painting in Europe—with a potential history stretching back to 100,000-plus years ago in Africa. However, the European rock art is the best known and most thoroughly explored. Fortunately, much has survived, for the European artists used cave walls as their canvases and durable antler and ivory, not wood and skins, as palettes.

The first appearance of cave art coincides with greater evidence for body ornamentation, especially with perforated carnivore teeth and seashells. This may have coincided with realizations that such adornments could define and communicate social roles—gender, group affiliation, and so on.

Niaux, France Painted cave with magnificent bison figures, dating to c. 15,000 years ago.

The surviving late Ice Age art of Europe and Eurasia is but a minor proportion of their artistic output, for the artists almost certainly used many perishable materials, including clay, wood, fiber, bark, hides, and bird feathers. Without question, too, they used red ocher and other pigments as body paint, for decoration. The surviving art occurs over a vast area from North Africa to Siberia, with major concentrations in northern Spain, southwestern France, and central and eastern Europe. On cave walls, the artists engraved and painted animals, occasional humans, and schematic patterns—lines, elaborate panels, and complex shapes. The same artists engraved antler, bone, and ivory with consummate skill. They created animals in the round and engraved bison with delicate strokes that etched in every detail of eyes, manes, and hair (see Figure 10.7). There are figurines of animals and humans in ivory, soft stone, and baked clay, such as the celebrated "Venus" figurines that depict women of all ages (see Figure 10.6a).

Trois Frères, France Magdalenian painted cave, famous for its sorcerer figures.

Le Tuc d'Audoubert, France Magdalenian ceremonial site famous for its clay bison figures.

Europe's Ice Age art is full of compelling images, many of them concentrated at major sites such as Lascaux and **Trois Frères** in southwestern France and Altamira in northern Spain (see Figure 3.4 on p. 76). These may have been places of unusual religious and symbolic importance. They were ritual shrines, not only for local groups, but also for people from far wider areas. Other locations were sacred places used occasionally for major ceremonies. These are illustrated dramatically by **Le Tuc d'Audoubert** cave in Ariège, France, where two carefully modeled clay bison lie in a remote, low-ceilinged chamber far from the entrance, placed against a rock (see Figure 10.7). The bison are about one-sixth the full size, shaped with a skilled artist's fingers and a spatula, the eyes, nostrils, and other features marked with a pointed object. Ancient human heel marks can be seen around the figures in this remote and dark chamber. In many other caves, paintings and engravings are far from daylight (see Box 10.2). There are several instances in which the footprints of both adults and children are preserved in damp clay, perhaps left by small parties of initiates who attended ceremonies in remote subterranean chambers. Some caves may also have been chosen for their echoes and other resonant effects.

Figure 10.7 A clay bison from Le Tuc d'Audoubert, Ariège, France. These sculptures lie in a deep chamber far from the open air.

Box 10.2 Discovery
Grotte de Chauvet, France

On December 18, 1994, three French cave explorers with an interest in archaeology crawled into a narrow opening in the Cirque d'Estre gorge in the Ardèche region of southeastern France. Feeling a draft flowing from a blocked duct, they pulled out some boulders and lowered themselves into a network of chambers adorned with exquisite calcite columns. To their astonishment, their lights shone on human hand imprints and then on paintings of mammoths, cave lions, and other animals. The three explorers were "seized by a strange feeling. Everything was so beautiful, so fresh, almost too much so. Time was abolished, as if the tens of thousands of years that separated us from the producers of these paintings no longer existed" (Chauvet, Deschamps, and Hillaire 1996, 42).

The **Grotte de Chauvet** is a series of painted and engraved chambers undisturbed since the late Ice Age. Hearths on the floor look as if they were only extinguished the day before. Flaming torches were rubbed against the wall to remove the charcoal so they would flare anew. More than 300 paintings adorn the walls. They include a frieze of black horses, wild oxen with twisted horns, and two rhinoceroses facing each other (see Figure 10.8). The horses have half-open muzzles; the eyes are depicted in detail. There are lions, stags, and engravings of an owl, animals never before seen in painted caves, covering an area of more than 10 meters (33 feet).

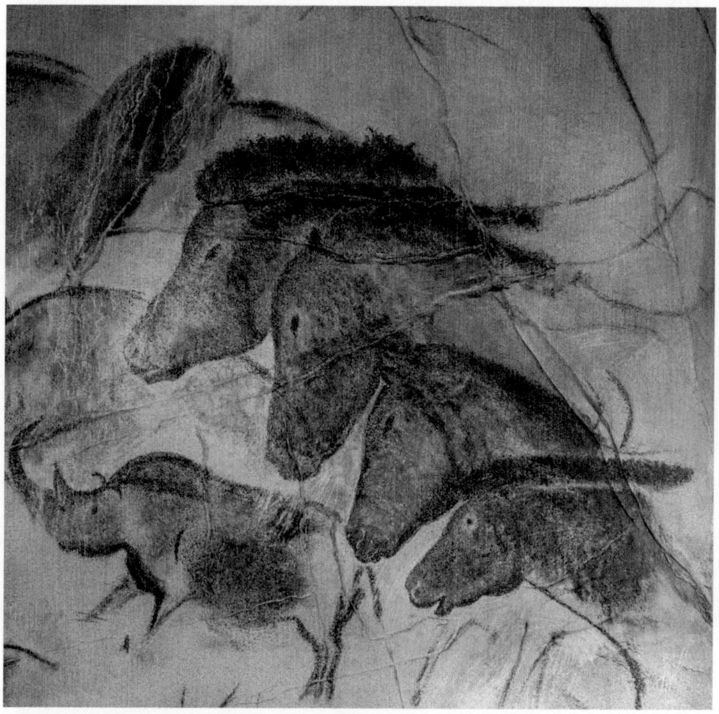

Figure 10.8 A horse frieze at the Grotte de Chauvet, Ardèche, France.
Source: Arterra Picture Library/Alamy Stock Photo.

A little farther on in the chamber lies a slab that has fallen from the ceiling. A bear skull has been set atop it. The remains of a small fire lie behind it. More than 30 calcite-covered and intentionally placed bear skulls surround the slab. A 10-meter (33-foot) frieze of black figures dominated by lions or lionesses (without manes), rhinoceroses, bison, and mammoths lies in an end chamber, a human figure with a bison head standing to its right. The discoverers wrote that it "seemed to us a sorcerer supervising this immense frieze" (110).

The artists were masters of perspective, overlapping the heads of animals to give the effect of movement and numbers. They even scraped some of the walls before painting them to make the figures stand out better. In spreading the paint with their hands over the rock, the artists were able to obtain values that showed dimension and color tonality.

The Grotte de Chauvet was a bear cave, a place where these powerful animals hibernated. Interestingly, many of the animals on the cave walls represent dangerous members of the late Ice Age bestiary: the bear and the lion, the mammoth, rhinoceros, and bison, and even occasionally the nimble and ferocious aurochs. Perhaps human visitors to the cave, with its claw marks, hollows, prints, and scattered bones, came to the chambers to acquire the potency of the great beast, whose smell probably lingered in the darkness.

Dating rock art is always difficult. Accelerator mass spectrometry (AMS) radiocarbon dates (see Box 11.2 on p. 353) from two rhinoceroses and a large bison point to a 1,300-year period around 37,000 years ago, making these paintings the earliest highly complex art in the world. Two torch smears on the walls are from around 26,500 years ago, and two charcoal samples on the floor gave readings of about 24,500 years ago, suggesting that humans visited Chauvet on several occasions over at least 6,000 or 7,000 years. Yet, some researchers, such as the UK's Paul Pettitt and Paul Bahn, argue that these very early dates are unreliable, and that they often simply relate to unconnected firing episodes rather than to the art itself. Moreover, they note that the sort of art found in Chauvet is quite unlike the rest of the known Aurignacian art corpus, which comprises technically simple outline paintings and engravings. In that sense, the Chauvet art is much more in keeping with later (after 20,000 years ago) artistic traditions. The truth will not be known until we can clearly establish the date of this art—perhaps something that will be achieved through more nuanced dating methods such as the uranium-thorium method, which dates stalactites over the art to produce minimum dates. Whatever its date, this prehistoric art comprises some of the most stunning artistic achievements in the world—then and now.

Grotte de Chauvet, France Painted late Ice Age cave with remarkable depictions of lions, rhinoceroses, and other animals.

Late Ice Age art defies easy interpretation, for the symbolic messages it communicates come from a world that is remote from our own. Yet the paintings and engravings still seem to come alive and appear larger than life when seen by modern candlelight flickering in the intense darkness. Did the artists paint art for art's sake, as some art historians and archaeologists believe? Or were they symbolically killing their prey before setting out on the chase? Such explanations are too simplistic, for we can be sure that the motivations for the art extended far beyond mere environmental and subsistence concerns.

Today, we know a great deal more about symbolic behavior and the art that goes with it and much more about how forager societies function. In such societies, visual forms are manipulated to structure and give meaning to existence. For Cro-Magnon artists, there were clear continuities between animal and human life and within their social world. Their art was a symbolic depiction of these continuities.

Some of the art may also have been associated with initiation rites, the journey through dark passages adding to the disorienting ordeal of initiation. Almost certainly, the art was a way of transmitting environmental and other knowledge to one another, and from one generation to the next. Australian Aborigines, for example, commit to memory vast quantities of information about their territory that is closely tied to the mythical and symbolic world of their ancestors. Much of this information is vital to survival, constantly imparted to the young in ceremonies and rituals.

shamans (from the Siberian Tungus word *saman*) Men and women who serve as intermediaries between the living and supernatural worlds and are thought to have magical powers; sometimes called *spirit mediums*.

Shamans, priests or spirit mediums (the term comes from the Siberian Tungus word *saman*, meaning "priest"), are important members of forager and subsistence farming societies all over the world. They are individuals perceived as having unusual spiritual powers, the ability to cross over into the world of the gods and ancestors. Through trance and chant, they communicate with the ancestors and define the order of the world and all Creation—the relationship between the living and the forces of the environment. Perhaps, argue some experts, much of the cave art was involved with shamanistic rituals, the animal figures being images of spirit creatures or the life force for the shamans.

Eurasia (35,000 to 15,000 Years Ago)

Mezhirich, Ukraine Late Ice Age forager camp with elaborate mammoth-bone houses on the Dnieper River, dating to about 17,000 years ago.

The open steppe and tundra plains that stretched from the Atlantic to Siberia were a far harsher environment than the sheltered valleys of southwestern Europe. To live there permanently, late Ice Age people had to find sheltered winter base camps, required the technology to make tailored, layered clothing with needles and thongs, and needed the ability to build substantial dwellings in a treeless environment. Only a handful of big-game-hunting groups lived in the shallow valleys that dissected these plains before the glacial maximum 18,000 years ago. Thereafter, the human population rose comparatively rapidly, each group centered on a river valley where game was plentiful and where plant foods and fish could be found during the short summers. It was here that the most elaborate winter base camps lay. One such base camp was at **Mezhirich** on the Dnieper River, a complex of well-built, dome-shaped houses fashioned of intricate patterns of mammoth bones. The outer retaining walls were made of patterned mammoth skulls, jaws, and

Figure 10.9 An artist's reconstruction of two mammoth-bone houses at Mezhirich, Ukraine. Source: SPUTNIK/Alamy Stock Photo.

limb bones. The completed oval-shaped dwellings were about 4.8 meters (16 feet) across, roofed with hides and sod and entered through subterranean tunnels (see Figure 10.9). The use of mammoth bone for houses was a logical strategy in a largely treeless environment. American archaeologist Olga Soffer has calculated that it would have taken some 15 workers about 10 days to build a Mezhirich dwelling: much more effort than would have gone into a simpler base camp or hunting settlement.

Soffer believes that these base camps were occupied by groups of about 30–60 people for about six months of the year. Mezhirich was but one of several important base camp locations in Ukraine, sites that contain the bones of a greater variety of game animals than at smaller, more specialized settlements. The mammoth-bone dwellings also yielded many bones from fur-bearing animals like the beaver, and exotic materials and ornaments such as shiny amber from near Kiev and shells from the Black Sea, far to the south. The items from afar exchanged between neighboring communities were predominantly nonutilitarian luxury goods that had social and political significance. Much of the trade may have been ceremonial, a means of validating important ideologies and of ensuring exchange of information and cooperation in daily life, just as it was elsewhere in the late Ice Age world at the time.

Late Ice Age groups settled much of the steppe and tundra plains as far east as Lake Baikal in Siberia, not through a deliberate process of migration, but as a result of the natural dynamics of forager life. The tundra hunters lived in small, flexible bands. As the generations passed, one band would coalesce into another, and sons and their families would move away into a neighboring empty valley. In time, a sparse human population would occupy thousands of square miles of steppe and tundra, concentrated for the most part in river valleys, at times venturing out on to the broad plains but always on the move. It was through these natural dynamics of constant movement, of extreme social flexibility and opportunism, that people first settled the outer reaches of Siberia and crossed into the Americas.

North and east of Lake Baikal, the steppe and tundra plains extend all the way to the Pacific, the home of late Ice Age hunting groups that are known from a handful of settlements along lakeshores and in river valleys. They are part of a widespread late Ice Age cultural tradition that reflects a varied adaptation by *H. sapiens* to an enormous area of Central Asia and southern Siberia from well west of Lake Baikal to the Pacific coast by 30,000 to 20,000 years ago. But where did these Siberian hunters come from? Did they originate in the West, or were their cultural roots in China, to the south? These questions have a direct bearing on one of the most debated questions of world prehistory—the date of the first Americans.

East Asia (c. 35,000 to 15,000 Years Ago)

We know enough about prehistoric Asia to realize that this was not a backward, peripheral region of the late Ice Age world. We cannot just argue that big-game hunters from Ukraine and the western steppe and tundra plains migrated steadily northeastward into Siberia and then into the Americas. Rather, the spread of modern humans into Central Asia, northern China, and the extreme northeast was a complex process that began at least 35,000 years ago.

While *Homo erectus* had roamed the area for hundreds of millennia before (arguably until 30,000 years ago, though the dates are contentious), it was not until just before 35,000 years ago that a few signs of AMH settlement appeared along the banks of the Huang He (Yellow) River in the arid grasslands of Mongolia. Open landscapes such as this and the neighboring plains could support only the sparsest of forager populations consisting of people who placed a high premium on mobility and portable tool kits. They were some of the first late Ice Age people to develop diminutive microliths.

microliths (from the Greek for "small stone") Diminutive stone artifacts manufactured on tiny blades and used as barbs and points for spears and later arrows; characteristic of the Ice Age and early Holocene societies.

Microliths (derived from the Greek *micros*, "small," and *lithos*, "stone") are highly distinctive artifacts manufactured on microblades struck from carefully prepared wedge-shaped, conical, or cylindrical cores (see Figure 10.10). By their very size, microliths were designed to be mounted in antler, bone, or wooden hafts to serve as spear barbs, arrow points, or small knives and scraper blades. Such diminutive artifacts came into use

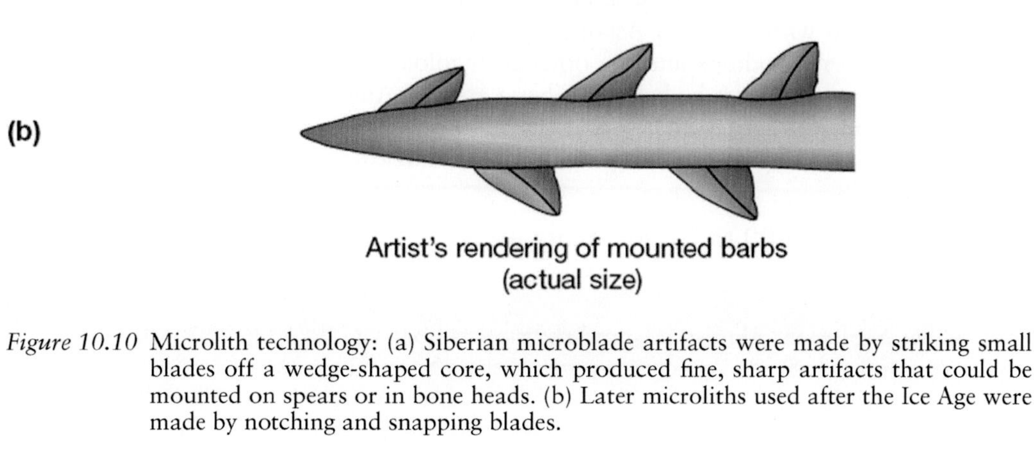

Figure 10.10 Microlith technology: (a) Siberian microblade artifacts were made by striking small blades off a wedge-shaped core, which produced fine, sharp artifacts that could be mounted on spears or in bone heads. (b) Later microliths used after the Ice Age were made by notching and snapping blades.

almost everywhere in the post-Ice Age world, for they were highly adaptive when used with slender wooden arrow shafts or with stout wooden handles. They first appeared in a crude form in northern China at least 30,000 years ago, were in widespread use by 25,000 to 20,000 years ago, and soon became popular in the arid open country of the steppe and tundra plains. A somewhat similar microblade technology developed in Siberia late in the Ice Age. We do not know, however, whether the first human inhabitants of northeastern Asia were people with such diminutive tool kits or whether they used heavier weaponry that included stone-tipped spears with sharp projectile points.

Unfortunately, the archaeology of northern China, northeastern Siberia, and Alaska is little known because harsh environmental conditions make fieldwork possible for only two months or so a year in many places. We can only guess at a possible scenario for first settlement of this vast area and of the Americas.

Sinodonty and Sundadonty

> **sinodonts** Siberian and Native American populations with a distinctive cluster of tooth features.

That the first Americans came from Siberia is unquestionable, but their ultimate ancestry is a matter of much debate. Christy Turner of Arizona State University studied the dental characteristics of Native American populations and compared them with other groups in the Old World. He showed that the crowns and roots of human teeth give clues to the degree of relationship between prehistoric populations. These tooth features are more stable than most evolutionary traits, with a high resistance to the effects of environmental differences, sexual distinctions, and age variations. In particular, he has focused on a pattern of specialized tooth features in Native American populations, whom he calls **sinodonts**.

> **sundadonts** Ancient Eurasian and European populations with shared tooth characteristics.

Sinodont hallmarks include incisor shoveling (the scooped-out shape on the inside of the tooth), double-shoveling (scooping out on both sides), single-rooted upper first premolars, and three-rooted lower first molars. Sinodonty is characteristic of all Native Americans. They share this feature with northern Asians, including northern Chinese. The morphological difference between sinodonts and the other Mongoloid populations, whom Turner labels **sundadonts**, is so great that he believes Siberia and the Americas were settled by sinodont populations from northern Asia. It was in China, he believes, that sinodonty evolved, at least 40,000 years ago. The problem is finding the archaeological sites to confirm his theory.

Siberia (Before 20,000 to 15,000 Years Ago)

> **Yana RHS, Siberia** (RHS stands for "rhinoceros horn site") 25,000–27,000-year-old hunting site at latitude 70 degrees north, on the Yana River.

If the ancestry of the first Americans lies in Siberia, what, then, is the earliest evidence for modern human settlement in extreme northeast Asia? The earliest known site in northeastern Siberia is north of latitude 70 degrees north, far above the Arctic Circle and 140 kilometers (87 miles) from the Arctic Ocean on the Yana River. Here the broken bones of mammoths, wild horses, reindeer, and birds lie with a variety of stone tools. A foreshaft made of wooly rhinoceros horn came from the site some years ago, hence its name: **Yana RHS** (Rhinoceros Horn Site). Yana RHS has been radiocarbon-dated to 25,000–27,000 years ago, which means that humans were living in extreme northeastern Siberia before the intense cold of the late Ice Age that began after 26,000 years ago.

It is important to note that Yana dates to a time when northeastern Siberia was somewhat warmer than it was during the height of the last glaciation, around 20,000 years ago. At that time, the entire northeast was an extremely cold and windy desert environment, exceptionally forbidding for any form of human settlement until sporadic warming began after 16,000 years ago. Over enormous areas, the landscape was vegetationless, offering little for animals or humans. Such human inhabitants as there were probably moved southward into more hospitable environments, just as they did in Eurasia, for Arctic deserts were just like the Sahara in one sense: they pushed out populations in cold, dry times and sucked them in when it was warmer and moister.

Diuktai Cave, Siberia Site of a widespread late Ice Age culture in northeastern Siberia that may have been the ancestor of some early Native American groups; dates to as early as 18,000 years ago.

Verkhene-Trotiskaya, Siberia Earliest known Diuktai-like site in Siberia, dating to about 18,000 years ago.

The earliest settlement after the warm-up began comes from the **Diuktai Cave** in the Middle Aldan valley. Russian archaeologist Yuri Mochanov found 14,000-to 12,000-year-old mammoth and musk-ox bones there, associated with flaked-stone spear points, burins, microblades, and other Upper Paleolithic tools. The earliest securely dated Diuktai-like site is **Verkhene-Trotiskaya**, also on the Aldan River, which has been radiocarbon-dated to about 18,000 years ago. Subsequently, microblades and characteristic wedge-shaped cores have been found over a wide area of northeast Asia, across the Bering Strait in Alaska, and as far south as British Columbia.

With its microblades and wedge-shaped cores, the Diuktai culture has plausible links with widespread microblade cultures to the south, in China. A case can be made, then, for linking Diuktai cultural traditions with northern China, where sinodonts have been found, as well as with microblade finds in Alaska and British Columbia. Were the Diuktai people thus the first Americans? Almost certainly not, for recent discoveries in Alaska have shown that foragers without microlithic tool kits flourished in the far north of North America just after the end of the Ice Age. Diuktai-style microliths appear later, by about 9000 B.C.

Beringia Ice Age landmass consisting of northeastern Asia, Alaska, and what is now the Bering Sea; dry land during the late Ice Age.

When Diuktai people or even earlier settlers first crossed the windy, steppe-and-tundra-covered land bridge that joined Alaska to Siberia (known to geologists as **Beringia**) remains a mystery. We do not even know how they subsisted, although it is likely that they preyed on all kinds of Arctic game. They might also have hunted sea mammals and taken ocean fish. Unfortunately, their settlements are deep beneath the waters of the Bering Strait.

The First Americans (By 15,000 Years Ago)

Throughout the last glaciation, the Bering land bridge joined extreme northeastern Siberia and Alaska. During warmer intervals, it was little more than a narrow isthmus; during the glacial maximum, it was a broad plain. It was therefore theoretically possible for humans without canoes to cross into North America from the Old World dry-shod for most of the past 100,000 years. Therein lies one of the great questions of world prehistory: When and how did the first human beings settle the New World?

The controversies that surround the first Americans are many. Years ago, linguist Joseph Greenberg proposed that most North American and all South American languages were part of a single, large "Amerind" family. Aleut-Eskimo and Na-Dene were quite separate linguistic groups, making a total of three for the whole of the Americas. Greenberg then spent years compiling a vast database on the vocabulary and grammar of the 140 families of American Indian languages, which confirmed his belief that there were three linguistic groups that corresponded to migrations into the Americas. Greenberg's large grouping of many languages into an Amerind family has been severely criticized by other linguists. Despite this drumbeat of criticism, some geneticists claim that the genetic evidence agrees with Greenberg's tripartite subdivision of Native American languages. Certainly, the genetic picture is complex. It suggests that the first people in America descended from an Ancient East Asian lineage that split from other East Asians before the Last Glacial Maximum. They also received geneflow from Ancient North Eurasians, a distinct Siberian population.

Settlement in the Americas before 30,000 Years Ago?

The chronology of first settlement divides archaeologists into two camps. Some argue passionately for a late Ice Age occupation before 30,000 years ago, perhaps as much as 15,000 years earlier. Their theories pit them against most American archaeologists, who believe that humans first crossed into Alaska at the very end of the Ice Age, after 20,000 years ago. We must examine these two viewpoints more closely.

The case for early settlement rests on a handful of sites, most of them in South America and none of them yielding much more than a scatter of alleged stone artifacts and sometimes animal bones. Therein lies the controversy, for what one archaeologist claims is a stone tool, another rejects out of hand. Unfortunately, most of the claims for early settlement are based not on fine-grained, scientific examination of the artifacts and their context in the surrounding deposits, but on an individual archaeologist's subjective belief that a handful of chipped stones is humanly manufactured rather than of natural origin. For example, if one finds 35,000-year-old "stone artifacts" deep in a hypothetical Peruvian cave, it is not sufficient to state that they were manufactured by humans. One must prove beyond all measure of reasonable scientific doubt that they were made by prehistoric people and not formed, for example, by stones falling from a cliff face or by pebbles being knocked together in a stream that once ran through the cave. Such research is extremely time-consuming and very difficult and has not yet been carried out at most of the sites where early settlement has been claimed. Let us briefly examine some of the early sites.

Monte Verde, Chile Streamside forager site in northern Chile dating to about 18,500 years ago.

In southern Chile, Tom Dillehay has uncovered a remarkable settlement on the edge of a stream. Foragers living in simple wooden dwellings occupied **Monte Verde** about 18,500 years ago (see Box 10.3). A 31,000-year-old lower level is said to contain split pebble and wood fragments, but to date, excavations in these levels have been relatively limited and insufficient to document the presence of human occupation at such an early date.

There is no theoretical reason why humans could not have moved south from Beringia well before 25,000 years ago, but we still lack credible proof of such early human settlement in the Americas. Whether this is because the Americas were still uninhabited or because the human population was so mobile and tiny that little or no material survived continues to be hotly debated. As an outside observer, African archaeologist Nicholas Toth has made the important observation that it is pointless to place too much

Box 10.3 Site
Monte Verde, Chile

Monte Verde lies in a small river valley in southern Chile, a streamside settlement covered by a peat bog, so that not only stone and bone but also wooden artifacts have survived (see Figure 10.11). A portion of the site has been excavated very thoroughly and has been radiocarbon-dated to about 18,500 years ago. The excavation so far has revealed two parallel rows of what are believed to be rectangular houses, joined by connecting walls. The animal-skin-covered houses measure 3–4 meters (9–13 feet) square, with log and crude-plank foundations and a wooden framework. Clay-lined hearths, wooden mortars, and large quantities of vegetable foods were found in the houses. A short distance away lies a wishbone-shaped structure associated with chewed bolo-plant leaves (used today to make a form of medicinal tea), mastodon bones, and other debris. This may have been a work area.

The Monte Verde people exploited a very wide range of vegetable foods, including wild potatoes; they also hunted small game and perhaps mammals such as now-extinct camels and mastodons. (It is possible that they scavenged such meat rather than hunting the animals.) Monte Verde was in a forest, with abundant vegetable foods year round. The site was almost certainly a long-term campsite. What is fascinating is that 90 percent of the stone artifacts are crude river cobbles. It is clear that wood was the most important raw material. Wood was certainly used for spears and digging sticks and for hafting stone scrapers, three of which have survived in their wooden handles. Sites yielding simple flaked-stone artifacts like those from Monte Verde have been found elsewhere in South America, as far south as Patagonia, but this is the first place that anyone has been able to make more complete discoveries.

Figure 10.11 Aerial view of the Monte Verde site, Chile.
Source: Kenneth Garrett.

reliance on isolated finds. Rather, we should be searching for patterns of very early human settlement—characteristic distributions of artifacts and human activity that occur over wide areas, which indeed reflect widespread early occupation. Such patterns document the very earliest human occupation on Earth. There is no theoretical reason why similar patterns should not turn up to chronicle the first Americans. So far, consistent distributions of human settlement in the New World date to after the Ice Age. We cannot rule out that earlier settlement may be found one day; so far, however, the evidence is unconvincing.

Settlement after around 20,000 Years Ago?

Most American archaeologists consider first settlement a much later phenomenon. Under the later scenario, a few families may have moved into Alaska during the very late Ice Age, perhaps around 15,000 years ago. Perhaps this group includes the people whose footprints have been preserved at **White Sands National Park**, and radiocarbon-dated, not without controversy, to 23,000 years ago. At that time, and for the millennia to come, time, vast ice sheets mantled much of northern North America, effectively blocking access to the midcontinent. However, after 14,000 years ago, these ice sheets retreated rapidly, allowing a trickle of human settlers to move on to the plains and into a new continent.

White Sands National Park, New Mexico Over 60 preserved human footprints alongside prints of megafauna like mammoths and giant sloths, dated not without controversy to 23,000 years ago.

Paisley Five-Mile Point caves, Oregon Evidence of human occupation in the form of feces dating to 12,300 years ago.

Debra L. Friedkin site, Texas A well-stratified Paleo-Indian site with a pre-Clovis occupation of around 13,000 years ago, underlying a later Clovis layer.

Meadowcroft Rock Shelter, Pennsylvania Long-occupied rock shelter, with possible evidence of human occupation as early as 14,000 years ago.

Fort Rock Cave, Oregon A site with possible evidence of human occupation in North America as early as 14,000 years ago.

Cactus Hill, Virginia A stratified Paleo-Indian and Archaic site with possible human occupation as early as 15,000 to 16,600 years ago.

Valsequillo, Mexico Site where mastodon bones and artifacts date to about 14,000 years ago.

Taima Taima, Venezuela Site with possible evidence of early human occupation in the 14,000 years ago range.

This hypothesis is based on the earliest indisputable archaeological evidence for human settlement, which dates to between 14,000 and 12,000 years ago. In North America, a handful of sites may lie within this time frame, among them the **Paisley Five-Mile Point** site in Oregon's Cascade Range, where a scatter of human feces date to 12,300 years ago, their genetic material akin to that of Native Americans. Another is the **Debra L. Friedkin** site north of Austin, Texas, where a large assemblage of stone artifacts date to between 13,100 and 12,800 years ago and lie below a well-defined Clovis occupation with quite different artifacts (see below). **Meadowcroft Rock Shelter** in Pennsylvania and **Fort Rock Cave** in Oregon may also belong in this time frame. A few other sites date to before 14,000 years ago; most of them are little more than artifact scatters, a reflection of highly mobile groups with portable tool kits who left little behind them. **Cactus Hill** in Virginia is said to have occupation levels that date to as early as 15,000–16,600 years ago. Scattered sites from Central and South America, among them **Valsequillo** in Mexico, **Taima Taima** in Venezuela, and Monte Verde in northern Chile, date to at least 12,000 years ago. All these sites have yielded small scatters of stone artifacts and occasionally a projectile point.

Paleo-Indian Generalized label given to the earliest forager cultures in North America from before 14,000 to 8,000 years ago.

After about 11,200 years ago, the trickle of archaeological sites turns into a flood. There are now traces of **Paleo-Indian** (*paleos* in Greek means "old") settlement between the southern margins of the ice sheets in the north and the Straits of Magellan in the far south. (The term *Paleo-Indian* is conventionally used to refer to the prehistoric inhabitants of the Americas from earliest settlement up to the beginning of the Archaic period about 8,000 years ago.)

How, then, did Paleo-Indians travel southward from the Arctic to the heart of North America? (See Figure 10.12.) Were they big-game hunters who followed small herds of

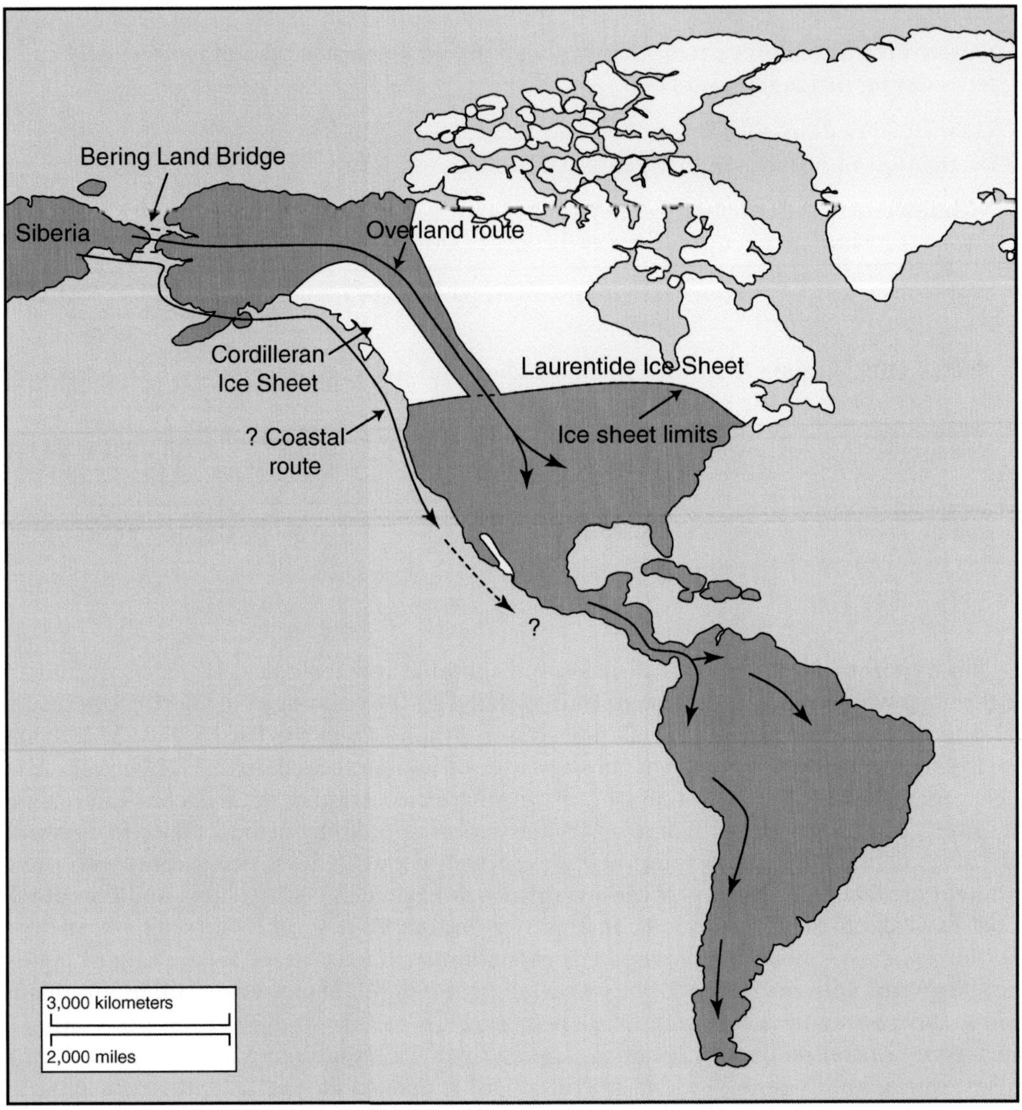

Figure 10.12 Hypothesized routes for the first settlement of the Americas. Coastal routes are now buried under the higher sea levels of modern times.

animals southward through a widening corridor between the two great North American ice sheets to the east of the Rockies as the ice sheets melted? Or were the first Americans expert sea-mammal hunters and fisherfolk who crossed from Siberia along low-lying coasts in canoes, while fishing and sea-mammal hunting? Did their successors then travel southward along the Pacific coast into more temperate waters? Again, fierce controversy surrounds what is virtually nonexistent archaeological evidence. Perhaps, both coastal settlement and terrestrial occupation took hold in the rapidly changing world of the late Ice Age. We simply do not know, partly because the coastal sites of the day are buried hundreds of meters below modern sea levels.

At present, the consensus of archaeological opinion favors a relatively late human occupation of the Americas at the very end of the Ice Age, but it is entirely possible that this scenario will change dramatically as a result of future research.

But why did first settlement take place? In all probability, the first Americans were behaving in the same way as animal predators. They spent their days tracking the game herds, and perhaps sea mammals, that formed an important part of their subsistence, and when Siberian game herds moved on to the Bering land bridge during the coldest millennia of the last glaciation, their human predators followed in very small numbers. The higher ground to the east—Alaska—formed part of the same hunting grounds.

The Clovis People (c. 13,050 to 12,750 Years Ago)

Hidden Mammoth, Alaska A hunting camp in central Alaska dating to about 11,700 years ago.

Mesa, Alaska Forager campsite in the Brooks Range of northern Alaska, occupied about 11,700 years ago.

The earliest well-documented Paleo-Indian settlement is associated with the distinctive Clovis fluted point (see Figure 10.13). The Clovis tradition, named after a town in New Mexico, once flourished in various forms over much of North and Central America from about 13,050 to 12,750 years ago. Clovis may be an indigenous North American cultural tradition, but its roots lie in northern forager cultures such as flourished in Alaska at locations, including the **Hidden Mammoth** and **Mesa** sites as early as 13,800 years ago, where foragers used simple bifacial spear points in the chase. These locations, little more than tiny scatters of bones, hearths, and stone artifacts, are the earliest evidence for human settlement in Alaska and have no direct equivalents in earlier traditions such as Diuktai in Siberia.

Clovis is best known (misleadingly so) from occasional mammoth and bison kills on the North American plains. These plains expanded at the end of the Ice Age, their short grasses providing ample feed for all kinds of big game, including bison, mammoths, and other

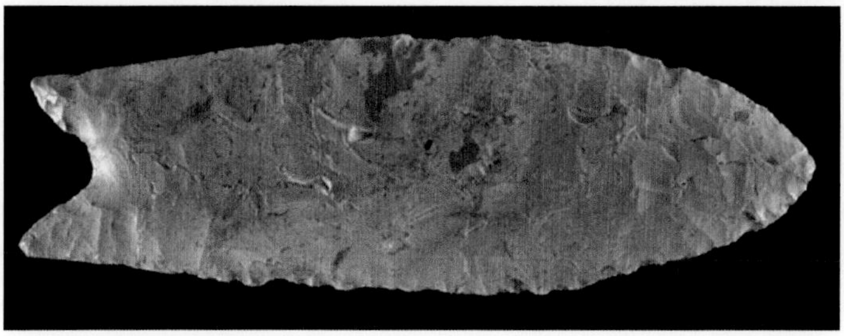

Figure 10.13 Clovis points from the Naco mammoth kill site, Arizona. Arizona State Museum, Tucson.

Source: Arizona State Museum, University of Arizona.

ruminants. Clovis bands on the plains preyed on these and many other game species, large and small. They were constantly on the move, often camping along rivers and streams and close to permanent water holes. Here they killed their prey, camping near to where the carcasses lay.

It would be a mistake, however, to think of the Clovis people as purely big-game hunters. They settled not only on open grasslands but also in woodlands, tundra, and deserts, and along seacoasts. In some areas, wild plant foods were probably at least as important as game. Fish and sea-mammal hunting may also have assumed great local importance, especially along rising coastlines. But wherever Clovis people and their contemporaries settled, large game was of importance, simply because it was a relatively abundant meat source.

atlatls Throwing sticks used by early North American hunters; *see* spear thrower.

Nowhere were Clovis populations large. Their tool kit was highly portable, based on an expert stone-flaking technology that produced fine, fluted-based points. The hunters mounted these on long wooden shafts, sometimes attaching the head to a detachable foreshaft that acted as a hinge. When the spear penetrated an animal, the foreshaft would snap off, ensuring that the lethally sharp point stayed in the wound. Like other later Paleo-Indian groups, and like Ice Age hunters in the Old World, the Clovis people hunted their prey on foot, relying on their stalking skill and the accuracy of their throwing sticks (***atlatls***) to dispatch their quarry.

The origins of the Clovis people remain a complete mystery. However, most experts believe that they derived from late Ice Age forager populations in Alaska and northeastern Asia. If the first Americans crossed into the New World before 15,000 years ago, then the peopling of the uninhabited continent took place remarkably quickly. By 12,000 years ago, Stone Age foragers occupied nearly every corner of the Americas. The overall human population probably numbered no more than a few tens of thousands, but they had adapted to every form of local environment imaginable.

By this time, the last glaciation was long over, and the great ice sheets of the north were in rapid retreat. Climatic conditions were warming up rapidly, and many species of Ice Age big game vanished. The descendants of the first Americans adapted to these new circumstances in very diverse ways, along trajectories of cultural change that led, ultimately, to the brilliant array of Native American societies encountered by Europeans in the late fifteenth century A.D. (see Chapter 14).

With the first settlement of the Americas, the great radiation of *H. sapiens* was nearly complete. This was the second great radiation of humanity, the climactic development of world prehistory. From it stemmed not only the great biological and cultural diversity of modern humankind, but also food production, village life, urban civilization, and the settlement of the Pacific Islands—the very roots of our own diverse and complex world.

Summary

- This chapter documented the permanent spread of *H. sapiens* into Europe, Eurasia, and Southeast Asia by 50,000 years ago, during the late Ice Age.
- By this time, there was increasing specialization and flexibility in human hunting and foraging as modern humans replaced pre-modern groups in many environments.

- Modern humans had inhabited New Guinea by at least 40,000 years ago, and soon afterward lived on adjacent offshore islands. Australia was settled by 50,000 years ago.
- The Neanderthals had disappeared by 40,000 years before present, as had all the other known hominin contemporaries, such as *Homo erectus* in Asia, and *Homo floresiensis* on the Indonesian island of Flores. For the first time in over 6 million years of human evolution, only one hominin remained on Earth: us, *H. sapiens*.
- The sheer diversity of the late Ice Age environment gave the modern humans of western Europe (sometimes known as Cro-Magnon people) great flexibility. They developed more complex societies and elaborate bone and antler technology, as well as an intricate symbolic life, reflected in their artistic traditions.
- These cultures reached their apogee in the Magdalenian culture, which flourished after 18,000 years ago, and for about 5,000 years.
- Late Ice Age hunter-gatherers also spread slowly on to the Russian plains, relying heavily on game of all kinds. Far to the northeast, western Siberia was settled at least by 25,000 years ago, but we only settled the extreme northeast in the very late Ice Age, perhaps as late as 18,000 years ago.
- The first humans to settle the Americas crossed from northeastern Asia, probably across or along the coasts of the Bering land bridge (Beringia), but the date of their arrival is highly controversial. Some scientists claim that archaeological evidence from South America proves that Native Americans were flourishing as early as 40,000 years ago.
- Most experts believe that first settlement occurred much later, perhaps at the very end of the Ice Age, no more than around 15,000 years ago. There is evidence for human occupation in Chile by 13,800 years ago, and the Clovis people of North America flourished between 13,050 and 12,750 years ago.

Key Terms and Sites

Sunda
Wallacea
Sahul
Liang Bua Cave
Jeremalai Cave
Huon Peninsula
Willandra Lakes
Cro-Magnon
Abri Pataud
burin
groove-and-splinter technique
blades
foreshaft
spear thrower
Magdalenian culture
Niaux
Trois Frères
Le Tuc d'Audoubert
Grotte de Chauvet
shamans
Mezhirich

microliths
sinodonts
sundadonts
Yana RHS
Diuktai Cave
Verkhene-Trotiskaya
Beringia
Monte Verde
Paisley Five-Mile Point caves
Debra L. Friedkin site
Meadowcroft Rock Shelter
Fort Rock Cave
Cactus Hill
Valsequillo
Taima Taima
Paleo-Indian
Hidden Mammoth
Mesa
atlatls

Critical-Thinking Questions

1. Why are the climate changes of the late Ice Age so important to human history? What developments in the great diaspora did they foster and hinder?
2. Discuss the implications of the more sophisticated technology of *H. sapiens* to their colonization of new areas. What contribution did this technology make to the human ability to adapt to environmental extremes?
3. What are the differences between the first human settlement of Australia and that of North America? Do you think that environmental conditions played an important role in such settlement?

Further Reading

People of the Earth by Fagan and Durrani (New York: Routledge, 2023) includes a more in-depth survey of the material covered in this chapter. Brian Fagan has also written an accessible overview and background of the lives of the first modern humans in Europe in his book, *Cro-Magnon* (New York: Bloomsbury Press, 2010). P. Bahn, *Images of the Ice Age* (Oxford: Oxford University Press, 2016) is an invaluable analysis of Stone Age European art. For Eurasia generally, see J. Hoffecker, *Desolate Landscapes* (New Brunswick, NJ: Rutgers University Press, 2001). For the controversies surrounding the first settlement of the Americas and the Clovis people, see D. Meltzer, *First Peoples in a New World: Colonizing Ice Age America* (Berkeley: University of California Press, 2009). T. Dillehay, *The Settlement of the Americas* (New York: Basic Books, 2000) is an important survey. See also J. Adovasio with Jake Page, *The First Americans* (New York: Random House, 2009).

Part 5

The First Farmers and Complex Societies

11 The Earliest Farmers

Chapter Outline

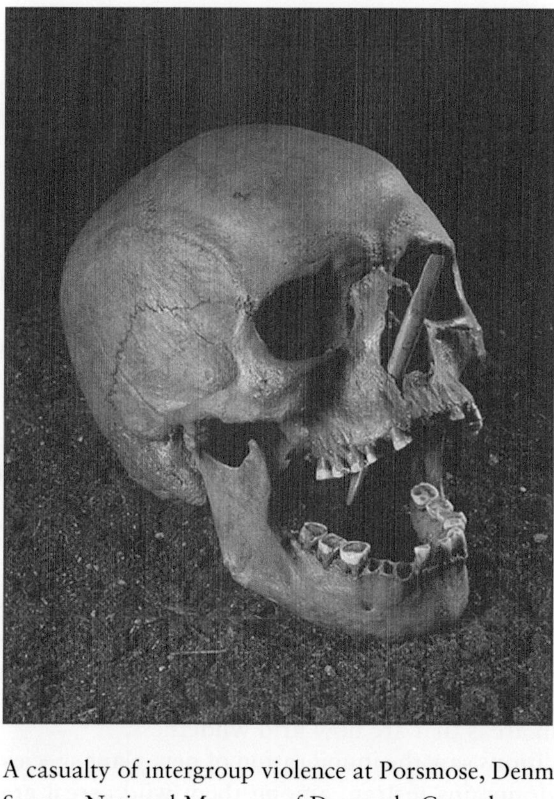

A casualty of intergroup violence at Porsmose, Denmark, c. 3000 B.C.
Source: National Museum of Denmark, Copenhagen.

DOI: 10.4324/9781003592754-16

The men climb high above the ground, lopping off small branches with their stone-bladed axes. The women and children gather up the foliage and pile it around the bare tree trunks. It is backbreaking work that goes on for days as the farmers watch the brassy sky for thunderclouds and signs of rain. A few spits of rain and building clouds bring hope of imminent showers. The people ignite the tinder-dry brush, which burns fiercely. The sky fills with dense brown smoke as far as the eye can see, as the women turn over the fresh ash into the cleared soil and plant their precious seed. Then, everyone waits for the life-giving rains to conjure bright green shoots from the soil.

food production Agriculture and animal domestication.

It is sometimes hard for us, buying our food from supermarkets, to imagine that for more than 99 percent of our existence as humans, we were hunters and gatherers, tied to the seasons of plant foods, the movements of game, and the ebb and flow of aquatic resources. **Food production**, the taming of animals and the deliberate cultivation of cereal grasses and edible root plants, is largely a phenomenon of the past 12,000 years. Animal and plant domestication had major consequences for all of humankind—new economies and great interdependence, permanent settlement, more complex social organization, accelerating population growth, and increasing social inequality, to mention only a few. Agriculture was the foundation for all early civilizations and, ultimately, for our own industrial world.

After the Ice Age

Holocene (from the Greek word for "recent") The era since the end of the Pleistocene (Ice Age), which occurred around 11,700 years ago.

After around 20,000 years ago, the great ice sheets began to retreat, at times very rapidly, marking the transition from the last Ice Age toward the present interglacial period, the **Holocene** (from the Greek *holos* "whole," and *kainos* "new," thus meaning "entirely recent"). At the same time, world sea levels rose dramatically, if irregularly, from their previous lows of over 90 meters (300 feet) below modern levels, leading to major changes in world geography. The chilly waters of the Bering Sea eventually flooded central Beringia and separated Siberia and Alaska. Sunda in Southeast Asia became an enormous archipelago. Great Britain became an island. The North Sea and the Baltic assumed their modern configurations.

The most striking climatic and vegetational transformations took place in northern latitudes, in areas like western and central Europe and in regions of North America contiguous to the great ice sheets. Only 7,000 years after the Scandinavian ice sheet began retreating, forests covered much of Europe. There were major vegetational changes in warmer latitudes, too. Rainfall patterns changed at the end of the Ice Age, bringing large, shallow lakes and short grasslands to the Sahara. As late as 6000 B.C., hunter-gatherer populations flourished in the desert, in areas that are now arid wilderness.

In southwestern Asia, warmer conditions saw the immigration of new plant species into highland areas such as the Zagros Mountains in Iran, among them wild cereal grasses. Their distribution now expanded dramatically, to the point that wild wheat and barley became important staples for forager groups in the highlands and fertile river valleys like the Euphrates. Far away, in Mexico, rising temperatures brought a rich forest of cacti and legume trees to mountain valleys of the central highlands. This thorn-scrub-cactus forest included many wild ancestors of domesticated plants, among them maguey, squash, beans, and teosinte, the wild grass that was probably the ancestor of maize. Maize became one of the staples of Native American life (see Chapter 14).

Changes in Hunter-Gatherer Societies

These and other Holocene climatic changes had profound effects on forager societies throughout the world, especially on the intensity of the food quest and the complexity of their societies. Natural population growth also affected forager societies. By 15,000 years ago, the world's forager population was probably approaching about 10 million people. Except in the most favored areas, like southwestern France or the Nile valley, late Ice Age environments were incapable of supporting anything but the sparsest of human population densities—well under one person per square mile. As a result, in early Holocene times, still-rising human populations began to match the ability of the world's environment to support them as foragers. It was no longer possible to solve a subsistence problem simply by moving elsewhere. People began to exploit a wider range of food resources with greater efficiency, both to avert starvation and to protect themselves from food shortages caused by short-term droughts and other unpredictable changes. In time, forager societies underwent profound changes and in some areas acquired greater complexity.

Nowhere can these changes be seen more clearly than in the Americas, settled by Stone Age foragers either during or immediately after the Ice Age. By 13,000 years ago, the big game that formed a staple part of their diet was extinct. The Paleo-Indians responded to changed circumstances by developing ever more intensive and specialized ways of exploiting local environments. The change was especially marked in areas of exceptional resource diversity like parts of the west coast of North America, the Peruvian coast, and the fertile river valleys of the southern midwestern and southeastern United States. In all these areas, forager populations became more sedentary, developed specialized technologies for hunting, foraging, and fishing, and in the process developed some form of social ranking.

Such intensive exploitation, processing, and storage were adaptive in environments where seasonal phenomena such as salmon runs, caribou migrations, or hickory nut harvests required not only efficient collection of quantities of food in a short time, but also their processing and storage for later use. Thanks to storage and the careful seasonal exploitation of game, plant, and aquatic resources like fish and waterfowl, Holocene foragers were able to compensate for periodic food shortages caused by short-term climatic change and seasonal fluctuations. For example, Native American societies developed a remarkable expertise with wild plant foods. They also used an array of simple pestles, grinders, and other tools to process seeds and other wild plant foods. Later, it was an easy matter to adapt these tool kits to new, specialized tasks such as farming.

More restricted territories, less mobility, rising population densities, unpredictable environmental variations, and seasonal flood fluctuations were problems common to Holocene foragers throughout the world. A few of these societies, especially those in areas with rich and diverse food resources that included fish and sea mammals, achieved a greater complexity than any Ice Age society, with some signs of social ranking.

Social Complexity among Hunter-Gatherers

Complex forager societies did not appear everywhere, but they developed in a remarkable variety of environments, from fertile river valleys to coastal deserts. Everywhere, however, certain general conditions were necessary. First, population movements had to be limited by either geography or the presence of neighbors. Second, resources had to be abundant and predictable in their seasonal appearance. Such resources included fish, shellfish, nuts, and seeds—species that are abundant and seldom exhausted. Dependable water supplies were likewise vital. Third, population growth could reach a point at which food shortages occurred and there was an imbalance between people and their food supply. Again, a solution was to intensify the food quest, an intensification that could result in a more complex society or, as we shall see, in food production (see Figure 11.1).

Social complexity was most common in areas where freshwater or marine fish, shellfish, or sea mammals were abundant. The full potential of marine and freshwater resources was realized only in a relatively few areas, like northern Europe, Peru, and western North America. Here, higher than normal population densities were concentrated in restricted territories circumscribed by geography or neighbors. These populations acquired a more varied diet by using more specialized tool kits and sophisticated food-storage systems and preservation techniques. These groups often lived in large, sedentary base camps ruled by important kin leaders who monopolized trade with neighboring groups (see Box 11.1).

Another example of increased complexity comes from southern California. The Chumash Indians of the Santa Barbara region were skilled fishers and sea-mammal hunters. Some Chumash communities numbered as many as 1,000 people, living under hereditary chiefs (*wots*). There was a small, elite group of ceremonial officeholders, shamans, and such experts as canoe builders. Chumash culture was a maritime adaptation made possible by a specialized fishing technology that included planked canoes (***tomols***) about 7.6 meters (25 feet) long (see Figure 11.2). Each community maintained exchange contacts with other coastal communities and with people living far in the interior.

tomol Planked canoe used by the Chumash people of southern California.

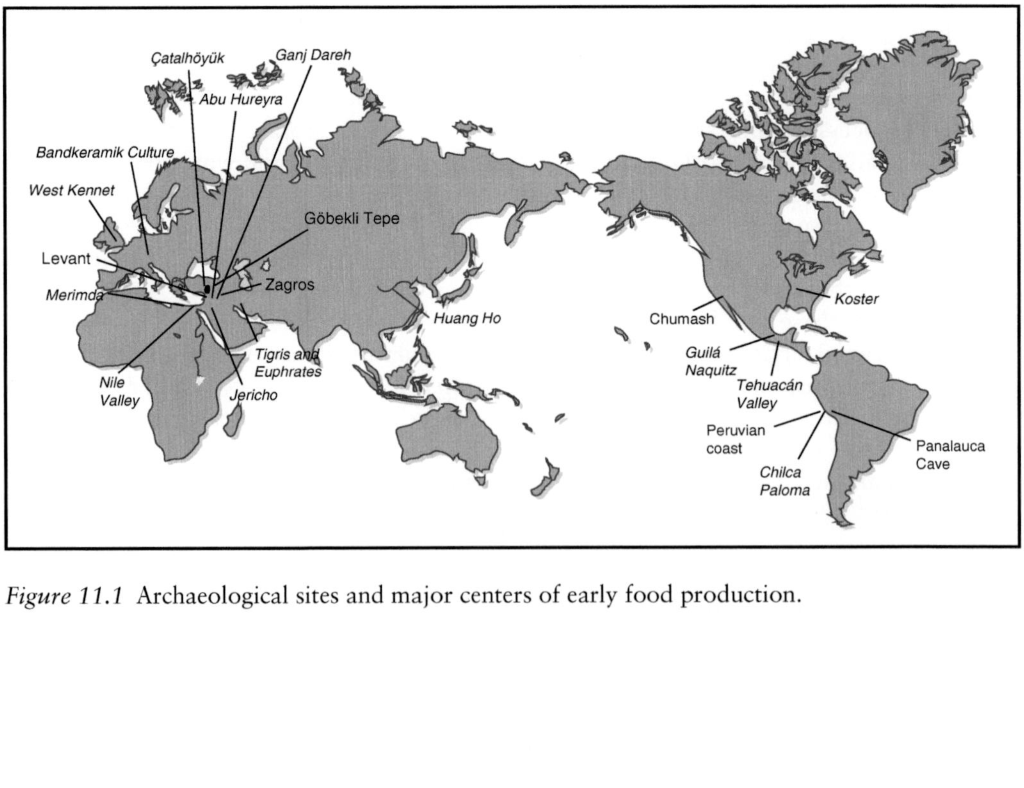

Figure 11.1 Archaeological sites and major centers of early food production.

Figure 11.2 Reconstruction of a Chumash Indian *tomol* (canoe), used on the waters of the Santa Barbara Channel, California.

Source: Courtesy of the Santa Barbara Museum of Natural History.

Modoc Rock shelter in Illinois that contains human occupation from about 8000 to 2000 B.C. Well known for its Archaic occupation levels.

Box 11.1 Discovery
Hunter-Gatherers at Modoc Rock Shelter, Illinois

The gradual shift from nomadic to more permanent hunter-gatherer settlements is well documented at numerous sites in the North American Midwest, among them Koster in the Illinois River valley (see Chapter 3) and **Modoc** rock shelter near the Mississippi River in Randolph County, Illinois. Modoc lies in a hickory-rich riverine environment about 150 kilometers (90 miles) southeast of Koster. Some 8.2 meters (27 feet) of midden accumulation spans human occupations dating from about 8000 to 2000 B.C. (see Figure 11.3). The first occupants were general hunter-gatherers, without any particular dietary focus. Early levels at Modoc show little use of aquatic resources before about 5600 B.C., when fish, mussels, and freshwater crayfish assume more importance, just as they did at Koster and other contemporary midwestern sites. The Modoc people also exploited many small mammals, including cottontail rabbits, muskrats, and squirrels, but few larger animals. White-tailed deer became a major food source in later times, before about 1600 B.C.

Figure 11.3 Excavations at Modoc rock shelter, Illinois.
Source: Illinois State Museum Archives.

At first, Modoc served as a short-term camp. But around 1600 B.C., selective use of food sources like hickory nuts increased and people used Modoc for longer periods of time. As fish and other bottomland foods came into greater use, Modoc probably became a base camp, used for much of the year. Later, it was a place used for more specialized activities, visited when people hunted deer on the nearby uplands and waterfowl in the shallow creeks and ponds nearby. These changes in Modoc's role may reflect more restricted mobility in many areas during a period of climatic change. But, in general, as sites like Koster and Modoc, and on the Little Tennessee River show (see Figure 14.3 on p. 440), there was conservative, seasonal exploitation of the Eastern Woodlands environment—even if we still know little of winter, spring, and summer activities. This seasonal exploitation required at least a degree of careful scheduling to maximize the potential of nut harvests, and to capitalize on the game that fed on the forest mast each fall.

Chumash culture achieved a degree of social elaboration that came close to the limit of such complexity possible without adopting agriculture. Why did such social complexity develop? Some scholars regard the ocean as a kind of Garden of Eden, an environment sometimes so productive that foragers could maintain permanent sedentary settlements and maintain high population densities. Perhaps, people turned to harvesting fish, shellfish, and sea mammals in a period of rapid environmental change, like that at the end of the Ice Age. Unfortunately, however, we do not know how decisive marine or riverine resources were in allowing dense populations and sedentary living, both essential prerequisites for social complexity.

Away from coasts, rivers, and lakeshores, and especially among groups inhabiting the edges of several ecological zones, people living in more or less permanent settlements in rich inland environments turned to another strategy. They experimented with the planting of wild plant staples to supplement food resources in short supply. The cultural changes forced on them by Holocene climate change made it easier for their descendants to adopt radically new economic strategies such as deliberate cultivation of the soil and animal domestication—food production.

Origins of Food Production

Victorian scientists believed that agriculture was a brilliant invention, fostered by a rare genius. One day, went the scenario, a solitary forager was carrying home a bundle of edible grasses when he stumbled, spilling some of his load on damp ground. A few days later, he passed the same way and noticed small green shoots sprouting from the soil. With startling insight, the man realized the potential of his new invention; he planted more seeds near his hut and fed his family off the bountiful harvest. Other families soon copied his example, and agriculture was born.

Such captivating scenarios offer simple explanations but have no foundation in scientific fact. First, no one ever "invented" agriculture, because all hunter-gatherers knew that grasses germinated each year. One can propagate root crops like the African yam simply by cutting off the top and placing it in the soil. Foragers living on the fringes of the African rainforest as early as 40,000 years ago may have planted yams in that way, but such practices are a far cry from the cultivation of cereal grasses, which began in the Old World and the New after the Ice Age. Reality was more complex than mere invention and is still little understood.

Nor did a single society "invent" agriculture, for farming appeared at different times in many parts of the world. Farmers in southwestern Asia's Euphrates and Jordan River valleys, and in southeastern Türkiye, cultivated wheat and barley by about 9000 B.C. Central American cultivators grew domesticated squashes by about the same date. Chinese villagers harvested rice by 6000 B.C., perhaps earlier. Most scientists believe that a set of complex cultural and environmental factors combined with population growth to cause societies in widely separated parts of the world to shift from foraging to food production, usually within a relatively short time, sometimes a few generations.

The emergence of agriculture was not in itself that important an event. What was of all-embracing significance was the transition from hunting and gathering to cultivation, which was the catalyst for all of the elaborate cultural developments of later millennia, of which urban civilization was but one. In strictly archaeological terms, we will never document the moment of invention, but over many years, we have chronicled the rapid spread of the new economies that soon reached all parts of the world where farming or animal herding were possible. Thanks to new cutting-edge research, we now know that the process of spread was very complex, involving long periods when people subsisted off wild foods and domestic crops as well as moments when the new economies spread rapidly.

At the end of the Ice Age, foragers in drought-prone subtropical zones such as southwestern Asia and highland Mesoamerica were exploiting potentially domesticable wild grasses and root plants with greater intensity. Dependence on such foods probably came earlier in these regions, where there were only a few forageable plant foods. Such dependence was essential to long-term survival, and led almost inevitably to experimentation with deliberate planting of wild cereals, and ultimately to cultivation. In contrast, populations in more humid, plant-rich tropical regions, like the African and Amazonian rainforests, probably did little more than plant a few wild species to minimize risk of starvation in lean years long after farming appeared in more temperate regions. Cereal agriculture came to tropical Africa only within the past 3,000 years, and it spread widely after the introduction of iron technology some centuries later (see Figure 11.4).

agricultural revolution (expression coined by Vere Gordon Childe) The beginnings of food production, prompted by drought and close associations among animals, humans, and plants.

In the 1930s, European archaeologist Vere Gordon Childe wrote of an **agricultural revolution** during what he thought was a time of drought at the end of the Ice Age. The arid conditions brought animals, humans, and plants into a close symbiosis (Greek for "life together"), creating favorable conditions for foragers to experiment with cereal grasses and with herding wild goats and sheep. These experiments revolutionized human existence and spread rapidly throughout southwestern Asia and further afield.

Figure 11.4 Dogon women from Mali in West Africa pounding millet.
Source: fiondavi/iStock via Getty Images.

Childe's "agricultural revolution" and other early theories have proved to be too simple in the face of today's multidisciplinary research. For example:

accelerator mass spectrometry (AMS) radiocarbon dating Method of radiocarbon dating that counts actual ^{14}C atoms; can be used to date items as small as individual seeds.

- Multidisciplinary studies of Holocene climatic change combine pollen samples from lakes and marshes with deep-sea and tree-ring data to produce a chronicle of large-and small-scale climatic change over the millennia. These data allow archaeologists to place early farming sites within much more precise environmental contexts.
- New botanical data acquired through systematic use of flotation methods (see Box 4.7 on p. 145) allow the recovery of large samples of wild and domesticated seeds from occupation levels.
- New DNA analysis has shown that many wild animals and wild plants were domesticated at several locations at different times. The transition to food production was much more complex than we have assumed.
- Major advances in zooarchaeology, the study of animal bones, are providing a wealth of new information on the domestication of cattle, goats, pigs, sheep, and other animals.
- **Accelorator mass spectrometry (AMS) radiocarbon dating**, which permits the dating of individual seeds, root fragments, or maize cobs (see Box 11.2), enables us to date early farming with high precision, as opposed to merely dating layers in which tiny seeds are found (and into which they may have fallen from higher levels).

This multidisciplinary research has spawned complex models for early food production. Many variables must be understood before we can reconstruct the conditions under which agriculture was first regarded as a profitable activity. We are searching for sets of conditions in which population pressure, the distribution of plants, the rate at which the environment was changing, and even the techniques of harvesting wild grasses all played their part in making agriculture work. Then, there were variations among the potentially domesticable plants and animals, some of which resisted domestication because of their long life span or because they spent much of their lives in areas remote from human settlement. The seasonal distribution of wild vegetable foods or game may also have prevented experiments in domestication, when the seasons during which these wild foods were exploited coincided with the times of year when it was important for experimenting farmers to stay near their growing crops. Under these circumstances, people would tend to pursue their traditional food-gathering habits.

Box 11.2 Doing Archaeology
Accelerator Mass Spectrometry (AMS) Radiocarbon Dating

Until about 30 years ago, dating the rate of decay (beta counts) from different radiocarbon samples had a calculated ratio that gave only approximations. Using carbon-14 (^{14}C) and carbon-12 (^{12}C), scientists could detect and count individual decay events with radiocarbon. They could observe the emission of beta particles to determine the rate of radioactive breakdown and so estimate the number of ^{14}C atoms remaining in the sample. Since only a small number of ^{14}C atoms break down over the many hours of the sample count, the samples had to be large enough to provide an adequate number of beta counts.

Back in the 1960s, archaeologists collected handfuls of charcoal from hearths in plastic bags, the rule being "the larger the sample, the better." Scientists could not date small objects like maize cobs or tiny wood fragments embedded in the sockets of prehistoric bronze spearheads. Furthermore, minute samples such as seeds can easily move upward or downward into other occupation layers, either through human agencies such as trampling or through natural phenomena such as burrowing animals. The development of a new radiocarbon method based on AMS in 1983 revolutionized radiocarbon chronologies and the study of early food production.

An accelerator mass spectrometer can date the age of sample material by counting the number of ^{14}C atoms present. Rather than counting decay events (beta counts), researchers estimate the remaining ^{14}C by directly counting ^{14}C atoms. By doing this, they can date samples 1,000 times smaller than the handful of charcoal used a generation ago.

The development of small, high-energy mass spectrometers solved a major problem: that of background noise from ions or molecules of a similar mass to the ^{14}C atoms masking their presence. The new instruments filter out background as a proportion of the sample's atoms are propelled through an accelerator toward a detector. Ionized carbon atoms from the sample are pulled in beam form toward the accelerator. A magnet bends the beam, so lighter atoms turn more sharply than heavier ones and move to the inside of the diverging beam. A filter blocks the passage of all charged particles except those of atomic mass 14. The accelerator pushes the stripped beam through a second beam-bending magnet, filtering out any last non-^{14}C particles. A magnetic lens focuses the beam as a ^{14}C detector counts the number of remaining ions, allowing the calculation of the sample age.

Consequences of Food Production

Once successful, food production spread rapidly, partly because subsequent population growth prevented people from reverting to hunting and gathering. Food production spread to all corners of the world, except where an environment with extreme aridity or heat or cold rendered agriculture or herding impossible, or where people chose to remain hunters and gatherers. In some places, food production was the economic base for urbanization and literate civilization, but most human societies did not go further than subsistence-level food production until the industrial power of nineteenth- and twentieth-century Europe led them into the machine age.

Food production resulted, ultimately, in much higher population densities in many locations. The domestication of plants and animals can lead to an economic strategy that increases and stabilizes available food supplies, although more energy is used to produce them.

Farmers used concentrated tracts of territory for agriculture and for grazing cattle and small stock if they practiced mixed farming. Their territory was much smaller than that of hunter-gatherers (although pastoralists needed huge areas of grazing land for seasonal pasture). Permanent villages replaced the temporary camps of earlier times. New social units came into being as more permanent home bases were developed; these social links reflected ownership and inheritance of land and led to much larger settlements that brought hitherto scattered populations into closer and more regular contact. Within a smaller area of farming land, property lines were carefully delineated as individual ownership and problems of inheritance arose. Shortages of land sometimes led to disputes and to the founding of new village settlements on previously uncultivated soil.

The technological consequences of food production were, in their way, as important as the new economies. A more settled way of life and some decline in hunting and gathering led to long-occupied villages, lasting agricultural styles, and more substantial housing. As they had done for millennia, people built their permanent homes with the raw materials most abundant in their environment. The early farmers of southwestern Asia worked dried mud into small houses with flat roofs; these were cool in summer and warm in winter. At night during the hot season, people may have slept on the flat roofs. Some less substantial houses had reed roofs. In the more temperate zones of Europe, with wetter climates, timber was used to build thatched-roof houses of various shapes and sizes. Early African farmers often built huts of grass, sticks, and anthill clay (see Figure 11.5). Nomadic pastoralists of the northern steppes had no concern with a permanent and durable home, yet they, too, took advantage of the related benefits of having a domestic food supply: they used animal skins to make clothing as well as tents to provide shelter during the icy winters.

Agriculture is a seasonal activity, with long periods of the year when the fields lie fallow or support growing crops. Any farmer is confronted with the problem of keeping food in ways the hunter-gatherer never has to ponder. Thus, a new technology of storage came into being. Grain bins, jars, or clay-lined pits became an essential part of the agricultural economy for stockpiling food for the lean months and against periods of famine. The bins may have been made of wattle and daub, clay, or timber (see Figure 11.5). Baskets and clay-lined silos protected valuable grain against rodents. In the Fertile Crescent, grain surpluses began around 8500 B.C. and are known from settlements including Nevali Çori in Southeastern Türkiye and Abu Hureyra in Northern Syria. Stored grain surpluses had far-reaching consequences. They allowed humans to build larger and more organized communities, ultimately setting the stage for the later development of cities and states (Chapter 12).

Yet while hunter-gatherers use skins, wood containers, gut pouches, and sometimes baskets to carry vegetable foods back to base, farmers face far more formidable transport problems: they must carry their harvest back to the village, keep ready-for-use supplies of foods in the house as opposed to in the storage bins, and store water too.

Figure 11.5 Permanent structures made from local raw materials: A farming village in Ethiopia, Northeast Africa.

Source: miroslav_1/iStock.

Figure 11.6 Removing fired pots from a kiln fueled with wood and cow dung, Mali, West Africa. Source: Irene Abdou/Alamy.

Early farmers began to use gourds as water carriers and, somewhat later in some areas, to make clay vessels that were both waterproof and capable of carrying and cooking food (see Figure 11.6). (The earliest known pottery is much earlier, made by hunter-gatherers in China and Japan.) They made pots by coiling rolls of clay or building up the walls of vessels from a lump and firing them in simple hearths. Clay vessels were much more durable than skin or leather receptacles. Some pots were used for several decades before being broken and abandoned.

For tens of thousands of years, people dug up wild edible roots with simple wooden sticks, sometimes made more effective with the aid of a stone weight. The first farmers continued to use the digging stick to plant crops a few inches below the surface, probably in readily cultivable soils. They also used wooden or stone-bladed hoes (and, much later, iron hoes) to break up the soft soil. These were fitted with short or long handles, depending on cultural preferences. European and southwestern Asian farmers made use of the oxdrawn plow in later millennia, at first with a blade tipped with wood, then with bronze, and later with iron. The plow was an important innovation, for it enabled people to turn the soil over to a much greater depth than ever before.

Every farmer has to clear wild vegetation and weeds from the fields, and it is hardly surprising to find a new emphasis on the ax and the adz. In southwestern Asia, more elaborate metal tools replaced the simple axes of earlier farmers by 2500 B.C. Present-day experiments in Denmark and New Guinea have shown that the ground and polished edges of stone axes are remarkably effective for clearing woodland and felling trees (see Figure 11.7). In later millennia, the alloying of copper and bronze and, ultimately, the development of iron cutting edges made forest clearance even easier. New tools meant

Figure 11.7 A Danish prehistoric stone ax with wooden handle, found perfectly preserved in a peat bog.

new technologies to produce tougher working edges. At first, the farmers used ground and polished stone, placing a high premium on suitable rocks, which were traded from quarry sites over enormous distances. Perhaps, the most famous ax quarries are in western Europe, where ax blanks were traded the length of the British Isles. Villagers traded yellow-brown Grand Pressigny flint over thousands of square kilometers of France. In southwestern Asia and Mexico, one valuable toolmaking material, not for axes but for knives and sickles, was obsidian, a volcanic rock prized for its easy working properties, sharp edges, and ornamental appearance. Early obsidian trade routes carried tools and ornaments hundreds of kilometers from their places of origin (see Chapter 5).

All of these technological developments made people more and more dependent on exotic raw materials, many of which were unobtainable in their own territory. Here we see the beginnings of widespread long-distance trading networks, which were to burgeon even more rapidly with the emergence of the first urban civilizations.

swidden agriculture Shifting agriculture in which farmers clear land, burn it off, plant crops, and then move on to new gardens when the land loses its fertility after several years.

Food production led to changed attitudes toward the environment. Expansion of agriculture meant felling trees and burning vegetation to clear the ground for planting. The same fields were then abandoned after a few years to lie fallow, and more woodland was cleared. The original vegetation began to regenerate, but it may have been cleared again before reaching its original state. This shifting pattern of farming is called slash-and-burn or **swidden agriculture**.

Domesticated animals stripped pastures of their grass cover, heavy rainfalls then denuded the hills of valuable soil, and the pastures were never the same again. However elementary the agricultural technology, the farmer changed the environment, if only with fires lit to clear scrub from gardens and to fertilize the soil with wood ash. In a sense, shifting slash-and-burn agriculture is merely an extension of the older use of fire to encourage regeneration of vegetation.

Food production resulted in high population densities, but disease, available food supplies, water supplies, and particularly famine helped limit population growth. Also, early agricultural methods depended heavily on careful selection of the soil. The technology of the first farmers was hardly effective enough for extensive clearing of the dense woodland under which many good soils lay, so potentially cultivable land could only be whatever was accessible. Gardens were probably scattered over a much wider territory than is necessary today. One authority estimates that even with advanced shifting agriculture, only 40 percent of moderately fertile soil in Africa is available for such cultivation. That figure must have been lower in the early days of agriculture, with simpler stone tools and fewer crops.

In regions of seasonal rainfall, such as southwestern Asia, sub-Saharan Africa, and other parts of Asia, periods of prolonged drought are common. Famine was a real possibility as population densities rose. Many early agriculturalists must have worriedly watched the sky and had frequent crop failures in times of drought. Their small stores of grain from the previous season would not have carried them through another year, especially if they had been careless with their surplus. Farmers were forced to shift their economic strategy in such times.

We know that the earliest farmers availed themselves of game and plant foods to supplement their agriculture, just as today some farmers are obliged to rely heavily on wild vegetable foods and hunting to survive in bad years. Many hunter-gatherer bands collect intensively just a few species of edible plants in their large territories. Aware of many other edible vegetables, they fall back on these only in times of stress. The less favored foods can carry a comparatively small population through to the next rains; a larger agricultural population is not so flexible and quickly exhausts wild vegetables and game in the much smaller territory used for farming and grazing. If the drought lasts for years, then famine, death, and reduced population can follow.

In the final analysis, some people probably turned to food production only when other alternatives were no longer practicable. The classic example is the Aborigines of extreme northern Australia, who were well aware that their neighbors in New Guinea were engaged in intensive agriculture. They, too, knew how to plant the top of the wild yam so that it re-germinated, but they never adopted food production simply because they had no need to become dependent on a lifeway that would reduce their leisure time and produce more food than they required.

We should never forget that humans have always been opportunistic, and the planting of food crops and the first taming of animals may have been the simple result. Whatever the complex factors that led to agriculture and animal domestication, the new food-producing economies proved dramatically successful. In 10,000 B.C., virtually everybody in the world lived by hunting and gathering. By A.D. 1, most people were farmers or herders, and only a minority were still hunter-gatherers, most of them living in environments where extreme cold or aridity prevented the growth of domesticated crops. The spread of food production throughout the world took only about 8,000 years.

The First Farmers in Southwestern Asia

The earliest known farmers flourished in southwestern Asia after the end of the last Ice Age, around 10,000 B.C. New agricultural economies appeared almost simultaneously in several areas—on the flanks of the Taurus and Zagros Mountains, in today's southeastern Türkiye and northern Iraq respectively, as well as in the Jordan and upper Euphrates valleys. At that time, only a few thousand foragers lived across the region but, over the following millennia, the population grew to the tens of thousands, all as a result of settled village life and farming.

Pollen samples from freshwater lakes in Syria and elsewhere tell us that forest cover expanded rapidly at the end of the Ice Age, for the southwestern Asian climate was still cooler and considerably wetter than today. Many areas were richer in animal and plant species than they are now, making them highly favorable for human occupation. At about 10,000 B.C., most human settlements lay in the Levant (the area along the Mediterranean coast) (see Figure 11.1) and in the Zagros Mountains of Iran and their foothills. Some local areas, like the Jordan River valley, the Middle Euphrates valley, and some Zagros valleys, were more densely populated than elsewhere. Here more sedentary and more complex societies flourished. These people exploited the landscape intensively, foraging on hill slopes for wild cereal grasses and nuts while hunting gazelle and other game on grassy lowlands and in river valleys. Their settlements contain exotic objects such as seashells, stone bowls, and artifacts made of obsidian, all traded from afar. This considerable volume of intercommunity exchange brought a degree of social complexity in its wake.

Thanks to extremely fine-grained excavation and extensive use of flotation methods, we know a great deal about the foraging practices of the inhabitants of Abu Hureyra in Syria's Euphrates valley. Abu Hureyra was founded in about 11,500 B.C., a small village settlement of cramped pit dwellings (houses dug partially in the soil) with reed roofs supported by wooden uprights (Figure 11.8). For the next 1,500 years, its inhabitants enjoyed a somewhat warmer and damper climate than today, living in a wooded steppe area where wild cereal grasses were abundant. They subsisted off enormous spring migrations of Persian gazelles from the south. With such a favorable location, about 300–400 people lived in a sizable, permanent settlement. They were no longer a series of small bands, but were a large community with more elaborate social organization, probably grouped into clans of people of common descent.

Figure 11.8 Abu Hureyra, Syria: Excavations in the earlier settlement revealed interconnecting pits that were roofed with poles, branches, and reeds to form small huts. Part of a later rectangular house can be seen at a higher level (*top right*).

Source: Andrew Moore.

The flotation samples from the excavations allowed archaeobotanist Gordon Hillman to study changing plant-collecting habits, as if he were looking through a telescope at a changing landscape. Hundreds of tiny plant remains show how the residents exploited nut harvests in nearby pistachio and oak forests. However, as the climate dried up, the forests retreated from the vicinity of the settlement. The inhabitants turned to wild cereal grasses, collecting them by the thousands, while percentages of nuts fell. By 10,200 B.C., drought conditions were so severe that the people abandoned their long-established settlement, perhaps dispersing into smaller camps.

Five centuries later, at about 9700 B.C., a new village rose on the mound. At first, the inhabitants still hunted gazelle intensively. Then, at about 9000 B.C., within a relatively short time, they switched to herding domesticated goats and sheep, and to growing einkorn, pulses, and other cereal grasses (see Box 11.3). Abu Hureyra grew rapidly until it covered nearly 12 hectares (30 acres). It was a close-knit community of rectangular, one-story mud-brick houses, joined by narrow lanes and courtyards, finally abandoned at about 6000 B.C.

rachis A hinge that joins a seed to a plant.

Jericho, Jordan valley Biblical city and famous archaeological site with evidence of an early fortified town of the eighth millennium B.C. and of farming settlements as early as 7800 B.C.

Box 11.3 Doing Archaeology
Domesticating Wheat and Barley

The qualities of wild wheat, barley, and similar crops are quite different from those of their domestic equivalents. In the wild, these grains occur in dense stands. You harvest them by tapping the stem with the hands and gathering the seeds in a basket as they fall off, or by uprooting the plant. The tapping technique is effective because the wild grain is attached to the stem by a brittle joint, or **rachis**. When the grass is tapped, the weak rachis breaks and the seed falls into the basket. (Not all wild rachises are brittle, so some seeds survive to regenerate the crop.)

The first cultivated wheat and barley crops were of the wild, brittle-rachised type, and the resulting crops would probably have been large enough to generate domestic-type mutants in the first two to five years (see Figure 11.9). Selection for the semi-tough rachised forms was an unconscious process during the earliest stages of domestication, perhaps accelerated by the use of sickles or uprooting of individual plants to harvest ripe seeds rather than merely tapping them into waiting baskets. Computer simulations have shown that domestic, semi-tough rachised forms may have been rare at first, but they would have been fully domesticated within 20–30 generations of plant growth—for these cereals, between 20 and 30 years. Even with less intense selective pressures than those assumed in the experiment, domestication could have been achieved within a century or two. Archaeobotanist Gordon Hillman believes that the farmers would have started conscious selection as soon as the domesticates became sufficiently common to be recognized—perhaps 1–5 percent of the crop. From then on, domestication would have been completed in three or four years.

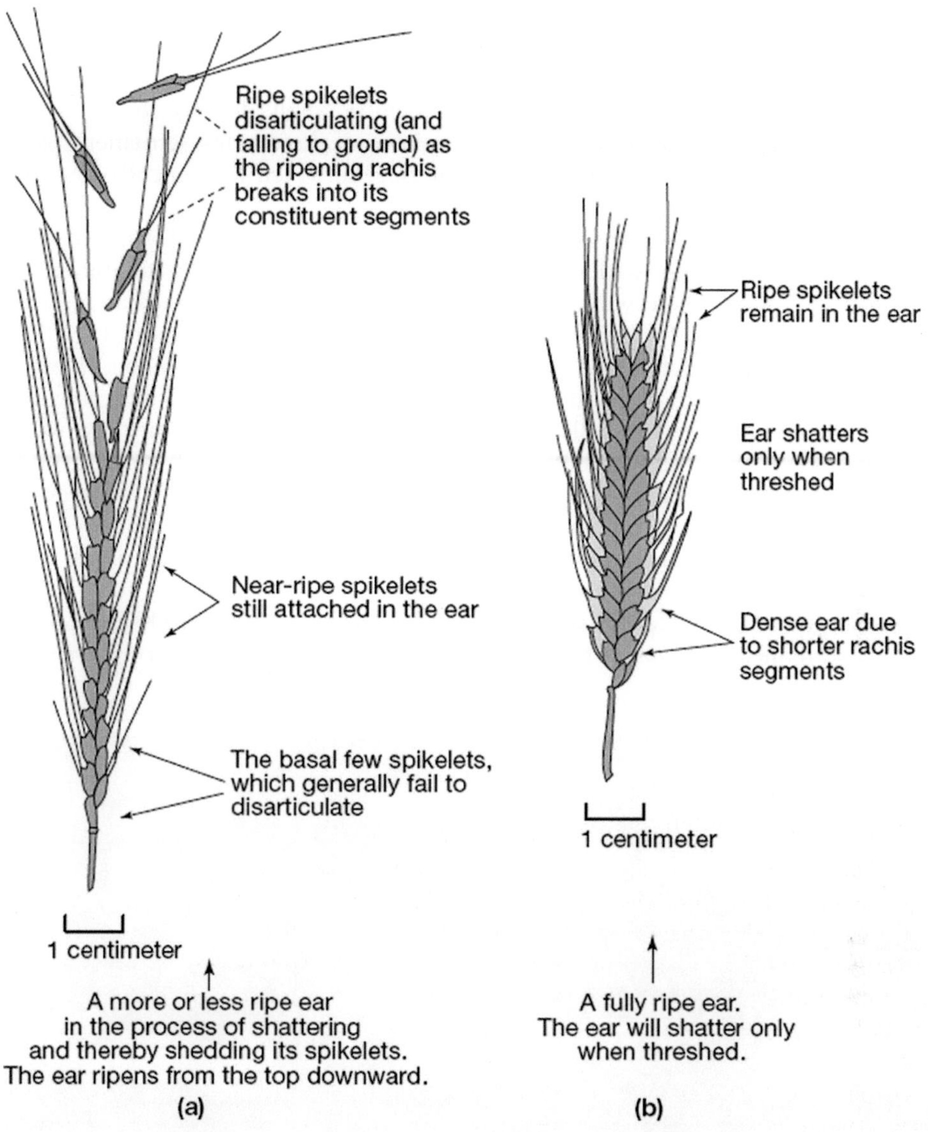

Figure 11.9 Wild and domesticated einkorn, showing brittle and tough rachises: (a) Wild einkorn's brittle ear and arrow-shaped spikelets are adapted for penetrating surface litter and cracks on the ground. (b) Domestic einkorn, with its tough rachised ear and plumper spikelets, has lost some key features necessary for self-implantation.

Although the broad outlines of the process of domestication can be reconstructed through controlled experimentation and computer simulation, it is unlikely that anyone will ever find "transitional" grains in archaeological sites that will document the actual process under way. Indeed, recent DNA studies have backed this up and shown that the shift from wild to domesticated wheat and barley occurred relatively quickly, with genetic changes occurring over a few dozen generations. This rapid domestication process means that, rather than finding grains with gradual changes, we are more likely to encounter wild seeds in one level and domesticated ones in the next.

Many complex factors led to the adoption of the new economies, not only at Abu Hureyra, but also at many other locations, such as 'Ain Ghazal, also in Syria, where goat toe bones showing the telltale marks of abrasion caused by foot tethering (hobbling) testify to early herding of domestic stock. Most settlements lay on low ground, near well-watered, easily cultivable land. Their inhabitants usually lived in small, densely clustered villages of circular or oval one-room houses. The most famous of these many settlements is at the base of the biblical city of Jericho, famous for the siege in which Joshua collapsed the city walls with the blast of trumpets.

A small camp flourished at the bubbling Jericho spring by at least 10,500 B.C., but a more permanent farming settlement quickly followed. Soon the inhabitants built massive stone walls complete with towers and a rock-cut ditch more than 2.7 meters (9 feet) deep and 3 meters (10 feet) wide around their settlement (see Figure 11.10). Their beehive-shaped huts were clustered inside the walls. The communal labor of wall and ditch building required both political and economic resources on a scale unheard of a few thousand years earlier. Why the walls were needed remains a mystery, but they may have been floodworks or for defense, resulting from competition from neighboring groups for scarce food resources, perhaps to protect their own grain stores. Jericho also yielded compelling evidence of ancestor worship in the form of human skulls with plastered faces, a clear sign that people enjoyed a close link with the supernatural and the land, guarded traditionally by the dead (see Figure 6.7 on p. 190).

The population of the Middle East increased considerably between 8000 and 6000 B.C., scattered in permanent villages as far east as the more arid Syrian plateau. Farmers now

Figure 11.10 The stone tower at Jericho.
Source: geothea/Fotolia.

grew emmer wheat, barley, lentils, and peas in small fields. They rotated crops with pulses to sustain soil fertility. Some communities like Jericho became important trading centers. The farmers were using obsidian from Türkiye, turquoise from Sinai, and seashell ornaments from the Mediterranean and the Red Sea. The volume of trade was such that many villages used small clay spheres, cones, and disks to keep track of commodities traded. These tokens are thought to have formed a simple recording system that later evolved into written script (see Chapter 12).

Ganj Dareh, Iran Seasonal foraging camp of 8500 B.C. in the Zagros Mountains.

Jarmo, Iran Early farming village in the Zagros Mountains occupied before 5000 B.C.

In the Zagros highlands of Iran, goat and sheep herding probably began somewhat earlier than in the lowlands. Here, open steppe was ideal country both for intensive hunting of wild goats and sheep and, after about 10,000 B.C., for herding them as well. At the village of **Ganj Dareh**, near Kermanshah in Iran, foragers occupied a seasonal hunting camp in about 10,000 B.C. About 1,500 years later, a small farming village of rectangular mud-brick houses stood on the same spot, a settlement based on goat and sheep herding and cereal horticulture. One of the best-known prehistoric farming villages in the Zagros is **Jarmo**, little more than a cluster of 25 mud houses forming an irregular huddle separated by small alleyways and courtyards. Jarmo was in its heyday in about 6000 B.C., by which time more than 80 percent of the villagers' food came from their fields or herds.

Egypt and the Nile Valley

Everywhere farming developed, local groups domesticated whatever potential domesticates were available, so the story of early food production varies from one area to the next.

The same dynamics of growing populations crowded into restricted territories due to climate change developed in the Nile valley as in the Levant. During the late Ice Age, the valley was a rich, diverse habitat, abounding in game, fish, and wild plant foods. Wild cereal grasses were important in the human diet from at least 15,000 years ago.

The Nile valley is unusual in that its water supplies depend not on local rains, but on floods from rainfall gathered far upstream in Ethiopia. The fluctuations in these yearly inundations had a profound effect on the pattern of human settlement downstream. The irregular cycles of higher and lower rainfall may have caused people to manage wild food resources very carefully. Like their southwestern Asian counterparts, they turned to the deliberate cultivation of wild barley and wheat.

Merimda Beni Salama, Egypt Farming settlement in the Egyptian delta dating to about 4500 B.C.

By 6000 B.C., dozens of farming villages flourished in the Nile valley, settlements that are now buried beneath deep layers of sand and gravel laid down by thousands of years of river floods. Only 1,500 years later, the inhabitants of the valley were subsisting almost entirely on agriculture, living in small villages like **Merimda Beni Salama**, near the Nile Delta. Merimda was a cluster of oval houses and shelters, built half underground and roofed with mud and sticks. The farmers planted barley and wheat as the annual floods receded while their animals grazed in flat river grasslands. Population densities were still low, so the average

Figure 11.11 Ancient Egyptian tomb painting showing a noble's estate workers reaping the harvest with sickles. Ancient Egyptian agriculture dates back to at least 6000 B.C. and probably began much earlier.

Source: Ancient Art & Architecture Collection Ltd/Alamy.

Nile flood allowed early Egyptian farmers to harvest grain over perhaps two-thirds of the river floodplain (see Figure 11.11). Thus, there was no need for irrigation works, which first appeared in about 3000 B.C., when Egypt became a unified state (see Chapter 12).

Early Agriculture in Anatolia

Anatolia (largely akin to modern Türkiye) was a diverse, favorable highland and lowland environment for human settlement from early in the Holocene. Food production probably began in this region at about the same time as it did in the Levant, though the processes involved are still being clarified. Some of the most exciting discoveries come from the southeast.

The upper reaches of the Euphrates and Tigris Rivers drain the tableland of the Urfa region of southeastern Türkiye. This is a place of arid limestone hills where the summers are hot and dry and the winters wet, with diverse soils that supported natural stands of wild cereals and eventually became ideal for farming. DNA researches have pinpointed the Karacadag Mountains in this area as the original homeland of domesticated einkorn.

Was the Urfa, then, the area where farming began, as opposed to the Euphrates and Jordan valleys to the south? The answer is that we do not yet know, but there are some fascinating archaeological sites that chronicle sophisticated ritual observances which coincide, in general terms, with the changeover from hunting and gathering to food production. For the first time, we find evidence for communal structures, for public areas where more elaborate structures served as a focus for the settlement (see Box 11.4).

Box 11.4 Site
Ritual Buildings in Southeastern Türkiye

Communal buildings, open spaces, monoliths, and sometimes human remains—convincing evidence for ritual comes from several early villages in southeastern Türkiye. At **Çayönü Tepesi** in southeastern Türkiye, occupied from about 8600 to 7000 B.C., the settlement lay on a terrace above a small river, the rectangular houses standing at right angles to the river. They formed an arc, with a large open space at the center. Three quite distinct buildings once stood in this plaza. One of them was continually rebuilt, with three stone-built cells crammed with human bones under one end of the structure. One contained a pile of over 40 human skulls. This "House of the Dead" also yielded a flat stone slab bearing traces of animal and human blood, as if some of the dead were sacrificial victims. Were the dead part of ancestor rituals, or were they war captives sacrificed after their capture? Our knowledge of religious beliefs at this early time is so incomplete that the question is still unanswerable. The remains of at least 400 people lay in the cells. Another of the public buildings was virtually square, with a floor made of small stones pressed into plaster and tall stone monoliths set into the floor.

Göbekli Tepe lies on the summit of a hill with a fine view over the surrounding landscape. In about 9600 B.C., at least four circular structures were cut partially into the limestone bedrock, so they were semisubterranean, almost crypt-like. Two huge stone pillars stood in the center of each crypt, with as many as eight other ones around the edges of each (see Figure 11.12a). Rectangular, with flat cross-sections, they were up to 2.4 meters (8 feet) high and weighed as much as 7 tons. Stone-cut benches lay between the pillars. The pillars bore carvings of game animals like wild boar, gazelle, and aurochs, as well as snakes and birds, but no domesticated animals or humans (see Figure 11.12b). One pillar bore a human arm, as if the columns were partially anthropomorphic. The pillars came from a quarry 90 meters (300 feet) away, where at least one still in place would have been 6 meters (20 feet) long and weighed 50 tons.

Göbekli Tepe is contemporary with early farming cultures to the south; however, its builders may have been hunter-gatherers rather than farmers, for there are no signs of any houses nearby, nor of any permanent settlement. Instead, Göbekli Tepe appears to have been a ritual center, visited from communities some distance away, perhaps a place where people reinforced beliefs and kin or other social ties.

What are we to make of these extraordinary sites, which apparently straddle the changeover from hunting and gathering to food production? They hint that elaborate rituals and more complex social organization predated agriculture in this region. Some experts argue that the religious beliefs behind these early carvings predated farming and may even have led to its adoption. How so? The elaborate construction and ritual activities at these sites would have required dozens, if not hundreds, of people. Feeding them would have required large quantities of wild grain, some of which would have fallen on the ground, germinated, and been gathered again—a form of domestication. In time, some of this high-quality Karacadag grain would have been carried back home and eventually been traded, like obsidian and seashells, to communities many kilometers away, perhaps even as far as Jericho. This hypothesis offers a speculative alternative to the common view that drought was a major contributor to the changeover to farming. The unresolved debate continues. But whatever the spur to early food production in this region, we can be sure that it resulted in major adjustments not only to society, but also to its complex relationship to the cosmos and the environment.

(a)

(b)

Figure 11.12 Ritual center at Göbekli Tepe, Türkiye: (a) In this view of the largest subterranean building under excavation can be seen the tops of two central T-shaped monoliths and other monoliths embedded in the dry stone wall at the edge of the building, where a bench emerges from the excavation. (b) A T-shaped monolith from the site bears a low-relief sculpture.

Source: National Geographic Image Collection/Alamy.

To add to the intrigue, another site with a ceremonial structure that includes stone pillars has recently been found at Boncuklu Tarla, some 300 kilometers (186 miles) east of Göbekli Tepe.

Çayönü Tepesi, Türkiye Early farming village with a shrine containing numerous human burials, 8600 to 7000 B.C.

Göbekli Tepe, Türkiye Hilltop shrine of circular structures, dating to about 9600 B.C.

Agriculture and animal domestication developed rapidly throughout Türkiye after 10,000 B.C. and spread from there into Greece, the Balkans, and temperate Europe. Between 9500 and 6000 B.C., long-distance exchange, especially of obsidian for ornaments and toolmaking, became a major factor in daily life. From Türkiye's Lake Van it traveled to the Levant and as far afield as the Persian Gulf. A few settlements like Çatalhöyük prospered by controlling the trade. In about 7000 B.C., Çatalhöyük covered 13 hectares (32 acres), where a settlement of numerous small mud-brick houses backed on to one another, the outside walls serving as a convenient defense wall. But the large village with its house shrines never became a full-fledged city. There were no powerful leaders who monopolized trade and production. Rather, it was a community of individual households and families that lacked the elaborate, centralized organization of a city (see Figure 11.13).

Figure 11.13 Artist's reconstruction of the town of Çatalhöyük, Türkiye, c. 6000 B.C. The houses were accessible through their roofs.

Source: De Agostini Picture Library/Getty Images.

European Farmers

At the time when Çatalhöyük was a bustling village, farming was already well established on the Aegean Islands of Greece and in parts of southeastern Europe. Since the end of the Ice Age, Europe had been the home of numerous scattered forager groups who lived off forest game, plant foods, and shellfish, fin fish, and mollusks. As in Asia, these populations were preadapted to cultivation and animal domestication, especially in areas where short-term population shifts and local environmental change may have required new subsistence strategies.

Domesticated animals and grains were probably introduced into southeastern Europe from Asia through local exchange and barter. DNA from ancient skeletons shows that the first farmers in Europe were closely related to populations from Anatolia and the Levant, where farming began. The early migrants intermingled with local hunter-gatherers as they moved north and west, blending genes and traditions over generations. The spread of farming was not a simple migration, but a complex process of population movement and integration.

The plants were cereals like emmer and bread wheat, demanding crops that extracted large quantities of nutrients from the soil. The farmers learnt how to carefully treat their land, rotating cereals with nitrogen-fixing legumes and revitalizing their fields with animal manure. Thus was born the European farming system that carefully integrated cultivation and animal rearing into a close-knit subsistence strategy based on individual households supplying their own food needs. Temperate Europe has year-round rainfall and marked contrasts between summer and winter seasons. With plentiful wood and cooler temperatures, timber and thatch replaced the mud-brick architecture of southwestern Asia.

Bandkeramik complex Cultural label describing the first farmers of central and northwestern Europe of about 6000 B.C.; distinguished on the basis of line-decorated pottery.

This expansion of Anatolian farming society into central and western Europe coincided with a cycle of higher rainfall and warmer winters around 5500 B.C. Within a thousand years, farming based on cattle herding combined with spring-sown crops developed over an enormous area of continental Europe. As farming groups spread across lighter soils, clearing forest for fields and grazing their animals in once-forested lands, many indigenous forager bands adopted the new economies. The best-known early European farming culture is named the **Bandkeramik complex** after its distinctive, line-decorated pottery. It first appeared in the middle Danube valley in about 5300 B.C. and then spread rapidly along sheltered river valleys far west to southern Holland and east into parts of Ukraine. Bandkeramik (Danubian) communities were well spaced, each with territories of some 200 hectares (500 acres). The people lived in long, rectangular timber-and-thatch houses measuring 5.5 to 14 meters (18–46 feet) long, presumably sheltering families, their grain, and their animals (see Figure 11.14). Between 40 and 60 people lived in Bandkeramik villages.

megaliths (from the Greek for "large stone") Stone-built graves, widespread during early farming times in western Europe, generally in the fifth millennium B.C.

As the centuries passed, the population rose rapidly, and the gaps between individual settlements filled in. In time, village territories became more circumscribed, their settlements protected by earthen enclosures. This was a time when communal tombs came

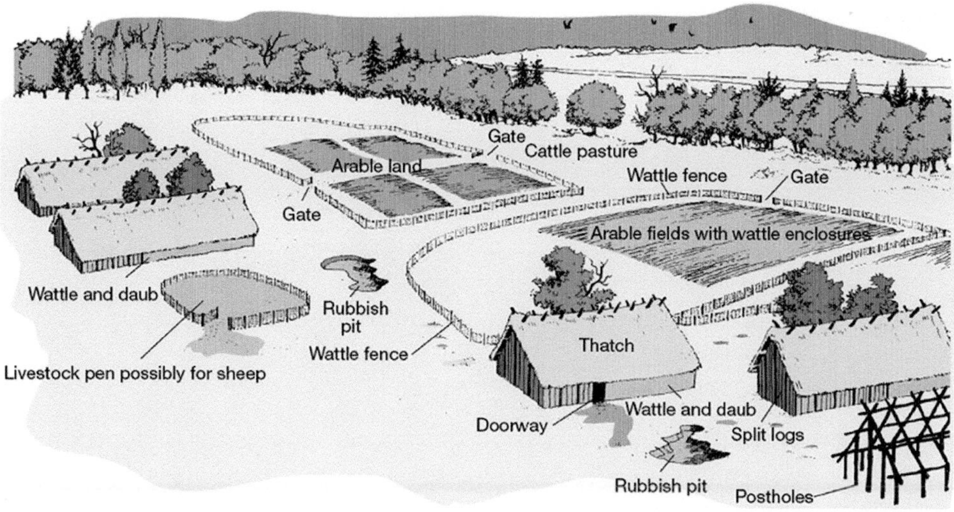

Figure 11.14 Reconstruction of a European Bandkeramik settlement around 5000 B.C. Source: Brian Fagan collection.

into fashion, among them the celebrated **megaliths** (Greek for "big stone") of western Europe. These were sepulchers fashioned from large boulders and buried under earthen mounds (see Figure 11.15). Such corporate burial places may have been locations where revered kin leaders were buried; people who had genealogical ties with the ancestors were of paramount importance to a group of farming communities with strong attachments to their fertile lands (see Box 11.5). Judging from modern analogies, the ancestors were seen as the guardians of the land, the links between the living and the forces of the spiritual world that control human destiny.

Easton Down, England A long, communal burial mound dating to c. 3200 B.C.

Early Agriculture in South and East Asia

Other major centers of plant domestication developed in southern and eastern Asia, where food production began almost as early as it did in eastern Mediterranean lands.

The Indus Valley

Mehrgarh, Pakistan Farming village and trading center west of the Indus River valley, dating to c. 6000 B.C.

By 6250 B.C., village farmers at **Mehrgarh**, west of the Indus River valley in what is now northwestern Pakistan, were cultivating western Asiatic wheat and herding goats, cattle and water buffalo. Genetic evidence confirms that these early farmers adapted crops and animals from the west but also developed key domesticated species locally. The presence of overland trade routes connected the Indus region to Mesopotamia, laying the foundations for the rise of the Indus Valley Civilization centuries later.

Figure 11.15 West Kennet long barrow, Wiltshire, England: A megalithic tomb buried under an earthen mound, the side chambers filled with burials. West Kennet was part of the Avebury sacred landscape.

Source: Skyscan Photolibrary/Alamy.

Box 11.5 Site
Easton Down and the Avebury Sacred Landscape, England

The great earthworks and megalithic monuments of western Europe did not stand alone. For example, the famous sacred circles at Avebury and Stonehenge in southern England (see Figures 3.1 on p. 72 and 3.9 on p. 85) lay at the center of vast, long-vanished sacred landscapes, which were marked by burial mounds, enclosures, charnel houses, and other sites for commemorating the ancestors.

Generations of archaeologists have excavated Avebury, but only recently have they paid close attention to its now-invisible landscape, very different from the rolling farmland of today. Obtaining evidence of ancient landscapes requires careful excavation and sample collection, most often of the original land surfaces under burial mounds and earthworks. When archaeologist Alisdair Whittle excavated some test trenches into a long burial mound at **Easton Down** in southern England, he exposed the original land surface and also the core of stacked turfs, chalk, and topsoil under the mound, which gave him an unusual opportunity to obtain a portrait of the local vegetation in about 3200 B.C.

First, Whittle turned to pollen analysis. Small amounts of pollen grains from the land surface were predominantly from grasses, showing that no woodland grew close to the tumulus when it was built. A well-sealed section of the premound soil yielded 11 mollusk samples, which chronicled a dramatic change from woodland to open grassland forms over a short period of time. Whittle located an ancient tree hollow under the mound, which, hardly surprisingly, contained woodland mollusks. A sudden increase in open-country mollusks followed, a change so rapid that human clearance of the land seems the only logical explanation. Interestingly, soil scientists found signs of lateral movement of the soil below the mound, which can have resulted only from cultivation before the mound was built.

Excavations such as Easton Down can only give us snapshots of the complex mosaic of cleared and uncleared land that characterizes any agricultural landscape. For example, mollusks and soil samples under nearby Avebury itself tell us that the great temple of 2550 B.C. rose on long-established but little-grazed natural grassland close to a forest that had regenerated after being cleared for farming.

This kind of environmental archaeology is now so precise that we can fix the exact seasons when monuments were built or buildings erected. For example, soil samples from carefully cut sod laid under the original ground surface of 40-meter (130-foot) Silbury Hill—built in about 2200 B.C., also close to Easton Down—show that the builders started work in the late summer, most likely after the harvest when people had time for construction work. We know this because the well-preserved sods contain ants and anthills. The ants were beginning to grow wings and fly away from their anthills, as they do in late summer.

As environmental and landscape studies continue, we will learn a surprising amount about the setting, and perhaps the meaning, of major religious sites like Avebury and Stonehenge.

Rice Cultivation in Southern China

Rice has long been the staple crop in the vast regions of southern and southeastern Asia and southern China. Today, it sustains over 3.5 billion people and provides approximately 20 percent of the total calories consumed by humanity. Genetic studies suggest that *Oryza sativa*—the most commonly cultivated rice species—was likely first domesticated in the Yangtze River Valley in China. Additionally, *Oryza glaberrima*, a different species, was independently domesticated in West Africa. While recent archaeobotanical findings and genetic sequencing have helped to clarify the origins of rice, the full story remains complex and subject to ongoing research.

Rice was one of the earliest plants to be domesticated in the northern parts of Southeast Asia and southern China. Botanists believe that the rices and Asian millets ancestral to the present domesticated species radiated from perennial ancestors around the eastern borders of the Himalayas at the end of the Ice Age. It is thought that the initial cultivation of wild rice likely took place in alluvial swamp areas, where there was plenty of water to stimulate cereal growth. The first form to be domesticated may have flourished in shallow water, where seasonal flooding dispersed the seed on the border zone between permanently dry and permanently inundated lands. This cultivation may have occurred under conditions in which seasonal flooding made field preparation a far from burdensome task. Such conditions have been found on the Ganges plain in India and in the mangrove swamps of Southeast Asia and southern China.

Perhaps, the first efforts to cultivate rice resulted from deliberate efforts to expand seasonally inundated habitats by constructing encircling dams to trap runoff. The dams could then be breached, flooding dry land that could be used for rice planting, thereby creating additional stands of wild rice. From there, it was a short step to deliberate sowing and harvesting in wet fields (paddies). Most likely, a sedentary lifeway based on the gathering of wild rice developed in low-lying, seasonally flooded areas at the beginning of the Holocene. Systematic cultivation resulted from a response to population growth, climatic change, or some other stress.

Diaotonghuan, China Early rice-farming settlement in the Yangtse River valley dating to between 8000 and 6000 B.C.

Xianrendong, China Early rice-farming site, c. 8000 to 7550 B.C.

During the early Holocene, warmer conditions may have allowed wild rice to colonize the lakes and marshes of the middle and lower Yangtse valley of southern China, when hunter-gatherer societies throughout China were exploiting a broad spectrum of animal and plant resources. The **Diaotonghuan** and **Xianrendong** caves in the lower Yangtse valley document the first appearance of rice cultivation between 8000 and 6000 B.C., during warmer, more humid conditions after a cold period some 10,000 years ago, when wild rice would have retreated southward to warmer environments.

Pengtoushan, China Farming settlement in the middle Yangtse River valley dating to between 6500 and 5800 B.C.

Bashidang, China Farming village with a defensive ditch in the Yangtse River valley dating to c. 7000 B.C.

With rice farming came much larger, permanent settlements. The **Pengtoushan** site, in the middle Yangtse valley, dates to between 6500 and 5800 B.C. and provides definite evidence of rice farming. This large settlement, with substantial dwellings and 19 graves, was a rice-farming village, occupied continuously for seven centuries when agriculture was spreading rapidly in southern China. The nearby and contemporary **Bashidang** site had a defensive ditch, and people lived in houses raised on piles and ate a wide range of plant foods. Both settlements were part of an agricultural culture that may have begun as early as 7000 B.C. and flourished for as long as 1,500 years. From southern China, rice farming appears to have spread into India and Southeast Asia.

By 3000 B.C., much more sophisticated agricultural societies were flourishing on the Yangtse River and farther afield. The archaeology of these traditions is known primarily from cemetery excavations that show slow changes in grave goods. The earliest graves indicate few social differentiations, but later sepulchers show not only a much wider variety of artifacts—pottery, bone and stone tools, jade objects, and other ornaments—but also an increase in the number of elaborately adorned burials. China specialist Richard Pearson, who has analyzed several cemeteries, argues that they demonstrate an increase in the concentration of wealth, a trend toward ranked societies, and a shift in the relative importance of males at the expense of females. The last trend may be associated with the development of more intensive agriculture, an activity in which males are valued for their major roles in cultivation.

The First Farmers in Northern China

A second great center of early Chinese agriculture lies nearly 650 kilometers (400 miles) north of the Yangtse, where the Huang He flows out of mountainous terrain into the low-lying plains of northern China. Northern Chinese agriculture was based on millet, whereas the southern staple was rice. The first northern agricultural communities were sited in the central regions of the Huang He valley. The area is a small basin, forming a border between the wooded western highlands and the swampy lowlands to the east. As in the south, the early Holocene saw a warming trend, followed by a cooler interval and then a more prolonged period of climatic amelioration. It was during the colder period, dating to after 6500 B.C., that the first well-documented sedentary farming villages appeared in the valley. However, farming may have started several thousand years earlier.

Yangshao culture, China Widespread farming culture in the Huang He valley of northern China after 5000 B.C.

The fine, soft-textured earth of the valley was both homogeneous and porous and could be tilled with simple digging sticks. Because of the concentrated summer rainfall, cereal crops, the key to agriculture in this region, could be grown successfully. The indigenous plants available for domestication included the wild ancestors of foxtail millet, broomcorn millet, sorghum, hemp, and mulberry. Many villages lay near small streams on lower river terraces, along foothills and plains. Ancient Chinese farmers developed their own cultivation techniques, which persisted for thousands of years. By far the best known of China's early farming societies is the **Yangshao culture**, which flourished over much of the Huang He basin—an area as large as the early centers of agriculture in Egypt or Mesopotamia—from before 4800 B.C. to about 3200 B.C.

Each Yangshao village was a self-contained community, usually built on a terrace overlooking a fertile river valley to avoid flooding or to allow maximal use of floodplain soils (see Figure 11.16). Using hoes and digging sticks, the farmers cultivated foxtail millet as a staple, mainly in riverside gardens that were flooded every spring. By 3000 B.C., Yangshao was a characteristic, and thoroughly Chinese, culture, with its own naturalistic art style. Expert potters made cooking pots for steaming food, the technique that forms the basis of much Chinese cuisine to this day. The Chinese language may have its roots in Yangshao as well.

Many regional variations of peasant farming culture developed throughout China. Agriculture developed over wide areas at about the same time, with people adapting their crops and farming techniques to local conditions. In time, the success of the new economies led to local population increases, more complex cultures, the concentration of wealth in privileged hands, and ultimately, the rise of early Chinese states.

Figure 11.16 Yangshao houses, a site museum display.
Source: JTB Media Creation, Inc./Alamy.

Navigators and Chiefs in the Pacific (2000 B.C. to Modern Times)

Food production in Asia had momentous consequences for the settlement of the offshore Pacific islands. By the end of the Ice Age some 15,000 years ago, *Homo sapiens* had reached nearly every part of the world, leaving only two regions remaining uncolonized: Antarctica, not even visited until the eighteenth century A.D., and the remote islands of Melanesia and Polynesia in the Pacific (see Figure 11.17).

> **Lapita cultural complex** A series of maritime societies that flourished and traded over an enormous area of the western Pacific, 1600 to 1000 B.C. and later.

In Chapter 10, we saw how late Ice Age foragers voyaged across open straits to colonize Sahul and the Solomon Islands. Small groups of them had settled on the islands close to New Guinea, in the Bismarck Archipelago of the southwestern Pacific, by at least 32,000 years ago. Here colonization paused for many thousands of years. The successful settlement of islands even farther offshore depended on the development of large oceangoing sailing craft and the ability to navigate far out of sight of land. It also hinged on the successful cultivation of root crops like taro and yam and also on small, portable animals like chickens and pigs that could be penned and transported in canoes. These conditions were

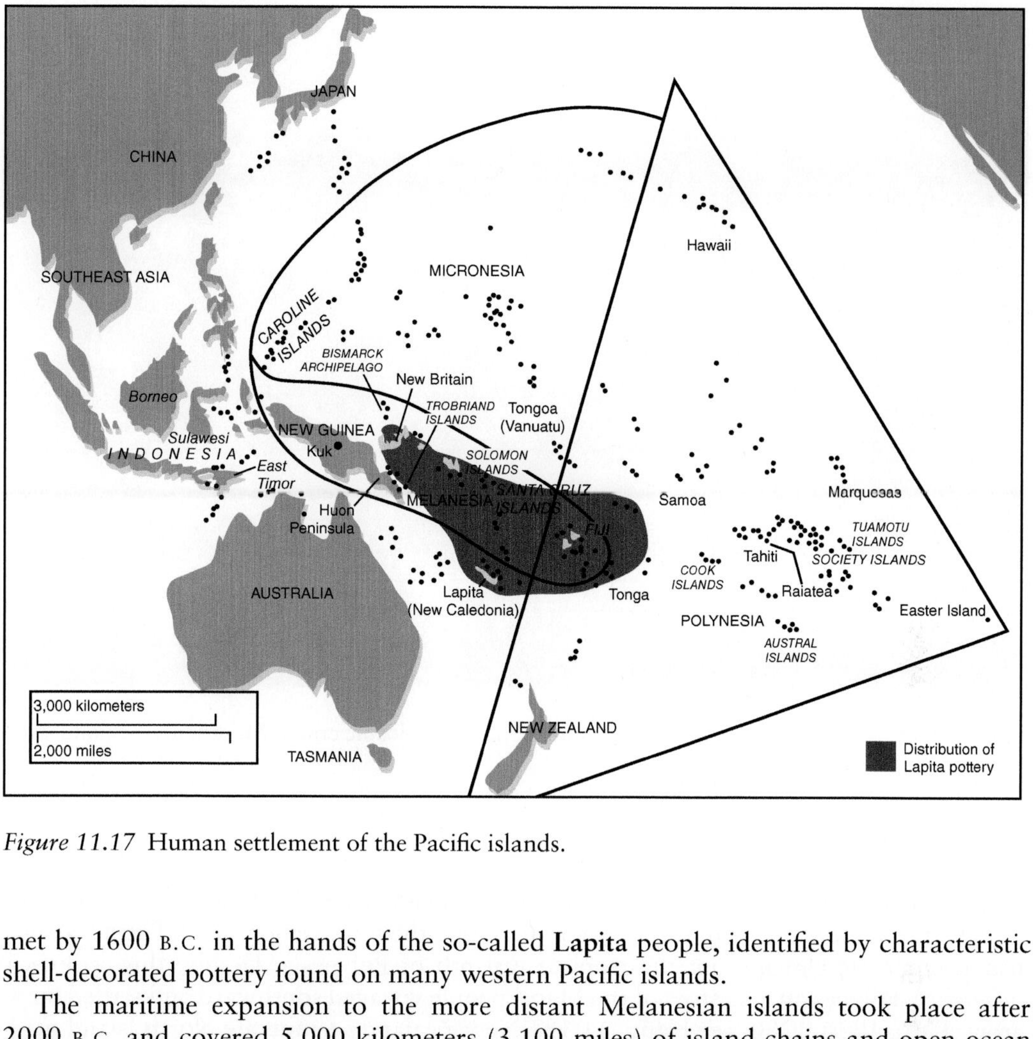

Figure 11.17 Human settlement of the Pacific islands.

met by 1600 B.C. in the hands of the so-called **Lapita** people, identified by characteristic shell-decorated pottery found on many western Pacific islands.

The maritime expansion to the more distant Melanesian islands took place after 2000 B.C. and covered 5,000 kilometers (3,100 miles) of island chains and open ocean during a period of six centuries. The voyages took place in oceangoing double-hulled canoes capable of carrying heavy loads (see Figure 7.3 on p. 219).

The rapid expansion to more remote islands occurred among people who lived in an island environment where short inter-island passages were an integral part of daily life. But the journeys to off-lying islands like Fiji and Tonga involved much longer passages, some as long as about 1,000 kilometers (600 miles). Here, one-way journeys may have been rare, and trade was at best sporadic. Navigation out of sight of land required expert skills. Canoe navigators became a respected and close-knit group who passed their knowledge down from generation to generation by word of mouth. Young apprentices acquired their skills over many years of sailing under expert supervision. They learned the angles of rising and setting stars, the trends of ocean swells, and the telltale phenomena that indicate the general direction and distance of islands.

From Melanesia, canoes voyaged from island to island through western Polynesia, taking the plants and domesticated animals of their homelands with them. Melanesians voyaged to Micronesia and Polynesia about 1,000 years ago. After a lengthy period of adaptation in western Polynesia, small groups settled the more remote islands within a remarkably short time. Canoes reached the Society Islands and Tahiti by A.D. 1035, the

Figure 11.18 Maori *pa*, a fortified village, built around a volcanic crater, Mt. Eden, Auckland, New Zealand.

Source: David Wall/Alamy Stock Photo.

Marquesas by 1200. The first canoes arrived in Hawaii around 1219 and at Easter Island by A.D. 1200. New Zealand, the largest and among the most remote of all Pacific islands, has a temperate climate, not the tropical warmth of Polynesia. Despite this ecological difference, Polynesian ancestors of the Maori people voyaged southward and settled there, around A.D. 1230–1280 (see Figure 11.18). New Zealand's temperate North Island made the cultivation of yams and other tropical island crops difficult, so the early settlers relied heavily on hunting, fishing, and foraging.

Technologically, Micronesia and Polynesia had no metals and relied heavily on stone axes and an elaborate array of bone and shellfish hooks. The crops people planted varied from island to island, but breadfruit, taro, coconut, yams, and bananas were the staples. By combining fish with simple agriculture, the islanders were able to accumulate significant food surpluses that were the basis of powerful chiefdoms. In Polynesia, as elsewhere in the world, agricultural surpluses generated on the larger islands were used as a form of wealth. This wealth, in turn, concentrated political power in the hands of a relatively small number of people.

When European explorers visited Tahiti in the mid-eighteenth century, they chanced on a center of a vigorous eastern Polynesian society. Here and elsewhere, powerful hierarchies of warlike chiefs and nobles ruled the islands, descendants of the canoe crews who had first settled the archipelago. The chiefs acquired prestige by controlling and redistributing wealth and food supplies, just as they did in Europe, North America, and elsewhere in the ancient world. Their formidable religious and social powers led, inevitably, to intense competition, to warfare, and to ever more ambitious agricultural projects.

Summary

- Many late Ice Age and early Holocene hunter-gatherer societies were preadapted to food production, as they were already exploiting some food resources intensively and living more sedentary lifeways.
- Most of these societies were in regions where food resources were diverse and seasonally predictable.
- In contrast to early theories that food production was a revolutionary development, modern hypotheses invoke social relations, population growth, ecological factors, and environmental changes as multiple causes of food production.
- Food production resulted in more sedentary human settlement, more substantial housing, elaborate storage technologies, and special implements for agricultural tasks.
- All these technological developments led to greater interdependence and to more long-distance exchange of raw materials, as well as increasing human social complexity.
- Southwestern Asia was cool and dry immediately after the Ice Age, with dry steppe over much of the interior. Farming began at Abu Hureyra on the Euphrates River in about 10,000 B.C. Sheep and goats replaced gazelle-hunting at the same site and other settlements after 9000 B.C.
- Farmers flourished in Egypt by at least 6000 B.C. Farming communities linked by long-distance exchange routes inhabited Anatolia (Türkiye) by at least 8500 B.C.
- Agriculture and animal husbandry developed in southeastern Europe because of a local shift to the more intensive exploitation of cereals and wild sheep, and because of a "drift" across from southwestern Asia of domestic animals and cereals. During the sixth millennium B.C., food production spread widely throughout Europe.
- Agriculture spread from the west into Pakistan's Indus valley by at least 6000 B.C.
- In southern China, rice may have been cultivated as early as 9500 B.C. and well established by 6500 B.C. The staple in the Huang He valley of northern China was millet, cultivated at least as early as 6500 B.C. and perhaps much earlier.
- The development of agriculture on the Asian mainland, combined with the invention of the double-hulled canoe, enabled the settlement of the offshore Pacific islands after 2000 B.C.

Key Terms and Sites

food production
Holocene
tomol
Modoc
agricultural revolution
accelerator mass spectrometry (AMS) radiocarbon dating
swidden agriculture
rachis
Jericho
Ganj Dareh
Jarmo
Merimda Beni Salama
Çayönü Tepesi
Göbekli Tepe
Bandkeramik complex
megaliths

Easton Down
Mehrgarh
Diaotonghuan
Xianrendong
Pengtoushan
Bashidang
Yangshao culture
Lapita cultural complex

Critical-Thinking Questions

1. Discuss the consequences of food production for human life. What, in your judgment, were the most important changes in human society that resulted?
2. Why do you think that accelerator mass spectrometry (AMS) radiocarbon dating is important to the study of early agriculture? Use specific examples of ways in which AMS refines our knowledge.
3. Why do you think the Pacific offshore islands were settled so late in prehistory?

Further Reading

G. Barker, *The Agricultural Revolution in Prehistory* (Oxford: Oxford University Press, 2006) is an authoritative, global synthesis with excellent theoretical insights. K. Flannery's, *Guilá Naquitz* (Orlando, FL: Academic Press, 1986), though written many years ago, is an exemplary monograph on this Central American rock shelter, which is essential reading, if for nothing else, for its hypothetical dialogues, which contain a multitude of wisdoms about archaeology and archaeologists. J. C. Scott's, *Against the Grain: A Deep History of the Earliest States* (New Haven, CT: Yale University Press, 2017), explores the origins of the first states, the staggering price we paid for civilization, and the centrality of grain to the story. P. Kirch, *On the Road of the Winds: An Archaeological History of the Pacific Islands before European Contact* (Berkeley: University of California Press, 2002) summarizes the first colonization of the Pacific Islands.

12 The First Civilizations

Chapter Outline

Shadow of a desert caravan, Sahara Desert.
Source: luisa puccini/Alamy Stock Photo.

DOI: 10.4324/9781003592754-17

Paul-Émile Botta was appointed the French consul in Mosul in northern Iraq in 1840, with one official objective: to dig the nearby mounds of biblical Nineveh. Botta had no archaeological qualifications whatsoever, except that he was an experienced traveler who spoke several western Asian languages. At first, he dug fruitlessly into Nineveh, finding nothing but inscribed bricks. Then, one of his workers told him of similar bricks that formed the chimney of his house at a village named Khorsabad, 23 kilometers (14 miles) away. To get rid of the man, he sent two of his laborers to investigate. A week later, they returned with stories of richly carved walls adorned with strange animals. Botta leapt on his horse and rode to Khorsabad, where he gasped at curious bas-reliefs of winged animals, wild beasts, and bearded men in long gowns. He moved his excavations to Khorsabad. Within a few weeks, he had uncovered room after room of sculpted limestone slabs, the wall decorations of a magnificent, exotic royal palace. "I believe myself to be the first who discovered sculptures which with some reason can be referred to the period when Nineveh was flourishing," he wrote excitedly of the palace (Fagan 2007, 102).

We know now that Botta had uncovered not Nineveh but Assyrian King Sargon's palace, constructed at great expense in the eighth century B.C. Even so, Botta's remarkable discoveries ushered in a classical era of nineteenth-century archaeology, which revealed to an astonished world not only the Assyrians, but also the Sumerians, the Maya, the Mycenaeans, and other long-forgotten civilizations (see Chapter 1).

state-organized societies Large-scale societies with strongly centralized governments and marked social stratification; also known as *preindustrial civilizations*.

Today, there are no more lost civilizations (or **state-organized societies**) to be unearthed, but archaeologists are still striving to understand the origins and workings of the world's earliest states. This chapter defines a state-organized society and describes the world's earliest civilizations in Egypt and Mesopotamia, which appeared after 3100 B.C. (see Figure 12.1).

What Is a State-Organized Society?

civilization Any complex, urbanized society organized as a state.

state Centralized political organization with institutionalized authority, usually governing a stratified population within a defined territory.

Everyone who has studied the prehistory of human society agrees that the emergence of **civilization** in different parts of the world was a major event in human adaptation. The word *civilization* has a ready, everyday meaning. It implies "civility," a measure of decency in the behavior of the individual in a civilization. Such definitions inevitably reflect ethno-centrism or value judgments because what is "civilized" behavior in one civilization might be antisocial or baffling in another. These simplistic understandings are of no use to students of early civilizations seeking basic definitions and cultural processes.

preindustrial civilizations State-level societies organized without the use of fossil fuels.

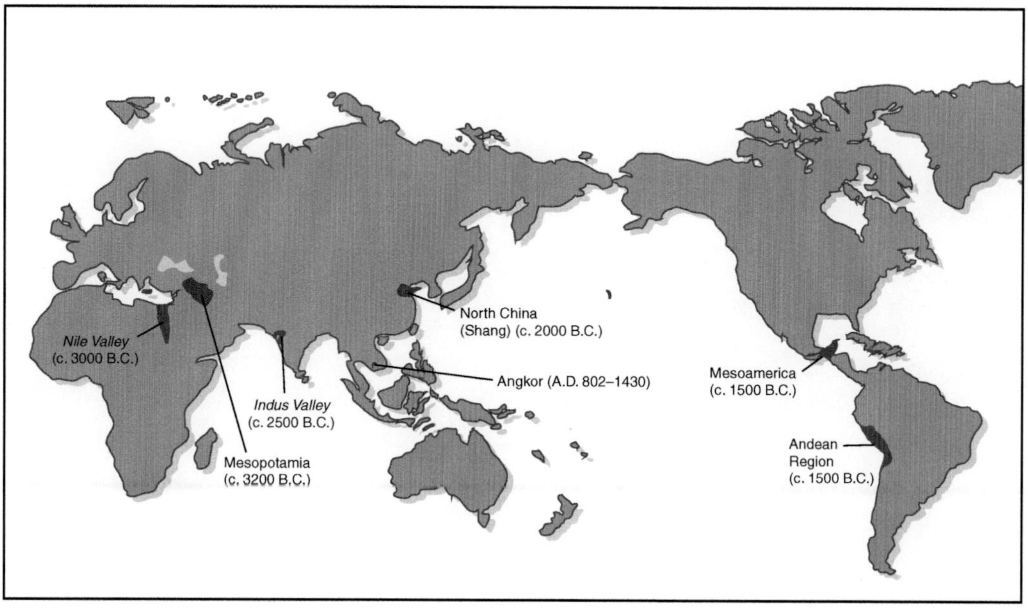

Figure 12.1 Areas of early state formation.

Often, archaeologists use the term *civilization* as shorthand for urbanized, state-level societies. Those described in these pages are sometimes called **preindustrial civilizations** because they relied on manual labor rather than on fossil fuels such as coal. There are many variations among the preindustrial civilizations, but the following features are characteristic of them all:

- Societies based on cities, with large, complex social organizations. The preindustrial civilization was invariably based on a larger territory, such as the Nile valley, as opposed to smaller areas owned by individual kin groups.
- Economies based on the centralized accumulation of capital and social status through tribute and taxation. For instance, Sumerian kings in Mesopotamia monopolized trading activity in the name of the state. This type of economy allowed the support of hundreds, often thousands, of non-food producers such as smiths and priests. Long-distance trade and the division of labor, as well as craft specialization, were often characteristic of early civilizations.
- Advances toward formal recordkeeping, science, mathematics, and some form of written script. This took many forms, from Egyptian hieroglyphs to the knotted strings used by the Inca of the Andes.
- Impressive public buildings and monumental architecture, such as Egyptian or Khmer temples and Maya ceremonial centers (see Figure 12.2).
- Some form of all-embracing state religion in which the ruler played a leading role. For example, the Egyptian pharaoh was considered a living god on Earth.

Cities

Early civilizations and cities go together. Today, the city is the primary human settlement type throughout the world, and it has become so since the Industrial Revolution altered the economic face of the globe. The earliest cities assumed many forms, from the compact, walled settlement of Mesopotamia to the Mesoamerican ceremonial center, with a core population

Figure 12.2 The Bayon Temple at Angkor Thom, Cambodia: an example of conspicuous public architecture.

Source: Jie Xu/Thinkstock.

in its precincts and a scattered rural population in villages arranged over the surrounding landscape. The palaces of the Minoans and Mycenaeans of Crete and mainland Greece functioned as secular economic and trading centers for scattered village populations nearby.

Population can define a city, which is generally larger and denser than a town or village. A general rule of thumb is a lower limit of 5,000 people for a city. However, numbers are not a sufficient definition. Economic and organizational complexity, as well as population size and density, distinguish the city from other settlement types. Cities were central places, providing services for the villages in the surrounding area and at the same time depending on those villages for food. Most cities had a marketplace where agricultural produce could be exchanged (see Figure 12.3). They boasted of monumental architecture such as temples or palaces and sometimes city walls; they were centers of government with centralized institutions such as a bureaucracy, priesthood, and royal family.

Here we must recognize an overlap between the concept of the city and the concept of the state. States also have centralized institutions. It may be possible to have states without cities, but it is hard to envisage a city that is not embedded within a state. The latter is a political unit governed by a central authority whose power crosscuts bonds of village kinship. Kin groups do not disappear, of course, but their power is reduced, and a new axis of control based on allegiance to a ruling elite emerges.

Theories of the Origins of States

The Victorians, like the Greeks and Romans before them, assumed that civilization had originated along the Nile, in the "Land of the Pharaohs." Eventually, early theorizing used a broader canvas, embracing both Egypt and southwestern Asia.

Figure 12.3 Mexican artist Diego Rivera's painting of the Aztec market at Tenochtitlán in the Valley of Mexico, said to have been visited by as many as 20,000 people a day.

Source: Robert Fried/Alamy © 2015 Banco de Mexico Diego Rivera Frida Kahlo Museums Trust, Mexico, D.F./DACS.

urban revolution Vere Gordon Childe's concept, based on the assumption that metallurgy, specialists, and food surpluses caused a revolution in human life and urban civilization.

Vere Gordon Childe (1892–1957), of "agricultural revolution" fame, wrote of a later **urban revolution,** which saw the development of metallurgy and the appearance of a new social class of full-time artisans and specialists who lived in much larger settlements: cities. However, the artisans' products had to be distributed and raw materials had to be obtained, often over long distances. Both needs reduced the self-sufficiency of peasant communities, Childe argued.

Agricultural techniques became more sophisticated as a higher yield of food per capita was needed to support a growing nonagricultural population. Scholars like Karl Wittvogel hypothesized that irrigation increased productivity, leading to centralization of food supplies, production, and distribution. Taxation and tribute led to the accumulation of capital, creating what he called "hydraulic civilizations," but more recent research has shown this view to be too simplistic. Ultimately, said Childe, a new class-stratified society came into being, based on economic classes rather than traditional ties of kin. Writing was essential for keeping records and for developing exact and predictive sciences. Transportation by land and water was part of the new order (see Figure 12.4). A unifying religious force dominated urban life as priest-kings and despots rose to power and monumental architecture testified to their activities.

Figure 12.4 Pharaoh Khufu's funerary boat, originally disassembled and buried near his pyramid at Giza and now reconstructed in a special gallery. Watercraft of all kinds were crucial to Egyptian civilization and also served as symbolic craft for transporting the king to eternity.

Source: Gemma Ivern/Thinkstock.

Childe considered technology and the development of craft specialization in the hands of full-time artisans to be a cornerstone of the urban revolution. With much more data to work with, modern scholars now know that three elements of Childe's urban revolution were of great importance in the development of all the world's early civilizations: (1) large food surpluses, (2) diversified farming economies, and (3) irrigation agriculture.

Most archaeologists agree that urban life and preindustrial civilization came into existence gradually, during a period of major social and economic change. Recent theories of the rise of states invoke multiple and often intricate causes and are frequently based on ecology and systems models (see Chapter 7). Archaeologists like Kent Flannery, who works in Mesoamerica, see the state as a complicated "living" system, the complexity of which could be measured by the internal differentiation and intricacy of its subsystems, such as those for agriculture, technology, or religious beliefs. The way these subsystems were linked and the controls that society imposed on the system were vital.

The management of a state is a far more elaborate and central undertaking than that of a small chiefdom. The most striking difference between states and less complicated societies is the degree of complexity in civilizations' ways of reaching decisions and in their hierarchic organization. Religion and control of information were key elements in the regulation of environmental and economic variables in early civilizations and, indeed, in any human society.

The ecological approach raises interesting questions. How, for example, does one tell which environments would foster state formation? Fertile floodplains like those in

Mesopotamia and Egypt? Coastal river valleys like those in Peru? Highland plateaus like those of Mesoamerica? Or areas where land is in short supply (also coastal Peru)? States have arisen in regions where there are few geographic constraints, like the Maya lowlands of Mesoamerica. What role did rapid population growth play? Economist Ester Boserup argued many years ago that it was the latter rather than food surpluses that was the incentive for more intensified agriculture and more complex societies. There is no question, however, that environmental factors were major players in a very complex process of cultural change and response.

More recently, archaeology has shifted toward a greater concern with individuals and groups and their influence on the course of history. Archaeologically, one can look at power in three domains: economic power, social and ideological power, and political power. Economic productivity, control over sources and distribution of food and wealth, the development and maintenance of the stratified social system and its ideology, and the ability to maintain control by force were the vital ingredients of early states.

Economic power depends on the ability to organize more specialized production and the diverse tasks of food storage and food distribution. In time, stored wealth in food and goods develops into relationships of dependency between those who produce or acquire the wealth and those who control and distribute it. A state comprises elites (the noble class), officials (the managers), and dependents (the commoners). The landowning class and land—whether owned by a temple, the ruler, or a private individual—provided security for the landowner's dependents. All early states developed from foundations where agricultural production became more intensified and diverse. At the same time, early states moved away from purely kin-based organization into centralized structures that cut across or overrode kinship ties.

Nubia The "Land of Kush," which lay upstream of Ancient Egypt in present-day Sudan.

Andean civilizations State-organized societies that developed in Peru and adjacent countries.

Economic power also rested in trade and long-distance exchange networks, which provided access to commodities that were not available locally. Sumer obtained its metal from Anatolia, Iran, and the Persian Gulf. Egypt acquired gold and ivory from **Nubia** (Sudan). Highland **Andean civilizations** imported fish meal from the Pacific coast. The acquisition of exotic commodities or goods on any scale required organization, recordkeeping, and supervision.

Social power means ideological power and comes from the creation or modification of certain symbols of cultural and political commonality. Such common ideology, expressed in public and private ceremonies, art, artifacts, architecture, and literature, served to link individuals and communities with common ties that transcended those of kin (see Figure 12.5). Individuals who created and perpetuated these ideologies were held in high regard and enjoyed considerable prestige, for they were often perceived as liaising with the spiritual world and the deities, and were sometimes even seen as divine themselves. The guardians of ideology were privileged members of society whose spiritual powers gave them special status and allowed them to perpetuate social inequality.

So important was ideology that one can speak of the Mesopotamian and Maya areas not in a political sense, for they were made up of patchworks of city-states, but in

Figure 12.5 Artifacts as ideological statements: A Moche ceramic vessel from coastal Peru, c. A.D. 400, depicts a seated anthropomorphic fox warrior with incised decoration on his chest.

Source: Peter Horree/Alamy.

an ideological one. Many great cities of the past, like Teotihuacán in the Valley of Mexico, were a combination of the spiritual and the secular. They all boasted powerful priesthoods and religious institutions. These owed their wealth to their ability to manage the spiritual affairs of the state and to legitimize rulers as upholders of the cosmic order. The temples and public buildings that they erected formed imposing settings for elaborate public ceremonies that ensured the continuity of human life and the universe.

Political power rested in the ruler's ability to impose authority throughout society by both administrative and military means. Individuals who held positions of authority in either the bureaucracy or the army did not come from the kin system, but were recruited from outside of it. This political power lay in foreign relations and in defense and making war. It also operated at a state-wide level, dealing with the resolution of major disputes among different factions. But a great deal of power lay outside the political realm, in the hands of community and kin leaders who handled many legal matters revolving around such issues as land ownership and family law.

The interplay among these three sources of power led to the development of new, society-wide institutions—supreme rulers and the state. There was no specific moment when civilization came into being, for social evolution did not end with the rise of the state. Preindustrial states functioned in an atmosphere of continual change and constant disputation. Some collapsed; others survived for centuries.

Every early civilization had a pervasive set of religious beliefs and philosophies that reached out to every corner of society. Such ideologies shaped society and ensured the conformity of its members, but to study such intangibles is a formidable task. Ideologies come down to us in distinctive art styles, like those of the Egyptians or the Moche art style of the Andes (see Figure 12.5). Such styles are visual reminders of a state's ideology, reinforcing the power of supreme rulers and their special relationships to the gods and the spiritual world. In societies where only a minority of members are literate—those with power or who have scribes in their employ—art and public architecture (see Figure 12.6) have powerful roles to play in shaping society and reinforcing ideology.

The Maya lived in cities like Copán and Tikal, which were depictions in stone, wood, and stucco of a symbolic landscape of sacred hills, caves, and forests. Here, great lords appeared before the people atop high pyramids in elaborate public ceremonies. Through ritual bloodletting and shamanistic trance, they entered the realm of the otherworld, the world of the deities and ancestors. These sacred rituals validated the world of the Maya and linked noble and commoner, ruler and humble village farmer, in a complex social contract. The leaders were the intermediaries, the people who liaised with the gods to guarantee plentiful crops and ensure the continued existence of human life. The ceremonial centers, with their pyramids, plazas, and temples, were reassuring settings where the dramas of life and death, of planting and harvest were played out against a backdrop of ever-changing seasons (see Figure 12.7). These ceremonies justified social inequality, the great distinctions between the ruler and the ruled.

With ideology comes factionalism. As we have seen, ancient societies were as diverse as modern ones, especially when their rulers traded with neighbors near and far. The state functioned for the benefit of a minority—privileged rulers and nobles to whom all wealth and power flowed. A ruler—almost invariably male—governed his domains by

Figure 12.6 The amphitheater at Hierapolis, Türkiye, a classic example of a public building used as a setting for religious ceremonies and entertainments.

Source: prmustafa/Thinkstock.

Figure 12.7 Palenque, Mexico, an important example of Maya ceremonial architecture.
Source: Marco Regalia/Thinkstock.

deputing governance to relatives and loyal followers who became provincial governors. But inevitably, some individuals were more ambitious than others, rebelling against authority and plotting to gain supreme power. Competing factions within local groups and in different regions triggered further social inequality and changing patterns of leadership, and increased specialization and the development of states. And once civilizations came into being, they would challenge royal successions, even trigger civil war, when a ruler was perceived as weak or indecisive. Competition and emerging factionalism were powerful catalysts in the development of many early states.

In recent years, there has been intensified discussion of what might loosely be called "fragility" in preindustrial civilizations. Current research is focusing on understanding how early cities and states struggled to survive and often did not. All early states had centralized power, at least in theory, but beneath the often spectacular structure of rulers and their officials were intricate strands of resistance to central authority.

Civilizations like those of Egypt and China were ruled by courts that were riven with factional rivalries for power, and over the succession, in eras when rulers could die without warning, often when very young. Many questions arise surrounding the longevity of ancient civilizations. How much control did rulers have over outlying territories in their domains? How efficient were their infrastructures and means of communication? How did they handle revolts and large-scale migrations, also famines? How powerful a ritual hold did self-proclaimed divine kings or individuals with claimed links to the supernatural really have in the long term?

All these, and many other factors, were major players in the world of preindustrial civilizations, where once-powerful states had often come to power, then collapsed abruptly. Even long-lived states like Egypt adjusted constantly to changing circumstances. The Egyptians were fortunate to have fertile soils and relatively reliable water supplies; others, like the Maya of Central America, confronted often less fertile soils and unreliable rainfall. We are slowly moving away from relatively straightforward evolutionary models to highly detailed studies of how preindustrial civilizations really worked, were successful in the long term, or failed. Such research is the challenge for future generations of archaeologists.

It is probably futile to search for a theory of state formation that can be applied to all civilizations. There are some common questions, however, that revolve around the implications of ecological variables in societies that became states: How was ecological opportunity or necessity translated into political change? What were the goals of the political actors who were pursuing their individual goals while states were coming into being? Which ecological variables were obstacles? Which were opportunities? The answers to these questions will come from sophisticated research that combines systems-ecological approaches with careful research into the "archaeology of mind," the elusive intangibles behind the material record of the past.

The Collapse of Civilizations

Many early civilizations are remarkable for their volatility, their sudden rise, and equally rapid collapse. An initial investment by a society in growing complexity is a rational way of trying to solve the needs of the moment. At first, the strategy works. Agricultural production increases through more intensive farming methods; an emerging bureaucracy functions well; expanding trade networks bring wealth to a new elite who use their authority and economic clout to undertake great public works such as pyramids and temples that validate their spiritual authority and divine associations.

As society runs out of viable options to satisfy its needs, it becomes imperative that new organizational and economic answers be found, which may have much lower yields and cost a great deal more. As these stresses develop, a complex society such as that of the Maya is increasingly vulnerable to collapse. There are few reserves to carry society through droughts, famines, floods, or other natural disasters. Eventually, collapse ensues, especially when important segments of society perceive that centralization and social complexity simply do not work anymore and that they are better off on their own. The trend toward decentralization, toward collapse, becomes compelling.

Collapse occurs when increasing stress requires some organizational change. Complete collapse can occur only under circumstances in which there is a power vacuum. In many cases, there may be a powerful neighbor waiting in the wings. In early times, numerous city-states traded and competed with one another within a small area. Sumerian cities, Mycenaean palace-kingdoms in Greece and the Aegean, the Maya in Mesoamerica—all lived in close interdependence. They traded, fought, and engaged in constant diplomacy. Under these circumstances, to collapse is an invitation to be dominated by one's competitors. There is only loss of complexity when every polity in the interacting cluster collapses at the same time.

The collapse of early civilizations may, then, be closely connected to declining returns from social complexity and to the normal political processes of climate change, factionalism, social unrest, succession disputes, and even civil war. With these general points in mind, we will now explore the world's earliest civilizations in Mesopotamia and the Nile valley (see Figure 12.8).

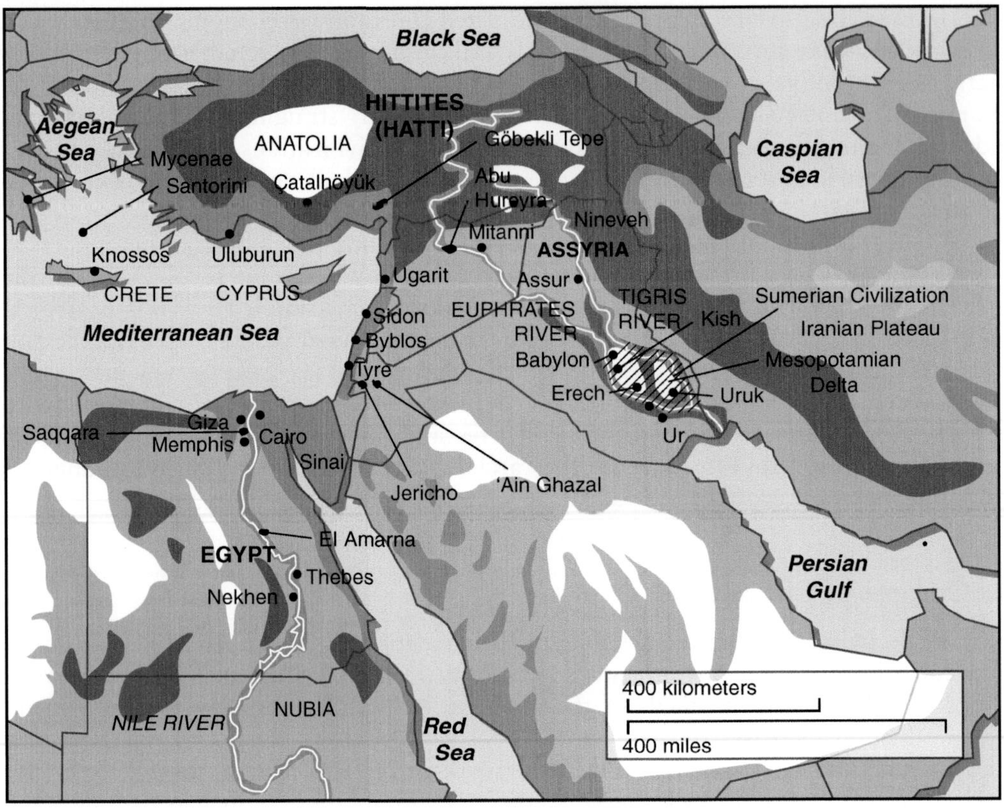

Figure 12.8 Archaeological sites in Egypt and Mesopotamia, with the borders of modern states superimposed.

Early Civilization in Mesopotamia (5500 to 3100 B.C.)

Controversy surrounds the first settlement of the land between the Tigris and Euphrates Rivers. Intensely hot in summer, bitterly cold in winter, the plains were far from a hospitable environment for village farmers. We know that by 5500 B.C., hundreds of small farming villages dotted the rolling plains of northern Mesopotamia upstream, settlements connected by long-distance trade routes that carried obsidian, finely painted pottery, and other goods over hundreds of miles, from Türkiye as far as southern Iraq. By this time, much of the trade, especially in pottery, was concentrated in the hands of a small elite who lived in key centers along water routes. However, we do not know whether the uninhabited plains were settled by village farmers from the north around 6000 B.C., as many scholars believe, or whether much earlier indigenous foragers adopted farming along the shores of the Persian Gulf at this time or even earlier.

Ubaid culture Early farming culture, of about 5000 B.C., in southern Iraq.

The first known farming communities date to around 5800 B.C.: small communities, linked by kin ties, located in clusters along the Euphrates River channels. As early as 5000 B.C., a few farming communities were diverting floodwaters from the Euphrates and Tigris on to their fields, then draining them away to prevent salt buildup in the soil. The largest of these clusters consisted of small rural communities located around a larger town that covered about 11.3 hectares (28 acres) and housed between 2,500 and 4,000 people. Some of these **Ubaid culture** settlements (named after a village near ancient Ur) boasted substantial buildings, alleyways, and courtyards. Others consisted of little more than humble mud-brick and reed huts.

We do not know anything about how the first inhabitants of the Mesopotamian floodplain acquired or developed the skills needed to survive in their harsh environment. Interdependence among members of the community was essential because raw materials suitable for building houses had to be improvised from the plentiful sand, clay, palm trees, and reeds between the rivers. Digging even the smallest canal required at least a little political and social leadership. The annual backbreaking task of clearing silt from clogged river courses and canals could only have been achieved by communal efforts. Distinctive social changes came from the more efficient systems for producing food that were essential in the delta. As food surpluses grew and the specialized agricultural economies of these Ubaid villages became successful, the trend toward sedentary settlement and higher population densities increased.

Eridu, Iraq One of the world's earliest cities, famous for its shrine, c. 4000 B.C. and later.

As Mesopotamian society grew rapidly in complexity, so did the need for social, political, and religious institutions that would provide some form of centralized authority. In time, the small village ceremonial centers grew. **Eridu**, a rapidly growing town, consisted of a mud-brick temple with fairly substantial mud-brick houses around it, often with a rectangular floor plan (see Box 12.1). The craftworkers lived a short distance from the elite, who were clustered around the temple, and still farther away were the dwellings of the farmers who grew the crops that supported everyone. By 4500 B.C., as many as 5,000 people lived in Eridu, while evidence for around 700 farms in the Eridu hinterland have been identified by archaeological surveys and remote sensing data.

The First Cities: Uruk

Uruk, Iraq The world's first city, flourishing from 4500 B.C. for more than 2,000 years.

Uruk began as a modest settlement on the southern Mesopotamian plain, surrounded by small farming villages. Over time, these scattered communities drew closer together, gradually merging into a single, growing town. By the fourth millennium B.C., Uruk had become a true city, sprawling across some 250 hectares (617 acres)—an immense area for its time. Satellite villages extended out at least 10 kilometers (6 miles), each with its own irrigation system and farmlands. All provided grain, fish, or meat for the growing urban population. Within Uruk, narrow alleys wove between clusters of mud-brick houses and shaded courtyards. The city may have been organized into quarters, home to extended families or skilled artisans like potters and sculptors. Rising high above this urban maze stood the ziggurat, a massive stepped pyramid visible for miles across the flat plain. More than a religious monument, the temple complex served as the beating heart of the city—a place of worship, but also a storehouse, a workshop, and the seat of civic authority.

Box 12.1 Discovery
The Temple at Eridu, Iraq

Sumerian legends called Eridu the earliest city of all, the dwelling place of Enki, God of the Abyss, the fountain of human wisdom. "All lands were the sea, then Eridu was made," proclaims a much later Mesopotamian Creation legend. Sumerians considered Enki's word to have created order from the chaos of the primordial waters. Eridu itself once lay in the heart of a fertile riverside landscape. Today, harsh desert surrounds the ancient city. Its ruined temple platform stands at one end of the great city mounds, now a low, flat mass of clay and sand with a dune forming downwind of the crumbling mound.

For generations, the desolate site defied some of the best archaeologists in the world, who lacked the expertise to distinguish sun-dried mud brick from the surrounding soil. British archaeologist Richard Campbell-Thompson dug into Eridu in 1918 and complained that he found nothing but loose sand. Thirty years later, Iraqi archaeologist Fuad Safar and his British colleague Seton Lloyd returned to the city with a large labor force and a small mining railroad, which enabled them to move enormous amounts of sand. They also had expertise in working with mud-brick structures, employing methods developed by German archaeologists at the great city of Babylon just before World War I, which used picks to "feel" different soil textures. To this simple technique they added brushes and compressed air, which proved an excellent way to clear mud brick. The two excavators removed enough sand to expose a small complex of mud-brick public buildings still standing about 2.4 meters (8 feet) high. Then, they embarked on a long-term project to decipher the history of the great shrine that had once stood at the heart of the city.

Safar and Lloyd soon found a solid brickwork platform extending from the base of the much later ruined ziggurat (temple). They spent two weeks piecing together scattered brick and reconstructed the foundations of a small, rectangular building surrounded by concentric brickwork triangles. After days of puzzlement, they realized that they were looking at a temple platform that had been extended again and again by the simple expedient of building another layer of brickwork around the shrine to build ever-larger, brilliantly decorated structures, culminating in the great ziggurat that adorned the city before it was abandoned (see Figure 12.9; see also Figure 3.18 on p. 96).

At least five temples had stood atop the one exposed by Safar and Lloyd. They dismantled the rectangular structure and penetrated deep toward bedrock, uncovering no fewer than ten earlier shrines, each built atop its predecessors. Temple XVI, dated to around 4500 B.C., lay on clean sand, and was a small mud-brick shrine 14 meters (45 feet) square, with one entrance, an altar, and an offering table. Hundreds of fish bones, including the complete skeleton of a sea perch, still lay on the offering table. Sea perch live in brackish water, like the shallow estuaries that were once close to Eridu.

Five hundred years later, Eridu's temple platform lay inside an approximately 180-meter (585-foot) square enclosure. A magnificent stepped ziggurat now rose in the center of the city, its façade adorned with brightly colored fired bricks. Residential quarters and markets crowded on the sacred enclosure, while the ziggurat was visible for kilometers around. Thanks to months of sophisticated and painstaking mud-brick excavation, we know that this imposing shrine was the descendant of much humbler temples that had commemorated the same sacred place.

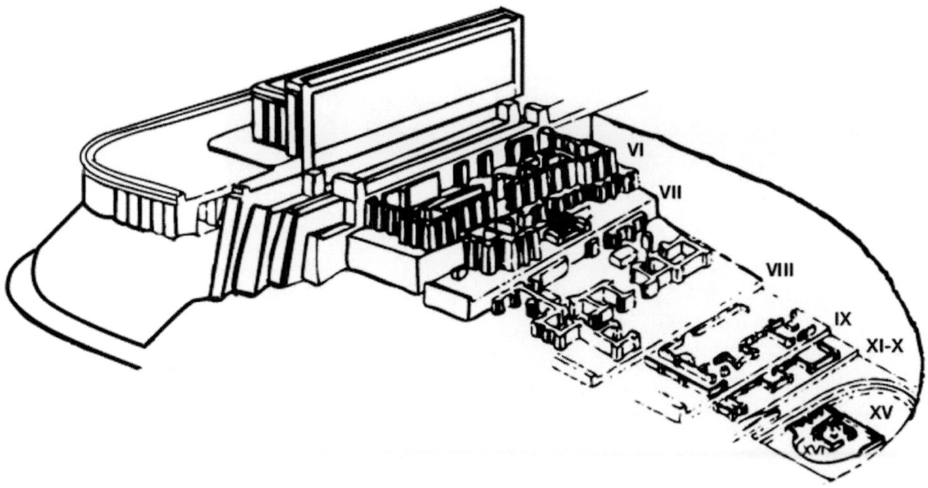

Figure 12.9 The temple at Eridu, reconstructed from excavations. The drawing shows successive shrines dating between 5000 and 3000 B.C. The lower temples are shown offset for clarity.

The ruler of Uruk, who was also the keeper of the temple, was both a secular and a spiritual ruler. His wishes were carried out by his priests and by a complex hierarchy of minor officials, wealthy landowners, and merchants. Tradespeople and artisans formed a lowlier segment of society. Under them were thousands of fisherfolk, farmers, sailors, and slaves that formed the bulk of Uruk's and other cities' growing populations.

By 3500 B.C., the Mesopotamian city had developed an elaborate system of management. This system organized and regulated society, meted out reward and punishment, and made policy decisions for the thousands of people who lived under it. Writing now appeared, born out of a growing need to track goods, people, and power. Yet the origins of written records date back even earlier, to a time soon after the adoption of agriculture, when rising trade between villages demanded a way to track transactions.

As early as 8000 B.C., people used clay tokens shaped to represent commodities, often carried on strings. By 5000 B.C., economic life had become so complex that these tokens gave way to small clay tablets, on which scribes scratched simple pictures of familiar items—pots, animals, tools—to keep accounts. These pictures evolved into more abstract, standardized signs, laying the groundwork for the cuneiform script (see Figure 12.10).

Recent research now suggests that writing may also have developed from the symbolic designs stamped onto clay using carved cylinder seals. These seals, dating back over 6,000 years, were used to mark ownership and record transactions. Some scholars argue that the images on these seals gradually took on meaning beyond their visual form and contributed to the emergence of proto-writing in cities like Uruk.

At first, specially trained scribes dealt almost entirely with administrative records—lists, inventories, and tallies. But before long, others began to see the broader possibilities of writing. Kings used tablets to proclaim victories. Fathers scolded wayward sons. Lawyers documented complex deals. And poets composed hymns, epics, and laments—giving voice to the earliest known literature in human history.

Cities like Eridu and Uruk were not isolated from other centers. Indeed, they were only too aware of their neighbors. For example, the city-states of Lagash and Umma were uneasy

Figure 12.10 A Sumerian cuneiform tablet, dealing with beer allocation, from Girsu, Mesopotamia, c. 2342 B.C.

Source: Prisma Archivo/Alamy.

neighbors and engaged in a tendentious border dispute that dragged on for three or four centuries. Cities soon had walls, a sure sign that they needed protection against marauders.

By this time, too, there were southern Mesopotamian "colonies" in what is now northern Iraq, at Susa across the Tigris, in the Zagros, and elsewhere on the northern and northeastern peripheries of the lowlands. Some of these colonies were entire transplanted communities; others merely yielded characteristic Uruk-style artifacts far from their Mesopotamian homeland. Artifacts and artistic styles characteristic of Uruk came from the Nile valley during the centuries when long-distance caravan trade was expanding rapidly in Egypt and across the Sinai.

The Sumerians (c. 3100 to 2334 B.C.)

With the emergence of the Sumerian civilization in about 3100 B.C., a new era in human experience began, one in which the economic, political, and social mechanisms created by humans began to affect the lives of cities, towns, and villages located hundreds, if not thousands, of kilometers apart. This was also the time of the first written literature (see Box 12.2).

By 3000 B.C., expanding trade networks linked dozens of cities and towns from the Mediterranean Sea to the Persian Gulf and from Türkiye to the Nile valley. By this time, city-states small and large flourished not only in Egypt and Mesopotamia, but also in the coastal Levant and in highland Iran. Each of them depended on the others for critical raw materials such as metal ore or soapstone vessels, timber, or even grain. In northern Mesopotamia, east of the Tigris, and in the Levant, expanding trade and a host of important technological innovations resulted not only from basic economic needs, but also from the competitive instincts of a new elite. All, however bitter their enmity, depended on their neighbors and more distant trading partners.

Box 12.2 Voices
The Sumerians

> When Enlil, like a big bull, set his foot on the earth,
> To make the good day thrive in abundance,
> To make the fair night flourish in luxuriance, to make grow tall the plants, to spread wide the grains.

Sumerian literature is the earliest in the world, rich in poetry and prose and also containing more prosaic documents: "Why do you idle about? Go to school, stand before your 'school-father,' recite your assignment, open your schoolbag, write your tablet." The voices of the ancient Sumerians speak to us over the millennia. The directive to the delinquent student, the love song, the agricultural directory, and the stirring epic—Sumerian literature vibrates with energy and perception. A bride sings to her royal bridegroom, Shu-Sin:

> Bridegroom, dear to my heart,
> Goodly is your beauty, sweetheart,
> Lion, dear to my heart,
> Goodly is your beauty, honeysweet.

A farming handbook gives pragmatic advice from a father to his son that fills 180 lines of tightly packed cuneiform. The author guides his heir through the yearly agricultural cycle, starting with the inundation of the fields by the great rivers in May and June:

> Plow 8 furrows to each strip of land about 6 meters (20 feet) wide. Keep an eye on the man who puts in the barley seed that he make the seed fall two fingers uniformly. On the day when the seed breaks through the ground, say a prayer to Ninkilim, goddess of field mice and vermin, so they do not harm the growing crop.

The handbook contains precise instructions on watering, adjuring the young farmer to "let your tools hum with activity."

The Epic of Gilgamesh is the most famous of all Sumerian epics, the saga of a man who loves and hates, weeps and rejoices, hopes and despairs. Gilgamesh is king of Erech, a restless hero famous for his tyrannical arrogance. His subjects complain to the gods, who send Enkidu, who has lived among the beasts, to tame Gilgamesh. The two heroes fight, then become fast friends and join forces to kill the formidable Bull of Heaven. Enkidu is sentenced to an early death by the gods. The grieving Gilgamesh then seeks immortality. Eventually, he fails in his quest and returns weary and disappointed to Erech to live out his days. The epic as we know it is a mixture of literary borrowings, but it is a masterpiece. Gilgamesh says to Enkidu:

> If now you will descend to the nether world,
> A word I will speak to you, take my word.
> Instruction I offer you, take my instruction.
> Do not put on clean clothes,

Lest like an enemy [the nether world]
stewards will come forth.
Do not anoint yourself with the good oil of the bur-vessel,
Lest at its smell they will crowd about you.

The Epic of Gilgamesh is still performed on the stage to this day. But the most vivid Sumerian voices are those of common folk, expressed in proverbs of the day: "We are doomed to die, let us spend; We will live long, let us save." "Friendship lasts a day, kinship endures forever." "You can have a lord, you can have a king, but the man to fear is the tax collector" (quotes from Kramer 1981, 304, 15, 246, 67–68, 196–197, 118, 121, 123).

Sumerian civilization came into being as a result of a combination of environmental and social factors. The Sumerians lived in a treeless, lowland environment with fertile soils but no metal, little timber, and no semiprecious stones. They obtained these commodities by trading with areas where such items were in abundance. Sumerian rulers controlled not only large grain surpluses that could be moved in river craft, but also a flourishing industry in textiles and other luxuries. The trade moved up and down the great rivers, especially the placid Euphrates. Ancient overland trade routes linked the Tigris and Euphrates with the distant Levant cities and ports. Even as early as Sumerian times, caravans of pack animals joined Anatolia to the Euphrates, the Levant to Mesopotamia, and Mesopotamia to isolated towns on the distant Iranian highlands to the east.

Bronze technology produced tougher-edged, more durable artifacts that could be used for more arduous, day-to-day tasks. One resulting innovation was the metal-tipped wooden plow, an implement dragged by oxen that was capable of digging a far deeper furrow than the simple hoes and digging sticks of earlier times. The plow, which, incidentally, was never developed in the Americas, came about as irrigation agriculture assumed greater importance in Sumer, and the combined innovations increased agricultural yields dramatically. These yields not only supported larger urban and rural populations, but also provided a means for the rulers of city-states both in Sumer and farther afield to exercise more control over food surpluses and over the wealth obtained by long-distance exchange. Eventually, Sumerian rulers became more despotic, controlling their subjects by military strength, religious power, and economic incentive. An intricate and ever-changing system of political alliances linked community with community and city-state with city-state.

Soon, a rapidly evolving economic system linked hundreds of southwest Asian societies all the way from eastern Iran and the Indus valley in Pakistan to Mesopotamia, the eastern Mediterranean, Anatolia, and the Nile valley with ever-changing cultural tentacles. By the third millennium B.C., this system not only embraced southwestern Asia, but also extended to Cyprus, the Aegean, and mainland Greece. City merchants began to handle such commodities as copper and lapis lazuli. They wholesaled goods, let contracts, and floated loans for individuals. After 3000 B.C., every city-state, and entire civilizations, came to depend on what we have called a nascent "world economic system," not so much for political stability as for survival.

As the Mesopotamian delta became an environment increasingly controlled by human activities and the volume of long-distance trade increased dramatically, competition over resources intensified. Both clay tablets and archaeological finds tell of warfare and constant bickering between neighbors. Each state raised an army to defend its water rights, trade routes, and city walls. The onerous tasks of defense and military organization passed

Figure 12.11 The reconstructed Sumerian ziggurat at Ur, Iraq, originally built about 2300 B.C.
Source: Thaer Jebur/iStock via Getty Images.

to despotic kings supposedly appointed by the gods. Such city-states as Erech, Kish, and Ur (see Figure 12.11) had periods of political strength and prosperity when they dominated their neighbors. Then, just as swiftly, the tide of their fortunes would change and they would sink into obscurity. There was a constant threat from nomadic peoples of the surrounding mountains and deserts, who encroached on settled Sumerian lands. At times, they disrupted city life so completely that any form of travel became impossible. In a real sense, city-states were the settings for economic and social strife in early Mesopotamia.

Some Sumerian cities nurtured powerful and wealthy leaders. British archaeologist Sir Leonard Woolley excavated a royal cemetery at Ur. He found the remains of a series of kings and queens who had been buried in huge graves with their entire retinue of courtiers. One tomb contained the remains of 59 people. Each wore his or her official dress and regalia. Woolley claimed that they had lain down to die in the correct order of precedence after taking a fatal dose of poison. Unfortunately, his excavation notes are incomplete, so we cannot verify his findings. In fact, some of the victims were clubbed on the head.

Inevitably, the ambitions of some of these proud Sumerian leaders led them to entertain visions bolder than merely the control of a few city-states in the lowlands. They were well aware that the control of lucrative sources of raw materials and trade routes was the secret of vast political power. In about 2400 B.C., a monarch named Lugalzagesi boasted of overseeing the entire area from the Persian Gulf to the Mediterranean. This boast was probably false. It is likely that Sumerian cities dominated the overland routes that linked Mesopotamia, Türkiye, and the Levant, but their influence was never permanent and their control was probably illusory. Lugalzagesi and others were characteristic of a tradition of Mesopotamian civilization: the combination of trade, conquest, ruthless administration, and tribute to create large, poorly integrated, and highly volatile empires. Each sought to control an enormous territory between the Mediterranean and the Persian Gulf.

The tenuous and sometimes more regular contacts maintained by Mesopotamia with dozens of city-states in Anatolia and along the eastern Mediterranean coast, foreshadowed the constant political and economic rivalry that was to dominate southwest Asian history during the second millennium B.C.—rivalry over control of Mediterranean coastal ports. The eastern Mediterranean coast had no natural harbors, so control of its overland routes was the key to dominating a vast area of the known world, resource-rich Anatolia and grain-rich Egypt. The history of this region was bound inextricably to the fortunes of the larger powers that surrounded it. Sumerian civilization became part of a larger kingdom based in Babylon to the north after 2334 B.C., but its cities, notably Ur, were still important political and trading centers. By this time, Mesopotamia was linked inextricably to a wider eastern Mediterranean world, including the Nile valley.

Ancient Egyptian Civilization (c. 3100 to 30 B.C.)

Ancient Egypt was the longest-lived and one of the world's earliest preindustrial civilizations, enduring for more than 3,000 years.

Predynastic Egypt: Ancient Monopoly? (5000 to 3100 B.C.)

By 5000 B.C., a patchwork of simple village farming communities lay along both banks of the Nile River, from the delta of Lower Egypt to the First Cataract at Aswan and even farther upstream. The river itself formed a natural highway between settlements near and far, the prevailing north winds allowing even sailing boats to stem the current. The villages soon became a patchwork of small kingdoms, each clustered under the rule of local leaders. Within 2,000 years, these small polities had become a unified state, at the time the largest literate civilization in the world.

At first, dozens of small communities, each with its own patchwork of farming land, competed and traded with their neighbors. This competition had long-term effects like those in a game of *Monopoly*. In *Monopoly*, each player maximizes the opportunities thrown out by the dice. In Egypt, both individuals and entire villages took full advantage of favorable locations, of their access to desirable resources like potting clay, and of chance breaks that came their way. At first, the communities, like *Monopoly* players, were basically equal, but inevitably, someone—or some hamlet—gained an unforeseen advantage, perhaps from trading expertise or unusually high crop yields. Equilibrium gave way to a seemingly inevitable momentum, in which some communities acquired more wealth and power than their neighbors—the prehistoric equivalent of building *Monopoly* hotels on Park Place. Their victory was inevitable, as they established a monopoly over local trade, food surpluses, and so on, which overrode any threat posed by other political or economic players.

In predynastic times, there were probably dozens of such "games" in progress. As time went on, the number of players grew fewer, but the stakes were higher as increasingly large chiefdoms vied for economic power and political dominance. Players changed over time, some acquiring great power and then losing it as charismatic individuals died or trading opportunities changed. The Egyptians also had a genius for weaving a distinctive ideology that imbued leadership and authority with elaborate symbols and rituals. These ideologies became a powerful factor in promoting unification.

Naqada, Egypt Predynastic Egyptian kingdom in Upper Egypt dating to the fourth millennium B.C.

Nekhen, Egypt Ancient Egyptian town, center of an important predynastic kingdom, c. 3500 B.C. Greek name is Hierakonpolis.

This, Egypt Predynastic Egyptian kingdom in Upper Egypt in the fourth millennium B.C.

By 3500 B.C., three predynastic kingdoms dominated the Nile: **Naqada, Nekhen,** and **This,** near Abydos in Upper Egypt. These little-known kingdoms were the nucleus of a unified Egypt. (Lower Egypt consists of the Nile Delta, bordering the Mediterranean Sea, and the valley to just beyond the modern city of Cairo. Upper Egypt extends from there upstream, and south, to the First Cataract at Aswan. The Ancient Egyptians themselves recognized this subdivision.)

Archaeology and myth combine to create a hypothetical scenario for unification: by 3500 B.C., the kingdoms of Upper Egypt may have had direct contact with southern Arabia and southwestern Asia, bypassing Lower Egypt. Mesopotamian cylinder seals came from Upper Egyptian sites, and gold was obtained from mines in the eastern desert. Conflict ensued, with the politically most developed center, Nekhen, emerging victorious. The rulers of Nekhen and then those of This finally embarked on a campaign of military conquest, which eventually engulfed all of Egypt.

By 3100 B.C., a semblance of political unity joined Upper and Lower Egypt in the symbolic linking of the gods Horus and Seth, depicted in later Egyptian art (see Figure 12.12). As these events unfolded, a new state came into being, founded on not only physical but also symbolic geography—a harmony achieved by balanced opposites of which Horus and Seth are but one manifestation. For thousands of years, the Egyptians were concerned with the potential of a world torn between chaos and order. They believed that disorder—disequilibrium—could be contained by the rule of kings and by the benign force of the power of the Sun. Thus, the Egyptians' intellectual view of the universe coincided with the structure of political power.

Unification was the pivotal and fundamental concept upon which the institutions of Ancient Egyptian civilization rested. Unification brought order, serenity, and peace to a confused world. The king's task as shepherd of the people was to preserve *ma'at*,

Figure 12.12 The Narmer Palette of about 3100 B.C., a slab carved on both sides with scenes commemorating King Narmer (Menes), whom legend credits with unifying Upper and Lower Egypt. He appears on the palette wearing the white and red crowns of these two regions, presiding over the conquest of the delta. The central design of entwined beasts (left) symbolizes harmony, balancing images of conquest above and below.

Source: Ivy Close Images/Alamy.

"rightness," derived in considerable part from unification, to maintain order in the face of a chaotic outside world.

The Egyptians themselves identified the first king as Narmer. (The term *pharaoh*, Egyptian for "great house," *par-aa*, came into use during the second millennium B.C.) A series of still unknown rulers, Narmer among them, may have completed the process of unification. Full unity took several centuries to achieve through a process of deft political alliance and continual warfare.

Dynastic Egyptian Civilization (c. 3100 to 30 B.C.)

Egyptologists conventionally divide Ancient Egyptian civilization into four broad periods: (1) Archaic Egypt and the Old Kingdom, (2) the Middle Kingdom, (3) the New Kingdom, and (4) the Late Period. The first three were separated by two intermediate periods that were interludes of political change and instability (see Table 12.1).

Archaic Egypt and the "Great Culture" (3000 to 2575 B.C.)

The first ruler of a truly unified Egypt was King Horus Aha, who reigned in about 3100 B.C. The next 450 years made up the Archaic period, which was a long time of consolidation when the pharaohs assumed the role of divine kings. They and their high officials invented Egypt's royal tradition, converting it into powerful architectural statements and artistic styles that endured for centuries. Just like Mesoamerican lords (see Chapter 15),

Table 12.1 Ancient Egyptian Civilization

Date	*Period*	*Characteristics*
30 B.C.	Roman occupation	Egypt an imperial province of Rome
332 to 30 B.C.	Ptolemaic period	The Ptolemies bring Greek influence to Egypt, beginning with conquest of Egypt by Alexander the Great in 332 B.C.
1070 to 332 B.C.	Late period	Gradual decline in pharaonic authority, culminating in Persian rule (525 to 404 B.C. and 343 to 332 B.C.)
1530 to 1070 B.C.	New Kingdom	Great imperial period of Egyptian history, with pharaohs buried in Valley of Kings; pharaohs include Rameses II, Seti I, and Tutankhamun, as well as Akhenaten, the heretic ruler
1640 to 1530 B.C.	Second intermediate period	Hyksos rulers in the delta
2040 to 1640 B.C.	Middle Kingdom	Thebes achieves prominence, also the priesthood of Amun
2134 to 2040 B.C.	First intermediate period	Political chaos and disunity
2575 to 2134 B.C.	Old Kingdom	Despotic pharaohs build the pyramids and favor conspicuous funerary monuments; institutions, economic strategies, and artistic traditions of Ancient Egypt established
2920 to 2575 B.C.	Archaic period	Consolidation of state
3100 B.C.	Unification of Egypt under Narmer-Menes and Scorpion	

the pharaohs made a great play of their rare public appearances, developing spectacular settings for major ritual events and festivals. They also created a centralized bureaucracy that directed labor, administered food storage, and collected taxes. In Egypt, the terms *father, king*, and *god* were metaphors for one another and for a form of political power based on social inequality that was considered part of the natural order established by the gods at the Creation.

The Archaic period saw the birth of Egypt's "Great Culture," a distinctive ideology that systematized Egyptian civilization over wide areas at the expense of local religious cults. Such an ideology was essential in a society where only a minority could read and write. Scribes held enormous power in all early civilizations, and Egypt was no exception. "Be a scribe ... You will go forth in white clothes, honored, with courtiers saluting you," a young man is advised. Writing was power, the key to controlling the labor of thousands of people.

Saqqara, Egypt Site of Djoser's Step Pyramid, c. 2650 B.C., and other major pharaonic burial places.

Old Kingdom (c. 2575 to 2134 B.C.)

The Old Kingdom saw society shaped into an image in which the well-being of the people depended on the ruler being supported by their labors. The new image of kingship developed after the death in 2649 B.C. of the pharaoh Djoser, whose architect Imhotep built the first pyramid as a royal burial place—the celebrated Step Pyramid at **Saqqara** (see Box 12.3).

Memphis, Egypt Royal capital of Ancient Egypt.

Box 12.3 Site
The Step Pyramid at Saqqara

Like other early Old Kingdom kings, Third Dynasty pharaoh Djoser (2668–2649 B.C.) grappled with internal political problems. He managed to extend his rule as far upstream as Aswan and laid great emphasis on his role as king and supreme territorial claimant, a role he celebrated within a large enclosure dominated by a unique structure: the Step Pyramid at Saqqara, opposite the royal capital at **Memphis.**

Djoser's vizier Imhotep devised the architecture of the Step Pyramid (see Figure 12.13). The great architect drew his inspiration from earlier royal tombs, rectangular structures like those at Abydos, which were eternal mansions for dead monarchs. Such tumuli (mounds) had associations with the primordial earthen mound that formed an integral part of the Egyptian legend of the Creation. Imhotep erected a stepped pyramid instead of a mound. It rose in six diminishing steps to over 60 meters (197 feet) above the desert, the stepped sides oriented to the cardinal points. The effect was like a giant double staircase rising toward heaven. A wall with a palace-like façade over 1.6 kilometers (1 mile) in perimeter surrounded the entire mortuary complex. The court before the pyramid was a setting for royal appearances, complete with ceremonial territorial markers, a throne platform, and

Figure 12.13 The Step Pyramid at Saqqara, Egypt, with part of the reconstructed temple complex in the foreground.

a token palace. On occasion, the pharaoh laid claim to his kingdom by striding around the limits of the court and its markers. The entire complex was an arena for the eternal pageantry of kingship on Earth.

The Step Pyramid was an area for the king's spirit. It consisted of six platforms, one atop the other. Each formed a bench, or *mastaba*, resembling earlier royal tombs, here built into a stepped pyramid. The substructure was a honeycomb of shafts and tunnels, many dug by tomb robbers after the time of Djoser, others containing large numbers of often exquisite stone vases. Some of them bore the names of earlier kings, as if Djoser had incorporated them into his pyramid as an act of piety toward his predecessors. Only a mummified left foot remains of the king himself. Other members of the royal family were buried in some of the shafts and tunnels. As the pyramid grew, these burial chambers were sealed off. Finally, the builders dug a new entrance for Djoser's burial chamber on the north side. They sealed it with a 3-ton granite plug.

A thick stone wall surrounded the pyramid, forming a huge courtyard, 108 by 187 meters (354 by 613 feet), with a main gateway at the southeastern corner. An entrance hall decorated with columns opened into a vestibule. The king's internal organs were buried in the so-called South Tomb facing the main pyramid on the south side of the enclosure. Thus, there were two sepulchers, one each for the two lands, Upper and Lower Egypt.

The Step Pyramid was an elaborate formal setting for the display of kingship and of the ruler himself, either to his courtiers or to the populace at large. Here the ruler could be seen by a large number of people, adorned in his ceremonial robes. The "appearance of the king" was an important occasion throughout Egyptian history.

The king was now absorbed into the mythic symbol of the Sun. The Sun God became a heavenly monarch; the pharaoh became the deity's representative on Earth. Upon his death, an Old Kingdom pharaoh "went to his double," joining the Sun God in heaven. Thus, it was that Djoser and his successors lavished enormous expenditure on their sepulchers—at first earthen mounds and then pyramids, which became symbolic ladders to heaven, their sloping sides representing the rays of the Sun widening after bursting through a gap in the clouds.

The court cemeteries and pyramid complexes of the Old Kingdom pharaohs extend over a 35-kilometer (22-mile) stretch of the western desert edge, mostly slightly north of the royal capital at Memphis.

The pharaohs lavished enormous resources on their pyramids, culminating in the reigns of Khufu and Khafre, who built the pyramid tombs of Giza (see Figure 3.3 on p. 75). In about 2528 B.C., Khufu built the Great Pyramid, one of the Seven Wonders of the Ancient World. It covers 5.3 hectares (13.1 acres) and is 146 meters (481 feet) high. Well over 2 million limestone blocks, some weighing 15 tons each, went into its construction. A long causeway linked each pyramid in the Giza complex to a royal mortuary temple. These were austere buildings that housed statues of the king. The nearby sepulchers vested these temples with great authority, for they associated the ruler with what was, in effect, a powerful ancestor cult that linked them to their predecessors and to the gods (see Figure 12.14).

We do not know why the pharaohs suddenly embarked on this orgy of pyramid construction, with all the accompanying demands that it made on the fledgling state. Their construction, like other major Egyptian public works, was a triumph of bureaucratic administration, of organizing and transporting food and building materials. Then, officials

Figure 12.14 The Sphinx at Giza, built by Old Kingdom pharaoh Khafre around 2500 B.C. Humanheaded lions (sphinxes) were important symbols of royal power.

Source: Sergey Khachatryan/Thinkstock.

marshaled skilled artisans and village laborers to quarry, dig, and drag stone into place. What is staggering is the efficient management overview, achieved without computers, deploying and supporting thousands of villagers for short periods of time as they fulfilled their annual tax-by-labor obligations to the state.

Perhaps, the pyramids were built as a means of linking the people to their guardian, the king, and to the Sun God, the source of human life and of bountiful harvests. The relationship between the king and his subjects was both reciprocal and spiritual. The pharaoh was a divine king whose person was served by annual labor. In short, pyramid building created public works that helped define the authority of the ruler and make his subjects dependent on him. Every flood season, when agriculture was at a standstill, the pharaohs organized thousands of peasants into construction teams. The permanent (year-round) labor force consisted of relatively few people, mainly skilled artisans, the fruit of whose work was placed in position on the main structure once a year. As far as is known, the peasants worked off tax obligations. Their loyalty to the divine pharaoh provided the motivation for the work.

Old Kingdom Egypt was the first state of its size in history. The pharaohs ruled by their own word, following no written laws, unlike the legislators of Mesopotamian city-states. The pharaoh had power over the Nile flood, rainfall, and all people, including foreigners. He was a god, respected by all people as a tangible divinity whose being was the personification of *ma'at*. *Ma'at* was far more than just literal "rightness"; it was a "right order" and stood for order and justice. *Ma'at* was pharaonic status and eternity itself—the very embodiment of the Egyptian state. As the embodiment of *ma'at*, the pharaoh pronounced the law, regulated by a massive background of precedent set by earlier pharaohs.

Old Kingdom Egypt was a time of powerful, confident rulers, of a virile state governed by a privileged class of royal relatives and high officials. Their talents created a civilization that was for the benefit of a tiny minority. It was for this privileged elite, headed by a divine king, that Egyptian merchants traded for the famed cedars of Lebanon, mined turquoise and copper in Sinai, and sought ivory, semiprecious stones, and mercenaries for Egypt's armies from Nubia.

A prolonged drought cycle after 2250 B.C. undermined the Old Kingdom rulers' absolute powers. Three hundred years of repeated famines led to anarchy and a diminution of pharaonic authority. Egypt splintered into competing provinces ruled by ambitious lords.

Thebes, Egypt Capital of Middle and New Kingdom Egypt after 1520 B.C. and a major center of the worship of the Sun God Amun; called *Wa-set* by the Egyptians.

Middle Kingdom (2040 to 1640 B.C.)

In about 2134 B.C., the city of **Thebes** (*Wa-set*) in Upper Egypt achieved supremacy and reunited Egypt under a series of energetic pharaohs. Middle Kingdom rulers were less despotic, more approachable, and less likely to see themselves as gods. They had learned lessons from the past and relied heavily on an efficient bureaucracy to stockpile food supplies and increase agricultural production (see Figure 12.15). For over three centuries, Egypt enjoyed great prosperity and political stability under a series of able pharaohs. Their decisive leadership expanded overseas trade as they secured Egypt's frontiers with vigorous military campaigns. The most able kings expanded irrigation agriculture and

Figure 12.15 Model of an estate granary belonging to a Middle Kingdom courtier named Meketre. Laborers fill bins with wheat, as scribes in a neighboring office record the amounts being stored.

Source: Werner Forman Archive/Getty Images.

worked hard to create a highly centralized, controlled state both by skillful leadership and by bureaucratic supervision.

Everything depended on charismatic leadership and a strong king. During the seventeenth century B.C., succession disputes engulfed the Theban court at a time when thousands of Asians were moving into the delta region. Egypt soon fragmented into two kingdoms centered on Lower and Upper Egypt. Lower Egypt came under the control of

Hyksos kings, nomadic rulers from Asia. This second intermediate period was a turning point in Egyptian history, for the Hyksos brought new ideas to a civilization that was slowly stagnating in its isolated homeland. They introduced more sophisticated bronze technology, the horse-drawn chariot, and new weapons of war. All these innovations kept Egypt up to date and ensured that subsequent pharaohs would play a leading role in the wider eastern Mediterranean world.

New Kingdom (1530 to 1075 B.C.)

The New Kingdom began when a series of Theban rulers fought and finally conquered the Hyksos, thereby reunifying the kingdom (see Box 12.4). An able pharaoh named Ahmose the Liberator turned Egypt into an efficiently run military state, tolerating no rivals, and rewarding his soldiers with gifts of land while keeping economic power and wealth in his own hands. Ahmose set the tone for the greatest era in Egyptian history. Now, the king became a national hero, a military leader who sat on a throne midway between the Asiatic world in the north and the African kingdoms of the Nile to the south. He was an imperial ruler, a skilled general, the leader of a great power. Egypt now became a major player in the shifting sands of eastern Mediterranean politics, competing for control of lucrative trade routes and seaports.

Box 12.4 Voices
Ahmose, Son of Ebana

The Ancient Egyptians boasted loudly on their tomb walls, to the point that one does not know what to believe. Their stories of unrelenting success are much too good to be true, but occasionally we come across a truly remarkable individual. A doughty warrior named Ahmose, son of Ebana, is a case in point. The old soldier must have been walking history. Ahmose was a soldier's son and followed in his father's footsteps, at first as a foot soldier, following the king as he "rode about on his chariot." His bravery was noted and "the gold of valor was given to him." This was the beginning of an illustrious military career. Ahmose served five pharaohs, witnessed the expulsion of the Asian Hyksos kings from Egypt, was present at the ravaging of their capital, Avaris, in the delta and at the siege of Sharuhen in Asia, and fought in several bloody Nubian campaigns. When the pharaoh Ahmose (no relative) laid siege to Avaris and fought three battles there, Ahmose (the soldier) "took captive there one man and three women, total four heads, and His Majesty gave them to him for slaves." After bitter fighting and the complete destruction of Avaris, Ahmose's armies chased the Hyksos into Palestine and laid siege to the town of Sharuhen, their stronghold in southern Palestine.

Fresh from the slaughter at Sharuhen, the victorious Theban king turned his attention to Nubia with Ahmose, son of Ebana, at his side. As Ahmose told it,

> Now when his majesty had slain the nomads of Asia, he sailed south … to destroy the Nubian Bowmen. His majesty made great slaughter among them, and I brought spoil from there: two living men and three hands. Then I was rewarded with gold once again, and two female slaves were given to me. His majesty journeyed north, his heart rejoicing in valor and victory. He had conquered southerners and northerners.

Ahmose served in several later Nubian campaigns, ending up as a crew commander on a warship, promoted for his skill in organizing the towing of his ship through a turbulent cataract: "I brought a chariot, its horse, and him who was on it as a living captive. When they were presented to his majesty, I was rewarded with gold."

After Nubia, the battle-scarred veteran relaxed in honored retirement, lavished with honor and land: "I let you know what favors came to me. I have been rewarded with gold seven times in the sight of the whole land, with many male and female slaves as well." Ahmose died honored and respected, his deeds remembered on the walls of his sepulcher: "The name of the brave man is in that which he has done; it will not perish in the land forever" (quotes from Lichtheim 1976, 12–14).

Karnak, Egypt Temple of the Sun God Amun during Egypt's New Kingdom.

Thebes (*Wa-set*) was now capital of Egypt, the "Estate of Amun," the Sun God. The Temple of Amun at **Karnak,** built mostly between the sixteenth and the fourteenth century B.C., was the heart of the sacred capital (see Figure 12.16). Amun was the "king of the gods," a solar deity who conceived the pharaohs and then protected them in life and death. The Estate of Amun extended to the western bank of the Nile opposite Thebes, where the pharaohs erected an elaborate city of the dead. They themselves were buried in secret, rock-cut tombs in the arid Valley of Kings. Their sepulchers became models of the caverns of the underworld traversed by the night-Sun.

Figure 12.16 The entrance to the Temple of the Sun God Amun at Karnak, and the avenue of sphinxes.

Source: Marcin Ciesielski/Thinkstock.

El-Amarna, Egypt Capital of the pharaoh Akhenaten, c. 1348 B.C.; occupied for only 17 years.

The New Kingdom witnessed a brief period of religious unorthodoxy in 1353 B.C., when a heretic pharaoh, Akhenaten, turned away from Amun to a purer form of Sun worship, based on the solar disk Aten. Akhenaten went so far as to found a new royal capital at **el-Amarna,** downstream of Thebes, on land associated with no established deity.

Akhenaten's innovations did not survive his reign. In 1333 B.C., his son, eight-year-old Tutankhamun, succeeded to the throne. He presided over a troubled kingdom, so his advisers took the only course open to them. They restored the old spiritual order, reverting to the dynastic traditions of the early pharaohs. Tutankhamun himself ruled for only about ten years, but achieved in death an immortality that transcends that of all other pharaohs, simply because Howard Carter and Lord Carnarvon found his intact tomb in the Valley of Kings (see Figure 12.17; see also Figure 1.1 on p. 4).

The Rameside pharaohs of 1307 to 1196 B.C. labored hard to elevate Egypt to its former imperial glory. Rameses II (1290–1224 B.C.) campaigned far into Syria, financing his military campaigns and an orgy of temple building with Nubian gold (see Figures 1.9

Figure 12.17 Lord Carnarvon (left), his daughter Lady Evelyn Herbert, and Howard Carter by the steps into Tutankhamun's tomb, 1922.

Source: David Cole/Alamy Stock Photo.

on p. 14 and 5.1 on p. 154). He met his match at the Battle of Kadesh in Syria, where the Hittites fought his army to a standstill. From then on, Egypt lost political influence in southwestern Asia and began a slow and at first barely perceptible decline.

Late Period (1070 to 30 B.C.)

With the death of Rameses III in 1070 B.C., Egypt entered a period of political weakness during which local rulers exercised varying control over the Nile. The pharaohs were threatened by Nubian rulers from the south, who controlled Egypt for a time in the eighth century B.C. Assyrians, Persians, and Greeks all ruled over the Nile for varying periods until Rome incorporated the world's longest-lived civilization into its empire in 30 B.C. The Greeks brought much of Egyptian lore and learning into the mainstream of emerging Greek civilization, ensuring that Ancient Egypt contributed to the roots of Western civilization.

Summary

- The world's earliest civilizations arose in Egypt and Mesopotamia. Civilizations are characterized by the state and the city. Vere Gordon Childe's "urban revolution" theory of civilization centered on the development of the city.
- Modern theorizing revolves around systems-evolutionary hypotheses and explanations involving environmental change.
- A new generation of social approaches, on the other hand, argues that the social structure of a society ultimately determined its transformation.
- Today, research on the development of civilization focuses on ecological variables and the opportunities they present to individuals pursuing political goals in different societies—individual agents of change.
- The Mesopotamian lowlands may have supported farmers before 6500 B.C., but the first traces of them appear in the Ubaid culture of the sixth millennium. A rapid evolution to urban life ensued, marked by fast population growth, the congregation of people in small cities, and the development of long-distance trade.
- By 2900 B.C., Sumerian civilization was in full swing and was part of a growing economic system that linked kingdoms as far afield as the Iranian plateau and the Indus in the east and the Mediterranean and the Nile valley in the west.
- Sumerian civilization flourished until about 2000 B.C., when it was eclipsed by Akkadian and then Babylonian power.
- Ancient Egyptian civilization resulted from the unification of the Nile valley in 3100 B.C.
- Egyptologists conventionally subdivide Ancient Egyptian civilization into four main periods: the Archaic and Old Kingdom, the Middle Kingdom, the New Kingdom, and the Late period, the first three of which were separated by brief intermediate periods of political chaos.
- The Old Kingdom was notable for its despotic pharaohs and its frenzy of pyramid construction, an activity that may be connected with pragmatic notions of fostering national unity.
- The Middle Kingdom saw a shift of political and religious power to Thebes and Upper Egypt.
- New Kingdom pharaohs made Egypt an imperial power.
- Ancient Egyptian civilization declined after 1000 B.C., and Egypt fell under Roman rule in 30 B.C.

Key Terms and Sites

state-organized societies
civilization
preindustrial civilizations
urban revolution
Nubia
Andean civilizations
Ubaid culture
Eridu
Uruk
Naqada
Nekhen
This
Saqqara
Memphis
Thebes
Karnak
El-Amarna

Critical-Thinking Questions

1. Do you think that charismatic leadership played a central role in the formation of state-organized societies? Were people important in the origins of civilization?
2. Why were temples and burial places important in the early civilizations of Mesopotamia and Egypt?
3. Discuss the major differences and similarities between Sumerian and Egyptian civilization. Are the similarities more striking than the differences?

Further Reading

C. Scarre and B. Fagan's, *Ancient Civilizations*, 5th ed. (Upper Saddle River, NJ: Prentice Hall, 2021) summarizes the world's early civilizations for beginning readers from a global perspective. Two definitive works: B. Trigger, *Understanding Early Civilizations: A Comparative Study* (Cambridge: Cambridge University Press, 2003) and N. Yoffee, *Myths of the Archaic State: Evolution of the Earliest Cities, States, and Civilizations* (Cambridge: Cambridge University Press, 2005). N. Yoffee, ed., *The Evolution of Fragility: Setting the Terms* (Cambridge: McDonald Institute for Archaeological Research, 2019) assesses recent research. Writing: A. Robinson's, *The Story of Writing*, 2nd ed. (London: Thames and Hudson, 2009) is a lavishly illustrated essay for beginners. S. Kramer's, *The Sumerians* (Chicago, IL: University of Chicago Press, 1963) is a deservedly popular classic. *The Sumerian World* edited by Harriett Crawford (Abingdon: Routledge, 2013) provides a comprehensive overview. I. Shaw's, *Ancient Egypt: A Very Short Introduction*, 2nd ed. (Oxford: Oxford University Press, 2021) is a concise account, while B. Kemp's, *Ancient Egypt: The Anatomy of a Civilization*, 3rd ed. (London: Routledge, 2018) is a specialized classic.

13 Early Asian Civilizations

Chapter Outline

A terracotta soldier from the precincts of Chinese emperor Shihuangdi's tomb, 210 B.C.
Source: Stanley Hong/Thinkstock.

DOI: 10.4324/9781003592754-18

Mohenjodaro, Pakistan Major city of the Indus Valley Civilization.

In 1950, the British excavator Sir Mortimer Wheeler assembled a team of young archaeologists, students, and local laborers to work on a confusion of mud bricks that projected out of a weathered citadel mound at **Mohenjodaro**, on the banks of the Indus River in Pakistan. The laborers removed load after load of sand; the few bricks grew into many, "until the stark walls of a huge platform began to emerge from the hillside. The aspect was of a fortress, towering grim and forbidding above the plain" (Wheeler 1968, 317).

Wheeler puzzled over the mass of brickwork. He saw a grid of narrow passages, signs of a timber superstructure, a carefully designed platform with an approach way. The enormous structure looked less and less like a fortress, but what was it? Suddenly a light went on in his mind. The narrow passages were ducts for air to dry the floor of the timber barn that once housed the city's grain, accessible only from the side, away from the teeming streets. The "fortress" was the municipal granary.

More recent excavations have thrown Wheeler's bold interpretation into doubt, but many details of the Indus civilization of South Asia, one of the world's least known, came from his classic investigations of more than half a century ago. Even today, much less is known of early Asian civilizations than of those in the West. This chapter describes how state-organized societies developed in South and Southeast Asia and China (see Figure 13.1).

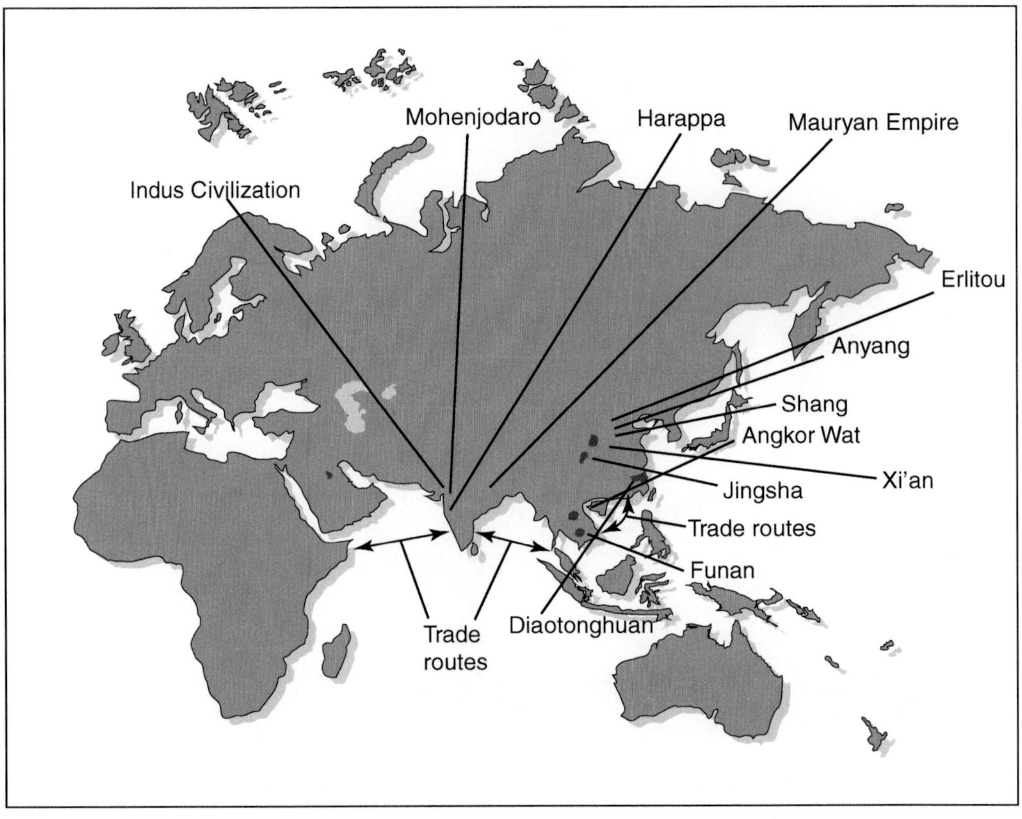

Figure 13.1 Asian sites and societies discussed in this chapter.

South Asia: The Indus Valley Civilization (c. 2700 to 1700 B.C.)

The Indus River, on the banks of which South Asian civilization began, rises in the snow-clad Himalayas of southern Tibet and descends 1,600 kilometers (1,000 miles) through Kashmir before emerging on to the Pakistani plains. Here, as in Mesopotamia and the Nile valley, fertile floodplain soils played an important role in the development of a state-organized society. Between June and September each year, the spring runoff from the distant mountains reaches the plains, inundating thousands of acres of good farming land and depositing rich flood-borne silts as a natural fertilizer, on soil soft enough to be cultivated without the aid of metal artifacts.

Hundreds of village settlements flourished across the Indus valley plains by 3000 B.C. Many of them were small, fortified towns with carefully laid-out streets, built above the highest flood level but as close to the river as possible. The next 500 years saw irrigation canals and flood embankments transform the Indus valley environment into an artificial landscape. The obvious leaders for these new communities were the chieftains, traders, priests, and kin leaders, who acted as intermediaries between the people and their gods. Their philosophy was that humans were part of an ordered cosmos that could be maintained by unremitting toil and a subordination of individual ambition to the common good. No one knows when this primordial philosophy developed, but it is probably as old as farming itself, always a risky undertaking in subtropical lands. By 2700 B.C., the most successful leaders of larger settlements presided over hierarchies of cities, towns, and villages.

Indus Valley Civilization Indigenous culture of the Indus valley of what is now Pakistan, c. 2700 to 1700 B.C.

The early stages of the **Indus Valley Civilization** date to between 3200 and 2600 B.C. The people lived in small villages covering only a few hectares, and there were no signs of social ranking. Their environment was somewhat like that of Mesopotamia, low-lying and hot with fertile soils but no metals. Thus, its inhabitants could not flourish in isolation. Long before the rise of Indus civilization in the valley, the peoples of the lowlands interacted constantly with their neighbors to the north and west, especially in the highlands of southern Baluchistan, in western Pakistan. Metals, semiprecious stones, and timber came from the highlands, where people depended on dry agriculture and sheep herding for their subsistence. Over the millennia, the relationship between lowlands and highlands was fostered not only by regular exchanges of food and other commodities, but also by seasonal population movements that brought enormous herds of goats and sheep down from mountain summer pastures in Baluchistan to the lowlands during the harsh winters. This interaction between Baluchistan and the Indus may have been a major catalyst in the rise of complex societies in both areas, a symbiosis that was vital not only in the Indus valley, but also in distant Mesopotamia.

Early Indus society was in sharp contrast to the complex, sometimes urban society that developed in the lowlands after about 2600 B.C. The transition was an indigenous one, with a short period of explosive growth over one or two centuries, ending about 2500 B.C. This contrasts dramatically with the long period of increasing social, political, and economic complexity in Egypt and Mesopotamia.

Dilmun, Bahrain Important transshipment port between Mesopotamia and the Indus valley in the Persian Gulf as early as 2500 B.C.

Magan An ancient region referred to in Sumerian cuneiform as the source of Mesopotamia's copper and diorite (likely within the area of modern UAE and Oman).

Meluhha The Sumerian name of a prominent trading partner, its identification remains unknown, but most scholars associate it with the Indus Valley Civilization.

Archaeologist Gregory Possehl believes that this growth may have coincided with a major shift in Sumerian trade patterns. After 2600 B.C., Mesopotamian city-states reorganized their trade in luxuries and raw materials and obtained many of their needs by sea from three foreign centers, which the Sumerian texts refer to as **Dilmun**, **Magan**, and **Meluhha**.

Dilmun was an important trading area, probably located (at least for some of its existence) on the island of Bahrain in the Persian Gulf. Some researchers believe its bounty was the inspiration for the Bible's Garden of Eden story, as told first in the Mesopotamian texts. Then there was Magan, a region rich in copper and diorite, which probably lay somewhere within today's United Arab Emirates and Oman, though archaeologists have also linked it with many other places, including Yemen, Egypt, Nubia, Sudan, and right over to Iran and Pakistan. Finally, Meluhha was the Sumerian name given to an important trading partner that provided ivory, oils, furniture, gold, silver, and carnelian, among other commodities. The Sumerians exchanged these goods for wool, cloth, leather, oil, cereals, and cedar wood. Though Meluhha's location is again unclear, most scholars align it with the Indus valley region. In about 2350 B.C., King Sargon of Agade in Mesopotamia boasted that ships from all of these locations were moored at his city. There are even records of villages of Meluhhans in Mesopotamia. This was a highly organized mercantile trade conducted by specialized merchants, a trade quite different from that of the exchange networks on the highlands far inland.

The sea trade increased the volume of Sumerian imports and exports dramatically. One shipment of 5,900 kilograms (13,000 pounds) of copper is recorded. The entire enterprise was very different from the basically noncommercial exchange systems of the Iranian plateau. The trade was under Mesopotamian control, much of it conducted through Dilmun, and, in Possehl's view, it had a major impact on the growth of Indus civilization. Interestingly, its beginnings coincide with the growth of urban centers in both Mesopotamia and the Indus valley. However, many scholars believe that overseas trade was less important than sometimes claimed and that Indus civilization was an entirely indigenous development.

Mature Indus Valley Civilization

The Mature Indus Valley Civilization developed and flourished over a vast area of just under 1.3 million square kilometers (500,000 square miles), a region considerably larger than modern Pakistan. The Indus and Saraswati valleys were the cultural focus of the Indus Valley Civilization, but they were only one part of a much larger and highly varied culture whose influences and ties extended over the lowlands of Punjab and Sind, from the highlands of Baluchistan to the deserts of Rajasthan, and from the Himalayan foothills to near Mumbai. The age-old relationship between highland Baluchistan and the Indus plains placed the Indus civilization within a larger cultural system, as did their maritime links with the Persian Gulf.

The Indus Valley Civilization was different from that of the predominantly urban Sumerians in Mesopotamia, covering a core area of more than 777,000 square kilometers (3 million square miles). Gregory Possehl makes an analogy with Egypt, where the Upper and

Lower Nile were part of the same civilization, but there were always administrative, cultural, and social differences between the two regions. There were major regional subdivisions of the Indus civilization, linked by common symbolism and religious beliefs, the foundations of a cultural tradition that endured, albeit in modified form, for many centuries.

Mohenjodaro and Harappa, Pakistan Major cities of the Indus Valley Civilization, c. 2500 B.C.

Like the Sumerians, the Indus valley people adopted the city as a means of organizing and controlling their civilization. We know of at least five major cities. The best known are **Harappa**, after which the civilization is sometimes named, and **Mohenjodaro**. Harappa and Mohenjodaro were built on artificial mounds above the floods through herculean efforts. Mohenjodaro is by far the largest of the cities, six times the area of Harappa, and was rebuilt at least nine times, sometimes because of disastrous inundations. Widely accepted population estimates, based on densities of somewhat similar modern settlements, place some 35,000–40,000 people at Mohenjodaro and 23,500 at Harappa.

The two cities are so similar that they might have been designed by the same architect. A high citadel lies at the west end of each city, dominating the streets below. Here lived the rulers, protected by great fortifications and floodworks (see Figure 13.2). Mohenjodaro's towering citadel rises 12 meters (40 feet) above the plain and is protected by massive flood

Figure 13.2 The citadel at Mohenjodaro, Pakistan, with the ceremonial bath in the foreground. Source: Robert Harding/Alamy.

embankments and a vast perimeter wall with towers. The public buildings on the summit include a pillared hall almost 27 meters (90 feet) square, perhaps the precinct where the rulers gave audience to petitioners and visiting officials. There are no spectacular temples or richly adorned shrines.

The rulers of each city looked down on a complex network of at least partially planned streets (see Figure 13.3). The more spacious dwellings, perhaps those of the nobility and merchants, were laid out around a central courtyard where guests may have been received, food was prepared, and servants probably worked. Staircases and thick ground walls indicate that some houses had two or even three stories. There were also groups of single-rowed tenements or workshops at both Harappa and Mohenjodaro where the poorest people lived, many of them presumably laborers. Some areas of Harappa and Mohenjodaro served as bazaars complete with shops.

Figure 13.3 Streets and houses at Mohenjodaro.
Source: Heritage Image Partnership Ltd/Alamy.

We do not know the names of the rulers who controlled the major cities like Harappa and Mohenjodaro. The anonymity of the Indus leaders extends even to their appearance (see Figure 13.4). These were not bombastic rulers, boasting of their achievements on grandiose palace walls. Archaeological evidence reveals that the rulers were perhaps merchants, ritual specialists, or people who controlled key resources or large areas of land. They seem not to have led ostentatious lives; there was a complete lack of priestly pomp or lavish public display. There was nothing of the ardent militarism of the Assyrian kings or of the slavish glorification of the Egyptian pharaohs.

One reason we know so little about Indus leaders is that their script still has not been deciphered. Almost 400 different pictographic symbols have been identified from their seals. Linguists do not even agree on the language in the script, but they know it is a mixture of sounds and concepts, just like Egyptian hieroglyphs. Indus seals may depict gods: one is a three-headed figure who sits in the yogic posture and wears a horned headdress. He is surrounded by a tiger, an elephant, a rhinoceros, a water buffalo, and deer. Some experts think that the deity was a forerunner of the great god Shiva in his role of Lord of the Beasts. Many seals depict cattle, which may be symbols of Shiva, who was worshipped in several forms. To judge from later beliefs, he may have had a dual role, serving as a fertility god as well as a tamer or destroyer of wild beasts. In part, he may have symbolized the unpredictable dangers of flood and famine that could threaten a village or a city. If the evidence of figurines and seals is to be believed, the symbolism of early Indus religion bears some remarkable similarities to that of modern Hinduism.

Figure 13.4 Sculpture of a bearded man from Mohenjodaro.
Source: Robert Harding/Alamy.

South Asia after the Indus Valley Civilization (1700 to 180 B.C.)

The Indus Valley Civilization reached its peak at about 2000 B.C. Three centuries later, Harappa and Mohenjodaro were in decline and soon abandoned. Their populations dispersed into smaller settlements over an enormous area. The reasons for this change are little understood but it may have been due to a variety of factors, among them possible flooding along the Indus, shifts in patterns of Mesopotamian trade, and changes in subsistence farming. One fundamental cause may have been major geological disturbances near the source of the all-important Saraswati River that caused the river to dry up and some tributaries to divert to new courses, thereby catastrophically disrupting farming life along its banks. Chronic deforestation and soil erosion may also have contributed to the demise of Indus cities.

Other changes followed soon after. By 1500 B.C., rice cultivation had taken hold in the Ganges Basin to the east, opening up a new environment for farming where conditions were unsuitable for wheat and barley cultivation. By 800 B.C., an indigenous iron technology was in full use throughout the subcontinent. Iron tools accelerated rice cultivation on the Ganges plain. Two centuries later, 16 major kingdoms were concentrated around urban centers on the Ganges plain.

City life in the Ganges valley marked the beginning of the classic period of South Asian civilization. The new cities became economic powerhouses and centers of great intellectual and religious ferment. Brahmanism was the dominant religion during the early first millennium, a form of Hinduism that placed great emphasis on ritual and sacrifice. But philosophers of the sixth century B.C., like Buddha and Makhali Gosala, challenged Brahmanism with revolutionary doctrines that militated against sacrifice. Buddhism, with its teachings of personal spiritual development, spread rapidly, becoming the dominant religion in the north within five centuries.

Mauryan Empire, India Early Indian empire centered on the Ganges River during the mid-first millennium B.C.

Meanwhile, outside powers eyed the fabled riches of the subcontinent. King Darius of Persia invaded the northwest in 516 B.C. and incorporated the Indus valley into the Persian Empire. Two centuries later, Alexander the Great ventured to the Indus River and brought Greek culture to the area. The great ruler Chandragupta Maurya of Magadha benefited from the power vacuum following Alexander's conquests and carved out the **Mauryan Empire,** which extended from Nepal and the northwest deep into the Deccan (see Figure 13.1). His grandson Asoka presided over the empire at its height between 269 and 232 B.C., seeking to unify its diverse people by a well-defined moral and ethical code based on Buddhist principles. As the Mauryan Empire came to an end in 185 B.C., South Asia had become part of a vast trading network that linked the Mediterranean world to all parts of the Indian Ocean and indirectly to new sources of raw materials across the sea to the east.

The Origins of Chinese Civilization (2600 to 1100 B.C.)

The origins of Chinese agriculture and the gradual elaboration of local society that resulted from cereal and rice cultivation were described in Chapter 11. By 3000 B.C., China was a patchwork of kingdoms large and small, ruled by chieftains buried in considerable splendor. Chinese civilization emerged in a volatile political environment of highly competitive kingdoms, some ruled from a single center, others comprising a network of smaller towns. Elaborate, ever-changing political alliances and exchange networks linked one polity to another, with rulers, who controlled such critical resources as copper ore, gaining considerable power. These many societies flourished at a time of environmental instability around 2000 B.C., when rising sea levels and cold, dry conditions appear to have contributed to political instability. Competition between rulers may have intensified, and worship of natural deities increased, as rulers developed ideological responses to environmental instability. Military activity escalated at a time when communal projects such as flood defenses became more commonplace as responses to ecological problems.

The origins of Chinese civilization in its traditional northern homeland are known only from legend. Popular stories tell us that the celebrated ruler Huang Di founded civilization in the north around 2698 B.C. There were three legendary dynasties of rulers: Xia, Shang, and Zhou (Shang oracle bones are described in Box 6.1 on p. 182).

Xia Early dynasty of northern Chinese rulers dating to before 1700 B.C., known from both archaeological evidence and legend.

What exactly do these legends mean? Who were the **Xia** and their successors, the Shang? In all probability, they were dynasties of local rulers who achieved lasting prominence among their many neighbors after generations of bitter strife. Every chieftain lived in a walled town and enjoyed much the same level of material prosperity, but each ruler came from a different lineage and was related to his competitors by intricate and closely woven allegiances and kin ties. Each dynasty assumed political dominance in the north in turn; but for all these political changes, Shang civilization itself continued more or less untouched, a loosely unified confederacy of competing small kingdoms that quarreled and warred incessantly, with executions and beheadings being commonplace (see Figure 13.5).

Figure 13.5 A Shang bronze ax.
Source: World History Archive/Alamy.

Royal Capitals

Erlitou, China Northern Chinese city occupied between 1900 and 1500 B.C., a key site in the early development of the Shang culture.

The city of **Erlitou** in the Yilou Basin south of the Huang He was an important player from 1900 to 1500 B.C.; at 300 ha (741 acres), it was the largest settlement in China at the time. Erlitou was the center of a strongly centralized kingdom. In the city itself, there was a huge chasm between the rich and the poor, with a large palace complex and a densely populated urban area, whose inhabitants engaged in agriculture and specialized crafts that included highly skilled bronze working. The latter was an innovation at Erlitou, although bronze had been used for ornaments for centuries. By 1700 B.C., Erlitou artisans were using multi-piece mold castings to fabricate elaborate ritual vessels. The foundry for these vessels lies close to the royal palace, reflecting their importance as symbols of economic, political, and religious power. Erlitou's rulers maintained tight control over a bronze culture that became a central part of later Shang civilization and required both highly skilled practitioners and control of reliable sources for the ore.

Erlitou lay amidst fertile agricultural land, but had to obtain all of its major timber, toolmaking stone, kaolin clay for the white pottery used by the elite, copper and tin, and salt from the kingdom's periphery. As a result, Erlitou's rulers expanded their domains and founded outposts as far as 200 kilometers (125 miles) away, in efforts to ensure reliable supplies of critical raw materials, especially copper, lead, tin, and salt. This territorial expansion came at a time of population increase, at least partly from immigration, as the kingdom became an elaborate hierarchy based on personal status, the acquisition of wealth, and control of production and trading of prestige artifacts. Erlitou became the founding kingdom behind later Shang civilization through its rulers' control of both the core and the economically important periphery. They created a network of kingdoms sustained by a common ideology based on ancestor cults that practiced ritual feasts, in which ritual bronze vessels were used. These rituals may have helped forge the common cultural tradition that underlay later Chinese civilization.

The same trends toward increasing complexity are thought to have occurred elsewhere in China at approximately the same time, for literate states may have emerged in the south and east as well. It seems likely that the Shang Dynasty was dominant from approximately 1766 to 1122 B.C., but that other states continued to grow at the same time. The larger area of Chinese civilization ultimately extended from the north into the middle and lower courses of the Huang He and Yangtse Rivers. In this account, we concentrate on northern Chinese civilization simply because more is known about the archaeology of the Shang than about any other early Chinese state.

Ao, China Shang culture capital in northern China, occupied c. 1560 B.C.

Shang rulers lived in at least seven capitals, situated near the middle reaches of the Huang He in the modern provinces of Henan, Shandong, and Anhui (see Figure 13.1). The sites of all these towns are still uncertain, but in approximately 1557 B.C. the Shang kings moved their capital to a place named **Ao**, which archaeologists have found under the modern industrial city of Zhengzhou, some 150 kilometers (95 miles) south of Anyang and close to the Huang He. The diggers have found traces of a vast precinct surrounded by an earthen wall more than 10 meters (33 feet) high, enclosing an area of 5 square kilometers (2 square miles). It would have taken 10,000 workers laboring 330 days a year for no fewer than 18 years to erect the fortifications alone. This walled compound housed the rulers, the temples, and the nobles. The residential quarters and craft workshops lay outside the Shang walls and included two bronze factories, one of them covering nearly a hectare (0.4 acre).

Xiao-tun, China Capital of the Shang culture, 1400 to 1122 B.C., located in the Anyang region of northern China.

In approximately 1400 B.C. the capital moved to the Anyang area, where it remained until the fall of the Shang more than 250 years later. This new royal domain was known as Yin and may have encompassed a network of compounds, palaces, villages, and cemeteries extending over an area of some 310 square kilometers (120 square miles) on the northern bank of the Huang He. The core of this "capital" was near the hamlet of **Xiao-tun**, 2.4 kilometers (1.5 miles) northwest of the modern city of Anyang. Years of excavations at Xiao-tun have revealed 53 rectangular foundations of stamped earth up to 36 meters (120 feet) long, 19.5 meters (65 feet) wide, and as much as 1.5 meters (5 feet) high, many of them associated with sacrificial burials of both animals and humans. One group of 15 foundations on the north side of the excavated area supported timber houses with mud and stick walls and was devoid of sacrificial victims. These are believed to be the royal residences that housed extended families of nobles living in large halls and smaller rooms closed off with doors.

Royal Burials

The Shang rulers at first buried their dead in a cemetery 1.7 kilometers (just over a mile) northeast of Anyang. Eleven royal graves from this cemetery were excavated during the 1930s. They were furnished on a lavish scale and date to between 1500 and 1200 B.C. The best-known grave is in the shape of a cross-like pit approximately 10 meters (33 feet) deep with slightly sloping walls. Four ramps lead from the surface to each side of the pit. The coffin of the ruler, which was placed inside a wooden chamber erected in the burial pit, was accompanied by superb bronze vessels and shell, bone, and stone ornaments. One ceremonial halberd has an engraved jade blade set in a bronze shaft adorned with dragons and inlaid with malachite. Slaves and sacrificial victims lay both in the chamber itself and on the approach ramps. Many had been decapitated, so their bodies lay in one place and their heads in another.

The Shang kings surrounded their sepulchers with hundreds of lesser burials. No fewer than 1,221 small graves have been dug up nearby, many of them burials of between 2 and 11 people in a single tomb. In 1976, archaeologists uncovered nearly 200 of these graves. Most of them contained decapitated, dismembered, or mutilated bodies. Some of the victims had been bound before death. These can only have been sacrificial offerings consecrated when the kings and their relatives died.

Bronze Working

The Shang people are justly famous for their bronze work, best known to us from ceremonial artifacts found in royal tombs. Gold was in short supply, so the prestigious metal was bronze. Most Shang bronze works are food or drinking vessels, some are weapons,

Figure 13.6 Shang ritual bronze vessel, twelfth century B.C.
Source: World History Archive/Alamy.

a few are musical instruments, and many are chariot and horse fittings. Bronze working was the guarded monopoly of the rulers, a complex art that the Chinese developed quite independently from the West before 2000 B.C. Their smiths produced some of the most sophisticated and elegant bronze objects ever crafted (see Figure 13.6). Their elaborate display pieces were copies of clay prototypes carefully sculpted around a baked clay core and encased in a segmented mold. Once the clay version was completed, the baked outer mold was removed, the model was broken away from the core, and the two parts were reassembled to receive the molten bronze. This complex technique remained in use for at least five centuries.

Shang Warriors

Every early Chinese ruler stayed in power by virtue of a strong army. Shang society was organized on what might be called military lines, so that the royal standing army could be supplemented with thousands of conscripts at very short notice. The kings were frequently at war, protecting their frontiers, suppressing rebellious rivals, or raiding for sacrificial victims. In a sense, every early Chinese state was an armed garrison that could call on armies of more than 10,000 men. Each kingdom was a sophisticated, permanent military establishment and a kin organization through which people were obligated to serve the king when called upon. The same basic organization persisted long after the fall of the Shang Dynasty around 1100 B.C.

Most surviving Shang weapons come from sacrificial chariot burials, such as the one excavated near Anyang in 1973. The archaeologists did not uncover the wooden chariot

Figure 13.7 Museum display of a chariot burial from the Shang royal cemetery near Anyang. The wooden parts of the chariot were excavated by following discolorations in the soil left by rotting wood.

Source: Dorling Kindersley Ltd/Alamy.

itself, but a cast of the wooden parts preserved in the soil (see Figure 13.7). They brushed away the surrounding soil with great care until they reached the hardened particles of fine sand that had replaced the wooden structure of the buried chariot. They were able to photograph not only the "ghost" of the chariot, but also the skeletons of the two horses. The charioteer had been killed at the funeral and his body had been placed behind the vehicle. The charioteer rode on a wicker and leather car measuring between 0.9 and 1.2 meters (3 and 4 feet) across and borne on a stout axle and two spoked wheels with large hubs adorned with bronze caps. In all probability, the nail-less chariot was held together with sinew lashings, adorned with bronze and turquoise ornaments, and perhaps painted in bright colors.

The War Lords (1100 to 221 B.C.)

Zhou Important Chinese dynasty that ruled over much of northern China after 1122 B.C.

The Shang Dynasty fell at about 1100 B.C. at the hands of the neighboring **Zhou**. The conquerors did not create a new civilization; rather, they took over the existing network of towns and officials and incorporated them into their own state organization, thus shifting the focus of political and economic power to the south and west, away from Anyang into the fertile Wei valley near the modern city of Xi'an. By this time, the influence of what may loosely be called Shang civilization extended far beyond the north, into the rice-growing areas of the south and along the eastern coasts. The Zhou divided their domains into various and almost independent provinces, which warred with one another for centuries. It was not until 221 B.C. that the great emperor Shihuangdi unified China into a single empire (see Box 13.1). His Han Dynasty successors traded with the Western world overland via the celebrated Great Silk Road across Central Asia and with newly powerful states in Southeast Asia.

Box 13.1 Discovery
The Burial Mound of Emperor Shihuangdi, China

King Zheng, the "Tiger of Qin," was the First Sovereign Emperor (Shihuangdi) of China. He became ruler of Qin at the age of 13 in 246 B.C., unifying China after a series of ruthless military campaigns in 221 B.C. Work may have begun on the emperor's tomb as early as 246 B.C., but it intensified after unification. The emperor considered himself unique, so his sepulcher was to be the largest ever built. Later court histories write of more than 700,000 conscripts, many of them convicts, who worked on the tomb, the capital, and the royal palace.

The great burial mound measures more than 335 meters (1,100 feet) on each side and rises 43 meters (140 feet) above the surrounding countryside 40 kilometers (25 miles) east of Xianyang on the banks of the Wei River. It is said that inside the mound lies a replica of the royal domains, with China's great rivers recreated in

Figure 13.8 Bronze cart with horses and driver, fabricated in cast bronze with silver inlay at one-third life-size, found near the tomb of Shihuangdi, first emperor of China.

Source: Hung Chung Chih/Shutterstock.

mercury flowing, by some mechanical device, into the ocean. The constellations of the heavens appear on the ceiling of the burial chamber, the Earth's geography beneath. Scale models of palaces and pavilions contain the emperor's personal possessions, while models of courtiers attend him in death. Many concubines, and also laborers who worked on the tomb, were sacrificed and buried inside the tumulus. Although Han Dynasty historians state that the mound was looted after the fall of the Qin line, Chinese archaeologists have detected unusually high concentrations of mercury in the soil chemistry of the mound and suspect that Shihuangdi's grave goods may be intact. They decline to excavate the tomb, as they say they lack the resources and skills to dig it properly and conserve the contents. The mound once lay in the middle of a large funerary park surrounded by a 6.4-kilometer (4-mile) outer wall.

In the 1970s, the Chinese excavated a regiment of terracotta soldiers to the side of the funerary mound—armed cavalrymen, kneeling archers, and their officers, perhaps a ceremonial guard assigned to protect the eastern side of the tomb (see chapter opener). The molded figures were finished with individual hairstyles, mustaches, and other features, and were fully armed. Other finds near the tumulus include two bronze chariots, made at one-third life-size, and their horses (see Figure 13.8), as well as underground stables, some with mangers containing horses buried alive.

Southeast Asian Civilization (A.D. 1 to 1500)

After 500 B.C., there are signs of major cultural and social change throughout Southeast Asia that coincide with the introduction of iron technology between about 600 and 400 B.C. The new metallurgy was grafted on to existing bronze technology, but it is uncertain whether ironworking was introduced from India, where forging (smelting in a small furnace) was used, or from China, where sophisticated casting methods were commonplace, involving molten iron at very high temperatures. Larger communities developed, usually centers for craft production. The appearance of larger settlements may have coincided with both irrigation and the advent of plowing, which greatly increased food production and produced much larger crop surpluses.

Toward the end of the first millennium B.C., some Southeast Asian societies had become highly ranked, centralized kingdoms, presided over by an aristocratic class to whom formal display, feasting, and ritual were of paramount importance. They ruled by virtue of their close relationships with their ancestors. The growing complexity of such societies came in part from the ability of their overlords to attract loyal followers and to organize people. In time, many such rulers aspired to even greater status by presiding over far larger kingdoms, carved out by force or charisma, or by the creation of magnificent palaces and temples to serve as the focus of elaborate public ceremonials and prestigious displays.

mandala Hindu conception of the state, applied to Southeast Asian archaeology.

Funan, Cambodia Prosperous city-state region in Southeast Asia between the third and sixth centuries A.D.

These Southeast Asian kingdoms were in a constant state of political flux and lacked fixed boundaries. Alliances developed between neighboring rulers. Everything revolved around the principal overlord, whose ability to cement alliances and deal with potential enemies dictated his relationships with his rivals. Some experts use a Sanskrit word, ***man-dala***, a Hindu conception of the state, to describe the relationships between these rulers, whose territories were thought of as circles. It is as if they were concertinas that expanded and contracted as different polities interacted with one another. Each society focused on its own center and on its own religious ruler and his retinue. The personal and spiritual qualities of each leader were important variables in a complex, ever-changing political equation. Divine kingship revolutionized social and political organization in Southeast Asia. Kingdoms flourished in riverine and lowland areas, along the lower Mekong, and in the middle Mekong valley, including the celebrated Tonle Sap plains, the homeland of Khmer. The Chinese called the lower Mekong region **Funan**, which meant "port of a thousand rivers," but the term has little real historical meaning. According to Chinese records, the ports of the delta handled bronze, silver, gold, spices, and even horses brought by sea from Central Asia. Chinese accounts of Funan extol its rich trade. They tell of a drainage and transport system that rapidly transformed much of the delta from barren swamps into rich agricultural land. The development of these fields took the communal efforts of hundreds of people living off the fish that teemed in the bayous of the delta. Most Funanese lived in large lake cities fortified with great earthworks and moats swarming with crocodiles. Each major settlement was a port connected to the ocean and its neighbors by a canal network.

Zhenla, Cambodia Major center of economic and political life on the middle Mekong River and Cambodia's Tonle Sap, sixth century A.D.

The coastal region prospered greatly during the third to the sixth century A.D., thanks to its long traditions of indigenous metallurgy and other crafts and trading expertise. But by the sixth century A.D., the center of economic and political gravity had shifted inland to the middle Mekong and the fertile Tonle Sap, an area the Chinese called **Zhenla.** Competing Zhenla rulers acquired sufficient food surpluses to embark on ambitious conquests and, eventually, to develop a new political concept of divine kingship that united their far-flung domains in a common purpose: the glorification of the god-king on Earth. Devotion to the Hindu creator, Shiva, became a mechanism that provided divine justification for kingship, as well as a focus for the loyalty and devotion of a ruler's retinue, who would endow temples in return for royal favors. Ambitious men would try again and again to rise above others and lead their kingdoms to supreme rule. Throughout the centuries, these were never states in the Western sense. Rather, the "concertina" effect of kingdom politics was constantly at work, with competing polities asserting independence at times and becoming tribute givers and vassals at others.

The Angkor State (A.D. 802 to 1430)

The overlords of the Tonle Sap all shared one ambition: to establish hegemony over as large an area as possible. The earlier kings were unable to hold the kingdom together until a dynamic Khmer monarch named Jayavarman II came to power in A.D. 802. He conquered his competitors and set up his new territories as tribute kingdoms, giving his loyal generals land grants.

Jayavarman II is said to have merged the cult of the ancestors with that of Shiva to consolidate his new kingdom. His subjects were taught to worship him as a god. All resources of an increasingly centralized government were devoted to the preservation of the cult of the god-king. Everyone, whether noble, high priest, or commoner, was expected to subordinate his or her ambitions to the need to perpetuate the existence of the king on Earth and his identity with Shiva in this life and the next. This remarkable leader reigned for 45 years, the first of at least three dynasties of Khmer rulers, who often came to power after vicious fighting and presided over an ever-changing state that reached the height of its prosperity between 900 and 1200.

Previous monarchs had encouraged the worship of Shiva in the form of the phallic image, but now Jayavarman II presented himself as the reincarnation of Shiva on Earth. He was the *varman*, the protector, and his priests were the instruments of practical political power. The high priests were invariably energetic, imposing nobles who presided over a highly disciplined hierarchy of religious functionaries. The ruler himself headed a bureaucracy of high-status families, which included generals and administrators who settled land disputes. The bureaucracy supervised every aspect of Khmer life, from agriculture to warfare, tax collection, and the rituals of the state religion. As always with preindustrial civilizations, there was a close link between food surpluses and the control of the enormous labor forces needed to construct temples, reservoirs, and other public works.

The custom of building a new majestic and holy temple to house the royal *linga* (phallic symbol) of each king was the most important of all the religious rituals. As a result, many of the 30 monarchs who followed Jayavarman II left massive religious edifices to commemorate their reigns. These were built on artificial mounds in the center of their capitals, the hub of the Khmer universe, an area known today as Angkor. The Khmer's unique form of kingship produced, instead of an austere civilization like that of the Indus, a society that carried the cult of wealth, luxury, and divine monarchy to amazing lengths. This cult reached its apogee in the reign of Suryavarman II, who built the temple of Angkor Wat in the twelfth century (see Box 13.2).

Angkor Wat, Cambodia Royal capital and shrine built by the Khmer rulers of Cambodia between A.D. 1000 and 1200.

Angkor Thom, Cambodia Royal capital and shrine built by the Khmer rulers of Cambodia between A.D. 1000 and 1200.

Angkor Wat taxed the resources of the kingdom severely at a time of increased strife with neighboring powers. In 1181, another ruler, Jayavarman VII, started building a huge new capital at nearby **Angkor Thom** (see Figure 12.2 on p. 382). A dark and forbidding 12.8-kilometer (8-mile) wall surrounded the capital. When visitors walked inside, they entered a symbolic Hindu world with the king's funerary temple at the center. The Grand Plaza of Angkor Thom was the scene of ceremonies and contests, vast military reviews, and massed bands.

Ta Prohm, Cambodia Khmer temple near Angkor Thom dedicated in the twelfth century A.D.

Box 13.2 Site
Angkor Wat, Cambodia

For four years after his succession in A.D. 1113, King Suryavarman II focused on building his masterpiece, an extraordinary shrine that is a spectacle of beauty, wonder, and magnificence—the largest religious building in the world. **Angkor Wat** is 1,500 meters (5,000 feet) by 1,200 meters (4,000 feet) across (see Figure 3.7 on p. 82). The central block measures 215 by 186 meters (717 by 620 feet) and rises more than 60 meters (200 feet) above the forest. It dwarfs even the largest Sumerian ziggurat and makes Mohenjodaro's citadel look like a village shrine.

Every detail of this extraordinary building reproduces part of the heavenly world in a terrestrial mode. The Khmer believed that the world consisted of a central continent known as Jambudvipa, with the cosmic mountain, Meru, rising from its center. The gods lived at the summit of Meru, represented at Angkor Wat by the highest

Figure 13.9 Bas-relief from Angkor Wat. Celestial females, naked to the waist, symbolize the delights of paradise after death.

Source: Sophie Dauwe/iStock via Getty Images.

tower. The remaining four towers represent Meru's lesser peaks; the enclosure wall depicts the mountain at the edge of the world, and the surrounding moat depicts the ocean beyond. Angkor Wat was the culminating attempt of the Khmer to reproduce a monument to the Hindu god Vishnu, the preserver of the universe.

Angkor Wat's bas-reliefs show Suryavarman seated on a wooden throne wearing an elaborate crown and pectoral. He receives his high officials as they declare their loyalty. Next, the king progresses down a hillside on an elephant accompanied by the high priest and his generals. The court rides with him through a forest, with noble ladies in litters, everyone protected by heavily armed soldiers. Scattered throughout Angkor Wat are scenes of battles and bas-reliefs of celestial maidens (*apsaras*). Naked to the waist, slender, and sensuous, the dancers wear skirts of rich fabric (see Figure 13.9). Their flowered background, the subtle rhythm of their gestures, and their jeweled necklaces and diadems bring to light the delights of paradise promised to the king after his death. Inscriptions also spell out the terrible punishments that awaited evildoers.

Angkor Wat was constructed using a Khmer unit of measurement known as a *hat*, equal to 0.435 meter (1.43 feet). The length and breadth of the central structure of the temple correspond to 365.37 *hat*, while the axial distances of the great causeway correspond to the four great eras of Hindu time. Someone standing in front of the western entrance on the spring equinox would be able to see the Sun rising directly over the central lotus tower. During his lifetime, Suryavarman used Angkor Wat as the place where he, as a divine monarch, communicated with the gods. When he died, his remains were placed in the central tower so that his soul entered his divine image and made contact with the royal ancestors. Here the immortal ruler became as one with Vishnu, master of the universe.

It is said that a million people once lived in or near Angkor Thom. One temple dedicated to the father of Jayavarman VII contained no fewer than 430 images, with more than 20,000 in gold, silver, bronze, and stone in the wider precincts. An inscription in the **Ta Prohm** temple nearby, dedicated to the king's mother in the image of the Buddha's mother, records that 306,372 people from 13,500 villages worked for the shrine, consuming 38,000 tons of rice a year (see Figure 13.10). Another inscription inventories a staff of 18 senior priests, 2,740 minor functionaries, 615 female dancers, and a total of 66,625 "men and women who performed the service of the gods." All this royal construction was designed to make merit for the king and his followers. He also built fully staffed hospitals and pilgrims' shelters to gain further credit. The result of Jayavarman's building projects was a totally centripetal religious utopia in which every product, every person's labor, and every thought was directed to embellishing the hub of the universe and the kings who enjoyed it.

The impression of prosperity and stability was illusory in a society in which the ruler's power depended on the granting of favors and on his successful patronizing of the major aristocratic families. The king mediated with the gods for rain, settled disputes, and used the rich resources of the land to redistribute wealth among his subjects. He sat at the center of the circle represented by the *mandala*, its boundaries defined only by the loyalties of the aristocrats who ruled the outlying areas. These provinces were vast: over the past two decades, various archaeologists, among them University of Sydney's Roland Fletcher, have led a series of remote-sensing projects combined with extensive fieldwork. This cutting-edge work has revealed a huge, low-density urban complex, that once stretched far around Angkor Wat itself. Known today as "Greater Angkor," this "mega city" of sorts once covered an area of about 1,000 square kilometers (386 square miles)

Figure 13.10 Banyan trees are gradually smothering the ruins of Ta Prohm.
Source: Singhatho/Shutterstock.

and contained an estimated 750,000 inhabitants. Yet the Khmer king's hold on the reins of power depended on the control of the center. Thus, when the central administration was weak, the kingdom tended to break up into regional units. In 1430–1431, Angkor Wat, and Greater Angkor, finally collapsed in the face of droughts caused by monsoon failures and ecological stresses, also, perhaps, as a result of pressure from ambitious neighbors.

Late in the thirteenth century, the strategic trade routes through the Malay Straits came under Islamic control in a new chapter of international trade. Melaka became an important port and stronghold on the northern shore of the straits. The rest of the kingdoms and ports of the islands soon adopted the new faith, which preached a message of religious egalitarianism in the face of centuries of Indian statecraft based on notions of divine kingship. Within three centuries, the rulers of inland Java had adopted Islam, perhaps to maintain control over their subjects, who were welcoming the new beliefs with open arms. Islam and trade went hand in hand in island Southeast Asia until the arrival of Portuguese gun-bearing sailing ships at Melaka in 1519.

The Khmer state is a classic example of how a combination of cultural processes and able individuals can lead to the appearance of powerful yet volatile states. Yet these same states constantly face the problem of controlling not only the center, but also the periphery, especially in times of weak rule and menacing competition from outside.

Summary

- State-organized societies on the Indian subcontinent developed from indigenous roots before 2700 B.C.
- The Indus Valley Civilization of the lowland Indus valley developed as the result of a major shift in Sumerian long-distance trade patterns and long-term interactions between the Indus culture of the lowlands and the people of the Baluchistan highlands.
- The Indus Valley Civilization flourished along the Indus for about 1,000 years. It was a highly sophisticated urban society with many smaller satellite settlements.
- After 1700 B.C., the major cities went into decline, but Indus society flourished in rural settings for a considerable time. The center of economic and political gravity moved eastward to the Ganges River valley, culminating in the Mauryan Empire of the first millennium B.C.
- Early Chinese civilization emerged independently of state-organized societies in the West. The Shang civilization of the Huang He valley is the best-known early Chinese state, flourishing from 1766 to 1122 B.C. It was probably the dominant state among several throughout northern China.
- Shang society was organized along class lines, with the rulers and nobles living in segregated precincts, whereas the mass of the population was scattered throughout townships and villages in the surrounding countryside.
- The Shang Dynasty was overthrown by Zhou rulers, who reigned over a wide area of northern China from 1122 to 221 B.C., when China was unified under the emperor Zheng (Shihuangdi).
- The process of forming Southeast Asian states began around the same time, but the first historical records of complex states date to the third century A.D.
- Many such states developed in and around the central Mekong valley and later in the central Cambodian basin. There, after A.D. 802, flourished the flamboyant Khmer civilization, a society based on divine kingship and strong notions of conformity.
- After six centuries of spectacular development, the Khmer civilization came in contact with expanding Islamic trade networks and new religious doctrines, which caused its partial demise.

Key Terms and Sites

Mohenjodaro
Indus Valley Civilization
Dilmun
Magan
Meluhha
Harappa
Mauryan Empire
Xia
Erlitou
Ao
Xiao-tun
Zhou
mandala
Funan
Zhenla
Angkor Wat
Angkor Thom
Ta Prohm

Critical-Thinking Questions

1. What is the most striking difference between early Chinese (Shang) states and that of the Egyptians? Use examples from Chapter 12 and this chapter.
2. The Khmer state flourished because it was completely centralized. What are the strengths and weaknesses of such centralization?
3. What, in your opinion, is the most striking feature of Indus Valley Civilization, compared with that of the Khmer?

Further Reading

The Indus: Lost Civilizations by A. Robinson (London: Reaktion Books, 2021) is a brilliant place to start your adventure into understanding the Indus Valley Civilization. For further reading, we recommend J. R. McIntosh, *A Peaceful Realm* (Boulder, CO: Westview Press, 2002), while R. Allchin's *The Archaeology of Historic South Asia* (Cambridge: Cambridge University Press, 1995) covers the Mauryan and later societies. K.-C. Chang's *Shang Civilization* (New Haven, CT: Yale University Press, 1980) is still authoritative. See also K.-C. Chang's *The Formation of Chinese Civilization: An Archaeological Perspective* (New Haven, CT: Yale University Press, 2005). L. Liu and X. Chen's, *State Formation in Early China* (London: Duckworth, 2003) provides a good overview, while G. Barnes's *China, Korea, and Japan* (London: Thames and Hudson, 1993) is a general summary in English. For Southeast Asia generally, see C. Higham, *Early Mainland Southeast Asia* (Bangkok: River Books, 2014); also see the same author and R. Thosarat's *Prehistoric Thailand* (Bangkok: River Books, 1998), which describes the excavations. M. D. Coe and D. Evans, *Angkor & The Khmer Civilization* (London: Thames and Hudson, 2024) is an excellent book on this important culture; or for a summary feature of work in the area, see *Current World Archaeology* (77) (2016): 14–20, by Fagan and Durrani.

Part 6

The Ancient Americas

14 North America

Chapter Outline

White House Ruins, Canyon de Chelly, Arizona, c. A.D. 1200.
Source: Robert Miramontes/Thinkstock.

DOI: 10.4324/9781003592754-20

In 1879, Frank Cushing, a young anthropologist from the Smithsonian Institution, arrived at Zuni Pueblo in the American Southwest on a mule. A pall of wood smoke covered the town as the sun set behind the settlement. The mud-brick walls melted into the landscape. He wrote, "It seemed still a little island of mesas, one upon the other, reared from a sea of sand, in mock rivalry of the surrounding grander mesas of Nature's rearing" (Cushing 1979, 45). A pioneer of the anthropological method known as participant observation, Cushing lived among the Zuni for four-and-a-half years, learning their language and recording their traditional life in great detail.

kivas Sacred ceremonial rooms built by prehistoric peoples in the American Southwest.

After three years, the Zuni initiated him into the secret Priesthood of the Bow. Cushing now dressed in Indian clothing. He spent many hours sitting in **kivas** watching "the blazes of the splinter-lit fire on the stone altar, sometimes licking the very ladder-poles in their flight upward toward the skyhole, which served at once as doorway, chimney, and window." He listened to "the shrill calls of the rapidly coming and departing dancers, their wild songs, and the din of the great drum, which fairly jarred the ancient, smoke-blackened rafters" (Cushing 1979, 48, 112).

Frank Cushing enjoyed the confidence of the Zuni, but died before he could set down more than a popular account of their culture. Cushing's observations have been of great value to archaeologists as they work back from the present into the remote southwestern past.

This chapter is a summary of North America after first settlement and generally tells the story of early food production in the Americas.

North America after First Settlement

As we saw in Chapter 10, *Homo sapiens* had settled in all parts of the Americas by 14,000 years ago (i.e. 12,000 B.C.). The exact date of first settlement remains uncertain, but within a remarkably short time, humans had spread throughout the hitherto uninhabited continent. Their numbers were small, but they adapted to all manner of natural environments, from arctic tundra to desert and tropical rainforest. By 11,000 B.C., the last of the great Ice Age animals (often called *megafauna*) that once inhabited the Americas became extinct, for reasons that are still little understood. An increasingly warmer and drier climate may have played a significant role in extinction. Humans may also have contributed by hunting slow-breeding animals like the mastodon.

Over the millennia that followed, ancient Native American societies diversified their lifeways greatly, at a time of profound environmental change in North America. As the great ice sheets retreated, woodland and forest moved northward, the Great Lakes came into being, and temperatures rose rapidly. Throughout the Americas, human groups responded by exploiting a broad range of small game and, especially, edible plant foods of every kind. They settled by rivers and on lakeshores, hunted sea mammals, and exploited inshore fisheries in estuaries and along open coasts (see Figure 14.1).

Only on the Great Plains did ancient big-game hunting practices endure. Paleo-Indians hunted now-extinct forms of bison, which thrived on the dry grasses of the presently much drier plains. They hunted their prey with stone-tipped spears, watching the herds closely and picking off isolated beasts. Occasionally, groups would drive entire herds into narrow

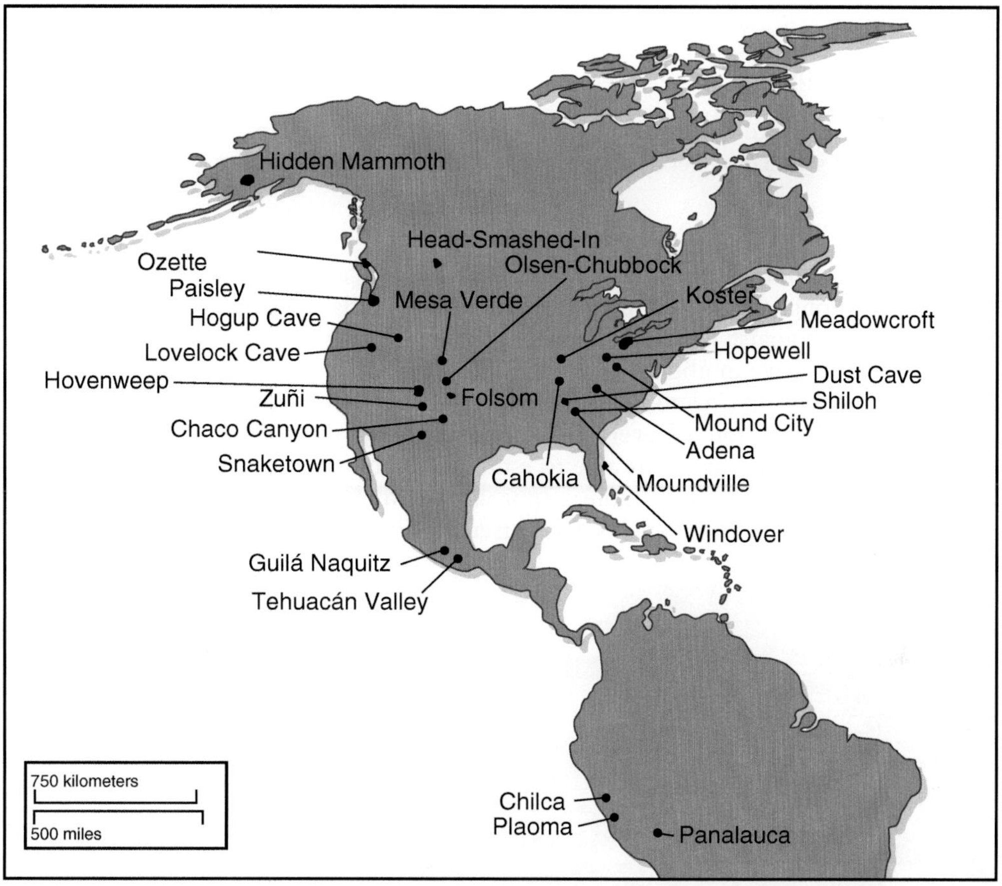

Figure 14.1 Sites discussed in Chapter 14.

gullies or over cliffs. These rare hunts yielded enough fresh and dried meat to feed several bands for months (see Box 14.1). We know of these people from their distinctive projectile points, which took many forms. Some of these can be ordered chronologically. All ultimately derived from the ancient Clovis point.

Olsen-Chubbock, Colorado Paleo-Indian kill site dating to c. 6000 B.C., the location of a mass bison kill involving over 150 beasts.

Fincastle, Alberta A bison ambush and kill site of 500 B.C., which provides detail on plains butchery methods.

In eastern North America, the Paleo-Indians adapted to progressively warmer and more diverse Eastern Woodlands environments. They hunted forest game like white-tailed deer, but relied increasingly on nuts and other edible plant foods. This basic subsistence pattern endured for thousands of years, with the fall nut harvest assuming increasing importance in many places. Hickories, pecans, and acorns were vital staples, and were easily stored for use in the winter.

Box 14.1 Sites
Plains Bison Kills

Mass bison kills were major events in the lives of Plains Indians. Many have been excavated and studied in detail. Here are two well-known examples.

Olsen-Chubbock, Colorado

The **Olsen-Chubbock** bison kill site in Colorado is a classic example of a game drive site. Although excavated many years ago, it remains a superb example of field research. Archaeologist Joe Ben Wheat's excavation tells the remarkable story of a successful bison drive in about 6000 B.C. With meticulous care, Wheat unearthed a pile of over 190 bison skeletons, packed tightly in a narrow gully (see Figure 14.2). By plotting the position of every bone and studying their orientation, and the butchering methods, Wheat was able to establish many details of the ancient hunt.

The hunt began when some hunters approached an unsuspecting bison herd from downwind. Stalking and driving bison is extremely difficult and requires consummate

Figure 14.2 Bison bones at the Olsen-Chubbock site, Colorado.
Source: University of Colorado Museum.

skill, as they are very nervous beasts. One can imagine the hunters watching the herd for days, gradually moving them into a strategic position upwind of the narrow gully that was to be their grave.

On the day of the hunt, the wind was blowing from the south. (We know this because the bison faced south in the gully.) Several bands probably took part in the hunt. The stalkers stood up, waved bison hides, and made bison calls, stampeding the frightened beasts toward the nearly invisible narrow defile. The leading animals stumbled and were swept on by the beasts galloping immediately behind them. The herd fell into the gully. Many animals were trampled to death; the hunters speared those that survived as they floundered in confusion.

When no animal remained alive, the band turned to butchering. With quiet efficiency, they maneuvered carcasses into a position where they could be cut up at the edge of the arroyo. The butchers worked in teams as they rolled the animals on their bellies, slit the hides down the back, and pulled them down the flanks to form carpets for the meat. Then, they removed the prime flesh from the back, also the forelimbs, shoulder blades, and other favored parts, eating the soft intestines as they worked and piling the bones to one side. This was almost industrial-scale butchering on a systematic basis, the aim being to acquire as much meat and as many hides as possible and then to dry the flesh for later use. Wheat estimated that the hunters butchered 75 percent of the animals they killed, acquiring about 24,752 kilograms (nearly 54,570 pounds) of meat in the process, much of which they probably dried. This was enough meat to feed 100 people for a month or more.

By any standard, bison drives were wasteful, but they were the only alternative to pursuing individual beasts. Mass hunts were rare endeavors, involving several bands who came together for the hunt. Hunting bison on foot and with spears continued into the eighteenth century A.D., when European fur traders witnessed hunters dressed in bison hides decoying a herd into a stout corral, bellowing like the animals themselves. As the great beasts entered the jaws of the compound, the decoys leapt to safety and the killing began. The methods used by these hunters dated back to Paleo-Indian times.

The Fincastle site, Alberta

Around 500 B.C., a sizable group of hunters ambushed a bison herd in a marshy area of southern Alberta in late summer or fall. At least 62 beasts were killed, probably more, the season of the kill determined from their teeth. The excavation was meticulous, with even tiny finds recorded in situ and entered in 1:5 scale graph paper plans. Careful excavation revealed a complex set of butchery activities, starting with the disarticulation of the carcasses, followed by stripping meat from the bones, removing the highly desirable tongues and extracting marrow and grease from the dead beasts. Much of the original bone bed was recovered.

Details of the kill strategy do not survive, but it may have revolved around a dune of windblown sand and a small pond where the beasts obtained water. The hunters used stone projectile points, most of which were made of Knife River flint, found in North Dakota, a toolmaking stone widely used across the northern plains. Maybe the hunters had close connections with the distant Middle Missouri region, where the flint occurs. Most likely, the hunt was opportunistic, in an area where bison congregated to feed. Here, as at Olsen-Chubbock and other plains bison sites, careful observation of the prey was a key element in the hunt.

The densest hunter-gatherer populations congregated in river valleys and on lakeshores, where food resources were both predictable and abundant. Freshwater fish, waterfowl, deer, and plant foods of all kinds made it possible to schedule different foraging activities for each season of the year. For example, a veritable carpet of oil-rich nuts and other foods covered upland forest floors each fall. White-tailed deer and other animals feasted on this "mast," so hunters could prey on them at the time of the nut harvest. As spring river floods receded, people came down from higher ground to spear fish in shallow pools. As long as food densities remained low, there was little incentive to exploit anything but a fairly narrow spectrum of animal, aquatic, and plant foods in favored locations (Figure 14.3).

For thousands of years, hunter-gatherer populations throughout the Americas remained thin on the ground, with different cultures being identified mainly by their changing projectile point forms. By 6000 B.C., population densities in more favored areas had risen to the point where group territories were more restricted. The Koster site in the Illinois River valley, briefly described in Chapter 3, documents thousands of years of increasingly restricted movement, to the point that by 5000 B.C., people found most of their food

Figure 14.3 Artist's reconstruction of a hunter-gatherer camp on the Little Tennessee River (c. 6300 B.C.), which gives a general impression of foraging lifeways in a woodland environment after the Ice Age.

Source: Courtesy of McClung Museum of Natural History and Culture, University of Tennessee, Knoxville; Artist is Greg Harlin.

within 5 kilometers (3 miles) of the settlement. By 4000 B.C., many river valley groups dwelt in more or less permanent base camps and exploited a relatively narrow spectrum of foods. Inevitably, as local populations rose, food supplies were in shorter supply. Some groups took the next logical step and began deliberately cultivating native grasses.

Lovelock Cave, Nevada Cave in the Great Basin occupied sporadically by hunter-gatherers from c. 7000 B.C. until recent times.

In the west, very sparse Paleo-Indian populations exploited large desert territories. Before 9000 B.C., some groups were settled along the southern California coast and on the offshore islands, which implies the use of at least simple watercraft. As in the east, the densest hunter-gatherer populations flourished in areas with the most diverse and predictable food resources. For thousands of years, forager bands in the arid Great Basin visited the same caves and rock shelters again and again because they lay close to marshlands and small lakes. Here they took waterfowl and small fish like chub, as well as edible plants; these foods were so reliable that they could return to the same location year after year for long periods of time. Hogup Cave in Utah and **Lovelock Cave** in Nevada were favored locations for more than 9,000 years.

The hunter-gatherers of the Great Basin and other arid regions maintained a highly mobile lifeway into modern times. After 4000 B.C., populations rose in favored locations, especially in California's inland river valleys, in the present-day San Francisco Bay area, and along the southern California coast. A combination of abundant and predictable food resources, increasingly efficient technology, and sedentary settlement gave rise to more complex hunter-gatherer societies along many parts of the Pacific coast in the last 1,000 years or so before European contact in the sixteenth to eighteenth centuries (see Figure 14.4).

In some areas like the desert west, the Pacific coast, and the far north, hunter-gatherer societies continued to flourish into recent times. Many of these groups were well aware of agriculture. Some of them even cultivated the soil on a sporadic basis, if it was advantageous to do so. But food production, especially the cultivation of maize, played a central role in the later history of many Native American societies.

The Story of Maize

For thousands of years after first settlement, Native Americans subsisted off hunting and gathering, developing an increasing expertise with wild plant foods of all kinds. In some regions, they exploited such resources intensively, especially in the Midwest and Southeast, where some groups were able to occupy more or less permanent settlements for many generations. In time, however, they also started planting wild native grasses as a means of supplementing wild plant resources. In time, too, this led to agriculture, especially in areas where wild grasses were plentiful.

By the time of Columbus, the ancient Americans had developed a truly remarkable expertise with all kinds of native plants, using them not only for food but also for medicinal and many other purposes. The most important staple crop was maize (Indian corn) which is the only significant wild grass in the New World to be fully domesticated. It remains the most important food crop in the Americas, and is used in more than 150 varieties as both food and cattle fodder. Root crops formed another substantial food source, especially in South America, and included manioc, sweet potatoes, and many varieties

Figure 14.4 Salmon fishing on the Columbia River, Pacific Northwest. Harvesting salmon runs required a carefully organized "production line" to process, dry, and store the fish as they were speared and netted by the thousands.

Source: North Wind Picture Archives/Alamy.

of the potato. Chili peppers were grown as a seasoning. Amaranth, sunflowers, cacao, peanuts, and several types of beans were also significant crops. In contrast to Old World farmers, the Indians had few domesticated animals. Among them were the llama of the Andes and alpacas, which provided wool. The ancient Americans also tamed the dog, the guinea pig, the turkey, and the Muscovy duck.

Most archaeologists now agree that there were at least three major centers of native plant domestication in the Americas, with ancient DNA (aDNA) research and the refined dating of material, adding important details and refining our understanding of the timing and geographic spread of these domestication events:

- Highland and lowland Central America for maize, beans, squash, and sweet potatoes.
- The highlands of the central Andes for root crops like potatoes and manioc.
- The southeastern United States for pepo squash, sunflowers, and other local plants.
- There were also four areas of later cultivation activity: tropical (northern) South America, the Andean area, Mesoamerica, and southwestern and eastern North America.

Mesoamerica: Guilá Naquitz and Early Cultivation

The process of plant domestication is becoming increasingly understood through a combination of archaeological, ecological, and genetic data. Archaeologist Kent Flannery's theories, initially grounded in ecological considerations (see Chapter 12), are now supported and refined by genetic evidence. Flannery suggested that plant cultivation began as a result of strategies designed to cope with continuous short-term climatic fluctuations and constant population shifts. Flannery cites his own excavations at the Guilá Naquitz rock shelter in the Valley of Oaxaca. Guilá Naquitz was occupied about six times over a 2,000-year period between 8750 and 6670 B.C. The tiny forager groups who visited the cave faced unpredictable climatic fluctuations due to periodic droughts in an area that could support very few people per square mile.

The Guilá Naquitz people foraged 11 different edible plant species over the year. In wet years, they experimented with deliberate planting of beans. Bean cultivation near the cave allowed people to collect more food and travel less. At first, the experiments were confined to wet years, but as time went on and they gained more confidence, plant yields rose and they relied more heavily on their own cultivation as opposed to foraging. In time, the Guilá Naquitz people simply added squash, beans, and a variety of maize to a much earlier foraging adaptation. Recent AMS radiocarbon dates put squash cultivation at the cave at about 8000 B.C., as early as cereal agriculture in other regions of the world, such as southwestern Asia. As Flannery proposed, ongoing scientific studies are indicating that this type of transition from foraging to farming likely occurred in many parts of Mesoamerica.

The Earliest Maize

The wild ancestor of maize (*Zea mays*) was a perennial grass called teosinte, which still grows in Central America today (see Figure 14.5). The process of domestication may have been unintentional. Foragers may have favored the most harvestable varieties of wild teosinte grasses, those whose seeds scattered less easily when ripe. This process may have led to selection for harvestable types of the grass and then to deliberate planting. In time, the favored types of teosinte would become established near campsites and in abandoned rubbish dumps. In time, too, people would remove weeds from these teosinte stands and then deliberately plant the more useful types. At first, the planted teosinte was no more productive than wild forms, but it was easier to harvest—a critical stage in the

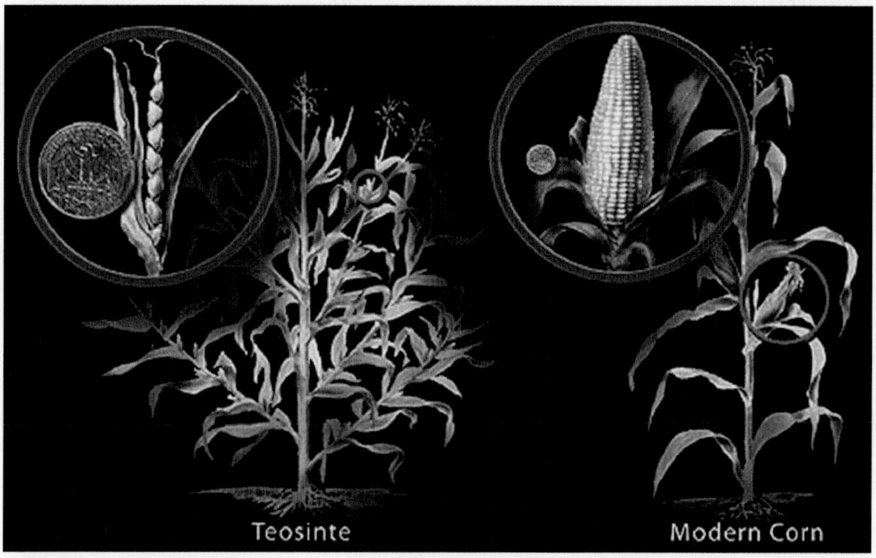

Figure 14.5 A comparison of teosinte (left) and maize (right).
Source: Randsc/Alamy.

process of domestication. Soon the grass became dependent on human intervention. Genetic adaptations ensured that teosinte's use as a human food had a selective advantage.

From its earliest introduction, maize would have been a more efficient source of calories than many wild forest plants, and hence a source of experimentation. No one knows exactly where maize was first cultivated. It may have been in the tropical lowlands, which did not have the richness of wild plant foods found in more open areas. Guilá Naquitz Cave in Oaxaca has yielded an AMS date on maize of 4250 B.C. There is indirect evidence of even earlier maize cultivation, before 5000 B.C., at San Andreas on the Gulf coast and elsewhere, but we lack the cobs or kernels to firmly establish this date. Further analysis suggests that maize domestication took place more than 250 kilometers (150 miles) west of Tehuacán, in river valleys that flow from the highlands into the Pacific—areas where the wild teosinte that is most biochemically similar to maize still grows today.

Tehuacán valley, Mexico Dry valley in southern Mexico where some of the earliest evidence for maize cultivation has been discovered.

San Marcos Cave, Mexico Important Tehuacán valley site for the early history of maize.

The best archaeological evidence for early maize cultivation comes from the dry caves and open sites of the dry highland **Tehuacán valley** in southern Mexico. Archaeologist Richard MacNeish found that the earliest Tehuacán people lived mainly by hunting deer and other mammals and also by collecting wild vegetable foods. MacNeish estimated that in 10,000 B.C., 50–60 percent of the people's food came from game. After 8000 B.C., the game population declined, and the people turned more and more to wild plant foods. By at least 4500 B.C., about 90 percent of the Tehuacano diet consisted of tropical grasses and such plants as cacti and maguey. So much grain was necessary that some form of cultivation or domestication of native plants may have been essential by this time. AMS radiocarbon samples from early maize cobs from **San Marcos Cave** date this staple to at least 3600 B.C.

Coxcatlán Cave, Mexico Rock shelter in the Tehuacán valley that yielded desiccated maize cobs dating to about 2000 B.C.

More than 24,000 maize specimens have come from the caves of the Tehuacán valley. They document a long sequence of maize evolution, beginning with 71 small cobs from the lowest levels of San Marcos Cave and from deep in **Coxcatlán Cave**. The cobs are about 5 centimeters (2 inches) long and lack the ability to disperse their kernels naturally, a clear sign of full domestication.

Maize was domesticated in Me soamerica well before the Great Pyramids of Giza were built along the Nile River (see Chapter 12). The primitive form of domesticated eight-rowed maize (*maiz de ocho*) represented at Tehuacán was the common ancestral corn that spread thousands of kilometers from its original homeland. Subsequent derivatives of this basic maize developed elsewhere throughout the Americas.

If Kent Flannery's hypothesis is correct, then plant domestication in Mesoamerica was not so much an invention in one small area, as a shift in ecological adaptation deliberately chosen by peoples living where economic strategies necessitated intensive exploitation of plant foods. Evidence from both Tehuacán and Guilá Naquitz bears out this hypothesis.

Andean Farmers

The story of plant domestication in Mexico shows that it was a deliberate shift in ecological adaptation. The same shift occurred in two areas of the Andean region: in the mountain highlands and along the low-lying, arid Pacific coast.

Eighteenth-century German naturalist Alexander von Humboldt was the first European scientist to explore the high Andes. He marveled at the great variety of wild plants and animals that thrived in the harsh and varied landscape of high peaks and mountain valleys. Only a handful of these many species had been tamed by the farmers living in the foothills of the great mountains. Five important Andean species were of vital importance to highland economies: the llama, alpaca, and guinea pig, the potato, and a grain crop, quinoa. Llamas were probably domesticated alongside quinoa, perhaps as early as 2500 B.C. (see Figure 14.6). Llama herding was widespread throughout the highlands and along the north coast of Peru by 900 B.C. Guinea pigs, which are actually rodents, were an important wild food for many thousands of years and may have been domesticated in high mountain valleys around 900 B.C. as well.

At the time of European contact in the sixteenth century A.D., Andean farmers used literally hundreds of potato varieties. Four major strains were domesticated in the highlands, of which one, *Solanum tuberosum*, is now grown all over the world. Wild potatoes were an important food for highland Andean foragers from the time of earliest settlement. Well-documented potato tubers come from midden sites dating to about 2000 B.C. at the mouth of the Casma valley on the Peruvian coast, but earlier specimens will undoubtedly

Figure 14.6 **Panalauca Cave**, near Lake Jumin, Peru. Excavations here have yielded evidence of early quinoa cultivation and llama domestication by 2500 B.C.

Source: Professor John Rick, Stanford University.

come to light in the south-central highlands, where other animal and plant species, including lima beans, were domesticated between 3000 and 2000 B.C.

The Peruvian coast forms a narrow shelf at the foot of the Andes, an arid desert strip dissected by river valleys with deep, rich soils and plentiful water for some of the year. For thousands of years, coastal communities lived off the incredible bounty of the Pacific and gathered wild plants in summer. Fishing may have assumed greater importance after 5000 B.C., when the climate was warmer and drier than it is today. By this time, the people were also cultivating some plant species like squash, peppers, and tuberous begonias.

Panalauca Cave, Peru Site that has yielded evidence of early quinoa cultivation and llama herding, dating to about 2500 B.C.

Chilca, Peru Semipermanent foraging settlement on the Peruvian coast dating to after 4000 B.C.

Paloma, Peru Large foraging settlement with limited agriculture on the Peruvian coast, dating to after 4000 B.C.

Generally, in more or less permanent coastal settlements like **Chilca** and **Paloma**, fish and mollusks were staples, but the inhabitants also ground up wild grass seeds into flour and grew squashes. By 3800 B.C., the Chilca people were growing several types of beans, including the ubiquitous lima, and squash. They lived in circular matting and reed huts erected on frameworks of canes or occasionally whale bones. The succeeding millennia saw many permanent settlements established near the Pacific with people combining agriculture with fishing and mollusk gathering. But fish and sea mammals were so abundant that agriculture remained a secondary activity much later than it did in Mesoamerica.

Within a remarkably short time, more complex farming societies developed out of the simple village communities of earlier centuries. In some regions, these developments led rapidly to the emergence of state-organized societies, the world's first civilizations. In others, egalitarian farming cultures became elaborate chiefdoms, remarkably effective adaptations to challenging environments.

The Southwest (300 B.C. to Modern Times)

Maize originated in Central America and was widely grown there by 3000 B.C. The new staple did not, however, spread northward across the Rio Grande into the North American Southwest until some centuries later. Both in the Southwest and in the South and Southeast, the arrival of corn led to major changes in indigenous society, but these changes varied greatly from one region to the next. In each area, highly variable ecological factors and social realities led to the development of complex farming societies.

Human occupation of the Southwest dates back to before 9000 B.C. For thousands of years, the descendants of these early southwesterners gathered many plant foods, including yucca seeds, cacti, and sunflower seeds, adapting skillfully to the harsh realities of desert living. They developed remarkable expertise with all kinds of plant foods, which preadapted them for maize agriculture. Maize, beans, and squash agriculture came to the Southwest from northern Mexico after generations of sporadic contacts between desert foragers and settled farmers. Knowledge of domesticated plants and even gifts of seeds or seedlings passed from south to north.

Climatic data from tree rings tell us that between about 2500 and 100 B.C., the southwestern climate was relatively stable, perhaps somewhat wetter than today (see Box 14.2). However, it was a semiarid environment where hunting and gathering were high-risk occupations, mainly because rainfall was always unpredictable.

Domesticated plants like maize and beans might have had low yields in these dry environments, but they had one major advantage: they were predictable food sources. Cultivators of the new crops could control their location and their availability at different

Box 14.2 Doing Archaeology
Dendrochronology (Tree-Ring Dating)

Most people are familiar with tree rings—concentric circles, each circle representing annual growth—visible on the cross-section of a felled tree's trunk. All trees form growth rings, but they vary in thickness, especially where seasonal changes in weather are dramatic, such as where wet and dry seasons alternate or where summer and winter temperatures are vastly different. Trees produce growth rings each year, formed by the cambium, or growth layer, lying between the wood and the bark. When the growing season starts, large cells are added to the wood. These cells develop thicker walls and become smaller as the growing season progresses; by the end of the growth season, cell production ceases altogether. This process occurs every growing year, and a distinct line is formed between the wood of the previous season, with its small cells, and the wood of the next, with its new, large cells. The thickness of each ring may vary according to the tree's age and annual climatic variations; thick rings are characteristic of good growth years.

Weather variations within a circumscribed area tend to run in cycles. A decade of wet years may be followed by five dry decades. One season may break a 40-year rainfall record. These cycles of climate are reflected in patterns of thicker or thinner tree rings, which are repeated from tree to tree within a limited area. Dendrochronologists have invented sophisticated methods of correlating rings from different trees so that they can build up long master sequences of rings from a number of trunks that may extend over many centuries.

Samples are normally collected by cutting a full cross-section from an old beam no longer in a structure. The researcher uses a special core borer to obtain samples from beams still in a building or V-cuts from exceptionally large logs. Once in the laboratory, the surface of the sample is leveled to a precise plane. Analysis of tree rings consists of recording individual ring series and then comparing them with other series. Comparisons can be made by eye or by plotting the rings on a uniform scale so that one series can be compared with another. The series so plotted can then be computer-matched with the master tree-ring chronology for the region (see Figure 14.7).

Extremely accurate chronologies for southwestern sites come from correlating a master tree-ring sequence from felled trees and dated structures with beams from Indian pueblos. The beams in many such structures have been used again and again, and thus some are very much older than the houses in which they were most recently used for support. The earliest tree rings obtained from such settlements date to the first century B.C., but most timbers were in use between A.D. 1000 and historic times.

Dendrochronology was once confined to the American Southwest, but is now widely used in many other parts of the world, including Alaska, Canada, parts of

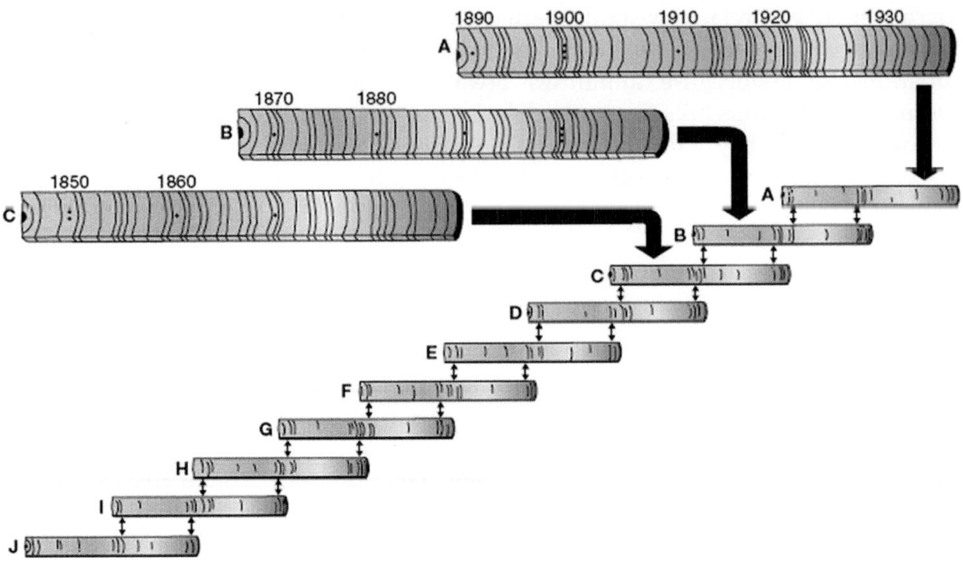

Figure 14.7 Dendrochronology: Building a tree-ring chronology. Boring A was taken from a living tree after the 1939 growing season. Specimens B through J were taken from old houses and progressively older ruins. The ring patterns match and overlap back into prehistoric times.

the eastern United States, England, Ireland, and continental Europe, as well as the Aegean islands and the eastern Mediterranean. The Europeans have worked with oak trees with ages of 150 years or more to develop master chronologies for recent times. Using visual and statistical comparisons, they have managed to link living trees to dead specimens serving as church and farmhouse beams and others found well preserved in bogs and waterlogged peats or prehistoric sites. The resulting tree-ring sequences go back at least 10,021 years in Germany and 7,289 years in Ireland. The Aegean Dendrochronology Project has developed a tree-ring sequence covering 6,000 of the last 8,500 years, which is leading to much more precise dates for the Minoan and Mycenaean civilizations than those suggested by cross-dating or radiocarbon readings. So precise are the master sequences that an expert can date even short ring cycles to within a few years.

Tree-ring chronologies provide records of short-term climatic change in areas such as the American Southwest, where cycles of wetter and drier weather can cause radical changes in settlement patterns. Southwestern chronologies are accurate to within a year, a level of accuracy rarely achieved with archaeological chronologies anywhere. The Laboratory of Tree Ring Research at the University of Arizona has undertaken a massive dendroclimatic study that has yielded a reconstruction of relative climatic variability in the Southwest from A.D. 680 to 1970. This enables researchers to study such phenomena as the Great Drought of A.D. 1276 to 1299, which caused many Ancestral Pueblo peoples to abandon their large pueblos. In 1276, the beginnings of the drought appeared in tree rings in the Northwest. During the next ten years, very dry conditions expanded over the entire Southwest before improved rainfall arrived after 1299.

seasons by storing them carefully. The people living in the southern deserts of the Southwest may have adopted maize and beans as supplementary foods not because they wanted to become farmers, but so that they could become more effective foragers and maximize the potential of their environment.

Maize first entered the Southwest during a period of higher rainfall between 2000 and 1500 B.C. The new crop spread rapidly throughout the region, especially when combined with beans after 500 B.C. Beans helped return vital nitrogen to the soil, maintaining fertility for longer periods of time. Maize farming in the dry Southwest was never easy, for the farmers were working close to the limits of the plant's range. They selected moisture-retaining soils very carefully, used north- and east-facing slopes that received little direct sun, planted near canyon mouths, and diverted water from streams and springs. They did everything they could to minimize risk, dispersing their gardens to reduce the danger of local drought or flood.

The appearance of maize did not trigger a dramatic revolution in southwestern life. The earlier maize varieties were not very productive, but more bountiful local forms soon became a vital staple for many southwestern groups who were now living in permanent hamlets and much smaller territories. They also led to more complex southwestern societies that adjusted to changing climatic conditions with remarkable flexibility.

Hohokam, Mogollon, and Ancestral Pueblo

Hohokam Widespread desert farming culture centered in southern Arizona, which flourished from c. 300 B.C. to A.D. 1500.

Mogollon Southwestern cultural tradition of about 300 B.C. to c. A.D. 1100; a highland farming culture without major population centers.

Ancestral Pueblo (Anasazi) Major American Southwestern cultural tradition centered on the Four Corners region, which reached its efflorescence after A.D. 1100.

By A.D. 300, many centuries of experimentation had produced much more productive domestic crops and a greater dependence on farming. The cultural changes of these centuries culminated in the great southwestern ancestral cultural traditions: **Hohokam**, **Mogollon**, and **Ancestral Pueblo** (formerly called Anasazi).

Snaketown, Arizona Major Hohokam settlement and ceremonial center located near the Gila River.

Hohokam people occupied much of what is now lower Arizona. They were desert farmers who grew not only maize and beans but also cotton, which flourishes in hot environments. Wherever they could, they practiced irrigation from flowing streams; otherwise, they cultivated floodplains and caught runoff from local storms with dams, terraces, and other devices. For centuries, much of Hohokam life and trading activity centered around **Snaketown**, a large settlement and ceremonial center near the Gila River (see Figure 14.8). The inhabitants maintained trading relationships with other parts of the Southwest, with the Pacific coast to the west, and with Mexico. The Hohokam obtained tropical bird

Figure 14.8 The Hohokam settlement at Snaketown, Arizona, during 1965 excavations, showing circular kivas and dwellings.

Source: Universal Images Group North America LLC/Alamy Stock Photo.

feathers, copper artifacts, and other exotic objects from the south, but scholars are sharply divided on the amount of Mexican influence on Hohokam culture and religious beliefs. The Hohokam people vanished after A.D. 1500; their cultural heirs are the O'odham people of today.

Mogollon was a more highland cultural tradition; it flourished mainly in what is now New Mexico from about 300 B.C. to between A.D. 850 and 1150. Mogollon farmers relied on direct rainfall and used little irrigation, living in small villages of pit dwellings with timber frames and mat or brush roofs. In only a few areas did more elaborate settlements develop, but by this time, Mogollon was becoming part of the western Ancestral Pueblo tradition.

Ancestral Pueblo culture developed from indigenous forager roots and was centered on the Four Corners area, where Utah, Arizona, Colorado, and New Mexico meet. Ancestral Pueblo people made heavy use of wild plant foods, even after they took up serious maize farming after A.D. 400. Most of their farming depended on seasonal rainfall, although they used irrigation where practicable.

pithouse Dwelling built partly into the subsoil, typically oval-shaped; common in the American Southwest, where the design provides good insulation.

At first, the Ancestral Pueblo lived in small **pithouse** villages but, after A.D. 900, much of the population congregated in above-ground settlements of adjoining rooms. These became the famous pueblos, often clustered in small arcs to make them equidistant from the subterranean ceremonial rooms, the kivas, in the middle of the settlement. The largest and most spectacular pueblos were located in densely populated areas like Chaco Canyon in New Mexico and Mesa Verde in Arizona. It was in areas like these that Pueblo society sometimes achieved a higher degree of complexity, with larger, densely populated towns that controlled large exchange networks.

Pueblo Bonito, New Mexico Major Ancestral Pueblo pueblo in Chaco Canyon, occupied in the twelfth century A.D.

Chaco Canyon, with its dramatic cliffs, was the center of a remarkable flowering of Ancestral Pueblo culture that lasted for two centuries after A.D. 900. During this time, the Chaco Phenomenon, as it is called, expanded from its canyon homeland to encompass an area of 65,000 square kilometers (25,000 square miles) of the San Juan Basin and adjacent uplands. The people constructed large, well-planned towns, subterranean ceremonial kivas, extensive road and water control systems, and outlying sites linked to the canyon by

Figure 14.9 A subterranean kiva at Pueblo del Arroyo, Chaco Canyon.
Source: Dale O'Dell/Alamy.

ceremonial roadways and visual communication systems (for **Pueblo Bonito**, the largest of these pueblos, see Figure 6.16 on p. 206. Kiva: Figure 14.9). The "great houses," or the large pueblos of Chaco Canyon, contained many luxury items, including turquoise from near Santa Fe, seashells, copper bells, and even the skeletons of macaws, colorful birds from the lowland rainforests of Mesoamerica much prized for their bright feathers.

When Chaco was in its heyday, between A.D. 1075 and 1115, the canyon was not only a focus for turquoise ornament manufacture, but also an important ceremonial center for dozens of outlying settlements. Chaco flourished during a period of uncertain rainfall, and the local farming land could never have supported more than about 2,000 people, although population estimates for the pueblos rise to as high as 5,600. Thus, archaeologists argue, Chaco may have had a relatively small permanent population and been a place where much food was stored and where large crowds of Ancestral Pueblo congregated for major ceremonial observances.

What, then, was Chaco? Was it a highly centralized chiefdom, controlled by a small but powerful elite of chiefs and nobles who had a monopoly over trade and important spiritual powers? Or was it what archaeologist Gwinn Vivian calls an egalitarian enterprise, a cooperative mechanism developed by dozens of communities living in a harsh and unpredictable environment? We do not know, but elaborately decorated burials were discovered in Chaco by early archaeologists. Recent DNA research suggests that some of these burials were of closely related people. The Ancestral Pueblo lived in a society where kin ties were all-important and everyone had complex obligations to fulfill, both to the community and to the clan. Without such obligations, it would have been impossible to carry large quantities of food to Chaco's storerooms or to transport the more than 200,000 wooden beams needed to build its large pueblos and kivas. Perhaps, the Chaco Phenomenon was an adaptive mechanism whereby local kin leaders regulated and maintained long-distance exchange networks and ceremonial life as a means of supporting far more people than the environment would normally carry. Perhaps, they used economic, social, and ritual ties among a scattered rural population to encourage cooperation among isolated communities in times of need.

Mesa Verde, Colorado Series of canyons in Colorado famous for their multiroom Ancestral Pueblo pueblos of the thirteenth and fourteenth centuries A.D.

Cliff Palace, Colorado Major Ancestral Pueblo site in Mesa Verde, which reached its greatest extent after A.D. 1200.

The Chaco Phenomenon reached its peak between 1100 and 1130, when a prolonged drought and environmental degradation caused the system to collapse. The Ancestral Pueblo moved away into more dispersed settlements, maintained alliances with one another, or flourished in scattered, independent pueblos. Perhaps the most famous of all Ancestral Pueblo cultural developments is that centered on the **Mesa Verde** canyon system in the northern San Juan Basin. By 1100, as many as 30,000 people lived in the nearby Montezuma valley, mainly concentrated in villages of 1,000 people or more. Only about 2,500 of them lived in Mesa Verde. Between 1200 and 1300, people moved from open locations into crowded pueblos. The **Cliff Palace**, the largest Mesa Verde settlement, had 220 rooms and 23 kivas (see Figure 14.10).

Both in Mesa Verde itself and in the surrounding countryside, large villages which were almost towns were home to between 1,000 and 2,500 people, living in room

Figure 14.10 The Cliff Palace at Mesa Verde.
Source: Brad Boserup/Thinkstock.

clusters associated with kivas and other ceremonial buildings. Everywhere in Mesa Verde, the emphasis was on individual communities. Judging from the numerous kivas, there was considerable cooperative and ritual activity, and there were numerous occasions when inhabitants of different communities organized large labor parties to carry out sophisticated water control works and other communal projects. This Ancestral Pueblo tradition was quite similar to that of Chaco Canyon, with its intricate mechanisms for integrating dispersed communities, or the chiefdoms of the South and Southeast, with their large centers and satellite villages.

The twelfth and thirteenth centuries saw the culmination of four centuries of rapid social and political development in the Mesa Verde region. About 1300, however, Pueblan peoples abandoned the entire San Juan drainage, including Mesa Verde. They moved in scattered groups southward and southeastward into the lands of the historic Hopi, Zuni, and Rio Grande pueblos, where their ultimate descendants live to this day. Following the abandonment of large areas of the Southwest in the late thirteenth and early fourteenth century, large settlements formed in previously sparsely inhabited areas. Some of these pueblos are recognized as those of direct ancestors of modern communities.

Southwestern Pueblo society never achieved the cultural complexity found in eastern North America or among the Hawaiians or Tahitians, but it achieved the limits of regional integration possible for an area where rainfall was irregular and the climate was harsh. Perhaps, the best way to describe much southwestern organization is as a theocracy, a government that regulated religious and secular affairs through individuals, like chiefs, and kin groups or associations (societies) that cut across kin lines. The basic social and economic unit was the extended family but, for hundreds of years, southwestern peoples fostered a sense of community and undertook communal labors like irrigation works using wider social institutions that worked for the common good.

Eastern North America (2000 B.C. to A.D. 1650)

No one knows exactly when maize spread across the southern plains into the Eastern Woodlands of North America, but at least sporadic corn cultivation may have diffused to the Mississippi River and beyond in the early first millennium A.D. Like all ancient Native Americans, eastern groups had developed great expertise with native plants of every kind soon after first settlement before 9500 B.C. The densest populations gathered by lakes and estuaries and in the fertile river valleys of the Midwest and Southeast. By 2000 B.C., local river valley populations in some areas had increased to the point that group mobility was restricted and periodic food shortages occurred. Under these circumstances, it was almost inevitable that some groups turned to the deliberate cultivation of native food plants like goosefoot (a group that includes spinach and beets) and marsh elder to supplement wild cereal grass yields.

At the same time, the first signs of social ranking appear in local burials. We also find an increasing preoccupation with burial and life after death. For the first time, individual communities and groups maintained cemeteries on the edges of their territories, which may have served to validate territorial boundaries. As the centuries passed, the funeral rites associated with death and the passage from the world of the living to that of the ancestors became ever more elaborate and important. This elaboration was associated not only with increasing social complexity and an explosion in long-distance exchange, but also with the building of ceremonial earthworks.

Adena and Hopewell

Thousands of years of long-distance exchange between neighboring communities had given certain raw materials and exotic artifacts high prestige value in eastern North American society. Such imports were scarce and hard to come by, important gifts exchanged between kin leaders and chiefs. They assumed great social value and significance in societies that placed a high premium on prestige. Hammered copper artifacts, conch shells from the Atlantic and Gulf coasts, certain types of stone axes—these became status symbols, buried with their powerful owners at death. By 500 B.C., the individuals who controlled these exchange networks were influential not only in life but also in death, for they were buried under large burial mounds.

Adena culture (Early Woodland) North American culture dating to between 500 B.C. and A.D. 400, centered on the Ohio River valley and famous for its elaborate earthworks.

The **Adena culture**, sometimes called the Early Woodland, which flourished in the Ohio valley between 500 B.C. and about A.D. 400, was one of the first to build extensive earthworks. The people lived in seasonal camps, relying not only on hunting and gathering, but also on the cultivation of squash and local starchy and oily plants. Major camps lay close to ceremonial burial mounds. The construction of even the largest mounds involved relatively few people. This mound building and other earthwork construction may have reflected a strengthening of group identity and the establishment of social and territorial boundaries, which were often marked by cemeteries.

At the same time, Adena groups developed large exchange networks that extended over enormous distances, the prototypes of even more elaborate trade routes in later centuries.

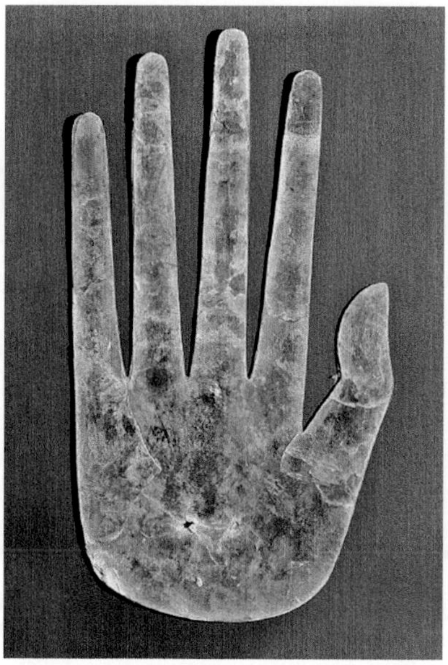

Figure 14.11 Hopewell sheet-mica ornament in the form of a human hand.
Source: Heritage Image Partnership Ltd/Alamy.

Powerful loyalties to local lineages caused the people to commemorate their dead not only with imposing burial mounds, but also with extensive earthworks.

Adena earthworks followed the contours of flat-topped hills and formed circles, squares, or other shapes, enclosing areas as much as 107 meters (350 feet) across. These were ceremonial enclosures rather than defensive works, sometimes built to surround burial mounds, other times standing alone. The most important people were buried in log-lined tombs under burial mounds, their corpses smeared with red ocher or graphite. Nearby were soapstone pipes and tablets engraved with curving designs or birds of prey. Some prestigious kin leaders were buried inside enclosures or death huts that were burned down as part of the funeral ceremony. Occasionally, the burial chamber was left open so that other bodies could be added later. The building of these mounds was invariably a communal effort, probably involving fellow kin from several settlements who piled up basketfuls of earth. The earthworks grew slowly as generations of new bodies were added. Apparently, only the most important people were interred in the mounds. Most Adena folk were cremated and their ashes were placed in the communal burial place.

Between 200 B.C. and A.D. 400, the Hopewell tradition, an elaboration of Adena with a distinctive religious ideology, appeared in Ohio. Hopewell burial practices were such a success that they spread rapidly from their heartland as far as upper Wisconsin and Louisiana and deep into Illinois and New York. The Midwest experienced a dramatic flowering of artistic traditions and of long-distance trade that brought copper from the Great Lakes region, obsidian from Yellowstone, and mica from southern Appalachia. The Hopewell people themselves dwelt in relatively small settlements and used only the simplest of artifacts in daily life. They wore leather and woven clothes of pliable fabrics. All of the wealth and creative skill of society was lavished on a relatively few individuals and their life after death.

At first glance, Hopewell exotic artifacts and ritual traditions seem completely alien to the simple indigenous culture of the area, but they were deeply rooted in local life. The cult objects buried with the dead tell us something of the social interactions of communities and kin groups. Some of the exotic grave goods, such as pipe bowls or ceremonial axes, were buried as gifts from living clan members to a dead leader. Others were personal possessions, cherished weapons, or sometimes symbols of status or wealth. Hopewell graves contain soapstone pipe bowls in the form of beavers, frogs, birds, bears, and even humans. Skilled artisans fashioned thin copper and mica sheets into head and breast ornaments that bore elaborate animal and human motifs (see Figure 14.11). There were copper axes and arrowheads, along with trinkets and beads fashioned from native copper nuggets, not smelted.

A few specialists manufactured most of these artifacts, perhaps in workshops within large earthwork complexes, themselves close to major sources of raw materials. Ceremonial objects of all kinds were traded from hand to hand throughout Hopewell territory along the same trade routes that carried foodstuffs and everyday objects from hamlet to hamlet. However, the prized manufactures may have passed from one person to another in a vast network of gift-giving transactions that linked different kin leaders with lasting, important obligations to one another.

The closest, but very far-fetched, modern analogy to such an arrangement is the famous *kula* ring exchange system of the Trobriand Islands of the southwestern Pacific. There, distinctive types of shell ornaments pass in perennial circles among individuals, linking them in lasting ritual and trading partnerships, in ties of reciprocal obligation. This kind of environment encourages individual initiative and competition, as kin leaders and their followers vie with one another for prestige and social status that is as transitory as life itself. Perhaps, somewhat similar practices were commonplace in Hopewell times. Once dead and buried with their prized possessions, the deceased were no longer political players, for their roles did not necessarily pass to their children or relatives.

Figure 14.12 Circular Hopewell mounds at Mound City National Monument, Ohio. Each covers a charnel house where cremated dead were deposited.

Source: Caitlin Mirra/Thinkstock.

Mound City, Ohio A Hopewell mound complex covering more than 5 hectares (13 acres) in the Ohio River valley.

Hopewell burial mounds are much more elaborate than their Adena forebears (see Figure 14.13). Some Hopewell mounds rise 12 meters (40 feet) high and are more than 30 meters (100 feet) across. Often the builders would deposit a large number of bodies on an earthen platform, burying them over a period of years before erecting a large mound over the dead. Hopewell burial complexes reached imposing sizes. The 24 burial mounds at **Mound City**, Ohio, lie inside an earthen enclosure covering 5.25 hectares (13 acres) (see Figure 14.12).

The Mississippian Tradition

The center of religious and political power shifted southward after A.D. 400 as the Hopewell tradition declined. It was then that the people of the densely populated and lush Mississippi floodplain realized the great potential of both native plants and maize as food staples. Much of the local diet always came from game, fish, nuts, and wild or cultivated native plants, but maize added a valuable new supplement to the diet. It was demanding to grow, but eventually maize became a vital staple, especially when combined with beans in the late first millennium A.D. Beans had the advantage of a high protein value, but also the asset of compensating for the nutritional deficiencies of corn. The new crops assumed greater importance as rising populations—and perhaps the insatiable demands of a small but powerful elite—were causing considerable economic and social stress.

Maize and beans may have been planted initially as supplementary foods, but they differ from native plants such as goosefoot in that they require more start-up labor to clear land. Within a short time, the river valley landscape was transformed in such a way that hunting and fishing provided less food for energy expended than farming. Major social and political changes and an entirely new economic pattern followed, changing eastern North American society beyond recognition. Thus was born the Mississippian tradition, the most elaborate prehistoric cultural tradition to flourish in North America.

Regional Mississippian societies developed in river valleys over much of the Midwest and Southeast and interacted with one another for centuries. Many Mississippian populations lived in fertile river valleys with lakes and swamps. They lived by hunting, fishing, and exploiting migrating waterfowl. Every family harvested nuts and grew maize, beans, squash, and other crops. The cultivation of native plants like goosefoot and marsh elder, as well as sunflowers—to mention only a few—was of vital importance. Theirs was a complex adaptation to highly varied local environments. Some groups flourished in small, dispersed homesteads, while others lived in compact villages, some so large that they might be called small towns. Thousands of people lived near locations like **Cahokia**, on the banks of the Mississippi opposite the modern-day city of St. Louis.

Cahokia, Illinois Major ceremonial center of the Mississippian culture built after A.D. 900.

Cahokia flourished on the so-called American Bottom, an extremely bountiful floodplain area with a great diversity of food resources and fertile soils. The greatest of all Mississippian

Figure 14.13 An artist's reconstruction of the central precincts of Cahokia, Illinois, in its heyday, around A.D. 1100.

Source: Painting by Lloyd K. Townsend. Courtesy: Cahokia Mounds State Historic Site.

centers, Cahokia presided over perhaps as many as 20,000 people or more in its heyday after A.D. 1000 (see Figure 14.13). Isotopic studies have revealed a remarkably diverse population, a significant proportion of them from afar. The great mounds and plazas of its ceremonial precincts dominated the countryside for many kilometers. Monk's Mound, at the center of Cahokia, rises 31 meters (102 feet) above the Mississippi floodplain and covers 6.5 hectares (16 acres). On the summit stood a thatched temple at the east end of an enormous plaza. Around the plaza rose other mounds, temples, warehouses, administrative buildings, and the homes of the elite. The entire ceremonial complex of mounds and plazas covered more than 1,618 hectares (4,000 acres) and depicted the ancient cosmos of the Eastern Woodlands, divided into four opposing segments and oriented toward the cardinal points of the compass.

Why did Cahokia achieve such political and religious importance? The great center lay at a strategic point close to the Mississippi River, near its confluence with the Missouri, and in a region where northern and southern trade routes met. The ruling families of Cahokia achieved enormous political and spiritual power within a few generations, perhaps by virtue of their supernatural abilities as mediators between the spiritual and living worlds, between those on Earth and the ancestors. At the same time, they must have been adept traders, with economic and political connections over a wide area. Their political power was sufficient to command the loyalty and labor of satellite settlements and religious centers throughout the American Bottom, to the point that elite families may have lived in subordinate centers, where they presided over critical rituals such as the annual Green Corn festival, a celebration of the new harvest. Sacred figurines and distinctive clay vessels bear motifs that are familiar in later Native American religious beliefs and have deep roots in more ancient cultures.

Cahokia was the most elaborate of all Mississippian chiefdoms, its core territory minuscule by, say, Ancient Egyptian standards. Politically volatile and based on ancient religious beliefs, its power and prosperity depended heavily on the authority, charisma, and ability of a handful of rulers. The great center imploded in A.D. 1250 and the population dispersed. Other polities to the south and east rose to a prominence that never rivaled that of the Mississippian's greatest chiefdom.

Cahokia was in the north of Mississippian lands. A major center also developed to the south, at Moundville in Alabama (see Box 14.3). Dozens of small centers and towns sprang

Box 14.3 Site
Moundville, Alabama

Moundville, by the Black Warrior River in west-central Alabama, flourished between A.D. 1250 and 1500. The site, with its 29 or more earthen mounds, covers more than 75 hectares (185 acres). The larger mounds delineate a quadrilateral plaza of about 32 hectares (79 acres) that is oriented on the cardinal directions. Some of the mounds supported public buildings or residences of important individuals; a few were associated with skull caches, a sweathouse, and a charnel structure for exposing the dead just outside the southern side of the plaza (see Figure 14.14). The three sides of the site away from the river were protected by a bastioned and much rebuilt palisade during some of Moundville's history. As at Cahokia, hundreds of people, perhaps as many as a thousand, lived within the general site area. Over 3,000 burials have been excavated at Moundville, with the highest-status interments lying in the mounds (see Figure 5.6 on p. 162).

In A.D. 900, a relatively small number of people lived in the Moundville area at a time of considerable political and economic unrest and increasingly circumscribed territory. These groups relied on nut harvests and other wild foods until maize production intensified between A.D. 950 and 1000. They dwelt in relatively small settlements, which seem to have grown in size as a response to higher agricultural production, increased production of freshwater shell beads, and warfare.

Between 1050 and 1250, the first platform mounds appeared at Moundville. This was a time when maize and bean agriculture assumed increasing importance, providing as much as 40 percent of the diet. The Black Warrior valley became an

Figure 14.14 Moundville, Alabama.
Source: Rosa Betancourt/Alamy.

important maize farming area as the population dispersed into smaller agricultural communities—some little more than farmsteads, some probably much larger. The site became an important ceremonial center, one of the only two in the valley.

In about 1250, the site changed completely in character from a dispersed settlement to a compact, highly formalized and fortified town. The inhabitants laid out a quadrilateral plaza with accompanying earthworks arranged in their proper order. They imposed a symbolic landscape on the natural one. At this point, Moundville had an east–west symmetry, a pairing of residential mounds with mortuary temple mounds, and a well-defined ranking of social spaces within the site; it resembled a compact, fortified town inhabited by up to 1,000 people living in tight groupings of square pole-and-mud houses. Moundville had expanded from an important ceremonial center to the capital of a single kingdom ruled by a paramount chief supported by tribute and engaged in long-distance exchange. The formal layout of public architecture in the heart of the site probably reflected the status relationships of different kin groups set in the context of a sacred landscape. And the paramount chief derived his power from both his supernatural authority and the power conferred on him by the sacred landscape.

After 1300, a firmly entrenched dynasty ruled Moundville for 150 years, reflected in a series of lavishly adorned burials in its burial mounds. The rulers' increasing power isolated them both symbolically and practically from their subjects as the population moved out of the hitherto compact town into the surrounding countryside. Only the elite and their retainers seem to have remained at the now unprotected site. No one knows why the people dispersed. It may have been the result of administrative decision, an adjustment to soil exhaustion, or a tactic to lessen the danger of attack. Whatever the cause, Moundville became a sparsely inhabited ceremonial center and a necropolis, with cemeteries occupying former residential areas. Many of the burials within them came from outlying communities. At the same time, the wide distribution of distinctive cult motifs on clay vessels seems to suggest that more people had access to the religious symbolism of chieftainship than ever before. Moundville went into decline after 1450, a century before Spanish contact. Elite burial ceased, although a nominal chief may have presided over the site. Perhaps, chronic factionalism and resistance to authority among lesser leaders led to the collapse of the once rigid Mississippian hierarchical system, resulting in a patchwork of local chiefdoms that may have shown some allegiance to a hereditary chief still living among the mounds of his ancestors. Some people still lived at Moundville when Spanish conquistador Hernando de Soto passed through the area in 1540, but we do not know whether a much-weakened, shadowy chiefdom still existed.

up between the two. More than just sacred places for annual planting and harvest ceremonies, all Mississippian centers were markets and focal points of powerful chiefdoms. For example, Cahokia owed some of its importance to the manufacture and trading of local salt and chert, a fine-grained rock used to make hoes and other tools.

Moundville, Alabama Major Mississippian town and ceremonial center after A.D. 900.

We know little about how Mississippian society functioned, but each major population center was probably ruled as a series of powerful chiefdoms by an elite group of priests and rulers who lived somewhat separated from the rest of the population. Unlike their recent predecessors, these individuals may have inherited political and economic power, also social position, as the offices of the elite were passed from one generation to the next. The chieftains controlled long-distance trade and were the intermediaries between the living, the ancestors, and the gods.

As in the Hopewell culture, high-ranking individuals went to the next world in richly decorated graves, with clusters of ritual objects of different styles that symbolized various clans and tribes. Excavations at burial mound 72 revealed at least 6 different burial events that involved 261 people—including 4 mutilated men and 118 women, who were probably retainers sacrificed to accompany a chief in the afterlife. One such chief lay on a layer of thousands of shell beads, accompanied by grave offerings from as far away as Wisconsin and Tennessee. Cahokia and most other larger Mississippian communities had more or less standardized layouts. The inhabitants built platform-like mounds and capped them with temples and the houses of important individuals. These mounds were grouped around an open plaza, and most people lived in thatched dwellings clustered nearby.

Mississippian graves and mound centers contain finely made pottery and other artifacts that bear elaborate designs and distinctive artistic motifs. These artifacts include stone axes with handle and head carved from a single piece of stone, copper pendants adorned with circles and weeping eyes, shell disks carved with woodpeckers and rattlesnakes, elaborately decorated clay pots, and engraved shell cups adorned with male figures in ceremonial dress (see Figure 14.15). The themes and motifs on these objects have many common features throughout the South and Southeast and as far afield as the borders of the Ohio valley. Many North American groups commonly used such motifs. Many Mississippian

Figure 14.15 An engraved shell gorget with a pair of figures. From the Rutherford-Kizer site, Tennessee. Dated to A.D. 1300–1400.

Source: Dr. David Dye, University of Missouri.

ceremonial artifacts served as badges of rank and status and as clan symbols. They were traded from hand to hand over long distances as symbolic gifts between widely separated chieftains who shared many common religious beliefs.

The Mississippian was an entirely indigenous cultural tradition, the climax of millennia of cultural change in eastern North America. Cahokia, Moundville, and other great Mississippian centers were past the height of their powers by the time European explorers reached the Mississippi valley in the sixteenth century. But numerous chiefdoms still flourished in the mid-South and Southeast right up to the time of European contact and beyond. It is interesting to speculate about what trajectory the successors of Mississippian society would have taken if Europeans had not arrived. Would they have evolved into a full-fledged, state-organized society, to rival those of the Maya and Aztec to the south? Experts believe that they would not have evolved in this manner, simply because the growing seasons for maize and beans in North America are too short and the climate is too harsh to support either specialized agriculture or high urban population densities under preindustrial conditions. It would have been difficult for any chieftain to accumulate the food surpluses necessary to maintain authority over more than a relatively limited area.

The most important cultural consequences of food production in North America were a long-term trend toward greater political elaboration, a degree of social ranking, and greater interdependence in a wide range of village farming societies.

Summary

- The hunter-gatherer societies that flourished in North America after first settlement exhibited great diversity and reflected many local environments. A long-term trend toward greater complexity and more sedentary settlement developed in areas of the most plentiful and varied food supplies.
- By 2000 B.C., some groups in eastern North America were experimenting with the cultivation of native plants.
- Maize was the most important cereal in the Americas, domesticated from a Central American native grass known as teosinte as early as 5000 B.C.
- Maize agriculture spread from southern Mexico and Guatemala thousands of miles to the north and south. There were farmers in the highland Andes and in coastal Peru by 3000 B.C., but maize and cotton did not become vital cultivated staples until about 1,000 years later.
- More complex societies also developed in the North American Southwest and Eastern Woodlands. Maize agriculture reached the Southwest by about 2000 to 1500 B.C.
- By 300 B.C., sedentary villages and a much greater dependence on farming were characteristic of the Southwest, leading to the emergence of the Hohokam, Mogollon, and Ancestral Pueblo cultural traditions, from which the ultimate ancestry of modern Pueblo peoples emerged.
- After 1000 B.C., a series of powerful chiefdoms arose in the Southeast and the Midwest, peoples among whom elaborate burial customs and the building of burial mounds and earthworks were commonplace.
- The Adena (Early Woodland) tradition appeared in about 700 B.C. and was overlapped by the Hopewell in approximately A.D. 100.
- Maize and bean agriculture arrived in the southeastern United States during the first millennium A.D.
- About A.D. 800, the focus of economic, religious, and political power shifted to the Mississippi valley and the Southeast with the rise of the Mississippian tradition. This tradition, with its powerful religious and secular leaders, survived in a modified form until European contact in the sixteenth century A.D.

Key Terms and Sites

kivas
Olsen-Chubbock
Fincastle
Lovelock Cave
Tehuacán valley
San Marcos Cave
Coxcatlán Cave
Panalauca Cave
Chilca
Paloma
Hohokam
Mogollon
Ancestral Pueblo (Anasazi)
Snaketown
pithouse
Pueblo Bonito
Mesa Verde
Cliff Palace
Adena culture (Early Woodland)
Mound City
Cahokia
Moundville

Critical-Thinking Questions

1. What are the similarities between the development of maize agriculture and the beginnings of farming in southwestern Asia? Give examples from Chapters 11 and 14.
2. Why is dendrochronology so important to the study of the peoples of ancient southwestern North America? What does it tell us about their lives beyond giving us a very accurate chronology?
3. Did the Mississippian develop into a full-fledged civilization like those of Egypt or China? Use examples from Chapters 12 to 14 for your discussion.

Further Reading

Maize: B. Smith, *The Emergence of Agriculture* (New York: W. H. Freeman, 1999) remains a useful summary. For everything you want to know (and perhaps don't want to know) about maize, turn to J. Staller, R. Tykot, and B. Benz, eds., *Histories of Maize* (New York: Academic Press/Elsevier, 2006). An overall summary of North America: B. Fagan, *Ancient North America: The Archaeology of a Continent*, 5th ed. (London: Thames and Hudson, 2019). Southwestern archaeology is well analyzed by L. Cordell and M. McBrinn, *The Prehistory of the Southwest*, 3rd ed. (Orlando, FL: Academic Press, 1999). For the Eastern Woodlands, see G. R. Milner, *The Moundbuilders* (London: Thames and Hudson, 2004), also T. R. Pauketat, *Ancient Cahokia and the Mississippians* (Cambridge: Cambridge University Press, 2004). T. R. Pauketat and S. M. Alt, *Medieval Mississippians: The Cahokian World* (Santa Fe, NM: School for Advanced Research, 2015) is a collection of valuable essays for a general audience.

15 Mesoamerican Civilizations

Chapter Outline

Maya incense burner with the features of an ancestor from Taclopa, Tabasco, Mexico. Source: World History Archive/Alamy Stock Photo.

DOI: 10.4324/9781003592754-21

> And when we saw all those cities and villages built in the water, and other great towns on dry land, and that straight and level causeway leading to Mexico, we were astounded. These great towns and pyramids and buildings rising from the water, all made of stone, seemed like an enchanted vision ... Indeed some of our soldiers asked whether it was not all a dream.
>
> (Bernal Díaz, quoted in Cohen 1963, 214–215)

Spanish conquistador Bernal Díaz was one of the 600 soldiers and adventurers who accompanied Hernán Cortés on his hazardous march from the Gulf Coast to the heart of the Aztec Empire. He was an impressionable youth when he gazed out over the Valley of Mexico in 1519 and saw the Aztec capital, Tenochtitlán, stretched out before him. Half a century later, he wrote, "I stood looking at it, and thought that no land like it would ever be discovered in the whole world, because at that time Peru was neither known nor thought of." Then, he added, "All that I then saw has been destroyed." Díaz knew he had witnessed a unique moment in history, a sight of a well-ordered preindustrial city at the height of its powers. His memories of his first sighting of the Aztec capital were as fresh in his seventies as they were when he glimpsed the Valley of Mexico for the first time (Cohen 1963, 214–215).

The roots of the Aztec state went back at least 1,500 years before the Spanish conquest and sprang from deep indigenous roots. This chapter tells the story of Mesoamerican societies from the Olmec to the Aztec Empire.

The Olmec (1500 to 500 B.C.)

Two great mountain chains form the backbones of Mesoamerica, running down the coastlines until they reach the east–west volcanic chain that forms the Mesa Central, the central plateau (see Figure 15.1). The inland basin of the Valley of Mexico, with its five lakes, forms the heart of the plateau, for thousands of years the center of political and economic life in highland Mesoamerica.

To the north, the serried mountains of the highlands give way to the low-lying limestone peninsula of the Yucatán, the so-called Maya lowlands. Highland climatic conditions contrast dramatically with those in the lowlands, where the climate is hot and humid throughout the year. The southern two-thirds of the Yucatán make up the Petén, hilly limestone formations covered with dense tropical forest intersected with lakes and swamps. The limestone plains of the northern Yucatán are much drier, with a drainage pattern based on underground water channels. The shores of the Gulf of Mexico are low-lying and hot: the low coastal plains of Veracruz and Tabasco, the Yucatán Peninsula, and the heavily forested coastal strip along the Gulf of Honduras.

By 2000 B.C., sedentary villages were common throughout Mesoamerica, dispersed in small communities across highly diverse agricultural environments in both lowlands and highlands. From the earliest times, barter networks linked village to village, lowland groups to people living on the semiarid highlands or in the Basin of Mexico. Therein lies a crux of complex Mesoamerican cultures: the constant interactions and exchanges of both commodities and ideas between people living in dramatically contrasting environments.

Preclassic era (Formative era) The early stages of Mesoamerican states and urban societies, c. 1000 B.C. to A.D. 250.

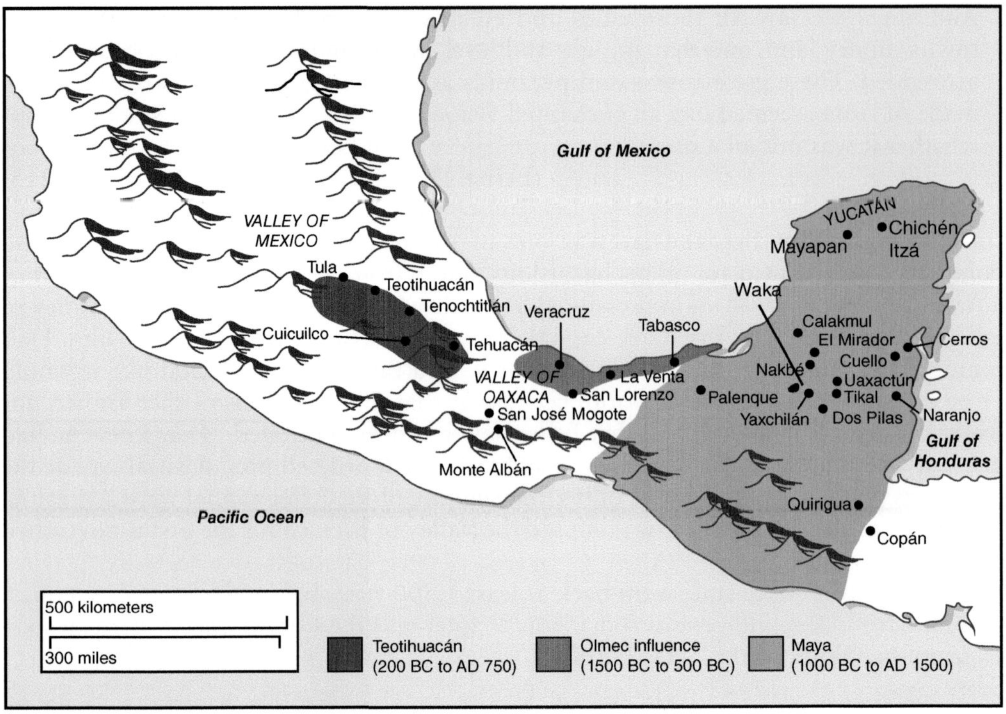

Figure 15.1 Map of sites discussed in this chapter.
Source: Chad Zuber/Thinkstock.

The first signs of political and social complexity appeared in many parts of highland and lowland Mesoamerica between about 2000 and 1000 B.C., during the so-called **Preclassic era (Formative era)**. In many regions, small but often powerful chiefdoms headed by a chief and a small nobility appeared. There was no one region where this emerging sociopolitical complexity occurred first. Rather, it was a development that took hold more or less simultaneously in many regions of Mesoamerica, not in isolation, but with each region interacting with others. The most famous of these early societies was the Olmec.

Olmec Lowland Mesoamerican art style and series of cultures that formed one of the foundations of later cultures in the region, c. 1500 to 500 B.C.

The Olmec occupied a revered place in the legend and lore of later Mesoamerican civilizations. Olmec peoples lived along the Mexican south Gulf Coast from about 1500 to 500 B.C. Their homeland was low-lying, tropical, and humid, with fertile soils. The swamps, lakes, and rivers teemed with fish, birds, and other animals—creatures that formed an important part of a new and remarkably sophisticated art style that was to leave a permanent imprint on Mesoamerican life.

San Lorenzo, Mexico Major Olmec center dating to c. 1250 B.C.

La Venta, Mexico Olmec ceremonial center dating to after 900 B.C.

The origins of the Olmec are a complete mystery, but their culture undoubtedly had strong local roots. Some of the earliest Olmec settlement comes from a platform at **San Lorenzo**, in the midst of frequently inundated woodland plains. By 1250 B.C., the people of San Lorenzo were farming both dry gardens and fields located on river levees, which produced exceptional crop yields. Soon San Lorenzo's leaders erected ridges and earthen mounds around their platform, on which they built pyramids and possibly ball courts. A century later, magnificent monumental carvings adorned San Lorenzo—apparently portraits of rulers—which were often mutilated by the Olmec themselves, perhaps when the person portrayed died (see Figure 15.2). The people of San Lorenzo traded obsidian and semiprecious stones with many parts of Mesoamerica until their center fell into decline after 900 B.C. and was superseded by **La Venta**, the most famous Olmec site, nearer the Gulf of Mexico.

Was Olmec society a large, homogeneous state or a series of smaller kingdoms linked together by kin, religious, and trading connections? Current opinion favors the second alternative, arguing that large kin groups originally owned villages over many generations. Under these circumstances, certain families probably acquired control of the most fertile lands and prime fishing and waterfowl hunting preserves. They became the dominant elite in Olmec society. To give symbolic and ritual expression to their newfound power, the new elite built awe-inspiring artificial mountains and strategically placed open spaces, designed to give an impression of overwhelming power. It was here that the rulers performed carefully staged public rituals and displays designed to confirm supreme authority. Those who ruled over these settings adorned their precincts with colossal statues of themselves. Nowhere are these buildings and sculptures more spectacular than at La Venta, built on a small island in the middle of a swamp. A rectangular earthen mound 120 meters long by 70 meters wide and 32 meters high (393 by 229 by 105 feet) dominates the island. Long, low mounds surround a rectangular plaza in front of the large mound, faced by walls and terraced mounds at the other end of the plaza. Vast monumental stone sculptures litter

Figure 15.2 The countenance of a huge Olmec statue depicting a ruler with snarling lips. Source: Chad Zuber/Thinkstock.

the site, including some Olmec heads bearing expressions of contempt and savagery (see Figure 15.2), perhaps portraits of actual rulers.

For about 400 years, La Venta's people traded ceremonial jade and serpentine from as far away as Costa Rica, during a time when Olmec ideas of kingship and religious ideology spread far across the lowlands and highlands. Then, sometime around 400 B.C., La Venta was destroyed, its finest monuments intentionally defaced.

One of the most important institutions to come into being in Olmec society was kingship, known to us only from distinctive art styles centered on a mysterious half-jaguar, half-human figure. Throne-like blocks at La Venta depict a seated figure, perhaps a ruler, emerging from a deep niche carved into stone (see Figure 15.3). The sides bear stylized depictions of jaguars, perhaps symbolizing the mythic origins of the rulers among such animals.

Olmec lords grafted the ancient ideology of the jaguar onto an emerging institution of kingship, where the ruler was a shaman-king with awesome supernatural powers. The Olmec rain god may have been a half-human, half-animal figure with snarling jaguar teeth, but it was only one of many combinations of mythical beasts that came from the hallucinogenic mind as opposed to the forest itself. Olmec artists added eagles' feathers and claws to serpents and other beasts to form mythical creatures, perhaps one of them Quetzalcoatl, the "Feathered Serpent," the most enduring of all Mesoamerican deities and central to highland states for many centuries.

Figure 15.3 An Olmec altar at La Venta, depicting a lord sitting below a schematic jaguar pelt. He emerges from a niche or cave holding a rope that binds prisoners carved on either side of the throne.

Source: stockcam/iStock.

Olmec society flourished during a period when art motifs, religious symbols, and ritual beliefs were shared among developing chiefdoms in many regions as a result of regular contacts between the leaders of widely separated communities and through day-to-day trade. Olmec art and artifacts have been found over an area 20 times that of the Gulf Coast heartland. This "lattice of interaction" over many centuries produced the complex and sophisticated traditions of Mesoamerican civilization that developed in later centuries.

By the time the classic Mesoamerican civilizations of the highlands and lowlands arose, dynasties of lords had been ruling Mesoamerica along well-established lines for nearly 1,000 years.

Early Maya (Before 1000 B.C. to A.D. 300)

Few ancient civilizations fire the popular imagination more than that of the Maya, which flourished in the lowlands before the time of the Roman Empire.

Beginnings

Maya civilization Major lowland Mesoamerican civilization from about 1000 B.C. until the sixteenth century A.D., with the Classic period ending c. A.D. 900.

Cuello, Belize Maya community and ceremonial center, in use before 1000 B.C.

Nakbé, Guatemala Early Maya ceremonial center of 600 to 400 B.C.

El Mirador, Guatemala Preclassic Maya center dating to between 250 and 50 B.C.

The roots of ancient **Maya civilization** lie in much earlier cultural traditions of the second millennium B.C. **Cuello,** a small Maya ceremonial center in northern Belize, was in use before 1000 B.C. and remained so for many centuries. But much larger Preclassic centers appeared elsewhere in the lowlands. The **Nakbé** ruins lie about 350 kilometers (215 miles) from Guatemala City, and 13.6 kilometers (8.5 miles) from the early Maya city at **El Mirador,** which covers 15.5 square kilometers (6 square miles). The two settlements were once linked by a causeway, but smaller Nakbé was occupied much earlier, by about 1000 B.C.

Between 650 and 450 B.C., Nakbé's leaders built huge platforms over their earlier ceremonial structures, raising pyramids with blank façades atop them. The pyramids themselves were crowned with three small temples clustered at the top of a steep stairway bounded with panels and masks. Nakbé's temple façades reflect the emerging notion of *ch'ul ahau*, divine kingship, in Maya society. In lavish public ceremonies, important lords donned the masks of gods, symbolizing their role as living divinities.

Calakmul, Guatemala Major Maya political and religious center from Preclassic times to A.D. 800.

Nakbé reached the height of its powers around 300 B.C., but slid into complete political and economic obscurity within a few generations as its neighbor, El Mirador, rose

Figure 15.4 The Tigre complex at El Mirador, Guatemala: A pyramid 55 meters (182 feet) high is surrounded by a plaza and smaller buildings.

Source: Al Argueta/Alamy.

to prominence. Between 150 B.C. and A.D. 50, the city of El Mirador grew rapidly (see Figure 15.4), and is yielding some of the earliest examples of Maya writing, inscribed on potsherds and occasionally on stucco sculpture. A raised road connected El Mirador with another important Preclassic center, **Calakmul**, 38 kilometers (24 miles) to the north.

El Mirador was an elaborate city and was probably controlled by a highly organized elite. They used artisans, priests, architects, and engineers, as well as traders and thousands of unskilled villagers. El Mirador lay in a depressed zone, where water could be trapped for later use during the dry season. By this time, reservoirs and other water storage systems were in common use in a society that was well aware of the need to plan for drought years. All of these public works, and the construction of ever more elaborate temples and palaces, led to an increasingly stratified society, where the elite distanced themselves from the commoners and competed with one another through diplomatic exchanges, gift giving, and long-distance exchange. Conspicuous consumption, the need to justify one's rule, and old-fashioned one-upmanship all played their parts in elaborating Maya society.

El Mirador collapsed suddenly about 2,000 years ago. The dynamics of this collapse are little understood, but are mirrored at other Preclassic Maya communities where the institution of kingship rose and was then abandoned.

Kingship

Kingship was at the heart of lowland Maya civilization. Maya rulers linked their actions to those of the gods and ancestors, sometimes legitimizing their descent by claiming their genealogy reflected mythical events. In a real sense, Maya history was linked to the present, the otherworld, and the legendary Olmec of the remote past. Society was embedded in a matrix of sacred space and time.

Maya kingship unfolded within an intensely sacred setting, artificial landscapes where complex ceremonies took place throughout the year and on longer cycles of time. The calendar was therefore vital to Maya life, for the complex geography of sacred time was just as important as that of space for determining political strategies and social moves (see Figure 15.5).

At the heart of Maya life lay both the calendar and the elaborate hieroglyphic script used, among other things, to calculate the passage of time and regular religious observances. Unlike Egyptian or Sumerian script, the Maya archive is limited in scope and confined to inscriptions on clay pots, monumental inscriptions on buildings, and stelae. Only four **codices** survived the Spanish conquest. There are public statements of royal accessions, triumphant military campaigns, and important ceremonies. The inscriptions are the political propaganda of Maya lords, the "politically correct" literature of a nobility intent on justifying its deeds and its ancestry. The surviving texts tell us that Maya rulers were bloodthirsty lords presiding over a patchwork of competing city-states and a constantly shifting quicksand of diplomatic marriages, political alliances, and brutal conquests.

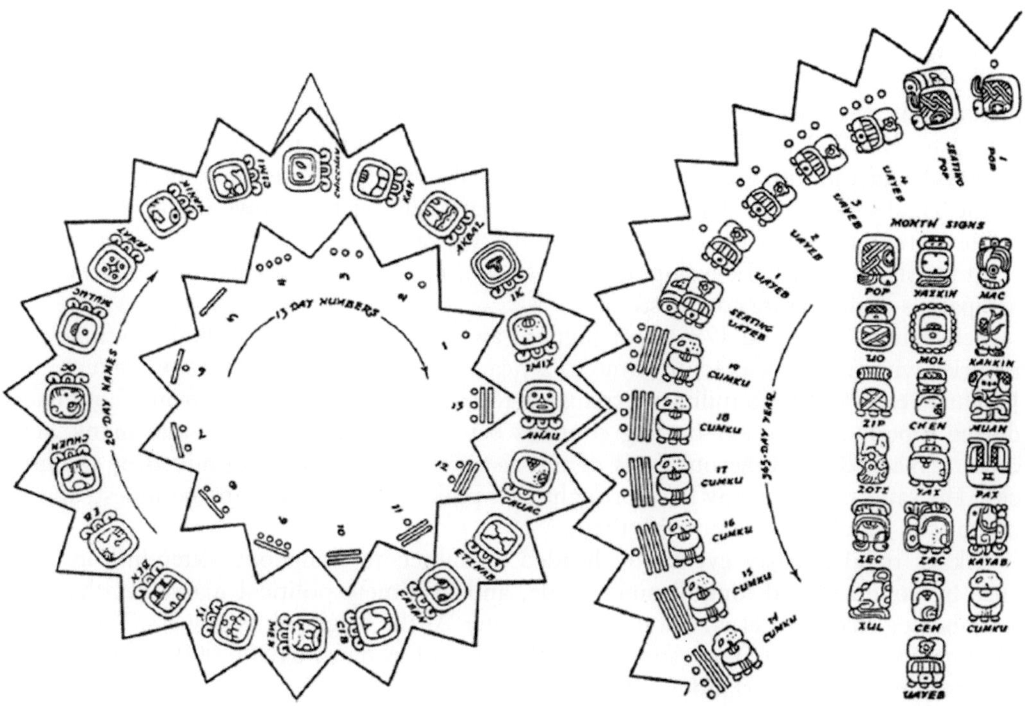

Figure 15.5 The Maya calendar, showing the two interlocking cycles. The left wheel is the 260-day *tzolkin*, the sacred calendar with 13 numbers (inner wheel) and 20 day names (outer wheel). The wheel on the right is the *haab*, the secular cycle, with 18 months of 20 days each.

codices (sing., codex) Documents on bark or deer skin prepared by ancient Maya and Aztec scribes.

Classic Maya (A.D. 300 to 900)

Tikal, Guatemala Classic Maya city that reached the height of its power in A.D. 200 to 600.

Uaxactún, Guatemala Classic Maya city in the Mesoamerican lowlands, defeated by its neighbor Tikal in A.D. 378.

Even as El Mirador collapsed, perhaps because its trading connections faltered, two other centers, **Tikal** and **Uaxactún**, stepped into the resulting political and economic vacuum. The two centers were less than 20 kilometers (12 miles) apart, too close for bitter rivals to coexist. Their rivalry coincided with the blossoming of Classic Maya civilization.

Tikal had expanded greatly during the first century B.C. as large public buildings rose on the foundations of earlier, more humble structures (see Figure 15.6). Clearly, the intent was to rival, and outdo, El Mirador's splendor.

Tikal's inscriptions are the chronicle of a remarkable dynasty that ruled one of the four Maya capitals from the early Classic era until the ninth century A.D. The earliest recorded monarch is Yax-Ch'aktel-Xok ("First Scaffold Shark"), who is thought to have reigned around A.D. 200 (although the city had a long and much earlier history). Tikal's hieroglyphic texts identify 31 rulers (18 known by name) after the founder, the earliest dating to A.D. 292 and the last known one to 869, making for 669 years of recorded history. Uaxactún also fostered a powerful royal dynasty whose monuments, like those of the Tikal kings, soon depicted rulers with sacrificial victims cowering at their feet or noble victims taken in hand-to-hand combat for later sacrifice in public rituals. These portraits signal a crucial development in Maya history: the increasing role of warfare and campaigns of deliberate conquest.

Between A.D. 320 and 378, Great-Jaguar Paw sat on the throne of Tikal at a time when rivalries with nearby Uaxactún came to a head. He defeated the armies of Uaxactún on January 16, 378. Tikal's military expansion took place with assistance from Teotihuacán during a period of regular trading contacts between the highland city and many Maya centers, marked by numerous finds of the distinctive green obsidian mined by the great city. The same contacts may have brought new philosophies of war and conquest, and the militaristic rituals associated with them.

Tikal's royal dynasty eventually headed a multicenter kingdom, extending its influence by conquest and long-distance trade, and by timely political marriages that gave neighboring rulers maternal kin ties to the center. At the height of its powers, Tikal's territory may have supported an estimated population of as many as 300,000 people, the city and its immediate hinterland 62,000.

Caracol, Belize Important Maya center in the seventh century A.D.; a rival of Calakmul and a major center of stone trade.

In about A.D. 557, Tikal went into decline after its defeat by the lord of a new rising state, **Caracol**, but then prospered anew during the late Classic era. Caracol commenced hostilities against Tikal in 557. The Caracol ruler, Lord Water, defeated Tikal, apparently capturing the city's ruler, Double Bird. Tikal now became a tribute dependency of Caracol,

Figure 15.6 The central precincts at Tikal, Guatemala.
Source: Diego Grandi/Alamy Stock Photo.

which grew in size and prestige as its vassal declined. Lord Water's successors dominated Tikal for at least 150 years and embarked on ambitious conquests against their neighbors. But eventually Caracol paid the price for its military adventures.

Calakmul, also in the southern lowlands, was another important city-state. At its height, Calakmul had a ceremonial precinct covering about 2 square kilometers (0.7 square miles) and a surrounding residential area that was over 20 square kilometers (7.7 square miles) in extent. At least 50,000 people lived in the urban core of this great city and important rival of Tikal between A.D. 514 and 814. Like Tikal, Calakmul sat astride an important overland trade route. The intense rivalry between the two cities may have been both a power play and a struggle for dominance of long-distance exchange.

Tikal had few allies in its immediate vicinity but maintained friendlier relations with two more distant city-states, Palenque and Copán. Palenque, a Maya capital in the western lowlands, is remarkable not only for its fine buildings (see Figure 12.7 on p. 388), but also for its rulers' obsession with their ancestry. Palenque's dynastic history began on March 11, 431, when Bahlum-Ku'k ("Jaguar-Quetzal") rose to power. Two Palenque rulers, Pacal the Great ("Shield") and his oldest son, Chan-Bahlum ("Snake-Jaguar"), who ruled in the seventh century A.D., stand out for their vision and wisdom. Toward the end of his long reign, which lasted 67 years, Pacal built the Temple of the Inscriptions, a masterpiece of Maya architecture under which his tomb lies (see Figure 15.7). The lid of his sarcophagus bears his royal genealogy. Palenque dominated the southwestern lowlands between A.D. 603 and 702.

Copán, in Honduras, is adorned with pyramids and plazas covering 12 hectares (30 acres), rising from the vast open spaces of the Great and Middle Plazas to an elaborate complex of raised enclosed courtyards, pyramids, and temples known to archaeologists as the Acropolis (see Figure 15.8). Here, successive rulers built their architectural statements atop those of their predecessors in an archaeological jigsaw puzzle of the first magnitude.

Copán, Honduras Major Maya center during the mid-first millennium A.D.

Quiriguá, Guatemala Small Maya center that briefly dominated nearby Copán, c. A.D. 738.

(a) (b)

Figure 15.7 (a) Temple of the Inscriptions, Palenque, Guatemala, which covers the tomb of the Lord Pacal, who died in A.D. 683. (b) A life-size stucco head of the Maya Lord of Pacal of Palenque.

Source: Alberto Loyo/ Thinkstock, © 2015. Photo Scala, Florence.

Figure 15.8 Artist Tatiana Proskouriakoff's reconstruction of the central precincts of the Maya city of Copán, Honduras.

Source: Gift of the Carnegie Institution of Washington. © President and Fellows of Harvard College, Peabody Museum of Archaeology and Ethnology, Harvard University, PM# 50–63-20/18487 (digital file# 60742852).

The earliest inscription at the site dates to December 11, 435, and was the work of ruler Yax-Ku'k-Mo' ("Blue Quetzal Macaw"), although there may have been earlier rulers. For four centuries, Blue Quetzal Macaw's successors formed a powerful dynasty at Copán and became a major force in the Maya world. At one point, Copán ruled over neighboring **Quiriguá**. More than 10,000 people lived in the surrounding valley. But on May 3, 738, the subordinate ruler of Quiriguá turned on his master and captured and sacrificed him. However, Copán seems to have maintained a measure of independence and survived. In A.D. 749, a new ruler, Smoke Shell, ascended to the throne of the once-great city. He embarked on an ambitious campaign of rehabilitation, even marrying a princess from distant Palenque. He also went on a building frenzy that culminated in the Temple of the Hieroglyphic Stairway, built in 755 and one of the oldest and most sacred of Copán's precincts (see Box 15.1). By this time, the city was top-heavy with privilege-hungry nobles and rife with political intrigue. Collapse was imminent.

The central institution of Maya civilization was still kingship, as outlined earlier, for it was the concept that unified society as a whole. Maya kings lived and carried out their deeds in the context of a history they recorded in building projects at Copán, Palenque, Tikal, and elsewhere. Maya elites lived out their lives in the context of the kings who ruled them, and in turn, thousands of commoners lived their lives on the terms of the nobility. We are only beginning to understand the tapestry of their history.

Box 15.1 Doing Archaeology
The Hieroglyphic Stairway at Copán

Archaeologists William and Barbara Fash combined both lines of evidence to reconstruct the Hieroglyphic Stairway at Copán, erected by the ruler Smoke Shell in 755 in

Figure 15.9 Tatiana Proskouriakoff's rendering of the Hieroglyphic Stairway at Cop á n, built by the ruler Smoke Shell in 755. More than 2,200 glyphs provide an elegant statement of the Maya kings' supernatural path. Portraits on the stairs depict Cop á n's lords as warriors carrying shields, with inscriptions recounting their deeds. The fi gure at the base of the stairway may be Smoke Shell himself.

Source: Gift of the Carnegie Institution of Washington. © President and Fellows of Harvard College, Peabody Museum of Archaeology and Ethnology, Harvard University, PM# 50- 63- 20/ 18489 (digital fi le#60741055).

one of the city's most sacred precincts (see Figure 15.9). In the 1930s, archaeologists of the Carnegie Institution restored much of the ruined stairway, replacing the glyph blocks in approximate order. They were unable to read the inscriptions, which made the task difficult. In 1986, a team of archaeologists and epigraphers headed by the Fashes set out to restore and conserve the building while establishing the true meaning of the stairway. Using meticulous excavation, the archaeologists recovered thousands of mosaic fragments from the structure, which were drawn and photographed and then pieced together in a precise reconstruction of the building. They recovered a powerful political statement.

More than 2,200 glyphs ascend the sides of the stairway and provide an elegant statement of the Maya kings' supernatural path. William Fash believes that the building was an attempt by Smoke Shell to relegitimize the conquered dynasty of earlier times. Portraits on the stairs depict Copán's lords as warriors carrying shields, with inscriptions recounting their deeds. A figure, perhaps Smoke Shell himself, stands where an altar serves as the base of the stairway, in the form of an inverted head of the Rain God Tlaloc. Tlaloc seems to be belching forth the inscriptions, his lower jaw forming the top of the stairs. Inside his head is an offering of decorated flints in the form of portraits and artifacts, perhaps used by Smoke Shell himself in the sacrificial and bloodletting ceremonies that dedicated the stairway. Unfortunately, the stairway was shoddily and hastily built. It soon collapsed, at a time when Copán was rapidly losing its political authority.

The Classic Maya Collapse

Maya civilization reached its peak after A.D. 600. Then, at the end of the eighth century, the great ceremonial centers of the Petén and the southern lowlands were abandoned, the long-count calendar was discontinued, and the structure of religious life and the state decayed. Within a century, huge sections of the southern lowlands were abandoned, never to be reoccupied. This is not to say that Maya civilization vanished completely, for new centers emerged in neighboring areas, taking in some of the displaced population. Maya civilization continued to flourish in the northern Yucatán until the arrival of the Spaniards in the sixteenth century.

All students of this ninth-century collapse agree that a multiplicity of factors—some ecological, some political and social—led to catastrophe in the southern lowlands. Population densities had risen to as many as 200 persons per square kilometer (518 per square mile) during the late Classic era over an area so large that it was impossible for people to adapt to bad times by moving to new land or emigrating. Failure of the agricultural base and environmental degradation resulting from forest clearance and soil erosion were important elements in the collapse at the local level. At the same time, severe drought cycles, documented in Mesoamerican lake sediments, played havoc with subsistence agriculture in an environment with only moderately fertile soils and overly dense populations. Such droughts may indeed have been the trigger that brought about the collapse in the southern lowlands. Surveys of Copán and its hinterland have shown how dramatic the settlement shifts were (see Box 15.2).

Ecological factors lay at the center of the collapse. The expanding Maya population was dependent on an agricultural system that made no allowance for long-term problems. Eventually, the system could produce no further riches, could not expand, and could only decline—with catastrophic results. But it would be a mistake to think of the Maya "collapse" as a universal phenomenon. Rather, the ninth-century collapse in the southern

Box 15.2 Doing Archaeology
Studying the Maya Collapse at Copán

How and why did Copán collapse? Archaeologists David Webster and William Sanders, and many colleagues working on a long-term investigation of the city, decided to investigate the collapse by studying changing settlement patterns and shifting population densities around the abandoned city. They developed a large-scale settlement survey—modeled after the famous Basin of Mexico survey of some years earlier—to examine more than 135 square kilometers (52 square miles) around the urban core. Using aerial photographs and systematic field surveys, the research team recorded more than 1,425 archaeological sites containing more than 4,500 structures. Team members mapped and surface-collected each location. A total of 252 sites were testpitted to obtain artifact and dating samples so that they could be placed within the general chronological framework for the valley.

As the data flowed into the laboratory, the researchers developed a classification of site types using size and other criteria, classifying them in a hierarchy from simple to complex as a way of developing a portrait of shifting landscape use over many centuries. At the same time, they obtained 2,300 dates from volcanic glass fragments using the obsidian hydration method. The survey yielded a bird's-eye view of dramatic population changes as human settlement expanded and contracted over the valley landscape.

The earlier sites found in the survey documented rapid population growth, especially in the city itself and nearby. There was only a small, scattered rural population. Between A.D. 700 and 850, the Copán valley reached its greatest sociopolitical complexity, with a rapid population increase to between 20,000 and 25,000 people. These figures, calculated from site size, suggest that the local population was doubling every 80 to 100 years, with about 80 percent of the people living within the urban core and immediate periphery. Rural settlement expanded outward along the valley-floor, but was still relatively scattered. Now people were farming foothill areas, as the population density of the urban core reached over 8,000 people per square kilometer (26,500 per square mile), with the periphery housing about 500 people per square kilometer (1,650 per square mile). Some 82 percent of the population lived in relatively humble dwellings, an indication of the pyramid-like nature of Copán society.

The survey showed dramatic shifts after A.D. 850. The urban core and periphery zones lost about half their population, while the rural population increased by almost 20 percent. Small regional settlements replaced the scattered villages of earlier times, a response to cumulative deforestation, overexploitation of even marginal agricultural land, and uncontrolled soil erosion near the capital. By 1150, the Copán valley population had fallen to between 2,000 and 5,000 people.

The Copán research does not explain why the city collapsed, but it chronicles the dramatic impact of rapidly growing populations on ecologically fragile landscapes. The evidence hints that environmental degradation was a major factor in the Maya collapse. Maya writings tell us that their lords considered themselves the intermediaries between the living and supernatural worlds. However, when the inexorable forces of environmental decline took hold, their authority evaporated, and a centuries-old spiritual relationship between farmers and an elaborate cosmic world vanished.

Figure 15.10 The Castillo at Chichén Itzá, the Temple of Kukulcán (Quetzalcoatl), a square, stepped pyramid about 23 meters (75 feet) tall, crowned with a temple, with stairways on all four sides. Acoustic research has shown that a speaker's voice can be projected effortlessly to a large audience with the front stairway as a backdrop.

Source: Medioimages/Photodisc/Thinkstock.

Chichén Itzá, Mexico Postclassic Maya center in the northern Yucatán, especially in the thirteenth century A.D.

lowlands was a marked episode in a long series of periodic flowerings and collapses characteristic of the Maya civilization—indeed, of Mesoamerican civilization generally.

Maya religious and social orders still endured in the more open country of the northern Yucatán. Just as Tikal and other famous cities collapsed, northern centers like **Chichén Itzá** in the northeast came into prominence during the Postclassic period (see Figure 15.10). During its heyday, this great city maintained contacts with the Maya of the Gulf Coast lowlands and through them with the Valley of Oaxaca and the highlands.

The Rise of Highland States (1500 to 200 B.C.)

The foundations of highland Mesoamerican states came both from Olmec roots and from developments in the Valleys of Mexico and Oaxaca. The warm, semiarid Valley of Oaxaca is the homeland of the modern-day Zapotec people. By 2000 B.C., maize and bean agriculture supported dozens of small villages and hamlets of 50 to 75 people. In time, some of these settlements grew to considerable size, with as many as 500 inhabitants, some of them nonfarming artisans and priests.

The evolution of larger settlements in Oaxaca and elsewhere was closely connected with the development of long-distance trade. Simple barter networks of earlier times evolved into sophisticated regional trading organizations in which Oaxacan and other village leaders controlled monopolies over sources of obsidian and its distribution. Soon magnetite mirrors (important in Olmec ritual), tropical feathers, and ceramics were traded widely between the highlands and lowlands. The influence of the lowlands was felt most strongly in Oaxaca, where Olmec pottery and other ritual objects appear between 1150 and 650 B.C. Many of them bear the distinctive human-jaguar motif of the lowlands, which had an important place in Olmec ideology.

San José Mogote, Mexico Important farming village, located in the Valley of Oaxaca, in the second millennium B.C.

In 1300 B.C., the largest settlement in the Valley of Oaxaca was **San José Mogote**, which lay at the junction of three side valleys. It was a village of thatched houses with about 150 inhabitants, sharing one lime-plastered public building. During the next century, San José Mogote grew rapidly into a community of 400 to 600 people living in rectangular houses with clay floors, plastered and whitewashed walls, and thatched roofs, over an area of about 20 hectares (50 acres). Clay figurines of masked, costumed dancers lie in San José Mogote's ceremonial buildings (see Figure 15.11). There are marine fish spines, too, almost certainly used in personal bloodletting ceremonies

Figure 15.11 These four figurines formed a ritual scene buried beneath the floor of a house at San José Mogote, Oaxaca, Mexico.

Source: Joyce Marcus and Kent Flannery, University of Michigan.

performed before the gods. By 400 B.C., there were at least seven small chiefdoms in the Valley of Oaxaca.

Monte Albán was founded in about 900 B.C. on a hill overlooking three arms of the Valley of Oaxaca, 400 meters (1,300 feet) below (see Figures 7.9 and 15.12). The new settlement grew rapidly, soon boasting more than 5,000 inhabitants. Monte Albán assumed great importance, becoming a major state by 150 B.C. Between 350 and 200 B.C., more than 16,000 people lived in the city, the population rising to a peak of 30,000 during the late Classic period, between A.D. 500 and 700.

Between 300 and 100 B.C., Zapotec rulers laid out the main plaza atop the artificially flattened hilltop. Monte Albán became an elaborate complex of palaces, temples, and plazas, some of which served as ritual settings and others as markets. The city straddled three hills, with at least 15 residential subdivisions, each with its own plazas. Most inhabitants lived in small houses erected on stone-faced terraces built against the steep terrain.

Monte Albán reached the height of its power after 200 B.C., when it rivaled another expanding state, Teotihuacán, to the north. The two great cities coexisted peacefully and traded with one another for centuries.

Figure 15.12 Monte Albán, Valley of Oaxaca, featuring an enormous ceremonial precinct centered around the paved main plaza. This ritual ward evolved over more than 1,000 years of continuous rebuilding and modification, which had the effect of progressively isolating the plaza and the people who lived around it from the rest of the city. The late Classic plaza of A.D. 500 to 720 was 300 meters long and 150 meters wide (975 by 480 feet), bounded on its north and south sides by 12-meter (37-foot) platform mounds with staircases leading to buildings atop them. The rulers and their families lived in a complex of buildings on the north platform, which also served as the formal setting for meetings with high officials and with emissaries from other states such as Teotihuacán.

Source: Nicolas Lecoz/Fotolia.

Teotihuacán (200 B.C. to A.D. 750)

Cuicuilco, Mexico A rival kingdom to Teotihuacán in the Valley of Mexico, destroyed by a volcanic eruption c. 100 B.C.

Teotihuacán, Mexico Major city in the Valley of Mexico that flourished from about 200 B.C. to A.D. 750.

As early as 600 B.C., a series of chiefdoms ruled over the Valley of Mexico. Five centuries later, two of them, **Cuicuilco** in the west and **Teotihuacán** to the east, were vying for leadership of the valley. Nature intervened with a major volcanic eruption that buried and destroyed Cuicuilco completely. Teotihuacán was the master of the Valley of Mexico and adjacent parts of the central highlands.

Teotihuacán grew rapidly during the ensuing centuries as thousands of people moved from outlying communities into the metropolis. Whether they moved voluntarily or as a result of conquest and compulsory resettlement is unknown. At least 80,000 people lived in the city by A.D. 100. Between 200 and 600, Teotihuacán's population grew to more than 150,000 people, making it similar in size to all but the very largest cities of contemporary western Asia and China.

A map of the city reveals an enormous community that grew over many generations according to a long-term master plan. Over more than eight centuries, the Teotihuacános built 600 pyramids, 500 workshop areas, a great marketplace, 2,000 apartment complexes, and precinct plazas, all laid out on a grid plan anchored by the Avenue of the Dead, 5 kilometers (3 miles) long, which bisected the city on a north–south axis (see Figure 15.13).

Figure 15.13 The Pyramid of the Moon and the Avenue of the Dead at Teotihuacán.
Source: Michael Rooney/Alamy Stock Photo.

Most people lived in standardized, walled residential compounds up to 60 meters (200 feet) wide on each side, connected by narrow alleyways and compounds. Some of these barrios (neighborhoods) were home to craftspeople like obsidian workers or potters. There were also military quarters. Foreigners from the Valley of Oaxaca, as well as lowland Veracruz, lived in their own neighborhoods (see Box 15.3). More important priests and artisans lived in dwellings built around small courtyards. Prominent nobles occupied elaborate palaces with central, sunken courts.

Teotihuacán's first, and very able, leaders planned their entire city as a symbolic landscape commemorating the Creation and the principal gods. Their architects laid out the Avenue of the Dead perpendicular to a Sacred Cave under the Pyramid of the Sun and built a small pyramid dedicated to what scholars call "the Great Goddess," associated with the Sun, on the site of the present Pyramid of the Moon, framing it with a sacred mountain on the horizon.

Box 15.3 Doing Archaeology
Life in Teotihuacán's Barrios

Teeming neighborhoods of single-story, flat-roofed, rectangular apartment compounds complete with courtyards and passageways lay beyond Teotihuacán's ceremonial precincts. Narrow alleyways and streets about 3.6 meters (12 feet) wide separated each compound from its neighbors. Each housed between 20 and 100 people, perhaps members of the same kin group. Judging from artifact patterns, some sheltered skilled artisans, obsidian and shell ornament makers, weavers, and potters.

What was life like inside Teotihuacán's anonymous neighborhood apartment compounds (barrios)? Mexican archaeologist Linda Manzanilla investigated one such complex close to the northwest edge of Teotihuacán, searching for traces of different activities within the complex. The stucco floors in the apartments and courtyards had been swept clean, so Manzanilla and her colleagues used chemical analyses of the floor deposits to search for human activities. Manzanilla developed a mosaic of different chemical readings, such as high phosphate readings where garbage had rotted and dense concentrations of carbonate from lime (used in the preparation of both tortillas and stucco) that indicated cooking or building activity. Her chemical plans of the compound are accurate enough to pinpoint the locations of cooking fires and eating places where the inhabitants consumed such animals as deer, rabbits, and turkeys. She was able to identify three nuclear families of about 30 people who lived in three separate apartments within this community inside a much larger community. Each apartment had specific areas for sleeping, eating, religious activities, and funeral rites.

Teotihuacán's barrios have revealed intense interactions between people who knew one another well and between these tight-knit communities and the wider universe of the city itself. Walking along one of the cleared streets, you can imagine passing down the same defile 1,500 years earlier, each side bounded by a bare, stuccoed compound wall. Occasionally, a door opens on to the street, offering a view of a shady courtyard, of pots and textiles drying in the Sun. The street would have been a cacophony of smells and sounds—wood smoke, dogs barking, the monotonous scratch of maize grinders, the soft voices of women weaving, and the passing scent of incense.

The Teotihuacános valued their foreign trade so highly that they allowed foreigners to settle among them in special barrios occupied over many centuries. Immigrants

Figure 15.14 Reconstruction of a Veracruz barrio at Teotihuacán, showing the distinctive architecture.

Source: Chuck Carter/National Geographic Creative.

from the Veracruz region of the lowlands lived in a neighborhood on the city's eastern side, identified from the remains of distinctive circular adobe houses with thatched roofs identical to those of the inhabitants' Gulf Coast homeland (see Figure 15.14). These people, easily identified by their orange-, brown-, and cream-painted pots, probably traded in exotic tropical luxuries such as brightly colored bird feathers. Another neighborhood, on the western side, housed Zapotec traders from the Valley of Oaxaca, 400 kilometers (250 miles) south of Teotihuacán. Potsherds from their segregated compounds allow us to identify their presence in the crowded city.

The broad avenue extends southward for 3.2 kilometers (2 miles), where it intersects an east–west avenue, thereby dividing the city into four quadrants. The huge square enclosure known as the Ciudadela, with sides over 400 meters (1,300 feet) long, is at the intersection. Here lies the Temple of Quetzalcoatl, the Feathered Serpent, a six-level pyramid adorned with tiers of inset rectangular panels placed over a sloping wall (see Figure 15.15). The façade is thought to depict the moment of Creation, when opposed

Figure 15.15 Faces on the façade of the Temple of Quetzalcoatl, Teotihuacán.
Source: Illia Gimyk/Alamy Stock Photo.

serpents, one representing lush greenness and peace and the other representing desert, fire, and war, cavorted in the primordial ocean, painted blue in the background. The Temple of Quetzalcoatl was built to the accompaniment of at least 200 human sacrifices, young warriors with their hands tied behind their backs sacrificed in groups of 18 individuals, perhaps one for each of the 20-day months of the Maya calendar.

Teotihuacán was a unique city, covering at least 21 square kilometers (8 square miles), and a major place of pilgrimage, a sacred city of the greatest symbolic importance. Its prosperity came from trade, especially in the green obsidian found nearby, which Teotihuacán's merchants exchanged for all manner of tropical products, including bird feathers, shells, and fish spines from the lowlands. Food supplies came from the intensive cultivation of valley soils and from acres of swamp gardens built up in the shallow waters of the nearby lakes. This was a brightly colored city, a landscape painted in every hue, the houses adorned with polished whitewash, which still adheres to wall fragments. But above all, the great city spoke a powerful symbolic language, which comes down to us in architecture, art, and ceramics. Its leaders perpetuated an origin myth that had their great city as the place where the cosmos and the present cycle of time began.

To be a Teotihuacáno was to be honored, for one dwelt at the very center of the world. But this honor carried important obligations to the city, the lords, and the gods. Every citizen served the state, through artisanship, through laboring on public works, and by serving in Teotihuacán's armies. These obligations were fulfilled through the ties of kinship that underlay every household, every apartment compound, and every royal palace, while linking everyone in the great city in the common enterprise of maintaining the cosmos. The great city was the heart of a large, loosely knit state about the size of the island of Sicily in the Mediterranean, some 26,000 square kilometers (10,000 square miles).

By A.D. 500, the secular ruler most likely governing Teotihuacán may have been looked on as a divine king of some kind. A class of nobles controlled the kinship groups that organized the majority of the city's huge population. In approximately A.D. 500–550, Teotihuacán was deliberately burned down, perhaps as a result of internal revolt and outside intervention. The very success of Teotihuacán may have accelerated its downfall. The new orders of society and politics spawned by the city may have been copied by other leaders, perhaps more aggressive and less tradition-bound than those of the mother city. No one knows exactly why this great city collapsed so suddenly. Its rapid development may have resulted in serious internal weaknesses that made Teotihuacán vulnerable to easy overthrow. A drought may also have weakened the city and provided an opportunity for jealous rivals to attempt an attack. Whatever the precise cause, by A.D. 700 the city's population had dropped sharply, although as many as 30,000 to 40,000 people lived around the old ceremonial precincts. Even as late as the sixteenth century, Teotihuacán was a city-state with a ruler and had as many as 10,000 subjects. The city remained a place of pilgrimage and sacred association into Aztec times. Indeed, the Aztecs believed that their world was created there, atop the Pyramid of the Sun.

The Toltecs (A.D. 650 to 1200)

Teotihuacán had acted as a magnet to the rural populations of the highlands for many centuries. When the great city collapsed, its inhabitants moved outward as other major Mexican cities expanded into the political vacuum left by its conquerors. Political authority passed rapidly from one growing city to the next. Eventually, one group—the Toltecs—achieved a semblance of dominance.

Early Toltec history is confusing at best, but like other highland peoples, the Toltecs were composed of various tribal groups, among them the Nahuatl-speaking Tolteca-Chichimeca, who were apparently semicivilized people from the fringes of Mesoamerica. (Nahuatl was the common language of the Aztec Empire at the time of the Spanish conquest.)

Tula, Mexico Capital center of the Toltec civilization, c. A.D. 900 to 1160.

A ruler named Topiltzin Quetzalcoatl, born in the year 1 Reed (each year had a label like "Reed"), or A.D. 935 or 947, moved the Toltec capital to Tollan, "the Place of Reeds" (the archaeologists' **Tula**), in its heyday a city of some 30,000 to 60,000 people, far smaller than Teotihuacán. Here, bitter strife broke out between the followers of the peace-loving Topiltzin Quetzalcoatl and those of his warlike rival Tezcatlipoca, "Smoking Mirror," who was the god of warriors, and of life itself, in human form. The Tezcatlipoca faction prevailed by trickery and humiliation. Topiltzin and his followers fled Tula and eventually arrived on the shores of the Gulf of Mexico. There, according to one account, the ruler set himself on fire decked out in his ceremonial regalia. As his ashes rose to heaven, he turned into the Morning Star. The Spanish conquistadors learned another version of the legend in which Topiltzin Quetzalcoatl fashioned a raft of serpents and sailed over the eastern horizon, vowing to return in another year 1 Reed in a future calendar cycle.

In the years following Topiltzin Quetzalcoatl's departure, the Toltec state reached its greatest extent, controlling much of central Mexico from coast to coast. By 900, Tula was a prosperous town of artisans that soon grew into a city of as many as 40,000 people covering 16 square kilometers (5.4 square miles) (see Figure 15.16). Tula's temples, pyramids, and ball courts were torn to the ground in about 1200, when the Toltec Empire fell apart.

Figure 15.16 Pyramid B at Tula, the Toltec capital, topped by colossal figures of warriors. Source: Prisma by Dukas Presseagentur GmbH/Alamy Stock Photo.

Aztec Empire (A.D. 1200 to 1521)

During the next century, a political vacuum existed in the Valley of Mexico, where a series of moderate-sized city-states prospered and competed. Into this settled and competitive world stepped a small and obscure group, the Azteca, or Mexica. Within a mere two centuries, these insignificant players on the highland stage presided over the mightiest pre-Columbian empire in the Americas.

The Aztecs' history, as they tell it, reads like a rags-to-riches novel. They claimed that they came from Aztlan, an island on a lake west or northwest of Mexico, migrating into the valley under the guidance of their tribal god Huitzilopochtli, "Hummingbird on the Left," who was soon reborn as the Sun God. This was the official version perpetuated by Aztec historians and recorded by the Spaniards. Such migration legends were common in ancient Mesoamerica and should not be taken at face value. The Aztecs had certainly settled in the valley by the thirteenth century, but they were unwelcome arrivals in the densely settled region. Eventually they settled on some swampy islands in the marshes of the largest lake in the valley, where they founded their capital, Tenochtitlán, "The Place of the Prickly Pear Cactus," sometime after 1325. Fierce and ruthless warriors, the Aztecs became mercenaries for the lord Tezozomoc of the expanding Tepanec kingdom in 1367.

After Tezozomoc's death in 1426, an Aztec ruler named Itzcoatl and his exceptionally able adviser Tlacaelel attacked the Tepanecs and crushed them in one of the great battles of Aztec history. The Aztecs became the masters of the Valley of Mexico and set out to reinvent society and rewrite history. Tlacaelel ordered all the historical codices of the Aztecs' rivals to be burned, creating a mythic, visionary history of the Mexica in their place. The Aztecs were now the chosen of the Sun God Huitzilopochtli, the true heirs of the ancient Toltecs and great warriors destined to take prisoners in battle to nourish the Sun in its daily journey across the heavens. A series of brilliant and ruthless leaders embarked on aggressive campaigns of conquest, designed to fulfill Aztec destiny. The greatest Aztec ruler was Ahuitzotl (1486–1502), the sixth *tlatoani*, or "speaker." His armies marched far beyond the valley to the borders of Guatemala. Just as in Teotihuacán and Tikal, the initial conquests rapidly delineated the broad outlines of their domains.

The Aztec Empire covered both highlands and lowlands and affected the lives of over 5 million people. A brilliant strategist and an able administrator, Ahuitzotl was a singleminded militarist who believed fervently in his divine mission to nourish the Sun God. Twenty thousand prisoners are said to have perished in 1487 when he inaugurated a rebuilt Great Temple of Huitzilopochtli and the Rain God Tlaloc in the central precincts of Tenochtitlán.

Tenochtitlán, Mexico Capital of the Aztec civilization from c. A.D. 1325 to 1521, estimated to have had a maximum population of about 250,000 people.

Tenochtitlán

In its late fifteenth-century heyday, Tenochtitlán was a sophisticated and cosmopolitan city with a social, political, and economic organization flexible enough to integrate large numbers of outsiders, merchants, pilgrims, foreigners, and laborers into its already large permanent population. The Aztec capital reflected a society that depended on military strength and on its ability to organize large numbers of people to achieve its end. Thousands of acres of carefully planned swamp gardens (*chinampas*) that intersected with canals provided food for the large urban population.

The city originally consisted of two autonomous communities, Tenochtitlán and Tlatelolco, each with its own ceremonial precincts. By 1519, Tenochtitlán was the center

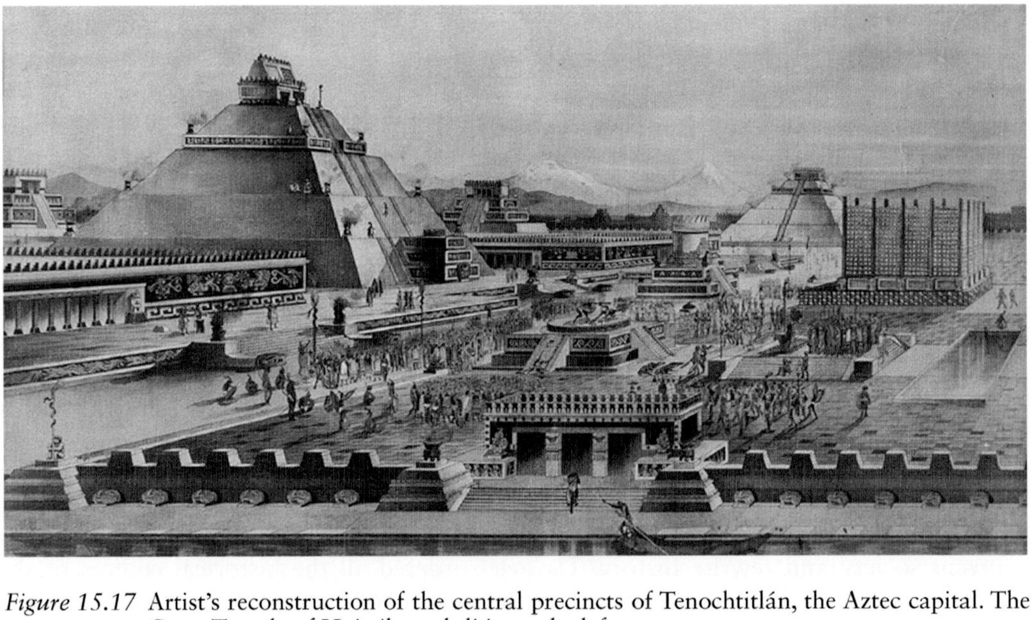

Figure 15.17 Artist's reconstruction of the central precincts of Tenochtitlán, the Aztec capital. The Great Temple of Huitzilopochtli is on the left.

Source: American Museum of Natural History.

of religious and secular power, and the main market was at Tlatelolco. The capital was divided into four quarters that intersected at the foot of the stairway to the Great Temple of Huitzilopochtli and Tlaloc within the central walled plaza (see Figure 15.17). The rectangular plaza was about 460 meters (1,500 feet) square, large enough to accommodate nearly 10,000 people during major public ceremonies.

Thanks to years of excavations by Mexican archaeologists, we know that the Great Temple stood on the north side of the plaza, and was a stepped pyramid with two stairways and two shrines, dedicated to Huitzilopochtli and Tlaloc, respectively (see Box 15.4). Tenochtitlán was the symbolic center of the universe, a city set in a circle of water—a re-creation of Aztlan itself, the mythic island surrounded by water.

The most important festivals of the Aztec world unfolded at the great pyramid, ceremonies marked by rows of brightly dressed prisoners climbing the steep stairway to their death. Each victim was stretched out over the sacrificial stone. In seconds, a priest with an obsidian knife slashed open his chest and ripped out his still-beating heart, dashing it against the sacrificial stone. The corpse rolled down the steep pyramid into the hands of butchers at the foot, who dismembered the body and set the skull on the great skull rack nearby (see Figure 15.18). Despite the Mexica's reputation for cannibalism, most experts believe that they consumed only small amounts of their sacrificial victims on ritual occasions, perhaps as acts of spiritual renewal.

The World of the Fifth Sun

The Aztecs were militaristic, but every deed, every moment of living, was filled with symbolic meaning and governed by ritual. They inherited the cyclical view of time, established by the movements of the heavenly bodies, which had been at the core of Mesoamerican civilization for millennia. Their 365-day secular calendar measured the passing of seasons and market days.

A ritual calendar on a 260-day cycle consisted of 20 "weeks" of 13 days each. Each week, each day, had a patron deity, all of them with specific good and evil qualities. Once every 52 years, the two calendars coincided, a moment at which time was thought to expire until rekindled by the priests lighting a sacred fire in a sacrificial victim's chest. Then, a new cycle began amid general rejoicing.

Aztec creation legends spoke of four Suns preceding their own world, that of the Fifth Sun. A cataclysmic flood destroyed the world of the Fourth Sun. Primordial waters covered the Earth. The gods gathered at the sacred city, Teotihuacán, where they took counsel. Two gods were chosen to represent the Sun and the Moon. They did penance for four days and then immolated themselves in a great fire in the presence of the other gods. They emerged as the Sun and Moon, blown on their cyclical courses by the Wind God Ehecatl. Thus was born the world of the Fifth Sun, a world doomed to inevitable, cyclical extinction. A strong sense of fatalism underlay Aztec existence, but they believed that they could ensure the continuity of life by nourishing the Sun with the magic elixir of human hearts. This was the reason why human sacrifice was so prevalent in Mesoamerican society; it was a means of returning food and energy from living people to the earth, the sky, and the waters. Feeding the Sun was warriors' business, for they were the chosen people of the Sun, destined to conquer or to suffer the "flowery death" (death on the sacrificial stone) when captured in battle. From birth, in formal orations, in schools, through art, architecture, and poetry, and even in dress codes, the Aztecs were told that theirs was a divine quest—to carve out an empire in the name of Huitzilopochtli.

Box 15.4 Site
The Great Temple at Tenochtitlán

The focal point of Aztec religious life was the Great Temple of the gods Huitzilopochtli and Tlaloc in the heart of Tenochtitlán (see Figure 15.17). The Spaniards demolished the final temple at the conquest and built Mexico City's cathedral on approximately the same site. In 1978, electricity workers digging a pit came across a gigantic oval stone, over 3.2 meters (10.5 feet) in diameter, not far from the cathedral. Reliefs carved on the stone depicted the dismembered body of the goddess Coyolxauhqui, who, according to myth, had been killed by her brother, Huitzilopochtli. Five years of excavations on the site led by archaeologist Eduardo Matos Moctezuma and his colleagues unearthed the remains of the Great Temple. Little survived of the final building razed by the Spaniards, but beneath it lay no fewer than six earlier phases of the temple, the second dating to about A.D. 1390, virtually complete.

The original temple structure had been a small and crude construction, later enclosed within successively larger pyramids each with its own shrines, sculptures, offerings, and other artifacts. In all, about 6,000 objects were excavated from 86 separate offering caches, some of them objects of Aztec manufacture, but the great majority clearly tribute or spoils of war from different parts of the empire buried there as a sacred expression of Aztec power and might. They included magnificent artifacts of obsidian, jade, and terracotta, and even ancient stone masks from Teotihuacán. Perhaps, the Aztecs were themselves amateur archaeologists who dug up the masks at this ruined city?

The Great Temple depicted the Aztec vision of the cosmos. The platform that supported the whole structure of the temple corresponded to the terrestrial level of existence. The four tapering tiers of the pyramid rose to the summit and represented the celestial levels. At the summit was the supreme level, with the two shrines to the gods Huitzilopochtli and Tlaloc. The underworld lay beneath the platform. Most of the offerings came from below it. These offerings included a very large number associated with Tlaloc—not just depictions of him, but also extraordinary quantities of fish and marine animal bones appropriate for this god of water and rain. According to the Aztecs, the Earth lay in the center of the universe, encircled by a ring of water. Above lay the heavens with the gods, and beneath lay the underworld. The terrestrial level of existence had a central point, located at the Great Temple, from which radiated the four directions of the Aztec world. The Great Temple was the symbolic pivotal point, the place where a vertical channel led both to the heavens and to the underworld. The symbolism went even further, for Tenochtitlán itself lay in the midst of a lake. Indeed, it was sometimes called Cemanahuac, "Place in a Circle of Water," thought of as a turquoise ring: as was Aztlan, the mythical Aztec island homeland to the northwest, surrounded by water. Thus, Tenochtitlán was the symbolic center of the universe and the place where the supreme ruler liaised with the gods.

Aztec State Organization

The Aztec Empire was a mosaic of ever-changing alliances, cemented together by an elaborate tribute-gathering machine and controlled by a tiny group of rulers, the lord of Tenochtitlán being principal among them. Everything was run for the benefit of a growing elite, who maintained their power by ruthless and efficient taxation campaigns, political

Figure 15.18 Aztec human sacrifice: A victim's heart is torn out at the Great Temple of Huitzilopochtli. Source: World History Archive/Alamy.

marriages, and the constant threat of military force. Tribute was assessed on conquered cities and taken in many forms, especially raw materials like gold dust, metal artifacts, or tropical bird feathers for ceremonial mantles and headdresses (see Figure 15.19). Twenty-six cities did nothing but provide firewood for one royal palace alone.

Under the highly visible and much-touted imperial veneer lay a complex foundation of small kingdoms, towns, and villages, all integrated into local economies. Many of them existed before the Aztec state or even earlier; civilizations came into being and continued after the Spanish conquest. At the same time, the economic and political patterns of the empire were highly variable, both regionally and socially, in everything from land tenure to craft specialization, patterns of urbanization, and merchants and markets.

Tribute and trade went together, for the Aztec Empire depended heavily on professional merchants (*pochteca*). The Aztec merchants formed a closely knit class of their own, serving as the "eyes and ears" of the state and sometimes achieving great wealth. Tenochtitlán's great market at Tlatelolco was the hub of the Aztec world, attended, so the Spanish chroniclers recorded, by at least 20,000 people a day, and by 50,000 people on market days. There were gold and silver merchants, dealers in slaves and tropical feathers, sellers of capes and chocolate and every other kind of merchandise imaginable. Appointed officials ensured that fair practices prevailed.

The state itself was run for the benefit of the rulers and the nobility, a privileged class who controlled land and had the right to make use of communal labor. An elaborate dress code covered everything from ornaments to cape and sandal styles: regulations designed

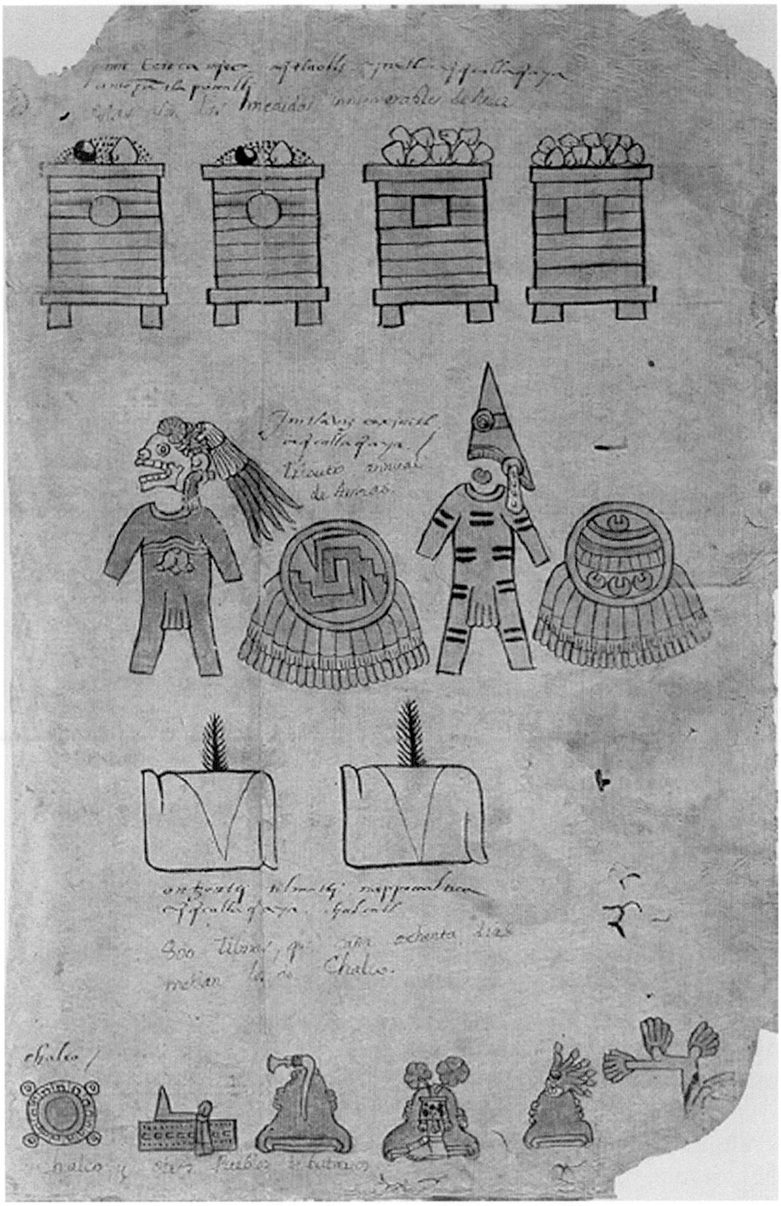

Figure 15.19 Aztec tribute: An inventory preserved in the *Codex Mendoza*, which was an account of Aztec society compiled after the Spanish conquest for the Viceroy of New Spain; it lists, among other items from the province of Tochtepec, "1,600 rich mantles, 800 striped red, white, and green mantles, 400 warrior's tunics and shorts." The tribute also included colored bird feathers, cacao, and tree gum.

Source: The Art Archive/Alamy.

to restrict the size of the nobility. The tribute and labor of tens of thousands of commoners supported the state. The humble commoners, with their coarse capes and work-worn hands, supplied a small number of people with an endless supply of food, firewood, water, fine clothing, and a host of luxury goods that came from all over the lowlands and highlands. Only slaves and prisoners were lower in the social hierarchy.

Every Aztec was a member of a *calpulli*, or "big house," a kin-based group of families that claimed descent through the male line from a common ancestor. The four quarters of Tenochtitlán were organized into neighborhoods based on such groups. The *calpulli* served as the intermediary between the individual commoner and the state, paying taxes in labor and tribute and allocating people to carry out public works. Most important, the *calpulli* held land communally and allocated it to its members. An elected leader maintained special maps showing how the land was being used and dealt with government tribute collectors. The *calpulli* provided a measure of security to every member of society while being an efficient device for the state to govern a teeming, diverse urban and rural population and to organize large numbers of people for armies or work projects at short notice. None of the Aztecs' social and political institutions were new. The Toltecs and the rulers of Teotihuacán had used them with ruthless success centuries earlier, even if, in the Aztec case, they worked within a more flexible and diverse milieu.

The Spanish Conquest

The Aztec Empire was at its height when the aggressive and militaristic ruler Ahuitzotl died in 1501. The following year, Moctezuma Xocoyotzin ("the Younger") was elected to the throne. He was a complex man, said to be a good soldier but given to introspection. When reports reached Tenochtitlán in 1517 of mountains (Spanish ships) moving on the Gulf of Mexico, of white-bearded visitors (conquistadors) from over the eastern horizon making contact with the Maya of the distant Yucatán, Moctezuma became obsessed with ancient Toltec legends, with the departure of Topiltzin Quetzalcoatl, who had sailed over the eastern horizon vowing to return in the year 1 Reed. By grotesque historical coincidence, Hernán Cortés landed in Veracruz in the year 1 Reed (1519), convincing Moctezuma that Topiltzin Quetzalcoatl had returned to claim his kingdom.

The story of the Spanish conquest that followed unfolds like a Greek tragedy. The conquest pitted an isolated, battle-hardened expeditionary force of about 600 men against a brave, driven people who were convinced, like their illustrious predecessors, that every act of war was imbued with deep symbolism. The Aztecs had long used war to feed the relentless appetite of the gods and to keep a loose patchwork of vassal states in order. With a skilled enemy exploiting their uneasy allies, they found themselves on their own. Inevitably, the war-hardened Spaniards prevailed and they destroyed Tenochtitlán in 1521.

Ten years passed before the whole of Mexico (New Spain) was under secure Spanish control. Tens of thousands of people died in bloody encounters, hundreds of thousands more from exotic diseases like influenza and smallpox introduced by the newcomers. Instead of the divine benevolence of Quetzalcoatl, the conquerors brought suffering, death, disease, and slavery. More than 3,000 years of Mesoamerican civilization passed rapidly into historical obscurity.

Summary

- Mesoamerican civilization extends back at least 4,000 years. The Preclassic period of Mesoamerican prehistory lasted from approximately 2000 B.C. to A.D. 300, a period of major cultural change in both the lowlands and highlands. Sedentary villages traded with each other in raw materials and exotic objects. Increasing social complexity went hand in hand with the appearance of the first public buildings and the evidence of social stratification.

- These developments are well chronicled in the Olmec culture of the lowlands, which flourished from approximately 1500 to 500 B.C. Olmec art styles and religious beliefs were among those that spread widely over the lowlands and highlands during the late Preclassic period.
- Religious ideologies, ritual organization, and extensive trading networks were key factors in the development of Maya society in the lowlands after 1000 B.C.
- Classic Maya civilization flourished from A.D. 300 to 900 and consisted of an ever-changing patchwork of competing states. Until about A.D. 600, the largest states were in northeast Petén, with a multicenter polity headed by the rulers of Tikal.
- Maya civilization reached its height in the southern lowlands after the seventh century, collapsing suddenly in the Yucatán after A.D. 900.
- After that, the focus of Maya civilization moved into the northern Yucatán, where Maya civilization flourished at Chichén Itzá and other centers right up to the Spanish conquest of the sixteenth century. Many Maya communities still flourish in the lowlands today.
- Highland Mesoamerican civilization stemmed from both indigenous and lowland roots. Olmec influence was strong, but small kingdoms developed in the Valley of Oaxaca by at least 1000 B.C. These coalesced into the Monte Albán state, which reached its heyday during the first millennium A.D. and coexisted with Teotihuacán on the edge of the Basin of Mexico.
- Teotihuacán was the dominant political and economic force in the highlands and in the Basin of Mexico for the first seven centuries of the first millennium A.D.
- The Toltec civilization, also based in the Valley of Mexico, filled the political vacuum left by the collapse of Teotihuacán but fell apart itself in A.D. 1200.
- By the fourteenth century, the Aztecs, who originated in the northwest of the basin, were becoming the dominant force in the highlands. Over the next two centuries, their rulers created a vast tribute-paying empire that extended into the lowlands and as far south as Guatemala. The empire was already showing signs of strain when Hernán Cortés and 600 conquistadors entered the Aztec capital, Tenochtitlán, in 1519.

Key Terms and Sites

Preclassic era (Formative era)
Olmec
San Lorenzo
La Venta
Maya civilization
Cuello
Nakbé
El Mirador
Calakmul
codices
Tikal
Uaxactún
Caracol
Copán
Quiriguá
Chichén Itzá
San José Mogote

Cuicuilco
Teotihuacán
Tula
Tenochtitlán

Critical-Thinking Questions

1. What were the most obvious similarities between all Mesoamerican complex cultures from the Olmec onward? Use examples from the chapter in your discussion.
2. What, in your opinion, was the central economic, religious, or social factor that held together Maya society? Was this ultimately a strength or a weakness?
3. What legacy did earlier Mesoamerican societies pass on to the Aztecs, and was this legacy a strength or a weakness for a society forced to confront the Spaniards?

Further Reading

The definitive summary is S. T. Evans, *Ancient Mexico and Central America*, 3rd ed. (London: Thames and Hudson, 2013). K. Flannery's edited, *The Early Mesoamerican Village* (New York: Academic Press, 1976) contains a rich foundation of wisdom about archaeology generally, as well as valuable information on early complexity in the Valley of Oaxaca. For the Olmec, see R. Diehl, *The Olmecs: America's First Civilization* (London: Thames and Hudson, 2004). See also C. Pool, *Olmec Archaeology and Early Mesoamerica* (Cambridge: Cambridge University Press, 2007). J. Marcus and K. Flannery's, *The Zapotec Civilization* (London: Thames and Hudson, 1996) is a richly illustrated account of Monte Albán and the origins of civilization in the Valley of Oaxaca. Teotihuacán is well described in René Millon, R. B. Drewitt and G. Cowgill's, *Urbanization at Teotihuacán* (Austin: University of Texas Press, 1974). The Maya: M. Coe and S. D. Houston, *The Maya*, 10th ed. (London: Thames and Hudson, 2022) is the most widely read summary. See also A. Demarest, *Ancient Maya: The Rise and Fall of a Rainforest Civilization* (Cambridge: Cambridge University Press, 2005). L. Schele and D. Freidel's, *A Forest of Kings* (New York: Morrow, 1990) is a popular synthesis of Maya history based on both archaeology and glyphs, which is seminal, if controversial in places. Their *Maya Cosmos* (New York: Morrow, 1993) discusses Maya astronomy and world views. The Aztecs: M. Smith, *The Aztecs (The Peoples of America)*, 2nd ed. (Oxford: Blackwell, 2002). Also R. Townsend, *The Aztecs*, 3rd ed. (London: Thames and Hudson, 2009). I. Clendinnen's, *Aztecs: An Interpretation* (Cambridge: Cambridge University Press, 1991) is a valuable analysis of Aztec history. For the Spanish conquest, see C. Dibble and A. Anderson's, *The Florentine Codex* (Salt Lake City: University of Utah Press, 12 vols., 1950–1975).

16 Andean Civilizations

Chapter Outline

DOI: 10.4324/9781003592754-22

Andean textiles: A costumed figure from Paracas wearing a cat-like nose ornament and carrying a trophy head.

Source: From Paracas; Cloth with procession of figures (detail); Peru, south coast, Paracas Peninsula, Nasca style (100 B.C.–A.D. 700); cotton, plain weave and pigment (field), camelid fiber, plain weave (border); 69.8 × 280.7 centimeter. © The Cleveland Museum of Art. The Norweb Collection, 1940.530.

The year was 1911. American explorer Hiram Bingham was high in the Andes, struggling along precipitous, densely forested paths, slipping ankle-deep in mud at every corner. Bingham was searching for Vilcabamba, the last refuge of the Inca ruler Manca Inca when he fled from the Spaniards in 1537. With a local farmer as a guide, he and his men climbed—on all fours in places—far above the tumbling Urubamba River. Suddenly, he emerged into the open, high atop a mountain ridge. There he found a granite stairway, which led to a plaza. From the plaza, Bingham wandered through "a maze of beautiful granite houses ... covered with trees and moss and the growth of centuries" (Bingham 1964, 212). He walked for hours among "walls of white granite ... carefully cut and exquisitely fitted together." Stone terraces climbed like giant staircases up the hillside. A twisting path led to ruined houses built with fine Inca stonework. The plaza that Bingham had reached via the granite stairway contained two temples, one with a large altar stone. "The sight held me spellbound," declared Bingham. On this mountain ridge, the Incas had built **Machu Picchu,** a settlement in such a remote, inaccessible setting that Bingham proclaimed it the "lost city of the Incas." For three years, Bingham worked at Machu Picchu, clearing, excavating, and mapping houses and temples.

Machu Picchu, Peru Inca settlement high in the Andes occupied before, during, and after the Spanish conquest.

Machu Picchu is one of the most spectacular archaeological sites in the world (see Figure 16.1), but it was never truly a lost city, for the local farmers were well aware of its existence. Bingham himself believed he had found Vilcabamba, but in 1964, explorer Gene Savoy identified the remote Inca settlement of Espiritu Pampa in the forested Pamaconas valley as the last Inca capital.

Tawantinsuyu Inca name for their empire, "The Land of the Four Quarters."

Figure 16.1 Machu Picchu, an Inca settlement and ritual center high in the Andes, Peru. Source: Jgz/Fotolia.

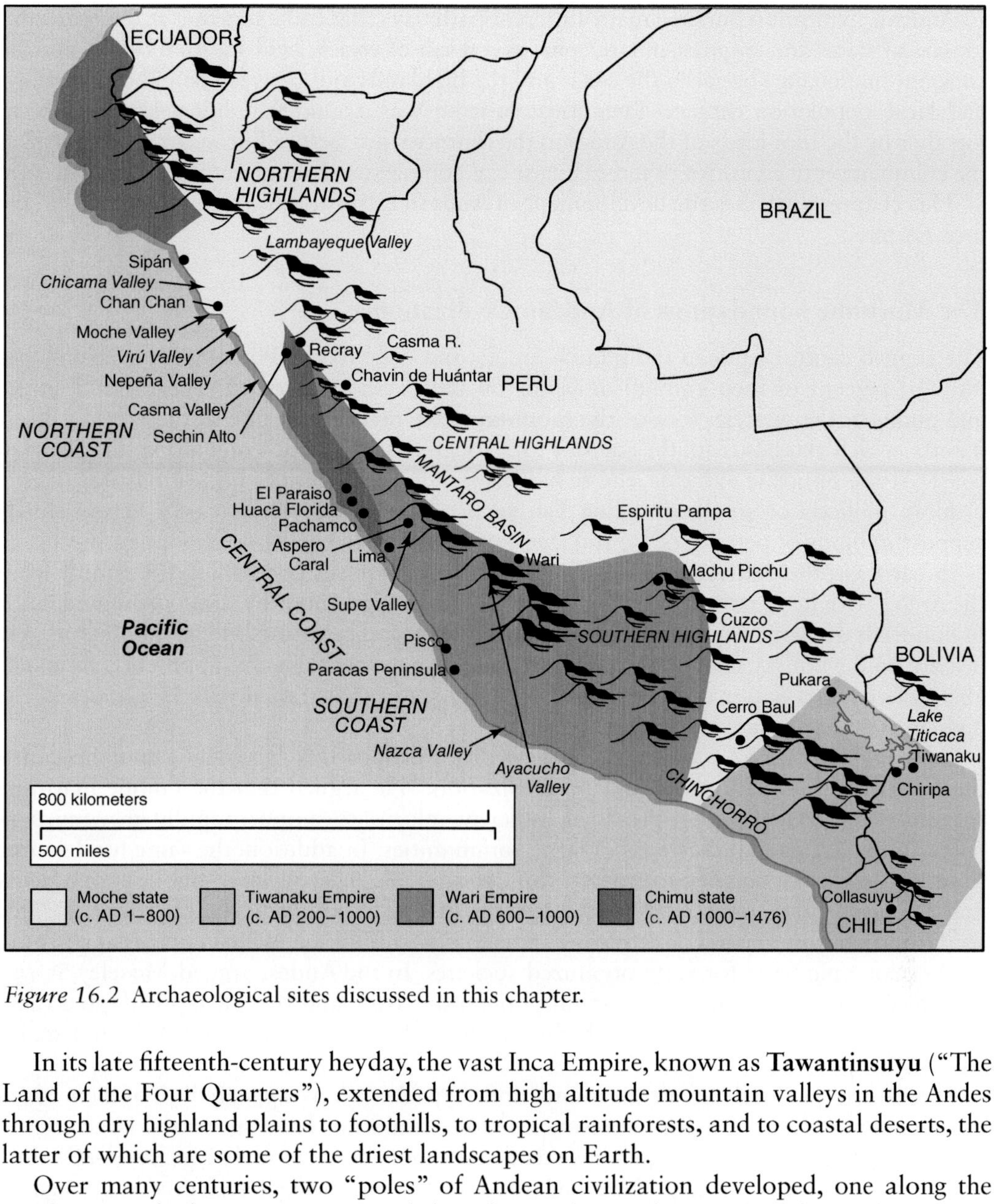

Figure 16.2 Archaeological sites discussed in this chapter.

In its late fifteenth-century heyday, the vast Inca Empire, known as **Tawantinsuyu** ("The Land of the Four Quarters"), extended from high altitude mountain valleys in the Andes through dry highland plains to foothills, to tropical rainforests, and to coastal deserts, the latter of which are some of the driest landscapes on Earth.

Over many centuries, two "poles" of Andean civilization developed, one along the north coast of what is now Peru and the other in the south-central Andes. Only the Inca succeeded in joining the two into one vast empire. The northern pole was centered on the bleak and effectively rainless Peruvian desert plain, which extends south nearly 550 kilometers (350 miles) along the coast as far as Collasuyu, reaching a width of up to 100 kilometers (62 miles) in the area of the Lambayeque River (see Figure 16.2). Some 40 rivers and streams fueled by mountain runoff flow across the plain, but they can only be used for irrigation in areas where the surrounding desert is low enough.

The southern pole embraced the high plains of the Lake Titicaca Basin, highland Bolivia, and parts of Argentina and northern Chile in the south-central Andes. Much of this region was too dry and cold to sustain dense human populations. The northern end of the Lake Titicaca Basin was somewhat warmer and better watered, making alpaca and llama herding, as well as potato and quinoa agriculture, possible.

Andean civilization pursued many different pathways that came together in a remarkable mosaic of states and empires, in large part as a result of widely held spiritual beliefs and via constant interchange between the coast and the highlands and between neighboring valleys and large population centers. Tawantinsuyu itself was a unique political synthesis sewn together by the Inca lords of the Andes in the centuries just before European contact. It was the culmination of centuries of increasing social complexity throughout the Andean area.

This chapter describes the development of Andean civilization, which culminated in the Inca Empire.

The Maritime Foundations of Andean Civilization

The rugged central Andean mountains are second only to the Himalayas in height, but only 10 percent of their rainfall descends on the Pacific watershed. The foothill slopes and plains at the western foot of the mountains are mantled by one of the world's driest deserts, which extends from the equator to 30 degrees south, much of it along the Peruvian coast. At the opposite extreme, the richest fishery in the Americas hugs the Pacific shore, yielding millions of small schooling fish such as anchovies. These easily netted shoals support millions of people today, and they supported dense prehistoric populations.

In contrast, the cultivation of this dry landscape requires controlling the runoff from the Andes with large irrigation systems that use long canals built by the coordinated labor of hundreds of people. Only 10 percent of this desert can be farmed, so its inhabitants rely heavily on the bounty of the Pacific Ocean. Surprisingly, perhaps, this apparently inhospitable desert was a major center of complex early states that traded with neighbors in the highlands and built large ceremonial centers.

In the 1970s, archaeologist Michael Moseley proposed a hypothesis that he called the "maritime foundations of Andean civilization." He argued that the unique maritime resources of the Pacific coast provided sufficient calories to support rapidly growing, sedentary populations that clustered in large communities. In addition, the same food source produced sufficient surplus to free up time and people to erect large public monuments and temples—work organized by the leaders of newly complex coastal societies. This scenario runs contrary to conventional archaeological thinking, which regards agriculture as the economic basis for state-organized societies. In the Andes, argued Moseley, it was fishing. For thousands of years, coastal populations rose, and their rise preadapted them to later circumstances, under which they would adopt large-scale irrigation and maize agriculture.

Several critiques of the maritime foundations hypothesis have appeared, all of them based on the assumption that maritime resources alone could not have supported large coastal settlements. Most of these critiques have tended to ignore the potential of anchovies. Overall, the maritime foundations hypothesis has stood the test of time well, seen as a component in a much broader evolutionary process that also took place inland, in the highlands, and in areas where the width of the coastal shelf precluded extensive anchovy fishing.

Richard Burger argues that changing dietary patterns in the highlands, where agriculture became increasingly important, would have created a demand among farmers for lowland products—salt, fish, and seaweed. Seaweed is rich in marine iodine and could have been an important medicine in the highlands for combating endemic goiter and other conditions. By the same token, carbohydrate foods like white potatoes that could not be grown on the coast have been found at sites in the Pacific lowlands. Thus, the formation of states in both the lowlands and highlands may have been fostered by continuous interchange between the coast and the interior.

Michael Moseley believes that the reliance on maritime resources led to a preadaptation in the form of large, densely concentrated populations whose leaders were able to organize the labor forces needed not only for building large ceremonial centers, but also for transforming river valleys with sizable irrigation schemes. Under this scenario, irrigation farming was in the hands of a well-defined group of authority figures who took advantage of existing simple technology and local populations to create new economies. This transformation, based as it was on trade, maize agriculture, and a maritime diet, acted as a "kick" for radical changes in Andean society. But the transformation was based on ancient fishing traditions, which can be documented thousands of years earlier at early coastal villages.

Coastal Foundations (3000 to 900 B.C.)

Agriculture remained a secondary activity in the lowlands. Nevertheless, sedentary villages of several hundred people flourished along the north coast of Peru. For centuries, communities large and small grappled with problems of political authority, emerging social inequality, and new definitions of the cosmos that were not to crystallize for a long time. This was a time of experimentation, accelerating change, and probably intense rivalries triggered by ambitious emergent rulers. The new beliefs manifested themselves in a wave of monumental construction in both the lowlands and highlands. At the same time, textiles, like those found in the Paracas cemeteries (see the chapter-opener photo), assumed great importance in Andean life.

Aspero, Peru Coastal community near the mouth of the Rio Supe on the Peruvian coast, dating to c. 3050 B.C.

Caral, Peru Coastal kingdom on the Rio Supe that cultivated cotton with irrigation agriculture, c. 2600 B.C.

We do not know when this experimentation began—when the first, more complex societies developed along the coast—but it was at least 5,000 years ago. At **Aspero**, near the mouth of the Rio Supe, a sprawling coastal community covered at least 15 hectares (37 acres), including platform mounds with buildings on top of them. One, Huaca de los Idolos, has been radiocarbon-dated to 3055 B.C. By 2600 B.C., a large kingdom ruled by a center named **Caral** developed in the hot Supe valley, about 200 kilometers (120 miles) north of modern-day Lima and 20 kilometers (12 miles) from the Pacific. There were as many as 17 centers in the Supe region, supported by cultivating beans, peppers, guavas, and other fruit grown with skilled irrigation agriculture. The farmers also grew cotton, but not maize or potatoes, the two later staples of Andean life. The kingdom may have prospered by growing and trading industrial crops like cotton for net manufacture and gourds for floats. Certainly, much of its subsistence came from anchovies, which have been found in desiccated feces from the site.

Caral is dominated by six large stone platforms with structures atop them built of quarried stone and filled in with cobbles from the nearby river (see Figure 16.3). The largest measures 152 by 137 meters (500 by 450 feet) and stands 18 meters (60 feet) high. There are three sunken plazas and eight sectors containing different types of dwellings—apartment complexes, modest houses, and grand stone-walled residences. Fortunately for science, the platform builders had carried their loads of cobbles in bags woven from reeds, which were added to the fill, carriers and all. Radiocarbon dates from the netting trace the construction, a task carried out in two efficiently organized stages, to about 2627 B.C.

Clearly, a small and authoritative elite governed this important kingdom, but we still know almost nothing about them or about the ways in which they commanded the loyalty

Figure 16.3 The major terraced structure at Caral in the Supe valley, the earliest Andean center. Source: Rudimencial/iStock.

of the hundreds, if not thousands, of people who built their imposing centers. Caral was abandoned for unknown reasons between 2000 and 1500 B.C., just as other kingdoms came into prominence along the coast to the north. This remarkable site, called by some a city, was the largest settlement in the Americas in its day, a full millennium and a half before Teotihuacán in Mexico. It rose in the Supe valley at the time when the Egyptian pharaohs were building pyramids on the other side of the world.

El Paraíso

A series of interacting chiefdoms emerged along the northern and central parts of the coast after 1800 B.C. Political units centered on the Moche, Casma, Chillón, and other river valleys, where irrigation agriculture developed. Centuries before, when pottery was unknown on the coast, but cotton had already been widely cultivated, communication networks had arisen that linked not only neighboring coastal river valleys, but also the lowlands and highlands. These trade routes, which straddled all manner of environmental zones, helped spread technology, ideology, pottery making, and architectural styles over large areas, creating a superficial sense of unity that was reflected in the widespread use of common art motifs.

El Paraíso, Peru Ceremonial center in Peru's Chillón valley dating to c. 1800 B.C.

Figure 16.4 El Paraíso, Peru.
Source: Ernesto Benavides/AFP/Getty Images.

During the Initial Period, coastal ceremonial buildings were greatly elaborated and new architectural devices were adopted. Among them was a distinctive U-shaped platform often associated with elaborate adobe friezes. **El Paraíso**, built close to the mouth of the Chillón River near Lima in about 1800 B.C., is the oldest of these U-shaped ceremonial complexes and the closest one to the Pacific (see Figure 16.4). This vast site consists of at least six huge square buildings constructed of roughly shaped stone blocks cemented with unfired clay. The people painted the polished clay-faced outer walls in brilliant hues. Each complex consisted of a square building surrounded by tiers of platforms reached by stone and clay staircases.

The largest is more than 250 meters (830 feet) long and 50 meters (166 feet) wide, standing more than 10 meters (33 feet) above the plain. The rooms were apparently covered with matting roofs supported by willow posts. Perhaps as many as 100,000 tons of rock excavated from the nearby hills were needed to build El Paraíso's buildings. There are few signs of occupation around them, though, as if they were shrines and public precincts rather than residential quarters. The two largest mounds of collapsed masonry lie parallel to one another, defining a vast, elongated patio covering more than 2.5 hectares (6 acres).

What is most surprising is that people from dozens of scattered villages erected these huge structures. For reasons not yet understood, they united in a building project that channeled most of their surplus energies into a vast monumental center, a place where few people lived but where everyone apparently congregated for major public ceremonies.

El Paraíso's U-shaped layout coincides with the florescence of similarly shaped ceremonial centers in the interior, at a time when coastal people began to consume much larger amounts of root crops, make pottery, and shift their settlements inland to river valleys. Some scholars believe that this move coincided with the introduction of large-scale canal irrigation. Perhaps, the spread of U-shaped ceremonial centers reflects a radical restructuring of society that accompanied major economic change.

What does this mean in ritual terms? In many parts of the Americas, the ritual manipulation of smoke and water served as a way of bridging stratified layers of air, earth, and bodies of water in the cosmos. The early ceremonial centers of the coast and highlands may reflect an ancient tradition of using these substances to maintain communication with the cosmos.

The Early Horizon and Chavín de Huántar (900 to 200 B.C.)

Chavín de Huántar, Peru Ceremonial center in Peru's Andes foothills dating from as early as 1500 B.C. and thriving until between 900 and 600 B.C.; source of much Andean art in the distinctive style known as Chavín.

Early Horizon, Peru Period marked by the widespread adoption of distinctive art and religious beliefs over much of highland and lowland Peru, c. 900 to 200 B.C.

Back in 1943, archaeologist Julio Tello identified a distinctive art style in stone, ceramics, and precious metals over a wide area of highland Peru, a style he named Chavín after a famous prehistoric ceremonial center at **Chavín de Huántar** in central Peru. Tello's research led to a long-held belief among Peruvianists that the widespread Chavín art style was a "mother culture" for all later Andean civilizations, somewhat equivalent to the Olmec phenomenon in Mesoamerican prehistory. This became a distinctive **Early Horizon** in Peruvian prehistory, dating to about 900 B.C., when there was a great expansion of indigenous religious belief through conquest, trade, and colonization—when civilization began.

Chavín de Huántar became an important shrine in Andean life. Like all great religious centers, the site has a long and complex history that is only now being unraveled, starting perhaps as early as 1500 B.C. (The site itself was occupied much earlier.) From small-scale beginnings, the builders expanded the center, adapting the local geology and topography by diverting the nearby Mosna River, using massive landfills to raise land surfaces, and erecting heavy foundations to stabilize plazas on swampy ground. At the same time, they used precisely cut and engraved stone plaques to adorn plaza walls, lintels, and terrace fronts. All of this culminated in the world-famous ceremonial buildings of Chavín after 900 B.C., a maze of plazas, stairways, and galleries, associated with a well-established and highly distinctive iconography that was to exercise a wide influence across the Andes.

The temple area is terraced with an impressive truncated pyramid, 10 meters (33 feet) high on the uppermost level (see Figure 16.5). The pyramid appears solid but is in fact hollow, a honeycomb of stone passages and rooms. Special rectangular tubes ventilate the galleries. The temple housed a remarkable carving of a jaguar-like human with hair in the form of serpents, the famous Lanzón, which may have served as an axis joining the heavens, Earth, and the underworld (see Figure 16.6). The deity seems to be acting as an arbiter of balance and order. The entire center was a place of mediation between the heavens and the underworld. Chavín's priests and religious functionaries served as intermediaries who linked the living and the supernatural. In this shaman-like role, they transformed themselves into supernatural jaguars and crested eagles.

Chavín art reflects these transformations. Jaguar motifs predominate: humans, gods, and animals have jaguar-like fangs or limbs, and snakes flow from the bodies of many

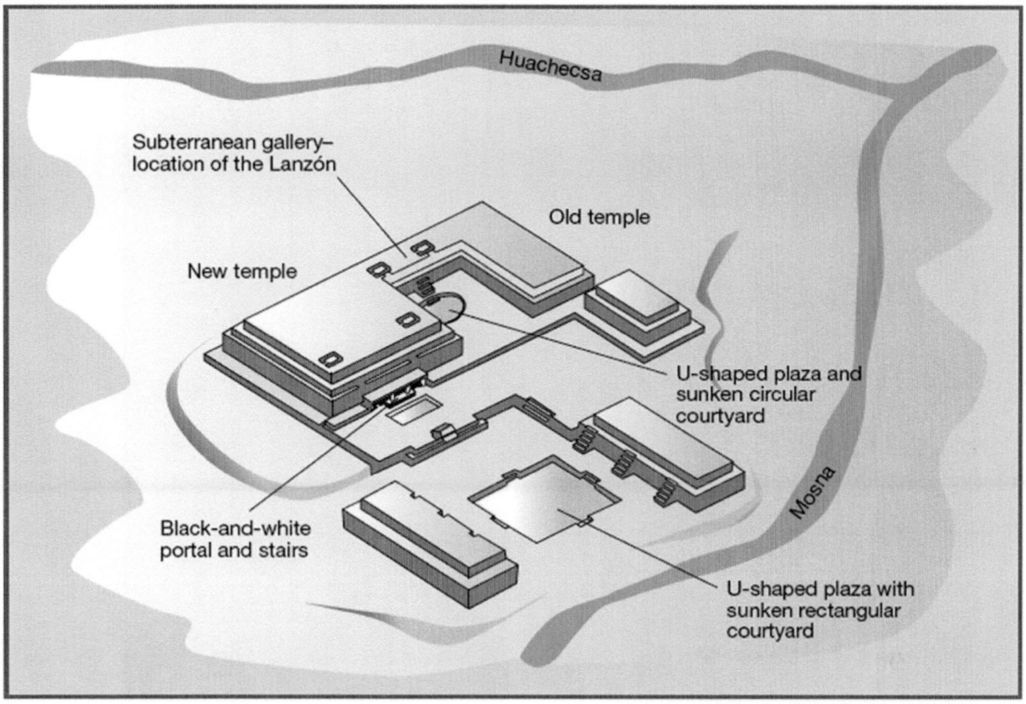

Figure 16.5 Plan of the ceremonial center at Chavín de Huántar, Peru, showing major architectural features.

figures (see Figure 2.2 on p. 42). The art is grotesque and slightly sinister. Many figures were carved in stone, others in clay or bone, with their nostrils dripping with mucus from ingesting hallucinogenic substances. The principal god may have been a nature deity, associated with thunder and other powerful meteorological phenomena of the nearby high mountains.

Richard Burger theorizes that, conceivably, Chavín de Huántar was a four-stage artificial mountain where rituals focused on the circulation of water.

According to these beliefs, the Earth floated on a vast ocean. From there, water circulated through mountains to the Milky Way in the heavens, where it became rain to water human fields before flowing back into the ocean. Peruvian archaeologist Luis Lumbreras has replicated the deep roaring sound of water flowing through the elaborate stone-lined tunnels and canals of the great shrine. He believes that the roar of the water would have echoed through the temple during the rainy season, a symbolic link between the rain-giving mountains, the temple, and the layers of the cosmos. Experiments have shown that conch-shell trumpets could produce a droning sound that resonated through the chambers, which would have added to the sense of awe and supernatural fear (see Box 2.2 on p. 41). The temple was a carefully contrived setting for elaborate ceremonies invoking the supernatural.

With its tangled animal and human motifs, Chavín art has all the flamboyance and exotic touches of the tropical forest. The animals depicted—cayman, jaguar, and snake—are all forest animals. The art may have originated in the tropical forests to the east of the Andes, but the Early Horizon Chavín temple is U-shaped, with a sunken central plaza, which is an architectural design documented centuries earlier at other coastal and highland sites.

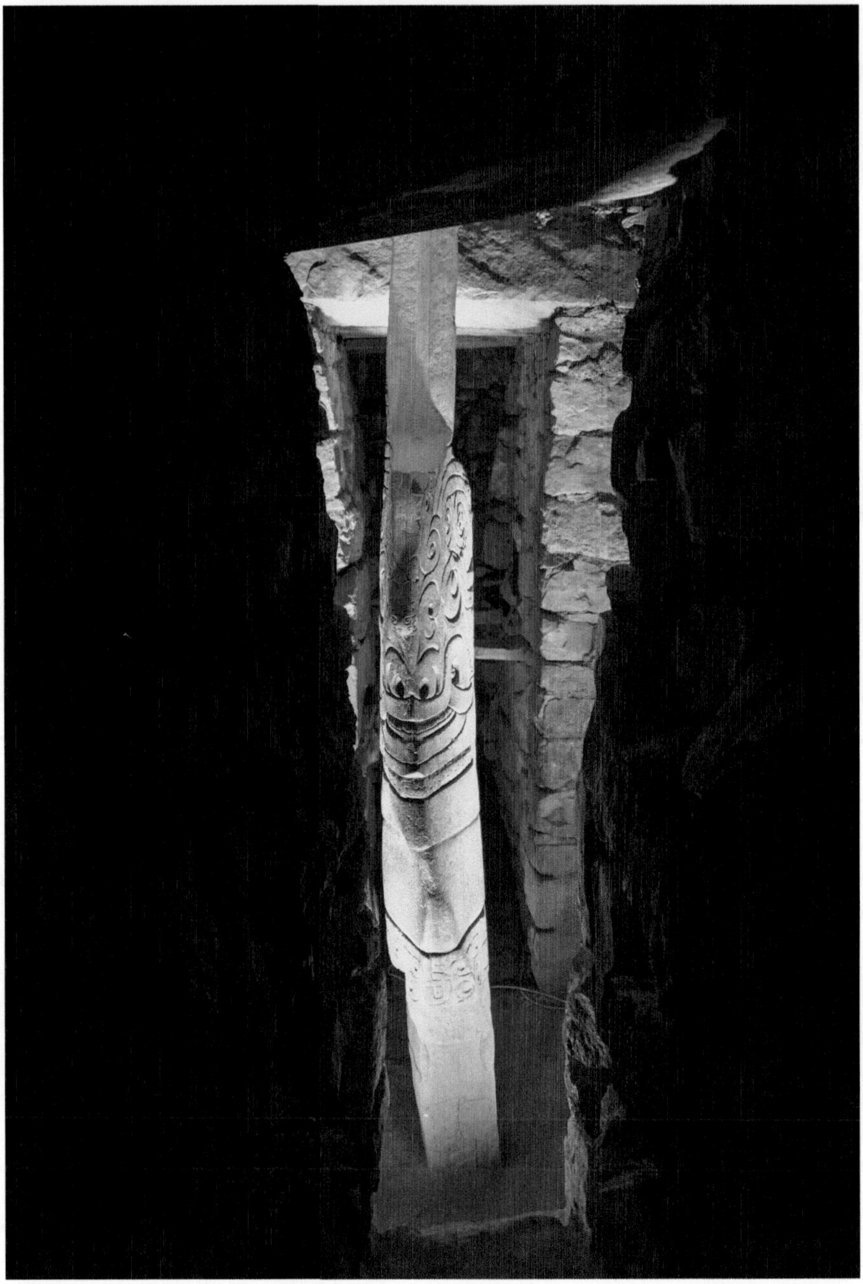

Figure 16.6 The Lanzón god, carved on a pillar in the interior of the temple at Chavín de Huántar.

By 600 B.C., the great shrine was in decline. Chavín was never a great city; only 2,000 to 3,000 people lived there in its heyday. As the shrine was abandoned, it became a modest village of squatters living in the shadow of once sacred precincts. Chavín de Huántar was certainly a large center, probably an influential place within its local area, and one of the largest settlements in Peru at the time of its occupation. It failed to expand into a fully developed urban center, however, and the nascent civilization that worshipped there collapsed, leaving nothing more than a village and a persistent art style and iconography.

Chavín represents a coalescence of traits and ideas from both the coast and the forest that formed a flamboyant cultural manifestation over a local area of the highlands. The Early Horizon may have been a long period of cultural change and political adjustment.

Inland Developments (1800 B.C. to A.D. 100)

In what archaeologists call the Initial Period (c. 1800–900 B.C.), distinctive coastal and highland societies emerged at either end of the Andean world, on the north coast and on the shores of Lake Titicaca far to the south. These developments continued into the Early Horizon (900–200 B.C.) and beyond, when regional centers became more elaborate and widely connected.

Irrigation Agriculture Inland (after 1800 B.C.)

By 1800 B.C., people had moved inland from the coast. The subsistence base changed from fishing to large-scale irrigation agriculture. Even the first farmers probably made some limited use of canals to water their riverside gardens. However, the new works were on a far larger scale, spurred by the availability of an army of workers fed by abundant Pacific fish, by the presence of gentle, cultivable slopes inland, and by the expertise of the local people in farming cotton, gourds, and many lesser crops such as squash and beans.

At first, each family may have worked together to irrigate its own sloping gardens, but gradually each community grew so much that essential irrigation works could be handled only by cooperative effort. Organized irrigation perhaps began as many minor cooperative works between individual families and neighboring villages. These simple projects eventually evolved over many centuries into elaborate public works that embraced entire inland valleys, controlled by a corporate authority that held a monopoly over both the water and the land it irrigated.

The Lake Titicaca Basin: Chiripa and Pukara (1000 B.C. to A.D. 100)

As Chavín de Huántar rose to prominence in the northern highlands, a separate Early Horizon tradition of complex society developed around Lake Titicaca far to the south. The plains landscape of the basin was gradually transformed by more intensive agriculture and herding.

Chiripa, Peru Ceremonial center near Lake Titicaca founded in 1000 B.C.

Tiwanaku, Bolivia Highland Andean state near Lake Titicaca, which traded with a wide region, dating to between A.D. 200 and 1000.

At **Chiripa**, on the southern shore of the lake, farming and herding were integrated into much earlier hunter-gatherer traditions. Chiripa itself remained a small village until about 1000 B.C., when a platform mound was built in the community, being was modified many times over the centuries. Eventually, carved stone plaques set into the walls depicted serpents, animals, and humans, the earliest appearance of a stone-carving tradition that persisted along the shores of the lake for many centuries. Sixteen rectangular buildings surrounded the court. Many features of the Chiripa shrine—especially the stepped doorways, sunken courts, and niche-like windows—can be seen in the later **Tiwanaku** architectural tradition, which used the same devices for its ceremonial buildings. The religious beliefs associated with this architecture have been grouped under the so-called Yaya-Mama religious tradition, which flourished for many centuries.

Pukara, Peru Center of a small kingdom in the north Lake Titicaca Basin in the early first millennium A.D.

Another major center flourished at **Pukara,** 75 kilometers (45 miles) northwest of Lake Titicaca, with a large residential area and an imposing ceremonial complex on a stonefaced terrace, complete with rectangular sunken court and one-room structures on three sides. Judging from the distribution of Pukara pottery styles, the kingdom's power was confined to the northern Titicaca Basin, but ceramics and other artifacts from as far afield as the north coast reflect widespread trade connections. At the time a smaller center than in later centuries, Tiwanaku presided over the southern shores of the lake between 400 B.C. and A.D. 100. There is no evidence that Pukara incorporated its southern neighbor.

From the Initial Period onward, the Andean region witnessed an extraordinary array of state-organized societies that displayed a remarkable diversity of culture, art, organization, and religious belief. At the same time, there were broad similarities in cosmology and culture that distinguished these societies from states elsewhere in the prehistoric world.

The Moche Culture (A.D. 1–800)

The **Moche culture** had begun in northern coastal Peru by around A.D. 1; it went on to flourish for around 800 years. Its origins lay in the Chicama and Moche valleys, with great ceremonial centers and huge irrigation works.

Moche culture, Peru Coastal Peruvian civilization centered on the Chicama and Moche valleys, dating from A.D. 1–800.

Sipán, Peru Major ceremonial center of the Moche people, celebrated for its spectacular royal burials and dating to after A.D. 100.

The spectacular discovery of undisturbed Moche tombs near the village of **Sipán,** about 680 kilometers (420 miles) northwest of Lima, has revolutionized our knowledge of Moche's elite (see Box 16.1). Peruvian archaeologist Walter Alva has excavated over 15 unlooted royal burials. The sepulchers included plank coffins holding the extended skeletons of men wearing gold nose and ear ornaments, gold and turquoise bead bracelets, and copper sandals. A ceremonial rattle, crescent-shaped knives, scepters, spears, and exotic seashells surrounded each body.

Comparing the objects found in the tombs with people depicted in Moche art, Christopher Donnan has identified the men as warrior-priests. Such individuals are depicted on Moche pots as presiding over sacrifices of prisoners of war (see Figure 16.9). Apparently, Moche warriors went to war specifically to take captives. They stripped captives of their armor and weapons and led them in front of the warrior-priest. Each prisoner's throat was cut, and the warrior-priest and others drank the blood of the slain victim while the corpse was dismembered. On pot after pot, the warrior-priest wears a crescent-shaped headdress atop a conical helmet—exactly the regalia found in the Sipán tombs. Such men were

Box 16.1 Discovery the Lords of Sipán, Peru

The discovery of the undisturbed Moche burials at Sipán, on Peru's northern coast, ranks as one of the greatest archaeological finds of all time. Peruvian archaeologist Walter Alva spent months painstakingly excavating the royal tombs, using conservation laboratories in Peru and Europe. The result is a triumph of scientific archaeology.

Tomb I held the body of a warrior-priest in his late thirties or early forties, in his full regalia (see Figure 16.7). The mourners had built a brick burial chamber deep in the pyramid (see Figure 16.8), building the sepulcher like a room with

Figure 16.7 A mannequin wearing a lord of Sipán's regalia.
Source: Realy Easy Star/Alamy Stock Photo.

Figure 16.8 Artist's reconstruction of Tomb I at Sipán, showing the lord in his regalia in his coffin, with male and female attendants.

Source: wening/Alamy.

solid mud-brick benches along the sides and at the head end. They set hundreds of clay pots in small niches in the benches. Priests dressed the dead lord in his full regalia, including a golden mask, and wrapped him in textile shrouds. Then, they placed him in a plank coffin and set it in the center of the burial chamber, the lid secured with copper straps. They laid out more ceramics, mainly fine-spouted bottles, at the foot and head of the coffin. Next, someone sacrificed two llamas and placed them on either side of the foot of the coffin. At some point, the priests also sat the body of a nine-or ten-year-old child in poor health at the head of the warrior-priest.

Five cane coffins were then lowered into the grave, each containing the body of an adult. The two male dead, perhaps bodyguards or members of the lord's entourage, were each laid on top of one of the llamas. One was a strongly built male, over 35 years old, adorned with copper ornaments and laid out with a war club. The other bore a beaded pectoral and was between 35 and 45 years old. Two of the three women's coffins lay at the head of the royal casket; in the third, at the foot of the coffin, the woman had been turned on her side. Interestingly, the women's disarticulated and jumbled bones suggest that they were not sacrificial victims, for they had died long before the lord and were partly decomposed at the time of their burial. Perhaps, they had been wives, concubines, or servants. Once the coffins had been positioned, a low beamed roof was set in place, too low for someone to stand inside the chamber. Then, the tomb was covered, a footless male victim being laid out in the fill. Finally, a seated body with crossed legs watched over the burial chamber from a small niche in the south wall, about 1 meter (3 feet) above the roof.

Figure 16.9 A Moche lord presiding over a parade of prisoners who are being sacrificed. This frieze from a painted pot was "unrolled" photographically.

Source: Fowler Museum of Cultural History, UCLA.

a priesthood of nobles living in different parts of the kingdom who enacted the sacrifice ceremony at prescribed times.

Moche society consisted of farmers and fisherfolk as well as skilled artisans and priests, who are depicted on pots with feline-like fangs set in their mouths and wearing puma-skin headdresses. A few expert craft potters created superb modeled vessels with striking portraits of arrogant, handsome men who can only have been the leaders of Moche society (see Figure 16.10). The potters modeled warriors, too, complete with shields and war clubs, well-padded helmets, and colorful cotton uniforms. Moche burials show that some members of society were much richer than others, such as those individuals found lying in graves filled with as many as 50 vessels, or with weapons or staffs of rank. We do not know exactly how Moche society was organized, but we can assume that the ruler wielded authority over a hierarchical state of warriors, priest-doctors, artisans, and the mass of the agricultural population. For instance, there was at least one Moche-style settlement in each subject valley. By this time, the coastal people were expert metalworkers. They had discovered the properties of gold ore and extracted it by panning in streambeds rather than by mining. Soon they had developed ways of hammering gold into fine sheets and had learned how to emboss it to make raised designs (see Figure 16.11). They had also worked out the technique of annealing, making it possible to soften the metal and then hammer it into more elaborate forms, joining the sheets with fine solder. The smiths used gold as a setting for turquoise and shell ornaments, crafted crowns, circlets, necklaces, pins, and tweezers.

The Moche domain was a multivalley state that may have consisted of a series of satellite centers that ruled over individual valleys, but owed allegiance to the great centers of the Moche valley. At one time, the Moche valley presided over the coast as far south as the Nepeña valley. Where possible, the Moche extended their ambitious irrigation systems to link several neighboring river valleys and then constructed lesser copies of their capital as a basis for secure administration of their new domains.

Cuzco, Peru Capital of the Inca Empire in highland Peru.

Like all Andean coastal societies, the Moche lived at the mercy of drought and El Niño. Michael Moseley believes that a series of natural disasters struck Moche domains in the late sixth century. The first may have been a devastating drought cycle between A.D. 564 and 594, identified from the growth rings of trees deep in mountain glaciers between **Cuzco** and Lake Titicaca. Crop yields in some valleys may have fallen as much as 20 per-cent. Sometime between 650 and 700, a great earthquake struck the Andes, choking rivers with debris from landslides. Within a century, Moche civilization had collapsed.

Figure 16.10 A Moche portrait jar.
Source: Danita Delimont/Alamy.

The Middle Horizon: Tiwanaku and Wari (A.D. 600 to 1000)

The Middle Horizon flourished between A.D. 600 and 1000 in the southern highlands. This period saw the beginnings of monumental building at a highland site—Tiwanaku—that would influence much of the Peruvian world.

Figure 16.11 Mastery in gold. A Chimu sacrificial gold knife representing the god Maymlap. Source: Prisma Archivo/Alamy.

Tiwanaku

Between A.D. 600 and 1000, the wealthiest highland districts lay at the southern end of the central Andes, in the high flat country surrounding Lake Titicaca. This was fine llama country; the local people maintained enormous herds of these beasts of burden and were also expert irrigation farmers. The *altiplano* supported the densest population in the highlands, and almost inevitably the Titicaca region became an economic and demographic pole to the prosperous northern coast.

By 450, Tiwanaku, on the eastern side of the lake, was becoming a major population center as well as an economic and religious focus for the region. The arid lands on which the site lies were irrigated and supported a population of perhaps 20,000 around the monumental structures near the center of the site. By 600, Tiwanaku was acquiring much

Figure 16.12 The Sunken Courtyard at Tiwanaku, Bolivia.
Source: Konstantin Kalishko/Thinkstock.

of its prosperity from trade around the lake's southern shores. Copper working probably developed independently of the well-established copper technology on the northern coast.

The great enclosure of Kalasasaya, dominated by a large earth platform faced with stones, testifies to the city's religious function. A nearby rectangular enclosure is bounded with a row of upright stones, and there is a doorway carved with an anthropomorphic god, believed to be the staff god, sometimes called Viracocha (see Figure 16.12).

A serious political vacuum arose in the south when Tiwanaku inexplicably collapsed into obscurity after 1200.

Wari

Wari, Peru Major highland Andean kingdom centered on an urban and ceremonial center of that name, c. A.D. 800.

Wari, in the Ayacucho valley, was a highland urban and ceremonial center that stood on a hill. It was associated with huge stone walls and many dwellings that covered several square miles. The Wari art styles showed some Pukara influence, especially in anthropomorphic, feline, eagle, and serpent beings depicted on ceramic vessels. Like their southern neighbors, the Wari people seemed to have revered a Viracocha-like being. By A.D. 800, their domains extended from Moche country in the Lambayeque valley on the northern coast to south of Nazca territory, down the Moquequa valley of the south-central Andes and into the highlands south of Cuzco. They were expert traders who probably expanded their domain through conquest, commercial enterprise, and perhaps religious conversion. Storehouses and roads were probably maintained by the state. As with the Inca of later centuries, the state controlled food supplies and labor.

Wari itself was abandoned in the ninth century A.D., but its art styles persisted on the coast for at least two more centuries. Both Wari and Tiwanaku were turning points in Peruvian prehistory, a stage when small regional states became integrated into much larger political units. There was constant and often intensive interaction between two poles of Andean civilization in the highlands and lowlands, each with quite different food resources and products. This interaction, long a feature of Andean life, was to intensify in the centuries ahead.

Sicán and Chimu (A.D. 700 to 1460)

Sicán, Peru Coastal Andean culture, c. A.D. 700 to 1375.

The highland states traded regularly with several emerging polities on the coast, each of them founded on extensive irrigation systems. The decline of the Moche in the Lambayeque valley left something of a vacuum, which was soon filled by the **Sicán** culture after A.D. 700. Sicán, a culture of expert irrigation farmers, reached its peak between 900 and 1100; it was centered on the Lambayeque valley and was remarkable for its magnificent gold work. A temple complex there contains a pyramid-shaped tomb filled with the skeletons of 33 women, some of whom had been tortured before becoming sacrificial victims.

Figure 16.13 Reconstructed gold mask of a lord of Sicán, Peru. The "drops" suspended from the nostrils represent mucus formed during hallucinogenic trance, an important part of Andean rituals. Height: 18 inch (46 centimeter).

Source: Peter Horree/Alamy.

In Sicán society, metals of all kinds served as markers of social status and wealth—and as a prestigious medium of political, social, and religious expression—since people's access to artifacts and ornaments in different ores was carefully limited according to rank. The so-called East Tomb at the Middle Sicán capital in the La Leche valley yielded the burial of a great lord of Sicán aged between 40 and 50, who had been mummified and dressed in his full regalia, including a gold mask (see Figure 16.13). His head had been detached and lay in front of the inverted body facing west. Sacrificial victims and elaborate grave ornaments in gold, gold and silver alloy, and bronze accompanied him, including a pair of golden gloves. The West Tomb nearby contained the remains of another person, 30 to 40 years old. Twenty women and other victims lay in the grave, divided—as indicated by DNA, health state, and dental traits—into two groups; one group was close kin of the deceased and the other diverse group was perhaps composed of victims from various parts of the Sicán domains. These two spectacular burials are part of an elite cemetery that remains unexcavated.

Chimu Lowland civilization in Peru's Lambayeque valley, which flourished between c. A.D. 1000 and 1476.

Between 1050 and 1100, El Niño caused widespread flooding and disruption. In 1375, an expanding **Chimu** state overthrew Sicán and absorbed its domains into a new empire. The Moche valley had long been densely cultivated, but the Chimu people now embarked on much more ambitious irrigation schemes: they built large storage reservoirs and terraced hundreds of kilometers of hillside to control the flow of water down steep slopes. So effective were these irrigation techniques that the Chimu controlled more than 12 river valleys with at least 50,000 hectares (125,000 acres) of cultivable land, all of it farmed with hoes or digging sticks.

Chan Chan, Peru Capital of the Chimu civilization, after A.D. 1000.

The focus of the Chimu state was **Chan Chan**, a huge complex of walled compounds lying near the Pacific at the mouth of the Moche valley (see Figure 16.14). Chan Chan covers more than 10 square kilometers (4 square miles), the central part consisting of nine large enclosures laid out in a sort of broken rectangle. Each enclosure probably functioned as the palace for the current ruler of Chan Chan, who probably built himself new headquarters near those of his predecessors. The adobe walls of these compounds once stood as high as 10 meters (33 feet) and covered areas as large as 200 by 600 meters (670 by 2,000 feet). The walls were not constructed to defend the rulers, but to provide privacy and some shelter from the ocean winds. Each enclosure had its own water supply, a burial platform, and lavishly decorated residential rooms roofed with cane frames covered with earth and grass. The same enclosure that served as a palace during life became the ruler's burial place in death. The common people lived in tracts of small adobe and reed-mat houses on the western side of the city. Similar dwellings can be seen on the coast to this day.

Oral traditions tell us that the Chimu rulers practiced the institution of split inheritance, whereby each ruler inherited no material possessions to finance his reign. (Split inheritance was to play a major role in the later Inca civilization as well.) Chimu rulers had access to and control of a huge labor pool. Powerful lords employed laborers to expand and maintain irrigation works. Commoners also served as soldiers to acquire new lands and expand the tax base.

Rulers soon learned the value of officially maintained roadways, which enabled them to move their armies from one place to the next rapidly. They constructed roads that

Figure 16.14 Chan Chan, the Chimu capital, showing a royal compound.
Source: Myriam B/Shutterstock.

connected each valley in their domain with the capital. These were the roads that carried gold ornaments and fine-hammered gold vessels to Chan Chan, and textiles and fine black-painted vessels throughout the empire. All revenues and tribute passed along the official roadways, as did newly conquered peoples being resettled in areas far from their homelands. This draconian resettlement tactic was so successful that the Inca adopted it. A ruler would install his own appointee in the new lands, in a compound palace that was a smaller version of Chan Chan itself.

The Chimu Empire, known as **Chimor**, extended far south, at least to Casma and perhaps reaching to the vicinity of modern Lima, for the main focus of civilization lay on the northern Peruvian littoral, where the soils were fertile and large-scale irrigation was a practical reality.

Chimor, Peru The domains of the Chimu civilization.

For all its wide-ranging military activities and material wealth, Chimor was vulnerable to attack from the outside. The massive irrigation works of the northern river valleys were easily disrupted by an aggressive conqueror, for no leader, however powerful, could hope to fortify the entire frontier of the empire. The Chimu were vulnerable to prolonged drought, too, for the storage capacity of their great irrigation works was sufficient to carry them over only one or two lean seasons. Perhaps, too, the irrigated desert soils became too saline for agriculture, so that crop yields fell drastically when population densities were rising sharply. Since the Chimu depended on a highly specialized agricultural system, once that system was disrupted—whether by natural or artificial causes—military conquest and control of the irrigation network were easy, especially for aggressive and skillful conquerors such as the Inca, who conquered the Chimu in the 1460s.

The Late Horizon: The Inca Empire (A.D. 1476 to 1534)

The Late Horizon of Peruvian archaeology was the shortest, dating from 1476 to 1534, the period of the Inca Empire. The Inca were born into an intensely competitive world, their homeland lying to the northwest of the Titicaca Basin in the area around Cuzco. They were a small-scale farming society living in small villages and organized in kin groups known as *ayllu*, groups claiming a common ancestry and also owning land in common.

The later Inca rulers clothed their origins in a glorious panoply of heroic deeds. It is likely, however, that the Inca were a fractious, constantly quarreling petty chiefdom. The chronicles of early conquest reflect the constant bickering of village headmen, and the earliest Inca rulers were probably petty war leaders (*sinchi*), elected officials whose success was measured by their victories and booty. To stay in office, they had to be politically and militarily adept so that they could both defeat and appease their many potential rivals. The official Inca histories speak of at least eight Inca rulers between 1200 and 1438, but these genealogies are hardly reliable.

During the fourteenth century, the Inca flourished in this competitive atmosphere because their leaders were expert politicians as well as warriors. A leader named Viracocha Inca rose to power at the beginning of the fifteenth century. Unlike his raiding predecessors, however, he turned to permanent conquest and soon presided over a small kingdom centered in Cuzco. Viracocha Inca became the living god, the first in a series of constant religious changes that kept the new kingdom under tight control.

Around 1438, a brilliant warrior named Cusi Inca Yupanqui was crowned Inca (the term *Inca* can refer to both the ruler and the people) after a memorable victory over the neighboring Chanca tribe. He immediately took the name Pachakuti ("He Who Remakes the World") and set about transforming the Inca state. In particular, he and his henchmen developed a form of royal ancestor cult. This in itself was not especially significant, since Pachakuti simply reworked an age-old Andean tradition, but the law of split inheritance that went along with it had a lasting and profound significance.

Figure 16.15 Inca ancestor worship: Two retainers carry the richly decorated mummy of an Inca so that he can participate in a religious ceremony.

Source: Heritage Image Partnership Ltd/Alamy.

Figure 16.16 Inca agricultural terraces in Pisac, Peru, testify to the intense nature of their farming.
Source: mariusz_prusaczyk/Thinkstock.

A dead ruler was mummified. His palace, servants, and possessions were still considered his property and were maintained by all of his male descendants except for his successor, normally one of his sons. The deceased was not considered dead. His mummy attended great ceremonies and would even visit the houses of the living (see Figure 16.15). Those entrusted to look after the king ate and talked with him, just as if he were still alive. This element of continuity made the royal mummies some of the holiest artifacts in the empire. Dead rulers were visible links to the gods, the very embodiment of the Inca state and of the fertility of nature.

mit'a Taxation through labor; imposed by Andean states, especially those of the Chimu and the Inca.

Meanwhile, the ascending ruler was rich in prestige but poor in possessions. The new king had to acquire wealth so that he could both live in royal splendor and provide for his mummy in the future—and the only wealth in the highland kingdom was taxable labor. Therefore, every adult in Inca country had to render a certain amount of labor to the state each year after providing for the basic subsistence needs of his own *ayllu*. This ***mit'a*** system repaired bridges and roads, cultivated state-owned lands, manned the armies, and carried out public works (see Figure 16.16). It was a reciprocal system as the state, or the individuals benefiting from the work, had to feed and entertain those doing it. Since the Inca rulers needed land to provide food for those who worked for them and the earlier kings owned most of the land near Cuzco, the only way a new ruler could obtain his own royal estates was by expansion into new territory. The conquest had to be permanent, the conquered territory had to be controlled and taxed, and the ruler's subjects had to be convinced of the value of a policy of long-term conquest.

A highly complicated set of benefits, economic incentives, rewards, and justifications fueled and nourished the Inca conquests. Inca rulers turned into brilliant propagandists, reminding everyone that they were gods and that the welfare of all depended on the prosperity of all rulers, past and present, and on constant military conquest. There were initial economic advantages, too, in the form of better protection against famine. Also, the rulers were careful to reward prowess in battle. Nobles were promoted to new posts and awarded insignia that brought their lifestyle ever closer to that of the king, and a brave warrior could become a member of the secondary nobility.

The Incas' successful ideology provided them with a crucial advantage over their neighbors. Within a decade of Pachakuti's accession, they were masters of the southern highlands. Their army had become an invincible juggernaut. In less than a century, the tiny kingdom had become a vast empire. Topa Inca (1471–1493) extended the Inca Empire into Ecuador, northern Argentina, parts of Bolivia, and Chile. Another king, Wayna Capac, ruled for 32 years after Topa Inca and pushed the empire deeper into Ecuador.

Tawantinsuyu, as the empire was known, was divided into four large provinces called *suyu* (quarters), each subdivided into smaller provinces, some of them coinciding with older, conquered kingdoms. Inca nobles held all the important government posts. The Inca rulers realized, however, that the essence of efficient government in such varied topography was efficient communication, so the road builders commandeered a vast network of age-old highways from the states they conquered. They linked them in a coordinated system with regular rest houses so that they could move armies, trade goods, and send messengers from one end of the kingdom to the other in short order.

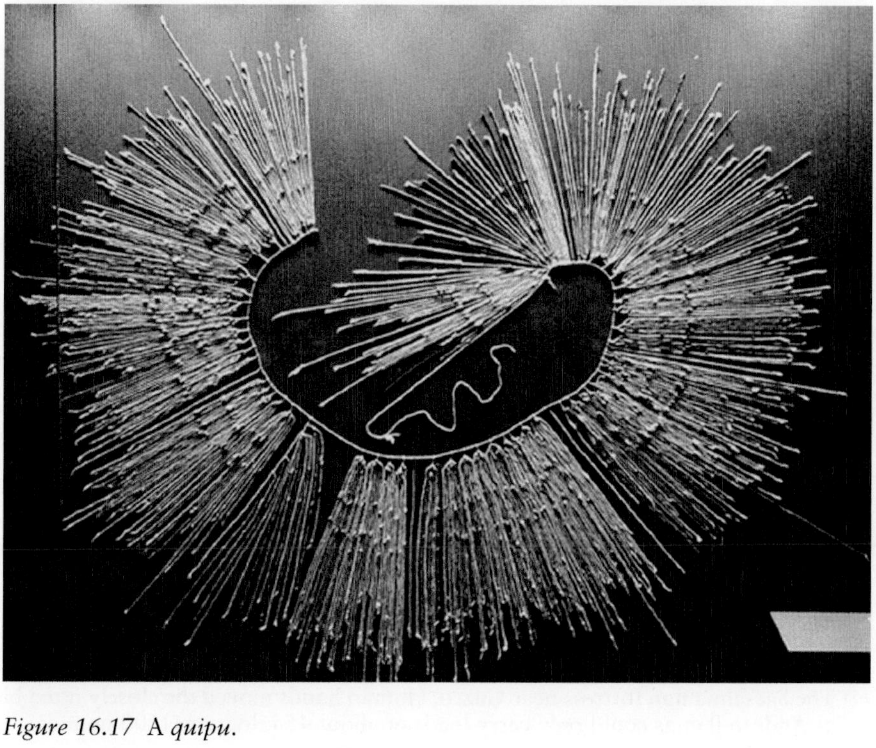

Figure 16.17 A *quipu*.
Source: little_monster/Stockimo/Alamy.

The Inca passion for organization impinged on everyone's life. Inca society was organized into 12 age divisions for the purposes of census and tax assessment; these were divisions based on physical changes like puberty and major social events like marriage. The most important stage was adulthood, which lasted as long as one could do a day's work. All of the census data and other data of the empire were recorded not on tablets but on knotted strings. These *quipu* constituted a complex and sophisticated recordkeeping system that seems to have been so efficient that it more than made up for the lack of writing (see Figure 16.17). They were also a powerful instrument for codifying laws and providing data for the state's inspectors, who regularly visited each household to ensure that everyone was engaged in productive work and living in sanitary conditions.

At the time of the Spanish conquest, the Inca controlled the lives of as many as 6 million people, most of them living in small villages dispersed around larger centers. Inca political and religious power was based on major ritual locations like Cuzco in the Andes, where the ceremonial precincts were built of carefully fitted stones (see Figure 16.18 and Box 16.2). The Inca ruler held court in Cuzco, surrounded by plotting factions and ever-changing political tides. One villain was the very institution of split inheritance that fueled Inca military conquest: every ruler faced increasingly complex governance problems as a result. The need for more and more conquests caused great military, economic, and administrative stress. The logistics of long-distance military campaigns were horrendous, and the soldiers had to be fed from state-owned land, not royal estates. Moreover, although their tactics were well adapted to open country, where their armies were invincible, the rulers eventually had to start fighting in forest country, where they fared badly.

Figure 16.18 The Sacsahuaman fortress near Cuzco. Human hands moved the closely fitted blocks, as Andean llamas could only carry loads of about 45 kilograms (100 pounds).

Source: Richard Maschmeyer/Alamy.

Box 16.2 Site
Cuzco, the Imperial Inca Capital

At the heart of Tawantinsuyu lay Cuzco, the home of the Sun God Inti, its patron. The royal families lived in the capital itself, they and their dependents numbering perhaps 40,000 people. An additional 200,000 people or so lived within 50 kilometers (30 miles), many of them artisans, minor officials, or engineers. The highest nobles had fine estates close to the city, the center of the universe that was Tawantinsuyu.

In the days of Pachakuti, a brilliant architect named Huallpa Rimachi Inca laid plans for a massive fortress to be built against a hill called Sacsahuaman ("Speckled Hawk") (Figure 16.18). The great rocky headland and its fort dominated Cuzco, looking eastward toward the rising Sun. Sacsahuaman was bathed in sunlight long before the rest of the city, so it was a logical place for the House of the Sun, Intihuasi. Intihuasi was the pukara, or place of refuge, for Cuzco. A close relative of the ruler commanded the fortress—a position of great trust, for he was responsible for the royal treasury and a vast array of weaponry stored in an armory close to the soldiers' barracks. The great walls that brood over Cuzco today are but a shadow of the original edifice, which was destroyed by the Spaniards soon after the conquest (Figure 16.19).

The Inca called the city Topa Cuzco, "Royal Cuzco." Their capital lay along the spine of a narrow ridge between two deep gullies, in a landscape shaped like a triangle facing the southeast. The great compounds of the living ruler and his deceased predecessors lay within this triangle. Each compound was a world unto itself, close to its neighbors yet separate, an invitation to the ardent factionalism that marked the Inca court.

The central plaza of Cuzco—today's Plaza de Armas—was called Huacaypata. The Inca plaza was about 120 meters (400 feet) on its long axis along the river

Figure 16.19 Close-fitting Inca masonry at Cuzco.
Source: TheImage/Alamy Stock Photo.

and 91 meters (300 feet) across. The Sapi River defined the southern side, paved with stone slabs to join Huacaypata with Cusipata, a square on the other bank. Huacaypata was where the four main roads of the empire met, defining the four quarters of Tawantinsuyu and merging them into the heart of the empire. Imposing buildings and royal palaces surrounded the plaza. Pachakuti's palace stood on the west side. The Yuchahuasi, or "House of Learning," adjoining the palace was the school for young nobles and scribes. The entire area was an architectural commemoration of Inca rulers and their deeds.

The Inca royal palaces were enlarged and elaborated versions of rural farm enclosures. The entrance led to a courtyard where a regiment of guards was stationed. Knights in ceremonial uniform bearing war clubs guarded the palace itself. The guard room led to an antechamber where high officials awaited their audiences in the nearby audience room. Here the Inca sat on the stool of state to receive ambassadors and delegations. The storage area and treasury were in the heart of the palace, where they were most protected. The "House of Spoils" contained trophies from the ruler's victories and sometimes the dried and stuffed bodies of conquered enemy leaders. The harem quarter, the most sequestered of all, was where the royal women lived, in adjoining, cell-like rooms, close to lush gardens and hidden from the outside world. Close by were the royal living quarters, where the Inca was looked after by carefully selected young women. During the Inca's life, the palace was a labyrinth of important happenings, ceremonies, and intrigue. When the ruler died, the palace continued to function as if nothing had happened, except that no one debated policy there.

The Coriancha was the largest palace of all, where the gods resided, each with his own thatched house and patio. At least 4,000 people were attached to the divine households, some 200 to 300 of them the virgin women (*manaconas*) who served as wives of Inti, the Sun God. They prepared his food and fermented maize beer, wove his clothes, and drummed for him at major festivals. The *manaconas* also symbolically satisfied Inti's sexual desires as his consorts. The walls of the Coriancha were built on precipitous terraces in the oldest part of the city. The tapered wall, with its beautifully fitted blocks, towered 3 meters (10 feet) above the highest level of the temple platform inside, giving a powerful illusion of height and strength. The temple itself was clad with gold sheet and housed the golden image of the Sun, with a garden of golden plants before the room where the symbol lay.

Cuzco was also a vast storehouse filled with the incredible wealth of the empire. The storehouses of Cuzco held gigantic stocks of raw materials and finished goods that poured into the capital from all corners of Tawantinsuyu. The stores bulged with stocks of cloaks, wool, weapons, metals, and food supplies neatly arranged in hundreds of stores.

Meanwhile, the empire had grown so large that communication became an increasingly lengthy process, compounded by the great diversity of people living within Inca domains. Under its glittering façade, Tawantinsuyu was becoming a rotten apple. In the end, the Inca Empire was overthrown not by Andeans, but by a tiny band of foreigners with firearms who could exploit the inherent vulnerability of such a hierarchical, conforming society.

The Spanish Conquest (A.D. 1532 to 1534)

The Inca Empire's vulnerability came home to roost in 1532, when a small party of rapacious Spanish conquistadors landed in northern Peru. When Francisco Pizarro arrived, the Inca state was in political chaos, its people already decimated by smallpox and other diseases introduced by the first conquistadors. Inca Wayna Capac had died in an epidemic in 1525. The empire was plunged into a civil war between his son Huascar and another son, Atahuallpa, half-brother to Huascar. Atahuallpa eventually prevailed, but as he moved south from Ecuador to consolidate his territory, he learned that Pizarro had landed in Peru.

The Spaniards had vowed to make Peru part of Spain and were bent on plunder and conquest. Pizarro arrived in the guise of a diplomat, captured Atahuallpa by treachery, ransomed him for a huge quantity of gold, and then brutally murdered him. A year later, a tiny army of Spaniards captured the Inca capital. The world's last preindustrial state was no more.

Summary

- The earliest complex societies of coastal Peru may have developed as a result of the intensive exploitation of maritime resources, especially small fish easily netted from canoes.
- In time, abundant food surpluses, growing population densities, and larger settlements may have preadapted coastal people to intensive irrigation agriculture. These societies were organized in increasingly complex ways.
- During the Initial Period, large monumental structures appeared, many of them U-shaped, just before and during the transition toward greater dependence on maize agriculture. This was also a period of continuous interaction and extensive trade between the coast and the highlands.
- The culmination of this trend is seen in various local traditions, among them the famous Chavín style. Chavín de Huántar, once thought to have been the source of Peruvian civilization, is now known to be a late manifestation of cultural trends that began as early as 2000 B.C., the so-called Early Horizon of Andean prehistory.
- After the Early Horizon ended, about 200 B.C., a series of coastal kingdoms developed between 200 B.C. and A.D. 700, the political and economic influence of which spread beyond their immediate valley homelands.
- These cultures included the Moche, remarkable for its fine pottery styles and expert alloy and gold metallurgy, which flourished between A.D. 1 and 800.
- About A.D. 1375, Chimu, with its great capital at Chan Chan on the northern coast, dominated a wide area of the lowlands. Its compounds reflect a stratified state with many expert craftspeople and a complex material culture.
- During the Late Horizon of Peruvian prehistory (1400 to 1534), the highlands and lowlands were unified under the Inca Empire, which may have emerged as early as 1200 and lasted until the Spanish conquest in 1532–1534.
- The Inca rulers were masters of bureaucracy and military organization and governed a highly structured state, but the state was so weakened by civil war and disease that it fell easily to the Spanish conquistador Francisco Pizarro and his small army of adventurers.

Key Terms and Sites

Machu Picchu
Tawantinsuyu
Aspero
Caral
El Paraíso
Chavín de Huántar
Early Horizon
Chiripa
Tiwanaku
Pukara
Moche state
Sipán
Cuzco
Wari
Sicán
Chimu
Chan Chan
Chimor
mit'a

Critical-Thinking Questions

1. Two "poles" of Andean civilization developed over the centuries. What salient features of the Andean environment caused this polarity?
2. The lords of Sipán are among the greatest archaeological finds of all time. What, in your opinion, is the significance of these remarkable burials?
3. Like the Aztec state, the Inca Empire owed much to earlier civilizations. Discuss the differences in the legacies inherited by these two societies. How similar and how different were they from each other institutionally?

Further Reading

M. Moseley's, *The Incas and Their Ancestors*, 2nd ed. (New York: Thames and Hudson, 2000) is an excellent summary of Andean archaeology for the general reader. So is J. Moore, *A Prehistory of South America: Ancient Cultural Diversity on the Least Known Continent* (Boulder: University Press of Colorado, 2014). See also J. Quilter, *The Ancient Central Andes* (London: Routledge, 2013). The Moche: J. Quilter, *The Moche of Ancient Peru* (Cambridge, MA: Peabody Museum Press, 2011). C. Donnan and W. Alva's, *Royal Tombs of Sipán* (Los Angeles: Fowler Museum of Cultural History, UCLA, 1994) is the definitive account of one of the most spectacular archaeological finds of the twentieth century. For Tiwanaku, see A. Kolata, *Tiwanaku* (Oxford: Blackwell, 1993). For an excellent overview see *The Inca: Lost Civilizations* by Kevin Lane (London: Reaktion Books, 2022); or G. McEwan, *The Incas: New Perspectives* (New York: W. W. Norton, 2008).

Part 7
Finale

17 What Remains to Be Done

Archaeology and You

Chapter Outline

Chumash rock art, Santa Barbara, California.
Source: Lisa Werner/Alamy Stock Photo.

DOI: 10.4324/9781003592754-24

Having gazed into the past, we end by looking into the future. Archaeology has made tremendous strides and is virtually unrecognizable today compared with a century ago. Back then, the number of archaeologists worldwide numbered in the hundreds (if that), and the field was more of an intellectual village—lacking radiocarbon dating and with little input from the sciences. Given limited resources available to them, our predecessors accomplished remarkable feats, and we owe them an enormous debt. Building on their efforts, we now have a comprehensive outline of the human past from its beginnings millions of years ago, until the appearance of the first preindustrial civilizations 5,000 years ago, and extending right into historic times.

Today, historical archaeology is a flourishing subfield, as it should be. At the same time, we can now rightfully speak of a truly global prehistory. World prehistory has come of age. But what remains to be done, and what is the future of archaeology? This final chapter looks at the archaeology of tomorrow, and at the careers that probably lie within it.

The Future of the Past

The modern world has witnessed the relentless destruction of archaeological sites and their priceless records on a scale that is truly frightening. Highway construction, massive expansion of cities and towns across the landscape, industrial-scale agriculture and deep plowing have torn apart sites large and small. Land reclamation has buried vital records of the past in places like Miami, San Francisco, and Shanghai. Even urban subway systems have torn apart the past. The tragic damage wrought by conflicts large and small, epitomized by the destruction at Nineveh and Palmyra, is beyond words.

We humans are destructive agents in other ways, too. The looting of archaeological sites has become a full-time job in parts of Italy and Peru, fueled by rural poverty and the insatiable demands of the illegal international market for antiquities. Ironically, too, while we accidently or deliberately destroy the record of the past, we also love it to excess. As we've seen, cultural tourism is the fastest segment of the international tourist industry, with major archaeological sites a huge attraction. Archaeology is a major contributor to the tourism industry in countries like Egypt, Guatemala, and Peru. The Pyramids of Giza and Egypt's Valley of the Kings are overwhelmed with winter crowds. Roman Ephesus is a circus of tourists; millions of visitors, many of them local Chinese, gaze on the terracotta regiment of Emperor Shihuangdi near Xi'an. The wear and tear on sites large and small, from Mexico's Teotihuacán to the stupendous ruins of Angkor Wat in Cambodia, is constant, unrelenting, and often inconspicuous. The French and Spanish have built magnificent replicas of painted caves like Chauvet, Lascaux, and Altamira. But how does one mitigate the damage at Angkor Wat and elsewhere? The answers are still being debated for there are no easy solutions. Divert visitors to lesser sites? Keep tourists away from key structures and ruins with fences? Build replicas? This is a major issue for future generations of archaeologists.

As we emphasized several times, we archaeologists, with the best will in the world, are also agents of destruction. All archaeological excavation destroys the very records it uncovers. As the American archaeologist Kent Flannery once memorably remarked, we're the only social scientists who murder our informants. He is ultimately correct, however conscientious our efforts to record and preserve what we find. One can legitimately, rather sweepingly, remark that the only archaeological sites that are not threatened are those that lie underground.

Two major trends are now fully embedded. Remote sensing, using sensing technologies, including satellite, drones, and LiDAR, is at the forefront of exploration. Thanks to these innovations, hundreds of previously unknown sites have been uncovered, such as those revealed through LiDAR surveys at Angkor Wat and various Maya centers. For the first time, we can gain a clearer understanding of the often-overlooked hinterlands that supported ancient cities, all while avoiding the destructive impact of excavation. However, much work remains to be done, especially in verifying satellite data through ground-based verification. Nonintrusive methods like these are playing, and will continue to play, a pivotal role in both academic and Cultural Resource Management (CRM) research.

The second trend is a shift from traditional fieldwork to laboratory-based research. This change is driven by remarkable advances in areas such as ancient DNA analysis, isotope and strontium studies, and residue analysis of pottery, which have illuminated aspects of ancient life, including the histories of beer and wine. We've covered many of these breakthroughs in earlier chapters, which have come at a time when many archaeologists are pursuing highly specialized, often interdisciplinary careers in these and other cutting-edge fields, many of them rooted in advanced science and technology. The revelations from this research can be truly fascinating, such as the life history of Ötzi the Iceman. For the first time, we are able to gain an extraordinarily intimate understanding of past peoples, thanks in part to groundbreaking bioarchaeological techniques like genome sequencing and facial reconstruction

A great deal of detective work in the laboratory is now reexamining old field notes and collections, many of them still unstudied from excavations of generations ago. This provides opportunities to make major discoveries. For example, a team reexamining fossils, previously through to be Neanderthal from Jebel Irhoud, in Morocco, found they were actually *Homo sapiens* fossils dating back at least 300,000 years—so pushing back the emergence of our species in the fossil record by 100,000 years.

Despite these groundbreaking developments, we also face significant challenges. Climate change is already beginning to affect archaeological sites, with rising sea levels threatening coastal sites, extreme weather events damaging fragile ruins, and changing weather patterns accelerating natural erosion. The increased intensity and frequency of wildfires, for example, have already led to the destruction of invaluable sites in places like Australia and the western United States. Preservation of these sites, both physically and digitally, will be a central concern for future archaeologists.

As we look to the future, it's clear that archaeologists will increasingly rely on collaboration with other disciplines—such as environmental science, engineering, and even artificial intelligence (AI). AI, in particular, has the potential to revolutionize our ability to analyze large sets of archaeological data, from identifying patterns in excavation sites to helping reconstruct ancient environments. And with advances in 3D scanning and virtual reality, we may soon be able to digitally "rebuild" sites that have been lost to time or conflict, allowing future generations to explore them in ways never before imagined.

Ultimately, the future of archaeology is bright, provided we realize that our highest priority for today and tomorrow is that of conserving and saving the past for the future. This is the responsibility of all of us, whether archaeologists or not. We are stewards of the past for future generations.

Conservation and Mitigation

The rhetoric is familiar and often repeated, but many of the now strenuous efforts to conserve the past and mitigate the damage take place far from the limelight. The weapons are diverse, some effective, others less so.

CRM in North America, and its equivalent in other countries across the world, began after World War II and accelerated dramatically during the 1960s. CRM is concerned with the management and assessment of the significance of cultural resources such as archaeological sites. It is now the dominant activity in North American archaeology and in many other countries. The fastest growing segment of archaeological employment is in the private sector. In 2020, more than a third of all American archaeologists working for private consulting firms were engaged in environmental monitoring and CRM, and the figure is climbing rapidly.

All this activity unfolds in the context of a battery of legislation in the United States both at the federal and state levels, which covers public lands. Private lands are unprotected owing to Constitutional guarantees, although they are in many other countries. These laws, and their equivalents elsewhere, govern the extent and scale of mitigation activities. These can range from controlled, total excavation of an important threatened site to merely sampling it. Sometimes, highways are rerouted or pipelines realigned. A network of UNESCO World Heritage Sites across the world protect exceptionally important prehistoric and historical locations, among them Stonehenge and Chaco Canyon, as well as a host of lesser-known locations. Significant numbers of CRM projects involve years of research (Box 17.1).

But there is a lot more to mitigation, including a constant struggle against the illegal antiquities business. This is far more than policing sites in the field, which is an obvious, but unfortunately expensive, proposition. There are now organizations that track auctions across the world where priceless artifacts are offered for bid. Notorious cases have involved sacred Native American artifacts. Meanwhile, in 2019, the Egyptian antiquities authorities attempted to halt the auction of a sculpted head of Tutankhamun, which sold to an anonymous bidder at Christie's auction house for $5.97 million. Year on year, further cases of contested sales and the repatriation of cultural artifacts continue to make headlines.

Museums worldwide are facing increasing pressure from countries seeking the return of stolen or illegally acquired objects. For example, in 2021, the Getty Museum returned a series of ancient Greek and Roman sculptures to Italy after years of legal battles. Former colonies continue to demand the repatriation of stolen items, such as the Benin Bronzes, looted from Nigeria during colonial wars in the nineteenth century. The people of Easter Island (Rapa Nui) continue to seek the repatriation of a *moiae* statue from the British Museum. By far, the most notorious case is that of the Elgin Marbles from the Parthenon, masterpieces fashioned by the classical Greek artist Phidias for the Parthenon in Athens, which were exported with scant legal justification by the seventh Earl of Elgin between 1801 and 1812. The Greek government has tried in vain to recover them for generations. They have even built a museum at the foot of the Acropolis in Athens for their eventual return. How the case will ultimately play out is uncertain.

Archaeology is not only under siege from humanity, but also from such natural phenomena as rising sea levels, also hurricanes and tropical cyclones that are inundating valuable coastal sites in places like Bangladesh and Louisiana, to say nothing of the vanishing islands of the South Pacific.

Then there's a siege that's our fault. The essence of scientific archaeology is publication, a permanent record of every field and laboratory project that provides information on the past. This is where many archaeologists have failed to fulfill their responsibilities. Thousands of excavations and surveys remain unpublished, represented only by finds in museums or in battered fieldnotes that cannot be easily deciphered except by the long-deceased excavator who wrote them. CRM projects require reports mandated by contract, but many of these merely satisfy legal requirements and lack many critical details. There are, of course, many notable examples, especially those executed by large private CRM companies, who have the budgets and resources to complete detailed analyses, to write everything up for professional audiences, and also produce an account that can be read by the general public.

The threats to the past are diverse, very difficult to counter, and are the most vital challenge for future generations of archaeologists.

Box 17.1 The Joint Courts Archaeological Project, Tucson, Arizona (CRM on a Grand Scale)

The Joint Courts Archaeological Project in downtown Tucson, Arizona, carried out by Statistical Research, a large CRM company based in the city, uncovered the Alameda-Stone historic cemetery, used between about 1862 and 1875. The cemetery was divided into a military section, surrounded by an adobe wall in about 1868, and the civilian portion, which had a wall on the western and northern sides. Excavations revealed a relatively orderly layout, with graves lying in meandering north–south rows. Many of the burials were apparently marked, the markers only being removed when the area was graded for residential construction after the cemetery was closed.

The project also involved the investigation of a large residential and commercial complex, and traces of early Native American settlement and early agriculture going back over 4,000 years. An area of 1.7 hectares (4.3 acres) was totally excavated, this to guarantee that all human remains in the area were recovered. The entire project was mind-bogglingly complex, not only archaeologically but because of the amount of advance planning, consultation, and archival research required, this in part because of the need to be respectful to the many stakeholders' interests and to comply with differing requirements for reburial and repatriation.

The Alameda-Stone cemetery housed the dead from many groups with a variety of different perspectives about how to treat the graves. The various cultural groups actively voiced their preferences regarding the treatment of disinterred individuals. Native American descendants preferred that the deceased be left undisturbed and in place. In the event that disinterred Native American individuals had to be moved—which they ultimately were—no photographs were to be allowed. Hispanic descendants welcomed scientific investigation so they could learn as much as they could about their forebears. They were also pleased that the cemetery was being moved from the heart of the present city to a specially set aside portion of a modern cemetery on the outskirts of town, where the dead could be memorialized and honored. Statistical Research developed as accurate and detailed records of the finds as possible, tracked them throughout the project, reported daily on burial discoveries, and carried out a comprehensive archaeological and biological analysis of the skeletal remains using state-of-the-art methods.

The bones of the dead were a mine of information on what was a hazardous place to live. Men's bones showed more stress on the back and elbows, women's on the knees. Hispanics showed more signs of stress from hard physical labor than Euro-Americans, who held most of the jobs. Broken and dislocated bones were commonplace in the cemetery, many of them resulting from hazardous physical activities, such as working around cattle and horses. What was unexpected was the low incidence of weapon injuries, given that Tucson was notorious for its gun violence. There was, however, evidence for injuries from stone projectile points, fired ammunition, knives, and blunt instruments. Historical records and the skeletons tell of a population subject to numerous imported, infectious diseases that spread easily through growing western cities. Women and children, in particular, experienced high mortality rates from childbearing and disease, but individuals of all ages were likely affected by the recurring epidemics and relatively poor sanitation common to many cities of the time.

The Joint Courts Archaeological Project is a remarkable example of a state-of-the-art CRM project carried out to the highest ethical and methodological standards. Tucson learned a great deal about a place that was used and reused over thousands of years and right into the twentieth century. At the same time, the project repatriated the people buried in the cemetery to their descendant groups and to the U.S. military.

Public Archaeology, aka Public Outreach

For generations, many professional archaeologists looked down on any efforts to communicate their research to wider audiences. The celebrated "publish or perish" culture that haunts academia regarded such activities as near-illegitimate. The situation has changed dramatically in the past quarter century. Every humanity, social science, and science is now concerned with what is often called public outreach—the need to communicate their findings to the widest possible audience. In archaeology, such activity, which has become much more prevalent in recent years, is called *public archaeology*.

Public archaeology covers an astonishingly broad range of activities, everything from Instagram feeds and Snapchat to blogs on the Web, radio and TV programs and series, articles in newspapers and magazines, books, and public lectures. At issue here is the need to communicate with the widest possible audience, especially with stakeholders, many of them members of local communities where research is taking place. Communicating a highly specialized field like archaeology to even knowledgeable audiences requires expert skills in communication and popular writing that are not necessarily those possessed by professional archaeologists with PhDs, accustomed to writing technical papers and monographs. Community archaeology in particular requires expert people skills and an ability to respect and become involved with cultures that are sometimes different from one's own.

We're not talking of the tomb of Tutankhamun, Angkor Wat, or Türkiye Uluburun ship, which have received international publicity ever since their discovery. What's involved here are such unspectacular sites as a shell midden on the South African or California coast, along with a long-forgotten African-American suburb in, say, Chicago, an early hominin camp site in East Africa, or complex, seemingly undecipherable Australian Aboriginal art. Long experience has shown that the only way of making such finds come alive in the mind of a casual beholder is by telling vivid—and accurate—stories about the people who were responsible for them. We can talk about bison hunts on the North American plains where we know the direction of the wind on the day of the hunt (from the orientation of the skeletons in the gully where they perished), or about the diseases suffered by the inhabitants of the 9,000-year-old Stone Age village at Çatalhöyük. Just for a moment, the curtain that hides the past comes alive and the people of the past resonates in an audience's mind, whether listeners or readers, perhaps visitors to an excavation in progress. This is what both community and public archaeology, public outreach if you will, is all about—connecting the past to the present for people who are stakeholders. Let's make it quite clear that pseudoarchaeology, briefly described in Chapter 1, tells *fictional* stories about the past, however vigorously their authors claim the tales they tell are historical fact.

Public archaeology has only recently become an integral part of archaeology, although there were celebrated practitioners who did it as a sideline. Leonard Woolley of Ur fame wrote a classic account of a Royal Burial at Ur in 2300 B.C. during the 1930s. (Unfortunately, details of his account have been disproven by more recent research, but that does not devalue his writing, which reached a huge audience.) Vere Gordon Childe of Urban Revolution fame wrote popular books between the 1930s and 1950s that treated

Figure 17.1 The Joint Courts Archaeological Project, Tucson, Arizona.
Source: Statistical Research, Tucson, Arizona.

prehistoric societies as actors in the play that was the past. The Historical Archaeologist Ivor Noël Hume electrified popular audiences with his accounts of colonial Williamsburg and an Indian raid on the village of Martin's Hundred nearby in 1622 (see Box 7.2 on p. 220, and Figure 17.1). The excavations on a Roman fort at Vindolanda near Hadrian's Wall in northern England with their sensational finds place a major emphasis on public outreach (Box 17.2). Magazines like *National Geographic* and *Smithsonian* popularized the hominin researches of Louis and Mary Leakey at Olduvai Gorge in East Africa.

Today, the focus has often shifted toward stakeholders and local issues and toward researches that involve close collaboration with Australian tribal groups and Native American communities, as well as urban neighborhoods such as Malay quarters in Cape Town, South Africa, and African-American areas in Alexandria, Virginia. We can only mention highlights here, but the long-term effects, combined with efforts to introduce archaeology into school curricula, are leading to a greater understanding of archaeology as an integral part of understanding ourselves and our history.

Our Responsibilities to the Past

All of us, whether professional archaeologist, avocational fieldworker, casually interested traveler, or basically uninterested citizen, share a common responsibility for the past. It is our collective cultural heritage, be it Stonehenge, Petra in Jordan, Cahokia, or the Inca trail in the Andes Mountains. This past extends back deep into human prehistory, more than 3 million years, a precious legacy of cultural achievement that is unique to humanity and something that we must cherish and pass on to generations still unborn. The word *steward* is overused, but we are as much stewards of the past as we are of the oceans, forests, and every part of the natural environment. Archaeology is different in one important respect: you cannot restore an archaeological site like a forest. Once destroyed, its archives can never be reconstructed; they are gone forever. Professional archaeologists subscribe to strict and explicit ethics in their dealings with the past, but in the final analysis, preserving the past for the future is the responsibility of us all.

The world's archaeological sites are under attack from many sources: industrial development, mining, and agriculture, as well as treasure hunters, collectors, and professional tomb robbers. Demand far exceeds the supply, so even modest antiquities fetch high prices in international markets. No government can hope to free the necessary funds to protect its antiquities adequately. And countries such as Egypt, Guatemala, and Mexico, with rich archaeological heritages, have almost overwhelming problems protecting even their well-known sites.

As long as there is a demand for antiquities among collectors and we maintain our materialistic values regarding personal possessions, the destruction of archaeological sites will continue unabated. Even the necessary legal controls to prevent the destruction of archaeological sites are just barely in force in most parts of the world. Yet, there is still hope, which stems from the enormous numbers of informed people who have gained an interest in archaeology from university and college courses or from chance encounters with archaeologists or the past. If sufficient numbers of laypeople can influence public behavior and attitudes toward archaeological sites and the morality of collecting, there is still hope that our descendants will have archaeological sites to study and enjoy. Imagine standing on a coastal shell midden in southern California, where one can think of planked canoes coming ashore on a fine summer evening. Such moments are deeply emotional, triggered by evocative sunsets, effects of cloud and light, and even by a chance thought. They help us remember that our past is utterly precious. We owe this legacy to our grandchildren.

Box 17.2 A Roman Barracks at Vindolanda, England

Vindolanda, the auxiliary fort just south of Hadrian's Wall, was under Roman occupation from roughly A.D. 85 to 370. Home to soldiers and their dependents, Vindolanda is perhaps best known for its hundreds of wooden writing tablets that tell of the everyday minutiae of life on the edge of empire—including chat about socks, underpants, beer, a birthday party, and work to be done at the bath-house.

Yet, one of the greatest, and most unexpected, discoveries was made in 2017. While investigating the foundations of Vindolanda's fourth-century fortress, the archaeologists lifted a small section of its concrete floor, only to be faced with a layer of sweet-smelling, perfectly preserved, anaerobic soil. Realizing this was peculiar, they removed more of the floor and began digging down. Some 3.5 meters (11.5 feet) beneath the floor, they discovered a series of eight rooms with stables for horses, plus living accommodation with ovens and fireplaces. Astonished, they realized they had discovered the remains of a very early cavalry barracks which may have housed over 1,000 soldiers and probably several thousand more dependents, including slaves.

The oxygen-free conditions created by the concrete meant that perishable items, such as wood, leather, and textile, were exquisitely preserved. The team has since uncovered thousands of artifacts, including two highly unusual cavalry swords, two wooden toy swords—one with a polished stone in its pommel, arrowheads, ballista bolts, combs, bath clogs, hairpins, brooches, swathes of fabric, more wooden writing tablets, and much else.

But what makes this find significant is not just its size, nor its pristine state, but its contribution to the chronology of Vindolanda and indeed Hadrian's Wall. To explain: the Emperor Hadrian did not begin building his bombastic barbarian-controlling (117-kilometer- or 73-mile-long) wall, until A.D. 122. Yet, this newly found barracks dates to A.D. 105 and had been sealed by A.D. 120. The fact that it was occupied two if not three decades before the wall indicates that the Romans already had a huge military presence in the area, undoubtedly to keep the local population under control.

So why had they abandoned their barracks and left so many things behind? Some of the items, such as the adults' swords, would have been very valuable. Perhaps the goods were left by soldiers and their families who were forced to flee, perhaps after the Roman emperor Trajan died in A.D. 117, and perhaps after a rebellion by the native Britons. Faced with saving your baby or your posh sword/shawl/comb/pot, it seems the Romans chose to save themselves. Vindolanda is unlocking the secrets of a turbulent time. A clear reading of the chronology is key to understanding what went on.

So You Want to Become an Archaeologist?

Archaeology has an aura of romance and spectacular discovery about it, which probably accounts for why many of you took the course that assigned this book in the first place. You learn pretty fast that modern-day archaeology, while often fascinating and sometimes conducted in remote lands, is a highly technical discipline. An Indiana Jones-like personality is certainly not a qualification for archaeology—indeed, it has never been. Today's archaeologist is about as far from Indiana Jones as you can get and probably works a long way from academia.

What, then, are the qualities that make a good archaeologist in these days of highly specialized research and wide diversity of career options? As you will see, qualities of character are as important as academic qualifications, for you will never become rich as an archaeologist. It is a profession that has unique rewards, but money is not one of them.

Anyone who wants to become an archaeologist needs far more than academic credentials. Quite apart from technical qualifications, you need a constellation of important qualities. A passion for archaeology and the past is all-important. The best archaeologists have a fire in their bellies that enables them to raise money, overcome major practical obstacles, and carry out their work. You need patience, the ability to carry out slow-moving, repetitive tasks. A mind that thrives on detail is a must, since a great deal of archaeology is minutiae—focusing on small attributes of stone tools and potsherds, analyzing computerized data,

Box 17.3 A Simple Code of Archaeological Ethics for All

- Treat all archaeological sites and artifacts as finite resources.
- Never dig an archaeological site without permissions.
- Never collect artifacts for yourself or buy and sell them for personal gain.
- Adhere to all federal, state, local, and tribal laws that affect the archaeological record.
- Report all accidental archaeological discoveries.
- Avoid disturbing any archaeological site, and respect the sanctity of all burial sites.

and studying tiny details of the past for weeks on end. Yes, there is sometimes adventure at the end of the rainbow, but you have to be adaptable and able to thrive on improvisation under difficult conditions. The list goes on, for you need good organizational skills—think logistics: field crews, site archives, and even camp kitchens. Don't forget your sense of humor, for sometimes everything that can go wrong does. Finally, cultural sensitivity and good people skills are essential. Many of archaeology's most successful practitioners invest enormous amounts of time cultivating people and communicating with local stakeholders. And don't become an archaeologist unless you are prepared to adhere to the ethical standards demanded of such professionals, some of which are spelled out in this book.

But what about jobs? Unless you truly have a passion for teaching, academia is shrinking. Less than a third of archaeologists in Europe and North America now work in academia. Many of these jobs involve highly technical research using esoteric scientific methods. Museum jobs are rare, especially research positions. Career opportunities as a professional archaeologist today are mainly in government or in the private sector, specifically in CRM or its equivalent in other countries. Some of the greatest potential lies in cultural tourism and heritage, where new career paths are opening up in everything from conservation and site management to tourist boards, even cruise ship companies. There are now emerging graduate programs in these areas.

Whatever career path you choose, you'll need more than an undergraduate degree in archaeology. A permanent position in archaeology requires a minimum of a Master of Arts (MA) degree. The MA may have a specialized slant, such as CRM, heritage, or historic preservation. It is the qualification of choice for many government and CRM or public archaeology positions. An MA degree gives you a broad background in archaeology, which is essential for any professional.

The PhD is a specialized research degree, which qualifies you to teach at a research university and at many institutions that stress teaching and not research. This is the professional "ticket" for academic archaeologists and is certainly desirable for someone entering government or the private sector, where complex research projects abound and management decisions are often needed. The typical U.S. PhD program requires at least two years of comprehensive seminar, course, and field training, MA papers, and a formal research proposal and period of intensive fieldwork that in written form constitutes the PhD thesis. The average U.S. doctoral program takes about seven years to complete and turns you into a highly specialized professional, with some teaching and research experience. After these seven years, you then have to find a job in a highly competitive marketplace. Yes, it is a daunting prospect to face seven years or more of genteel poverty, but the intellectual and personal rewards are considerable for someone with a true passion for archaeology and academic research. If you want to be competitive in the academic marketplace, we strongly recommend that you acquire not only a specialized PhD degree, but a broad general background for teaching purposes.

But why become a professional? You can have a very satisfying role as an avocational (amateur) archaeologist and a volunteer. In these days of highly specialized research and professional scholarship, it is easy to assume that there is no place for amateurs, but that would be untrue. Amateurs bring an extraordinary range of skills to archaeology. Your talents are valuable, so don't take no for an answer! We showed this passage to a colleague, who pointed out that some of her students have gone on to highly successful and lucrative careers in business. Their quiet philanthropy has endowed professorships, paid for excavations, and supported students. And, having trained in archaeology, they can continue to help by influencing other people's attitudes toward the past, and by supporting the code of ethics that all archaeologists live by (see Box 17.3).

Many people develop an interest in the past, which comes to the fore when they travel. Their background in archaeology, obtained as an undergraduate, enables them to visit famous sites all over the world as an informed observer and to enjoy the achievements of ancient peoples to the fullest. An informed public is vital to the future of the past.

Summary

- The future of the past lies in conservation and management of the finite record of the past. This involves heritage management, CRM, and vital mitigation strategies.
- Public Archaeology (Public Outreach) has become a major part of today's archaeologists, much of it involving work with local stakeholders in the past.
- All of us have ethical responsibilities to the past: not to collect artifacts; to report new finds; and to obey federal, state, and tribal laws that protect archaeological sites. Unless we all take our responsibility to the past seriously, the past has no future.
- Career opportunities for professional archaeologists can be found in universities, colleges, museums, government service, and private businesses, in the United States and abroad.

Critical-Thinking Questions

1. What, in your opinion, are our collective responsibilities to the archaeological record of the past?
2. This chapter lays out a simple set of ethics for all of us. Discuss how you would integrate these principles into your future life.
3. What are the most important qualities needed by an archaeologist in the twenty-first century? To what extent are these qualities unique to pursuing a career as an archaeologist?

Further Reading

For the general issues in this chapter, see B. Fagan and N. Durrani's, *Bigger Than History: Why Archaeology Matters* (New York: Thames and Hudson, 2020). For life after college, see C. Ellick and J. Watkins', *The Anthropology Graduate's Guide: From Student to a Career,* 2nd ed. (New York: Routledge, 2023). K. Vitelli and C. Colwell-Chanthaphonh, ed., *Archaeological Ethics* (Lanham, MA: AltaMira Press, 2010) is a standard work. Finally, be sure to tune into the *CRM Archaeology Podcast*, which covers all aspects of life as a CRM archaeologist.

Glossary

Abri Pataud, France Rock shelter used by Upper Paleolithic foragers in southwestern France during the late Ice Age; famous for its evidence of reindeer hunting.

Abu Hureyra, Syria Village site by the Euphrates River occupied first by foraging groups in about 11,500 B.C. and then by very early farmers; famous for its excellent botanical evidence for agricultural origins.

Abu Simbel, Egypt Temple built overlooking the Nile by the pharaoh Rameses II to honor himself and the major deities of Egypt, c. 1240 B.C.

Abydos, Egypt Ancient Egyptian town, famous for its cemeteries and shrines, thought to be the site of an entrance to the underworld, c. 3000 B.C. and later.

accelerator mass spectrometry (AMS) radiocarbon dating Method of radiocarbon dating that counts actual ^{14}C atoms; can be used to date items as small as individual seeds.

Acheulean stone technology A technology (named after the town of St. Acheul in northern France) based on hand axes, cleavers, and flake artifacts that flourished in Africa, Europe, southwestern Asia, and parts of Southeast Asia between about 1.7 million and 200,000 years ago.

adaptive radiation A burst of evolution, when a single species fills a number of ecological niches, the result being several new forms.

Adena culture (Early Woodland) North American culture dating to between 500 B.C. and A.D. 400, centered on the Ohio River valley and famous for its elaborate earthworks.

agricultural revolution (expression coined by Vere Gordon Childe) The beginnings of food production, prompted by drought and close associations among animals, humans, and plants.

Allia Bay, Kenya Site near Lake Turkana that yielded *Australopithecus anamensis*, c. 4 Ma.

Altamira, Spain Magdalenian painted cave dating to about 15,000 years ago; famous for its polychrome bison paintings.

Ambrona, Spain Acheulian butchering site dating to between 200,000 and 400,000 years ago.

analogy A process of reasoning whereby two entities that share some similarities are assumed to share many others.

analysis The process of classifying and describing archaeological finds.

Ancestral Pueblo (Anasazi) Major American Southwestern cultural tradition centered on the Four Corners region, which reached its efflorescence after A.D. 1100.

Andean civilizations State-organized societies that developed in Peru and adjacent countries.

Angkor Thom, Cambodia Royal capital and shrine built by the Khmer rulers of Cambodia between A.D. 1000 and 1200.

Angkor Wat, Cambodia Royal capital and shrine built by the Khmer rulers of Cambodia between A.D. 1000 and 1200.

anthropoids Members of the taxonomic suborder of apes, humans, and monkeys.

anthropology The study of humankind in the widest possible sense.

Anyang, China Central core region of the Shang civilization of northern China between 1400 and 1122 B.C.

Ao, China Shang civilization capital in northern China, occupied c. 1560 B.C.

Aramis, Ethiopia Site on the Awash River where *Ardipithecus ramidus* was discovered and dated to 4.4 Ma.

arboreal Living in trees.

archaeological data The natural materials recognized by the archaeologist as significant evidence, all of which are collected and recorded as part of the research.

archaeological record Artifacts, sites, and other human-manufactured features or results of ancient human behavior and their matrices, or the contexts in which they are found.

archaeological theory A body of theoretical concepts providing both a framework and a means for archaeologists to look beyond facts and material objects for explanations of events that took place in prehistory.

archaeological types Groupings of artifacts created for comparison with other groups, based on tool types, which may or may not reflect the use of the tool as intended by the original manufacturers.

archaeology The study of the human past using the surviving material remains of human behavior.

artifact assemblage All the artifacts found at a site.

artifacts Objects manufactured or modified by humans.

Aspero, Peru Coastal community near the mouth of the Rio Supe on the Peruvian coast, dating to c. 3050 B.C.

association The relationship between an artifact and other archaeological finds and a site level or another artifact, structure, or feature at the site.

astroarchaeology The study of ancient astronomical knowledge using archaeological methods.

Atapuerca, Spain Cave system that has yielded fossils dating to about 430,000 years ago, often attributed to *Homo heidelbergensis* or an early Neanderthal population.

atlatls Throwing sticks used by early North American hunters; *see* spear thrower.

attributes Individual features of artifacts.

attritional age profile Distribution of ages at death of animals in a population that were killed by selective hunting or predation.

Avebury, England A stone circle complex dating to c. 2500 B.C. that lies at the heart of a Stone Age sacred landscape.

Babylon, Iraq Major early city-state and later capital of the Babylonian Empire under King Nebuchadnezzar in the sixth century B.C.

band An egalitarian association of families knit together by close social ties.

Bandkeramik complex Cultural label describing the first farmers of central and northwestern Europe of about 6000 B.C.; distinguished on the basis of line-decorated pottery.

Bashidang, China Farming village with a defensive ditch in the Yangtse River valley dating to c. 7000 B.C.

Behistun, Iran Carved and polished rock face that commemorates a victory by the Persian King Darius over rebel leaders in 522 B.C.

Benin, Nigeria West African forest kingdom, with a capital of the same name, which flourished from at least the fourteenth century A.D. until recent times.

Beringia Ice Age landmass consisting of northeastern Asia, Alaska, and what is now the Bering Sea; dry land during the late Ice Age.
bipedal Walking upright on two feet.
blades Long, parallel-sided flakes produced from preshaped cores with the aid of a punch; characteristic of many Upper Paleolithic peoples.
Blombos Cave, South Africa Cave site with evidence of art and *Homo sapiens*-style artifacts dating to as early as 100,000 years ago.
Boxgrove, England Hunting site in southern England used by *Homo heidelbergensis* some 500,000 years ago.
burin Chisel-like stone tool made on a blade used for grooving stone, antler, bone, and wood and for making rock engravings.
Butser, England Modern replica of an Iron Age settlement used to experiment with prehistoric farming methods and technology.
Cactus Hill, Virginia A stratified Paleo-Indian and Archaic site with possible human occupation as early as 15,000–16,600 years ago.
Cahokia, Illinois Major ceremonial center of the Mississippian culture built after A.D. 900.
Calakmul, Guatemala Major Maya political and religious center from Preclassic times to A.D. 800.
Caracol, Belize Important Maya center in the seventh century A.D.; a rival of Calakmul and a major center of stone trade.
Caral, Peru Coastal kingdom on the Rio Supe that cultivated cotton with irrigation agriculture, c. 2600 B.C.
carbon isotope analysis Analysis of isotopic ratios in human bones to discern ancient diet.
Çatalhöyük, Türkiye Early farming town that prospered from the obsidian trade between 7000 and 5000 B.C.
catastrophic age profile Distribution of ages at death of animals in a population that died of natural causes.
Çayönü Tepesi, Türkiye Early farming village with a shrine containing numerous human burials, 8600 to 7000 B.C.
ceramic analysis The study of pottery (ceramics).
ceramics Vessels and other objects made of clay.
Cerén, El Salvador Maya village destroyed by a volcanic eruption in the sixth century A.D.
Chaco Phenomenon Generic name given to the Ancestral Pueblo sites and associated phenomena of Chaco Canyon, New Mexico, in the eleventh and twelfth centuries A.D.
Chan Chan, Peru Capital of the Chimu civilization, after A.D. 1000.
characterization studies Studies of sources of raw materials used to make artifacts.
Chavín de Huántar, Peru Ceremonial center in Peru's Andes foothills dating from as early as 1500 B.C. and thriving until between 900 and 600 B.C.; source of much Andean art in the distinctive style known as Chavín.
Chichén Itzá, Mexico Postclassic Maya center in the northern Yucatán, especially in the thirteenth century A.D.
Chilca, Peru Semipermanent foraging settlement on the Peruvian coast dating to after 4000 B.C.
Chimor, Peru The domains of the Chimu civilization.
Chimu Lowland civilization in Peru's Lambayeque valley, which flourished between c. A.D. 1000 and 1476.
Chiripa, Peru Ceremonial center near Lake Titicaca founded in 1000 B.C.

chronological types Types defined by form that are time markers.
chronometric dating Dating in calendar years before the present, often called absolute dating.
Chumash Maritime and interior-adapted hunter-gatherers of the Santa Barbara Channel region of southern California, celebrated for their elaborate maritime culture.
civilization Any complex, urbanized society organized as a state.
cladistics A method of analyzing evolutionary relationships that stresses diversity.
classical archaeologists Individuals engaged in the study of classical Greek and Roman civilizations.
Cliff Palace, Colorado Major Ancestral Pueblo site in Mesa Verde, which reached its greatest extent after A.D. 1200.
Clovis tradition Widespread Paleo-Indian tradition associated with some of the earliest well-documented human settlement of North America, dating to c. 13,050–12,750 years ago.
codices (sing., codex) Documents on bark or deer skin prepared by ancient Maya and Aztec scribes.
cognitive archaeology The "archaeology of mind," using archaeological methods to study human motives, ideologies, and intangibles.
cognitive-processual archaeology An approach to archaeology that combines the methods of processual and postprocessual researchers.
compliance In cultural resource management, the process of complying with federal and state laws affecting the archaeological record.
components All the artifacts from one occupation level at a site.
composite tools Artifacts with more than one component, such as a stone spear point and wooden shaft.
conchoidal fracture The fracturing tendency of igneous rocks that allows the manufacture of flakes, blades, and hence stone artifacts.
context In archaeology, the exact location of a site, artifact, or other archaeological find in time and space.
Copán, Honduras Major Maya center during the mid-first millennium A.D.
coprolite Human (or animal) feces.
core In archaeology, a lump of stone from which humanly struck flakes have been removed.
Coxcatlán Cave, Mexico Rock shelter in the Tehuacán valley that yielded desiccated maize cobs dating to about 2000 B.C.
Cro-Magnon, France Rock shelter near Les Eyzies in southwestern France where remains of the first late Ice Age people (Upper Paleolithic people of western and central Europe, often called Cro-Magnons) were found in 1868.
Cuello, Belize Maya community and ceremonial center, in use before 1000 B.C.
Cuicuilco, Mexico A rival kingdom to Teotihuacán in the Valley of Mexico, destroyed by a volcanic eruption c. 100 B.C.
cultural ecology The study of the ways in which human societies adapt to and transform their environments.
cultural landscape A landscape as defined by a culture that dwells in it.
cultural process The ways in which human cultures change over time.
cultural resource management (CRM) Conservation and management of archaeological sites and artifacts as a means of protecting the past.
cultural selection Process that leads to the acceptance of some culture traits and innovations that make a culture more adaptive to its environment; somewhat akin to natural selection in biological evolution.

cultural system The multifaceted mechanism that humans use to adapt to their physical and social environment.

culture The primary nonbiological means by which humans adapt to their natural environment.

culture areas Arbitrary geographic or research areas in which general cultural homogeneity is found.

culture history Descriptions of human cultures derived from archaeological evidence.

cuneiform From the Greek word *cuneus*, "wedge"; Mesopotamian script made by stamping clay tablets with a wedge-shaped stylus, long used as an international diplomatic script in the ancient eastern Mediterranean world.

Cuzco, Peru Capital of the Inca Empire in highland Peru.

debitage Waste by-products produced while working stone.

debitage analysis The study of debitage as a way of examining ancient stone technologies.

Debra L. Friedkin site, Texas A well-stratified Paleo-Indian site with a pre-Clovis occupation of before 13,000 years ago, underlying a later Clovis layer.

deductive reasoning Forming specific implications from a generalized hypothesis.

dendrochronology Tree-ring dating.

descriptive (inductive) research methods The development of generalizations about a research problem based on numerous specific observations on artifacts and other finds.

descriptive types Types based on the physical or external properties of an artifact.

Diaotonghuan, China Early rice-farming settlement in the Yangtse River valley dating to between 8000 and 6000 B.C.

diffusion The spread of ideas over short or long distances.

Dilmun, Bahrain Important transshipment port between Mesopotamia and the Indus valley in the Persian Gulf as early as 2500 B.C.

Diuktai Cave, Siberia Site of a widespread late Ice Age culture in northeastern Siberia that may have been the ancestor of some early Native American groups; dates to as early as 18,000 years ago.

Dmanisi, Georgia Site dating to c. 1.8 Ma that has yielded crania of *Homo erectus*-like people, the earliest known in Europe and Eurasia.

Dust Cave, Alabama Cave site occupied between about 8000 and 1600 B.C., with evidence of extensive plant exploitation and fishing activity.

Early Horizon, Peru Period marked by the widespread adoption of distinctive art and religious beliefs over much of highland and lowland Peru, c. 900 to 200 B.C.

East Turkana, Kenya Location where fossil hominins and their sites date to c. 2.5 to 1.6 Ma.

Easton Down, England A long, communal burial mound dating to c. 3200 B.C.

ecofacts Archaeological finds that are of cultural significance but were not manufactured by humans, such as bones and vegetal remains; not a commonly used term.

El-Amarna, Egypt Capital of the pharaoh Akhenaten, c. 1348 B.C.; occupied for only 17 years.

El Mirador, Guatemala Preclassic Maya center dating to between 250 and 50 B.C.

El Paraíso, Peru Ceremonial center in Peru's Chillón valley dating to c. 1800 B.C.

Epidauros, Greece Small Classical state, famous for its theater, dating to the fourth century B.C. and later.

epiphyses The articular ends of limb bones that fuse at adulthood in animals and humans.

Eridu, Iraq One of the world's earliest cities, famous for its shrine, c. 4000 B.C. and later.

Erlitou, China Northern Chinese city occupied between 1900 and 1500 B.C.; one of the founding kingdoms of the Shang civilization.

ethnicity In archaeology, the study of different ethnic groups within a society.

ethnoarchaeology The study of living societies to aid in the interpretation of ancient ones.

ethnographic analogy Analysis of living societies to aid in understanding and interpreting the archaeological record.

ethnohistory The study of history using oral and other traditional sources.

exchange systems Systems for exchanging goods and services between individuals and communities.

experimental archaeology Conducting controlled experiments with ancient technologies and other methods to provide a basis for interpreting ancient human behavior.

faunal analysis The study of animal bones.

features Artifacts such as storage pits or postholes that cannot be removed from a site; usually only recorded.

feces Body waste.

Fincastle, Alberta A bison ambush and kill site of 500 B.C., which provides detail on plains butchery methods.

flakes Stone fragments removed from cores, often used as blanks for finished artifacts.

flotation A method of recovering plant remains by passing them through screens and water.

Folsom, New Mexico Paleo-Indian kill site dating to c. 8000 B.C.; a location providing the first definitive evidence of the association of humans with extinct animals in the Americas.

food production Agriculture and animal domestication.

foreshaft A short staff on which a projectile point or harpoon was mounted, the foreshaft then hafted to a long stave. (When the weapon hit its quarry, the foreshaft would break off in the wound, allowing the hunter to rearm his weapon, as well as causing a more serious injury to the quarry.)

form The physical characteristics—size and shape or composition—of any archaeological find; an essential part of attribute analysis.

Fort Rock Cave, Oregon A site with possible evidence of human occupation in North America as early as 14,000 years ago.

Funan, Cambodia Prosperous city-state region in Southeast Asia between the third and sixth centuries A.D.

function The way in which an artifact was used in the past.

functional types Types based on cultural use or function of artifacts rather than on outward form or chronological position.

functionalism The notion that a social institution within a society has a function in fulfilling all the needs of a social organism.

Ganj Dareh, Iran Seasonal foraging camp of 8500 B.C. in the Zagros Mountains.

Garrison Plantation, Maryland Plantation of the eighteenth century A.D. where the excavated slave quarters are famous for their artifacts of African inspiration.

general systems theory The notion that any organism or organization can be studied as a system broken down into many interacting subsystems or parts; sometimes called *cybernetics*.

geographic information system (GIS) A system for mapping archaeological and other data in digitized form, thereby allowing the data to be manipulated for research purposes.

geometric excavation Excavation in arbitrary levels.

Gesher Benot Ya'aqov, Israel 800,000-year-old site that has yielded the first evidence for the controlled use of fire.

gift exchanges Exchanges of goods and commodities between two parties, marked by the ceremonial giving of gifts that signify a special relationship between the individuals involved.

Giza, Egypt Major pyramid site of Old Kingdom Egypt, dating to c. 2600 B.C.

Göbekli Tepe, Türkiye Hilltop shrine of circular structures, dating to about 9600 B.C.

groove-and-splinter technique Longitudinal grooving of antler and bone to produce long, parallel-sided grooves for making spear points, harpoons, and other artifacts; used by Upper Paleolithic and Mesolithic peoples.

Grotte de Chauvet, France Painted late Ice Age cave with remarkable depictions of lions, rhinoceroses, and other animals.

ground stone Technique used for manufacturing artifacts by pecking the surface and edges with a stone and then grinding them smooth to form sharp working edges; often used to make axes and adzes employed for felling trees and woodworking.

Guilá Naquitz Cave, Mexico Cave occupied by a small band of foragers between 7350 and 6670 B.C.; important for the study of early bean and squash cultivation.

Hadar, Ethiopia Location where *Australopithecus afarensis* has been found, dating to about 3 Ma.

Hadrian's Wall, England Frontier wall and forts across northern England built by the Roman emperor Hadrian to keep out Picts from the north in A.D. 122 to 130.

Hadza people, Tanzania East African group who still live by hunting and plant gathering.

Hallstatt culture, Austria An Iron Age culture widespread over central and western Europe, c. 750 B.C.

Harappa, Pakistan Major city of the Indus Valley Civilization, c. 2500 B.C.

Head-Smashed-In, Canada Major bison kill site on the plains of Alberta, used as early as 5,500 years ago.

Herculaneum, Italy Roman town buried by an eruption of Mt. Vesuvius in A.D. 79.

Herto, Ethiopia Site of three 160,000-year-old *Homo sapiens* skulls.

Hidden Mammoth, Alaska A hunting camp in central Alaska dating to about 11,700 years ago.

hieroglyphs Pictographic or ideographic symbols used as a written record or language in Egypt, Mesoamerica, and elsewhere.

historical archaeologists Individuals engaged in the study of the past by combining archaeology with historical records.

history The study of past human societies using written records.

Hogup Cave, Utah Long-occupied cave in the Great Basin, with levels extending back to at least 7000 B.C.

Hohokam Widespread desert farming culture centered in southern Arizona, which flourished from c. 300 B.C. to A.D. 1500.

Holocene (from the Greek word for "recent") The era since the end of the Pleistocene (Ice Age), beginning about 11,700 years ago (c. 9700 B.C.).

hominins Primates of the family Hominidae, which includes modern humans, earlier human subspecies, and their direct ancestors.

hominoids Members of the primate superfamily that includes apes and hominins.

Hopewell tradition Religious and burial cult centered in Illinois and the eastern United States that flourished from 100 B.C. to A.D. 500.

horizons Widely distributed sets of culture traits and artifact assemblages whose distribution and chronology allow researchers to assume that they spread rapidly; often formed of artifacts that were associated with widespread, distinctive religious beliefs.

horizontal excavation Excavation of a large horizontal area, designed to uncover large areas of a site, especially houses and settlement layouts. Also known as *area excavation* or *block excavation.*

Hovenweep, Colorado Ancestral Pueblo pueblo and observatory of the late twelfth to mid-thirteenth century A.D.

Huanchaquito-Les Llamas, Peru Site of a mass sacrifice of children and juvenile llamas overlooking the Pacific near the city of Chan Chan, c. A.D. 1400–1450.

Huon Peninsula, New Guinea Site where 40,000-year-old ground stone axes offer early evidence of human settlement on the island.

ideologies of domination Overarching philosophies or religious beliefs used by rulers or entire civilizations to focus their power and ensure conformity among their subjects.

ideology The knowledge or beliefs developed by human societies as part of their cultural adaptation.

inductive reasoning Using specific observations to form general conclusions.

Indus Valley Civilization Indigenous civilization of the Indus valley of what is now Pakistan, c. 2700 to 1700 B.C.

inevitable variation Cumulative culture change due to minor differences in learned behavior over time.

interpretation Conclusions drawn from data collected in the context of an original theoretical model, developed and modified as a project proceeds.

invention New ideas that originate in a human culture by accident or design.

Isamu Pati, Zambia Village mound occupied by cattle herders and cereal farmers from c. A.D. 600 to 1200; major site of the Kalomo culture of southern Zambia.

Jarmo, Iran Early farming village in the Zagros Mountains occupied before 5000 B.C.

Jebel Irhoud, Morocco Site of the earliest known *Homo sapiens* in the world.

Jeremalai Cave, East Timor A cave visited by tuna fishers at least 42,000 years ago, early evidence for the human occupation of Wallacea off Southeast Asia.

Jericho, Jordan valley Biblical city and famous archaeological site with evidence of an early fortified town of the eighth millennium B.C. and of farming settlements as early as 7800 B.C.

Jingsha, China Important center of the Shu kingdom, c. 1000 B.C.

Kabwe (Broken Hill), Zambia Site in Central Africa where a robust form of early *Homo sapiens* was discovered, exact age unknown.

Kalambo Falls, Zambia Lakebed site where Acheulian occupation levels over 200,000 years old were found.

Kanapoi, Kenya Site near Lake Turkana that yielded *Australopithecus anamensis*, c. 4 Ma.

Kanesh, Türkiye Hittite settlement founded in the seventeenth century B.C., famous in later centuries for its Assyrian trading quarter.

Karnak, Egypt Temple of the Sun God Amun during Egypt's New Kingdom.

Khok Phanom Di, Thailand Pottery-making community famous for its fine burials, c. 2000 to 1400 B.C.

Khorsabad, Iraq Palace and capital of Assyrian King Sargon, dating to the eighth century B.C.

Kingsmill Plantation, Virginia Plantation of the eighteenth century A.D. famous for artifacts excavated from its slave quarters.

Kish, Iraq Early Sumerian city-state of about 2800 B.C. and later.
kivas Sacred ceremonial rooms built by prehistoric peoples in the American Southwest.
Klasies River Cave, South Africa Stone Age cave, c. 100,000 years ago, where some of the earliest modern human remains have been found.
knuckle walking Specialized way of getting around on four limbs, using the backs of the hands for supporting body weight.
Koobi Fora, Kenya Location of some of the earliest traces of stone manufacture in the world, c. 2.5 Ma.
Koster, Illinois Stratified site in the Illinois River valley of the North American Midwest inhabited from about 7500 B.C. to A.D. 1200 by foragers and then maize farmers.
Koto Toro, Chad *Australopithecus afarensis* site south of the central Sahara dating to about 3.0 to 3.5 Ma.
kula ring Ceremonial shell-ornament exchange system in the southwestern Pacific involving gifts of shell necklaces between important individuals.
La Ferrassie, France Rock shelter near Les Eyzies, Dordogne, where evidence of Neanderthal burials was found.
La Madeleine, France Rock shelter near Les Eyzies, Dordogne, where early traces of the Magdalenian culture were discovered.
La Venta, Mexico Olmec ceremonial center dating to after 900 B.C.
Laetoli, Tanzania Site where hominin footprints were preserved in hardened volcanic ash 3.7 Ma.
Langebaan Lagoon, South Africa Site where 117,000-year-old footprints of an anatomically modern human are preserved in a fossilized sand dune.
Lapita cultural complex A series of maritime societies that flourished and traded over an enormous area of the western Pacific, 1600 to 1000 B.C. and later.
Lascaux Cave, France Major site of Magdalenian cave painting in southwestern France, dating to about 17,000 years ago.
Le Tuc d'Audoubert, France Magdalenian ceremonial site famous for its clay bison figures.
Liang Bua Cave, Flores Site that yielded a series of diminutive human skeletons, *Homo floresiensis*, dating to between 100,000 and 60,000 years ago.
LiDAR Light Detection And Ranging, a remote sensing technology that uses laser light to measure distances and create detailed, high-resolution maps of surface features.
lithic analysis Analysis of ancient stone technologies.
Lomekwi 3, Kenya Site in West Turkana, Kenya; home of earliest known, crudely chopped, stone tools, dated to 3.3 Ma.
Lovelock Cave, Nevada Cave in the Great Basin occupied sporadically by hunter-gatherers from c. 7000 B.C. until recent times.
Machu Picchu, Peru Inca settlement high in the Andes occupied before, during, and after the Spanish conquest.
macrobotanical remains Easily recognizable plant remains such as pine nuts, maize cobs, charred nuts, or seeds.
Magan An ancient region referred to in Sumerian cuneiform as the source of Mesopotamia's copper and diorite (likely within the area of modern UAE and Oman).
Magdalenian culture Late Ice Age culture (named after La Madeleine) with sophisticated technology and art tradition found in southwestern France, parts of central Europe, and northern Spain; flourished between 15,000 and 12,000 years ago.

Maiden Castle, England Iron Age hill fort in southern Britain attacked by the Romans in A.D. 43.

mandala Hindu conception of the state, applied to Southeast Asian archaeology.

market A permanent place where trading or exchange takes place; usually centered in a large village, town, or city.

Martin's Hundred, Virginia Colonial settlement of the early 1620s on the shore of the Chesapeake Bay.

Matuyama–Brunhes boundary Moment of reversal of the Earth's magnetic field, c. 780,000 years ago.

Mauryan Empire, India Early Indian empire centered on the Ganges River during the mid-first millennium B.C.

Maya civilization Major lowland Mesoamerican civilization from about 1000 B.C. until the sixteenth century A.D., with the Classic period ending c. A.D. 900.

Meadowcroft Rock Shelter, Pennsylvania Long-occupied rock shelter, with possible evidence of human occupation as early as 14,000 years ago.

megaliths (from the Greek for "large stone") Stone-built graves, widespread during early farming times in western Europe, generally in the fourth and third millennia B.C.

Mehrgarh, Pakistan Farming village and trading center west of the Indus River valley, dating to c. 6000 B.C.

Meluhha The Sumerian name of a prominent trading partner, its identification remains unknown, but most scholars associate it with the Indus Valley Civilization.

Memphis, Egypt Royal capital of Ancient Egypt.

Merimda Beni Salama, Egypt Farming settlement in the Egyptian delta dating to about 4500 B.C.

Mesa, Alaska Forager campsite in the Brooks Range of northern Alaska, occupied about 11,700 years ago.

Mesa Verde, Colorado Series of canyons in Colorado famous for their multiroom Ancestral Pueblo pueblos of the thirteenth and fourteenth centuries A.D.

Mesoamerica The area of the Central American highlands and lowlands where state-organized societies (civilizations) developed.

Mezhirich, Ukraine Late Ice Age forager camp with elaborate mammoth-bone houses on the Dnieper River, dating to about 17,000 years ago.

microliths (from the Greek for "small stone") Diminutive stone artifacts manufactured on tiny blades and used as barbs and points for spears and later arrows; characteristic of the Ice Age and early Holocene societies.

middens Accumulations of domestic garbage, shells, or other occupation debris.

migration The deliberate movement of people from one area to another.

Mimbres Regional variant of the Mogollon tradition of the southwestern United States, famous for its magnificent painted pottery, early to mid-first millennium A.D.

Minoan civilization Bronze Age kingdom centered on Crete that reached its height between 1900 and 1400 B.C.

Mississippian societies Maize-and bean-farming cultures in the midwestern and southeastern United States dating from A.D. 900 to 1500, remarkable for their large ceremonial centers, elaborate religious beliefs, and powerful chiefdoms.

mit'a Taxation through labor; imposed by Andean states, especially those of the Chimu and the Inca.

mitochondrial DNA Genetic material inherited through the maternal line, often used in studies of human ancestry and prehistoric population movements.

Moche state, Peru Coastal Peruvian civilization centered on the Chicama and Moche valleys, dating A.D. 1–800.

Modoc Rock shelter in Illinois that contains human occupation from about 8000 to 2000 B.C. Well known for its Archaic occupation levels.

Mogollon Southwestern cultural tradition of about 300 B.C. to c. A.D. 1100; a highland farming culture without major population centers.

Mohenjodaro, Pakistan Major city of the Indus Valley Civilization.

monophyletic Descended from a single ancestor.

Monte Albán, Mexico Major city and state in the Valley of Oaxaca during the first millennium A.D.

Monte Verde, Chile Streamside forager site in northern Chile dating to about 18,500 years ago.

Mound City, Ohio A Hopewell mound complex covering more than 5 hectares (13 acres) in the Ohio River valley.

Moundville, Alabama Major Mississippian town and ceremonial center after A.D. 900.

Mousterian Name applied to a stone tool technology associated with Neanderthal peoples of Europe, Eurasia, and the Near East after about 160,000 years ago, based on carefully prepared disk cores; named after the French village of Le Moustier.

multilinear cultural evolution Cultural evolution along many diverse tracks.

Must Farm, England Settlement site with exceptionally good preservation, dated to the Late Bronze Age (1000–800 B.C.).

Nakbé, Guatemala Early Maya ceremonial center of 600 to 400 B.C.

Naqada, Egypt Predynastic Egyptian kingdom in Upper Egypt dating to the fourth millennium B.C.

Nariokotome, Kenya Site on the west shore of Lake Turkana, and findspot of "Turkana boy," an almost complete specimen of *Homo erectus* (or *Homo ergaster*), dated to around 1.5 Ma.

Nekhen, Egypt Ancient Egyptian town, center of an important predynastic kingdom, c. 3500 B.C.; Greek name is Hierakonpolis.

Nelson's Bay Cave, South Africa Late Stone Age coastal cave dating to after 8000 B.C.

Nevado Ampato, Peru Site of the discovery of a 14-year-old Inca girl who died in about A.D. 1480, killed as a sacrificial victim at an altitude of 6,210 meters (20,400 feet) in the Peruvian Andes.

Nguni people, South Africa Offshoot of the Zulu people of South Africa, who spread widely northward into Zimbabwe and eastern Zambia in the early nineteenth century A.D.

Niaux, France Painted cave with magnificent bison figures, dating to c. 13,000 years ago.

Nimrud, Iraq Capital of Assyrian Kings Esarhaddon (680–669 B.C.) and Ashurbanipal (668–627 B.C.).

Nineveh, Iraq Capital of the Assyrian Empire under King Ashurbanipal, c. 630 B.C.

nonintrusive archaeology Archaeological field research conducted without excavation and without disturbing the archaeological record.

normative view of culture A view of human culture arguing that one can identify the abstract rules regulating a particular culture; a commonly used basis for studying archaeological cultures through time.

Nubia The "Land of Kush," which lay upstream of Ancient Egypt in present-day Sudan.

Nunamiut people, Alaska Modern Alaskan hunters who prey on seasonal migrations of caribou.

obsidian Volcanic glass.

Oldowan Earliest known widespread human stone tool technology, based on simple flakes and choppers, which appeared about 2.6 Ma and remained in use for nearly a million years; named after Olduvai Gorge.

Olduvai Gorge, Tanzania Site where stratified early hominin archaeological sites are associated with long-dried-up Lower and Middle Pleistocene lakes dated to between 1.75 million and 100,000 years ago.

Olmec Lowland Mesoamerican art style and series of cultures that formed one of the foundations of later civilizations in the region, c. 1500 to 500 B.C.

Olsen-Chubbock, Colorado Paleo-Indian kill site dating to c. 6000 B.C. which was the location of a mass bison kill involving more than 150 beasts.

opal phytoliths Minute silica particles from plant cells.

oral traditions Historical data transmitted from one generation to the next by word of mouth.

Ozette, Washington A Makah Indian village dating to the past 1,000 years.

Paisley Five-Mile Point caves, Oregon Evidence of human occupation in the form of feces dating to 12,300 years ago.

Palenque, Mexico Maya city and ceremonial center ruled by the Shield dynasty for many centuries and powerful in the seventh century A.D.

paleoanthropologists Individuals engaged in the multidisciplinary study of the behavior, culture, and evolution of the earliest humans.

paleoethnobotanist A scientist who studies ancient plant remains and their relationships with ancient peoples.

paleoethnobotany The study of ancient botanical remains.

Paleo-Indian Generalized label given to the earliest forager cultures in North America from before 14,000 to 8,000 years ago.

Paloma, Peru Large foraging settlement with limited agriculture on the Peruvian coast, dating to after 4000 B.C.

palynology (pollen analysis) The study of ancient vegetation by using minute pollens preserved in organic deposits.

Panalauca Cave, Peru Site that has yielded evidence of early quinoa cultivation and llama herding, dating to about 2500 B.C.

Paracas, Peru Coastal cemetery near the modern city of Pisco, famous for its mummies and fine textiles, dating to the past 4,000 years.

Pecos Pueblo, New Mexico Important Pueblo settlement from about A.D. 1140 to 1540, the deposits of which yielded a long sequence of Pueblo culture that became a yardstick for a wide area; subsequently became a major Catholic mission center.

Pengtoushan, China Farming settlement in the middle Yangtse River valley dating to between 6500 and 5800 B.C.

petrological analysis The study of the mineral contents of stone or stone tools.

petrology The study of rocks; in archaeology, analysis of trace elements and other characteristics of rocks used to make such artifacts as ax blades, which were traded over long distances.

phases Archaeological units defined by characteristic groupings of cultural traits that can be identified precisely in time and space, that last for a relatively short time and are found at one or more sites in a locality or region, and that have cultural traits that are clear enough to distinguish one phase from other phases.

Phylakopi, Greece Mycenaean town famous for its shrine, 1390–1090 B.C.

pithouse Dwelling built partly into the subsoil, typically oval-shaped; common in the American Southwest, where the design provides good insulation.

Pleistocene The last geological epoch, sometimes called the Ice Age or Quaternary epoch.

Pompeii, Italy Roman town buried by an eruption of Mt. Vesuvius in A.D. 79; layers of ash preserved evidence of life in the community intact.

pongids Members of the family of nonhuman primates closest to humans.

postprocessual archaeology Approaching the past by examining ideology, motives, and nonenvironmental aspects of culture change.

potassium-argon dating Radiometric dating method that establishes the ages of geological strata and early archaeological sites from volcanic rocks; used to date prehistory from the earliest times up to about 100,000 years ago.

potsherds Fragments of broken clay vessels.

Preclassic era (Formative era) The early stages of Mesoamerican civilization, c. 300 B.C. to A.D. 250.

prehistorians Individuals who study prehistory.

prehistory The study of ancient human societies without writing.

preindustrial civilizations Societies organized without the use of fossil fuels.

primary context An undisturbed association, matrix, and provenance.

primates Mammals belonging to the order that includes tree-living placental mammals.

processual archaeology Studying the process of culture change using a systems or environmental approach.

prosimians Members of the taxonomic suborder of primates that includes lemurs, tarsiers, and other so-called premonkeys.

provenance Position of an archaeological find in time and space, recorded three-dimensionally.

public archaeology Archaeological activity aimed at creating an informed public and conserving the archaeological record.

Pueblo Bonito, New Mexico Major Ancestral Pueblo pueblo in Chaco Canyon, occupied in the twelfth century A.D.

Pukara, Peru Center of a small kingdom in the north Lake Titicaca Basin in the early first millennium A.D.

Puruchucho-Huaquerones, Peru Inca cemetery on the outskirts of Lima (A.D. 1438–1532), famous for its mummy burials.

Quaternary The geological epoch also known as the *Pleistocene*.

Quiriguá, Guatemala Small Maya center that briefly dominated nearby Copán, c. A.D. 738.

rachis A hinge that joins a seed to a plant.

radiocarbon (14C) dating Radiometric dating method based on the decay rates of radiocarbon isotopes; highly effective for dating developments over the past 50,000 years.

reciprocity Obligations between individuals or fellow kin members or groups, involving the expectation that the other party will respond when called on to do so.

redistribution The passing out of foodstuffs, goods, or commodities by a central authority such as a chief, thereby ensuring even distribution throughout a community or wider group; often used to refer to the redistribution of exotic goods traded from afar.

reductive (subtractive) technology Stoneworking technique in which stone is shaped by removing flakes until a desired form is attained.

refitting The reconstruction of ancient stone technologies by refitting flakes and blades to cores; also known as *retrofitting*.

regions Areas defined by natural geographic boundaries that display some cultural homogeneity.

relative chronology Time scale developed by the law of superposition or artifact ordering.

remote sensing Reconnaissance and site survey methods using such devices as aerial photography and satellite imagery to detect subsurface features and archaeological sites.

research design A carefully formulated and systematic plan for conducting archaeological research.

Sahul The landmass consisting of Australia, New Guinea, and the surrounding continental shelf during the late Ice Age.

sampling excavation Excavation using sampling methods to place trenches, usually random sampling.

San José Mogote, Mexico Important farming village, located in the Valley of Oaxaca, in the second millennium B.C.

San Lorenzo, Mexico Major Olmec center dating to c. 1250 B.C.

San Marcos Cave, Mexico Important Tehuacán valley site for the early history of maize.

Saqqara, Egypt Site of Djoser's Step Pyramid, c. 2650 B.C., and other major pharaonic burial places.

Schöningen, Germany Stone Age archaeological site about 300,000 years old that yielded the earliest known wooden spears.

scientific method Method of inquiry based on the formal testing of hypotheses, cumulative research, and replicable experiments.

secondary context A context of an archaeological find that has been disturbed by subsequent human activity or natural phenomena; often applies to burials.

settlement archaeology The study of changing ancient settlement patterns in the context of their environments.

shamans (from the Siberian Tungus word *saman*) Men and women who serve as intermediaries between the living and supernatural worlds and are thought to have magical powers; sometimes called *spirit mediums*.

Shang civilization Early civilization centered on the Huang He River of northern China, dating from c. 1766 to 1122 B.C.

Shiloh Mound A, Tennessee Mississippian earthworks occupied about A.D. 1000.

Shiloh Mound Complex, Tennessee A Mississippian center on the Tennessee River, dating from c. A.D. 1000 to 1350.

Shoshone people, Nevada Hunter-gatherer peoples of the Great Basin, famous for their mobility.

Sicán, Peru Coastal Andean culture, c. A.D. 700 to 1375.

sinodonts Siberian and Native American populations with a distinctive cluster of tooth features.

Sipán, Peru Major ceremonial center of the Moche people, celebrated for its spectacular royal burials and dating to after A.D. 100.

site Any place where ecofacts, features, or objects manufactured or modified by humans are found; may range from a living site to a quarry location, and can be defined in functional and other ways.

slip A fine, wet finish applied to a clay vessel before it is decorated and fired.

Snaketown, Arizona Major Hohokam settlement and ceremonial center located near the Gila River.

social ranking In ancient human societies, evidence of differences in social status, usually detected in burial ornamentation.

social stratification In archaeology, evidence of different social classes, usually arranged hierarchically.

sourcing The study of the sources of traded commodities, such as obsidian, using spectrographic analysis and other scientific approaches.

spear thrower A hooked and sometimes weighted stick or equivalent device used for hurling spears.

Star Carr, England Mesolithic hunter-gatherer site of 11,000 years ago, famous for its wooden artifacts.

state-organized societies Large-scale societies with strongly centralized governments and marked social stratification; also known as *preindustrial civilizations*.

stelae (sing., stela) Commemorative columns or uprights.

Stonehenge, England Circular stone complex with associated sacred landscape first established before 3000 B.C.; its heyday was c. 1800 B.C.

stratigraphic excavation Excavation that involves exposing individual layers.

stratigraphy Observation of the superimposed layers at an archaeological site.

subsistence Ways in which humans feed themselves.

subsurface radar Radar used to detect subsurface features such as houses and pits without or in advance of excavation.

Sunda Continental shelf of Southeast Asia during the late Ice Age.

sundadonts Ancient Eurasian and European populations with shared tooth characteristics.

superposition Relationship between two objects, structures, or layers in the vertical plane.

Sutton Hoo, England Site of the ship burial of the Anglo-Saxon king Raedwald, who died c. A.D. 625.

Swanscombe, England Thames valley site that yielded Acheulian hand axes and a skull of an archaic hominin, c. 400,000 years old.

swidden agriculture Shifting agriculture in which farmers clear land, burn it off, plant crops, and then move on to new gardens when the land loses its fertility after several years.

Ta Prohm, Cambodia Khmer temple near Angkor Thom dedicated in the twelfth century A.D.

Taima Taima, Venezuela Site with possible evidence of early human occupation in the 14,000 years ago range.

Taung, South Africa Quarry in which the first *Australopithecus africanus* fossil was found in 1924.

Tawantinsuyu Inca name for their empire, "The Land of the Four Quarters."

Tehuacán valley, Mexico Dry valley in southern Mexico where some of the earliest evidence for maize cultivation has been discovered.

temper Coarse material such as sand or shell added to fine potting clay to make it bond during firing.

Tenochtitlán, Mexico Capital of the Aztec civilization from c. A.D. 1325 to 1521, estimated to have had a maximum population of about 250,000 people.

Teotihuacán, Mexico Major city in the Valley of Mexico that flourished from about 200 B.C. to A.D. 750.

test pits Cuttings of limited size sunk into archaeological sites for sampling purposes, to establish stratigraphy or to define the limits of a site.

Thebes, Egypt Capital of Middle and New Kingdom Egypt after 1520 B.C. and a major center of the worship of the Sun God Amun; called *Wa-set* by the Egyptians.

This, Egypt Predynastic Egyptian kingdom in Upper Egypt in the fourth millennium B.C.

Tikal, Guatemala Classic Maya city that reached the height of its power in A.D. 200 to 600.

Tiwanaku, Bolivia Highland Andean state near Lake Titicaca, which traded with a wide region, dating to between A.D. 200 and 1000.

Tollund Man Iron Age body of a man, a criminal or a sacrificial victim who was strangled with a cord, dating to some time between 375 and 210 B.C.

tomol Planked canoe used by the Chumash people of southern California.

Torralba, Spain Acheulian butchering site dating to between 200,000 and 400,000 years ago.

total data station An electronic and optical theodolite integrated with an electronic distance meter to read slope distances and other archaeological data.

traditions Persistent technological or cultural patterns identified by characteristic artifact forms that outlast a single phase and occur over a wide area.

transformation processes Processes (which can outlast a single phase and can occur over a wide area) that change an abandoned settlement into an archaeological site through the passage of time.

Trinil, Java, Indonesia Gravel deposits up to 1.8 million years old that have yielded the fossil remains of *Homo erectus*.

Trois Frères, France Magdalenian painted cave, famous for its sorcerer figures.

tuff Volcanic bedrock.

Tula, Mexico Capital center of the Toltec civilization, c. A.D. 900 to 1160.

typology Classification of archaeological types.

Uaxactún, Guatemala Classic Maya city in the Mesoamerican lowlands, defeated by its neighbor Tikal in A.D. 378.

Ubaid culture Early farming culture of about 5000 B.C. in southern Iraq.

Uluburun, Türkiye Bronze Age shipwreck site off southern Türkiye, dating to the fourteenth century B.C.

underwater archaeology The study of archaeological sites under water using special excavation methods, although the objectives of the research are similar to those for sites on land.

Ur (Ur-of-the-Chaldees), Iraq Biblical Calah, a major city of the Sumerian civilization in the third millennium B.C.

urban revolution Vere Gordon Childe's concept, based on the assumption that metallurgy, specialists, and food surpluses caused a revolution in human life and urban civilization.

Uruk, Iraq The world's first city, flourishing from 4500 B.C. for more than 2,000 years.

use-wear (edge-wear) analysis Microscopic analysis of artifacts to detect signs of wear on their working edges.

Uxmal, Mexico Maya city in the northern Yucatán that flourished c. A.D. 900.

Valsequillo, Mexico Site where mastodon bones and artifacts date to about 14,000 years ago.

Verkhene-Trotiskaya, Siberia Earliest known Diuktai-like site in Siberia, dating to about 18,000 years ago.

vertical excavation Excavation undertaken to establish a chronological sequence, normally covering a limited area.

Waka, Guatemala Maya center founded in c. 500 B.C. and at the height of its importance between A.D. 400 and 800.

Wallacea Sulawesi and Timor, Southeast Asia, during the late Ice Age.

Wari, Peru Major highland Andean kingdom centered on an urban and ceremonial center of that name, c. A.D. 800.

Whole-genome DNA Nuclear DNA inherited from both parents, now widely used in ancient DNA research to reconstruct human ancestry, population history, and prehistoric migrations.

Willandra Lakes, Australia Shell middens and campsites dating from about 45,000–20,000 years ago.

Windover, Florida Archaic hunter-gatherer site of c. 3000 B.C., remarkable for the preservation of human remains.

world prehistory The global study of human prehistory.

Wroxeter, England Major Roman city in west-central England that assumed great importance in the second century A.D.

Xia Early dynasty of northern Chinese rulers dating to before 1700 B.C., known from both archaeological evidence and legend.

Xianrendong, China Early rice-farming site, c. 8000 to 7550 B.C.

Xiao-tun, China Capital of the Shang civilization, 1400 to 1122 B.C., located in the Anyang region of northern China.

Yana RHS, Siberia (RHS stands for "rhinoceros horn site") c. 30,000-year-old hunting site at latitude 70 degrees north, on the Yana River.

Yangshao culture, China Widespread farming culture in the Huang He valley of northern China after 5000 B.C.

Zhenla, Cambodia Major center of economic and political life on the middle Mekong River and Cambodia's Tonle Sap, sixth century A.D.

Zhou Important Chinese dynasty that ruled over much of northern China after 1122 B.C.

Zhoukoudian, China Cave site famous for its *Homo erectus* fossils, some dating to before 600,000 years ago.

ziggurat Mesopotamian temple mound.

zooarchaeology The study of ancient animal bones found at archaeological sites.

References

Belzoni, Giovanni Battista. 1820. *Narrative of the Operations and Recent Discoveries within the Pyramids, Temples, Tombs, and Excavations in Egypt and Nubia*. London: John Murray.

Bingham, Hiram. 1964. *Lost City of the Incas*. New York: Atheneum.

Carver, Martin. 2009. *Archaeological Investigation*. London: Routledge.

Chauvet, Jean-Marie, Éliette Brunel Deschamps, and Christian Hillaire. 1996. *Dawn of Art: The Chauvet Cave*. New York: Harry Abrams.

Clendinnen, Inga. 1991. *The Aztecs: An Interpretation*. Cambridge: Cambridge University Press.

Cohen, John Michael, trans. 1963. *The Conquest of New Spain*. Baltimore, MD: Pelican Books.

Cushing, Frank. 1979. *Zuni*. Lincoln: University of Nebraska Press.

Fagan, Brian. 2007. *Return to Babylon: Travelers, Archaeologists, and Monuments in Mesopotamia*. Rev. ed. Boulder: University Press of Colorado.

Flannery, Kent, and Joyce Marcus. 1993. "Cognitive Archaeology." *Cambridge Archaeological Journal* 3 (2): 260–267.

Foley, Robert. 1995. *Humans before Humanity*. Oxford: Blackwell.

Gamble, Clive. 2001. *The Palaeolithic Societies of Europe*. Cambridge: Cambridge University Press.

Joyce, Rosemary. 2009. *Ancient Bodies, Ancient Lives: Sex, Gender, and Archaeology*. New York: Thames and Hudson.

Kramer, Samuel. 1981. *History Begins at Sumer*. Philadelphia: University of Pennsylvania Press.

Leakey, Mary D., and Jack Harris. 1990. *Laetoli: A Pliocene Site in Northern Tanzania*. Oxford: Oxford University Press.

Lichtheim, Miriam. 1976. *Ancient Egyptian Literature: A Book of Readings*. Vol. 2: *The New Kingdom*. Berkeley: University of California Press.

Malone, Caroline. 1989. *Avebury*. London: Batsford.

Noël Hume, Ivor. 1982. *Martin's Hundred*. New York: Alfred Knopf.

Scarre, Christopher, Brian M. Fagan, and Charles W. Golden. 2021. *Ancient Civilizations*. 5th ed. Upper Saddle River, NJ: Prentice Hall.

Shackleton, Nicholas J., and Neil D. Opdyke. 1983. "Oxygen Isotope and Paleomagnetic Stratigraphy of Equatorial Pacific Ocean Core V28-238." *Quaternary Research* 3: 38–55.

Stringer, Christopher B. 1984. "The Origin of Anatomically Modern Humans in Western Europe." In Fred Smith and Frank Spencer, eds., *The Origins of Modern Humans*, pp. 51–136. New York: Liss.

Swann, Brian, ed. 1994. *Coming to Light*. New York: Random House.

Tylor, Edward. 1871. *Anthropology*. London: Macmillan.

Wheeler, Mortimer. 1968. *The Indus Civilization*. 3rd ed. Cambridge: Cambridge University Press.

Wood, Bernard, and Mark Collard. 1999. "The Human Genus." *Science* 284: 65–71.

Index

Note: **Bold** page numbers refer to tables and *italic* page numbers refer to figures.

For Product Safety Concerns and Information please contact our EU representative GPSR@taylorandfrancis.com Taylor & Francis Verlag GmbH, Kaufingerstraße 24, 80331 München, Germany

Batch number: 10499522

Printed by Printforce, the Netherlands